Encyclopedia of Jewish Folklore and Traditions

Volume 2

Raphael Patai, Founding Editor
Haya Bar-Itzhak, Editor

M.E.Sharpe
Armonk, New York
London, England

On the cover: Seder (dinner on the feast of Passover).
The father is reading passages from the Haggadah. Ukraine XIX century. Anonymous artist.

Library of Congress Cataloging-in-Publication Data

Encyclopedia of Jewish folklore and traditions / Raphael Patai, founding editor; Haya Bar-Itzhak, editor.
2 v.; p. cm.
Includes bibliographical references and index.
ISBN 978-0-7656-2025-5 (hardcover : alk. paper)
1. Jews—Folklore—Encyclopedias. 2. Jews—Social life and customs—Encyclopedias.
I. Patai, Raphael, 1910–1996. II. Bar-Yitshak, Hayah.

GR98.E56 2012
398.20892′4—dc23 2012042203

Printed in the United States of America

The paper used in this publication meets the minimum requirements of
American National Standard for Information Sciences
Permanence of Paper for Printed Library Materials,
ANSI Z 39.48-1984.

∞

EB (c) 10 9 8 7 6 5 4 3 2 1

Contents

VOLUME 2

List of Color Plates

Volume 2 (following page 458)

Ashrei, the first word in Psalms 1:1, Italy, fifteenth century.

Painted papercut, by Moshe ben Aharon. Poland, ca. 1875.

Embroidered Sabbath tablecloth showing the Western Wall. Jerusalem, 1928.

New Year card with a Taslich scene. Likely Polish, 1910s.

Adar poster. Paper cutout from Germany.

Farewells of Abou Zayd and Al Harith before the return to Mecca. Illustration by Al-Wasiti, from al-Hariri's *Māqāmat* (Assemblies or Entertaining Dialogues), Baghdad, ca. 1240.

"Moses Receives the Torah from Sinai." Illustration to the first chapter of "Avot," Italy.

Ornamental plate showing Samson tearing down the pillars of the Temple. Ceramics painted with gold rim, Hebrew inscription, from Bohemia.

King Solomon judges two harlots who claim the same child. From The North French Hebrew Miscellany (folio 518a), written and illustrated in northern France, ca. 1278.

Encyclopedia of Jewish Folklore and Traditions

Volume 2

M

Ma'aseh Book (Mayse Bukh)

The *Ma'aseh Book,* or *Mayse Bukh* (Story Book), a compilation of stories in Old Yiddish, is one of the most important literary phenomena of Jewish fiction in Ashkenaz from the Middle Ages to the seventeenth century. The book, in its multiple editions, contains the entire range of characters, metaphors, and major tales based on the talmudic and midrashic legends; the narrative collections translated from the East and disseminated in Central Europe; and the medieval exempla and hagiography.

The *Mayse Bukh* was printed in Basle (present-day Basel), Switzerland, in 1602. Consisting of 257 stories, it is the largest anthology ever published in Old Yiddish. It was published by Jacob ben Abraham of Mezhirech, a bookseller who also printed books written in Hebrew and Yiddish in Basle between 1599 and 1603. Although the sources of this comprehensive narrative collection are varied and numerous, three major literary corpora stand out: (1) stories culled from ancient sources, particularly from the Talmud and the Midrash, with which the copyists were familiar, especially through Jacob ben Ḥaviv's "Ein Ya'akov" as indicated in the titles of some of the stories; (2) hagiographic tales about Rabbi Samuel the Pious and his son, Rabbi Judah the Pious, which were composed by the medieval pietists of Ashkenaz, as well as stories related to the history of Ashkenazi Jews and exemplary characters—such as the stories about Solomon ben Isaac of Troyes (known as Rashi), Rabbi Simeon the Great (well known as Rabbi Shimeon Ben Yitzhak of Mainz, 950–1020), Rabbi Meir ben Rabby Yitzhak Shatz, Rabbi Yeḥiel of Paris, Rabbi Amnon of Mainz, and Rabbi Amram of Cologne.

These stories are saturated with mystical and magic motifs that match the Jewish culture of the German pietists in the twelfth and thirteenth centuries. Some of these stories found their way into the *Mayse Bukh* through postmedieval sources, such as *Shalshelet ha'Kabbalah,* by Gedaliah ibn Yahya (printed in Venice in 1587). This corpus is grounded in medieval European fiction, an aspect discussed at length by the Yiddish scholars Max Erik and Yisrael Zinberg, though modern scholarship attributes this phenomenon to the indirect influence of Hebrew sources; (3) stories of the Middle Ages and later sources that were composed or copied close to the printing of the book and were taken from various collections, such as *Ḥibbur ha'Ma'asiyyot* and *Midrash Aseret ha'Dibberot* (printed in Constantinople in 1519) and *Midrashim u'Ma'asiyyot she'ba'Talmud* (printed in Venice in 1544), or the first Hebrew rendition of *Ḥibbur Yafeh meha'Yeshu'ah* by Rabbi Nissim ben Jacob of Kairouan (printed in Ferrara in 1557), which was originally written in Judeo-Arabic in the eleventh century. This corpus also contains stories that scholars believe were taken from *Sefer ḥasidim* (Book of the Pious), whose first printed editions date somewhat earlier than the *Mayse Bukh* (Bologna, 1538, and Cracow, 1581) and *Kaftor Va'Feraḥ* (Basel, 1581) by Ya'akov ben Rabbi Yitzhak Luzzato.

The narrative collections in ancient Yiddish originate in manuscripts such as MS London, the British Library, Add. 18695 (Mestre, Italy, 1504), written by Menaḥem Oldendorf; MS Paris, Bibliothèque Nationale, Héb. 589 (Northern Italy, 1579), written by Anshel Levi; MS Munich No. 100, copied by Isaac Reutlingen and containing twenty-two stories; and especially MS Munich Cod. Hebr. 495, with 117 stories (Northern Italy, late sixteenth century) and MS Jerusalem, National Library Heb. 8° 5245 (Innsbruck 1596), which was written by Samuel ben Zelikman Bak and contains 109 stories.

The development of these narrative collections of stories into the first collection in print (Basle, 1602) was studied starting early in the twentieth century by the scholars of Yiddish literature and its folklore: Max Erik and Jacob I. Maitlis, Chone Shmeruk, and, finally and most importantly, Sara Zfatman, who mapped this development beginning with the manuscripts and up to the late editions of the book. Also, Erika Timm offered the first seminal description of the Innsbruck's manuscript within the context of both the genre of the *mayse* in Ashkenazi culture and the Latin and Italian tradition of the exemplum and the novella, with a full correspondence with the *mayses* kept in this manuscript and those included in the Basel printed edition.

There are early and late printed editions of the *Mayse Bukh,* both in the original language and in translation. The first edition, printed in Basle (1602), was followed by others: Prague (1665); Wilhelmsdorf (1674); Frankfurt on the Oder (1677–1700); Amsterdam (1701); Frankfurt (1703); Frankfurt on the Oder (1709); Dyhernfurth (1709); Berlin (1709); Amsterdam (1723); Hamburg (1727); Rödelheim (1753); and Nuremberg (1763).

A digest of the stories, published in two volumes, was produced by Moses Gaster in his *Ma'aseh Book* (Philadelphia, 1923). A digest in Germany of the *Mayse Bukh* tales was produced by Bertha Pappenheim in her *Allerlei Geschichten Maasse-Buch* (Frankfurt, 1929), the title of which is borrowed from the Amsterdam edition (1723).

The various editions of the *Mayse Bukh* differ in their range of stories. The changes resulting from incorporating new stories and excluding others were mapped in detailed charts by Sara Zfatman, Yoav Elstein, and Ariela Krasny.

The *Mayse Bukh* left its imprint on the development of the Jewish story first in Yiddish, in the literature preceding and following World War I, and in modern Hebrew literature, where it exerted a strong influence on writers such as S.Y. Agnon.

Avidov Lipsker

See also: Anthologies.

Bibliography

Dan, Yoseph. "Manuscript Beit Ha'Sefarim 803182 and the Story of the Jersualamite." *Kiryat Sefer* 51, 1966 (in Hebrew).

Grünbaum, Max. *Jüdischdeutsche Chrestomathie: zugleich ein beitrag zur kunde der hebräischen literatur.* Leipzig: F.A. Brockhaus, 1882.

Heller, Bernhard. "Neuere Schriften zum Maase-Buch." *Monatsschrift für Geschichte und Wiessenschaft des Judentums* 44, 1936.

Meitlis, Jacob. *Das Ma'assebuch: Seine Entsteung und Quellengeschichte.* Berlin: Buchhandlung R. Mass, 1933.

———. *Midrash to Pirke Avot in Old Yiddish by Anshel Levi.* Jerusalem: Israeli Academy of Sciences, 1969 (in Hebrew).

Timm, Erika. "Zur Frühgeschichte der yiddischen Erzählprosa: Eine neuaufgefundene Maise-Handschrift." *Beiträge zur Geschichte der deutschen Sprache und Literatur* 117, 1995.

Yaari, Abraham. "R. Eliezer Paver, Life and Works." *Kirjath Sepher,* 35 (1959–1960): 499–520 (in Hebrew).

Zfatman, Sara. "The Mayse Bukh: An Old Yiddish Literary Genre." *Ha'Sifrut* 28 (1979): 126–152 (in Hebrew).

"Ma'aseh Yerushalmi," The Story of the Jerusalemite

"The Story of the Jerusalemite" is a medieval story (according to the versions of the story known to modern scholars) that brings together the folk motif of the marriage of a man to a female demon with the exemplary element of the punishment of those who break an oath. The relationship between these two elements varies among the many versions of the story, and so, too, does its genre characterization, which on occasion tends to be classified as a legend and, at other times, a folktale.

The basic plot concerns the tribulations of the son of a wealthy merchant who breaks his oath to his dying father that he would not travel on a boat, the hardships that lead him to his marriage to a demoness, and finally his death at her hands. The dramatic turns in the plot are indicated by the repeated violations of the hero's obligations, the high point being the violation of his oath to the king of the demons, who had granted him his patronage, and then to his daughter, whom the king had given to him in marriage. Each of these instances drives the protagonist further and deeper into the world of the demons. At the end of the story, the hero, who wishes to free himself from the demonic reality, obtains permission from his demon wife to visit his human wife and son, whom he had left in the human realm upon sailing. When he refuses to abide by his promise to return, she goes to his town in order to compel him to do so. At this point, the versions of the story diverge. In some, the hero generally succeeds in releasing himself from the demoness and permanently returning to human reality (sometimes at the cost of the death of his human wife at the hands of the demon one); in others, the demoness is compelled to accept a bill of divorce from him but then she kills him with a farewell kiss. Many versions of the story conclude with a motif in which the demon leaves their child, the fruit of coupling between humans and demons, in the father's community, with the demand that he be brought up in it and even that he rule over it.

In some versions, the motif of the violation of the oath is left aside and the son of the merchant is portrayed as an unfortunate victim of a chain of events, on account of which he is trapped in the world of demons and in the marriage with the daughter of their king. His attempt, as the hero of a magical folktale, to slyly escape from the demonic grasp and return to his natural world appears morally appropriate. In one variation, he even gains his freedom through recitation of the Shema. However, in most versions, the exemplary element is crucial and the motif of breaking the oath is prominent. In this case there is no salvation for the protagonist, and his death, from a kiss of death by the demoness who claims him, is perceived as justified.

Although the story was among the most popular medieval Jewish stories (and it also has a distant Christian medieval parallel), its history and origin remain uncertain. Scholars disagree as to its date (between the tenth and thirteenth centuries), provenance (whether in the Middle Eastern communities or from the circle of Ashkenazi Ḥasidim), and whether it is basically a literary work or a folk composition. It is now known in many versions, some in manuscript form and others in printed editions (beginning with the Constantinople edition of 1516), and still others are oral versions. Widespread mainly in Hebrew, the story was also translated into other Jewish languages, and such translations are still known to exist.

The different versions vary in the degree to which they portray the demonic reality and the life of the chief protagonist. The more detailed versions paint a world of Jewish demons, studying the Torah and observing the divine commandments, with wives, rabbis, houses of study, and synagogues, and whose king (Ashmedai) heads a large army. Their complex relationship with the man finds expression in their primal aspiration and their power to kill him, on the one hand, and in the high estimation with which their sages and king hold the value of his study of the Torah, the climax of which is the demon king's hope to have his daughter marry him, on the other. The expansion of cosmology in Jewish culture to the extent of including demons attains, therefore, a radical formulation in this story, which basically consists of correlated and symmetrical social, religious, and ethical systems in both the demonic and human worlds. The pinnacle is reached with the unification of the worlds through the creation of a family and the marital relations between the representatives of the two realms and with the birth of a demonic-human descendent. (Marital relations between humans and demons, along with humans' giving birth to demons, was a popular motif in medieval Jewish folklore; for its occurrences in international folklore cf. AT 424; Stith Thompson's *Motif-Index of Folk-Literature,* F302, T111.) Despite the substantial distance between these two realms, their unity and continuity as well as the protagonist's moves between them, underline the ease with which one can precariously slip from the human to the demonic. It is here that the exemplary power of "The Story of the Jerusalemite" is located.

Yuval Harari

See also: Asmodeus; Demon.

Bibliography

Alexander, Tamar. "Theme and Genre: Relationships Between Man and She-Demon in Jewish Folklore." *Jewish Folklore and Ethnology Review* 14:1/2 (1992): 56–61.

Ben Amos, Dan, ed. *Mimekor Yisrael: Classical Jewish Folktales.* Coll. M.J. Bin Gorion, trans. I.M. Lask, pp. 218–231. Bloomington: Indiana University Press, 1990.

Dan, Joseph. "Five Versions of the Story of the Jerusalemite." *Proceedings of the American Academy of Jewish Research* 35 (1967): 99–111.

———. *The Hebrew Story in the Middle Ages.* Jerusalem: Keter, 1974 (in Hebrew).

———. "Manuscript Jerusalem 8 3182 and 'Ma'aseh Yerushalmi.'" *Kiryat Sefer* 51 (1976): 492–498 (in Hebrew).

———. "The Version of 'The Story of the Jerusalemite' in 'Tales of Sendebar.'" *Hasifrut* 4 (1973): 355–361 (in Hebrew).

Gaster, Moses. "The Story of the Jerusalemite." *Folk-Lore* 42 (1931): 156–178.

Kagan, Zipora. "Marriage of Humans and Female Demons in Legends and in Folk-tales (Oral Versions of 'Ma'aseh Yerushalmi')." In *Proceedings of the Fourth World Congress of Jewish Studies,* vol 2. Jerusalem, 1979 (in Hebrew).

Shenhar, Aliza. *The Folk-Story of Israeli Communities.* Tel Aviv: Cherikover, 1982 (in Hebrew).

Zfatman, Sara. *The Marriage of a Mortal Man and a She-Demon.* Jerusalem: Academon, 1987 (in Hebrew).

Zlotnik, Yehuda, ed. *Ma'ase Yerushalmi (The Story of the Jerusalemite) Attributed to R. Abraham ben Maimon.* Jerusalem: Israeli Institute of Folklore and Ethnology, 1964 (in Hebrew).

MAGIC

Magic has deep roots in Jewish cosmology, which reserves a place of honor for supernatural forces, especially those associated with language, the Torah, the names of God, and His agents. In folklore studies, the term "magic" is identified with the inexplicable and the supernatural. It involves concrete attempts to employ rituals and spells in order to modify reality as well as elements of wonder in fantastic tales. Following a chronological progression, this survey draws on a broad spectrum of sources to move between these two spheres: texts and objects produced within Jewish magical culture and narrative, historical, and halakhic traditions.

Any study of Jewish magical culture, in both its imaginary and tangible aspects, comprises two groups of sources: "insider" ones, which are part of the culture of practical magic, and "outsider" ones, which are not magical per se but refer to magic. Both types are important for illuminating the role of magic in Jewish culture. The "insider" sources, which are largely performative in nature, attest to the existence and reveal the nature of a long-standing and unbroken Jewish magical culture from the First Temple period until the present and illuminate its contours. They can be divided into three categories: (1) Magical objects: These are amulets, incantation bowls, adjuration skulls, magical gems and pendants, and various objects and artifacts that became charms by virtue of a spell or blessing. What is important about these objects, of which thousands are known, is that they are evidence of concrete magical practices. They also teach us about spells (and through them about the essentials of magical cosmology), the goals of the practices, and something about their material aspects. (2) Magical recipes: Thousands of prescriptions survive for magical rites, recorded from antiquity to the present. The professional literature of magic, in which they were written, copied, revised, and repeatedly updated, is a broad and well-documented genre. The importance of these prescriptions is evident in the extremely broad spectrum of objectives to which they are applied and in the linguistic, material, and ritual means that the magical literature offers professional as well as occasional users. (3) Magical treatises: The relatively few works of this sort are, at base, collections of recipes. Their particular importance for the contemporary scholar lies in the theoretical framework that informs the recipes and reflects a comprehensive worldview in which magic is a rational practice and by no means absurd.

The "outsider" sources, which were not produced as part of Jewish magical activity, provide two types of information. On the one hand, they greatly expand scholars' knowledge of Jews' fantasies about magic and increase their understanding of where magic fits into the Jewish cosmology. On the other hand, these sources locate magic, especially the denunciation of magic, within the broad web of power struggles waged by various elites (priests, talmudic sages, rabbis, secular rationalists) against alternative agents of power. In these struggles, labels that establish a binary distinction, between the permitted and the forbidden, between religion and magic, between miracles and witchcraft, between saint and sorcerer, between truth and worthless fiction, were often employed to draw a sharp line between "us" and "them." The campaign against magic and its agents was presented as essentially a matter of ideology and, consequently, as the war of the rabbis or the rationalists, defending the true foundations of Judaism, against the ignorance and deviance of backward classes (which the research literature generally identifies with "the people"). This campaign, however, was not immune to political considerations.

During the biblical period, ritual power was practiced by the prophets as well as by foreign practitioners ("magicians"). In later periods, it was employed by the members of the rabbinic elite itself as well as by educated professionals who were proficient in broad sectors of ritual, halakhic, and esoteric Jewish knowledge.

The Biblical Period

The only magical objects that have survived from the biblical period are two amulets, which date from the late seventh or early sixth century B.C.E. (that is, the First Temple period). They were unearthed in a burial hoard found on the slope of the Hinnom Valley in Jerusalem. The two amulets are made of thin strips of silver leaf, which were rolled up after an incantation was engraved on them. In both cases, the incantation includes the Priestly Benediction (Num. 6:24–26), which served as an apotropaic text in biblical ritual as well. The biblical and priestly use of this text did not necessarily predate its magical use. Scholars have proposed the contrary sequence, namely, that the Bible borrowed the formula from its popular apotropaic use and converted it into a canonical blessing.

Everything else historians know about magic in the biblical age comes from the Bible itself. The Bible consistently and vigorously rejects magic and its agents (Deut. 18: 9–11) and pronounces a severe sanction against them: "You shall not let a sorceress live" (Exod. 22:17 [RSV v. 18]). It presents magic as a paradigmatic sin, which it sometimes associates with fornication and adultery (e.g., 2 Kgs. 9:22; Isa. 47:9, 12; Nah. 3:4; Mal. 3:5) and ascribes it to the "other" priests, Egyptians (Exod. 7:11ff.), or Persians (Dan. 2:2). In any case, their power, like that of Balaam, who was hired by the Moabite Balak, the son of Zippor, to curse the Israelites (Num. 22–24), is always inferior to that of God and His earthly representatives. However, at the same time, the Bible itself prescribes an unmistakable magical ritual: the ordeal of the woman suspected of adultery, carried out in the tabernacle by the priests (Num. 5:11–31). The priest wrote a curse on a scroll, which he then dissolved, along with dirt from the floor of the sanctuary, in holy water contained in an earthen vessel. The woman drank the water; if she was guilty of adultery, she succumbed to its effects immediately. In this case, the clearly magical element of testing the woman by means of a curse introduced into her body is combined with normative ritual elements: the priest, the tabernacle, the altar, a meal offering, holy water, and God, Who is depicted as testing the woman. The Bible apparently alludes to another ordeal conducted by Moses in order to determine who among the people were implicated in the sin of the golden calf (Exod. 32:19–20). This passage, however, lacks details concerning the ritual elements of the trial, and no verbal formula is employed in this case.

Two main elements of the Jewish magical culture are touched on in the Bible: the campaign against evil spirits and the use of the divine name (both were developed extensively in later sources). The Bible has very little to say about demonology. Evil spirits appear infrequently (Judg. 9:23; 1 Sam. 16:14, 23; 1 Kgs. 22:19–22); other demons, such as Reshef, Ketev, and Dever, are mentioned almost in passing (Deut. 32:24; Psalm 91). Satan (the "adversary" or "accuser"), too, plays only a bit part (Zech. 3:1; Job 1–2; 1 Chr. 21:1). In only one instance do we hear of a human attempt to repel these baneful entities—David's playing the lyre to soothe Saul. This is the only place where the Bible mentions an actual practice intended to exorcise an evil spirit (sent by God to torment Saul). Invocation of the divine name is likewise mentioned infrequently. Proclaiming God's name as a means of expressing fealty to Him is frequent, but its use as a blessing (Deut. 21:5; 2 Sam. 6:18; Ps. 129:8), a means of healing (2 Kgs. 5:11), a curse (2 Kgs. 2:24), or an oath (1 Kgs. 22:16) is rare. Taken together, however, these passages indicate that the infrastructure for such uses, which became very common in the later magical literature, already existed in Israel during the biblical age.

Many narrative traditions tell of biblical heroes' recourse to supernatural forces. The most conspicuous of these wonderworkers are Moses and Aaron, Elijah, and Elisha. They are not referred to as magicians, of course, and the marvels they work are represented as miracles rather than as magic. Nevertheless, if one penetrates the veil of the biblical redaction of the stories, one gains a strong sense of the magical traditions that underlie them. Even though the Bible distinguishes between the "spells" performed by the Egyptian sorcerers and "the finger of God" that is active on the side of Moses and Aaron (so that they are not implicated in magical arts), the story of their duel in Pharaoh's court has clear overtones of a combat among magicians, which some folklorists believe was almost certainly its nature before it was recast as the biblical version. In antiquity Egypt was known as the cradle of magic and its priests were accounted powerful wizards. There is little doubt that the story of Moses's victory in the magicians' "home court" was originally a popular account that highlighted the great power of the national hero who liberated the people from bondage. The biblical versions strongly downplay the element of practical magic in Moses's supernatural deeds. What remains is the wonder itself and the object used to perform it—his rod. Moses uses it to smite Egypt (Exod. 7–11), to extract water from a rock (Num. 20:7–11), to split the sea so that the people of Israel can cross and to make the water come back upon the Egyptians (Exod. 14:15–28), and even to affect the outcome of the battle between the Israelites and Amalekites at Rephidim (Exod. 17:8–13). The motif of the miraculous rod is also found in legends about Aaron. The rod that Aaron casts to the ground in Pharaoh's court turns into a serpent and swallows up the staff-serpents of the Egyptian magicians (Exod. 7:10–12). During the Israelites' wandering in the wilderness, it blossoms miraculously to signal God's choice of Aaron and his sons to serve Him (Num. 17:16–24). A third staff associated with Moses in the Exodus cycle is the one atop which he mounted a brazen serpent; looking at it healed those who had been bitten by a serpent (Num. 21:8–9).

But Moses's powers did not depend on the rod, for he effected miracles even without it: He afflicted the Egyptians with boils by casting soot into the air (Exod. 9:8–10) and sweetened the waters of Mara by casting a tree into them (Exod. 15:23–25). In two cases Moses conveys ritual knowledge that saves the people from mass death. In Egypt he teaches the Israelites to protect themselves against the destroying angel by using a bunch of hyssop to smear blood on the doorposts and lintels of their houses (Exod. 12). In the wilderness he instructs Aaron how to use incense to halt the plague that the Lord sent against the people (Num. 17:9–13). In the last case, the brothers employ the power of ritual to counteract a decree by God himself. In the other cases, they are acting in accordance with a directive by God, Who works the miracle. This strips the ritual element of its performative meaning, leaving only a gesture whose role is to provide a human sign of the divine intervention in the physical world. In this way, the biblical rejection of magic is expressed in the very editing of popular Israelite legends throughout the process of their incorporation into the canon.

This tendency can also be found in the hagiographical legends about Elijah and Elisha. The wonders they perform, which, in the biblical telling, are frequently associated with or highlight a request for divine intervention, are examples of wondrous deeds performed by wandering agents of ritual power. By means of words, ritual gestures, and various items and materials (a robe, salt, flour, a piece of wood), the two—master and student—were capable of instigating and ending a drought, causing water to flow in a dry streambed, turning a small amount of food into an unending feast, covering vast distances in almost no time, crossing a river on dry land, making the water of a spring potable and spoiled food edible, causing iron to float, summoning wild animals to harm others, infecting a person with leprosy, blinding enemies, helping barren women conceive, reviving the dead, and more (1 Kgs. 17 to 2 Kgs. 13). Elisha, who inherited his teacher Elijah's powers and wonder-working mantle, surpassed him in the scale of his miracles and even performed one posthumously (2 Kgs. 13:21). For later generations, Elijah, who ascended to heaven in a whirlwind, borne by a chariot and horses of fire, was a legendary hero, a miracle worker who moves back and forth between the upper and lower worlds, revealing secrets to human beings, rebuking them, and, especially, guarding and protecting the people.

The Second Temple Period

Literature of the Second Temple era (third century B.C.E. to first century C.E.) provides some information about magical beliefs and customs among the Jews of those centuries. Much of it relates to protection against demons and spirits—the demonology of the Second Temple period is much more developed than that of the Bible. The best-known magical artifacts from the period are several fragmentary antidemonic texts from Qumran and the knotted shirt from the Cave of Letters (in the Judean desert). The Qumran fragments indicate an intensive clash with demons, fought by means of spells and adjurations (4Q560, 4Q510–511, 11Q11, 8Q5). The child-size linen shirt, with small tied-up pockets containing minerals and seeds, evidently attests to an apotropaic practice based on these items. These pockets may be the "bindings" or "knots" in which boys may go out into the public domain on the Sabbath, mentioned in the Mishnah (*Shabbat* 6:9) or those mentioned later in the Babylonian Talmud by Abbaye's foster mother as means for protection and cure (*b. Shabbat* 66b).

These "insider" sources are supplemented by several narrative and historical testimonies. Here one must distinguish between traditions of a mythic character and those based on daily life. In the former category, the apocryphal Book of 1 Enoch is of special importance. In it, magic is said to be derived from the lore brought down to earth by angels, which they transmitted to the women with whom they coupled (1 En. 7). The Book of Jubilees, which also tells the myth of the angels, traces the source of demons to spirits that came out of the bodies of the Nephilim, the offspring of the angels and human women, after they killed one another. Noah was given antidemonic medical treatises of heavenly origin after he entreated God to protect his sons against the demons (Jub. 10:1–14). This is the first known mention of antidemonic magical literature. The earliest discussion of practices of exorcism is found in the Book of Tobit. The angel who accompanies Tobias on his journey to Rages tells him that when he enters the bridal chamber with Sarah, he must burn the heart and liver of the fish that he caught, in order to expel the demon. The trick works, and the demon, who slew Sarah's seven previous grooms before they could consummate the marriage, flees to the remotest corner of Egypt, where an angel chains and imprisons him (Tob. 6–8).

Josephus recounts that he saw a certain Eleazar exorcise an evil spirit in the presence of Vespasian, his sons and generals, and many of his soldiers. This scene, in which Eleazar placed a ring that contained "a root of one of those sorts mentioned by Solomon" under the madman's nostrils and ordered the spirit to overturn a basin of water to prove that it had exited the man's body (*Ant.* 8.45), is almost certainly based on public exorcisms that Josephus had heard about or perhaps had even witnessed. This story is supplemented by the tradition about the miraculous *baaras* root, which Josephus quotes elsewhere (*J.W.* 7.6.3). He reports that this root gives off light and shrinks away from those who try to pull it out of the ground. To touch it means certain death, unless one employs special precautions, but all desire it because of its ability to exorcise demons. It is possible that it was among the roots from which "root amulet" were made (see below). Josephus traced Eleazar's powers to incantations composed by Solomon to alleviate illness and cast out evil spirits. This is early evidence of the tradition that Solomon ruled over the demons. More developed versions of this tradition are found in the Testament of Solomon, a demonological work whose Jewish origins can be seen beneath the Christian redaction in which it survives, in the Babylonian Talmud (*b. Gittin* 68) and in later Jewish, Christian, and Muslim narratives.

The laying on of hands is also mentioned as an effective means of exorcising spirits. The Genesis Apocryphon relates that Abraham employed this method when he was summoned to Pharaoh's court to expel the evil spirit that had struck the king and his household as punishment for his seizure of Sarah (1QapGen 20:16–29. Cf. Gen. 12:10–20).

We hear very little about magic outside the context of demonology. Book 2 of Maccabees alludes to defensive magic—the idol-amulets that the Jewish warriors wore on their bodies when they went into battle (2 Macc. 12:39–42). Josephus mentions offensive magic in his account of the intrigues at Herod's court, where women in general and the ladies of the court in particular were accused of compounding drugs (*pharmaka*) to serve as love potions or poison (e.g., *Ant.* 15.223–231; *J.W.* 1.29.2, 1.30.1). The interweaving by a (male) historian of women, intrigues, and sorcery goes very well with the mythic image, noted above, of women as the transmitters of baneful heavenly magical lore to earth.

The many miracles attributed to Jesus in the Gospels provide additional evidence of how Jewish society of late antiquity conceived of wonders. The traditions about Jesus's expelling evil spirits and healing the sick, feeding the masses with a small amount of food and turning water into wine, stilling a tempest and walking on water, restoring the sight of the blind and resurrecting the dead are used to support Jesus's religious and spiritual message (in its Pauline version), but their foundations lie in a Jewish society that believes in miracles and considers them proof of holiness. The scribes' allegation that Jesus is employing the powers of Be'elzebul (Mark 3:22) points to the political underpinnings of the charge of sorcery—labeling the miraculous power of the "other" as illegitimate. Recipes in Greek magical papyri of the first half of the first millennium C.E. indicate the place of the miraculous-magical traditions about Jesus in the cross-cultural magical lore of the eastern Mediterranean basin in late antiquity.

The First Millennium C.E.: The Age of the Mishnah, the Talmud, and the Geonim

Diverse magical sources from the first millennium C.E. include a broad range of magical objects, produced for their clients by professional adjuration writers, as well as the texts on which these professionals drew. The rabbinic corpus, too, provides indications of the nature of contemporary Jewish magic, its role in Jewish culture, and the use that the sages made of the theme of magic in the *beit ha'midrash* (House of Study) discourse. Karaite and Rabbanite writings of the ninth and tenth centuries reflect mainly the rejection of magic—rabbinic magic, which the Karaites censured, and popular magic, which the Rabbanites condemned. They also provide supplementary evidence of what Jewish society thought about magic.

The Jews of that era believed in the power of various objects to protect them, cure disease, and improve their success in a number of areas, both for profit and for mischief making. The potency of these objects came from the spell written in them. To benefit from its properties, Jews (like their non-Jewish neighbors) commissioned writers of charms and spells to make amulets, incantation bowls, and other performative artifacts. The inventory of surviving objects, some of them discovered in proper excavations and accurately dated, depends, of course, on the durability of the material of which they are made. This means that it is limited to objects of metal, ceramics, precious stones, and bone. According to the Tosefta, there were also talismans made of roots (*t. Shabbat* 4:9). It is possible that the small metal cases with attached loops through which a thread could be inserted, found in Israel and Transjordan and containing some unidentified substance, were talismans of this type. In metal amulets, texts were engraved on thin strips of bronze, silver, and gold, which were rolled into a tight cylinder and sometimes placed inside a metal case. Some of them, unearthed in scientific excavations, were found in synagogues, sometimes at the location of the ark. This may reflect the notion of the synagogue as a sacred place and of the ark as the holy of holies, the point of contact between this world and the other, through which both public and private petitions rise to heaven.

The writing of amulets was part of a broader ceremonial process, which is outlined in the professional recipe literature; for example, love amulets were inscribed on soft pottery and thrown into the fire to complete the sympathetic process described in the spell: As the shard burns, so shall the heart of the one charmed by it burn after the one for whom it was made. Instructions for making amulets include detailed rituals of purification and writing to guarantee that they work properly. There were diverse ways to use amulets. The recipes suggest burying them (e.g., in the house or by the side of the road in order to influence someone who lives or passes there or between the roots of a tree to kill pests), casting them into the sea (to calm its waves), throwing them into a river (to increase a fisherman's catch) or a fire (to arouse love), hurling them at enemies (to frighten them away or make oneself invisible to them), or hanging them on the wall of one's shop or home, chair, or bed (for success or protection). But most amulets, especially those intended for healing and protection, were worn on one's person or, in special cases (such as easing childbirth), placed on or under the body.

The sages, too, recognized the power of amulets. Hence they ruled that an amulet that has been proven—meaning one that has healed three times or whose author has done so—may be carried on the Sabbath (*t. Shabbat* 4:9; *b. Shabbat* 61). Their debates on this topic indicate the widespread use of amulets to cure animals, as well as the medicinal use of grasshopper eggs, the teeth of foxes, and nails from a crucifix as a cure (*m. Shabbat* 6:10 and parallels), and of a "preserving stone" to prevent miscarriages (*t. Shabbat* 4:12; *b. Shabbat* 66b).

Magical gemstones were widespread in the Greco-Roman world in the first half of the first millennium; judging by the magical materials available; however, they do not seem to have gained popularity among Jews.

The situation with regard to magic bowls is quite different. This antidemonic practice was common among all groups in Mesopotamia during the fifth to seventh centuries C.E.; Jews were among the most prominent writers and users thereof. The recourse to such bowls was rooted in a cosmology that saw failure, disaster, sickness, and death as the work of demons. Jews in Babylonia went to great lengths to protect themselves against these evil spirits, which acted on their own or were compelled by magical means to wreak harm on people. Although the Babylonian Talmud quotes a number of incantations to be recited against demons in general and against certain demons in particular (*b. Shabbat* 67a), it never mentions magical bowls. More than 1,000 Jewish incantation bowls are extant today. Made of simple and undecorated pottery, they derived their performative power from the text that was written on them in ink, in a spiral moving from the center toward the rim. The circle, which closes and bounds, separates and binds, is seen in the shape of the vessel, in the inscribed text, and in the circles frequently drawn on the bowl's inside and rim, where they often frame images of demons—men and women, birds and monsters, often bound in chains. This is indeed the bowls' purpose, as the spell, too, makes plain: binding, overcoming, and chasing away demons. The adjurations on the bowls reflect a combination of a well-developed demonology with a deep knowledge of Jewish lore: the Bible, the Mishnah, the liturgy, and mystical traditions. The frequent references to Rabbi Hanina ben Dosa and Rabbi Joshua ben Perahiah are evidence that magical traditions about the sages circulated outside the House of Study. The five skulls on which adjurations were written in Aramaic indicate that Jewish charm makers had no qualms about making use of the dead when necessary.

The magical artifacts are evidence of the actual practice by the Jews of both Palestine and Mesopotamia of magical rituals based on adjurations. The two largest books of recipes from the first millennium, *Sefer ha'Razim* (The Book of Mysteries) and *Harba de'Moshe* (The Sword of Moses), greatly expand scholars' knowledge of Jewish magical culture. The former anchors magic in a cosmology known also from the apocryphal literature as well as from the early mystical writings—the *Hekhalot* (palaces) and *Merkavah* (chariot) literature. It enumerates seven heavens, each divided into several levels (except for the seventh, which is the place of God), with camps of angels headed by their own officers. Each camp is appointed over a particular realm—healing, injury, love, success, knowledge, and so on—and can be enlisted to achieve diverse aims within its province by means of the rituals and adjurations presented in the book. *Harba de'Moshe* describes a heavenly hierarchy of thirteen archangels who command the angelic hosts. In accordance with an explicit request by God that they honor the divine name by which they are adjured, human beings can control the angels through the use of the sword of the divine names brought by Moses from Mount Sinai. At the conclusion of a long and arduous ceremony of purification, prayer, and adjuration, they can employ the names enumerated in this treatise to work the many spells—for health, love, social and economic success, harm to others, protection, and so on—described in detail at its end.

The magical recipes for healing, protection, and warding off demons presented by the talmudic literature fit the evidence of the magical texts. There is no doubt that the sages believed that human beings could compel the universe to act contrary to the laws of nature. As was their wont, however, they meticulously distinguished, classified, and qualified. The official halakhic stance on magic is an absolute prohibition; its practitioners are to be stoned (*m. Sanhedrin* 7:4). Beyond this, however, the sages' discourse about magic is diverse and polyphonic and provides information both about the lineaments of the magical culture and on their own use of magical traditions for didactic as well as political ends. Some of their dicta deny that human beings have the ability to create living creatures (*Avot de'Rabbi Nathan* A12); but other traditions recount that a certain rabbi actually created an anthropoid (golem), and for others a calf was created during their study of secret knowledge (*b. Sanhedrin* 65b). They reject customs such as tying a pendulum to the thigh or a red thread around the finger, throwing a piece of iron into a cemetery, or spilling water in the public domain and pronouncing *ḥd'* or saying *dgn krdn* or *dny dnw*; all of these are categorized as "Ways of the Amorites," that is, heathen worship (*t. Shabbat* 6–7). But they pragmatically accept "whatever is proved to be of cure" (*b. Shabbat* 67a) and Judaize certain practices of sympathetic magic by giving them normative explanations (*b. Ḥullin* 72b–73a).

There is mockery in stories about the magical powers of gentiles, along with accounts of the sages' combat with them and defeat of their charms (*y. Sanhedrin* 7:11). There are many traditions about women who practice magic and narratives of the sages' power to defeat them (e.g., *Mekhilta de'Rabbi Shimon bar Yoḥai* 22:17; *y. Ḥagigah* 2:2; *y. Sanhedrin* 7:11; *b. Pesaḥim* 110a–111a; *b. Sanhedrin* 67b). There is abundant information about the origin of the demons, the dangers that they pose, the places that they frequent, and rituals to protect oneself against them, as well as stories of the sages' overcoming them (e.g., *m. Avot* 5:6; *Pirqe de'Rabbi Eliezer* 18; *b. Eruvin* 18b; *b. Shabbat* 77a; *b. Pesaḥim* 111b–113a; *b. Ḥullin* 105b; *b. Qiddushin* 29b). There are expressions of a belief in the power of curses (*b. Berakhot* 56a; *b. Bava Qamma* 93a; *b. Mo'ed Qatan* 17) and of the evil eye (*Gen. Rab.* 56:11; *b. Pesaḥim* 26a; *b. Bava Metzi'a* 107b; *y. Sanhedrin* 1:2; *b. Berakhot* 55b). There is also a profound recognition of the power of the Divine Name to act in the world and of the danger latent in its irresponsible use (*Avot de'Rabbi Nathan* A 12; *y. Yoma* 3:8; *Exod. Rab.* 1:29; *Eccl. Rab.* 3:11). In all of these, as well as many other matters, the sages' discussions of magic enrich our knowledge of Jewish magical culture and of the rabbinical establishment's attitude toward it.

Both types of information can also be extracted from later texts. In the late first millennium, the leaders of the Karaites accused the Rabbanites of employing magic through loathsome sacrificial rites, amulets, and pure and impure names to inspire love and hate, gather demons, heal illness, walk on fire, calm the sea, darken the sun and keep the moon from becoming smaller, shorten journeys, and so on. In their polemics they refer by name to several books of magic, later copies of which turned up in the Cairo Geniza. At the end of the millennium, the rabbis of Kairouan (in present-day Tunisia) asked the halakhic authority Rabbi Hai Gaon for his opinion of similar matters, such as the case of a man who employs certain practices of writing to conceal himself from robbers or beat them away, to calm a storm at sea, or to kill someone. These rabbis also refer to the books of magic that were evidently circulating at the time in the Mediterranean basin. The Gaon's answer was twofold, combining derision and approval: All these things are possible, he wrote, but can be accomplished only by the totally righteous and are no longer feasible in our own generation. Thus magic, which is, of course, not referred to by that name, is not totally barred from the Jewish milieu but is deflected out of the time, the cultural space, or the normative borders of contemporary society.

The situation is totally different in the *Hekhalot* and *Merkavah* literature. Both the learning and the use of adjurations and holy names are essential elements of these writings of early Jewish mysticism. In these texts, visionary aspects are interwoven with magical aspects into an amalgam that can no longer be broken down into its components: seals and holy names serve the mystic in his way up toward the Throne of Glory and his vision of God; at the same time, the visionary experience is woven into these texts in other contexts involving the use of adjurations, chiefly in order to master esoteric lore and study the Torah.

The Middle Ages and Early Modern Era (Eleventh to Seventeenth Centuries)

Magical documents from the Cairo Geniza (storage of writings), dating mainly from the eleventh through the thirteenth century, bear witness to the continuity between the Jews of the Muslim world and the magical ideas and practices of earlier times. The influence of their Arab environment, which provided them with new practical knowledge and theoretical terminology, is evident, however. The Geniza documents include a few thousand fragments relevant to magic, among them many passages from magical treatises and books of recipes and dozens of amulets. Like those of earlier centuries, these amulets were used mainly for healing, protection, love, knowledge, and success; but amulets on parchment, paper, and cloth that were deposited in the Geniza from this period survive. The performative aspect of the amulets remained the same, with adjurations based on holy names, letters, and signs. Addressed to heaven, they aimed to gain control over angels, names, letters, stars, and constellations, and sometimes demons, to enlist them in the service of the person employing the charm and compel them to act on his behalf, effectively and swiftly. Textual parallels among the amulets and recipes from the Geniza make it possible to study the link between theoretical knowledge and its application, conventional formats, and the creative freedom available to the authors of such charms. The great advantage of the Geniza is the extremely broad diversity of the recipes and magical works found there, which allow scholars to trace the continuity and changes in Jewish magical culture over the generations; some of them are copies of earlier texts.

The Geniza provides a broad and sometimes highly systematic literature that makes magical use of both canonical and noncanonical materials. The treatise *Shimmush Tehilim* (Use of Psalms), for example, turns the various chapters of Psalms into charms, with recommendations for their use in diverse rituals to achieve specified purposes (protection, love, harming others, escaping prison, finding a thief, healing animals, sobering up, etc.). Similarly, the treatise *Shimmush 18 berakhot* (Use of the Eighteen Benedictions) turns the blessings of the "Amidah" prayer (in the Eretz Israel rite) into incantations, which it incorporates into charms that are to be recited eighteen times in various rituals, each in pursuit of a goal appropriate to its content. The biblical trial of the woman suspected of adultery (Num. 5:11–31) finds a magical counterpart in a treatise titled *Inyan Sotah* (Case of the Adulteress). Pure and impure names are listed systematically, along with magical practices and illusions according to "four elements." Works referred to only by their titles elsewhere are actually quoted here. Works of astral magic develop the practical aspects of the link between stars and angels, astrology and magic. The hundreds of charms and materials (e.g., minerals, metals, rocks, seeds, leaves, oils, bones, internal organs, meat, animal heads, skin, blood, hair, sweat, sperm) and many rituals that appear in the magic documents from the Geniza create an extensive system of theory and practice, of texts and symbolic gestures whose purpose is to compel the world to act in the service of human beings through sympathetic means (i.e., according to the "laws" of similarity and contagion). As in earlier works, the range of practices offered by this professional literature is much broader than what can be found in amulets. Nevertheless, there is almost no trace of sheer fantasy. In an overwhelming majority of cases, the magical literature reflects logical and pragmatic thinking and offers metaphysical assistance to help human beings achieve what they might be able to achieve even without magic.

If the Geniza reflects the continuity of ancient Jewish magic in Palestine and adjacent regions (and a local Muslim influence), Ashkenazi practice represents a mixture of Babylonian and Palestinian traditions (along with a local Christian influence). Of particular importance here is the literary evidence of the migration of traditions from the East to the West, such as the work known as the *Alphabet of Ben Sira,* which originated in the Babylonian and Persian cultural sphere and circulated in later recensions in medieval Europe. It notably includes the myth of Lilith, according to which this archdemon took an oath not to cause injury wherever the names of the angels who captured her are mentioned. The narrative, which relates to fragmentary ideas about Lilith in the rabbinic literature, has clear parallels in ancient historiolae (brief stories incorporated into charms) from both Palestine (amulet) and Babylonia (magic bowls). The archaeological and literary findings are thus complementary and produce a comprehensive picture in which demonological beliefs and magical practices illuminate each other. Another important example of the links between East and West is the text known as the *Scroll of Aḥima'atz* (Italy, eleventh century). This family genealogy is full of legends of wonder and magic that recount the subjugation of wild beasts, magical shortcuts, knowledge of the arcane, resurrection of the dead, preventing the decomposition of a corpse, propelling a ship and halting it on the high seas, and more. This is a literary reflection of the milieu in which medieval Jews (and their neighbors) employed charms and holy names, a milieu that is documented in professional writings from the other side of the Mediterranean. But whereas the Geniza documents reflect a rich magical culture that employs diverse rituals, the heroes of the *Scroll of Aḥima'atz* work their wonders almost exclusively through words, by invoking divine names. As might be expected from an "outsider" source, Ahima'az also echoes the fear of the magical powers of the "other"—in this case, the harmful and sometimes predatory witchcraft of women.

Most of these elements of Jewish magical culture, as well as its reflection in nonmagical literature, are found in medieval texts from the Rhineland and northern France. Here, though, the picture is somewhat different. First, there is no physical evidence of practical magical activity, because no amulets or other magical artifacts from this period have survived. Consequently, what scholars know about the magical culture of those centuries is based chiefly on recipes and magical treatises in manuscript, frequently in combination with mystical traditions from the *Hekhalot* and *Merkavah* literature. In these works, the relative poverty of the ritual in which the charm is embedded (time and place of performance, material elements, ritual gestures), compared with what scholars know from older works, stands out. Performance practices are reduced chiefly to the use of names and incantations. Mystical and magical speculations in Ashkenazi manuscripts, produced by circles that were interested in names and their theoretical and practical significance and that are associated with the arcana of prayer and arcana of benedictions, with success in one's studies and a good memory, are based almost exclusively on the use of names and adjurations. This phenomenon is even more marked in the narrative and magical traditions that are not associated with performance.

Medieval Jewish literature is full of the marvelous and supernatural. It features monsters, demons, corpses, and witches, which are active in a dimension that exists alongside human beings and influences their destiny. Magic is the most important means that human beings can employ to deal with these creatures and avert the threat that they pose. Sometimes, as in demonological tales and exempla about the dead, the element of performative magic is marginal. Sometimes, though, it is the key to the story, as in accounts of battles against "others"—most often, representatives of the hegemonic Christian establishment—and in legends of Jewish saints. This genre flourished in Jewish folklore, with no thought given to the heroes' real-life opinion of magic. Hence Maimonides is one of the outstanding wielders of divine names, for his own sake and on behalf of his people, as are Solomon ben Isaac of Troyes (known as Rashi), Moshe ben Nachman (called Nachmanides), Abraham Ibn Ezra, Judah the Pious and his father Samuel, Menahem Recanati, Isaac (Yitzhak) Luria (known as Ha'Ari), and many others. In the popular mind, all of them spoke, wrote, engraved, carried, or hurled divine names consisting of four, twenty-two, forty-two, or seventy-two letters. These powerful names of God were employed by them to resurrect the dead, animate a golem, make buildings fly through the air, defeat enemies, exorcise ghosts and demons, make ships move with the speed of lightning, travel long distances in no time, render themselves invisible, and so on.

In the Middle Ages, a new esoteric doctrine emerged and took shape in Europe, the Kabbalah. It gradually became entrenched and expanded its influence over Jewish thought and practice. Embedded in the Kabbalah was a mythic demonology in which the Sitra Aḥra (the "other side" of the godhead) and the forces that serve it in the world replace the haphazard appearances of demons and spirits as the source of evil in the world. A broad demonological system, with Samael and Lilith at its head, was deemed to spread through the world, bringing enduring and almost independent evil to it. Correspondingly, the battle against evil took on a messianic aspect as an attempt to bring redemption to the Jewish people by eradicating cosmic evil (the story of Yosef dela Reina). Alongside theoretical Kabbalah, practical Kabbalah also developed. Practical Kabbalah (as its name suggests) is the system of rituals and "intentions" (*kavanot*) anchored in theosophical Kabbalah, whose crux is exerting a theurgic influence on the godhead in order to repair it, on the one hand, and to draw the emanations and powers down into the world to amend and improve it, on both the national and individual planes, on the other. Although all manifestations of magic and the use of divine names came to be called practical Kabbalah, only a relatively limited branch of Jewish magical practice actually reflects the influence of kabbalistic ideas (such as references to the Sitra Aḥra or the *sefirot*—the ten "aspects" or "powers" of the godhead—as part of the baneful or beneficial cosmic forces). The bulk of the literature of charms and adjurations remains untouched by the new doctrine and continues and develops pre-Kabbalah magic. This literature was collected from diverse sources and copied passage by passage, sometimes word for word and sometimes with revisions, in both Europe and the Muslim world. Some of the manuscripts created in this fashion are merely compendia of magic, which offer a mix of folk remedies, charms, treatises on magic, exorcism, the use of psalms and prayers, and so on. Others were carefully edited to produce systematic lists that could serve as the basis for the books of charms and remedies that were widely composed, copied, printed, and circulated at the beginning of the modern age.

The Modern Era

The use of holy names was a widespread practice at the beginning of the modern era and remains so today. The books of charms and remedies (*segulot u'refu'ot*) composed and at times printed since the seventeenth century are written evidence of a living phenomenon among Jews in both Europe and the Muslim world. In the seventeenth and eighteenth centuries many *ba'alei shem* (Masters of the [Divine] Name) flourished in Europe (chiefly, Eastern Europe). Some of them were members of the rabbinical elite, rabbis, and heads of yeshivas for whom magical activity was only a sideline. Others were itinerant specialists who made the rounds of the towns and villages to help their residents by means of names and charms. Their practices were based on professional knowledge amassed from various sources, which they sometimes edited into systematic treatises. These volumes provide evidence of the extremely broad range of aspirations and goals entertained by the *ba'alei shem,* which strongly recall what scholars know from much older sources as well: healing, protection against fire, conception and pregnancy, easing childbirth, protecting infants, shortcuts, invisibility, protection against enemies or harming them, recovering stolen objects, freeing prisoners from jail, warding off the effects of sorcery and the evil eye, exorcising demons and dybbuks (spirits that had taken control of a living person), and so on. Some of these men became the protagonists of legends that recount the marvels worked for them or that they effected for others. The most famous of them was, of course, Israel ben Eliezer, known as the Ba'al Shem Tov (or Besht), the founder of Hasidism. The professional activities of the Ba'al Shem Tov, who was widely known as a miracle worker, incorporated the use of charms, divine names, and adjurations along with standard medical practices, such as cupping and the application of leeches. The legends about him expand his powers beyond mere technical abilities and recount his wondrous capability of far-seeing, predicting the future, discovering the past (metempsychosis), hearing voices, and understanding the speech of birds and animals. He became famous for his victorious duels with demons, dybbuks, and even the angel of death. Special powers were attributed to his prayers. He employed all of these in his magical-miraculous activities, especially in his work as a healer.

Hasidic literature attributed similar marvelous abilities, although not on the scale of the Ba'al Shem Tov, to many of the rebbes who followed him. At the same time, experts in the use of divine names and amulets continued to be active in Europe and even in North America among non-Ḥasidim and among Jews in the Muslim world. There, too, many engaged in healing through words and rituals, frequently in close contact with the Muslim environment with regard to both the sources of their lore and their clientele. Several families, such as the Abuḥatseras, the Pintos, and the Ben Barukh Ha'Cohen family in Morocco, became known for the power of the *baraka* (heavenly grace and blessing) that was passed down among them from father to son and for the professional lore contained in their family manuscripts, which combined to produce extraordinary ritual performative power. Others, according to popular belief, acquired their knowledge and "efficacious hand" from their extreme piety and study of the exoteric and esoteric. In Morocco, Yemen, and Iraq, many of these holy men copied and composed manuscripts of practical Kabbalah, of which dozens survive. Many others (such as Rabbi Ya'akov Vazana) acquired their magical knowledge and powers from their Muslim neighbors and even, it was said, from demons. In North Africa, especially in Morocco, these pious men were known for working miracles even after death. Their tombs became annual pilgrimage sites for groups and individuals in quest of blessings and assistance.

This living magical activity, in both East and West, is documented in narrative traditions as well as in the diverse texts and objects produced by it, which provide evidence of its theoretical and professional underpinnings as well as of its wares, which were employed by the people. The professional aspect is reflected in dozens of manuscripts of charms and remedies composed in Europe, Iraq, Yemen, and North Africa by various *ba'alei shem* for practical use. These texts are in various languages—Hebrew, Aramaic, Yiddish, Ladino (Judeo-Spanish), Judeo-Arabic—depending on the local language of author or copyist. The influence of the Christian or Muslim environment is frequently evident in the terminology and sometimes also in the practices. In general they are arranged in a professional manner, divided into sections by topics and sometimes alphabetically by purpose; some of them even have indexes to make it easier for users to find what they need. Many such manuscripts contain treatises on casting lots—a diagnostic method employing various calculations based on the names of the client and his or her mother and on his or her birthdate. The result of the calculation is used to diagnose the real problem that underlies the patient's overt symptoms of disease or misfortune—sorcery, a demon, or the evil eye—and to treat it specifically. Some of these collections of charms have been printed, a few in multiple editions, and can be found in bookstores today. They have ornate title pages, rabbinical approbations, forewords, and sometimes indexes. In many cases, the authors incorporated narrative passages: memorates, fabulates, legends, and exempla concentrating on holy men and miracles, whose purpose is to corroborate and validate the magical knowledge they contain.

The consumer side of this activity is reflected in thousands of amulets from all over the Jewish Diaspora that are in private hands or public collections. Because of the durability of the material (and collectors' preferences), the vast majority of the amulets surviving from the past three centuries are made of metal. These amulets, especially those fashioned for protection and success, were meant to be worn as pendants; hence many have the form of or are incorporated into jewelry. Because of the amulets' small size, the texts are generally limited to holy names and to combinations of letters taken from biblical verses and standard spells. The amulets are ornamented with typical performative symbols such as the Star of David, a fish, an eye, and the seven-branched menorah; frequently they also incorporate purely decorative elements. Sometimes the piece of jewelry incorporates a container for a slip of parchment or paper, which was rolled up or folded and placed inside. These amulets come in diverse shapes. No single pattern seems to be dominant in Europe. In Muslim countries, by contrast, the outstretched hand pointing downward, the *ḥamsa,* is widespread and serves as a prophylactic device in its own right. The apotropaic use of the *ḥamsa* is common in the Muslim world; its use by Jews is a good example of a magical tradition borrowed from the non-Jewish environment, which is then adapted and Judaized.

The texts for amulets were written on paper or parchment and, as necessary, on other materials as well, such as wood, leather, cloth, bone, and leaves. Many of these amulet texts survive in handwritten and in an ever-increasing number of printed versions (generic texts written in advance to be given to customers). Some are meant to be folded or rolled up and worn on the body. Others are hung on the walls of homes or businesses, to ensure protection and success. Those in the last category are relatively large and often have a striking design. Sometimes the design is just a matter of aesthetics, but in other cases it has a performative significance. An extremely common pattern in both Middle Eastern and European communities is the prophylactic talisman known as the *Shiviti-menorah.* It features a seven-branched candelabrum in the center, composed of the words of Psalm 67 along with the first half of Psalm 16:8, whose first word is "*shiviti*": "I am ever mindful of the Lord's presence." The wide and public distribution of such plaques in homes and synagogues in the modern era has generated many textual as well as visual variations of the artifact based on its two basic elements. Pictorial and textual elements have been added to the plaques in keeping with local traditions and the artists' fancy. The *Shiviti-menorah* plaque is a good example of the multiple existence of an object in which content, form, beliefs, and ritual are inseparably merged ("conglomerate") and that lies on the fine line between normative religion and folk custom. This is also the location of magical beliefs and customs associated with the intrinsic powers of Torah scrolls and their associated paraphernalia: the case, the finials and crown, the dedication plaques, and the ark curtain. All of these, as well as the cloths tied to the Torah scroll or left briefly in the ark, or water poured into the hollow finials, have been considered charms for wealth, success, and protection, activated by touching them, being in their presence, or simply by donating them to the synagogue.

These object-agents of holiness, with performative powers, were frequently employed in ceremonies to exorcise evil spirits and dybbuks. Belief in the dybbuk, a type of trance possession in which, according to popular belief, the ghost of a dead person that cannot find rest enters and takes over the body of a living person, can be traced back to the sixteenth century. It spread widely in Jewish communities in subsequent centuries. In addition to attempts to negotiate with the dybbuk and persuade it to evacuate its victim voluntarily, exorcising it was based on vigorous and sometimes violent techniques applied against the ghost (in practice, against the possessed individual) and the use of adjurations. The latter were intended to force the ghost to escape the near-presence of holy names by leaving the body. The technique involved introducing the names into the body of the possessed in various ways: through the ears, by reading the adjurations aloud; through the mouth, by dissolving them in water, which the possessed drank; or through the nose, by burning them and having the possessed person breathe in the smoke. The battle that ensued inside the possessed person's body between the ingested holiness and the indwelling ghost was reinforced by various external agents of holiness: the synagogue, the rabbi-exorcist, and ritual objects such as a shofar, a tallit, candles, a Torah scroll—all of them endowed with performative powers. These, supplemented by blows and other forms of pressure, could ultimately banish the dybbuk and with it the impurity and deviant behavior and remove them out of the community—although they sometimes left the patient dead.

All these customs, beliefs, and ceremonies, so common in Jewish communities in the modern era, were the target of harsh criticism by the *maskilim* (those who took part in the Enlightenment ideology). They wanted to discard "folk" magic, as they called it, and purge it from "authentic" historical Judaism. They portrayed magic as an empty practice foreign to Judaism and the various *ba'alei shem* as ignoramuses at best and charlatans at worst. This attitude was similar to that of earlier elites; this time, however, the process was propelled by secularization (or at least a distillation of Jewish religion into ethical principles and rational thought). The dichotomy of religion and magic, exploited by earlier elites to place themselves and their values at the center and the "other" on the margins, was now joined by science, which frequently rejected both religion and magic. The proponents of the Wissenschaft des Judentums viewed and explicated magical beliefs and practices as the backward and decadent nadir of folk Judaism, an extreme manifestation of the decay of the spiritual and moral messages that are the core and essence of the true Jewish religion.

Of course, this idea, which was shared by the first academic scholars who studied Jewish magic, could not eradicate the magical elements from Judaism, and they still flourish today. Healing and prophylactic powers are associated with objects that were once owned by kabbalists and illustrious rabbis, such as Rabbi Menachem Mendel Schneerson (the Lubavitcher rebbe), Rabbi Yitzhak Kadouri, Rabbi Yisrael Abuḥatsera (known as the Baba Sali), and others, or received their blessing. Dozens of famous and lesser-known *ba'alei shem* are active in Israel and the Diaspora even today. The more professional among them rely on traditional modes of diagnosis (various forms of casting lots) and heal chiefly by means of incantations, blessings, and amulets. They attribute their powers to two sources: meritorious family lineage and professional expertise, which they employ on behalf of the Jewish masses, whether religious or not, who knock on their doors. Some of these practical kabbalists go beyond the use of divine names and spend years collecting and reworking the magical literature. In our own generation, too, Jewish magical knowledge, which draws on ancient sources, proliferates and develops.

To date, magical literature, both old and new, is available in bookstores and sold to all comers. Dozens of titles about practical Kabbalah, charms and remedies, incantations, divination, and magic have been published in Israel since the late twentieth century. The Internet has become a new arena for discourse and commerce of spiritual, ritual, and material aspects of magic. Many Web sites offer objects of practical Kabbalah: amulets, books of charms, precious stones, all sorts of preparations, jewelry with special powers, and paraphernalia such as cups, watches, and keychains that have been empowered in one way or another and are vaunted to possess the capacity to improve human life. Many of the wares hawked in this typical postmodern market amalgamate Jewish and non-Jewish traditions and interweave elements of traditional Jewish magic with others taken from Christianity, Buddhism, and various tribal cultures. In the multicultural spiritual fusion typical of the New Age, healing (individual, social, and global) and empowerment occupy center stage. Magic, with its many traditional and new manifestations, is considered a legitimate form of thought and action, whose attraction and hold keep increasing.

Yuval Harari

See also: Amulets; Charms, Books of; Demonology; Dybbuk; Kabbalah.

Bibliography

Bahruzi, Niza, Shalom Sabar, and Hagit Matras. *The Hand of Fortune: Khamsas from the Gross Family Collection and the Eretz Israel Museum Collection.* Tel Aviv: Eretz Israel Museum, 2002.

Bilu, Yoram. *The Saints' Agents: Dreamers, Healers and Holy People in the Israeli Urban Fringe.* Haifa: University of Haifa Press, 2005 (in Hebrew).

———. *Without Bounds: The Life and Death of Rabbi Ya'aqov Wazana.* Detroit: Wayne State University Press, 2000.

Bohak, Gideon. *Ancient Jewish Magic.* New York: Cambridge University Press, 2008.

Chajes, Jeffrey Howard. *Between Worlds: Dybbuks, Exorcists, and Early Modern Judaism.* Philadelphia: University of Pennsylvania Press, 2003.

———. "Rabbis and Their (In)Famous Magic: Classical Foundations, Medieval and Early Modern Reverberations." In *Jewish Studies at the Crossroads of Anthropology and History,* ed. Ra'anan S. Boustan, Oren Kosansky, and Marina Rustow, pp. 58–79. Philadelphia: University of Pennsylvania Press, 2011.

Goldish, Matt, ed. *Spirit Possession in Judaism: Cases and Contexts from the Middle Ages to the Present.* Detroit: Wayne State University Press, 2003.

Harari, Yuval. *Early Jewish Magic: Research, Method, Sources.* Jerusalem: Ben-Zvi Institute, 2010 (in Hebrew).

———. "The Sages and the Occult." In *Compendia Rerum Iudaicarum Ad Novum Testamentum II/3b—The Literature of the Sages, Second Part: Midrash and Targum, Liturgy, Poetry, Mysticism, Contracts, Inscriptions, Ancient Science and the Language of Rabbinic Literature,* ed. Joshua Schwartz, Peter J. Tomson, Zeev Safrai, and Shmuel Safrei, pp. 521–564. Assen: Fortress, 2007.

Idel, Moshe. "Jewish Magic from the Renaissance Period to Early Hasidism." In *Religion, Science and Magic in Concert and in Conflict,* ed. J. Neusner, E.S. Frerichs, and P.V.M. Flesher. New York: Oxford University Press, 1989.

Jeffers, Ann. *Magic and Divination in Ancient Palestine and Syria.* Leiden: E.J. Brill, 1996.

Montgomery, James A. *Aramaic Incantation Texts from Nippur.* Philadelphia: University of Pennsylvania Press, University Museum, 1913.

Naveh, Joseph, and Shaul Shaked. *Amulets and Magic Bowls.* Jerusalem: Magnes, 1987.

———. *Magic Spells and Formulae.* Jerusalem: Magnes, 1993.

Petrovsky-Shtern, Yohanan. "The Master of an Evil Name: Hillel Ba'al Shem and His *Sefer ha'Ḥeshek.*" *AJS Review* 28 (2004): 217–248.

Sabar, Shalom. "Childbirth and Magic: Jewish Folklore and Material Culture." In *Cultures of the Jews: A New History,* ed. David Biale, pp. 671–722. New York: Schocken Books, 2002.

Schäfer, Peter, and Shaul Shaked. *Magische Texte aus der Kairoer Geniza,* vols. 1–3. Tübingen: J.C.B. Mohr, 1994–1999.

Schiffman, Lawrence H., and Michael D. Swartz. *Hebrew and Aramaic Incantation Texts from the Cairo Genizah.* Sheffield, UK: JSOT Press, 1992.

Scholem, Gershom. "Practical Kabbalah." In *Kabbalah,* pp. 182–189. Jerusalem: Keter Publishing House, 1974.

Schrire, Theodore. *The Hebrew Amulets: Their Decipherment and Interpretation.* New York: Behrman House, 1966.

Schwartz, Dov. *Studies on Astral Magic in Medieval Jewish Thought.* Leiden: Brill, 2005.

Thompson, R. Campbell. *Semitic Magic: Its Origins and Development.* London: Luzac, 1908.

Trachtenberg, Joshua. *Jewish Magic and Superstition: A Study in Folk Religion.* New York: Behrman's Jewish Book House, 1939.

Veltri, Giuseppe. *Magie und Halakha: Ansätze zu einem empirischen Wissenschaftsbegriff im spätantiken und frühmittelalterlichen Judentum.* Tübingen: J.C.B. Mohr, 1997.

Vukosavović Filip. *Angels and Demons: Jewish Magic Through the Ages.* Jerusalem: Bible Lands Museum, 2010.

Manger, Itzik (1901–1969)

The Yiddish poet and author Itzik Manger published in Europe, Israel, and the United States, and his poetry is celebrated for its rich combination of humor, sadness, and nostalgia. Jewish folklore plays a prominent role in his works, which are frequently based on folk motifs, familiar folk literature plots, and symbols drawn from folk literature. His poetic mission, as he saw it, was to collect and preserve these motifs and symbols in a vanishing lyrical and folklore tradition.

Manger was born in Czernowitz, the capital of Bukovina (present-day Chernivtsi, Ukraine), on May 28, 1901. His father, Hillel, was a tailor, jester, and rhymester; his mother, Ḥava, was gifted with a rare ability to sing folk songs and recount folktales and legends. His childhood was spent in severe poverty. The entire family—parents and three children—lived in a single room and sometimes in a cellar. His first education was at the Czernowitz *cheder*; later he graduated from the German elementary school and attended the German Royal High School there. In his childhood Manger absorbed melodies from the old plays of the Yiddish playwright Abraham Goldfaden, the carefree singing of troupes of the Broder Singers, which he overheard at the tavern in town and the hostel behind it, and gypsy tunes from the wine cellars. Later, when he attended the German high school, he was exposed to the elegant poetry of Johann Wolfgang von Goethe, Friedrich Schiller, and Heinrich Heine. Because of his proclivity for pranks, which offended the teachers, Manger was expelled before graduation from the school. He studied tailoring with his father and began writing poetry in German. In 1914, with the beginning of World War I, he moved to Iaşi, and in 1918, at the end of the war, he returned to Czernowitz. Then he wrote poetry in Yiddish. His ballad "Portrait of a Girl" was published in the Romanian-Yiddish periodical *Kultur* in 1921. From then on, he published articles and ballads in various Romanian periodicals as well as in magazines published in Warsaw and New York.

In 1928 Manger toured Poland, lecturing on Jewish and European literature and on folklore, especially Jewish humor. He enthralled his large audiences. By the time he returned to Poland in 1929, he had already earned a reputation as one of the leading lights of Yiddish poetry. His poems and ballads circulated among all strata of people. Most of his poems, a play, and some of his best-known prose works were written during his decade in Poland (1928–1938).

When World War II broke out, Manger fled to London, where he came into contact with local poets who appreciated his talents. At the end of the war, he published two volumes of poetry: elegies for the murdered Jews of Europe. In 1948 he returned to Poland as a representative of the International PEN Club. He was traumatized by the experience of a Poland without Jews: "In every other nation, the people go on pilgrimage to the graves of poets; among the Jews, poets visit the graves of the people" (Besser 1998).

In 1951 Manger immigrated to the United States, where he published his collected poems as *Lid un balade* (Poems and Ballads, 1952). Some of the works from this collection were translated to English (Shmeruk, 1984): Nathan and Maryann Ausubel (1957); Sarah Zweig Betsky (1958); Joseph Leftwich (1961); Ruth Whitman (1966); Irving Howe and Eliezer Greenberg (1969). Other

Itzik Manger by Arthur Kolnik (1890–1972).

works were translated by Leonard Wolf (2002). Manger joined the editorial board of the Socialist paper *Der Veker* and wrote for *Di Goldene keyt* and *Vogshol.*

In 1958 Manger first visited Israel, where he was received with open arms by those who appreciated his poetry, as well as by his sister, Sheindel, whom he had not seen for twenty-one years. Several of his works were included in an anthology of world poetry published by UNESCO in Brussels in 1961; they also appeared in various periodicals in English, French, German, Polish, Romanian, Latvian, and Dutch translations. In 1962 he paid another visit to Israel, where he was again received enthusiastically, but illness forced him to return to the United States. He was already seriously ill when he made his fourth trip to Israel, this time to settle permanently, in 1967, and remained bedridden until his death on February 21, 1969.

Manger's works exemplify the charm of the Yiddish language, with its tenderness, humility, fondness, sadness, and humor. In his essay "Folklore and Literature" (Paris, 1939), Manger offered a concise definition of the aesthetic and national function of Jewish folklore and demonstrated how Jewish literature and Jewish folklore had been linked in every age. He asserted that the greatness of Jewish literature derives from its tie to Jewish folklore. The thesis at the core of the essay is that living literature is impossible without a foundation in folklore.

Manger also maintained that the history of culture shows that any attempt to foster a literature that lacks solid roots in folklore is doomed to failure. From this he concluded that the greatness of Yiddish literature lies in its link to Jewish folklore (Bar-Itzhak 2009).

Exploiting a modern historical consciousness, Manger made deliberate anachronism a major element in works such as *Khumesh Lider* (Bible Songs), *Megile Lider* (Scroll Songs), *Rus,* and *Dos bukh fon Gan-Eyden* (The Book of Paradise), in which he reset the biblical stories in the Jewish world of Eastern Europe.

Tamar Eyal

Bibliography

Bar-Itzhak, Haya. *Pioneers of Jewish Ethnography and Folkloristics in Eastern Europe.* Ljubljana: Scientific Research Center of the Academy of Science and Arts, 2010.

Besser, Yakov. "Yehudit Hendel: The Last Jewish Poet." *Iton* 77 (May 1998): 28–31 (in Hebrew).

Gamzu, Yossi. "Bible Songs or Bible Profanation." *Zehut* 5 (1987): 90–95 (in Hebrew).

Manger, Itzik. *The Book of Paradise: The Wonderful Adventures of Shmuel-Aba Abervo*, trans Leonard Wolf. New York: Hill and Wang, 1986, c1965.

———. "Folklore and Literature." *Shriftn in proze* (Prose Works), pp. 327–334. Tel Aviv: Farlag I.L. Peretz, 1980 (in Yiddish).

———. "Introduction to Arieh Merzer." In *Biblical Images: Sixteen Reliefs in Metal.* Safed: Kiryat Hatzayarim, 1960.

———. *The World According to Itzik: Selected Poetry and Prose,* trans. and ed. Leonard Wolf. New Haven, CT: Yale University Press, 2002.

Sadan, Dov. *Threshold Stones: Essays on Yiddish Writers.* Tel Aviv: Peretz, 1961 (in Hebrew).

Shaanan, Avraham. *A Dictionary of Modern Hebrew and World Literature.* Tel Aviv: Yavneh, 1959 (in Hebrew).

Shmeruk, Chone. "*Medrash Itsik* and the Problem of Its Literary Traditions." In *Medrash Itsik*, by Itzik Manger, 3d rev. ed., pp. v–xxix. Jerusalem: Magnes, 1984 (in Hebrew).

Wasserman, Leib. "Itzik Manger." In *Leksikon fun der yidishe literatur* 5 (1963): 257–268.

Yonatan, Natan. "Itsik Manger and Folk Poetry." *Al Hamishmar,* July 21, 1967 (in Hebrew).

MA'OZ TSUR

See: Ḥanukkah

MĀQĀMA

The *māqāma* (pl., *māqāmat*)—"assembly" in English—is a rhymed prose literary genre, popular in Hebrew literature since the twelfth century. The name "*māqāmat*" derives from the Arabic *māqāma,* meaning "a gathering place" where stories were told. It translates as *maḥberet* in Hebrew (from *ḥever*—a group of people together) and received its fame and was disseminated by oral recitation in such gatherings. From its inception, the Hebrew *māqāmat* took two forms: classical and nonclassical (Andalusian).

The classical *māqāma* emulates the Arabic classical genre, which originated with Badi al-Zaman al-Hamadh ̄anī (Persia, 967–1007), and his follower, al-Ḥarīrī (Iraq, 1054–1122). According to this classical form, the components that determine a *māqāma* are style, characters, and structure. The style involves an eloquent ornamental rhymed prose, interspersed with monorhymed metrical poems. There are two permanent characters: a narrator (*maggid*), who enables readers to see the hero, as their paths intersect, and a hero, portrayed as the antihero—a vagabond rogue and master of disguise who is capable of obtaining whatever he wishes from others, thanks to his wit, shrewdness, folklore, and outstanding rhetorical ability. The classical *māqāma* is structured as a short frame story. It has a standard opening and closing, portraying the characters' meeting and departing, and a variable body, conveying the hero's deeds. Often, the opening describes the hero as a storyteller, and the body itself is the story he recites to his listeners. The body of the *māqāmat* is varied both in content and in rhetorical method. Any topic can be expressed in a *māqāma,* including lowly, even bawdy themes and scenes taken from the everyday life of common folk, as the *māqāma* was intended for a middle-class audience from its origin—unlike the courtly literature that preceded it. The *māqāma* also varies in the literary genres conglomerated in it, consisting of tales, fables, legends, jokes, memoirs, proverbs, and epigrams, as well as riddles, prayers, sermons, debates, and more. Each book of classical *māqāma* is a compilation of fifty independent *māqāmat*, presented in what scholars believe is an arbitrary order. In all these components, Hebrew *māqāma* follow the Arabic model. Yet, while the goal of the Arabic *māqāma* is to entertain, the Hebrew *māqāma* involves didactic, mainly satirical intentions, aiming to teach and to instruct through laughter. This major difference is most likely due to Christian influence, to which Hebrew *māqāma* writers were exposed.

The main and most famous classical *māqāma* writer in Hebrew is Yehudah al-Harīzī (Toledo, 1165–Halab, 1225), who wrote *Maḥberot Iti'el* (Iti'el's *māqāmat*)—a translation-redaction of al-Ḥariri's book of *māqāmat*; and *Sefer Taḥkemoni* (Book of Taḥkemoni), which became the defining model of the classical Hebrew *māqāma.* Other classical *māqāmat* are *Māqāmat Akhituv ben Taḥkemoni* and *Māqāmat il-Tajnis* (*Māqāma* of Homonyms), by Yosef ben Tanchum Hayerushalmi (Cairo, end of thirteenth century), *Sefer ha'Musar* (Book of Ethics); by Zechariah al-Ḍahiri (Yemen, sixteenth century); and *Sefer ḥizzayon* (Book of Revelation), by Itzḥak Satanov (Berlin, eighteenth century). There was a renaissance of the classical genre in the eighteenth century. Still, few writers wrote in this specialized form.

The nonclassical form of the Hebrew *māqāma* is a narrative containing satirical elements, written in rhymed prose, not always including poetry. The other components of the classical *māqāma* are not compulsory, and the authors chose from them to suit their needs. The sketchiness and generality of this definition is the cause of a polemic between scholars, with some claiming that only a handful of classical *māqāmat* may properly take that name. Notwithstanding, this is the accepted definition. In the twelfth to fifteenth centuries, the nonclassical *māqāma* became the favored genre of Hebrew belles lettres in Spain, France, and Italy, at the expense of poetry. The first *māqāma* written in Hebrew is *Neum Asher ben Yehudah* (Asher ben Yehuda's Oration), by Shlomo ibn Zakbel (first quarter of the twelfth century), a short humorous narrative, embedded in a milieu like that in the *Arabian Nights*. This is one of the rare *māqāmat* written under the Muslim regime. Even so, it has Christian influences and differs in many ways—including a didactic morale—from the classical, Arabic *māqāma*. The second *māqāma* known to scholars, already written under Christian rule, is *Sefer Sha'ashuim* (Book of Delight), by Yoseph Ibn Zabara (Barcelona, twelfth century)—a compilation of animal stories, fables, proverbs, folktales, medical lore (such as rules on how to maintain good health), popular knowledge in other sciences and additional topics, all gathered in a frame story of two characters—the narrator and a devil—going from the narrator's hometown to the devil's home. This is considered the first picaresque novel in Hebrew. *Sefer Sha'ashuim* includes also many misogynistic sayings and tales, a topic that became popular in *māqāma* literature, until a polemic for and against women took place in it, such as in the *māqāmat MinḥatYehudah Sone ha'Nashim* (The Offering of Yehudah the Women Hater), by Judah [Yehudah] ibn Shabbethai (Toledo, 1208), and in *Ezrat Nashim* (The Aid of Women) and *Ein Mishpat*, by Isaac (Burgos, 1210).

The nonclassical medieval *māqāma* had a didactic purpose and helped spread ideas in Christian Europe, where poetry became subordinated to philosophy and was justified only if it was edifying or moralistic. Thus, in *Sefer Ha'Mevakesh* (Book of the Seeker), by Shem Tov ibn Falaquera (Tudela, thirteenth century), the hero, pursuing the best path in life, questions seventeen experts in different fields (such as a wealthy man, warrior, craftsman, physician, pious man, poet, mathematician, astronomer, logician, and physicist) until he finds the ultimate way—in philosophy. Another didactic, moralistic yet entertaining *māqāma* is *Meshal ha'Qadmoni* (The Fable of the Ancient), by Isaac ibn Sahula (1281). *Ma'ase ha'Rav* (Deed of the Master), by Shem Tov ben Isaac Ardutiel (1345), appears to be a humorous debate between a pen and scissors that argue which of them is more suitable for writing, after the writer has used the scissors for cutting letters, thus writing a letter on a cold winter night in which he could not use the pen because the ink had frozen. Yet even this entertaining argument might be allegorical and conceal political satire (Colahan 1979). Even the facetious *Maḥberot Immanuel*, by Immanuel Ha'Romi (end of thirteenth century), contains didactic teachings.

The decision to use the *māqāma* genre for bestowing knowledge upon the readers is a testimony to its popularity. The genre became so popular that it was chosen as the model for translation into Hebrew, including works that were not originally written as *māqāmat,* such as *Mishle Shu'alim* (Fox Fables), Berechiah ha'Nakdan's translation of Marie de France's animal fables (about 1200); and *Kalila Ve'Dimna*, by Ya'akov ben Elazar, and *Ben Ham'elekh ve'ha'nazir* (The King's Son and the Ascetic), by Abraham ibn Hisday—both adaptations of Indian works from their Arabic translation. Thus, the *māqāma* genre became a central means of transferring folk literature from other cultures into Hebrew.

The modern era of the *māqāma* genre begins with Bialik's *Aluf batzlut ve'aluf shum* (1928). Poet Shimshon Meltzer used it as a format for folktales in *Sefer hashirot ve'habaladot* (Book of Poems and Ballads), and Ḥaim Ḥefer wrote satirical *māqāmat* weekly in the daily newspaper *Yediot Aḥronot* from the 1960s until 2001. A significant transformation in contemporary *māqāma* is that it sometimes replaces the satirical element with mere humor. Thus, it is a preferred medium for writing festive greetings (recited at birthdays, weddings, etc.) and children's books.

Ayelet Oettinger

Bibliography

Al-Hariri, *The Assemblies of al-Hariri*, trans. Thomas Chenery. Farnborough, UK: Gregg, 1969.

Alharizi, Judah. *The Book of Taḥkemoni: Jewish Tales from Medieval Spain.* Translated, explicated, and annotated by David Simha Segal. London: Littman Library of Jewish Civilization, 2001.

Badi' al-Zaman al-Hamadhani. *Maqamat*, trans. W.J. Prendergast. London: Curzon, 1973.

Berechiah Ben Natronai, ha'Nakdan. *Fables of a Jewish Aesop,* trans. Moses Hadas. New York: Columbia University Press, 1967.

Colahan, Clark. "Santob's Debate: Parody and Political Allegory." *Sefarad* 39 (1979): 87–107, 265–308.

Falaquera, Shem Tov ben Joseph. *The Book of the Seeker (Sefer hamebaqqesh) by Shem Tob ben Joseph ibn Falaquera*, trans. and ed. M. Herschel Levine. New York: Yeshiva University Press, 1976.

Oettinger, Ayelet. "A Research of the Satirical Mode in Yehudah al-Harizi's 'Book of Taḥkemoni.'" Ph.D. dissertation, Haifa University, 2003 (in Hebrew).

Ratzaby, Yehuda. *An Anthology of the Hebrew Maqama.* Jerusalem: Bialik Institute, 1974 (in Hebrew).

Sahula, Isaac ben Solomon. *Meshal haQadmoni: Fables from the Distant Past; A Parallel Hebrew-English Text*, trans. and ed. Raphael Loewe. London: Littman Library of Jewish Civilization, 2004.

Schippers, Arie. "The Hebrew Maqama." In *Maqama: A History of a Genre,* by Jaakko Hämeen-Anttila, pp. 302–327. Wiesbaden: Harrassovitz, 2002.

Zabara, Yoseph ben Meir. *The Book of Delight*, trans. Moses Hadas. New York: Columbia University Press, 1960.

Marek, Pesaḥ

See: Anthologies; Poland, Jews of; Russia, Jews of

Marriage

Procreation is the first commandment given by God to humankind (Gen. 1:28, 9:1). Jewish law mandates that the sexual relationship between a man and a woman in order to fulfill this commandment is permissible only after a ritual marriage ceremony. Consequently, the wedding ceremony became a central occasion in the Jewish life cycle and is one of the major "rites of passage" in that cycle. The development of the ritual has a complex evolution, spawning a variety of ceremonies strongly influenced by the surrounding cultural milieus. The basic elements of the ritual, its historical development, and its attendant customs have been studied and documented by scholars throughout history.

There is little evidence as to the nature of marriage during the biblical period. The act of marriage, called "taking" (*lekiḥah*) (Deut. 24:1; Exod. 2:1), seems to have included processions for the bride and groom (Ps. 78:63, of Macc. 9:39) and to have been followed by a week of feasting (Gen. 29:22, 27).

In the talmudic period and probably earlier, the marriage cycle comprised two separate events. First was the betrothal, called *kiddushin* or *erusin,* during which the bridegroom presented the bride with a coin (of minimal value, *peruta*) or a ring (as the Romans did), reciting two benedictions, one over wine and the other for the actual act. Second, at some later date, a marriage ceremony, in which the bride was led to the groom's house or, later, to a *ḥuppah* (canopy), symbolizing her new home, and a ceremony (called *"sheva berakhot")* took place in which (six or) seven benedictions were recited. Between the first and the second events, which until the Middle Ages could be separated by a year or even more, the bride and groom could have no sexual relations. Only after the *nisuin* (the second stage of the marriage process) were they fully married and liable to the responsibilities and privileges accorded them by their new status. In the Middle Ages, these two events were unified, and in order to distinguish them, the *ketubbah* (marriage contract) is read out loud between them.

The actual ceremony is a joyful one and even in early times included dancing before the bride, even by rabbis (*Ket.* 16b–17a), who occasionally danced with the bride perched upon their shoulders (ibid.). At the end of the ceremony, the groom would shatter a glass, either in memory of the destruction of the Temple, or to reduce the unseemly hilarity of the proceedings (*Ber.* 31a), or as a means of protection against evil spirits. In medieval Germany, the glass would be hurled against the *ḥuppah Stein,* a special stone set in the (northern) wall of the synagogue.

The wedding took place before a minimal quorum of ten adult males and in the presence of two competent witnesses, followed by seven days of festivities, during which the seven special marriage benedictions were recited at meals.

Marriages did not take place during the period of the Omer, from after Passover to Lag Ba'Omer (Sephardim) or from the first of Iyar until before Shavuot (Ashkenazim). It was considered preferable to hold the wedding ceremony at the beginning of the month or during the full moon but not during the waning of the moon. The preferred day for a wedding during talmudic times was Wednesday, because the courts sat on Thursday, and this would allow the husband to complain to the court immediately, should he discover that his bride was not a virgin (*Ket.* 1:1). Wednesday was also considered a lucky day. However, later (mainly among Ashkenazim), having the wedding on Friday was more popular because it reduced costs, since the Sabbath meal was the first of the meals of the *sheva berakhot.* In modern times, Sunday is often the most convenient time for weddings.

Many customs are connected with the marriage ceremony. In Ashkenazi communities, on the Sabbath before the wedding (*spinholz*), the groom is called up to recite the blessings over the Torah (*Aufrufren*); among Sephardim he is called up on the Sabbath after the wedding (*Shabbat ḥatan*). It is customary for the bride and groom not to see each other for the week before their wedding, and they usually fast on their wedding day, until the actual ceremony. At the ceremony itself, the bride is dressed in white and her face is covered with a veil. Just before the ceremony, the groom lifts up the veil to see his bride's face (to make sure she is indeed his betrothed) and then lets it down again, in a ceremony called the Veiling of the Bride (*Badeken* or *Bedeckung*). The bride and groom are often brought by the Torah-bearing parents to the *ḥuppah,* and in Ashkenazi communities the bride is led in seven circuits around the groom, symbolically to create a protective circle to ward off all malignant forces. The bride then stands to the right of the groom, and the ceremony commences, conducted by an officiating rabbi. Often the seven benedictions are pronounced by family members, close friends, or distinguished guests. Traditionally, the groom hands over a ring (which must belong to him) and places it on the forefinger of her right hand, declaring her by this to be his lawfully wedded wife, according to the law of Moses and Israel. In some modern Conservative, Reform, and Egalitarian communities, there is an exchange of rings between the two parties. A peculiar custom found both in Eastern Europe and in some Middle Eastern communities is for the bride and groom to try to tread on each other's foot under the *ḥuppah*, signifying that the one who succeeded would become dominant in the marriage.

In some Middle Eastern communities, the husband would then take his newly wedded wife directly to the bridal home (suite) and carry her over the threshold, or he would enter her new home, treading over broken pottery and through water from an earthen pitcher poured down by the husband from the roof (Djerba, Libya). Furthermore, in Djerba the bride smeared broken eggs on the doorposts of the house, while in Georgia butter was similarly used, as powerful protective measures. In Afghanistan, a fowl was slaughtered to mark the occasion. Thus, the marriage cycle, on the one hand, was a time of great rejoicing but, on the other hand, it combined this joy with an element of tension and fear of the evil forces that lay in wait of the opportunity to jeopardize the couple's activities or harm them physically. For this reason, a broad variety of protective measures developed in the various communities, usually influenced by local practices, giving rise to a large number of local customs, which included elements of magic, superstition, and folklore.

Daniel Sperber

See also: Demon; Egg; India, Jews of; *Ketubbah*.

Bibliography

Epstein, Louis M. *The Jewish Marriage Contract: A Study in the Status of the Jewish Women in Jewish Law.* New York: Jewish Theological Seminary, 1927.

Hacohen, Menachem. *Jewish Life Cycle: Marriage.* Jerusalem: Keter, 1986–1993 (in Hebrew).

Klein, Moshe. *Wedding Traditions of the Various Jewish Communities.* Tel Aviv: Peretz, 1994.

"Marriage." In *Encyclopedia Judaica,* vol. 11, p. 1051. Jerusalem: Keter, 1971.

Sabar, Shalom, ed. "The Jewish Wedding in Art and Tradition of the Jewish Communities." *Rimonim* 6–7. Jerusalem: Society for Jewish Art, Hebrew University of Jerusalem, 1999.

Sperber, Daniel. *The Jewish Life Cycle: Custom, Lore and Iconography—Jewish Customs from the Cradle to the Grave.* Ramat Gan: Bar-Ilan University Press, 2008.

Meir Ba'al Ha'Nes, Rabbi

Rabbi Meir Ba'al Ha'Nes (Master of the Miracle), also known as Rabbi Meir, was a Jewish sage and *tanna* (teacher of the Mishnah) who lived during the time of the Mishnah, the collection of Jewish oral traditions compiled circa 200 C.E. and included in the Talmud. According to tradition his grave is located in the southern part of the city of Tiberias and is one of the most sacred, famous, and revered shrines among Jews in Israel and the Diaspora.

Unlike most of the sages of the Mishnah and the Talmud, whose lineage is known, neither his father's name nor the birthplace of Rabbi Meir is known. His common name was Rabbi Nehoray (Aram., light), and he is said to have been called Rabbi Meir because he lit up the eyes of the *ḥakhamim* (sages). The present popular view is that the *tanna* Rabbi Meir is the one buried in Tiberias, but the identification is problematic and has been contested by historians up to the present. In the thirteenth century, several pilgrims mentioned that Rabbi Meir Katzin was buried in Tiberias. The burial place has also been associated with Rabbi Meir ben Ya'akov, who came to Eretz Israel with Rabbi Yeḥiel of Paris, as well as with Rabbi Meir ben Yitzhak, the author of the *Akdamot for Shavuot*. The testimonies of other pilgrims refer to the grave of Rabbi Meir in Gush Ḥalav near Safed. With time, the Gush Ḥalav grave disappeared and people connected Rabbi Meir with Tiberias.

The first pilgrims to tour the Holy Land, Rabbi Benjamin of Tudela and Rabbi Petahiah of Regensburg, mention the grave of Rabbi Meir in Khila in Iraq. A folk tradition in northern Morocco mentions that Rabbi Meir Ba'al Ha'Nes is buried in Ksar El-Kebir, by the grave of the local saint Rabbi Yehudah Zabali. Rabbi Moshe Bassola, who visited Eretz Israel in 1522, described a grave of erected stones on a plateau in Tiberias, where people gathered in the evenings and mornings to pray and said that there was buried a certain Rabbi Meir, who had sworn not to sit down and thus had been buried standing up, but who was not Rabbi Meir of the Mishnah. Rabbi Isaac Luria (Ha'Ari), the greatest of the kabbalists, who used to visit Tiberias and the holy graves there, spoke about the grave of the *tanna* Rabbi Meir and that he was buried in a standing position. This determination by the Divine Ari of the place of the tomb of the *tanna* Rabbi Meir was followed and respected by the majority of the sages of his time and thereafter. Extensive folklore support has strengthened this determination and the tomb in Tiberias is recognized today as Rabbi Meir Ba'al Ha'Nes's grave.

Beginning in the thirteenth century the graves of Rabbi Meir Ba'al Ha'Nes in Tiberias and Rabbi Shimeon Bar Yoḥai in Meron became the most popular sites among

Jews in Eretz Israel and in the Diaspora. The expulsion of the Jews from Spain in 1492 and the development of Safed as an important kabbalistic center in the sixteenth century greatly contributed to attracting pilgrims to holy places in Eretz Israel. From this time onward, there was a significant increase in the veneration of saints among the Jews in North Africa. The different emissaries from Eretz Israel touring the Jewish communities in the Diaspora contributed to the divulgation of the great importance that Rabbi Meir Ba'al Ha'Nes's blessing holds for protection against all kinds of ailments and dangers. An almsbox in the name of Rabbi Meir could be found in almost every Jewish house, synagogue, and yeshiva and served for supporting the poor and the Jewish scholars in the Holy Land.

Rabbi Meir, a disciple of Rabbi Akiva and Rabbi Ishmael, played an important role in spreading the study of the Torah in the generation following the second-century Bar Kochba revolt, a failed Jewish revolt against Roman rule. Rabbi Meir also made a major contribution to the compilation of the Mishnah. According to tradition, every anonymous saying in the Mishnah is attributed to him. Apart from his great understanding of the Halakhah (Jewish religious laws), Rabbi Meir also excelled in the Aggadah. He was an accomplished orator beloved by all social classes. He divided his sermons into three portions: one-third Halakhah, one third Aggadah, and one-third fables. Rabbi Meir was versed in 300 fox fables. The sages said: "After Rabbi Meir passed away, the fable tellers disappeared."

Rabbi Meir's residence was in Tiberias. When the Roman edicts against the sages who ordained their disciples as rabbis became intolerable, Rabbi Meir was forced to flee to Asia Minor, where he joined his teacher, Rabbi Akiva, who also fled there due to the Roman persecutions.

Rabbi Meir was married to Beruriah, the daughter of Rabbi Ḥananiah ben Teradion, one of the ten martyrs. Beruriah is the only female mentioned in the Talmud as a female sage who participated in debates about the Halakhah with the talmudic sages. Her sayings were compared to those of the *tannaim*. Legend has it that for three years she studied 300 Halakhot (laws) a day from 300 great scholars. The Gemara tells about her wisdom with regard to ruffians who lived near Rabbi Meir and upset him frequently. Rabbi Meir wished them a merciful death. Beruriah said to him: "It is written 'Let the sins be consumed out of the earth' (Ps. 104:35), not sinners. Thus you should ask for compassion for them so they will repent." Rabbi Meir did so, and they repented.

The deed that crowned Rabbi Meir as a miracle maker for generations, and earned him the appellation of "Ba'al Ha'Nes" relates to saving Beruriah's sister, who had been taken to Rome and forced into a brothel. Beruriah asked Rabbi Meir to go and redeem her sister. He went there and said: "If no misdeed was done to her, a miracle will happen to her." He addressed the guard and asked him to free her. The guard said: "I am afraid that the authorities will kill me." Rabbi Meir said: "Take this money, give half of it as a bribe and keep the other half for yourself." The guard said: "When there is no more money, what shall I do?" He told the guard: "say: 'God of Meir, answer me,' and you will be saved." And the guard asked: "Who will guarantee that it will happen this way?" Rabbi Meir answered: "Now, you will see. Look, there are man-eating dogs over there. I will go there." Rabbi Meir took a branch and threw it at them. The dogs came running, ready to devour him. He said: "God of Meir, answer me," and they left him in peace. The guard believed Rabbi Meir and handed the woman over to him. When it became known, the authorities came to take the guard. He said: "God of Meir, answer me." They asked: "What is that?" He told them the story. They let him go, and he was saved.

Rabbi Meir died in Asia Minor. As mentioned in the Talmud, Rabbi Meir asked the local people to inform the people of Eretz Israel that a *tanna* had died there and that they should bring his body to the Holy Land. Rabbi Meir also requested that his coffin be placed by the seashore so that the waves could carry the coffin to Eretz Israel.

For generations, the rabbis advised the Jews that in times of trouble they should make a vow to Rabbi Meir Ba'al Ha'Nes in these words: "God of Meir, answer me." In 1695 Rabbi Eliyahu Hacohen from Izmir wrote: "If someone loses an object and then vows to provide oil for lighting lamps in honor of Rabbi Meir, he will immediately find the lost object." Rabbi Ḥaim Abulafia, who renewed the Jewish community in Tiberias in 1742, decreed that "he who makes a vow in the name of Rabbi Meir will find it is not fulfilled if it is paid in his own city, but only if the charity is donated solely to the holy city of Tiberias, so that Torah students in Tiberias are provided for." All Sephardic Jews in the Diaspora followed his decree.

In the book *Keter Shem Tov* it is said that in the name of the Ba'al Shem Tov (the founder of Hasidism) "if a person is in danger and in need of a miracle, he should give eighteen coins for candles for the synagogue and say wholeheartedly: 'I vow eighteen coins for candles for the soul of Rabbi Meir Ba'al Ha'Nes; God of Meir, answer me! God of Meir, answer me! God of Meir, answer me! May it be your will our God and God of our fathers, in the same way you heard the prayer of your slave Meir and performed miracles for him, please do the same for me and all your people Israel, who are in need of visible and hidden miracles. Amen, may it be your will." The Ḥasidim believed that a person tempted by bad thoughts could be relieved by placing a coin in an almsbox for Eretz Israel or for Rabbi Meir Ba'al Ha'Nes.

In 1866, at the site of Rabbi Meir's grave, the sages of Tiberias erected a shrine with two white domes overlooking the Sea of Galilee, a yeshiva, a synagogue, and rooms for pilgrims. For generations, the sages of Tiberias honored the tradition of visiting the grave on predetermined dates in order to pray and ask for mercy for all Jews. They published and distributed prayers and liturgies said at the grave of Rabbi Meir. When the shrine was completed in 1867, a *hillulah* (ritual celebration) in honor of Rabbi Meir was held on the fourteenth of Iyar, called a "second Passover." An impressive procession with Torah scrolls departed from the old synagogue Etz Ḥaim in the Old City, led by the rabbis of Tiberias, its sages, and representatives of the Ottoman authorities. Large amounts of money were collected in an auction of different mitzvot. The determination of the date of *hillulah* was strongly contested by the Ashkenazi community. Despite heavy protests, the *hillulah* continued to develop and to attract more and more pilgrims over the years. Large donations collected at the end of the twentieth century changed the nature of the site. The grave has been completely rebuilt, the yeshiva has been enlarged, and the shrine is bustling with pilgrims throughout the year.

The vast usage in folk art of the dome of Rabbi Meir's shrine, scenic pictures of Tiberias and the Sea of Galilee in *tashmishei kedushah* (Jewish ceremonial objects), *ketubbot*, pamphlets praising the *tanna*, tablecloths, mural paintings, and *parokhot* (curtains over the Ark) in synagogues, calendars, book covers, sukkah decorations, and others, along with the spreading in Eretz Isreal and in the Diaspora of stories and legends telling the miracles of Rabbi Meir, have undoubtedly contributed to his glorification. His presence in the daily life of Jews of different communities and their frequent appeals to him have established and strengthened the popularity of Rabbi Meir Ba'al Ha'Nes as one of the greatest saints of the people of Israel.

Issachar Ben-Ami

Bibliography

Ben-Ami, Issachar. *Saint Veneration Among the Jews in Morocco.* Detroit: Wayne State University Press, 1998.

Bier, Aharon. *Jewish Holy Places in Eretz Israel.* Jerusalem: Keter, 1988.

Eisenstein, Yehuda David, ed. *Otzar Yisrael.* Jerusalem: Sefer, 1972.

Vilnai, Zeev. *Holy Graves in Eretz Israel.* Jerusalem: Ahiever, 1986.

Weiss, Shraga. *Jewish Holy Sites in Eretz Israel.* Jerusalem: R. Mass, 1992.

Memorial Day

Observed on the fourth of Iyar, Yom Ha'zikaron (Memorial Day) commemorates those who died in the 1948 War of Independence and other wars in Israel.

The need for an official day to honor those who have fallen in Israel's wars was apparent soon after the War of Independence and became more acute with the subsequent wars and their victims; however, setting an appropriate date for this holiday was not without controversy. On the one hand, holding the holiday close to Independence Day on the fifth of Iyar would emphasize the contribution of the fallen to the establishment of the State of Israel. On the other hand, combining the two was potentially problematic, and bereaved parents stated that they preferred to keep them separate. In 1951, state officials decided that Memorial Day would be observed the day before Independence Day. This highlights the two holidays' intrinsic connection—the soldiers who gave their lives were responsible for the existence of Israel as an independent state—but keeps Independence Day from being a solemn occasion.

All over Israel, a siren blares in the evening to mark the start of the observance. Unlike Independence Day, which begins with an official state ceremony on Mount Herzl, Memorial Day did not originally start with an official ceremony in a specific place. Although there was an attempt to hold an opening ceremony on Mount Zion, the first official national observance at the start of Memorial Day was not introduced until after the Six-Day War of 1967, when the Western Wall plaza was designated for the ceremony.

In the evening, worshipers light memorial candles in the synagogue; candles are also lit in cemeteries and in private homes. In public places, the flag is lowered to half-mast. All places of entertainment are closed, by law, for twenty-four hours, starting in the evening. Radio and television broadcast programs featuring elegiac songs, classical music, stories of heroism, and personal accounts by soldiers, along with letters and excerpts from their writings.

The main events on Memorial Day are state ceremonies in military cemeteries, with the participation of government representatives. Various local communities hold their own commemorative observances, each in tune with its ideals and values. These events, too, are usually held by the graves of the fallen, adjacent to monuments to the dead, or in a room dedicated to their memory. In secular kibbutzim, it was long the custom to avoid religious texts, which were replaced by secular passages, including a *yizkor* (memorial prayer) written by Berl Katznelson, one of the leaders of the prestate labor movement, that make no reference to God. Over the years, the opposition to religious texts has diminished, and today they are generally part of local ceremonies.

Memorial Day concludes with a special recitation of the *yizkor* at Mount Herzl, immediately preceding the festivities for Independence Day. After the prayer, the national flag is raised to the top of the staff, as a sign for the start of the Independence Day celebrations.

Nili Aryeh-Sapir

Bibliography

Azaryahu, Maoz. *State Cults: Celebrating Independence and Commemorating the Fallen in Israel, 1948–1956.* Sede Boker: Ben-Gurion Heritage Center, 1995 (in Hebrew).

Ha'Cohen, Dvora, and Rabbi Menahem Ha'Cohen. "Independence Day." *Celebrations and Holidays,* vol. 5. Jerusalem: Keter, 1981 (in Hebrew).

Levinski, Yom Tov, ed. "Independence Day." In *The Book of Holidays,* vol. 7. Tel Aviv: Oneg Shabbat, 1956 (in Hebrew).

Shashar, Michael. *Sambation: Essays on Jewish Holidays.* Tel Aviv: Yediot Aharonot, 1992 (in Hebrew).

Sole, Moshe Zeev. *The Festivals of the Year.* Jerusalem: Keter, 1986 (in Hebrew).

Menorah

The menorah (Heb., lamp or candelabrum) is the golden seven-branched Temple candelabrum, one of the Tabernacle (or "tent of meeting," the movable sanctuary built in the desert) implements, and an important cultic vessel in the First and Second Temples. The shape of the seven-branched menorah is the central symbol of Judaism and a recurring symbol-motif in Jewish culture and art since the Temple period.

In the first Solomonic Temple, there were ten lamps (1 Kgs. 7:49; 2 Chr. 4:7). Some scholars claim that there was one cultic lamp, as in the Tabernacle, and ten additional lamps to light the space. In the Second Temple, there was one lamp, as in the Tabernacle. This lamp was removed in 169 B.C.E. by Antiochus Epiphanes IV. Judah Maccabee cleansed the Temple after the desecration and built a new lamp, which remained there in Herod's Temple until its destruction in 70 C.E. (1 Macc. 4:44; 2 Macc. 10) by Titus, who conquered Jerusalem (*J.W.* 5:216–217; 7:148–149). The raiding of the menorah and its transportation to Rome, along with the other Temple implements, on the shoulders of Roman soldiers is depicted on the triumphal arch built in Rome on the via Sacra some twelve years later in Titus's honor.

A detailed description of the menorah, including its material shape and construction, is given in the instructions transmitted to Moses on Mount Sinai to build the Tabernacle in the desert (Exod. 25:31–40) and in the description of Bezalel actually constructing the menorah according to the divine directions (Exod. 37:17–24).

The instructions specify the material, weight, and form of the menorah, but do not give measurements, as are given to other furnishings. According to the instructions, the menorah should be cast or carved of pure solid gold and its weight a talent. It should have six branches—three on each side—and a central shaft, but it is not specified whether it should have a stand. The branches are decorated with cups, knobs, and flowers: three "almondlike cups" shaped as almond blossoms, with each divided into a knob, and a flower on each side of every branch.

Though detailed, the description of the menorah is somewhat complicated and enigmatic. For instance, it is not clear what the "almondlike cups" or the knobs are. Furthermore, because the menorah of the Tabernacle or the First Temple has not survived, it is very difficult to know its exact shape in detail. Its form is studied today from early visual depictions, some in archaeological finds, none earlier than the First Temple period, in conjunction with the textual descriptions; some details, such as the form of its base, are hotly debated by scholars.

Other points of discussion are the veracity of these depictions and whether they correspond to the Tabernacle menorah, whose descriptions in Exodus are claimed by scholars to be later texts, or to the Second Temple menorah.

The difficulty encountered in understanding the structuring details of the menorah are reflected in the midrashim to the following verse:

> And this is the work of the candlestick was of beaten gold: unto the shaft thereof, unto the flowers thereof, was beaten work: according unto the pattern which the Lord had showed Moses, so he made the candlestick. . . . Now this was how the lampstand was made, out of hammered work of gold. From its base to its flowers, it was hammered work; according to the pattern that the Lord had shown Moses, so he made the lampstand (Num. 8:4).

The word מקשה is interpreted in its two senses, one as one piece of gold, and the second referring to קשה (difficult), describing the difficulties Moses had in implementing the instructions to build the lamp. It is related in the Midrash that God helped Moses by showing him a visual model (and other aids), but in the end he did not overcome this difficulty and passed on the task to Bezalel, who actually built it without seeing the model. (Bezalel is considered the exemplary artist and patron of artists) (*Bam. Rab.* 15:4; *Tanḥuma* Beha'alotkha 11; *Yalqut Shimoni* Beha'alotkha 8).

Early depictions of the menorah date back only to the first century B.C.E. (incised menorah on a plaster fragment; a coin of Antigonus, the last Hasmonean king [40–37 B.C.E.]; and others). They vary in form and detail, though they display some identical features, such as the six curved branches.

As different opinions prevail as to the date of the texts, especially those describing the Tabernacle lamp, it is uncertain to which candelabrum the depictions refer.

The best-known depiction of the menorah is the Titus Arch relief, which was discussed by many scholars (Narkiss, Sperber). This is probably the only one made as a realistic historic image of the actual Temple lamp transported to Rome. But it has a heavy octagonal stand that does not correspond to any of the descriptions; therefore it is conjectured that its original stand was broken and that this is an additional base.

In the Tabernacle the menorah stood in front of the curtain *parokhet*, which separated the Holy of Holies, containing the Ark, from the Holy (Exod. 26:35). Its lamps (*nerot)* using pure olive oil were lit by the high priest every evening (Exod. 27:20; 30:7–8; Lev. 24:2). This light is called the perpetual light (*ner ha'tamid).* Hence it became the prototype for the *ner ha'tamid* lit later in synagogues in front of the Ark in remembrance of the Temple. If it was extinguished, it was considered a bad omen for the future, just as it was for the lamp from which the *ner ha'tamid* was lit every day *(ner ma'aravi).*

The Menorah as Symbol

Apart from being an actual cultic vessel in the Temples, the seven-branched gold menorah functions as a constant symbol in Jewish culture from biblical times to the present, including its role as the symbol of the State of Israel (modeled after the Titus Arch menorah).

Even by the time of the Temple, the menorah alone or together with other cult objects was considered a metonym for the Temple, for Jerusalem, and for the Land of Israel. From the various depictions dating from the time of the Temple, it is evident that the menorah was much more important for its symbolic significance than for its precise depiction.

It should be noted that reproduction of the menorah imitating that of the Temple was prohibited (*b. Rosh Hashanah* 24a; *Menahot* 28b; *Avodah Zarah* 43a), but apparently this did not apply to depictions of the menorah.

Both collectively and individually, the menorah served as an identifying symbol of Judaism. It is found in synagogues, on tombs, and on objects belonging to Jews, such as clay oil lamps and jewelry. The menorah acquired multiple meanings, some of them in the mystical and magic traditions; it served as a symbol of God and His light, of the light of the Torah, of the sun and the planets, of the tree of life, and, in particular, of redemption and salvation, both national and personal.

The menorah as a symbol of redemption and messianic hope features in the vision of the prophet Zachariah, who lived in the time of the rebuilding of the Second Temple (520 B.C.E.) (Zach. 4:2–12). In his vision, he saw a gold menorah with a bowl above it (Gullah) feeding it with olive oil, flanked by two olive trees. The vision is explained as a good omen, promising the help of God in rebuilding the Temple. In later texts—rabbinic exegesis to Zachariah's prophesy, by Rashi (Solomon ben Isaac of Troyes), Abraham Ibn Ezra and others—this vision is understood in a far wider context as a symbol for God's promise for redemption in messianic times and is considered an eschatological symbol.

In the third-century Syrian synagogue of Dura Europos, the menorah features along with the shofar (ram's horn trumpet) and *lulav* (palm branch) on the central panel along with the sacrifice of Isaac (on Mount Moriah, identified with the Temple mount) and the depiction of the Temple where it symbolizes the past Temple, the covenant between God and Abraham, and the hope for a future rebuilding of the Temple. A similar meaning is conveyed in the mosaic floors of synagogues in the land of Israel dating from the fourth to sixth centuries C.E. (Hammat Tiberias Beit Alpha and others). There the menorah is represented along with a depiction of a Temple façade and with other implements as a reminder of the Temple and of hopes of the future rebuilding of the Temple.

As in synagogue decoration, the menorah expresses collective redemption; its appearance on funerary art on gravestones, sarcophagi, and catacombs (in Israel's Beit She'arim, in the Diaspora Catacombs in Rome) expresses the hope for individual redemption: resurrection of the dead expected to follow the arrival of the messiah.

In a similar way, it features in conjunction with the Tabernacle implements on the first page of hand-written Bible manuscripts from Egypt (tenth century) and from Spain called מקדשיה (thirteenth to fifteenth centuries), symbolizing the connection to the past temples and hope for future rebuilding of the Temple. These Bibles are called מקדשיה and thus are compared to the Temple themselves.

In medieval kabbalistic literature, the menorah was interpreted as a mystical and magical symbol. The mystical interpretation went in two main directions. The first views the menorah as representing the celestial bodies, following Josephus Flavius (*Ant.*, 111144–146). The second, more widespread, sees the menorah as representing God in its structural composition. The first kabbalist known to have given this interpretation is Rabbi Asher Ben David of Provence in the first half of the thirteenth century and later spread by others. According to this view, the menorah represents at the same time the absolute unity of God as it was made of one piece of solid gold, מקשה אחת, and the multiplicity of the divine aspects of the divine entity, the *sefirot* as represented by the branches of the menorah. The seven *sefirot* in the menorah are *tiferet* (beauty) in the middle, *hod* (majesty), *ḥesed* (love), *malkhut* (kingdom), *yesod* (foundation), *netsaḥ* (victory), *gevurah* (strength), three on each side.

In practical Kabbalah magical properties were attributed to the menorah, such as those ascribed to the menorah in Psalm 67. Around the fifteenth century, an interesting exchange of symbols occurred. The menorah, considered a magical symbol and believed both to have been engraved on the shield of King David and to have helped him to win his wars, is exchanged gradually for the six-pointed star, considered a magical protective symbol and called the Shield of David. Later in the nineteenth century, the star took the place of the menorah as a Jewish identity symbol.

Esther Juhasz

See also: Jerusalem and the Temple; Shiviti-Menorah; Symbols.

Bibliography

Israeli, Yael, ed. *In the Light of the Menorah, Story of a Symbol.* Jerusalem: Israel Museum, 1999.

Narkiss, Bezalel. "A Scheme of the Sanctuary from the Time of Herod the Great." *Journal of Jewish Art* 1 (1974): 6–15.

METHUSELAḤ

See: Age and the Aged; Noah

MESSIAH AND REDEEMER

In folk tradition the messiah is the savior born of the seed of David who will appear on earth one day, bringing the longed-for redemption. The term "*messiah*" (Heb., *mashiaḥ*) stems from the Hebrew root משח—anointed with oil—meaning the man chosen by God to be king (e.g., 1 Sam. 9–10). The yearning for the revelation of a supreme power, bringing security, might, abundance, and peace, intensified in times of political stress, enslavement, exile, and suffering, giving rise to tales about a supernatural figure that would redeem the people of Israel and revive its glory: the messiah.

In the course of centuries, yearning for a messiah was expressed in various writings, exposing tensions between diverse perceptions concerning the nature of the days of the messiah, the characteristics of the messiah, the messiah's role in the process of redemption, and the time of redemption. These tensions are also embedded in the folktales and reflect the cultural contexts in which they were created.

There is a specific typology of the way redemption and redeemers appear in descriptions, tales, and visions throughout Jewish history. The prototype of the descriptions and tales of redemption is the first story of redemption, that is, the Exodus, and the model for the redeemer is the figure of Moses. The figures of redeemers and their struggles are depicted in the various writings by analogy with the Exodus in the Bible and the Aggadah (in the Talmud). The utopian images of the world to come stem from portrayals of the glorious past of the people of Israel in the days of the kingdom of David and Solomon, who attained exceptional idealization.

The Development of the Messianic Tale

Although rabbinic messianic sayings frequently mention premessianic tribulations—his wars, his origin, names, and the nature of the Days of Redemption—there is no complete narrative or portrayal of the messiah from his birth to the successful completion of his endeavor. It was only in the Middle Ages that the story of the messiah appeared as a complete and coherent narrative in the apocalyptic *Book of Zerubavel,* apparently written in the first half of the seventh century in the Land of Israel. This work describes, in great detail the coming of the messiah at the appointed time, referring to his deeds, wars, enemies, and helpers, until his success in establishing a perfect reality, a world based on new principles, and his bringing Celestial Jerusalem down from heaven.

The *Book of Zerubavel* presents the tradition of the messianic precursor, the messiah son of Joseph, from the tribe of Ephraim, who will die in the battlefield shortly before the appearance of the messiah son of David. The messiah son of Joseph is a mortal warrior, fighting against the forces of evil, and he even succeeds in preserving the independence of the kingdom of Judea for a certain period of time but dies in the decisive battle against evil. It is only after his death that the messiah son of David appears in the Arbel Valley by the Sea of Galilee, reveals himself to the elders of the people of Israel, and proves that he is the messiah. Then he brings the dead to life and heads their army in the last battle. The messiah son of David does not stain his hands with blood; he annihilates evil by spiritual means only.

This narrative model continues to feed folk imagination, but other narrative patterns have developed alongside it, stemming from new beliefs and schools. With the spread of the ideas of Rabbi Isaac Luria in the sixteenth century and the proliferation of stories praising him, a form of messianic tale developed, featuring a hero who is not the mythical messiah set to appear at the end of days but a saintly human being, mediating between heaven and earth, who might hasten the coming of the messiah and of redemption. In these tales the holy man tests the faith of his disciples. They fail the tests, and their failure postpones the coming of redemption. An outstanding example of this type of narrative is the story about Rabbi Isaac Luria, who invited his disciples to go up to Jerusalem on Sabbath Eve (*Shivḥei Ha'Ari*). This type of plot reappears also in the stories about the mystical rabbi Israel ben Eliezer (called the Ba'al Shem Tov), the prominent kabbalist Rabbi Ḥaim ben Atar, and other holy men.

Alongside the story of the mythical messiah and the tales about holy men, an additional type of narra-

Detail from "Meeting the Messiah" (Łódź, 1935), from the Szyk Haggadah. *(The Robbins Family Collection. Reproduced with the cooperation of The Arthur Szyk Society, Burlingame, California, www.szyk.org)*

tive developed, about a wise man who tries to destroy evil by practicing Kabbalah mysticism and thus hasten the coming of the messiah and with him national and cosmic redemption. However, the human limitations of the wise man cause him to fail badly, and even empower evil. This type of narrative developed around the figure of the kabbalist Rabbi Yosef dela Reina.

Three basic folk narrative patterns developed over time, each telling about the redeemer and his struggle against evil, and each representing a different perception of redemption and of the messianic endeavor: the pattern portraying the mythical messiah, fighting mythical evil until redemption; the pattern portraying the holy person with supernatural knowledge, who tests his disciples' faith, their failure, and eventual delaying of redemption; and the pattern portraying a wise man, well-versed in the practical aspect of the Kabbalah, who tries to subdue mythical evil by means of oaths but fails because of his human limitations and as a result sins and causes others to do so. These three patterns are models, leading to the development of other messianic tales that continue to appear at times of increasing messianic expectations, such as the mythical tales about Shabtai Zvi and Nathan of Gaza, the stories about David Alroy and Shlomo Molkho, as well as stories praising the *tzaddikim* (Hasidic rabbis), who tried to reform the world and hasten redemption.

One might perceive these patterns as a theme composed of three elements of plot: the redeemer's decision to bring about redemption, the struggle against evil, and success or failure. These elements take various forms in the different patterns. The decision to bring about redemption appears in three different versions: (a) the mythical one, in which the time of the supernatural redeemer's arrival is determined by a supreme power; (b) the version in which the redeemer, a holy man, decides to make use of an opportune time revealed to him by supernatural knowledge; and (c) the version in which a human redeemer, wise and knowledgeable about the secrets of practical Kabbalah, decides to compel the supreme powers to do his bidding.

The struggle against evil appears in two main versions: (a) the mythical one, displaying a physical struggle occurring in many stages, with the assistance of various helpers and holy objects; and (b) tales about holy men, in which the struggle is mainly spiritual and rarely described.

Success or failure is portrayed in three ways: (a) as mythical, in which the messiah succeeds in bringing about redemption; (b) in tales about holy men, who fail as the result of their disciples' improper conduct and the insufficient faith of their generation; and (c) in the version in which the wise man fails due to his own weaknesses when adjuring and subduing the supreme powers, and through his failure sins and causes others to sin, delaying redemption.

Hebrew literature since the beginning of the twentieth century continued to weave the tale of the messiah and of redemption into its works, attempting to link modern events to Jewish history and tradition. Most literary attempts to confront historical events of utmost importance to the Jewish people incorporate the theme of redemption and the figure of the messiah as a recurring essential element in Jewish thought and as an all-powerful motive for the endeavors of the Jew in modern times. But what used to be permeated with innocent faith, which confirmed and empowered social and religious institutions as well as life patterns, has been replaced by doubt and frustration in modern Hebrew literature, as it is unwilling to adopt the previously prevalent religious, harmonic perception. The Jewish revolutionary, whether Zionist or socialist, is deeply influenced by his affinity with the figures of redeemers in folk literature, but this affinity is always dialectical and displays doubt and disillusionment alongside hope and prospects for the future (e.g., *Stories of the Revolution,* by H. Hazaz; *Days and Nights,* by N. Bistricki). The narrative pattern of the redeemer, which reflects the presence of God and the messiah in Israeli tradition, changes its features in the modern era and becomes, in most works, the symbol of the futile search for divine transcendental presence (e.g., the heroes of Ya'akov Shabtai and some of the heroes of *The Last Jew,* by Yoram Kaniuk).

Yael Poyas

See also: Elijah the Prophet.

Bibliography

Patai, Raphael. *The Messiah Texts.* Detroit: Wayne State University Press, 1979.

Saperstein, Marc, ed. *Essential Papers on Messianic Movements and Personalities in Jewish History.* New York: New York University Press, 1992.

Sharot, Stephen. *Messianism, Mysticism and Magic.* Chapel Hill: University of North Carolina Press, 1982.

Silver, Abba Hillel. *A History of Messianic Speculation in Israel.* Boston: Beacon, 1959.

MEZUZAH

The *mezuzah* is the parchment scroll inscribed with particular Hebrew verses from the Torah affixed to the doorpost of the entrance to Jewish homes and rooms within it. In the Bible, *mezuzah* simply means "doorpost" (Exod. 12:7), but later it acquired the meaning of the actual object placed on the doorpost. The biblical commandment to "write *them* upon the *mezuzot* [doorposts] of your house and upon the gates" is given twice (Deut. 6:9 and 11:20) but does not specify which exact words of God are meant by "them." Rabbinical tradition employs words in Deuteronomy 6:4–9 and 11:13–21; the Samaritans (see: Samaritans) who carve their *mezuzot* on large stones, use different texts—in particular, the Ten Commandments.

Other laws concerning the preparation of the *mezuzah* were set by the rabbis in the talmudic period and later elaborated in such works as the Jewish philosopher and Torah scholar Maimonides's *Mishneh Torah.* According to these rules, the *mezuzah* is prepared from the skin of a kosher animal (size not indicated) and inscribed by a *sofer* (a Jewish scribe who transcribes prescribed texts) upon one side, with the above passages, in square letters, commonly occupying twenty-two lines. It should be affixed to the doorpost of every residential room; rooms such as bathrooms or storage rooms are excluded. Ashkenazi Jews affixed it also to their synagogues' entrances, while the Sephardim did not. Today it is common to affix it as well in other public buildings. Commonly, the *mezuzah* is affixed in the upper third of the right side of the doorpost and should slant inward—actually representing a compromise between the vertical (Rashi [Solomon ben Isaac of Troyes]) and horizontal (Rabenu Tam [Ya'akov ben Meir, 1100–1171]) positions common in the Middle Ages. Halakhah further specifies that a blessing should be recited when the *mezuzah* is attached to the doorpost and that it must be inspected twice within seven years.

The practice of protecting the house against evil spirits with written formulas or other magic objects is known from the folklore of many people in antiquity as well as the modern era. Early Jewish sources and modern scholars thus disputed whether the *mezuzah* is a protective amulet. While the Talmud occasionally refers to the protective powers of the *mezuzah* (see *y. Pe'ah* 1:1), Maimonides claimed that those "foolish hearts" who believe so "turn a commandment" whose purpose is to emphasize the love of God "into an amulet" (*m. Sefer Ahavah, Tefillin* 5:4). Believing in the potency of the *mezuzah* as a protection against evil spirits (*shedim*), Jews in the Middle Ages used to inscribe on the parchment kabbalistic formulas and names of protective angels, and draw magical designs. But Maimonides's decision finally became the norm, and no such formulas were added on the face of the *mezuzah.* However, to this day the back of the parchment is inscribed with two powerful names of God, familiar also from standard Hebrew amulets. Most common is the name Shaddai (Almighty), which is inscribed so that it is visible when the parchment is rolled up. The name Shaddai is considered especially powerful in protective formulas, but in the context of the *mezuzah* it is traditionally interpreted as standing for שומר דלתות ישראל ("Guardian of the doors of Israel" [i.e., Jewish homes]). The second name is the so-called fourteen-letter name כוזו במוכסז כוזו, usually written on the back of the parchment. This name is derived by one of the forms of the system called *temurah* (substitution), according to which every letter represents the one preceding it in the Hebrew alphabet (thus, the hidden name is יהוה אלוהינו יהוה).

The belief in the power of the *mezuzah* led some authorities to strongly recommend appropriate codes of behavior toward the *mezuzah.* The most prevalent custom is to kiss the *mezuzah,* or touch it with bare fingers and

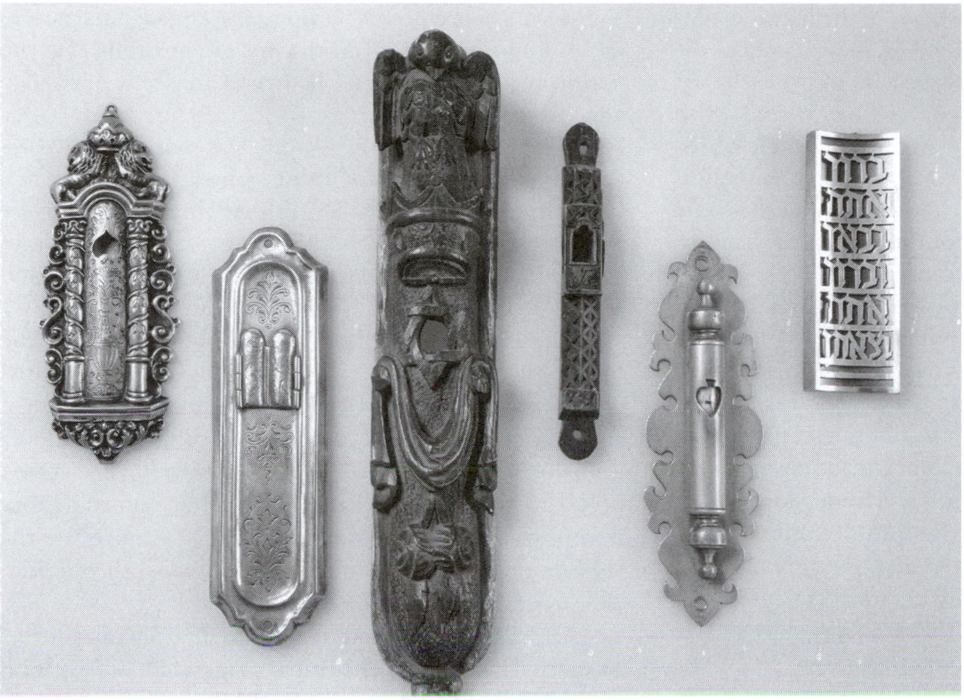

Assorted *mezuzah* cases. *(Jewish School/The Bridgeman Art Library/Getty Images)*

kiss them, every time one enters or leaves the room or apartment. This custom is mentioned in *Minhagei Maharil*, the book of customs of the German rabbi Jacob ben Moshe Moelin Halevi (called the Maharil; 1360?–1427). Another German authority, Rabbi Meir of Rothenberg (called the Maharam; ca. 1215–1293), urged his fellow Jews to place in their homes many *mezuzot,* as "no demon can have power over a house upon which the *mezuzah* is properly affixed" (*Responsa Maharam,* Cremona, 1557, no. 108). To this day there are rabbis who claim that car accidents or other misfortunes can be prevented if the *mezuzot* are properly written and periodically inspected.

It became customary in the talmudic period to encase the rolled parchment in a receptacle, which the Talmud called a שפופרת (tube). As Rabbi Judah (third century C.E.) objected to this practice, one may assume it was a new custom at the time (*Mezuzah* 2:10). But despite the objection, the custom was apparently widely accepted early on and later adopted by many Jewish communities, East and West. It is assumed that the talmudic tube was plain and no decorations adorned its face—whether made of wood, metal, or, more likely, simple reed. The tradition of using reeds was still prevalent in the Italian communities of the Renaissance and Baroque period, as is testified by Rabbi Judah Leon de Modena (1571–1648), who in his work *Historia de riti hebraici* (Venice, 1638, II,2) calls it *canna* (reed).

European *mezuzah* cases were made of a variety of materials reflecting the status of their owners and their artistic tastes. In both the Sephardic and Ashkenazi worlds, plain *mezuzah* cases were most common; however, the highly ornamental *mezuzah* case was much more at home among the Ashkenazim, especially high-ranking members of the community and large synagogues, in Central and Eastern Europe. Extant examples are exquisitely carved of wood in a style and technique familiar from other objects (e.g., Torah pointers), and there are some decorative silver cases, executed by skilled silversmiths, who at times even embedded them with semiprecious stones. As a rule, Ashkenazi (and other) cases have a small opening to show the word "Shaddai," inscribed on the rolled parchment. On some East European cases the aperture has tiny doors, at times inscribed with another "name" of God associated with Shaddai, that is, קרע שטן (lit., "rend Satan"). Other decorative symbols include designs familiar from local Jewish ceremonial objects, such as the Torah crown, the Ten Commandments, the four "holy animals" (lion, tiger, deer, and eagle—the latter commonly shown as double-headed), twisted pillars (generally standing for Jachin and Boaz, the two pillars that stood at the entrance vestibule of Solomon's Temple [I Kgs 7:21; II Chr 3:17]), and floral designs. In some cases German examples featured human figures as well (e.g., praying Jews).

Italian *mezuzah* cases were at times made in the shape of rectangular thin brass boxes, with a circular aperture covered with glass through which the word "Shaddai" is visible. In Eretz Israel of the Old Yishuv, olive wood cases gained widespread popularity and were decorated with holy sites, most often the Western Wall and Rachel's Tomb, the visual hallmarks of the Holy Land.

Most attractive and unusual are the *mezuzah* covers of Moroccan Jews. The custom in Morocco had been to hang over the *mezuzah* at the entrance of the house an embroidered cover in the form of a shield, reminiscent of the Moroccan tefillin (phylacteries) case. The cover is made of velvet and embroidered in gold or silver threads with typical designs: flowers, *ḥamsa* (see: Symbols) elements, protective pairs of birds, and so on. Most remarkably is the name of the mistress of the house, which is centrally embroidered in the upper part of the cover, just beneath the word "Shaddai" at the top center.

In modern times, the *mezuzah* covers feature old designs and familiar motifs, but many new materials and modern decorative features have been adopted. Side by side with traditional materials, *mezuzah* cases today are made of Jerusalem stone, glass, fiberglass, plexiglass, ceramic, plastic, molded rubber, mold-made paper (handmade paper actually produced on a cylinder machine or a cylindrical mold), anodized titanium, ceramic alpaca, and combinations of various materials. A common feature of the modern *mezuzot,* especially in Israel, is the replacement of the word "Shaddai" with the enlarged letter *shin* (though sometimes both are used). Craftsmen in the United States and Israel create *mezuzah* covers often aimed at particular sectors of the Jewish population, clearly reflected in the combination of materials and designs. In addition to covers made for the various Jewish denominations, some are made for special groups, such as those for children's rooms, which are designed in the shape of a car, Noah's Ark, or other toylike motifs. Though halakhically unnecessary, another recent phenomenon is the car *mezuzah.* In Israel some institutions and sectors, such as the army or police, produce their own *mezuzah* cases, embedded with their familiar logos or emblems.

Shalom Sabar

See also: Amulets; Samaritans; Symbols.

Bibliography

Gordon, Martin L. "Mezuzah: Protective Amulet or Religious Symbol?" *Tradition* 16:4 (1977): 7–40.

Landsberger, Franz. "The Origin of the Decorated Mezuzah." *Hebrew Union College Annual* 31 (1960): 149–166.

Rosenbaum, Belle. *Upon Thy Doorposts: The Law, the Lore, the Love of Mezuzot. A Personal Collection.* New York: Jacob and Belle Rosenbaum Foundation, 1995.

Shachar, Isaiah. *Jewish Tradition in Art: The Feuchtwanger Collection of Judaica.* Jerusalem: Israel Museum, 1981.

Trachtenberg, Joshua. *Jewish Magic and Superstition: A Study in Folk Religion.* New York: Behrman's Jewish Book House, 1939.

MIDRASH

Midrash (Heb., מדרש) is a particular genre of rabbinic literature comprising four major forms: (1) biblical exegesis; (2) halakhic discussion; (3) aggadic narrative; and (4) public sermon. Midrashic literature is also the main source for Jewish folk literature from antiquity and late antiquity.

The noun "midrash"—from the root *drsh* (דרש)—appears only twice in the Bible (2 Chr. 13:22 and 24:27), both times meaning "book" or "writing." This narrow meaning evolved in Second Temple writings and later in rabbinic literature to primarily mean "to search," "to seek," "to examine," and "to investigate."

The *darshan,* the individual who interprets the biblical verse, might decide not to uncover the original context or meaning of the biblical verse. While aware of these, he can choose to invent new readings that validate his own needs or the needs of his generation. The verse's polysemy—and its potentially different or contradictory meanings—enable the *darshan* to use or manipulate the verse in order to support his own religious, theological, ideological, or halakhic ideas.

Midrash is divided into two major subgenres: Midrash Halakhah and Midrash Aggadah. In Midrash Halakhah, the sages usually interpret biblical verses to support their innovative halakhic positions, while in Midrash Aggadah they offer literary interpretations, having no direct halakhic implications, upon the verses. Scholarship traditionally dates Midrash Halakhah to the Tannaitic period (first two centuries C.E.) and Midrash Aggadah to the Amoraic period (approximately the third to sixth centuries C.E.); however, as many scholars have shown, this historical division is not absolute, as much aggadic material appears in the tannaitic corpus.

During the Tannaitic period, two main textual corpuses make use of midrashic material: the Mishnah and the Tosefta, and the *Midreshei ha'Tannaim.* The pre-eminent third-century halakhic work known as the Mishnah is traditionally attributed to Rabbi Yehuda ha'Nasi's redaction. The Tosefta, a large collection of segments that were left out of the Mishnah and collected over the following two centuries, is structurally similar to the Mishnah. The category of *Midreshei ha'Tannaim* is a scholarly designation used to describe a series of tannaitic compositions interpreting both the halakhic and literary sections of the Torah. The compositions follow the order of the Torah, skipping over Genesis and beginning with Exodus: *Mekhilta de'Rabbi Yishmael* and *Mekhilta de'Rabbi Shimon Bar Yohai* are dedicated to Exodus; the *Sifra,* also known as *Torat Kohanim,* is dedicated to Leviticus; *Sifrei Bamidbar* and *Sifrei Zuta* are dedicated to Numbers; and *Sifrei Devarim* is dedicated to Deuteronomy.

Significantly, midrashic material can also be found in several other sources: Second Temple literature, the writings of Jewish Hellenist authors such as Josephus Flavius and Philo of Alexandria, and early Christian writings, particularly the New Testament.

During the Amoraic period, the sages reached a peak of creativity, composing hundreds of brief literary texts. These texts can be divided into two major groups: exegetical narrative expansions of the biblical story, in which the sages rewrite the original text in light of their own theological, philosophical, and cultural understandings, and biographical narratives of the sages (Heb., *Ma'ashe ḥakhamim*), in which the sages recount variegated tales about their colleagues and daily life in Palestinian and Babylonian Jewish communities of late antiquity. These stories not only describe the house of study (Heb., *beit ha-midrash*) and the sages who studied in it but also grant a hearing to the diverse spectrum of voices usually unheard during antiquity and late antiquity, including those of women, children, and slaves.

The midrashic material from the Amoraic period is collected in two large corpuses: the Talmuds and the aggadic Midrash compilations. There are two Talmuds: the Talmud Yerushalmi (the Palestinian Talmud), created primarily in the Galilee at the beginning of the fifth century C.E., and the Talmud Bavli (the Babylonian Talmud), known also as the "Talmud" or Gemara, created in Babylonia and edited around the seventh century C.E. The aggadic Midrash compilations include the "Classical Midrash," mainly collected and edited in Palestine during the Amoraic period, and the "Postclassical Midrash," collected in many different locales, including Babylonia, the Balkans, and southern Europe, from the end of the Amoraic period until the end of the first millennium. Chief among midrashic compilations are *Midrash Rabba* and *Pesiqta de'Rav Kahana. Midrash Rabba* gathers ten distinct compilations, which were collected at different times in different places, under one name; five contain aggadic homilies on the five books of the Torah, and five contain aggadic homilies on the five scrolls (Song of Songs, Ruth, Ecclesiastes, Esther, and Lamentations). *Pesiqta de'Rav Kahana* is unique in that it is structured upon the annual cycle of sections from the Torah that the prophets publicly read on festivals and specially designated Sabbaths. The largest homiletical compilations from the postclassical period are the *Tanḥuma,* a midrash on the five books of the Torah; *Avot de'Rabbi Nathan,* which follows tractate *Avot* of the Mishnah; and *Pirqe de'Rabbi Eliezer,* the latest compilation, written after the rise of Islam and containing a rewrite of the book of Genesis and of the first part of Exodus.

Ever since the Middle Ages, the midrashic traditions have been retold again and again, and they are found in all the important story anthologies such as *Midrash Aseret ha'Dibberot, Alphabet of Ben Sira,* and *Ḥibbur Yafe min ha'Yeshua.*

Haim Weiss

See also: Rabbinic Literature.

Bibliography

Frenkel, Yona. *The Ways of the Aggada and Midrash.* Ramat Gan: Yad La'Talmud (Massada), 1991 (in Hebrew).

Hasan-Rokem, Galit. *Web of Life: Folklore and Midrash in Rabbinic Literature.* Stanford, CA: Stanford University Press, 2000.

Yassif, Eli. *The Hebrew Folktale: History, Genre, Meaning,* trans. J.S. Teitelbaum. Bloomington: Indiana University Press, 1999.

MIMUNA FESTIVAL

The Moroccan-Jewish Mimuna festival is a metamorphosis of one of the oldest festivals in human history, dedicated to celebrating the renewal of nature in the spring and its regeneration after the winter hibernation. This festival, held in communities throughout Israel and Morocco, has become a significant new festival for North African immigrants and others in Israel and shows how ethnic behavior succeeds in perpetuating itself in a new cultural environment. As a festival with deep roots in the Jewish tradition, it contributes to preserving some features of Jewish cultural identity and original communal values.

Roots in an Agrarian Society

In the biblical tradition, Passover was normally designated for this celebration, but the constraints that were thereafter imposed on Passover ceremonies and food consumption—especially on ordinary bread and other foods, in the rabbinical tradition—changed the substance of this ancient and central Hebrew festival. It morphed from a celebration of the cycle of life to a national and a religious festival. In numerous Mediterranean Jewish communities, and especially among North African Jews, the night and day following the end of the Passover festival were used for the reappropriation of some ancient spring traditions and the return to ordinary food and bread consumption after the Passover interruption. However, nowhere other than Morocco did this new celebration acquire such an institutionalized and enlarged set of ceremonies and behaviors, for historical and sociocultural reasons. In Moroccan-Jewish communities, the Mimuna took on numerous new cultural meanings—from economic, livelihood, and daily life meanings to friendship between Jews and Muslims and messianic aspirations.

Mimuna, or *Maymuna* (the feminine form of *Maymun*), is an Arabic word that means "lucky," "fortunate," "blessed," and the traditional blessing said at the festival is: "May you earn and be fortunate." The blessing is derived from the traditional agricultural calendar: The Mimuna takes place at the beginning of the crucial harvest season, on which the livelihood of both individuals

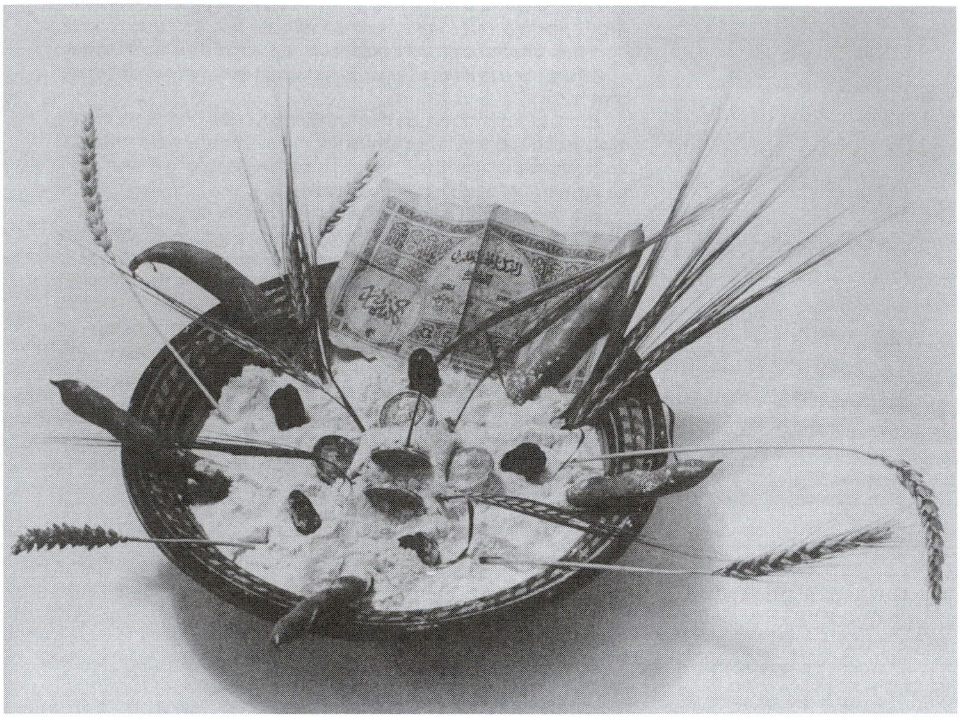

A Mimuna plate, Morocco. The items in the plate are symbols of fertility and wealth. *(Courtesy of the Israel Museum, Jerusalem. Photo by Reuben Milon)*

and the community depends. A Moroccan-Jewish proverb hints at the importance of the agricultural calendar: "Who didn't make good benefits between Passover and Pentecost would find where to die," that is, he is very unlucky; this emphasizes the link between spring agriculture and economic success. The food and drinks served during the night ceremonies of Mimuna, including fresh beans, ears of barley or wheat, branches of blooming fruit trees such as fig or pomegranate, milk and butter, drinks and liquors, and plates of fine flour and sweets, homemade cookies, and marmalade, also have symbolic and agricultural implications. These ceremonies include the rendition of some biblical verses from the Book of Proverbs and paragraphs from the mishnaic Chapters of the Fathers, and the tasting of the goodies by large groups of family members, friends, and neighbors, who visit numerous houses on this night. In some families, they also prepare a kind of unsalted and unleavened fried bread, called *mofleta,* which is served with butter and honey to relatives and guests and is often accompanied by glasses of green tea.

The night ceremonies end with the preparation of dough for the new bread to be baked and consumed on the following day. On this occasion, the mistress of the house kneads the dough and performs blessings for the young girls and boys of the family and friends, wishing them good luck in marriage and placing some coins and light jewels on the surface of the dough. Thus, this ceremony is also a good occasion for bringing together boys and girls from large families and of acquaintances and giving them an opportunity to meet each other in the hope of possible marital arrangements. On this festival, betrothals also were celebrated.

Multidimensional Aspects

Apart from these communal family, friendship, and hospitality aspects, the Mimuna festival encourages and exemplifies good relations between Jews and Muslims. According to some scholars, beginning at the end of the seventeenth century, after a period of violent conflict between Muslims and Jews, numerous Moroccan Jews, especially in rural communities, would visit the home of their Muslim acquaintances before the night ceremonies. During these visits, Jews offered their Muslim neighbors typical Jewish delicacies, including Passover *matzah* (unleavened bread), cookies, and cooked food. The Muslims looked forward to and welcomed these traditional visits, offering tea and other beverages in return and providing their guests with milk, butter, honey, eggs, fresh beans, and ears of wheat, and sometimes also fine flour and yeast for the new dough to be put on the Mimuna table.

On the following day, families would go, separately or in small groups, to parks, forests, or gardens with picnic baskets to enjoy nature. Later, the mistress would return to her house to bake another batch of bread, whose dough had risen overnight and during the day.

An additional meaning of the Mimuna festival is evident in a mixed Hebrew and Judeo-Arabic song performed at the evening ceremonies. It speaks longingly of the hope of every Jew to be in the Holy Land the following year and to enjoy all its promised abundance, symbolized by the

Mimuna table and its abundance. Moreover, the common Hebrew blessing "Next year in Jerusalem" was repeated so often on this occasion that communities of southwestern Morocco called the evening of Mimuna by a mixed Judeo-Arabic and Hebrew name, "Lilt Shanah Habba," that is, the night of the blessing "in next year." In rabbinical circles, the name "Mimuna" even has a messianic meaning: The word is said to be a deformation of the Hebrew word *emunah* (faith). From this point of view, Mimuna ceremonies refer to the messianic hope of redemption during the month of Nissan, according to the midrashic saying "In Nissan they were liberated [from Egypt] and in Nissan they will be liberated [by the messiah from exile]."

In Israel, rabbis attributed another meaning to the Mimuna. They established a link between the festival name and Rabbi Maimon, the father of the celebrated Jewish philosopher Maimonides (Rabbi Moses ben Maimon), who found refuge with his family and his notorious son for five years in Fez, Morocco, after fleeing the persecutions of Almohad fundamentalists in Cordoba in 1160. However, there is no trace of this rabbinical meaning in the festival ceremonies or in the texts performed at them.

After the mass immigration of many Moroccan Jews to Israel, their cultural habits and behaviors were disrupted. This was due to the dispersal of their natural communities and their scattering around the country, as well as to the new cultural ideology of "the melting pot" adopted by the leadership of the new Jewish state in order to shape a common Israeli identity and culture. This disruption also affected the Mimuna ceremonies, and only a few families continued to celebrate them in the 1950s and the early 1960s. In 1964, a Moroccan-Jewish political leader initiated a public gathering of immigrants from North Africa, especially Morocco, in a Jerusalem park on Mimuna day, for a great picnic, accompanied by Moroccan-Jewish music and food, and invited social and political leaders to welcome the guests. Thereafter, a new tradition of Mimuna was born in Israel, with great public and sociopolitical significance and ceremony.

Mimuna Today

Since the 1980s, Mimuna has become a new official festival in Israel, about which local and national newspapers and the electronic media report and deliberate and even special radio and TV programs are produced. The evening ceremonies open with a festive event that occurs at a public and cultural space in Jerusalem or in the home of a political figure from the Moroccan-Jewish community and to which numerous political, diplomatic and religious figures, including the prime minister and the chief rabbis, are invited for official greetings and tasting the sweet *mofleta,* which has become the new symbol of the Mimuna in Israel. Elsewhere in the country, local ceremonies are also organized in public spaces or in the homes of Moroccan Jews, gathering local leaders and guests from among their neighbors and Ashkenazi acquaintances. The slogan transmitted by the national organizers of the ceremonies to Moroccan-Jewish families is "Open House," requesting that these families open their houses to guests from other Israeli communities in order to make the Mimuna festival one of friendship and brotherhood for all Israeli society.

Not all Moroccan Jews celebrate the family ceremonies of the Mimuna. This is true not only for young generations born in Israel but for the older generation as well. The festival has become a special event organized by a few families in every Israeli settlement and includes plenty of cookies, beverages, and a great amount of *mofleta.*

The following day, the ceremonies take place all over Israel; picnics are held in parks, with grill pans and various foods. In some places, principally those with a great number of Moroccan Jews, municipal authorities organize entertainment, including official greetings and the performance of Moroccan-Jewish music. Until the beginning of the 2000s, a great gathering was organized, at the national level, at a large park in Jerusalem, where thousands were invited to picnic and participate in the traditional ceremony of greetings, addressed by the president of the state, the prime minister, and important ministers. A musical program was also offered with the performance of famous Middle Eastern and other singers and groups.

Hence, the Mimuna festival slowly became an important sociopolitical arena in Israel, at which political leaders meet and greet future voters. With the communal and cultural aspects of the festival, the event has evolved from a pure folk festival to an official national celebration.

Joseph Chetrit

See also: North Africa, Jews of.

Bibliography

Ben-Ami, Issachar, "The Mimuna Festival of the Moroccan Jews." In *Le Judaïsme marocain: études ethno-culturelles.* Jerusalem: Rubin Mass, 1976 (in Hebrew).

Chetrit, Joseph. "In This Manner We Celebrated the Mimuna at Tarudant in the Sus Valley." In *Mimuna,* ed. Moshe Elkaiam. Tel Aviv: Histadrut, 1982, 1983 (in Hebrew).

Einhorn, I. "The Mimuna: Its Origin and Substance." *Tarbiz* 41 (1972): 211–218 (in Hebrew).

Elkaiam, Moshe, ed. *Mimuna.* Tel Aviv: Histadrut, 1982, 1983.

Goldberg, Harvey E. "The Mimuna and the Minority Status of Moroccan Jews." *Ethnology* 17 (1978): 75–87.

Maman, A. "Mimuna: The Name Meanings and the Festival Habits." In *Recherches sur la culture des juifs d'Afrique du Nord,* ed. I. Ben-Ami, pp. 85–95. Jerusalem: Committee of the Western in Jerusalem, 1991 (in Hebrew).

MINHAG (CUSTOM)

The word "*minhag*" (custom) has two different meanings in Jewish tradition and folklore: (1) a postbiblical religious custom; and (2) a version of a liturgical rite.

A Postbiblical Religious Custom

In talmudic times the structure of the Halakhah (Jewish law) had a fairly clear hierarchy. The laws that had biblical authority (*mi'de'oraita*) were the most stringent. Transgressions of them carried the heaviest penalties, and they could hardly ever be changed or modified. The laws based on rabbinic authority (*mi'derabbanan*) were more lenient, bore lighter sanctions, and were more open to being modified or overturned. (They are usually called either "*gezerot*" or "*takkanot*" [negative or positive enactments].) The class of practices with the least authority in the hierarchic structure was the *minhag*.

One does not say a prayer on carrying out a *minhag*, because it has not been "commanded": The benediction usually begins with: "Blessed art Thou . . . who has *commanded* us to . . ." Likewise, transgression of a *minhag* exacts no serious sanction. *Minhag* is more amenable to change and cancellation. In many cases, customs are of a local nature, limited to a country, a town, or even a single family, as opposed to the other categories of Halakhah, which for the most part devolve upon the whole community. However, with the passage of time, and as a result of threats from different groups (Karaites, Reform Judaism, etc.), which attacked and rejected certain customs as baseless, the *minhag* was given greater authority and status. Thus the Tosafot (*Menahot* 20b) state that "custom is Torah" and on occasion had precedence over law (based on *y. Yevamot* 12.1, *y. Bava Metzi'a* 7.1, *Soferim* 14:18), while the revered Torah scholar Maimonides classified *minhagot* (pl.) with *gezerot* and *takkanot*, thus suggesting the three had equal status. The early-nineteenth-century rabbi Moses Sofer ruled that any attempt to innovate, that is, to change or annul customs, was forbidden by Torah law (*ḥadash assur min ha'Torah*), thus limiting rabbinic flexibility in dealing with archaic and obsolete practices.

Over the generations, there has been a blurring of the distinction between different classes of customs, such as those that a community adopted probably following the personal practice of a renowned sage or, on the other hand, a non-Jewish practice that somehow penetrated from the surrounding cultural milieu. The former usually fell into two categories: (1) a stringent practice "to distance oneself from transgressions," such as making the Sabbath begin early, adding to the days a woman must abstain from relations with her husband after her menstrual period ended, or extending the period between the eating of meat and milk products, and (2) "making mitzvot more endearing" (*ḥibbuvei mitzvah*), such as kissing a *mezuzah,* a Torah scroll, or elaborate decoration of ritual objects (*hiddur mitzvah*). The latter class often reflects local folk beliefs and was not infrequently called into question by rabbis as falling into the category of *ḥukkat hagoyim* (idolatrous practice). For example, early medieval *mezuzot*—even one written by Rabbi Judah the Pious—in addition to having the canonic biblical texts, had in their margins divine names, angels' names, characters, magical symbols, and verses from the Psalms. With regard to such *mezuzot,* Maimonides wrote that he who has them would have no part in the world to come. In a similar vein, Rabbi Tam of the twelfth century pointed out that if one reverses the Hebrew letters in *minhag* (מנהג; custom), one arrives at *Gehinnom* (גהנם; hell), indicating that sages should not uphold foolish customs.

These additions to the "classic" *mezuzah* were intended to increase its power to protect the house against malignant forces. Indeed, the biblical name of God, Shaddai, inscribed on the parchment was understood to be an acronym for *shomer daltot (or dirot) Israel* (guardian of the door, or houses, of Israel). Many such folk customs arose out of the belief that one required protection against evil spirits. Thus, in North African Jewish communities the use of the Islamic *ḥamsa* (hand of Fatimah) was widespread, a Torah scroll was placed in the room of a woman in childbirth to protect her, and a knife was placed under her pillow for the same purpose. Salt and iron were used as protective devices, and amulets, such as the famous one preventing the female demon Lilith from killing newborn babies, found in the early *Sefer Raziel ha'Malakh*, were hung on walls, above beds, or around the neck. These practices, which entered the halakhic literature (including the authoritative *Tzara'at* [will] of Rabbi Judah the Pious), have their roots in the folk superstitions of the surrounding culture. Rabbinic literature is copiously interspersed with such customs, which belong to the realm of folk religion.

At the other extreme, some customs took on the status of real law. Thus, although originally the second day of the foot-festivals (*yom tov sheni shel galuyyot*) was imitated in the Diaspora because of doubt as to where the new month begins, and emissaries sent out by the Sanhedrin could not reach distant communities to inform them in time, when the calendar became fixed by astronomical calculations, this consideration no longer applied and the practice of keeping the Second Day should have become obsolete. The Talmud (*b. Betzah* 4b) asks: "Now that we are acquainted with the calendar, why do we observe two days?" And the answer given is: "Because they sent a directive from Jerusalem stating: Adhere to the *minhag* of your ancestors that was transmitted to you." In this way, many customs assumed a status of sacredness by virtue of long usage and were treated with greater reverence than those from Halakhah, such as eating apples and honey on Rosh Ha'Shana and Kapparot on the eve of Yom Kippur.

Historically there has been a remarkable diversity of customs in Jewish practice and there was a clear tendency by rabbis to attempt to amalgamate various customs into a harmonic whole, so as to "cover all the options" (*latzet yedei kol hadeot*). Likewise the rabbis went out of their way to justify even the strangest practices (*lemashkunei nafshei lehatzdik haminhagim*). Hence numerous obsolete customs have been contracted into a composite unit.

Liturgical Rite

The basic foundations of the liturgy are found in the Talmud (tractate *Berakhot*). However, over the generations numerous conditions and modifications were made in different communities, so significant variations developed between the rites of various countries and communities. Most notably, the Ashkenazi ritual evolved from Palestinian practice, whereas the Sephardic one was based on Babylonian usage. Within these broad distinctions are a multitude of local variant *minhagim:* Byzantine, Italian, Polish, German, Yemenite, and North African, to mention but a few. The Palestinian ritual was largely forgotten during the period of the Crusaders (eleventh and twelfth centuries), when few Jews arrived to live in Palestine. Thus, the Palestinian triennial Torah-reading cycle fell into abeyance and the Babylonian annual cycle took over; the twenty-four fasting days listed in Palestinian Byzantine *Megillat Ta'anit Zuta* (or *Batra*), though cited in the legal codices, are no longer kept. Current liturgy is based primarily on the Babylonian *siddur Rav Amram Gaon,* and only remnants of the Palestinian rite survive, mostly in the Ashkenazi rite.

With the advent of printing, the versions became more standardized and consolidated and three major rituals emerged: *Nusaḥ Ashkenaz* (the European version), *Nusaḥ edot ha'Mizraḥ* (the version employed in North African communities), and *Nusaḥ Sepharad.* The latter is an amalgam of the Spanish (Sephardi) rite initiated by the school of the Ari, Rabbi Isaac Luria, in late-sixteenth-century Safed, and the Ashkenazi–Polish rite, a combination adopted by the Ḥasidim in the late eighteenth century. Considerable modification of the traditional liturgy has been introduced under Reform, Conservative, and Reconstructionist influence. In the State of Israel, especially in the Israeli army, an attempt has been made to consolidate unified prayers–rites, acceptable to all communities (*Nusaḥ Ahid*), based primarily on the *Nusaḥ Sepharad.*

Daniel Sperber

See also: Folk Belief; Folk Medicine.

Bibliography

Elbogen, Yitshak Moshe. *The Prayer in Israel and Its Historical Development.* J. Heinmann. Tel Aviv: Dvir, 1972 (in Hebrew).

Elon, Menachem. *The Hebrew Law, Its History, Sources, Principles,* vol. 8. Jerusalem: Magnes, 1973 (in Hebrew).

———. "Minhag." In *The Principles of Jewish Law,* ed. Menachem Elon. Jerusalem: Encyclopaedia Judaica, 1975.

Fleischer, Ezra. *The Prayer and the Customs of Prayer in the Land of Israel in the Genizah Period.* Jerusalem: Magnes, 1988 (in Hebrew).

Gelbard, Shemuel Pinhas. *The Treasure of Customs: Sources and Explanations to Laws and Customs.* Petach Tikva: Mifal Rashi, 1995 (in Hebrew).

Halamish, Moshe. *Kabbalah in Liturgy. Halakhah and Custom.* Ramat Gan: Bar-Ilan University Press, 2000 (in Hebrew).

Mack, Hananel. *Introduction to Jewish Prayers.* Tel Aviv: D.O.D., 2001 (in Hebrew).

Reif, Stefan C. *Judaism and Hebrew Prayer: New Perspectives on Jewish Liturgical History.* Cambridge, UK: Cambridge University Press, 1993.

Roth, Joel. "On Custom in the Halakhic System." In *The Halakhik Process: A Systemic Analysis.* New York: JTS Press, 1986.

Sperber, Daniel. *Jewish Customs: Sources and History.* 8 vols. Jerusalem: Urim, 1989–2007 (in Hebrew).

———. *The Jewish Life Cycle: Custom, Lore and Iconography: Jewish Customs from the Cradle to the Grave.* Ramat Gan: Bar-Ilan University Press, 2008.

———. *On Changes in Jewish Liturgy: Options and Limitations.* Jerusalem: Urim, 2010.

———. *Why Do What They Do? The History of Jewish Customs Throughout the Cycle of the Jewish Year.* Hoboken, NJ: KTAV, 1999.

Ta-Shma, Yisrael Moshe. *Ancient Ashkenazi Custom.* Jerusalem: Magnes, 1992 (in Hebrew).

———. *Halakha, Custom and Reality in Ashkenaz.* Jerusalem: Magnes, 1996 (in Hebrew).

Trachtenberg, Joshua. *Jewish Magic and Superstition: A Study in Folk Religion.* Philadelphia: Jewish Publication Society of America, 1961.

Wieder, Naphtali. *The Crystallization of the Prayer Style in West and East.* Jerusalem: Ben Zvi Institute, 1998 (in Hebrew).

MINHAG BOOKS (BOOKS OF CUSTOM)

Minhag books, devoted to the collection of Jewish customs (*minhagim*), fall into three major categories: (1) those that address customs of individual communities or of notable authorities; (2) those that celebrate customs relating to specific events, such as weddings, funerals, circumcision, and festivals; and (3) studies of customs to reveal their background and origins and (among the kabbalists) their innermost meanings. Since customs represent life patterns of societies and individuals, which are not normally recorded, the need for such books arose as a result of contacts between communities that had varying customs, usually to demonstrate the legitimacy for each community to follow its own tradition and that each set of customs was binding upon its own locale.

In the Tannaitic period (first–second centuries C.E.) there existed such a list of the differences in marriage customs between Judea and the Galilee (*t. Ketubbot* 1:4). However, the earliest significant compilation of this nature is *Sefer ha'Ḥillukim* which lists the differences between Palestinian and Babylonian liturgical usage, compiled during the Geonic period (seventh–eighth centuries C.E.?, critically edited by M. Margaliot, Jerusalem 1938). Provence, in southern France, was an area in which the Franco-German and Spanish customs frequently clashed with one another, and several collections of customs were composed there, such as *Sefer ha'Manhig,* by Abraham ben Nathan (ed. Y. Raphael, Jerusalem, 1978), and *Sefer ha'Minhagot,* by Asher ben Saul Lunel, both from the early thirteenth century, listing customs of Lunel, Narbonne, Catalonia, and other areas, and their sources. In the late thirteenth century Menaḥem Meiri produced the work *Magen Avot*, defending Provençal customs against the attacks of Spanish authorities, primarily the disciples of Ramban, who tried to force the Spanish rite upon them. Germany had many small scattered communities, each of which developed its own customs.

From the early fourteenth century onward, there exists an entire genre of *minhag* literature, beginning with the followers of Rabbi Meir of Rothenberg (called the Maharam). The most important of these works are the *Tashbetz* of Rabbi Samson ben Zadok and the *minhag* books of Rabbi Avraham Klausner, Rabbi Jacob ben Moshe Moelin Halevi (called the Maharil), and Rabbi Isaac Tyrnau (of Hungary). In the sixteenth century a new form of *minhag* book emerged, for popular use, designed primarily for women and children, in Yiddish and with simple woodcut illustrations. The earliest was printed in Venice in 1593, based on Shimon Ashkenazi's publication in 1590. In modern times *minhag* literature has been enriched by studies that sought to give reasons for each Central Term. Among the most popular works are *Ta'amei ha'Minhagim,* by A.I. Sperling (1896), and *Otzar kol minhagei Yeshurun,* by A.E. Hirshkovitz (1917). The fullest digest published to date is *Otzar Ta'amei ha'Minhagim,* by S.P. Gelbart (1995). In many of these works the reasons given for inclusion are imaginative and far-fetched, and the late twentieth century saw a number of critical analyses published on the historical developments of customs.

Daniel Sperber

See also: *Minhag* (Custom).

Bibliography

Lewy, Joseph. *Minhag Yisrael Torah.* 5 vols. Brooklyn, NY: Pink Graphic, 1994–2002.

Rapeld, Meir, and Joseph Tabory. *Custom, Its Offshoots and Research: A Selected Bibliography.* In *Jewish Customs: Sources and History,* ed. D. Sperber, vol. 4. Jerusalem: Urim, 1994 (in Hebrew).

Sperber, Daniel. *Jewish Customs: Sources and History.* 8 vols. Jerusalem: Urim, 1989–2007 (in Hebrew).

Yassif, Eli. *Jewish Folklore: An Annotated Bibliography.* New York: Garland, 1986.

MINYAN

In Jewish law, the minimum requirement of individuals for a variety of liturgical purposes is a minyan (מנין), a quorum of ten males age thirteen or older. Certain sections of communal prayer, such as *Barekhu* (meaning, "bless," the opening word of the call to worship), *Birkat Cohanim* (the priestly benediction), and the reader's repetition of the Amidah (Standing Prayer), can be recited only in the presence of a minyan. So, too, the reading of the Torah and of the *haftarah,* and the recitation of *sheva berakhot* (the seven benedictions) of a wedding ceremony and marriage feast require such a minyan.

This notion, that ten adult males constitute a community *(edah)* and are therefore required for community ritual activities, was variously derived by the sages ("This evil community," Num. 14:27), referring to the ten spies who brought back to Joshua a negative report from Jericho (*b. Ber* 216, *b. Megillah* 23b), or from Genesis 18:32, where it is related that ten righteous men could have saved the evil city of Sodom (*b. Ber.* 6a). The Talmud (*b. Ber.* 6b) cites the third-century Palestinian sage Rabbi Yoḥanan as stating, "When God comes to a synagogue and does not find a minyan there, He is angry, as it is said, 'wherefore, when I came, was there no man? When I called, was there none to answer?'" (Isa. 50:2).

Some communities that find it difficult to raise a quorum for prayer employ paid "minyan men" regularly to attend services. In modern-day egalitarian congregations, usually of the Conservative or Reform denominations, women worshipers may be counted as part, or all, of the quorum. In emergency situations, one may also form a minyan consisting of nine adult males and one boy holding a Bible (*Shulḥan Arukh Ḥayyim* 55:4).

Daniel Sperber

See also: Hebron.

Bibliography

Elbogen, Ismar. *Jewish Liturgy: A Comparative History,* trans. Raymond P. Scheindlin. Philadelphia: Jewish Publication Society of America; New York: Jewish Theological Seminary of America, 1993.

MITTEILUNGEN DER GESELLSCHAFT FÜR JÜDISCHE VOLKSKUNDE

See: Germany, Jews of; Grünwald, Max

MIZRAḤ

Mizraḥ (Heb., east) might refer to the eastern wall of the synagogue, which faces toward Jerusalem, where the holy ark is situated. This wall is also called *kotel ha'mizraḥ* (lit., "eastern wall"), and the seats against it are considered the most honorable seats in the synagogue.

In Jewish folklore, *mizraḥ* is the name of a plaque that includes this word as a central feature; it is hung in synagogues and Jewish homes, in Eastern and Central Europe, in Germany and Alsace, to indicate the direction of Jerusalem and, hence, the direction for prayer. (The direction of Jerusalem from Eastern and Central Europe is more to the south, but it has become the custom to refer to the direction of Jerusalem as east in this context.) Rabbinical texts state that one should direct one's heart in the direction of Jerusalem, the direction of the Temple, in the time of prayer (*m. Berakhot* 4; 4–5, *b. Berakhot*). Thus, the *mizraḥ* was more prevalent in homes, where it served as an indicator of the direction for prayer, though it also featured in synagogues, where it was mainly combined with the *shiviti* plaque, which is placed in front of the reader's desk.

The word "*mizraḥ*" is also interpreted as an acronym for the phrase "from this side the spirit of life." Psalm 113:3, referring to the direction of the Temple and the divine presence. A phrase commonly inscribed on *mizraḥ* plaques, "From the rising of the sun to its setting, the name of the Lord is to be praised," refers to the glorification of God from the east. Other verses and benedictions and devotional or moral texts are often added. A very common combination is that between the word "*mizraḥ*" with the verse "I have set the Lord always in front of me" (Ps. 16:8).

*Mizraḥ*s were made sometimes by scribes or by yeshiva students as a pastime. They were painted or printed on parchment or paper or embroidered on textile, and many were made as papercuts. They are colorful and decorative, bearing symbolic images such as the rising sun, rampant lions flanking a crown, the four animals from the saying in *Pirqe Avot* (The Ethics of the Fathers; 5:20) "Be bold as the leopard and light as the vulture/eagle, swift as the gazelle, and powerful as the lion to do the will of your father in heaven" and many others.

Mizraḥ plaques became signs of Jewish homes, were associated with the creation of a new home, and were given as wedding presents.

Esther Juhasz

See also: Jerusalem and the Temple; Papercut; Shiviti-Menorah.

Bibliography

Yaniv, Bracha. "The 'Mizrach' Papercut." *Jerusalem Studies in Jewish Folklore* 3 (1982): 105–112.

MLOTEK, CHANA

See: Anthologies

MONSTERS AND OTHER MYTHOLOGICAL CREATURES

In Jewish folklore, monsters and other mythological creatures have played a role ever since biblical times. The origin of many of these creatures is vague, and scholars assume that many of them are of non-Jewish origin.

In the Bible a few mythological creatures, such as Leviathan (meaning "snake") (Isa. 27:1) and Behemoth (Job 40:15–24) (maybe meaning "hippopotamus"), are mentioned. The prophet Ezekiel saw a creature combining human and nonhuman segments (Ezek. 10). Giants are known from the Bible as well (Gen. 6:4; Deut. 3:11), and modern scholars argue that the role of such creatures was greater in antiquity, when God was believed to have subdued Rahav, the Canaanite sea monster (Ps. 89:11; Ps. 26:12).

In pseudepigrapha literature one reads about the phoenix (3 Bar. 6:1–13), two types of gigantic birds combined of several beasts' segments. Dragons appear as well (Add. to Dan.; Add. to Esth.).

In talmudic literature there are all sorts of monsters, some already known from earlier sources, such as a giant man (*b. Nid.* 24b), a gigantic bird (*Gen. Rab.* 19:4; *b. Bek.* 57b), the phoenix, a gigantic fish, the unicorn, and a Capricorn. The siren is mentioned in connection to halakhic (legal) matters (one is not allowed to eat a siren, because it is human, but its corpse is pure because it is a fish). Centaurs are mentioned in rabbinic text (*Bereshit*

Rab. 23:6) and also appear on synagogue ornaments. The *tannaim* (teachers of the Mishnah) believed (as did Aristotle) that there is a mouse made half of flesh and blood and half of soil (*m. Ḥul.* 9:6). The rabbis were aware of the reality of all sorts of human deformations and believed that a woman could give birth to a demon, a beast, or a snake (*m. Nid.* 3:1).

In *Hekhalot* literature—that is, Jewish mystical literature from the fourth through the seventh century—(Seder Rabba deBereshit 32 = Schäfer, Synopse # 452), there is a description of six heavenly beings that resemble a kind of Egyptian or Babylonian pantheon. In the Middle Ages Jews became aware of the legends concerning Alexander and were exposed to dwarfs and *acephalos* (headless) persons. Jews believed that a holy person could create a humanlike creature, known as the golem, a homunculus or anthropoid, which has become the most prominent Jewish monster in Jewish folklore.

In his commentary to Gen. 49:27, Rabbi Ephraim of Regensburg (twelfth century) took the legend about a werewolf as a Jewish tradition and wrote a charm about how to be saved from it.

Meir Bar-Ilan

See also: Jerusalem and the Temple.

Bibliography

Bar-Ilan, Meir. "Fabulous Creatures in Ancient Jewish Traditions." *Mahanaim* 7 (1994): 104–113 (in Hebrew).

Gutmann, J. "Leviathan, Behemoth and Ziz: Jewish Messianic Symbols in Art." *Hebrew Union College Annual* 39 (1968): 219–230.

Niehoff, M.R. "The Phoenix in Rabbinic Literature." *Harvard Theological Review* 89:3 (1996): 245–265.

Toaff, Ariel. *Mostri giudei*. Bologna: Mulino, 1996.

Month

The Jewish calendar is lunar, so the length of a month is based on the moon's circumnavigation of the earth. The month starts with the first appearance of the crescent, while the moon is positioned between the sun and the earth. This moment is called "*molad*" (Heb., birth), or "new moon." The moon takes approximately 29-1/2 days (precisely 29 days, 6 hours, 44 minutes, and 3-1/3 seconds) to travel around the earth. To prevent a new month from starting in the middle of the day, the half day is either omitted or added to the next month. Therefore, in the Jewish calendar a month may be either 29 or 30 days.

The names of the months in use today originated in Babylonian sources and are mentioned in the Talmud (*y. Rosh Ha'shanah* 1:2). Other names (1 Kgs. 6,1; 6, 38; 8, 2) and a numerical system (Exod. 12:2; Num. 29:16) are found in the Bible, but were not retained.

The custom of Kiddush Levanah (the sanctification of the new moon). Woodcut from *Sefer Minhagim*, Amsterdam, 1727.

The Jewish calendar year comprises twelve lunar months. The length of the first seven alternates: The first month, Nissan, always has 30 days; Iyar always has 29 days; Sivan, 30; Tammuz, 29; Av, 30; Elul, 29; and Tishrei, 30 days. The next two months, Heshvan, and Kislev, vary in length. Some years they are full (30 days) or abbreviated (29 days), and some years they alternate: Heshvan 29 days; and Kislev, 30 days. This flexibility is imposed to ensure that certain holidays will occur on fixed days. The following months, Tevet and Shevat, always have 29 and 30 days, respectively. In a regular year, Adar has 29 days, but in leap years (which are always the 3d, 6th, 8th, 11th, 14th, 17th year in a 19-year cycle), an entire additional month is added. Adar I has 29 days, and Adar II has 30 days.

Ceremonies and celebrations observed every month mostly refer to the first day, Rosh Ḥodesh (lit., head of the month), when the crescent of the new moon appears. Some of the festivals related to nature (Sukkot, Passover, Tu Be'Av) occur on the full moon, in the middle of the month. In the Bible, trumpets were sounded to announce the first day of the month (Num. 10:10), when gatherings and banquets were set (1 Sam. 20:5), and when offerings and sacrifices were made (Num. 28:11–15).

In the Mishnah, the proclaiming of the new month is described in detail (*m. Rosh Ha'shanah* Ch. 2). The oldest method was used by a rabbinic court, which questioned at least two witnesses who claimed to have seen the crescent. A meal was offered to those who came to testify. After the testimony was accepted and agreed upon, the new month was announced throughout the country and the Diaspora by way of bonfires on hilltops. Due to controversies among sects, such as the Kutim (*m. Rosh Ha'shanah* 2:2) regarding the calendar, several cases of false testimonies and deceptive fires occurred, as a result of which this custom was altered. The court was charged with announcing the beginning of the month, and messengers were sent to the Diaspora. As these journeys were dangerous and at time failed, this method was abandoned as well. The calendar was finally fixed around 360 C.E. by Hillel the Second.

Since the sixteenth century, a custom developed of fasting on Rosh Ḥodesh eve and reciting Selihot (Supplication prayers usually recited daily during the month of Elul, before Rosh Ha'Shana). This fast is called Minor Yom Kippur.

Several customs related to the first day of the month existed among the different Jewish communities, such as paying a respectful visit to the rabbi, offering money to the *melamed* (traditional teacher), and abstaining from shaving. Tunisian women would whitewash graves. But many of these customs did not prevail or spread among all the Jewish people.

Although the calendar is fixed, the month's length is announced in the synagogue. On the first day of the month, prayers and blessings are recited. The traditional blessing dedicated to the new moon, "Birkat ha'Levana," is read by moonlight.

An ambivalent relationship exists between women and the first day of the month. In a positive context, women celebrate the day by abstaining from working. This custom has its source in the Midrash, in which it is told that women do not work on this particular day as a reward for not participating in the sin of the golden calf from the time of Moses (*Pirkei de'Rabbi Eliezer* 41). In a negative context, women are not allowed to participate in the blessing of the moon. This custom is based on an ancient Apocryptic tradition in which the moon assisted Eve by giving her light to commit the sin of eating the forbidden fruit.

Idit Pintel-Ginsberg

Bibliography

Eisenberg, Yeudah. *The Hebrew Calendar.* Jerusalem: Bar Ilan and T.A.L., 2001 (in Hebrew).

Ginzberg, Louis. *The Legends of the Jews,* vol. 1, p. 80. Philadelphia: Jewish Publication Society of America, 1966.

Levinsky, Yom Tov. *The Book of Festivals,* vol. 5. Tel Aviv: Agudat Oneg Shabbat, 1954 (in Hebrew).

Ushpizay, Dvora. "About Rosh Ḥodesh." *Mehkarey Hag* 9 (1999): 21–37 (in Hebrew).

Moses

Moses—whom the Bible attests brought the Jewish people out of Egypt, led them through the desert, brought the tablets down to them from heaven, gave them the Torah, and died before himself entering the Promised Land—is the hero of innumerable legends in the apocryphal literature, the Midrash, and the literature of the Middle Ages and the modern era. These narratives fill the gaps in the scriptural account and go on to recount not only Moses's birth and life's work as leader of the people in Egypt as told in the Book of Exodus but also those years between these two periods of his life, about which the Bible offers scant information. The Hellenistic literature presents Moses as an ideal figure—a leader, military man, and architect of the culture. The rabbinic literature, by contrast, offers a more complex figure, one in keeping with the biblical portrayal: The sages viewed Moses as a human being with limitations and weaknesses yet also as the greatest of the prophets and one who possessed superhuman traits. The collections of expanded biblical stories of the Middle Ages, such as *The Chronicles of Moses* and the sixteenth-century *Sefer ha'yashar* (The Book of the Just), weave Moses's life story into an all-embracing epic, adapting the Hellenistic sources and the apocrypha disallowed in the rabbinic literature, the Midrash, and narrative material of their time. As it usually does in fashioning the characters of culture heroes, legend details several stages in the life of Moses. Scholars distinguish between legends before his birth, legends about his life, and legends set after death. Legend makes no mention of Moses's descendants; it was Joshua, his disciple, who took his place as spiritual leader of the Jewish people.

Legends Preceding and the Story of Moses's Birth

Noble parentage, an elderly mother, advance knowledge possessed by either the enemy or the family, the appearance of light, a painless delivery, unnatural growth, and various miracles in connection with the baby are all characteristic motifs of the typical birth model of cultural heroes. Legend adds many details to the biblical description of the birth of Moses as outlined in Exodus 2:1–2. According to Josephus, the pharaoh knew in advance, courtesy of his astrologers, of the birth of the Israelites' redeemer, who would one day defeat him. According to medieval sources, such as *The Chronicle of Moses* and *Sefer ha'yashar*, the pharaoh dreamed of a scale with a little lamb on one side and the elders and ministers of Egypt on the other; the lamb outweighed the rest. When he learned that the dream attributed the future destruction of Egypt to an Israelite soon to be born, the pharaoh took Balaam's advice and commanded that every male child born to the Israelites be thrown into the Nile.

Consequently, according to the rabbinic sources, Amram divorced his wife, Jocheved, so as not to have to send more sons to their death. It was his daughter, Miriam, who persuaded him to remarry and continue to have children lest the males of the nation die out. In full view of the entire people, Amram, head of the Sanhedrin, remarried Jocheved as she sat on a bridal litter beneath a wedding canopy. Jocheved became young again, conceived a child, and gave birth to Moses in the sixth month of her pregnancy without labor pains. She and Amram both knew the nature of the fetus she bore: In a dream, the Almighty revealed himself to Amram and told him. At the time of Moses's birth, the house was filled with a light like that of the sun and the moon. Other miraculous signs of the birth are: Moses was born already circumcised and he was given the power of speech and the ability to walk at birth.

Legends About Moses's Life

Accounts of the scene in which the pharaoh's daughter—Thermuthis, according to the Greek sources, and Bitya, according to the rabbinic sources (Exod. 2:3–10)—pulled Moses out of the Nile report that there was such blistering heat that day that the princess went to the river with her handmaidens to cool off. Other explanations detailed in the Hellenistic and rabbinic sources for the princess's descent to the Nile are: her sadness at being barren, her desire to purify herself from her father's idols, or her wish to find a cure for leprosy. The Bible's ambiguous use of the word *"amatah"* ("her forearm" or "her maidservant") is resolved in the post-biblical literature and art in two ways: One explanation is that the princess's forearm lengthened so that she could reach the basket. The paintings of Dura Europas, from the third century, bear out this interpretation and express the positive view of the rabbinic sources toward Bitya. The translations into Greek and Latin (the Septuagint and the Vulgate), by contrast, opted for the second possibility. It was Bitya who named Moses after pulling him out of the water. Philo and Josephus offer a detailed Egyptian etymology for the name. The angel Gabriel also had a hand in rescuing Moses from the Nile: He struck Moses to make him cry and to arouse the princess's compassion. He also killed all her handmaidens save one because they advised her against violating her father's decree. After Moses was drawn out of the water, his sister, Miriam, appeared. She had been waiting nearby and suggested to the princess that the baby be brought to a Hebrew nursemaid. Consequently, he was brought to Jocheved's house.

Moses. From *Maḥzor Rödelheim* by Wolf Heidenheim (ca. 1800).

Moses in Childhood

Moses stayed in his mother's house for two years, at which time he was weaned and brought to Bitya, in the pharaoh's palace. A critical event in Moses's childhood occurred, according to Josephus in his *Chronicle of Moses,* when he reached for the royal crown, grasped it, and stepped on it or, alternatively, placed it on his own head. This act was perceived as a bad omen, and Moses was put through a test to prove his innocence: Hot coals and an onyx stone were placed in front of the child; when Moses reached for the onyx, Gabriel deflected his hand toward the burning coals, and everyone deemed the taking of the crown merely a child's act. Ailianos cites a Greek variant to this story.

Moses as a Youth

The Bible (Exod. 1:11–12) recounts Moses's involvement in the fate of his brethren. Upon witnessing an Egyptian beat an Israelite to death, he killed the Egyptian and buried him in the sand. The postbiblical traditions related to this act in one of three ways, all intended to prevent the creation of a precedent allowing a Jew to kill a gentile oppressor: Josephus ignores it in deference to a target audience that dictated an apologetic orientation; the rabbinic sources presented it as a one-time event emerging from unique circumstances: the killing of the Egyptian was the calculated implementation of Heaven's sentence against the Egyptian oppressor, who had committed adultery with the wife of an Israelite overseer. Moses killed him with assistance from above and not with a conventional weapon. The late source *Petirat Moshe rabbeinu* (The Death of Moses) from the eleventh century in Byzantium is the only one to criticize Moses. It presents this act as the reason that Moses is sentenced to die and forbidden to enter the Land of Israel.

After killing the Egyptian, Moses had to flee Egypt. Two Israelites who were fighting each other (Exod. 2:13), identified in the rabbinic sources as Dotan and Aviram, informed on him to the pharaoh. Moses was in fact saved from death when the pharaoh's messengers tried to behead him: His neck became as hard as marble, and thus he was impervious to harm but still had to leave Egypt.

Hellenistic as well as medieval sources recount the legend of Moses in Ethiopia. This is an example of how legendary traditions passed from the apocryphal and Hellenistic literature to the medieval literature of expanded biblical tales, skipping over the talmudic and midrashic sources. (One rabbinic reference to the legend, in an Aramaic translation of the Bible attributed to the second-century sage Jonathan ben Uzziel, bears mention.) While the sages identify the "Ethiopian woman" about whom Miriam told Aaron (Num. 12:1) as Zipporah, these traditions identify Moses's wife as the queen of Ethiopia, whom he wed after a brilliant victory on the battlefield. In the passage from the Hellenistic period to the Middle Ages, Egyptian mythological elements were repressed in a process of adaptation (Shinan 1977; Yassif 1994, 106–107).

After leaving Ethiopia, Moses arrived in Midian, where Jethro, his future father-in-law, lived. *Pirqe de'Rabbi Eliezer* and several works from the Middle Ages cover this chapter of Moses's life. They describe the chain of events that led to the marriage of Moses and Zipporah, and Moses's period of training in Midian as the future redeemer of Israel. According to the topos found also in Arthurian legends, Moses succeeded in uprooting God's staff, which had been stuck in Jethro's garden, a feat unmatched by any of the local heroes. Consequently, he was rewarded with the hand of Zipporah (Aarne-Thompson folktale classification system, Thompson H310). The fashioning of Jethro's character in these sources is particularly interesting: Sometimes he is neutral; at other times, negative.

The turning point in Moses's life was the revelation of the Almighty in the burning bush, a thornbush on fire that was not consumed by the flames. There Moses is commanded to return to Egypt, stand before the pharaoh, and demand that he let the Israelites depart (Exod. 3:1–22). But, according to the eleventh-century work *Gedulat Moshe* (The Greatness of Moses), before he returned to Egypt, Moses ascended to Heaven, his physical form becoming a flaming torch—like an angel, he reached the seventh heaven and toured paradise and hell. This is one of three ascents Moses makes to Heaven: at the start of his career, before receiving the Torah, and before his death.

One difficult event at this stage of Moses's life took place along the journey, with Zipporah and his children, to Egypt (Exod. 4:18–26). The angel of God nearly killed him, and would have, had not Zipporah hurriedly taken a sharp stone and circumcised their son. She is the heroine of the story, like Jocheved, Miriam, and Bitya, the other prominent women in the first two chapters of Exodus.

The continuation of the story of Exodus describes the completion of the mission imposed on Moses against his will: Moses meets with the pharaoh, who stubbornly refuses to let the children of Israel leave Egypt, even after the ten plagues have rained down on them (Exod. 11:10). Three events constitute the climax of Moses's life as leader of the nation: the exodus from Egypt, receiving the Torah, and building of the Tabernacle *(mishkan)*, the portable dwelling place for the divine presence during the period of the wanderings of the Israelites in the expanse of the wilderness (Exod. 25:1–20).

The motif of a halo, expressed in the description of Moses's radiant face (*qaran or panav*) upon descending from the mountain with the tablets of the Ten Commandments in hand (Exod. 34:29–35), is embodied in midrashic accounts that clarify the origin of Moses's radiant face. A mistranslation, however, by Jerome, refers to an actual horn. This mistranslation was Michelangelo's source of inspiration for his sculpture of Moses.

The most tragic event in Moses's life was undeniably the verdict that he had to die before the children of Israel entered the Promised Land, because of his transgression at the water of *Meriva* (Num. 19:7–14). His pleas to be permitted to enter the Land of Israel as a bird on the wing over the Jordan or as a fish beating its fins in the water were in vain, for the ruling had been decreed and the time had come for Joshua to lead the nation. Midrashic accounts from the eleventh century on elaborate extensively on Moses's final moments: his argument with the Almighty in an effort to reverse the decree; the exchange of roles with Joshua in his suddenly becoming the latter's apprentice and acolyte; his clash with the angel of death, who chased after him with a staff engraved with the name of God; his conversation with his soul, which refused to leave his pure body; and, ultimately, how God concealed and preserved Moses with a kiss. The Bible itself offers an ambiguous account of Moses's death, stating that the place of his burial is unknown and, at the same time, specifying its location precisely: in the valley in the land of Moav, opposite Beit Pe'or. This ambivalence remains unresolved in the dozens of versions that flesh out the biblical story, expressing an oxymoronic conception of the death of Moses as one who both died and was simultaneously secreted away by God.

"Moses by the Well" is a late theodicean story, type AT 759 (Aarne-Thompson folktale classification system). Moses witnessed an act of vengeance against one who seemed to him to be clearly innocent of wrongdoing, while the true villain was saved from all harm. Upon wondering at the ways of the Lord, he is exposed to facts of which he was previously ignorant, which brings him to acknowledge God's justice in His rulings.

One unusual tale about Moses, apparently of non-Jewish provenance, is "The Picture." A portrait of Moses, painted for an Arab king, revealed extremely negative character traits. This was incompatible with the familiar image of Moses. To the king's astonishment, Moses explained that the artist had rendered an accurate portrait—that he, Moses, had been born with those vices but through personal diligence had succeeded in overcoming his nature and raising himself to a higher level.

Another story about Moses, also of non-Jewish origin (apparently of Arab provenance), type B121, touches on the period of his sojourn in the house of Jethro, as a shepherd. It concerns an angel in the form of a wolf who sought to test the measure of Moses's dedication to his flock.

Arab legend is also the source for "The Man of the Tenth Generation," type 785 (see *Mimekor Yisrael*, Ben Amos ed., #12). A wicked and dishonest man accompanied Moses to Mount Horeb, stole cake from his provisions, and then denied it. Moses, with the power of the divine staff in hand, forced him to admit what he had done. Ultimately, he received his due punishment: Along the journey, Moses performed various miracles with his staff, even reviving the dead; the scoundrel tried to reproduce the miracles but naturally failed, and this led to his capture.

Legends Set After Moses's Death

One episode in the Talmud regarding the disappearance of Moses's burial place describes a delegation of Romans who set out to find it. Once in the vicinity, they found that regardless of where they stood, the grave appeared to be elsewhere; the phenomenon recurred even when they split up (*Sotah* 13b).

The numerous legends about Moses at various stages of his life, gathered from biblical and mostly postbiblical sources to refill narrative gaps, establish his figure as a collective cultural hero. In sum, Moses is portrayed as both a distanced, unattained persona and a human figure with whom one can identify.

Rella Kushelevsky

See also: Aaron; Magic; Zipporah.

Bibliography

Amnon, Mordechai. "On Moses' Shining Face and the Viel." *Beit Mikra* 31 (1986): 186–188 (in Hebrew).

Be'er, Haim. "The Names of Moshe Rabbeinu." *Mahanayyim* 115 (1967): 140–147 (in Hebrew).

Bin-Gorion, Emanuel. *The Paths of Legend.* Jerusalem: Bialik Institute, 1970 (in Hebrew).

Bin-Gorion, M.J. *Mimekor Yisrael: Classical Jewish Folktales,* ed. Dan Ben-Amos, trans. I.M. Lask. Bloomington: Indiana University Press, 1990.

Flusser, David. "Moses, the Man of God." *Mahanayyim* 115 (1967): 16–19 (in Hebrew).

Gil, Ya'akov. "The Skin of Moses' Face Shone." *Beit Mikra* 30 (1985): 341–344 (in Hebrew).

Ginzberg, Louis. *The Legends of the Jews,* trans. H. Szold and P. Radin. 7 vols. Philadelphia: Jewish Publication Society, 1909–1938.

Hacohen, Mordechai. "Moses' Face." *Mahanayyim* 115 (1967): 20–31 (in Hebrew).

Kushelevsky, Rella. "Aaron's Rod: An Exploration of One Criterion for Establishing a Thematic Series." *Jerusalem Studies in Jewish Folklore* 13–14 (1992): 205–228 (in Hebrew).

———. *Moses and the Angel of Death.* New York: Peter Lang, 1995.

Leiman, S. "The Portrait of Moses." *Tradition* 24 (1989): 91–98.

Noy, Dov. "Moses in Folk Narratives." *Mahanayyim* 115 (1967): 80–91 (in Hebrew).

———. "Rabbi Shalom Shabazi in the Folk Narratives of the Jews of Yemen." In *Bo'i Teiman: Studies and Documents on the Culture of Yemenite Jewry,* ed. Yehuda Ratzhabi, pp. 106–133. Tel Aviv, 1967 (in Hebrew).

Pardes, Ilana. "Zipporah and the Bridegroom of Blood: Women as Midwives in the Book of Exodus." *Theory and Criticism* 7 (1995): 89–97 (in Hebrew).

Raglan, Lord. "The Hero of Tradition." In *The Study of Folklore,* ed. Alan Dundes, pp. 142–157. Upper Saddle River, NJ: Prentice Hall, 1965.

Schwarzbaum, Haim. *Jewish Folklore Between East and West: Collected Papers,* ed. Eli Yassif. Beer Sheva: Ben-Gurion University of the Negev Press, 1989.

———. *Studies in Jewish and World Folklore.* Berlin: Walter de Gruyter, 1968.

Shalev-Eini, Sarit. "The Finding of Moses and the Rebirth of Pharaoh's Daughter." *Rimonim* 5 (1997): 8–14 (in Hebrew).

Shinan, Avigdor. "Between Martyrdom and Judicial Execution: Various Stances in Ancient Jewish Literature on the Story of Moses and the Egyptian." In *Martyrdom and Self-Sacrifice*, ed. Isaiah Gafni and Aviezer Ravitzky, pp. 55–68. Jerusalem: Merkaz Shazar, 1993 (in Hebrew).

———. "The Birth of Moses in the View of Rabbinic Literature." *Rimonim* 5 (1997): 4–7 (in Hebrew).

———. "*The Chronicle of Moses:* The Time, Origins and Nature of a Medieval Hebrew Tale." *Hasifrut* 24 (1977): 100–116 (in Hebrew).

———. "From Artapanus to *Sefer ha'yashar*: On the History of the Legend of Moses in Ethiopia." *Eshkolot* n.s. 2–3 (1977–1978): 53–67 (in Hebrew).

Vilnay, Zev. "Moses in Place Names in the Land of Israel and Sinai." *Mahanayyim* 115 (1967): 100–107 (in Hebrew).

Yassif, Eli. *The Hebrew Folktale. History, Genre, Meaning.* Trans. from Hebrew by Jacqueline S. Teitelbaum. Bloomington: Indiana University Press, 1999.

Yassif, Eli, ed. *The Book of Memories: The Chronicle of Jerhameel.* Tel Aviv: Chaim Rosenberg School of Jewish Studies, Tel Aviv University, 2001 (in Hebrew).

Mother (Ḥannah, Miriam) and Her Seven Sons

The legend of the mother and her seven sons is probably one of the most popular and widely disseminated legends among Jews in varied cultural contexts. In addition to Hebrew and Aramaic, it has been narrated both orally and in writing in Yiddish and in a number of local variants of Judeo-Arabic, Judeo-Spanish (Ladino), and Judeo-Persian, and it is still recounted today. In ancient and medieval times it was associated with the memorial day of the destruction of the Temple of Jerusalem, Tisha Be'Av (the Ninth of Av), a connection retained in most early modern and modern occurrences among Jews of the Middle East and North Africa. Later traditions, especially among the Jews of Central and Eastern Europe, associate it with Ḥanukkah. It gained much importance and wide distribution in medieval Europe, particularly in the wake of various pogroms and atrocities against Jews, such as those related to the Crusades. It is still very popular in educational contexts and may have been the script of the first Hebrew school theater performance in Jerusalem at the end of the nineteenth century.

The Plot

In the legend, seven brothers sacrifice themselves by refusing to comply with a decree that orders the transgression of some of the most central Jewish laws, for example, eating a forbidden food or worshiping an imperial statue. The plot usually highlights the sacrifice of the youngest son as well as the encouragement of the mother. In some versions the mother follows her sons to death by committing suicide. The legend, from its earliest formulations, may be considered the prototype of Jewish martyrological legends that exemplify women's role in martyrology in general.

The name Ḥannah is a rather late but dominant addition to the tradition of the legend of the mother and her seven sons, explicitly mentioned in the circa tenth-century south European *Yosippon*, but, as suggested by the editor of the text, David Flusser, possibly rooted in the grouping of the tale of the mother of seven with a number of barren women who were blessed with sons, among them the biblical Ḥannah, mother of Samuel (1 Sam.), in an earlier text: the *Pesiqta Rabbati.* In many earlier sources she is anonymous, referred to simply as "the woman" or is called Miriam, Tanḥum's daughter (in some late printed variants, also Nahtom's [baker's] daughter). The sons are anonymous as well, except for some early modern and modern Judeo-Arabic variants in which the youngest son bears the name Ezra or Azar.

The Sources

The earliest written document including the legend of the mother of the seven sons is 2 Maccabees, apocryphal in Jewish tradition, included in the Septuagint (LXX) translation of the Hebrew Bible that was extant among the Jews of Hellenistic Egypt and possibly also in contemporary Palestine. This was the dominant ancient version of the tale that fed into later traditions, both Jewish and Christian. The events are historically contextualized by being set during the period of religious oppression by the Seleucid ruler Antiochus Epiphanes, and this particular story is the one preceding, and perhaps also motivating, the outbreak of the Hasmonean rebellion leading to another—short—period of Jewish independence including the reinstitution of the Temple of Jerusalem.

The tale of the woman and her sons follows the account of the martyrdom of the priest Eleazar, whose name is possibly reflected later in the above-mentioned name of the younger son. In this version the woman and all her sons are anonymous and the transgression that they resist is being "compelled by the king, under torture with whips and cords, to partake of unlawful swine's flesh" (RSV 7:1), which may be understood as part of a sacrificial ceremony. The seven sons all behave with utter stoicism and nobility while subjected to detailed acts of torture, the seventh and presumedly youngest son is highlighted, and the mother joins her sons in death. Although the text is Greek, the story explicitly stresses the linguistic as well as the religious particularity of the Jewish martyrs. The story, however,

The Courage of a Mother. Illustration by Gustave Doré, from Doré's English Bible (1866).

has also been paradigmatic for the Christian martyrological tradition.

The much longer, less narrative and more philosophical version of 4 Maccabees was not taken up in later tradition. Talmudic-midrashic sources crystallize into two main versions, one in the Palestinian aggadic Midrash compilation of Lamentations Rabbah (*Eikha Rabba*), the other in the Babylonian Talmud tractate *Gittin*. In both cases the legend is embedded in a longer chain of narratives all pertaining to the period of religious oppression stretching from the destruction of Jerusalem and the Second Temple by the Roman emperors Vespasian and Titus to the "decrees of Hadrian" specifically prohibiting Jewish religious practices such as circumcision and intellectual practices such as learning their own traditions. The transgression resisted is the imperial worship of the emperor's icon, and, according to the poetics of the corpus, the sons all quote biblical passages to justify their act. Torture is less emphasized than in the Hellenistic versions, although it does appear in yet another midrashic rendering of the tale in the *Pesiqta Rabbati,* which in other details resembles both main traditions.

The two main versions differ in some significant details: In the Lamentations Rabbah version, the woman is named Miriam (in most manuscript traditions, "Tanḥum's daughter"), in an associative linking with a number of adjacent martyrological tales of women bearing the same first name, with a possible inter-religious narrative dialogue with Christianity in mind (Miriam = Martha = Mary), whereas in the Talmud she remains anonymous. Lamentations Rabbah seems the dominant version in later tradition, contrary to the usual dominance of the Babylonian Talmud traditions, especially in its stronger emphasis on the mother's role—including also a scene of breast feeding the youngest son—characteristic of many of the medieval European versions. Christian parallels abound, such as the famous narratives of saints Perpetua and Felicitas.

The Cultural Context

The conjunction of the name Ḥannah as well as the origin in the Book of Maccabees may explain the consistent association between the legend of the mother of seven sons and the celebration of Ḥanukkah, which, for instance, can account for the fact that the tale provided the theme for one of the first known Hebrew theater performances in modern times, in a Jewish school in Ottoman Jerusalem. The topic itself explains the solitary reading as well as performance of prose and poetry versions in various Jewish languages on Tisha Be'Av, commemorating the destruction of both temples of Jerusalem.

Galit Hasan-Rokem

See also: Av, Ninth of (Tisha Be'Av); Ḥanukkah.

Bibliography

Hasan-Rokem, Galit. *Web of Life: Folklore and Midrash in Rabbinic Literature.* Stanford, CA: Stanford University Press, 2000.

Mother, Jewish

See: United States, Jews of

Mountain Jews

See: Russia, Jews of

Mourning

See: Death; *Qinah* (Lament); Women in Rabbinic Literature

Moykher Sforim, Mendele (1835–1917)

Mendele Moykher Sforim (also Moicher; Sfarim) was the pseudonym of the writer, critic, and essayist Sholem Yankev (Jacob) Abramovitsh (Abramovich), a major figure in both Yiddish and Hebrew literature. In the field of modern Hebrew literature, Abramovitsh's formidable presence and influence are noticeable both in the period of the Haskalah (Jewish Enlightenment) and in the subsequent period of Jewish national renaissance. While Abramovitsh assumed the literary figure of "Mendele the Book Peddler" as his pen-name for his literary works since the appearance in Yiddish of *Dos Kleyne Mentshele* (The Little Fellow, 1864), his given name, Sholem Jacob, was used in the essays he published before and after his literary persona became popular.

Abramovitsh was born in the small town of Kapulye (Kopyl) (Belarus; exact date not available), and at the age of thirteen traveled extensively in the Pale of Settlement, where Jews were permitted to live in the Russian Empire. He spent the first decade of his literary career in Berdichev, moving in 1869 to Zhitomir in order to enroll in the Haskalah-oriented, government-sponsored rabbinical seminary, and then spending most of his later years (1881–1917) in Odessa. In Berdichev, Abramovitsh published *Mishpat shalom* (Judgment of Peace, 1860) and *Ein mishpat* (Fountain of Judgment, 1867), two volumes that assembled his early essays in literary social and educational criticism.

In addition, Abramovitsh published an important polemical letter ("Lehashiv et Mordechai" [Repudiating Mordechai], *Ha'Melitz* 38–39 [1861]), which called on Haskalah literature to reorient itself toward social and political issues, as well as works of popular science (*Toledot ha'teva* [History of Nature], 1862–1873). Most crucially, however, in Berdichev, Abramovitsh made his debut as a writer of both Hebrew fiction (*Limmedu heitev* [Learn to Do Good], 1862, later published as *Ha'avot ve'habanim* [Fathers and Sons], 1868) and Yiddish fiction (*Dos Kleyne Mentshele* and *Dos Vintshfingeril* [The Magic Ring], 1865). The Yiddish stories combine a depiction of the grim realities of Jewish daily life with a critique of the passive and false hope for supernatural redemption. *Dos Vintshfingeril,* for example, severely criticizes the popular passion for a miraculous "magic ring" and recommends, instead, that modern Jews pursue active, scientific knowledge of nature. Taking the new path of criticism and enlightenment should push the Jewish people from mysticism to an active exploitation of nature, he argued. His Hebrew publications of the period are also indicative of his affinity with the Haskalah movement. In them, he champions contemporary *maskilic* (enlightened) ideas in the realm of social and educational reform and calls for an incisive critique of religion, tradition, and metaphysics.

Abramovitsh's early essays are an important milestone in the history of Hebrew literary criticism and theory. In the realm of criticism, they call for a stringent and impersonal standard of literary taste. In the realm of literary theory and aesthetics, those texts prescribe a realist and socially committed reference (*hityahassut*) to the actual reality of the Jews in the Russian Empire. Philosophically, the publications in Hebrew of the Berdichev period raise a clear voice in favor of retaining the basic tenets of Jewish religious belief while harmonizing them with the new, European culture of Enlightenment.

Abramovitsh's poignant articulation of this familiar *maskilic* idea was directed against the moderate Lithuanian *maskil* Eliezer Zvi Zweifel (1815–1888). Abramovitsh claimed that Zweifel's version of Haskalah was a lukewarm and opportunistic blend of religious faith and secular Enlightenment. Zweifel ignored the Jewish Enlightenment's crucial call for a critical reassessment of religious belief. For Abramovitsh, true Haskalah must dare to submit all "accepted traditions" (excluding the "words of God" or the written and oral Jewish law [Torah]) to a strict epistemological reevaluation. The final outcome of Haskalah criticism should be a stable and reliable amalgam of traditional faith and rational knowledge. Zweifel's entire *maskilic* endeavor epitomized for Abramovitsh an indecisive limping between two opposing opinions, that is, between modern rationality and traditional faith. Abramovitsh's espousal of moderate and reflective *maskilic* ideology is also apparent in the novel *Ha'avot ve'habanim,* a love story, which presents the younger generation's infatuation with the Haskalah as a central aspect of its spiritual and political maturity.

Abramovitsh's attempts to revitalize the thought and practice of the Jewish Enlightenment took a markedly social turn in the late 1860s. He wrote *Di Takse* (The Tax, 1869), a socially minded play that criticizes the power structures that held sway in the large Jewish town of Berdichev. In addition, Abramovitsh published the first version of *Fishke der Krumer* (Fishke the Lame, 1869), which became—after many revisions, in both Yiddish and Hebrew—the mainstay of Abramovitsh's bilingual oeuvre. Together with the aforementioned *Dos Vintshfingeril, Fishke der Krumer* appeared in an enlarged Yiddish version in 1888; both were translated into Hebrew, respectively, as *Be'emek ha'bakha* (In the Valley of Tears, 1904) and *Sefer ha'Kabbtsanim* (Book of Beggars, 1909). They incorporate the most representative and memorable aspects of Abramovitsh fiction: a curious mixture of scathing social criticism of the shtetl (village) with a sentimental empathy for its inhabitants.

During the 1870s, in the town of Zhitomer, Abramovitsh published a short social allegory under the title *Di Klyatshe* (The Nag, 1873) and an allegory of Jewish history,

Mendele Moykher Sforim. *(Courtesy of the Library of the Jewish Theological Seminary)*

titled *Dos Yidl* (The Little Jew, 1875). In 1878 he published the picaresque novel *Kitser masoes Binyomin ha'shlishi* (Travels of Benjamin the Third), which he translated into Hebrew in 1896. Those texts study the situation of the Russian Jews within the tumultuous international power structure of Europe. The stress Abramovitsh placed on the historical and political position of the Jews in Europe separates his 1870s works from his earlier, *maskilic* attention to their spiritual and educational situation.

Abramovitsh's deep commitment to the wide popular reach of Haskalah ideology was the motivation behind the publication of a Yiddish translation—complete with popular scientific commentary—of two traditional Jewish religious texts, *Zemirot Yisrael* and *Perek shirah* (1875). The latter is a long, laudatory ode that describes the natural world as a harmonious, teleological system. In his commentary, Abramovitsh employed passages from his own *Toldot ha'teva* for establishing a wholesome picture of the natural world, where scientific knowledge of nature operates in tandem with the traditional praise for the Creator's unfailing wisdom.

The so-called Zhitomer years (1869–1881) were crucial for Abramovitsh's development as a Hebrew publicist and essayist. His essays of that period are ambitious, in both scale and thematic reach. Setting aside the polemics with various rival *maskilim*, the new essays of the Zhitomer period evoke more radical questions about the material and metaphysical measures that should be undertaken in order to change the historical and social situation of the Jews in Europe. The essays treat various issues, such as the attitude toward women in Jewish education, the metaphysics and politics of Jewish sovereignty in Europe, and the advantages and limitations of nationalism (e.g., "Ma annu?" [What Are We?], *Ha'shaḥar* 6, 1875; "Hagoy lo nichsaf" [Nation Not Desired], *Ha'maggid* 19–23, 1875; and "Ahava le'umit ve'toldotea" [History of Patriotism], *Ha'melitz* 6–7, 10–12, 15, 1878). The critique of Haskalah in *Di Klyatshe,* taken together with the materialist and utilitarian worldview advocated in the Hebrew essays, account for Abramovitsh's deep acceptance of the materialist and positivist trends that flourished in Russian philosophy and literature at that time.

The last period in Abramovitsh's long writing career (Odessa, 1881–1917) is dominated by his decision to join forces with the growing body of Hebrew literature, written under the aegis of Jewish national renaissance. Abramovitsh forcefully and famously returned to the sphere of Hebrew literature with the story "Beseter ra'am" (The Secret Place of Thunder, 1886), a daring attempt to come to terms with both the anti-Semitic pogroms of the early 1880s and the cultural and political upheavals that came in their aftermath within the Jewish world. "Be'seter ra'am" was the first of a few short Hebrew stories that together consolidated his canonic stature as the genius-creator of the post-*maskilic* Hebrew-literary idiom. This *nusaḥ* (style) has since been celebrated by many critics (e.g., Alter 1988, Bialik 1954) as better suited to realistic literature, mainly due to its flexible syntax and multilayered vocabulary. Politically, however, Abramovitsh was highly skeptical of the newly emerging public infatuation with the pre-Zionist Hibbat-Zion movement, which called for a celebration of Jewish life in the Land of Israel. His stories refuse to adopt a strictly progressive view of history (i.e., the inevitable move from Haskalah to nationalism), preferring, instead, to evoke deep suspicion vis-à-vis the consequence, dangers, and seductions of the rise of modern nationalism. Abramovitsh died in Odessa on December 8, 1917.

The most important aspect of Abramovitsh's participation in the production of Jewish folklore lies in the nature of his literary persona, Mendele the Book Peddler, and in his specifically "Mendelean" representation of the shtetl. Over the course of the twentieth century, various scholars analyzed and theorized both aspects of Abramovitsh's literary career. The consequence of this extensive scholarly endeavor can be described as consisting of three major, consecutive phases: (1) the prestructuralist phase (the "aesthetics of ugliness"); (2) the structuralist phase (from the 1960s onward); and (3) the current and emerging poststructuralist reading of

Abramovitsh, which has resulted in numerous volumes of literary criticism.

Dan Miron's classical study of the Mendele's persona (1996, first published in 1973) is instrumental in defining the aesthetic ideology of the first phase, as well as its radical critique and ultimate displacement in the second phase. Together with other scholars, most notably Gershon Shaked (1965) and Menahem Perry (1968), Miron sets out to defend Abramovitsh's literary artifice from what he defined as "the fallacy of "folk archetype." Critics who took the folk-archetypal path interpreted Abramovitsh's Mendele as a common man, a "positive plebian," "one of the common people," or a person through which "the soul of the people speaks." As such, Mendele became an epitome of "the aesthetics of ugliness," an aesthetic attitude that defined the merits of Yiddish literature solely in terms of its ability to represent the abnormality, absurdity, and self-destructive particularity of the Jewish people in Eastern Europe. As an aesthetic depiction of Jewish abnormality, Yiddish literature in general—and Abramovitsh's work in particular—did nothing more than replicate the deformed particularities of Jewish life. Within this framework, some critics argued that Abramovitsh's work is a radical attack on the very existence of the Jewish shtetl (Brenner 1967; Kariv 1950), while others believed that his work is a "pleasing idiosyncrasy," as Miron put it, or a nostalgic preservation of the shtetl (Frishman 1914).

In both cases, however, the literary imitation of the folklore element is reduced to a "comic mimesis," that is, an imitation that flouts—critically or nostalgically—the incorrigible ugliness or abnormality of the social world it represents. According to this aesthetic ideology (its main speaker was, according to Miron, Sholem Aleichem), Yiddish literature is capable only of "externalistic, mimetic, comic perception of reality" (Miron 1996, 72). The reason for this limitation lies in the nature—or rather, the stereotype—of the Yiddish language. Due to its verbal gesticulations and elasticity, the Yiddish literary artifact tends to impersonate and *become* the folkloric subject matter it imitates. The oral, communal, and particularistic characteristics of Yiddish literature turn it, for better or worse, into an embodiment, an authentic replication of "the Jew" in Eastern Europe. However, in the process of impersonating the archetypal Jew, Yiddish literature loses it *literary* value as a universal medium of criticism and transcendence. In the "aesthetics of ugliness" the imitator is said to be incapable of guarding against losing his or her own autonomy vis-à-vis the contagious and seductive powers that dwell in the social reality he or she set out to imitate.

The folk-archetypal reading of Abramovitsh typically stresses, first, the oral-conversational character of its language; second, its reach toward the communal (rather than individual or psychological) aspects of Jewish life; and, third, its deviation from any universal norm of truth, common sense, or beauty. This led critics of the first phase to believe that Abramovitsh's literature is inherently circumscribed by the "chains of ordinary life" (*avotot ha'havay;* Tzemach 1968) and that, consequently, it lacks "expressive" literary value.

This view has been challenged from a structuralist viewpoint, which stresses the authority of the literary text vis-à-vis the social world. Critics like Miron, Perry, and Shaked raised forceful objections against the first phase of Abramovitsh's reception. Rather than a simple mimetic replication of Jewish communal and linguistic practices, the new reading of Abramovitsh stresses Mendele's dual *re*presentational competence, that is, his ability to give voice to the old shtetl and, at same time, his ability to judge and criticize that form of life from a modern, secular, and Europeanized point of view. Readers in the second phase believe that Mendele knows very well how to inspire the typical Jewish merchant or trafficker (such as Alter) to talk. However, these critics also point out that Mendele is very quick and adroit in expressing the critical view of "common sense" (Shaked) or in voicing the verdict of the "universality of common humanity" (Miron) as he encounters and represents the Jewish form of life. If the prestructuralist phase of Abramovitsh's reception was monolithic in its stress on Mendele's gesticulating mimicry of the communal-folkloric elements, the structuralist reading of him turns our attention to Mendele's ability to be in two places at one time. Mendele is a go-between, a "ventriloquist" who is able to assume the voice of the common Jews (in fact, to be the common Jew) while commenting and passing scathing judgments vis-à-vis that very social and cultural existence. Whereas the first phase of Abramovitsh criticism presented the folkloric elements as if they existed "outside" the literary work, the structuralist phase stresses Mendele's double act of representation and criticism. Mendele ventures into the old world in order to transform and "modernize" it, by means of his emphatic representation and criticism. For critics of the second phase, Mendele's literary genius is marked by his daring ability to delve into the depths of Jewish exilic experience, in order to emerge back with it as a symbol of modernized Jewish identity.

The nascent poststructuralist phase challenges the notions of transcendence, normalization, and secularization, which informs and motivates the structuralist reading of Abramovitsh. The third phase returns to the old mimetic model but denies its Platonic negative assessment as a mere replication of the social world. The poststructuralist readers of Abramovitsh believe that Mendele indeed loses himself in the act of impersonating the shtetl, but they argue that there is nothing wrong with that. The gesticulatory mimesis of the shtetl is stripped of its "debased" character as an abnormality and becomes active and independent force of critique: This time, however, it serves as a critique of modernity, European universality, and secularism (Banbaji 2009; Schwartz 1991). Politically, then, the poststructuralist readers of Abramovitsh deny the secularist or transcendent character of Abramovitsh's representation of the shtetl. In other words, while structuralist critics maintained that the folkloric, Jewish subject matter is a figure that the Abramovitsh's work is capable of framing and criticizing, the poststructuralist critics believe that his work—specifically Mendele's character—is a tableau that accommodates an undecided strife between two allegorical figures or, indeed, between "two Mendeles," the first being a typical Jew and the second a universal, Europeanized symbol of a modern Jewish identity. The latter Mendele, which was held as a figure of normalcy and universal judgment, is dethroned in the poststructuralist reading of Abramovitsh, but not for the sake of a nostalgic return to the old "aesthetics of ugliness." Reintroducing the old archetypal Jew as an equal participant in the literary imagination of the shtetl, the poststructuralist critics turn the readers' attention to Mendele's irredeemably fractured consciousness of Jewish modernity.

Amir Banbaji

Bibliography

Alter, Robert. *The Invention of Hebrew Prose.* Seattle: University of Washington Press, 1988.

Banbaji, Amir. *Mendele and the National Narrative.* Beer Sheva: Heksherim and Ben Gurion University Press, 2009.

Bialik, Hayyin Nahman. "The Inventor of Hebrew Style." In H.N. Bialik, *Divre Sifrut*, pp. 170–175. Tel Aviv: Dvir, 1954 (in Hebrew).

Brenner, Yosef Hayyim. "Self-Criticism in Abramovitsch's Three Volumes." In *Kol kitve Y.H. Brenner,* vol. 3, pp. 57–58. Tel Aviv: Ha'kibbutz, Ha'meuḥad, 1967 (in Hebrew).

Frishman, David. "Mendele Mokher Sefarim: Biography, Evaluation and a Survery of His Books." In *Kol kitve Mendele Mokher Sefarim,* vol. 2, pp. 3–29. Odessa: Vaad Hayovel, 1914 (in Hebrew).

Mendele Project at the Hebrew University of Jerusalem. *Mendele Mokher Sepharim: Bibliography of His Works and Letters*. Jerusalem: Magnes Press, 1965 (in Hebrew and Yiddish).

Miron, Dan. *Between Vision and Truth.* Jerusalem: Mosad Bialik, 1979 (in Hebrew).

———. *A Traveler Disguised: The Rise of Modern Yiddish Fiction in the Nineteenth Century.* 2d ed. Syracuse, NY: Syracuse University Press, 1996.

Kariv, Avraham. *Speaking My Heart.* Tel Aviv: Am Oved, 1950 (in Hebrew).

Perry, Menahem. "The Role of Analogies in the Structure of Mendele Mokher Sefarim's Novels." *Hasifrut* 1 (1968): 66–100 (in Hebrew).

Schwarz, Yigal. "Initial Remarks for a New Reading of *Sefer hakabtsanim.*" *Achshav* 57 (1991): 144–168 (in Hebrew).

Shaked, Gershon. "Between Laughter and Tear." Ramat Gan: Makor, 1965 (in Hebrew).

Tzemach, Shlomo. "Under the Spell of Ordinary Life." In *Massot u'reshimot,* pp. 39–61. Ramat Gan: Massada, 1968 (in Hebrew).

Museums (Vernacular) in Israel

The publication of *Museums of Israel* (Rosovsky and Ungerleider-Mayerson, 1989), an English-language guidebook to Israeli museums, marked the public recognition given to vernacular museums in Israel, that is, local heritage museums established through largely nonprofessional, grassroots efforts. These museums reflect Israelis' passion for preserving and interpreting the past. Since the late twentieth century, this widely recognized popular interest in local heritage has given rise to the establishment of more than a hundred local museums across the country, about one-third of them in kibbutzim (collective settlements) and others in moshavim (noncollective settlements), small towns, and urban centers.

Taken together, the local heritage museums that dot the country inscribe various strands of the metanarrative of the Zionist enterprise of place-making and nation-building. They provide object-rich arenas in which stories are told and retold of ancient national roots that can be gleaned through archaeological finds; attachment to place that is expressed through the collection of local flora and fauna; or territorial claims that are reflected in the commemoration of foundational acts of settlement. Many of these vernacular museums were first informally established by a charismatic enthusiast (referred to locally as *meshuga ladavar),* often aided by a small group of followers. Once established, they became locally institutionalized through the vote of the kibbutz general assembly, or the decision of some other governing body, and only later received the recognition (and, at times, financial support) of national authorities, such as the Ministries of Culture, Education, Tourism, or Defense (the Museum Act legally regulating the museum field was passed in 1983).

The development of the Israeli local museum scene before the 1970s was gradual and involved mainly the establishment of museums centered on regional archaeological collections and nature-related environmental displays. In addition, a few local museums were devoted to Israeli art (e.g., Ein Harod, in the Jezreel Valley near Mount Gilboa in northern Israel), and some were devoted to the memory of the Holocaust (e.g., Ghetto Fighters' House Museum in western Galilee). The development of the museum scene that took place in Israel during the last quarter of the twentieth century involved the establishment of dozens of museums concerned with the history of pre-Independence Zionist settlement, the history of building Israel's military force, and the history of the relationship between Israel and the Jewish Diasporas, usually framed in terms of the project of the Ingathering-of-the-Exiles, that is, the national effort to bring Jews from all over the world to the Land of Israel. These various thematic agendas ground the establishment of immigration, settlement, and military museums. They reflect the core Zionist metanarrative, whose tripartite concerns are Jewish immigration (aliyah, ideologically perceived as "ascendance"), settlement of the land, and self-defense through military means. Their proliferation in the later part of the twentieth century marks a change in the Israeli idiom of cultural legitimization. Notably while archaeological museums celebrate the Jews' ancient link to the land of Israel, settlement and military museums commemorate the foundational acts of place-making and self-defense. The nostalgic celebration of the nation-building era in the dozens of vernacular museums established around the country in the 1970s and 1980s is an intriguing cultural phenomenon, as it began just when the West Bank settlement movement turned acts of settlement into a highly contested political issue. It can be seen as a grassroots movement of cultural self-interrogation as well as reaffirmation that grew at a time when the troubled present was felt to cast a doubtful shadow on what mainstream Israelis believed to be a cherished past.

While the nation-building narrative presented by the majority of local museums tends to focus on the Land of Israel as the telos of a secular Israeli civil religion, the several ethnographic museums established during the same period are devoted mainly to the display of the cultural heritage of Jewish ethnic groups, such as Iraqi, Yemenite, Italian, German, or Hungarian Jews. The objects displayed in these museums are not the traces of a local, mostly agricultural past but the shreds of a partly lost cultural heritage authenticated through its links to a once-thriving diasporic center. They feature traditional Jewish ritual objects that are almost totally absent from settlement museums but are found in Judaica collections in Jewish museums worldwide. They tell a story of Jewish continuity in the Diaspora and through immigration to Israel, rather than narrating the implications of the Zionist revolution for the lives of pioneering communities and individuals.

The twenty-first century has seen the further institutionalization and professionalization that have taken place in Israeli vernacular museums, which have become thriving centers of educational activities for both children and adults. Some new museums have been established, for example, the Centers for the Heritage of the Jews of Libya and Turkey in the towns of Or Yehyda and Yahud, respectively, which display and narrate additional pieces of the Jewish-Israeli past. Some older museums, such as the first settlement museum in Israel located in Kibbutz Yifat in the Jezreel Valley, have renewed their exhibitions in line with new pedagogical approaches. Nonetheless, the oral guided tour in and through which past events and actions are continuously reassessed by live narrators in the light of the present remains the main source of a dynamic cultural dialogue in Israeli heritage museums.

Tamar Katriel

Bibliography

Inbar, Yehudit, and Ely Schiller, ed. *Museums in Israel.* Jerusalem: Ariel, 1990 (in Hebrew).

Katriel, Tamar. *Performing the Past: A Study in Israeli Settlement Museums.* Mahwah, NJ: Lawrence Erlbaum, 1997.

Rosovsky, Nitza, and Joy Ungerleider-Mayerson. *The Museums of Israel.* New York: Abrams, 1989.

Schiller, Ely, ed. "Museums in Kibbutzim." *Ariel* 60 (1988) (in Hebrew).

Museums, Jewish

Since their earliest incarnations at the end of the nineteenth century, Jewish museums have celebrated the folklore of the Jewish people. Starting in the mid-twentieth century they transitioned from being vehicles for the display of collections of ritual or folk objects to being much more varied in their approach and to having a particular story to tell. Many of the stories focus on local history and on Jews' social and cultural adaptations to the local environment, while still emphasizing some of the common aspects of Jewish life throughout the ages and in different lands.

Early History

The first Jewish exhibitions and museums, which were opened toward the end of the nineteenth century, focused on the display of Jewish ritual objects. This trend was set by the spectacular display of the Isaac Strauss collection at the Paris World's Fair in 1878. The objects from the collection were selected for their outstanding aesthetic merit, but they displayed according to the kind of ceremonial function for which they were originally designed. Thus, all Ḥanukkah lamps were displayed together, all Torah crowns together, and so forth. As scholars such as J.D. Feldman have expressed, this helped to recontextualize such objects in terms of ritual function and Jewish observance while still retaining the narrative of artistic achievement.

This method of display was evident in the earliest Jewish museums, in Vienna in 1895, Prague in 1906, and Frankfurt in 1922, and remained canonical for most subsequent displays of Jewish collections until the 1970s. The influence of such an approach can still be observed today in more recent museums, whether they be in Venice, Amsterdam, or Israel, as seen in the Israel Museum in Jerusalem.

In these museums, the dominant mode of display focused on the manner in which the Jewish communal leadership and leading families were able to integrate and make an important contribution to the welfare of the country in which they found themselves. The tone for such an approach was set by the Anglo-Jewish Historical Exhibition in London in 1887. The exhibition stressed the positive contribution made by British Jews and included letters, mementos, and portraits of distinguished persons. By stressing the way that Jews were similar to members of the wider society, the exhibition was staking a claim for Jews to be rightfully recognized as loyal British subjects.

Other exhibitions, however, sought to emphasize cultural distinctiveness and focused much more on folk art and folk costumes. One such exhibition, held in Cincinnati, Ohio, in 1913, portrayed Jews as coming to the United States from many different lands. The exhibition featured Jews who came from twenty-seven countries, each in their own booths, with men and women dressed in picturesque costumes. This exhibition was specifically designed to promote the idea of cultural pluralism as a positive feature of American society, at a time when there was mounting pressure to restrict immigration to the United States from Europe. Another example in this vein, but in a different political context, is represented by the An-Ski exhibition held in 1914, in St. Petersburg. This exhibition was based on materials gathered in the course of folklorist S. An-Ski's 1912 expedition in Ukraine and neighboring countries for the purpose of recovering items of Ashkenazi material culture. The exhibition displayed mainly objects obtained from peasant and rural households so as to place Jewish art within the same context as other so-called folk traditions within the Russian Empire, emphasizing the contributions made by ordinary people as opposed to those of the elite.

A few collections, such as the one in Danzig (present-day Gdánsk, Poland), combined both ritual objects and items of folk art, and in 1939, the Jewish community of Danzig sent its collection of Jewish folk art to the Jewish Museum in New York for temporary safekeeping, where it has remained. Most collections at the time, however, focused on Jewish ritual objects.

It is also in the 1930s that a new facet of Jewish art began to be displayed in Jewish museums: artwork by contemporary Jewish artists within the framework of a Jewish museum. The Jewish Museum in Berlin took the lead, when, under the directorship of Karl Schwartz, it opened in January 1933, with works by artists such as Max Liebermann and Jacob Steinhardt. But the experiment was short lived, and the museum was forced to close after the Nazi-initiated pogroms known as Kristallnacht in November 1938 vandalized or destroyed many Jewish cultural centers.

Nevertheless, the seed had been sown, and after World War II, when European Jews sought to rebuild from the ashes of the Holocaust, the Museum of Jewish Art was established in Paris in 1948. It was set up with the specific mission of collecting and displaying Jewish works of art, both religious and secular. The permanent exhibition included religious artifacts, reproductions of Jewish tombstones from Prague, and reproductions of synagogue mosaics. It also included a large collection of contemporary art, including works by Marc Chagall, Emmanuel Mane-Katz, Ben Benn, and Jacques Lipschitz. In 1988, the museum's collection was transferred to newer and grander premises at the Museum of Jewish Art and History in Paris.

Emphasis on Storytelling

By the 1960s, a tradition of exhibiting Jewish artifacts in European and American cities had already become well established and was becoming increasingly diversified, starting with a display of Jewish ritual objects and increasingly also taking note of folk art and of contemporary Jewish artists. However, the greatest change in the manner in which Jewish culture was displayed came in the 1970s and 1980s, with a new emphasis on history and storytelling.

Indeed, many Jewish museums began to change their displays and narratives in order to accommodate a more general trend emphasizing communal histories by focusing on the lives of ordinary people. The U.S. civil rights and women's movements led to a reassessment of the rights of indigenous and minority groups, as well as of the manner in which history was taught and retold. Exhibitions and displays began to celebrate cultural difference as something to be admired in its own right. Thus, the Jewish Museum in New York arranged exhibitions on the history of Jews on the Lower East Side of Manhattan, from the 1870s onward, as well as on the Yiddish theater.

Moreover, nation-states are increasingly promoting themselves as pluralistic and multicultural, which in turn is transforming modes of display. In the 2000s, Jewish folk and ritual objects are displayed in order to tell a story that illustrates a Jewish way of life, often focusing on Jewish festivals and the Jewish life cycle. Hence there is an increasing use of thematic displays in Jewish museums, with items laid out in such a way as to re-create a scene, for example, a table set out for a Friday evening meal or a Seder, as in the Jewish Museum in London, or a *ḥuppah* (wedding canopy) and a wedding scene or items associated with the burial society, as in the Jewish Museum in Prague.

The Jewish Museum in Berlin, which opened in September 2001, combines Jewish social history and way of life in an overarching story of the Jews. The permanent exhibition explores the interaction of Jews and gentiles in Germany over the past 2,000 years. The story includes courtly Jews and more humble rural dwellers, urban socialites and street hawkers, entertainers, scientists, artists, and businessmen. There are also portraits of Jews by Jewish artists and the display of books and articles written by Jews about their views on religion, society, child rearing, and other topics.

The exhibition focuses on the theme of tradition and change and, among other things, explores the transformations in the role of Jewish women in the process of social change. The exhibition tells the story of women such as the seventeenth-century businesswoman Glückel of Hameln, who kept a diary concerning her daily life; Henriette Herz, who initiated a literary salon in the early nineteenth century; Bertha Pappenheim, who led the Jewish women's movement in the early twentieth century; and Regina Jonas, the first woman ordained as a rabbi.

Over the past few decades, there has been an increasing emphasis on storytelling and narrative. Yet the most exciting developments still lie ahead. Many leading Jewish museums, whether in Jerusalem, London, or Warsaw, are boldly facing the challenge of going beyond narrative and are seeking to engage their audiences in encounters and discussions.

David Clark

Bibliography

Cohen, Richard I. *Jewish Icons: Art and Society in Modern Europe.* Berkeley: University of California Press, 1998.

Feldman, Jeffrey D. "Die Welt in der Vitrine und die Welt außerhalb: Die soziale Konstruktion jüdische Museumsexponate." In *Wiener Jahrbuch für Jüdische Geschichte, Kultur und Museumswesen,* vol. 1, pp. 39–54. Vienna: Christian Brandstätter, 1994.

Kirshenblatt-Gimblett, Barbara. "American Jewish Life: Ethnographic Approaches to Collection, Presentation and Interpretation in Museums." In *Folklife and Museums: Selected Readings,* ed. P. Hall and C. Seeman, pp. 143–161. Nashville: American Association for State and Local History, 1987.

———. *Destination Culture: Tourism, Museums and Heritage.* Berkeley: University of California Press, 1998.

Kushner, Tony. "The End of the Anglo-Jewish Progress Show: Representations of the Jewish East End, 1887–1987." In *The Jewish Heritage in British History,* ed. T. Kushner, pp. 78–105. London: Frank Cass, 1992.

N

Name, Naming

See: Circumcision; Folk Belief

Narkiss, Mordechai

See: Folk Art

New Year Cards

Every year hundreds of thousands of Jewish New Year cards are mailed throughout the world. Contrary to a widely held opinion, the origin of this custom predates by centuries the sending of Christian New Year cards, which have been popular in Europe and the United States since the nineteenth century.

The custom is first mentioned in the *Book of Customs* of Rabbi Jacob Moelin Halevi (called the Maharil; ca. 1360–1427), the spiritual leader of German Jews in the fourteenth century (*Minhagei Maharil* [Sabionetta, 1556]). Based on the familiar talmudic dictum in the tractate *Rosh Ha'shanah* 16b concerning the "setting down" of one's fate in one of the three Heavenly books that are opened on the Jewish New Year, the Maharil and other German rabbis recommended that letters sent during the month of Elul should open with the blessing "May you be inscribed and sealed for a good year." Other than in Germany and Austria, not many in the Ashkenazi world followed this custom before the modern era. In fact, other than the Sephardim and Jews in Islamic lands, Jews did not undertake the practice of sending New Year cards until relatively recently.

The German-Jewish custom reached widespread popularity, however, only with the invention—in Vienna, in 1869—of the postcard. This invention won immediate success, and within a few years the plain cards were enriched with illustrations, which attracted the public to buy more and more cards, festooned with beloved and familiar themes. The high period of the illustrated postcard, called in the literature "The Postal Card Craze" (1898–1918), marks also the flourishing of the Jewish New Year card in Europe and the United States. During these years, cards were printed in three major centers: Germany, Poland, and the United States (chiefly New York). The German cards are frequently illustrated with biblical themes, such as the Giving of the Law or the Binding of Isaac, which were popular also among the general public. The urban makers of the Jewish cards (mostly in Warsaw), however, preferred nostalgic depictions of the religious life of Eastern European Jews, often using photography. Though the photographs on their cards were often theatrically staged in a studio with amateur actors, they preserve the visual reality—how things looked at the time the postcards were produced—and customs lost in the Holocaust. Moreover, some of the cards depict customs (such as "Krishme bei den Kimpterin" [The Reading of the Shema Prayer for a Woman in Childbirth]) that provide the folklorist with the only visual testimony of the said practice. The mass immigration of Jews from Eastern Europe to the United States in the first decades of the twentieth century gave a new boost to the production of the cards. Colorful and elaborate cards frequently depicted America as the new homeland, widely opening its arms for the new immigrants. At the same time, other American cards emphasized the Zionist ideology and depicted contemporary views of Eretz Israel.

Even before the invention of the postcard, tablets of varying sizes bearing wishes and images for the new year were in wide use by the Jews of nineteenth-century Eretz Israel ("The Old Yishuv"). These tablets depicted the holy sites of the "four holy cities" in the Holy Land, in particular, those in and around Jerusalem. A popular biblical motif was the *Akedah,* the Binding of Isaac, often "taking place" against the background of the Temple Mount and accompanied by the prayer for Rosh Ha'Shana, which mentions the *Akedah.* Also common were interior and exterior views of yeshivas or buildings of the various organizations that produced these tablets. The tablets were commonly sent abroad for fund-raising purposes.

With successive waves of new immigrations (*aliyot*), the images on the cards changed dramatically, almost without a transitional stage. Instead of the religious sentiments of the Diaspora communities and the Old Yishuv, in the 1920s and 1930s the cards highlighted the land that was purchased and settled by Jews—that is, the new settlements, such as farm lands, villages, and towns, including Tel Aviv and Petaḥ Tikvah; the tilling of the land; and "secular" views of the proud new pioneers. At the same time, the very growth in the consumption and production of these cards attests that the traditional and basically religious custom continued and even became increasingly popular. Moreover, the new cards demonstrate a burst of creativity and originality not only in the new subject matter but also in their innovative graphic designs and the texts accompanying them. Thus, the wishes on the cards call for "A year of conquering our land," "A year of construction and immigration," "A year of flourishing of our homeland," "A year of the revival of our people," "A year of the triumph of light over darkness," and so forth.

In the years preceding the establishment of the State of Israel, the cards called for the development of the country, the expansion of its borders, and the ingathering of the exiles from all corners of the world. One card bears the wish "A new generation will come to the Land [of Israel] that will never know the yoke of Diaspora." The hardship of life in the transition camps and the strains of shortages during the 1950s are reflected in many cards from these years, depicting images of fruits and other foods and accompanied by the wish for "a year of abundance and plenty." This period also witnessed the beloved images of proud soldiers bravely guarding their young homeland. This tendency increased after the Six-Day War. The heroes of the war, political leaders, and soldiers depicted against the background of the liberated holy sites, filled the stalls selling New Year cards in Israeli streets. These images were replaced in the 1970s by views of the "ideal Israeli family," shown fashionably dressed in its well-appointed apartment.

Most recently, the custom of mailing New Year cards has declined in Israel. Instead, many now prefer to call or send e-mail messages. In other countries, especially the United States, cards with traditional symbols, which are sent by postal mail, are still common. The new cards, however, are much more elaborate and use a variety of techniques, including pop-ups and papercuts. Thus, the simple and naive New Year cards, which are commonly discarded after the holiday, vividly reflect the dramatic changes in the life of the Jewish people through the generations.

Shalom Sabar

See also: Rosh Ha'Shana.

Bibliography

Arbel, Rachel, ed. *Blue and White in Color: Visual Images of Zionism, 1897–1947.* Tel Aviv: Beth Hatefusoth, 1997.

Branska, Joanna. *"Na Dobry Rok badzcie zapisani": Zydowskie karty noworoczne firmy Jehudia* (You Will be Written for a Good Year: Jewish New Year Cards). Warsaw: Biblioteka Narodowa, 1997.

Goodman, Philip. "Rosh Hashanah Greeting Cards." In *The Rosh Hashanah Anthology,* ed. P. Goodman, pp. 274–279, 356. Philadelphia: Jewish Publication Society of America, 1970.

Sabar, Shalom. "Between Poland and Germany: Jewish Religious Practices in Illustrated Postcards of the Early Twentieth Century." *Polin: Studies in Polish Jewry* 16 (2003): 137–166.

———. "The Custom of Sending Jewish New Year Cards: Its History and Artistic Development." *Jerusalem Studies in Jewish Folklore* 19/20 (1997/1998): 85–110.

———. "Introduction." In *Past Perfect: The Jewish Experience in Early 20th Century Postcards,* pp. 5–13. New York: Library of the Jewish Theological Seminary of America, 1999.

Smith, Ellen. "Greetings from Faith: Early Twentieth-Century American Jewish New Year Postcards." In *The Visual Culture of American Religions,* ed. David Morgan and Sally M. Promey, pp. 229–248, 350–356. Berkeley: University of California Press, 2001.

Tartakover, David. *Shanah Tovah: 101 New Year Cards.* Jerusalem: Keter, 1978 (in Hebrew).

Tzur, Muki, ed. *The Next Year: New Year Cards from the Kibbutz.* Giv'at Haviva: Yad Yaari, 2001 (in Hebrew).

NIGER, SHMUEL

See: Poland, Jews of

NITL NAKHT

See: Ḥanukkah

NOAH

The story of Noah and the Flood, recounted in Genesis 6–9, is a tale of cosmic destruction and re-creation after the first attempt at creation failed. The similarity between the biblical narrative and Mesopotamian myths, especially the Epic of Gilgamesh, is striking, although Mesopotamian-polytheistic motifs are transformed so as to serve the monotheistic worldview of the Bible. The biblical account of both the cataclysmic event and its human protagonist, Noah, is rather terse and at times opaque, leaving much to the imagination of later interpreters. Alternatively, the biblical narrative itself can be viewed as concealing circulating traditions of ancient time that resurfaced in later, Second Temple and postbiblical, writings. Two aspects implicit in the biblical account of the flood appear explicitly in extracanonical traditions: the analogy between the flood as re-creation and the first creation of humankind as portrayed in Genesis 1–2, and the breaching of sexual categories within which the biblical account of the flood is framed.

Noah's Moral Stature

The biblical Noah is cast in ambivalent terms. On the one hand, he is the person chosen by the Almighty to be the sole survivor of humanity. Scripture explicitly states that "Noah found favor with the Lord" and that "Noah was a righteous man; he was blameless in his age; Noah walked with God" (Gen. 6:8–9). On the other hand, Noah's shameful behavior in which he is exposed naked to his son Ḥam in a state of drunkenness (Gen. 9:18–26) presents him as a flawed model. In fact, when Scripture describes him as "blameless in his age," it might be qualifying his piety by contextualizing it in a comparative (to his age) manner. Second Temple texts, as well as rabbinic writings, oscillate between these two views of his character. The Babylonian Talmud articulates this dual image vividly (108a): "Noah was a righteous man; he was blameless in his age. Rabbi Yoḥanan said: In his age, but not in other ages. And Resh Lakish, said: In his age, how much more so in other generations. Rabbi Ḥanina said: To what may Rabbi Yoḥanan's view be likened? To a barrel of wine that is laid in a cellar of vinegar. In its place [compared to the vinegar], its odor is fragrant; not in its place, its odor will not be fragrant. Rabbi Oshaya said: To what may Resh Lakish's view be likened? To a dish of perfume that is laid in a place of filth. In its place, its fragrance spreads and how much more so in a place of perfume."

Noah's Birth

Accompanying the view of Noah as a cultural hero (and possibly addressing textual hints in Gen. 5:29), some traditions provide details on his birth, imbuing it with the necessary miraculous elements. According to 1 Enoch 106:2–16, when Noah appeared, "His body was like snow and red like the flower of the rose, and the hair of his head [was] white like wool . . . and his father, Lemech, was afraid of him and fled and went to his father, Methuselaḥ. And he said to him: 'I have begotten a strange son; he is not like a man, but is like the children of the angels of heaven . . . and I am afraid lest something extraordinary should be done on the earth in his days.'" Methuselaḥ then turns to the heavenly figure of his father, Enoch, who reassures him that the child and his sons will be saved from destruction. In the Genesis Apocryphon (column 5, 12–13), Lemech describes the newborn Noah, saying that "his eyes shone like the sun . . . this youth is on fire." In *Midrash Ha'gadol* (Gen. 5:29), Noah's miraculous birth is signaled by the fact that he was born already circumcised, thus associating him with other outstanding individuals such as Moses and David, who are said to have been born circumcised. The Genesis Apocryphon and 1 Enoch also refer to Lemech's anxieties regarding his paternity, situating Noah in surprising proximity to other cultural heroes such as Jesus, Samson and even Isaac.

Noah, Animals, and Sexual Transgressions

Assuming that humankind was indeed deserving of annihilation, how could the animals be accused of mortal sin? According to some traditions, the animals were guilty of sexual sins similar to those practiced by humanity. They, too, were copulating with members of other species (*Tanḥuma Buber,* Noah 11), analogous to the marriage of the sons of God and the daughters of men (Gen. 6:1–4, preceding the verse that recounts God's realization of the wickedness on earth). Sexual motifs appear in the biblical story—in the paragraph preceding the decree of the flood and in the postflood scene in which Noah's nakedness is exposed. Extracanonical traditions further develop the theme of sexual transgression, expanding it to the realm of the animals, for example, animals that violated the rule of sexual abstinence in the ark were punished. Such was the fate of the dog that was punished by remaining attached to its partner, the raven who was condemned to spitting, and Ḥam (hereby associated with the animal realm) who was inflicted with a dark complexion (*b. Sanhedrin* 108b).

Immoral conduct and divine retribution thus form the crux of this etiological tradition. The raven's licentious character is explicitly linked to his untrustworthy behavior as Noah's first messenger (Gen. 8:6). According to the Talmud, when Noah sends the raven away, the latter protests that not only is it rendered an unclean animal, hence there are only two of his kind in the ark, but now Noah chooses it for a dangerous mission. By so doing, claims the raven (rightfully), Noah is endangering the future of the species. However, the raven goes on to accuse Noah of coveting its (the raven's) "wife." Noah's furious answer alludes to the fact that he has remained abstinent throughout the period.

The Arc and the Garden of Eden

That Noah's interaction with the raven becomes so intimate should not be surprising, for Noah had spent almost an entire year on board in close quarters with representatives of the animal kingdom. We are told of the sleepless nights and hard toil that were entailed in taking care of the varied needs and routines of the different animals (e.g. *Tanḥuma Buber,* Noah 2). A few specific incidents are reported: The lion, for instance, attacked Noah as a result of which he began to limp (*Tanḥuma,* printed edition, Noah 9). The lion's ungrateful behavior stands in contrast to that of the *urshana* (a dove or pigeon), which displayed gracious conduct for which he was blessed with the phoenix motif of eternity (*b. Sanhedrin* 108b). Here, it is worth noting that another rabbinic version of the phoenix myth appears in relation to the Garden of Eden, where the bird declines the forbidden fruit of the tree of knowledge, which Eve offers to Adam as well as the animals. His refusal, in turn, saves him from the overarching principle of existence, namely, mortality (*Gen. Rab.* 19:5). That these two rabbinic versions appear in connection with the paradisic phase of the first creation and in the context of the womblike ark emphasizes the conception of the flood as a modified reenactment of the first, failed, effort at creation.

The threads leading from the Garden of Eden to the ark are made visible by the tradition that explains Noah's vine as having originated there (*Pirqe de'Rabbi Eliezer* 23). The miraculous vine bore fruit on the very same day it was planted, but turned out to cause great damage. Not only did drunkenness trigger Noah's immodest conduct, but, having awakened from his stupor, he realizes Ḥam's indiscretion and curses the latter's son, Canaan (Gen. 9:20–27). Noah, as the archetypal drunk, plays the lead role in the following didactic tale: "When Noah came to plant a vineyard, Satan came and stood before him . . . what did Satan do? He brought a sheep and killed it beneath the vine . . . a lion and killed it . . . a pig and killed it . . . a monkey and killed it beneath the vineyard and sprinkled their blood . . . and they irrigated it with their blood. God indicated [by these] that before a man drinks wine behold he is as innocent as that sheep . . . when he has drunk aplenty, behold, he is as bold as the lion . . . when he has drunk too much, he becomes like a pig . . . when he has gotten drunk, he becomes like a monkey: standing, and dancing and uttering obscenities before all and unaware of what he is doing" (*Tanḥuma,* printed edition, Noah 13). This tale is also one of the early versions of the tale type "The Devil in the Ark" (AT 825).

Modern Traditions

Modern oral narratives, as recorded in the Israel Folktale Archives (IFA) at the University of Haifa, attest to the ongoing appeal of Noah's story. While some narratives rely on earlier, written sources, others offer expansions, introducing into the biblical framework novel motifs and generic structuring. Satan's role in planting the vine is, according to one tale (IFA 13715), the endpoint of a longer scheme. According to this tale, Satan tricked his way into the ark and put his hand on the grapeseeds that he found there. Noah, who had his own plans for planting a vineyard, agreed to a pact with Satan and entered into partnership with him. Another tale (IFA 11435) builds on the above-cited tradition of the lion's attacking Noah, but adds that the lion felt deep remorse and earned Noah's forgiveness. The repenting lion is thus rewarded by being placed on King Solomon's chair. A seemingly popular tale (IFA 660, 15081, 5024) deals with Noah's shortage of daughters (in the biblical narrative we hear of none; here he has one) in light of three prospective grooms, either his own sons or strangers. The solution is found in the transformation of a dog and a donkey into the two missing brides. The tale suggests that most wives are beastly, in one way or another. A few tales are etiological in their treatment of relationships between animals, providing a drama that has its roots in the ark (IFA 2371, 7422). In other tales the emphasis is on Noah as a model of redemption in which he is presented as motivated by selfish concerns and is measured vis-à-vis other models, associated with figures such as Abraham and Moses (IFA 15986, 7864).

Dina Stein

See also: Animals; Ararat.

Bibliography

Dundes, Alan, ed. *The Flood Myth.* Berkeley: University of California Press, 1988.

Ginzberg, Louis. *Legends of the Jews,* vol. 1. Baltimore: Johns Hopkins University Press, 1998.

Kugel, James L. *Traditions of the Bible.* Cambridge, MA: Harvard University Press, 1998.

Levenson, Jon D. *Creation and the Persistence of Evil: The Jewish Drama of Divine Omnipotence.* San Francisco: Harper & Row, 1988.

Niehoff, Maren R. "The Phoenix in Rabbinic Literature." *Harvard Theological Review* 89:3 (1996): 245–265.

Patai, Raphael. *The Children of Noah: Jewish Seafaring in Ancient Times.* Princeton, NJ: Princeton University Press, 1999.

Sarna, Nahum M. *Understanding Genesis: The World of the Bible in the Light of History.* New York: Jewish Theological Seminary of America/Schocken, 1966.

Shinan, Avigdor, and Yair Zakovitch. *Once Again: That's Not What the Good Book Says.* Tel Aviv: Yediot Ahronot, 2009 (in Hebrew).

Yassif, Eli. *The Hebrew Folktale: History, Meaning, Genre.* Bloomington: Indiana University Press, 1999.

NORTH AFRICA, JEWS OF

According to archaeological sites, Jewish communities settled in North Africa beginning in at least the third century B.C.E. The most ancient of these sites are in Libya and the most recent ones (third century C.E.) in Morocco, which seems to support scholars' hypothesis that Jews came to North Africa from ancient Israel after a stay in Egypt and scattered progressively from East to West, from the Middle East to the Atlantic in the Hellenic-Roman Empire. Another thesis, which was influential in the twentieth century, argues that North African Jewry descends essentially from Zenata Berbers, who were converted by Jewish missionaries before the Arab conquest and organized resistance in the Algerian Aures Mountains to Arab troops, headed by the so-called Judeo-Berber queen, the Kahina. But serious sustained and detailed epigraphic and historical research showed the weakness of this thesis, which was presented in the fourteenth century by the Arab philosopher Ibn Khaldun, who referred to Arab traditions originating in the eleventh century. It is also probable that some Eastern Jewish groups came to North Africa accompanying Arab troops and after the Arab conquest was completed. All these Jewish groups created a rich and diverse folklore, at times influenced by the broader North African culture, and have sustained elements of that folklore to this.

Islamic Rule in the Middle Ages

Beginning in the eighth century, North African Jews developed their own culture and forged their history under the patronage and control of Islamic civilization, which imposed on them the humiliating regime of the *dhimma* (protection). Under this status, their existence in Dar al-Islam (House of Islam) was tolerated and their life and properties secure in exchange for their recognition of Muslim state superiority; payment of a communal tax, the *jizya;* and acceptance of other constraints and daily humiliations. Under these sociopolitical conditions, North African Jews developed urban centers of great reknown, such as Gabes, Kairouan, and Mahdia (in present-day Tunisia); Tahert and Qal'at Hammad (in present-day Algeria); and Walili, Fez, and Sijilmasa (in present-day Morocco), where they engaged in economic activities as merchants, goldsmiths, and craftsmen and studied and created halakhic (legal) and linguistic treatises in Hebrew as well in Judeo-Arabic. They were in close contact with the Middle Eastern Jewish communities of Iraq, Egypt, and the Holy Land and had regular exchanges with the Jewish communities of medieval Spain, which were ruled at that time by the same North African Berber tribes. With these communities, they developed the rich written Judeo-Arabic culture, in the fields of philosophy and medicine as well as of biblical and talmudic exegesis.

This intense Jewish creativity reached its climax in the eleventh century in Kairouan and Fez. In Kairouan, figures such as Rabbi Ḥanan'el ben Ḥushi'el and Rabbi Nissim ben Jacob ibn Shahin were heads of yeshivas in the first half of the eleventh century and wrote talmudic treatises. Rabbi Nissim also gathered the first anthology of old and new Jewish talmudic and folktales, in Middle Classic Judeo-Arabic, which thereafter was widespread in the Jewish world. In Fez, Hebrew grammarians and poets—as well as great talmudic scholars such as Rabbi Isaac ben Jacob Alfasi Hacohen (called the Rif), whose supplements to talmudic jurisdiction (the *Tosafot*) influenced the development of halakhic law and the blossoming of the Jewish cultural center of Spain—were among the heads of the Spanish Golden Age. Nonetheless Rabbi Moshe ben Maimon (Maimonides; 1135–1204) left Granada to go to Fez with his family in 1160 and stayed there for five years in a famous yeshiva. This intense Jewish existence was abolished by the destruction of Kairouan in 1056 with the invasion of North Africa by Egyptian Bedouin tribes. In the second half of the twelfth century, the persecutions imposed by the fundamentalist Almohad dynasty, which left southern Morocco and conquered all of North Africa and Islamic Spain, forced Jewish communities to convert to Islam or die, and thus destroyed all the Jewish communities there. Until the rise of the Merinid dynasty at the beginning of the fourteenth century, many Jewish families lived as Muslims in the open but honored their Jewish traditions and lifestyle secretly, allowing for the restoration of a Jewish communal life thereafter.

Jews in the Early Modern Era

At the end of the fourteenth century and in the fifteenth century, Jews who were refugees from Spain and Portugal settled in North African urban communities and contributed to the broader culture. They were able to maintain their Jewish identity and economic life thanks to their culture developed over some six centuries. In 1392, because of the Christian persecutions of Jews in northern Spain, great rabbinical Spanish figures settled in Algeria and founded important Jewish centers of Halakhah, Hebrew poetry, and exegesis. Thus numerous rabbinical figures settled in Algiers and Tlemcen, with hundreds of refugees, and led the recovering Jewish communities of North Africa. In Tlemcen, Rabbi Ephraim Ankawa (1359–1442) was considered a holy man and his tomb became a place of pilgrimage. In Algiers, Rabbi Shimon ben Semah Duran (1361–1444) and Rabbi Yitzhak bar Sheshet Perfet (called the Rivash; 1326–1407) were respected rabbinical scholars, renowned *dayyanim* (judges), and great Hebrew poets as well. Their descendants led the community of Algiers for centuries.

Those expelled from Spain in 1492 (and from Portugal in 1496) (*megorashim*) found a precarious refuge in northern Moroccan and Algerian ports before they scattered in local or inland Jewish communities, such as Oran, Honein, and Tlemcen in western Algeria; Larache, Sale, Tetuan, Tangier, Fez, Meknes, Sefru, and even Marrakesh, in Morocco; or before their emigration to other places in Europe (primarily Italy) or in the Ottoman Empire, especially the Holy Land. Some of them suffered casualties from local potentates upon their arrival, but thereafter they gained the protection of central powers, such as the kings of the Moroccan Saadian dynasty, who saw them as a new, valuable social group, capable of contributing to the economy of their country or their region. In some communities, such as Fez and Marrakesh, tensions developed between the *megorashim* and the indigenous Jewish communities, due to their different Jewish habits and traditions and to their Spanish or Andalusian culture. They even constituted separate communities, with rabbinical leaders and synagogues of their own for a period. Yet these Castilian rabbis and merchants soon became the leaders of their merged communities, and their descendants led them until their dispersion in the second half of the twentieth century.

In the fifteenth and sixteenth centuries, descendants of *megorashim* who settled first in Italy, especially in Livorno, continued to emigrate to North African communities, and principally to Tripoli and Tunis, where they occupied important positions in the fields of international trade and internal commerce, and were called Grana (newcomers from Livorno). In Tunis, their large number and close links with Italian interests brought the Grana to separate themselves progressively from the autochthonous community (the Twansa) and to maintain their own Jewish religious and social institutions. This situation created great tensions between the two communities, which disappeared only after the dispersal of the whole community.

In spite of these tensions, the settlement of thousands of *megorashim* in Jewish urban centers largely contributed to the regeneration of North African Jews after the severe persecutions of the Middle Ages and permitted them to develop their Jewish identity in close relation to the Sephardic heritage until the dispersion of the communities in the second half of the twentieth century. However, in some halakhic domains, such as the inheritance rights of the widow as laid down in the *ketubbah* (marriage contract), there developed two traditions in some communities, one pertaining to the indigenous communities and the other to the Castilian tradition. This Sephardic culture prevailed especially in yeshiva learning (talmudic study), which was based essentially on family recruitment, and in halakhic jurisprudence based on communal *Taqqanot* (ordinances) and *She'elot u'teshuvot* (Shu"t), or halakhic questions addressed to the great rabbinical figures of the time, whose answers were regarded as legitimate decisions and binding rules. In fact, all the written North African Jewish intellectual contributions in Hebrew, Judeo-Arabic, and Judeo-Spanish (Ladino) were influenced by Sephardic sources and canons—kabbalistic and mystical creation or exegetic and homiletic literature as well as Hebrew poetry. Moreover, a majority of the writers who distinguished themselves during the previous five centuries in various fields of Jewish learning and creativity were descendants of refugees from Spain. Some families, such as Serfati or Monsonego in Fez and Berdugo or Toledano in Meknes, held the communal *ḥazaqa* (monopolistic right) in certain communal affairs, such as the *sheḥita* (the ritualistic and halakhic slaughter) or the *dayanut* (the status of rabbinical judges).

With the settlement and integration of those who had been expelled, there developed several kinds of Jewish communities in North Africa, with implications for the local Jewish identity and communal life based on the Jewish language and culture that prevailed there, with binding relations to the non-Jewish culture of their Muslim environment, from the Arabized or the Berber stock. The first—and the most important—kind includes autochthonous urban and rural communities that always spoke Judeo-Arabic. The second includes urban mixed communities, in which those expelled from Spain initially formed separate communities that spoke Judeo-Spanish but finally merged with the Judeo-Arabophone group and thereafter took leadership of the communities, as happened in Tripoli, Tunis, Algiers, Oran, Fez, Meknes, and Sale. The third type of community is composed of new communities that developed in northern Morocco, such as Tetuan, Tangier, Larache, and Alqsar-Kebir, and spoke Judeo-Spanish until the twentieth century, with a rich oral culture in a dialectal variety locally named *haketia.* A fourth category included isolated rural and small communities scattered in the High Atlas and Anti-Atlas Mountains of Morocco among Berber tribes, which spoke only Judeo-Berber or Berber, or Judeo-Arabic and Berber, and followed Berber oral culture in their social life. It is this great diversity of intermingling between the ancient Jewish tradition and the neighboring Islamic cultures, based on Arabic or Berber practices, that forged the various modes of life and identities of the North African Jews.

In the nineteenth and twentieth centuries, these varied traditional facets of Jewish life and Jewish identity experienced modernization and change due to pressure from the European colonial powers on the North African countries and to the educational networks instituted by Jewish European benevolent and educational organizations, such as the Alliance Israélite Universelle of Paris and the Anglo-Jewish Association of London in the second half of the nineteenth century. In Algeria, the French military and political occupation that began in 1830 and lasted until 1962 ended the Ottoman domination of the country. For Jewish communities, early French schools and the abolition of Jewish judicial autonomy led to a regime that culminated in the 1870 Crémieux Decree, which gave French citizenship to Algerian Jews (but not to Algerian Muslims). As a result, Hebrew and Judeo-Arabic writing decreased in Algeria in all traditional Jewish fields. In Tunisia, the French Protectorate of 1881 and the Alliance's scholar network initiated in Tunis in 1879 as well as the introduction of Hebrew printing gave birth to a worthy and original internal Jewish modernization movement. Judeo-Arabic and Hebrew writings and journals blossomed between 1875 and 1914 but were thereafter challenged by French writing. In Libya, imperialistic ambitions led Italy to occupy the country militarily in 1911, ending its long subordination to the Ottoman Empire, and accorded some civil rights to Jewish communities. In Morocco, the large network of schools inaugurated by the Alliance in Tetuan in 1862 and the French Protectorate of 1912 contributed to training a valuable French-speaking elite in the great urban centers, who played an important administrative and economic role during the French colonization of the country. Yet the rabbinical position of power did not

Postcard of École de l'Alliance Israélite, Tetuan, Morocco. *(Gross Family Collection, Tel Aviv)*

suffer from this change. On the contrary, the reforms introduced by the French Protectorate creating communal committees and official rabbinical courts with a High Rabbinical Court at Rabat contributed to improving the jurisprudential tradition of the great communities and led to valuable rabbinical efforts to adapt the world of Halakhah to modern changes. In line with these processes of modernization, there also developed in the urban communities a new appraisal of the neighboring Arabic culture by the traditional Jewish elites, which led them to strengthen their performance and practice of medieval Andalusian music, adapted to the society's new cultural needs.

As for Jewish culture in North Africa, apart from its Jewish religious assets, oral and written, which had developed and changed after the Arab invasion, it was essentially a syncretic culture, integrating cultural elements from the neighboring Berber and Arab Muslims as well as from Spanish, Italian, and French colonial culture. In all aspects of everyday material culture, the influence of the rural or urban environment on Jewish life was obvious, from the houses typical of Andalusian and Berber architecture to public hygiene and men's and women's clothing (with some distinctive aspects), to Mediterranean dietary rules and foodways except for the strict religious rules of *kashruth* that still governed Jewish life. In the various verbal arts, Jewish borrowings from Arabic traditions (and Berber traditions in Moroccan rural communities) were extensive, including hundreds of folktales and folk songs and thousands of proverbs and sayings, as well as routines of daily interaction, based on the practice of Jewish languages and dialects, which were similar to those of their neighboring environment. Even the intense veneration of saints, with hundreds of rabbinical and miraculous figures, and of holy places such as the ancient synagogue known as El Ghriba, on the Tunisian island of Jerba, continued after the mass departure from North Africa, reinforced by similar Berber traditions.

These cultural and behavioral borrowings were reinterpreted and given new meaning and status through their integration into Jewish life, such that they appeared to the Jewish communities as their own. The modernization processes introduced North African communities to new technologies, rational knowledge, individualistic trends, and European languages. The educated Jewish elites largely adopted these new values, but, with the exception of some small elitist groups in Algeria, who shifted completely to French in the twentieth century, these communities continued to merge their new values with their traditional life in a hybrid and syncretic manner.

Jewish Life Today

During the second half of the twentieth century, this intense and rich Jewish life abruptly ceased, almost entirely. The independence of the four North African countries—Libya, Tunisia, Morocco, and Algeria—and their political involvement in the Arab-Israeli conflict against Israel led the Jewish masses to emigrate, to the new Jewish state, France, Canada, and other countries in Europe and South America, leaving behind thirteen centuries of life under Islamic rule. Today, approximately 3,000 Jews live in Morocco, mostly in Casablanca, compared with more than 250,000 in 1950. In Tunisia, there are some 1,500 Jews today, approximately 800 of them in Jerba, compared with more than 105,000 before the great emigration. In Algeria, there are fewer than 100 elderly Jews, the last rem-

Talit holder, Algeria, 1936. *(Gross Family Collection, Tel Aviv)*

nants of some 165,000 who lived in the country in the 1950s, and in Libya there is not one Jew today, compared with the 35,000 who lived there in 1950. Due to this massive emigration, the original North African communities dismantled, and their scattered members were forced to create new communal structures and construct new Jewish identities for the survival of their communal traditions, adapted to their new Jewish life in Israel, Europe, and America. Today, like millions of other displaced Jews, more than 1.5 million Jews originating in North Africa are seeking new forms of cultural integration that will allow them to preserve their cultural memory and identity.

Joseph Chetrit

See also: Circumcision; Folk Songs and Poetry, North African; Illuminated Manuscripts; Languages, Jewish; Mimuna Festival; Pinto, Rabbi Ḥaim, and the Pinto Family; Spain, Jews of.

Bibliography

Abitbol, Michel. *The Jews of North Africa During the Second World War.* Detroit: Wayne State University Press, 1989.

Attal, Robert. *Les juifs d'Afrique du Nord: Bibliographie.* Jerusalem: Institut Ben-Zvi et Université Hébraique, 1993.

Bahloul, Joelle. *La maison de mémoire. Ethnologie d'une demeure judéo-arabe en Algérie (1937–1961).* Paris: Editions Métailié, 1992.

———. *Le culte de la table dressée; rites et traditions de la table juive algérienne.* Paris: A.M. Métailié, 1983.

Ben-Ami, Issachar. *Culte des saints et pélérinages judéo-musulmans au Maroc.* Paris: Maisonneuve & Larose, 1990.

———. *Le judaïsme marocain; études ethno-culturelles.* Jerusalem: Rubin Mass, 1975.

Chetrit, Joseph. "Ambivalence et hybridation culturelle; interférences entre la culture musulmane et la culture juive au Maroc." *Perspectives* 9 (2002): 102–124.

———. *Diglossie, hybridation et diversité intra-linguistiques. Etudes socio-pragmatiques sur les langues juives, le judéo-arabe et le judéo-berbère.* Louvain–Paris: Peeters, 2007.

———. "National Hebrew Modernity Against French Modernity in North Africa at the End of the Nineteenth Century." *Miqqedem Umiyyam* 3 (1990): 11–76 (in Hebrew).

———. *Written Judeo-Arabic Poetry in North Africa, Poetic, Linguistic and Cultural Studies.* Jerusalem: Misgav, 1994 (in Hebrew).

Chouraqui, André. *Between East and West: A History of the Jews of North Africa.* Philadelphia: Jewish Publication Society of America, 1968.

———. *Histoire des juifs d'Afrique du Nord.* Paris: Hachette, 1985.

Deshen, Shlomo, and Moshe Shokeid. *The Predicament of Homecoming; Cultural and Social Life of North African Immigrants in Israel.* Ithaca, NY: Cornell University Press, 1974.

Dugas, Guy. *La littérature judéo-maghrébine d'expression française; entre Djéha et Cagayous.* Paris: L'Harmattan, 1991.

Elbaz, André E., and Ephraim Hazan. *Tehilla Le'David. Poèmes de David Ben Hassine, le chantre du judaïsme marocain. Edition critique et annotée.* Ramat Gan/Lod: Bar-Ilan University, 1999.

Felice, Renzo de. *Jews in an Arab land; Libya 1835–1970.* Austin: University of Texas Press, 1985.

Goldberg, Harvey E. *Cave Dwellers and Citrus Growers: Jewish Community in Libya and Israel.* Cambridge, UK: Cambridge University Press, 1972.

Hakohen, Mordechai. *The Book of Mordechai, a Study of the Jews of Libya: Selections from the Higgid Mordechai,* ed. and trans. H. Goldberg. Philadelphia: Institute for the Study of Human Issues, 1980.

Hazan, Ephraim. *The Hebrew Poetry in North Africa.* Jerusalem: Magnes, 1996 (in Hebrew).

Hirschberg, Haim Zeev. *A History of the Jews in North Africa,* vols. 1–2, ed. E. Bashan and R. Attal. Leiden: E.J. Brill, 1981–1982.

Laskier, Michael M. "The Evolution of Zionist Activity in the Jewish Communities of Morocco, Tunisia, and Algeria 1897–1947." *Studies in Zionism* 8 (1983): 205–236.

Rouach, David. *Imma ou rites, coutumes et croyances chez la femme juive en Afrique du Nord.* Paris: Maisonneuve & Larose, 1990.

Sebag, Paul. *Histoire des juifs de Tunisie; des origines à nos jours.* Paris: Editions L'Harmattan, 1991.

Stillman, Norman A. *The Jews of Arab Lands: A History and Source Book.* Philadelphia: Jewish Publication Society of America, 1979.

———. *The Jews of Arab Lands in Modern Times.* Philadelphia: Jewish Publication Society of America, 1991.

Udovich, Abraham L., and Lucette Valensi. *The Last Arab Jews; The Communities of Jerba, Tunisia.* Chur, UK: Harwood Academic, 1984.

Vassel, Eusèbe. *La littérature populaire des israélites tunisiens avec un essai ethnographique et archéologique sur leurs superstitions.* Paris: E. Leroux, 1904–1907.

Zafrani, Haim. *Kabbale, vie mystique et magie; judaïsme d'occident musulman.* Paris: Maisonneuve & Larose, 1986.

———. "La vie intellectuelle juive au Maroc de la fin du XVe au début du XXe siècle; première partie: la pensée juridique et et les environnements socio-économiques." Ph.D. dissertation, Université de Paris, 1970.

———. *Littératures populaires et dialectales en occident musulman: l'écrit et l'oral.* Paris: Geuthner, 1980.

———. *Pédagogie juive en terre d'Islam; l'enseignement traditionnel de l'hébreu et du judaïsme au Maroc.* Paris: A. Maisonneuve, 1969.

NOY, DOV (1920–)

Dov Noy was the first person to establish folklore as an academic discipline in Israel, initially, in 1955, at the Hebrew University in Jerusalem, and subsequently at Haifa University. From 1956 to 1982, Noy established and then directed the Israel Folktale Archives (IFA), within the framework of the Haifa Ethnological Museum and Folklore Archives. The IFA, a comprehensive repository of more than 23,000 folktales from more than 70 ethnic groups, was transferred to the University of Haifa in 1983 and was renamed in Noy's honor in 2002.

Noy was born on October 20, 1920, in Kolomyja, Poland. In 1938 he immigrated to Palestine to study at the Hebrew University (HU) of Jerusalem. In 1941–1945 he served in the British Army (Royal Engineers). In 1946 he received his M.A. (Bible, Talmud, and Jewish history) and enrolled as a Ph.D. student at the HU.

In 1947–1948 Noy headed the cultural and educational activities in the Cyprus Refugee Camps, where so-called illegal Jewish immigrants to Palestine were detained by the British. Through his encounter with Holocaust survivors in Cyprus, Noy listened to many narratives referring to the Holocaust and to the destruction of Jewish culture in Europe, including its folkloric infrastructure. In 1949–1952, along with Shimshon Meltzer, the widely read Hebrew poet, who had been his teacher of Hebrew in Kolomyja, Noy coedited the children's weekly magazine *Davar le'yeladim.*

After completing his studies at Indiana University (folklore, comparative literature, and anthropology) and his 1954 Ph.D. dissertation under Professor Stith Thompson, Noy taught at Indiana University in 1954 in the Departments of Folklore and of Slavic Studies.

Noy began to teach Aggadah (post-biblical oral tradition) at the HU in 1955, and the folkloristic methodology he acquired there provided him with fresh insight into the study of Aggadah literature, especially the talmudic-midrashic narratives, which he believes belong more to the realm of folklore than to that of written literature. Thus the genres of Jewish folk narratives should be defined and described according to the accepted universal ethnopoetic classification, established by A. Aarne and S. Thompson (Type- and Motif-indexes).

Noy believed that in the absence of reliable material, he could not face the challenge that modern folklore imposes on scholars, who demand a clear and unequivocal formulation of the questions concerning the continuity of oral tradition; the existence of specific national, ethnic and local traits; and the problems of intercultural contacts and acculturation. As a result, he established the IFA to aid scholars in accessing the folklore and cultures of Jews who immigrated to Israel from various countries. The IFA continues to collect folktales extant in Israelis' oral tradition.

Noy saw the collecting of folktales as the first stage in organizing the archives. His 1967 paper "Collecting Folktales in Israel" was followed by the annual *A Tale for Each Month* (TEM) reports. The second stage involved the annotated (documentation of the "chain of tradition" and comparative notes) publication of as many narrative texts as possible. Noy started to publish authentic texts, mainly in the IFA Publication Series (IFAPS), which consisted of story collections, in which the folktales were accompanied by comparative notes, data on the collectors and narrators, English summaries, indexes, and so on. The series (1962–1978) included forty-two booklets (among them fifteen TEM booklets)—twenty of which were edited by Noy.

During the early years of the IFA, Noy saw the IFAPS—as well as the "From the Folk-Mouth" section, which he established in 1954 in the Hebrew daily *Omer* intended for newcomers to Israel, and his series in the Israel Broadcasting Service—as tools to encourage collectors, some of whom were editors of their collections.

With the establishment of a wide collectors' network, during the mid-1960s Noy founded another series of collections whose purpose was to reflect and promote the study of Jewish ethnic communities and their contribution to the ethnopoetic heritage. Each collection consisted of seventy-one folktales extant in a particular ethnic community that faithfully reflected its ethnic "ego" and its rich narrative tradition.

The third stage involved synthesizing research and scholarly conclusions. Noy created a new methodological path in the study of folk literature. The major trends in his academic work, which combines written and oral literary sources, touch on almost all periods and aspects of Jewish culture.

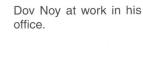

Dov Noy at work in his office.

Noy's folklore views were affected having grown up in a multicultural and multilingual home and were strengthened by his experiences in World War II and the Holocaust, in which he lost his family. For him, the folklore of East European Jews became memory rather than living reality, a task of reconstruction rather than of documentation. In some of his studies, he acted as an "agent," trying to associate the former generation of European Jewish folklorists and the young generation of Israeli folklorists, most of whom are his disciples. This is evident in *Yiddish Folksongs from Galicia* (1971). In his 1982 paper on S. An-ski, "The Place of S. An-sky in Jewish Folkloristics," Noy combines the history and the classification of Ashkenazi folklore and ethnography, of which S. An-ski can be considered the "founder." Noy's 1969 comparative-structural study of Yiddish folk balladry is probably also influenced by the same view, as is "The Model of the Yiddish Lullaby" (1986).

In a variety of studies, Noy demonstrated that the national cultural heritages of the non-Jewish neighbors among whom the Jews lived and created throughout their wanderings have been assimilated into Jewish folklore. While mutual intercultural contacts are evident in many realms, Jewish folklore has certain specific traits common to Jews of the East and the West (Ashkenazi, Sephardic, Middle Eastern), which are characteristic of the creative "ego" of the Jewish people in general. According to Noy's analysis, the Judaization and adaptation of universal traditions (the oicotypification in narratives) bear witness to the qualities, trends, and hopes of the Jewish "tradents," who transmitted the tales while adapting and Judaizing them, and by the Jewish "audiences" that listened to them.

Noy formulated four rules of Jewish oicotypification: (1) changes at the beginning and at the end of the tale; (2) use of biblical verses and allusions; (3) Hebrew wordplay, allusions, and analogies; and (4) Jewish folkways in Jewish space and Jewish time.

In his discussions of the issues of Jewish hagiography, Noy used authentic Yemenite materials, which have been transmitted orally from generation to generation. In his papers on the Yemenite-Jewish poet and folk hero Rabbi (Mori) Shalem Shabazi, he created a model for the analysis of a Jewish hero's folk biography as extant in Jewish folk narratives.

Noy emphasized that Jewish folklore is not transmitted through a single medium, but combines the following three categories, one of which usually dominated: (1) oral: folk literature and folk music; (2) visual: arts and crafts, costumes, ornaments, and material culture; and (3) cogitative, including popular beliefs, which bring about customs and rites. Each category is exemplified by a single bibliographical entry.

While working to establish the IFA, in 1968 Noy founded and directed the HU Folklore Research Center and was the editor of its *Studies* (8 volumes). In 1974 he held the newly founded M. Grünwald Chair of Folklore at the HU.

The University of Haifa granted Noy an honorary Ph.D. in 1999. In 2002, he was granted the prestigious

Bialik Prize for Life Achievement, of which he regards his contribution to the study of Aggadah and folklore as the most important component. In 2004 he was awarded the most prestigious prize in Israel, the Israel Prize for literary research.

Noy succeeded in inspiring public and community institutions to deal intensively with the study of folklore of all sectors of the population, especially (in the 1950s and 1960s) of the Middle Eastern and Sephardic ethnic groups, which, compared with the Ashkenazi groups, were until then neglected with regard to their cultural heritage. His institutional leadership and his pluralistic approach contributed to his stature as the single most influential folklorist in Israel and in universal Jewish folklore throughout the world.

Edna Hechal and Aliza Shenhar

See also: Israel Folktale Archives.

Bibliography

Hasan-Rokem, Galit, and Eli Yassif. "The Study of Jewish Folklore in Israel." *Jewish Folklore and Ethnology Review* 11:1–2 (1989): 2–11.

Hechal, Edna. "Bibliography of Dov Noy's Research Papers in Folklore and in the Talmudic-Midrashic Aggada." *Folklore Research Center Studies* 7 (1983): 11–30 (in Hebrew).

———. "Bibliography of Dov Noy's Writings in Folkloristics and in Talmudic-Midrashic Literature (Second List)." *Jerusalem Studies in Jewish Folklore* 13–14 (1992): 11–18 (in Hebrew).

Noy, Dov. "The Aggadic Endings in the Mishnaic Tractates." *Mahanayim* 57 (June 1961): 44–59 (in Hebrew).

———. "Archiving and Presenting Folk Literature in an Ethnological Museum." *Journal of American Folklore* 75 (1962): 23–28.

———. "Between Jews and Non-Jews in Folk Legends of Yemenite Jews." In *Studies of Communities and the Geniza,* ed. Sh. Morag and I. Ben Ami, pp. 229–295. Jerusalem: Hebrew University Magnes Press, 1981 (in Hebrew).

———. "The Death of R. Sh. Shabazi in the Folk Legends of Yemenite Jews." In *The Legacy of the Jews of Yemen: Studies and Researches,* ed. J. Tobi, pp. 132–149. Jerusalem: Come Yemen, 1976.

———. "Folklore." In *Encyclopaedia Judaica,* vol. 6, pp. 1374–1410. Jerusalem: Keter, 1974.

———. *In the Dispersion,* vol. 7, pp. 151–167. Jerusalem: Jewish Agency, 1967.

———. "The Jewish Versions of the 'Animal Languages' Folktale (AT 670): A Typological-Structural Study." In *Scripta Hierosolymitana,* vol. 22, pp. 171–208. Jerusalem: Hebrew University, 1971.

———. "Kings' Parables of R. Shimeon Bar-Yohay." *Mahanayim* 56 (June 1961): 73–87 (in Hebrew).

———. "The Legend of R. Israel Ba'al-Shem-Tov in the Carpathian Mountains." *Mahanayim* 46 (June 1960): 66–73 (in Hebrew).

———. "The Maiden and the Robber: A Comparative-Structural Study in Yiddish Folk-Balladry." In *Haifa Yearbook for Literature and Art,* ed. M. Kroshnits, vol. 5, pp. 177–224. Haifa: Dept. of Culture, Haifa Municipality, 1969 (in Yiddish).

———. "The Model of the Yiddish Lullaby." In *Studies in Yiddish Literature and Folklore,* vol. 7, pp. 208–235. Jerusalem: Hebrew University, 1986.

———. *Motif Index of Talmudic-Midrashic Literature.* Unpublished dissertation, Bloomington, IN, 1954.

———. "Motif Index to Our Folk Literature." In *The Israel Almanac on the Tenth Anniversary*, ed. Josef Shchavinski, pp. 151–155. Tel Aviv: 1958 (in Hebrew).

———. "On the Origin of the 'Guests' Custom." *Mahanayim* 50 (September 1960): 42–47 (in Hebrew).

———. "The Place of S. An-sky in Jewish Folkloristics." *Jerusalem Studies in Jewish Folklore* 2 (1982) 94–107 (in Hebrew).

———. "R. Sh. Shabazi in the Folk Legends of Yemenite Jews." In *Come, Yemen,* ed. Y. Ratzahbi, pp. 106–133. Tel Aviv: Afikim, 1967 (in Hebrew).

———. *Seventy-One Lybian Jewish Folktales.* Jerusalem: Jewish Agency, 1967 (in Hebrew).

———. *Seventy-One Moroccan Jewish Folktales.* Jerusalem: Jewish Agency, 1964 (in Hebrew).

———. *Seventy-One Tunisian Jewish Folktales.* Jerusalem: Jewish Agency, 1966 (in Hebrew).

———. "Simpleton's Prayer Brings Rain." *Mahanayim* 51 (November 1960): 34–45 (in Hebrew).

———. "The Tree of Life Among Jews and Gentiles." In *Studies in Problems of Culture, Education and Society, in Memory of Naftali Ginton,* vol. 4, pp. 142–162. Tel Aviv, 1972 (in Hebrew).

———. *Yiddish Folksongs from Galicia, Collected by Shmuel Zanvel Pipe.* In *Folklore Research Center Studies,* vol. 2. Jerusalem: Hebrew University, 1971 (in Yiddish).

Shenhar, Aliza. "Israel." In *Enzyklopaedie des Maerchens,* vol. 7, pp. 329–336. New York: Walter de Gruyter, 1992.

Shenhar, Aliza, and Edna Hechal. "Noy (Neuman), Dov." In *Enzyklopaedie des Maerchens,* vol. 10, pp. 150–154. New York: Walter de Gruyter, 2000.

O

Olswanger, Immanuel (1888–1961)

Immanuel Olswanger was a folklorist, Yiddishist, linguist, Zionist activist, poet, and translator (into Hebrew) of world-famous folklore works.

Born in Grajewo, Poland, in 1888, Olswanger attended school in nearby Suwałki and later studied at the Universities of Königsberg (in Eastern Prussia) and Bern, Switzerland, where he studied languages and literature. In Switzerland, he began to develop an interest in Jewish folklore and acted as the secretary of the Jewish Section of the Swiss Folklore Association. In Switzerland he met Ludwig Lazarus Zamenhoff, the creator of the international auxiliary language of Esperanto, and became an avid user and distributor of Esperanto. Olswanger's two main areas of interest, languages and folklore, later became the basis of his folklore and translation projects.

In the early 1930s, Olswanger was active in the Zionist movement and was founder of the student Zionist organization He'ḥaver, as well as acted as emissary of Keren Ha'yesod, the United Jewish Appeal, the financial arm of the World Zionist Organization. He emigrated to Eretz Israel in 1933 and settled in Jerusalem, where he worked as writer, editor, and translator at Tarshish Press in Jerusalem. He published a book of verse titled *Bein Adam le'kono* (Between Man and God) in 1943 as well as a book of poetry in Esperanto, *Eternal Yearnings,* and children's literature. He was among the first to translate into Hebrew Asian literary texts and collections written in languages such as Sanskrit (*Bhagavad Gita* [Song of God], a part of the *Mahabharata,* attributed to Lord Krishna) and Japanese (the ancient story collection *Mukashi banashi*).

The uniqueness of this work lies, among other things, in the Latin transcription Olswanger used, which made his work accessible to a wide audience. He translated from European languages, including German, Italian, and Spanish, as well. He translated poems by Goethe, Boccaccio's *Decameron,* and Dante's "Divine Comedy," to which he added notes and wrote an introduction. In addition, he edited collections of Yiddish folklore, mainly proverbs, jokes, and anecdotes: *Röyte pomerantsen* (Red Oranges; 1947, republished and subtitled *Or How to Laugh in English,* with an introduction by Harry Goldin, 1965), and *Lechayim* (To Life; 1949). These works describe in a humorous way the lives and worlds of ordinary East European Jewish characters, such as peddlers, wagon drivers, and beggars. Olswanger's Yiddish collections augment the work of renowned earlier Yiddish writers such as Mendele Moykher Seforim (Shalom Ya'akov Abramovich, 1836–1917), Sholem Aleichem (Solomon Rabinovitch, 1859–1916), and Olswanger's contemporaneous Alter Druyanow (1870–1938), especially with regard to Druyanow's voluminous *Book of Jokes and Witticisms.*

Olswanger died in Jerusalem on February 7, 1961.

Ilana Rosen

Bibliography

Cornfield, Peretz. *Palestine Personalia.* Tel Aviv: Palestine Personalia, 1947 (in Hebrew).

Lazar, David. *Rashim in Yisrael.* Tel Aviv: Amichai, 1955 (in Hebrew).

Oring, Elliott (1945–)

Elliott Oring is a prominent American folklorist distinguished by his contributions to the analysis and interpretation of Jewish humor. He regards humor as an expressive genre that is basic to the formation and reflection of Jewish identity.

Born in New York City on April 20, 1945, Oring earned his Ph.D. in folklore at Indiana University in 1974. His career as an educator (1971–2004) was spent in the Department of Anthropology at California State University, Los Angeles. He also served as visiting professor at the University of Texas, Indiana University, and the University of California campuses in Los Angeles and Berkeley, and as Fulbright scholar at the University of Iceland.

Oring's field-based dissertation, revised into the book *Israeli Humor* (1981), explores the content and structure of the *chizbat* (Arab., "lies") of the Palmach. *Chizbat* were humorous narratives about characters and situations in the Palmach commando units that operated underground during the British Mandate in Palestine. Oring saw the narratives as crucial to the construction of a nascent Israeli identity in which traits of the cocky, secular, Levantine *sabra* (native-born Jews of Palestine) were contrasted with those of immigrant European Jews.

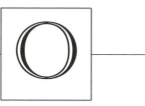

Oring has frequently dealt with jokes by and about Jews as signs of identity. The most sweeping study of this phenomenon is *Jokes and Their Relations* (1992), in which he analyzes the idea of "Jewish humor." Pointing out that the conceptualization of Jewish humor was a modern invention, he proposed several hypotheses to explain how this notion came into being. In the nineteenth century, humor had come to be viewed as a sign of a civilized humanity, and Jews felt it necessary to demonstrate that they had participated in this humanity since their emergence as a people. But because the humor of the Jews was borne of a history of suffering, rejection, and despair, this history could be reconciled with humorous expression in only a limited number of ways. Consequently, in both scholarly and popular sources, Jewish humor was regarded as transcendent, defensive, or pathological. Other chapters in the volume address the hypothesis of self-hating humor, Jewish-American song parodies, and the Jewish jokes of Sigmund Freud (which is the subject of an entire volume [1984]).

Oring has been critical of psychodynamic interpretations of humor as aggression and favors a consideration of the social, individual, and historical conditions under which jokes are created and told. He has developed a concept of humor as "appropriate incongruity": the perception of an appropriate interrelationship of elements from domains that are generally regarded as incongruous. In his interpretations of humor, he has analyzed the categories that are brought into incongruous opposition and the means by which they are made appropriate.

Simon J. Bronner

See also: Humor; Joke.

Bibliography

Oring, Elliott. *Engaging Humor.* Urbana: University of Illinois Press, 2003.

———. *Israeli Humor: The Content and Structure of the Chizbat of the Palmah.* Albany: State University of New York Press, 1981.

———. *Jokes and Their Relations.* Lexington: University Press of Kentucky, 1992.

———. *The Jokes of Sigmund Freud: A Study in Humor and Jewish Identity.* Philadelphia: University of Pennsylvania Press, 1984.

OSEH PELE

Oseh pele is a collection of ninety-four tales compiled by Joseph Shabbetai Farhi, who was born in Jerusalem in 1802. In 1843 Farhi moved to Livorno, Italy, and lived there as a writer and religious leader until his death in 1882.

Oseh pele was published in three different volumes in 1845 and in 1869; in 1870 it was published in one volume and then was republished many times in this form. This book has influenced generations of storytellers, in particular, and Jewish folk literature, in general. The main reasons are its content, sources, genre, and style. The book comprises stories from Hebrew sources of different times, including canonic sources (midrashic and talmudic legends, collections of folk stories from the Middle Ages and modern times). It offers central social and national themes for Jewish culture, including conflicts between Jews and non-Jews; social class differentiation (poor and rich); family relationships (fathers and sons); the cycle of life (birth, marriage, and death); and the Jewish year cycle (Sabbath and holidays). It also represents different literary genres such as myths, fairy tales, novellas, legends, anecdotes, and parables. All the stories are written in biblical style (some of them rhyme) and end with a clear moral statement explaining the meaning and the function of the story according to the author.

The tales included in the book are from three different sources: (1) famous Jewish folktales elaborated from written sources such as the Book of Judith, in which Judith decapitated the enemy and saved the Jews (apocryphal literature); the story of Teraḥ and Abraham, who smashed the idols (Midrash); and the "Story of the Jerusalemite," who broke his oath to his father and found himself married to a she-demon (Middle Ages); also from the same sources are stories about famous sages, saints, and rabbis such as Rabbi Akiva, Rabbi Meir, Rabbi Ḥanina ben Dosa, Rabbi Isaac Luria Ashkenazi (called Ha'Ari; founder of the Lurianic Kabbalah), or the Sephardic rabbi Abraham Galante; (2) oral sources—that is, stories that the author heard, as he writes, "from wise people more precious than pearls"; and (3) original stories by the author that are sometimes based on non-Jewish sources, including "The Beloved Friend and a Half," about a true friend who hides a friend who, he thinks, is a murderer, and "The Woman Whose Upper Half Looked Like a Beast," though she was very wise. At the end with the help of her son, she turns beautiful and regains her husband, who had run away from her when he saw her face right after the wedding.

The author's aim of the book was to draw young Jews back to traditional Jewish literature in the context of the Jewish cultural crisis of the nineteenth century: the tendency toward secularization and the Haskalah (Enlightenment) movement in European Jewish communities.

This book illustrates traditional rabbinic Jewish norms and values. It became popular especially in the Sephardic and Middle Eastern Jewish communities (in which the book was translated into Judeo-Spanish and Judeo-Arabic). It serves as a source of oral stories told to this day.

Tamar Alexander

See also: Anthologies.

Bibliography

Alexander-Frizer, Tamar. The *Heart Is a Mirror—The Sephardic Folktale.* Detroit: Wayne State University Press, 2008 (translation and elaboration of the Hebrew version).

Yassif, Eli. "The Influence of *Oseh Pele* on Jewish Folk Literature." *Jerusalem Studies in Jewish Folklore* 3 (1982): 47–66 (in Hebrew).

P

Papercut

The art of papercut, or cutting designs in paper or in parchment, is a traditional Jewish creative art form. The earliest record of papercuts dates back to a humorous text from 1345: "Milḥemet ha'et ve'ha'misparaim" (The Battle of the Pen and the Scissors) written by Rabbi Shem-Tov ben Yitzhak ben Ardutiel of Spain. Then it is mentioned in seventeenth and eighteenth centuries regarding the development of papercut in Central Europe. *Ketubbot* and the Book of Esther embellished with papercuts, common among Italian Jews, came from that period. This art form reached its peak in the nineteenth century due to the widespread use of paper at every social stratum. Papercuts from that period come mostly from Ashkenazi Jews living in Central and Eastern Europe and from Sephardic Jews living in the Ottoman Empire, especially in Turkey. This art was known to the Jewish population living in North Africa as well as to Jews from Iraq and Syria; alas, only a few items from that population survive. At the turn of the nineteenth and twentieth centuries, the art of papercut was introduced to the United States by immigrants from Eastern Europe, where the art form began to disappear by the mid-twentieth century. The tradition was revived in the 1960s in Israel and in the United States and, later, in Poland and continues to develop.

The basic function of a papercut in traditional Jewish society was *hiddur mitzvah* (enhancing the Commandments through aesthetics), and to that end, both the motifs and the embedded texts were always subordinate to the Commandments. Far less common were papercuts used as amulets or as decoration.

Among the most renowned traditional papercuts were those produced by Eastern European Jews. Its makers were individuals with a profound knowledge of Judaism, which enabled them to enhance the artistry of papercuts by imbuing them with meaningful content, widely used abbreviations, in pattern layout, or in ornaments. Both the layout and the most commonly used motifs came from traditional art, often a synagogue decoration. Among recurring motifs are menorahs, crowns symbolizing the Torah crown, Decalogue (Ten Commandments) tablets, and the Tree of Life. The most common and most monumental are *mizraḥ* papercuts, hung on the eastern wall of the house, that is, pointing toward Jerusalem—a sacrum that one would pray to—and *shiviti* papercuts, often encountered in synagogues. In addition, papercuts would often announce special events, namely, holidays like Purim or Shavuot, or decorate the walls of a sukkah (booth) during the festival of Sukkot or the calendar used for counting the Omer. The papercuts were made of white paper, often a rectangular page taken out of a school notebook. The artist would then fold the page in half along its vertical axis, draw a pattern with a pencil, affix it to a wooden board, and cut the pattern with a sharp knife. After unfolding it, he would color the papercut with various water-based paints and then put it on a paper, often with a contrasting color, to create a background.

Another group of papercuts in that region were *Roizeleh,* most often round and cut from colorful shiny paper; they would be used to decorate building and synagogue windows during the holiday of Shavuot. Both the pattern and the paper from which it was made as well as the cutting technique indicate that it drew on local non-Jewish art.

The second most renowned and numerous group of papercuts were those created by Sephardic Jews living in the Ottoman Empire, especially in Turkey. They were created in conditions that were diametrically opposed to those in Eastern Europe. Their development reached a peak, according to known sources, earlier than in Eastern Europe. Scholars are aware of papercuts made by Turkish Jews as early as the beginning of the nineteenth century. After continuous development throughout the nineteenth century, papercut was on the wane in the first half of the twentieth century. In order to properly evaluate that art, it is significant to mention that the art of papercut was widely developed in Turkey, a non-Jewish society. There, shops sold papercuts, and their creators were organized in craft guilds.

The art of papercut was also taught in school in the 1920s. Historians have no information whether there were Jewish papercut artists for whom this activity was their profession and their sole source of income. Among these papercuts, we encounter a diversity of materials. Paper was widely used, as was cardboard and sometimes even plywood. The paper was often colored, dyed at printing houses, and the colors used were intense: red, dark blue, sometimes a gold. In addition, colored pencils were used. The use of water-based paint was rare. The cutting technique was also different; both scissors and knives were used. In addition, the technique most commonly used was cutting a single element of a pattern and then attaching it to the background or to an existing composition. The technique would create multilayer papercuts, often creating a sort of three-dimensional effect. An artist would use pattern elements cut from various printed texts. The papercut artists were men familiar with Judaism, as indicated by their use of commonly used texts. The basic function a papercut played was consistent with *hiddur mitzvah.* The most common were *shiviti* papercuts, papercuts functioning as amulets, papercuts that would decorate a sukkah during Sukkot holidays, wedding blessings, and *ketubbot.* The strong influence of local non-Jewish art can be seen in the decorative elements in Jewish papercuts in the Ottoman Empire, such as the use of a rich plant ornamentation, especially flowers, architectural elements, and illustrations of holy places that pilgrims would visit in the Holy Land. Affinity to Jewish art can be seen in widely used texts and abbreviations, and in single-pattern elements. The most common are the Torah crown, the Decalogue tablets, menorah, and the Star of David. It is worth noting that in a pattern layout, the center of the ground is emphasized, and there is the completion of the wholeness. The papercuts do not usually display symmetry in their design elements.

Papercuts now produced in Israel do not involve their traditional function but, instead, are often created for tourists as souvenirs. Thus their objective is to satisfy the buyer's sense of aesthetics and desire for an art object with Jewish affiliation. They are intended as decorations for a residence or for a festivity. This tendency is becoming more common as seen in the number of types of papercuts: less use of traditional texts and more use of secular texts. The papercut motifs are still traditional, although new ones are being introduced from nature and Israel's contemporary symbolism. In contemporary Israel, as in the Diaspora, the artists creating papercuts are both men and women gifted in the fine arts and employing this art form to depict Jewish culture and key events in their history.

Olga Goldberg-Mulkiewicz

See also: Frenkel, Gizela; Goldberg-Mulkiewicz, Olga; Mizraḥ; Shiviti-Menorah; Symbols.

Bibliography

Frankel, Giza. *The Art of the Jewish Papercut.* Jerusalem: Modan, 1996 (in Hebrew).

Juhas, Esther. "Papercut." In *Sephradi Jews in the Ottoman Empire.* Jerusalem: Israel Museum (in Hebrew).

Shadur, Joseph, and Yehudit Shadur. *Traditional Jewish Papercuts: A History and Guide.* Hanover, NH: University Press of New England, 2002.

Parable

The Biblical Parable

"Parable" is the standard translation of the Septuagint for the Hebrew word *mashal*. In the Bible *mashal* designates an array of genres—parables, fables, riddles, proverbs—all of which require decoding of their figurative language or symbolic representation, as shown by two famous examples.

The first is Nathan's rebuke to King David, in which he presents him with the following parable:

> There were two men in the same city, one rich and one poor. The rich man had very large flocks and herds, but the poor man had only one little ewe lamb that he had bought. He tended it and it grew up together with him and his children: it used to share his morsel of bread, drink from his cup, and nestle in his bosom; it was like a daughter to him. One day, a traveler came to the rich man, but he was loath to take anything from his own flocks or herds to prepare a meal for the guest who had come to him; so he took the poor man's lamb and prepared it for the man who had come to him. (2 Sam. 12:2–4)

The second is Jotham's parable, in which he turns to the people of Shechem, who have just appointed his murderous brother as king. In this parable, it is the lowliest and most damaging thornbush that accepts the offer made by the trees of the forest to rule over them, after the worthy trees had all turned it down (Jud. 8–15). In both instances the parable is used as a rhetorical device by a speaker, who acts in a sensitive, even perilous, power structure in which indirect, coded speech is required.

The Rabbinic Parable

Compared with its biblical predecessor, the rabbinic *mashal* is more restricted in its meaning and relates mainly to parables and fables, although it is difficult to identify these latter terms with the culturally specific term "*mashal.*" Rabbinic parables may be traced to the same environment that produced the synoptic parables, thus rendering them an important tool for reconstructing the dialogue and polemic between the two emerging religions, Judaism and Christianity. There are few examples of Aesopian or Aesopian-like fables in rabbinic literature: the fox who enters a vineyard through a hole in the fence and, having stuffed himself for three days, cannot exit (*Ecclesiastes Rab.* 5:14) or the bird that removes a bone from the throat of a lion only to learn that not having been swallowed by the beast is in itself the biggest reward it could have hoped for (*Gen. Rab.* 64:10).

Indeed, rabbinic literature lists the study or knowledge of parables, including fox parables, as a separate discipline alongside legal and ethical (aggadic) studies (*b.Sukkah* 28a; *BavaBatra* 134a; *Sanhedrin* 28b). It also alludes to different social contexts in which parables were delivered, such as wedding celebrations (*Leviticus Rab.* 28:2). However, it is the exegetical context that forms the main, almost exclusive, framework for the hundreds of parables in rabbinic texts. That the rabbis saw the parable as a key hermeneutical tool is attested not only by their prominence throughout the rabbinic corpus but also in explicit statements (or rather in metaparables) that compare the parable to handles that allow the basket of fruit (the Torah) to be carried or to a thread that provides a way out of the (interpretational) maze (Song of Song Rabbah 1:1). Parables are usually introduced by the formula *"mashal le'mah ha'davar domeh"* (*mashal* to what it is like), or in abbreviated forms. Rabbinic parables went through a process of standardization in which earlier parables employ a wider stock of characters (a man, a field owner, a proprietor) that in the classical rabbinic period (in amoraic compilations) are often subsumed in the single persona of a king. The figure of the king is modeled after the courtly setting of the Roman emperor.

The other component that becomes a regular feature of parables in later midrashim is the inclusion of the *nimshal*—an explication and the corresponding biblical citations. The King parables entertain basic plot-character structures anchored in familial and stately relationships: a king who leaves his wife (or his consort: a matron, a woman of high statue); a king who despairs of his sons' upbringing; a king who prepares a banquet for his citizens; a king who marries off his daughter. While the king always symbolizes God, the identity of the other characters may vary. Thus, the daughter may stand for the Torah (and her implied groom, for the Israelites). The rabbinic parable functions hermeneutically through its dual nature: It is both a fictional story and exegesis.

The following example illustrates the rabbinic parable's complex rhetorical power:

> Abba bar Kahana said: It is like a king who married a woman and wrote her a large dowry (*ketubbah*). He wrote to her: So many chambers I make for you, so much jewelry I make for you; so much gold and silver I give you. Then He left her for many years and journeyed to the provinces. Her neighbors used to taunt her and say: Hasn't your husband abandoned you? Go, marry another man. She would weep and sigh, and afterward, she would enter her bridal chamber and read her marriage settlement and console herself. Many days later the king returned. He said to her: I am amazed that you have waited for me all these years! She replied: My master, O king! If not for the large dowry you wrote to me, my neighbors would have led me astray long ago. Likewise: The nations of the world taunt Israel and say to them: Your God does not want you. He has left you. He has removed His presence from you. We will appoint you to be generals, governors and officers. And the people of Israel enter their synagogues and houses of study, and there they read in the Torah, "I will look with favor upon you, and make you fertile. . . . I will establish My abode in your midst, and I will not spurn you" (Lev. 26:9, 11), and they console themselves. In the future when the redemption comes, the Holy One, blessed be He, says to Israel: My children! I am amazed at how you have waited for Me all these years. And they say to Him: Master of the universe! Were it not for the Torah you gave us, in which we read when we entered our synagogues and house of study, "I will look with favor upon you . . . and I will not spurn you," the nations of the world would have led us astray long ago. That is what is written, "Were not your teaching my delight, I would have perished in my affliction (Ps. 119:92). Therefore it says, "This I call to mind; therefore I have hope" (Lam. 3:21).

This elaborate parable functions on several levels: It serves as an intertextual binder of remote biblical verses by providing them with a "plot-structure," through which the addressees—the people of Israel—are praised for their loyalty in desolate times, a loyalty that is guaranteed by the dowry (Torah). At the same time, the fictional narrative and its relation to the *nimshal* suggest inexplicable gaps that carry deep theological anxiety and queries: Why did the king (God) desert his wife (Israel), and how does one reconcile the difference in tenses between the parable—in which the "happy ending" is included—and its explanation, which refers to an imagined future? It is the multifaceted nature of the *mashal,* its ability to provide both a clear message (e.g., praise and comfort) and reflect on the limits of its exegetical enterprise, that endows it with such hermeneutical power.

Post-Rabbinic Parables

Whereas in the rabbinic period the parable was the most prominent explicitly fictional genre, the post-rabbinic periods gave rise to other fictional narratives, such as the exemplum. Post-rabbinic parables, while often employing traditional imagery of the rabbinic parable, now function in novel ways: They serve as an illustrative rhetorical device for conveying complex ideas (e.g., in *Seder Eliyahu,* ninth to tenth century), thus assuming a clear didactic role; alternatively, they convey and conceal esoteric concepts (e.g., Gnostic notions in *Sefer ha'bahir,* twelfth century). Later medieval Jewish philosophers, as well as mystics, continue to use human characters in their parables, at times in the mode established by earlier post-rabbinic literature, transforming the parable into an allegorical, illustrative tool. Indeed, in the poetic lexicon of the later Middle Ages the word *"mashal"* becomes a technical term for allegory. Parables appear in ethical and homiletic literature (Bahya ibn Paquda, *Duties of the Hearts,* twelfth century); in medieval rhymed prose of different character (Joseph ibn Zabara, *Sefer Sha'shuim,* end of twelfth to beginning of thirteen century; Isaac ben Solomon ibn Sahula's *Mashal ha'qadmoni,* thirteenth century). Parables also figure in Hasidic writings and preaching. Early Hasidic writings often refer to tales of the Ba'al Shem Tov (the eighteenth-century founder of Hasidism) as *meshalim,* although poetically they bear stronger affinities to the exemplum. The tales of Rabbi Nachman of Bratslav (late eighteenth to early nineteenth century) not only make use of traditional parables and fables but also invite allegorical interpretations that in turn render their overall fictional character a "parable" of sorts. Modern folk-narratives, documented in the Israel Folktale Archives (IFA) at the University of Haifa, include several parables, some of which rely on earlier written sources (midrashic works as well as later folk-narrative books such as the *Oseh Pele*).

A structuralist-functionalist approach to the "parable" (cf. Kirshenblatt-Gimblett 1975) identifies the parabolic aspects of a given narrative as contingent on the context in which it is performed. Thus, multiple discourses could be characterized as "parables" provided that they bear implied structural analogies to a tension-ridden social situation in which they are applied and on which they comment. As the contexts change, so does the meaning of the parable. This performance-oriented definition of the "parable" allows the inclusion, in addition to traditional "parables" and "fables," of other fictional narratives. It also provides a theoretical model for reconsidering traditional Jewish "parables" and "fables," beginning with their first appearance in the Bible.

Dina Stein

See also: Fable.

Bibliography

Ben Amos, Dan, and J.R. Mintz, ed. and trans. *In Praise of the Baal Shem Tov: The Earliest Collection of Legends About the Founder of Hasidism.* Northvale, NJ: Jason Aronson, 1993.

Boyarin, Daniel. *Intertextuality and the Reading of Midrash.* Bloomington: Indiana University Press, 1990.

Flusser, David. *Judaism and the Origins of Christianity.* Jerusalem: Magnes, 1998 (in Hebrew).

Hasan-Rokem, Galit. *Tales of the Neighborhood: Jewish Narrative in Dialogue in Late Antiquity.* Berkeley: University of California Press, 2002.

Kirshenblatt-Gimblett, Barbara. "A Parable in Context: A Social Interactional Analysis of Storytelling Performance." In *Folklore: Performance and Communication,* ed. D. Ben-Amos and K. Goldstein, pp. 105–130. The Hague: Walter de Gruyter, 1975.

Saperstein, Marc. *Jewish Preaching 1200–1800: An Anthology.* New Haven, CT: Yale University Press, 1989.

Stern, David. *Parables in Midrash: Narrative and Exegesis in Rabbinic Literature.* Cambridge, MA: Harvard University Press, 1991.

———. "The Rabbinic Parable and the Narrative of Interpretation."*The Midrashic Imagination: Jewish Exegesis, Thought, and History,* ed. M. Fishbane, pp. 78–95. Albany: State University of New York Press, 1993.

Yassif, Eli. *The Hebrew Folktale: History, Genre, Meaning,* trans. J.S. Teitelbaum. Bloomington: Indiana University Press, 1999.

PARADISE (*GAN EDEN*)

See: Afterlife

PASCHELES, WOLF

See: Anthologies

PASSOVER

Passover (Heb., Pesaḥ) is the first of the three pilgrimage festivals on the ancient calendar. It starts on the eve of the fifteenth of Nisan and lasts seven days, from the fifteenth to the twenty-first of Nisan. The seven-day festival was commanded by God in order to commemorate the events described in Exodus 12:1–42.

The Story of the Exodus

According to the biblical story, God instructed the Israelites to slaughter a lamb on the twilight of the fourteenth of Nisan and apply its blood to the lintel and side posts of their doors, using hyssop leaves, in order to indicate that their households should be "passed over," hence the name given to the festival (Exod. 12:27). This so-called paschal lamb was to be roasted later that night and eaten together with unleavened bread and bitter herbs. That night God killed all the Egyptians' firstborn children (the tenth plague) but bypassed the houses marked with paschal blood. Led by Moses and Aaron, the Israelites left Egypt in haste and thus had to form their bread from dough before it was leavened. The unleavened cakes they made are called "*matzot*" (sing., *matzah*). Thus in the Bible the festival is also called *Ḥag Hamatzot* (Feast of the Unleavened Bread). During the seven days of the festival, only unleavened bread is permitted.

Because the story of Passover took place in the springtime, the third name given to this festival is the *Ḥag Ha'Aviv* (Feast of Spring). It was the Bible that related the historical events to the spring. The newly settled Israelite society in Canaan (roughly corresponding to present-day Syria, Lebanon, part of Jordan, Palestine, and Israel) was agricultural, and Nisan, the first month of the Hebrew year that fell during the spring, symbolized the renewal of nature as well as the renewal of the Hebrew nation. In Leviticus (23:10–11) the Israelites are instructed to bring a sheaf (*omer*) of the first fruit of their harvest to the priest, who will wave it on the sixteenth of Nisan. While laying the foundations for the new nation, the Bible binds together its history—the end of slavery and the Exodus promised to Abraham, the first patriarch (Gen.

Seder plate. Spain, fifteenth century. Gift of Jakob Michael, New York, in memory of his wife, Erna Sondheimer Michael. 134/57; 483–12–65. *(© The Israel Museum, by Nahum Slapak)*

15:13–14)—and its new reality in Canaan. In the Book of Exodus, the slaughtering and eating of the Passover lamb are part of a family feast to which a needy neighbor was to be invited (12:3–4); it is not a sacrifice to God.

The Feast of Passover in the Bible

The Bible does not mention observance of Passover with respect to the Israelites' years of wandering in the desert after they left Egypt. Only after crossing the Jordan River and arriving at Gilgal did the Israelites celebrate their first Passover in Canaan, eating *matzot* and roasted corn (Josh. 5:10–11). 2 Chronicles 30 relates to the feast of Passover at the time of King Hezekiah, who restored the Temple worship after it was desecrated by King Ahaz, his father. The king sent posts throughout Judea and Israel to summon the people to the Temple. Priests performed the slaughtering of the Passover offering on the fourteenth of Nisan. The feast of the *matzot* was celebrated, as ordered by God, seven days (30:21). 2 Chronicles 35:1–18 describes Passover during the reign of Josiah: The king distributed to the people 30,000 lambs and kids for the Passover offering. Priests and the Levites performed the slaughter, and, after the burnt offerings, intended to God, were removed, the meat was given to the people to be roasted and eaten. After the exile to Babylonia, and the destruction of the Temple and of Jerusalem by Nebuchadnezzar (2 Kings, 25:1–17), the prohibition against building the Temple outside Jerusalem (Ezek. 20:40) put an end to the sacrifices. The celebration of Passover is mentioned again at the time of Ezra, when, after Cyrus's decree, the Israelites returned from the Babylonian exile and rebuilt the Temple in Jerusalem (Ez. 6:16–22). On the fourteenth of Nisan the priests slaughtered the Passover offerings for the people returning from exile.

Passover During the Time of the Second Temple

The Mishnah (*Pesaḥim* 9:5) called the paschal lamb the Egyptian Passover (*Pesaḥ mitzrayim*). The lamb was also called "Passover throughout the ages" (*pesaḥ dorot*).

At the time of the Second Temple, although the paschal lamb was slaughtered in the Temple, it was not performed by priests, as was the case earlier, but by the people themselves, while the Levites were reading the *Hallel* (Psalms 113–118; *t. Pesaḥim* 3:11). According to the Tosefta (*Pesaḥim* 4:14), each person arrived at the Temple with his lamb and his knife. After the slaughtering, the meat was distributed to the pilgrims, who roasted it throughout the city and ate it in groups (*m. Zevaḥim,* 5:8). During this period, thousands of pilgrims from Israel and the Diaspora went to Jerusalem to celebrate the Passover. The Passover offering was eaten together with *matzah*, bitter herbs, and *ḥaroset.* The benediction over the wine and grace after the meal were accompanied by the drinking of wine, but the Talmud and other sources make no mention of the drinking of four cups of wine, as was later to become standard at a Seder (see below). One reads the *Hallel* and nothing points to the telling of the story of the Exodus. Even though thousands of Jews still made the pilgrimage to Jerusalem, most Jews celebrated the eve of Passover, like every other feast—a meal, a benediction over wine, and grace after the meal—at home.

Passover After the Destruction of the Second Temple

In the generations after the destruction of the Temple, the Passover observance took another form. The Seder, celebrated on the eve of the fifteenth of Nisan, became the main feature of the feast. The foundations of the Seder as we know it today were laid in the Mishnah (*Pesaḥim* 10). Unlike most of the tractate *Pesaḥim,* which refers to the celebration at the time of the Temple, chapter 10 mentions the sages of Yavneh. Because Yavneh became the spiritual center after the destruction of the Temple, Shmuel Safrai and Ze'ev Safrai, in *Haggadah of the Sages: The Passover Haggadah* (1998), infer that this chapter was incorporated into the Mishnah after the destruction of the Second Temple by the

Romans in 70 C.E. The word "Seder" (lit., "order") does not derive from the Mishnah, but was coined by Rashi (Rabbi Solomon ben Isaac of Troyes) (*Sefer ha'oraḥ* 53) in the eleventh century.

The prohibition against eating leavened bread or other foods considered forbidden for Passover (*ḥametz*) during the seven days of the festival gave rise to a tradition, observed to this day, that begins long before the Seder itself and consists of a thorough cleaning of the house to remove any leaven and preparation of the *matzot.* According to the symbolic ceremony, on the eve of the fourteenth of Nisan one hides crumbs of leavened bread in one's home, then searches for them by candlelight. The crumbs found are burned early on the morning of Passover eve, along with the rest of the leavened bread in the house. In Israel all the *ḥametz* is symbolically sold to a non-Jew for the seven days of the festival.

The Seder

The Seder, like the biblical event, takes place on the eve of the fifteenth of Nisan. Its essence is the reading of the Haggadah—a book consisting of the story of Exodus and of halakhic and midrashic texts, psalms, liturgical hymns, benedictions, and prayers—and the performance of symbolic rituals related to the story of the Exodus, which are followed by a festive meal. According to the custom already established in the Mishnah (*Pesaḥim* 10), the participants in the Seder are to recline, as was the habit among the Greeks and the Romans.

The Seder intends to commemorate and partially reenact the biblical events. It takes place around the table on which lies the Seder plate, containing a roasted bone commemorating the paschal lamb and Passover sacrifice, called "*zroa,*" and an egg recalling the special sacrifice (*korban ḥagigah*) offered by the pilgrims in the Temple in Jerusalem. The Italian Haggadah attaches to the roasted bone and the egg an eschatological meaning while stating that the roasted bone is a reminder of the leviathan and the egg refers to a legendary bird called "*ziz.*" Both animals will be eaten in the righteous meal in paradise, with the arrival of the messiah. The *maror* (bitter herbs) symbolize the bitter slavery in Egypt and recall the bitter herbs that the Israelites ate with the lamb on the eve of the Exodus. The *ḥaroset* (a mixture of chopped fruits, wine, and spices) resembles the clay with which the Israelites worked in Egypt. *Karpas* (various green leaves, according to the custom) is dipped in salt water or in vinegar. This custom originates in the Greek and Roman practice of starting a meal with hors d'œuvres, unlike the Jews who would start it with bread. The Italian Haggadah adds to the plate roasted grains, nuts, sweets, and fruit, meant to keep the children awake and to persuade them to ask the Four Questions in the Haggadah (chiefly, "What makes this night different from all other nights?"). In addition, the Seder plate features three *matzot,* of which two fulfill the requirement for *leḥem mishneh* (the double portion of bread also served on the Sabbath) and the third, placed in the middle, is called "*afikoman*" (the name derives from the Greek *epikomen,* or "entertainments after the meal"). Half of the *afikoman* is hidden at the beginning of the Seder and is eaten at the end. An Ashkenazi custom, which became a common practice, is for the children in attendance to search for the hidden portion and "redeem" it at the end of the Seder in exchange for a present. The Seder cannot be terminated until after the *afikoman* is eaten, after which nothing further is eaten. In addition, the Seder includes the drinking of four cups of wine at specified points in the ceremony. In some communities, it is customary to fill a cup for the prophet Elijah and open the door to await his arrival.

Passover in Art

The importance of the festival together with the *mitzvah* of embellishing ritual objects gave rise to a tradition of decorating objects related to the Seder. Some of these objects are used on other occasions, and it is the decoration that identifies their particular function. Wine cups and goblets, for example, are inscribed with the word "Pesaḥ," sometimes with quotations from the Haggadah, and are often decorated with motifs related to the festival. It is customary to decorate Elijah's Cup.

An object made especially for the Seder is the Seder plate. This tradition was most elaborated in the Jewish communities of Europe, but plates were also made in Iran, Syria, and Israel. The earliest Seder plate known today is a faience plate from the fifteenth century. The plates, also made of silver, pewter, brass, and olivewood, were decorated with text taken from the Haggadah and scenes related to the story of the Exodus and Passover customs.

In addition to the special plate, the Seder ceremony has produced silver vessels for the *ḥaroset,* embroidered cases for the *matzot,* and special covers for the cushion on which reclines the person who conducts the Seder. The creation of decorated ritual objects continues.

The most richly decorated object is the Haggadah. The earliest decorated *Haggadot* date to the thirteenth century. Many decorated *Haggadot* have been printed since the invention of movable type. The special iconography of the Haggadah includes text, rituals, and biblical illustrations. The printed *Haggadot* of the twentieth century often include illustrations that refer to events of the time of their creation.

Yael Zirlin

See also: Egg; Food and Foodways; Haggadah of Passover; Seder Plate.

Bibliography

Davidovitch, David. "Ceramic Seder Plates from Non-Jewish Workshops." *Journal of Jewish Art* 2 (1975): 50–61.

Goldschmidt, Daniel. *The Passover Haggadah: Its Sources and History.* Jerusalem: Bialik Institute, 1977 (in Hebrew).

Kanof, Abraham. *Jewish Ceremonial Art and Religious Observance.* New York: Harry N. Abrams, 1969.

Kasher, Menachem M. *Haggadah Shelemah. The Complete Passover Haggadah.* Jerusalem: Torah Shelema Institute, 1967 (in Hebrew).

Rapel, Yoel. *Encyclopedia of Jewish Holidays.* Tel Aviv: Mod, 1990 (in Hebrew).

Safrai, Samuel, and Ze'ev Safrai. *Haggadah of the Sages: The Passover Haggadah.* Jerusalem: Carta, 1998 (in Hebrew).

Shachar, Isaiah. *Jewish Tradition in Art: The Feuchtwanger Collection of Judaica.* Jerusalem: Israel Museum, 1981.

Patai, Raphael (1910–1996)

Raphael Patai's scholarly works represent a synthesis of anthropological-folkloristic theories and methods with the historical study of Jewish and Arab cultures and of the Jewish communities that experienced the world of Islam. In numerous books and essays spanning more than sixty years, Patai drew upon major folkloristic and anthropological approaches of the twentieth century, such as cross-cultural comparative methods, myth and ritual theory, and theories of cultural contact and acculturation to analyze the ancient Israelite religion, post-biblical and medieval Jewish literature, and the cultures and traditions of Jewish ethnic groups from predominantly Muslim lands. Within Jewish folklore, his studies examine biblical beliefs in the context of the ancient Middle East, highlight the mythic dimensions of the Aggadah, and broaden scholars' initial concern with east European communities to include Jewish ethnic communities from Arab lands.

Early Life and Education

Patai was born in Budapest, Hungary, on November 22, 1910. Following the spirit of Hungarian nationalism, his father, Jozef (1882–1953), had changed his last name from Klein to Patai, alluding to his childhood village Pata. His father and his mother, Edith Patai (née Ehrenfeld) (1886–1976), belonged to Hungarian Jewish-Zionist intellectual circles. Both were scions to long lines of rabbinical families and became poets and writers in Hebrew and Hungarian. Raphael Patai began his education in a modern school and continued in the newly established high school of the Israelite Congregation of Pest. After graduation in 1928, he briefly studied mechanical engineering at Budapest's Technical University but, because of its blatant anti-Semitism and his own interest in other areas, transferred to the yeshiva in Montreux, Switzerland, which combined an east European Jewish curriculum with a Western setting. Having attended the yeshiva for only a few months, he enrolled at the Rabbinical Seminary of Budapest in September 1929, after explaining to his father that he was nonetheless not intending to pursue a rabbinical career. He was, at the same time, enrolled at the University of Budapest (now called Eötvös Loránd University). At the seminary, he came under the influence of Bernard Heller (1871–1943), a prominent scholar of Jewish and Arabic folklore. During the academic year 1930–1931, he attended the Jüdisch-Theologisches Seminar in Breslau and the University of Breslau, and then returned to Budapest to complete his studies.

After graduation from the University of Budapest in 1933, Patai moved to Palestine and enrolled as a "research student" at the Hebrew University. Even as a young student, he demonstrated his dedication to folklore by publishing the essay "Ha'folklor ma hu?" (What Is Folklore?) in the Jerusalem daily *Do'ar ha'Yom* on March 15, 1935.

In 1936, after completing his dissertation, "Ha'Mayim: Mehqar leyediat ha'aretz ulefolklor eretziyisraeli bitequfot hamiqra vehamishna" (Water: A Study in Palestinology and Palestinian Folklore in the Biblical and Mishnaic Periods), Patai became the first student to receive a Ph.D. at the Hebrew University. After it was published, his dissertation was awarded the prestigious Bialik Prize for 1936. He followed this study by exploring the theme of "man and land," prominent in the discourse of the Yishuv (settlement) period, in his book *Adam ve'Adamah* (Man and Land).

As an extension of his doctoral research, Patai published *Ha'sappanut ha'ivrit: meḥkar betoldot hatarbut ha'eretz yisraelit beyemei kedem* (Jewish Seafaring: A Study in Ancient Jewish Culture) (1938), to which he returned at various points later in his life. It was one of the last subjects on which he worked at the end of his life, and the revised text was published posthumously as *The Children of Noah: Jewish Seafaring in Ancient Times* (1998).

Research and Life Work

Very early in his career Raphael Patai recognized the significance of systematic research in folklore and anthropology among the diverse Jewish ethnic groups that were gathering in Palestine and began recording information about the culture and history of several ethnic groups. An exemplary ethnographic-historical and folkloric research project employing this method was his study of the Crypto Jews of Meshhed, begun in Jerusalem in 1946 and completed sixty years later

Raphael Patai, ca. 1993. *(Courtesy of Daphne Patai)*

and published posthumously as *Jadīd al-Islām: The Jewish "New Muslims" of Meshhed* (1997). In Jerusalem, Patai was the major moving force in the formation of the Palestine Institute of Folklore and Ethnography (1944) and the founding editor of its journal, *Edot: A Quarterly for Folklore and Ethnology* (1945–1948), and its monograph series "Studies in Folklore and Ethnology," which comprised five volumes between 1946 and 1948.

In 1947 Patai received a research fellowship in the United States from the Viking Fund (later the Wenner-Gren Foundation for Anthropological Research) and left for a year, but unable to obtain an academic appointment in Israel, his departure lasted a lifetime. Supported by the Wenner-Gren Foundation, he conducted field research among the Jewish community (which had intermarried with the local indigenous Indian tribe) in the village of Venta Prieta, Mexico, in summer 1948 and revisited the village in 1964. With his report on this field research, Patai entered an arena in which the level of controversy was unexpectedly high. These papers were republished in Patai's volume *On Jewish Folklore* (1983) and again, with additional essays on the subject, in volume 18 of the *Jewish Folklore and Ethnology Review* (1996).

In the United States Patai taught anthropology at Dropsie College (1948–1957) and Fairleigh Dickinson University (1966–1975) and was a visiting professor at Columbia University, New York University, Ohio State University, the University of Pennsylvania, and Princeton University. In 1956 he became the director of research at the Herzl Institute, New York, and a year later he became also the editor of the Herzl Press. In 1988 he founded and edited, at Wayne State University Press, the monograph Series in Jewish Folklore and Anthropology, which after his death was renamed the Raphael Patai Series in Jewish Folklore and Anthropology."

A prolific scholar in Hungarian, Hebrew, and, above all, English, who wrote about a broad range of subjects, Patai introduced into Jewish studies anthropological and folkloric theories of the twentieth century. He selected some of his key articles for republication in his volume *On Jewish Folklore* (1983). During the first phase of his research, he drew upon the comparative, evolutionary, and cultural anthropology of James Frazer, and later he shifted to the Cambridge school of "myth and ritual," and its applications to the Mediterranean societies in the ancient Middle East and Greece. His book exploring this approach, *Man and Temple in Ancient Jewish Myth and Ritual* (1947), led years later to a collaboration with Robert Graves. Their joint book, *Hebrew Myths: The Book of Genesis* (1964), recast Genesis and midrashic narratives about biblical figures and events as Hebrew myths, long before other scholars applied the concept of myth to Jewish traditions and Jewish mysticism. The influence of this collaboration is also apparent in such works as Patai's *The Hebrew Goddess* (1967, 1978, 1990, 2011). Among his best-known works are *The Arab Mind* (1973, 1983, 2003, 2007, 2010) and *The Jewish Mind* (1977, 2007). He provided the first detailed exploration of the role of Jews in alchemy in his book *The Jewish Alchemists: A History and Source Book* (1994).

At the end of his life, Patai turned his attention to the country of his birth and published *The Jews of Hungary: History, Culture, Psychology,* which appeared in 1996, a few months before his death. He also wrote several autobiographical volumes. His last published book was *Arab Folktales from Palestine and Israel,* which appeared posthumously in 1998.

Patai's final project consisted of planning, outlining, and initiating the writing of the *Encyclopedia of Jewish Folklore and Traditions* (2013).

Dan Ben-Amos

See also: Alchemy; *Edot: A Quarterly for Folklore and Ethnology*; Hungary, Jews of; Sea.

Bibliography

Ben-Amos, Dan. "Raphael Patai (1910–1996)." *Journal of American Folklore* 110 (1997): 314–316.

Graves, Robert, and Raphael Patai. *Hebrew Myths: The Book of Genesis.* Garden City, NY: Doubleday, 1964.

Haskell, Guy H. "The Development of Israeli Anthropological Approaches to Immigration and Ethnicity, 1948–1980." *Jewish Folklore and Ethnology Review* 11 (1989): 19–26.

Hirschler, Gertrude. "Bibliography of the Published Writings of Raphael Patai." In *Fields of Offerings: Studies in Honor of Raphael Patai,* ed. Victor D. Sanua, pp. 29–53. Cranbury, NJ: Associated University Presses, 1983.

Patai, Raphael. *Apprentice in Budapest: Memories of a World That Is No More.* Salt Lake City: University of Utah Press, 1988.

———. *The Hebrew Goddess.* 3d enlarged ed. Detroit: Wayne State University Press, 1990.

———. *Israel Between East and West: A Study in Human Relations.* Philadelphia: Jewish Publication Society of America, 1953.

———. *Jadīd al-Islām: The Jewish "New Muslims" of Meshhed.* Detroit: Wayne State University Press, 1997.

———. *Journeyman in Jerusalem: Memories and Letters, 1933–1947.* Salt Lake City: University of Utah Press, 1992.

———. *Man and Land: A Study in Customs, Beliefs and Legends Among the Jews and the Nations of the World.* 2 vols. Jerusalem: Hebrew University Press, 1942–1943 (in Hebrew).

———. *Man and Temple in the Ancient Jewish Myth and Ritual.* Edinburgh: Thomas Nelson, 1947.

———. *On Jewish Folklore.* Detroit: Wayne State University Press, 1983.

———. *Robert Graves and the Hebrew Myths: A Collaboration.* Detroit: Wayne State University Press, 1992.

———. *The Science of Man: An Introduction to Anthropology.* 2 vols. Tel Aviv: Yavne, 1947–1948 (in Hebrew).

Patai, Raphael, ed. and trans. *Between Budapest and Jerusalem: The Patai Letters, 1933–1938.* Salt Lake City: University of Utah Press, 1992.

Patai, Raphael, and Jennifer Patai Wing. *The Myth of the Jewish Race.* New York: Charles Scribner's Sons, 1975.

Schwarzbaum, Haim. "The Oeuvre of Raphael Patai." In *Fields of Offerings: Studies in Honor of Raphael Patai,* ed. Victor D. Sanua, pp. 19–28. Cranbury, NJ: Associated University Presses, 1983.

PERETZ, ISAAC LEIB (1851–1915)

Isaac Leib Peretz was an author, poet, playwright, critic, and translator and an advocate of the collection, study, and use of folklore in literary works. A central figure in the public and cultural life of Jewish Warsaw, he wrote in both Hebrew and Yiddish and is considered the father of modern Yiddish literature, as well as a major influence on its authors.

Born on April 18, 1851, in Zamość to Yehuda and Rivka Peretz, he received a religious education but was also exposed to *maskilic* circles when he was in his teens. At eighteen he was married to Sara Lichtenfeld, the daughter of the *maskilic* author and mathematician Gabriel Judah Lichtenfeld. The couple had two sons, Jacob, who died young, and Eliezer (Lucjan). After the marriage ended in divorce, Peretz married Helena (Nechama) Ringelheim in 1878. After spending two years in Warsaw (1876–1877) he returned to Zamość, where he studied law. He supported himself as an attorney until 1887, when his license was revoked after he was accused of promoting Polish nationalism and socialism. He moved to Warsaw with his wife and son. In 1890, at the recommendation of Naḥum Sokolov, Peretz joined the statistical expedition financed by the philanthropist Jan Bloch, which investigated the economic plight of the Jews in Poland; this took him to the towns and villages of the Tomaszów district. In 1891 he became a member of the Warsaw community council. Peretz continued in this capacity, dividing his time between this job and his writing and cultural activity, until his death in 1915.

The Works

At the start of his literary career, in the 1870s, Peretz wrote in Yiddish—satirical poems on local Zamość affairs, some of them set to popular melodies. But, like the poems he wrote in Polish during the same years, they were never published. In the late 1870s and throughout the 1880s he wrote chiefly in Hebrew, with his work appearing in the periodicals *Ha'Shahar, Ha'Boker,* and *Ha'Zefirah. Sippurim Be'Shir ve'shirim shonim* (Stories in Verse and Selected Poems), his first published collection (1877), was a co-production with his father-in-law, Gabriel Judah Lichtenfeld. It was not until 1888 that his first important work in Yiddish, the poem "Monish," saw the light of day, in *Di yidishe folksbibliotek,* a periodical edited by Sholem Aleichem. From then on, Peretz published in both Hebrew and Yiddish, gradually switching to the latter. Many of the stories of these years were realistic, with a positive angle on the social aspects of Jewish life. Peretz also became the editor and publisher of four journals: *Di yidishe bibliotek,* with a *maskilic* orientation, in which he published, among other pieces, his impressions of his travels in the Tomaszów district; *Literatur un lebn; Ha'Hetz*; and *Yontev bletlekh.* The last of these, which followed a radical socialist line, evaded the censor by pretending to focus on the Jewish holidays. Peretz also attended conferences of Jewish workers and published stories and essays with socialist sympathies in Eastern Europe, London, and New York. In 1899 he was jailed for three months for socialist activity. After his release, a four-volume collection of his work in Hebrew was published by Tushiya.

Collection of Jewish Folklore

In the 1890s Peretz began collecting folk songs, tales, and sayings. Although he prepared forty-two folksongs for publication in *Yontev bletlekh* in 1896, it was only in 1898 that his first work on the subject appeared, in the German-language *Am Urquell.* His interest in Jewish folklore became more intense around the turn of the century. In 1900–1902 Peretz published many of the stories later collected in *Khasidish* (In the Hasidic Manner). Beginning in 1904 he wrote a series of treatments of folktales, which appeared initially in the journal *Der fraynd* and later in the first edition of his *Folkstimlikhe geshikhtn* (Folktales) in 1909. Additional stories in the series were written between 1912 and 1914.

At the same time, starting in 1903, Peretz turned to writing for the stage. His most famous works in this genre are *Di goldene keyt* (The Golden Chain, 1909) and *Baynakht oyfn altn mark* (At Night in the Old Market, 1907). In 1904 Peretz resumed publication of *Di yidishe bibliotek* as a monthly and became the unofficial spokesman of the Yiddishists. A ten-volume collection (the last in 1913) of his writings was published by the Warsaw publishing house Progress.

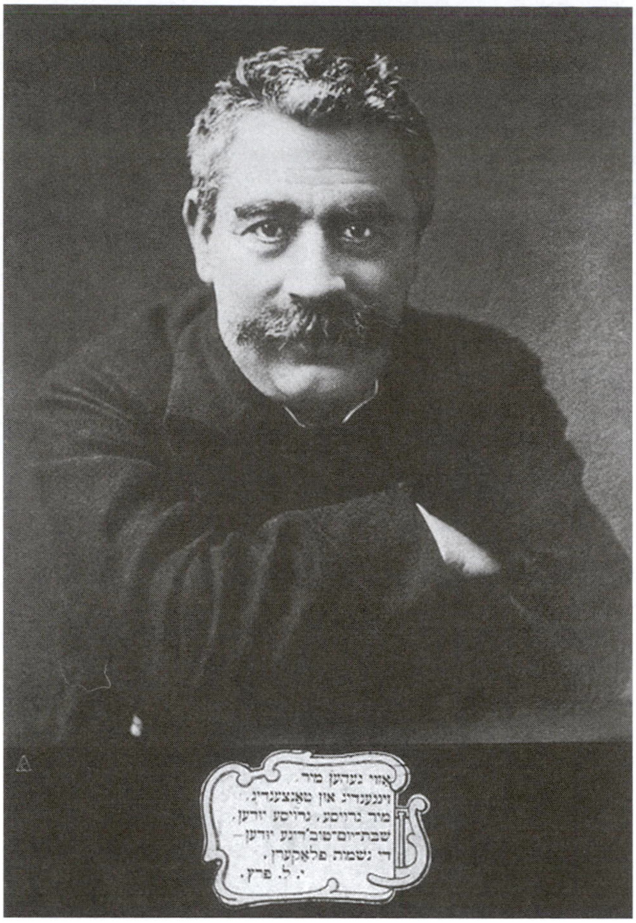

Isaac Leib Peretz, postcard.

Literature and Folklore in the Service of Ideology

The aesthetic ideals of the Haskalah (Enlightenment) are evident in Peretz's works of the 1870s, 1880s, and first half of the 1890s. Although they drew on Jewish folklore, their perspective was critical and motivated by an interest in ethnography, as in the *Bilder fun a provints-rayze* (Pictures from a Provincial Journey), based on his experiences in the Tomaszów district, published in *Di yidishe bibliotek* in 1891. In these sketches Peretz described the folklore of the shtetl (village) and its inhabitants, but added trenchant social and cultural criticism, informed by an anticlerical socialism, of the people and their customs. He presented himself as a modern Polish Jew, urban and secular, remote from the people and their folkways, and a sharp contrast to the conservative and disintegrating shtetl. Nevertheless, by this time Peretz was feeling a certain attraction to folklore and compassion for the shtetl Jews. His attitude toward Yiddish, too, the language in which the *Bilder* were written, began to change.

In 1888, when he published the poem "Monish," Peretz told Sholem Aleichem that he wrote in Yiddish for his own pleasure and not to educate the people. This was a bold attitude toward that language: not a despicable jargon, dismissed by the *maskilim* as a linguistic and cultural excrescence whose sole merit was as a tool to educate the common folk, but a vehicle that could convey aesthetic values, a language of belles-lettres in which the common folk, too, could have an experience, in his words, "of beauty, of the spirit hovering above the poem." This view of Yiddish went together with a rejection of the pragmatic character of Haskalah literature, a farewell to its social themes, and the turn to an expressive literature that deals with the inner world of individuals and the community. Whereas the Haskalah authors who wrote in Yiddish in the nineteenth century had no use for the older Yiddish literature (the *teḥinot* [supplications], the ethical treatises [*musar*], and the *bobbe meises* [romances; lit., grandma stories]) and ignored the existence of contemporary Yiddish writing (such as collections of legends) and Yiddish folk literature, Peretz was the first important writer who attempted to connect to the storytelling tradition of the revival of the old Yiddish language and turned toward the Jews' recent Yiddish-speaking past: the folksongs, the Hasidic legends, and the *teḥinot* for women.

In Peretz's oeuvre, the use of Yiddish and reliance on folklore developed in parallel. Peretz changed his mind about the national and aesthetic status of Yiddish and also about the national and aesthetic status of folklore. The national awakening all over Europe, including Poland; the Jewish national revival (the First Zionist Congress met in 1897); and the emergence of ethnography and folklore studies led Peretz to recognize the national significance and aesthetic value of folklore. He went on to exert great influence on his contemporaries and inspired them to accept folklore as a national treasure. Peretz presented their folklore as evidence that the Jews were a nation with their own culture, language, and history. He saw folklore as a means of preserving the culture of the past and shaping a modern secular Jewish identity for the future and as a symbol of the national spirit. In his evocations of folk beliefs and folk customs he highlighted the supernatural and mystical elements. He depicted the people's moral and spiritual elevation and their inherent love of beauty and poetry. Jewish folksongs, he held, demonstrated the Jews' sensitivity to nature, to music, to beauty, to dance, and to love. Although folkloric elements can be found throughout his oeuvre, most of the stories written in a folk or Hasidic vein are in the two collections *Khasidish* and *Folkstimlikhe geshikhtn.* Because of Peretz's strong attraction to folklore, his editors could not always decide how to categorize various works; hence the stories included in the successive editions of *Folkstimlikhe geshikhtn* changed over the years. In a 1915 letter to Jacob Dinezon, for example, H.N. Bialik wondered whether "we should perhaps add some of Peretz's Hasidic stories in Hebrew—which also have a folk origin—to *Folkstimlikhe geshikhten,* in order to pad the size of the volume."

Both Yiddish and folklore served Peretz as a tool for consolidating modern Jewish nationalism. During the last decade of his life, Peretz was at the forefront of the campaign, which reached its high-water mark at the Czernowitz Conference of 1908, to make Yiddish a national language of the Jews. He advocated cultural autonomy for the Jews of the Diaspora and wanted to crystallize a Jewish national culture for the Jews living in the Diaspora that would be secular, humanist, and ethical. Peretz did not see the Land of Israel and the Zionist idea as a feasible solution for the entire Jewish people; he believed that it was impossible to create "a spiritual center far from the center of the people's life," as Ahad Ha'am (pseudonym of Asher Ginsberg, 1856–1927) proposed. Consequently he favored implanting a strong secular national culture in the Diaspora, to replace the tradition of the religious past and prevent the assimilation catalyzed by loss of faith. One way to achieve this, Peretz maintained, was by forging a national literature based on all facets of the Jewish tradition, both written and oral. In the essay "What Does Literature Lack?" (1910) he phrased it in the clearest possible terms: "We must get out of the ghetto and see the world, but with the eyes of a Jew. . . . I am speaking to those who are fighting for our right to have our own culture, for the right to create Jewish cultural values. Here again it is not enough to speak Yiddish—you have to say something, too. . . . But someone who has neither past nor future wanders through the world like a foundling, with no father or mother, with no tradition, and with no obligations to what is still to come, to the future and eternity." Peretz died on April 3, 1915.

Limor Weissman Ravid

See also: Poland, Jews of.

Bibliography

Bar-Itzhak, Haya. *Pioneers of Jewish Ethnography and Folkloristics in Eastern Europe.* Ljubljana: Studia Mythologica Slavica—Supplementa, Scientific Research Center of the Academy of Science and Arts, 2010.

Gottesman, Itzik Nachmen. *Defining the Yiddish Nation: The Jewish Folklorists of Poland.* Detroit: Wayne State University Press, 2003.

Mayzel, Nachman. *Yitskhok Leybush Perets un zayn dor shrayber* (I.L. Peretz in His Writer's Generation). New York: Iḳuf, 1951.

Niger, Shmuel. *Y.L. Perets: Zayn lebn* (I.L. Peretz: His Life). Buenos Aires: Argentiner optayl fun Alveltlekhn Yidishn kultur-kongres, 1952.

Roskies, David G. "I.L. Peretz." In *A Bridge of Longing: The Lost Art of Yiddish Storytelling.* Cambridge, MA: Harvard University Press, 1952.

Shmeruk, Chone. *Peretses yiesh-vizye* (Peretz's Vision of Despair). New York: YIVO, 1971.

Wisse, Ruth R. *I.L. Peretz and the Making of Modern Jewish Culture.* Seattle: University of Washington Press, 1991.

Pinto, Rabbi Ḥaim (1748–1845)

Rabbi Ḥaim Pinto the Great was the first in a family dynasty to achieve recognition throughout Morocco and abroad. Due to his renowned erudition, the numerous miracles he performed and recounted all over the country, and his humbleness and great worry to the well-being of his people, his sons and their descendants have acquired the status of sainthood. He was the first of the Moroccan *tzaddikim* whose miracles and deeds were described in a book titled *Shevaḥ Ḥaim.*

The Pinto family is one of three large families (the two others are Abuḥatsera and Ben Barukh Ha'Cohen) to produce several saints and illustrious rabbis. To this day, the families are considered holy, and their descendants share this distinguished reputation. The migration of these families to Israel and a dramatic change in the general framework of saint veneration among Moroccan Jews in Israel have altered the relative influence of these families.

The Pinto family originated in a small town of the same name in the area of Madrid, Spain. After the expulsion of the Jews from Spain in 1492 and from Portugal in 1496–1497, several Pinto families migrated to Morocco as well as other countries. According to a Pinto family tradition, Rabbi Yosef Pinto immigrated to Damascus, Syria. One of his descendants, Rabbi Yoshiyahu Pinto (1565–1648), became famous as a rabbi. Rabbi Yoshiyahu's daughter married the son of Rabbi Ḥaim ben Joseph Vital, a prominent disciple of Rabbi Issac Luria Ashkenazi (Ha'Ari). Members of the Pinto family stress this link to Rabbi Luria and view Rabbi Yoshiyahu as the head of the family dynasty.

The Pinto families that moved to Morocco settled in Tangier, Agadir, and Marrakech, where they had an important role in leading the local community and the rabbinate. Rabbi Ya'akov Pinto, a disciple of Rabbi Abraham Azulay, became a famous kabbalist and published a commentary to the Zohar. His son, Rabbi Abraham Pinto, was a *dayan* (religious judge) in Marrakech. The last Pinto to live in Tangier was Rabbi Shlomo Pinto, who dedicated his life to the study of the Torah, with the support of his first wife's brother, a wealthy merchant named Rabbi Khalifa Malka. After his first wife's death, Rabbi Shlomo traveled to Marrakech and married a woman from the Benbeniste family. The couple returned to Agadir, where their son, Ḥaim, later known as Rabbi Ḥaim Pinto the Great, was born in 1748. Rabbi Shlomo died in 1761, when Ḥaim was only 12 years old.

That same year, there was an earthquake in Agadir, and many of its inhabitants moved to Mogador. The young Ḥaim arrived in Mogador and stayed with Rabbi Ya'akov Gedalia, one of the city's richest residents. When he learned that one of his relatives, Rabbi Meir Pinto, lived in the city and worked at the French embassy, Ḥaim contacted him. Rabbi Meir registered Ḥaim in the yeshiva headed by Rabbi Ya'akov Bibas. Ḥaim excelled in his studies, and, after Rabbi Ya'akov Bibas died in 1769, Ḥaim, now a rabbi himself, was appointed head of the yeshiva and a *dayan,* together with his friend Rabbi David Ben Ḥazan. Rabbi Ḥaim Pinto served as the chief rabbi of Mogador until his death in 1845.

Among the legends about Rabbi Ḥaim Pinto is that he studied with the prophet Elijah. Every night, Rabbi Ḥaim would wake up to study and his disciple and servitor, Rabbi Aharon Ben-Ḥaim, would serve him a cup of coffee. One night, Rabbi Aharon heard two voices and brought in two cups of coffee. When Rabbi Ḥaim inquired, the servitor answered that he had brought two cups of coffee because he had heard two voices and thought that there was a guest present. Rabbi Ḥaim said to him: "Happy are you that you have seen the prophet Elijah, but now you must swear that you will reveal this secret only after my death." And so it was that Rabbi Aharon revealed the secret after Rabbi Ḥaim's death.

Another legend recounts that when he was young, Rabbi Ḥaim would pray in the synagogue of a rich man. Every Saturday afternoon, before the Minḥa prayer service, he would give a lesson until the rich man would ask him to stop. On one occasion, Rabbi Ḥaim gave a sermon that excited those in attendance. Rabbi Ḥaim continued his sermon and ignored the rich man's orders, agreeing to stop only after his third request. In the Minḥa prayer, Rabbi Ḥaim implored God to help him find financial support for building his own synagogue. The next day a man about to travel abroad asked Rabbi Ḥaim to hold on to a large sum of money for him until his return. Rabbi Ḥaim asked the man for permission to use the money until his return, and the man agreed. Rabbi Ḥaim then called skilled workmen and built a magnificent synagogue. The man never returned to claim the money, and Rabbi Ḥaim understood that God had sent the prophet Elijah to help him.

Another story tells that while Rabbi Ḥaim was in the middle of teaching a lesson at the yeshiva, he suddenly went and stood at the entrance to the building. His disciple and servitor followed him. A rich man, known to be a miser, passed by, and Rabbi Ḥaim asked him to give alms for the poor. The rich man refused. Then Rabbi Ḥaim asked his servitor to follow the man to his house and recite the Shema. When the rich man reached his door, he suddenly dropped dead as the servitor finished reading the prayer. Upon his return, the servitor told the rabbi what had happened. The rabbi then disclosed that he had seen the Angel of Death dancing in the town around the rich man. Since he had found out what was going to happen, the rabbi tried to save him from death by performing an act of charity. Because he was unable to persuade the rich man to perform an act of charity, he ensured that he had a proper death as a Jew by reciting the Shema.

Rabbi Ḥaim had four children: Rabbi Yehuda (also known as Rabbi Hedann), Rabbi Yosef, Rabbi Yoshiyahu, and Rabbi Ya'akov. Rabbi Hedann became particularly famous as a saint and a performer of miracles. It is told that when he walked through a market, both Jews and Muslims would kiss his hand and ask for a blessing, which they accompanied with a donation. He supported his family from these donations and also gave money to the poor.

It is said that when Rabbi Ḥaim Pinto the Great died, his sons mourned him for seven days. During the day, the four brothers would take light naps. During one of these naps, Rabbi Hedann closed his eyes but remained awake. When he opened his eyes, he saw his father of

Cover page of the book *Shevaḥ Ḥaim* by Makhluf Mazal Tarim. (Casablanca, no date)

blessed memory about to enter the house. Rabbi Hedann shouted loudly, waking up his brothers, and told them that he saw their father entering the house. At night, his father came to him in a dream and said that he had intended to come to him while he was awake, but now that he had revealed the secret, he would be able to come to him only in his dreams.

A legend tells that at the time of Rabbi Hedann, a Jewish merchant named Messann Bohbot decided to travel to Amzat village in the region of Taroudant, where he used to buy citrons that he would later sell in Mogador. After purchasing the merchandise, he was on his way to his hometown when he encountered bandits on the road. He had 500 douro in his wallet. He knew that the bandits would most likely murder him and take his money, so he vowed to donate all his money to Rabbi Hedann if he were saved. Miraculously, he was saved but regretted making the vow and considered giving Rabbi Hedann only 100 douro. That night, Rabbi Ḥaim Pinto the Great appeared to his son in a dream and told him what happened to Messann and instructed him not to accept less than 500 douro. In the morning, Messann went to the house of Rabbi Hedann and gave him 100 douro and five citrons. Rabbi Hedann said, "I will not accept less than 500 douro, because that was your vow," and told Messann about Rabbi Pinto the Great's appearance in his dream. Messann was shocked to hear that Rabbi Hedann knew everything and immediately handed him all the money.

Another story describes how one year there was a drought and people from the community came to Rabbi Hedann, asking him to pray for rain. Surrounded by the crowd, he went and stood by his father's house. He did not even have time to complete the prayer for rain when the rain started and all the people returned home wet.

A prominent son of Rabbi Hedann, Rabbi Ḥaim Pinto, was born in Mogador in 1865 and died on the fifteenth of Ḥeshvan (October 20) 1937 in Casablanca. He is buried in the old Jewish cemetery of Casablanca, where he was a very popular saint. He is sometimes called Rabbi Ḥaim Pinto Ha'Katan (the Younger), to distinguish him from his illustrious grandfather, Rabbi Ḥaim Pinto the Great.

It is said that around 1924, Rabbi Ḥaim Pinto the Younger was saying the "Birkat ha'Levanah" (the blessing of the new moon). When he finished the blessing, he told the people who were with him: "What did we say in the blessing? *Ke'shem she'anaḥnu meraqqedin* . . . [as we dance toward thee, but cannot touch thee]. I promise you that some of you will live to see the day when man will go up to the moon and dance there." The people who were with him asked: "How can such thing come about?" He told them: "It will happen."

Rabbi Ḥaim Pinto the Younger had four children: Rabbi Moshe-Aharon, Rabbi Ḥaim-Shimon, Rabbi Raphael, and Rabbi Meir. The last two were brutally murdered by Muslims in 1980 in Casablanca. The most eminent of the four brothers was undoubtedly Rabbi Moshe-Aharon Pinto. He was considered a *tzaddik*. He secluded himself for many years in the family house in Mogador and was there when his father died. Moshe-Aharon and others in Mogador did not immediately receive the message about their father's impending death. Several followers of the Pinto saints left for Casablanca, knowing that they would not arrive there in time. They invited Rabbi Moshe to join them, but he declined. Upon their arrival, they were astonished to see Rabbi Moshe already observing the shiva mourning rituals with his brothers and were even more amazed to learn that he had attended the funeral. When Rabbi Moshe was asked about it by his son Rabbi Ḥaim, he answered that some things are best left unsaid.

Rabbi Moshe-Aharon immigrated to Israel, became famous in Morocco and in Israel, and was associated with many miracles. He died in Ashdod when he was seventy-three years old and is buried there. His grave, a domed structure ornamented with colored glass, is a site of pilgrimage for many of the Pinto family followers in Ashdod and elsewhere in Israel. The most distinguished of his sons, Rabbi David, is responsible for leading the rabbinical activities in France, where he teaches and spreads the Torah. He also leads a large group of followers in Los Angeles. His name is also associated with many miracles.

The eldest son of Rabbi Moshe, Rabbi Ḥaim Pinto, is married to the granddaughter of the famous Baba Sali (Rabbi Yisrael Abuḥatsera) of the Abuḥatsera family. He lives in Ashdod and thus is sometimes called Rabbi Ḥaim Pinto of Ashdod. He serves as the chief rabbi of Kiryat Malakhi. He oversees a broad range of activities in Ashdod and Kiryat Malachi and makes frequent visits to followers of the Pinto family's saints around the world. Rabbi Ḥaim Pinto is the present keeper of a holy Torah scroll famous for its miracles. The scroll was written by Rabbi Yoshiyahu following the instructions of Rabbi Ḥaim Vital and was completed by Rabbi Ḥaim Pinto the Great on the day of his death, the 26th of Elul (September 28) 1845. Rabbi Ḥaim of Ashdod frequently travels abroad presenting the holy Torah scroll to different communities. In a ceremony held in Ashdod one year after Rabbi Moshe-Aharon's death, with the participation of a large crowd, *hakafot* were performed with the Torah scroll according to the tradition of the family. On the fourth encircling, dedicated to Rabbi Moshe-Aharon, water started flowing from the grave, a phenomenon considered a miracle and signifying the presence of the saint buried in the grave. People hurried to touch the water. As the fourth encirclement ended, the water stopped coming out of the grave.

Rabbi Ḥaim Pinto of Ashdod has six sons and daughters. The most prominent of his sons are Rabbi Yoshiyahu and Rabbi Shlomo. Their distinction and status enabled them to develop and expand the Pinto family's activities to several continents. In the past decade, there has been a significant increase in the number of followers and in the inherent ability of some of the followers to provide massive support to strengthening and broadening the family's activities.

Saint veneration among Moroccan Jews in Israel has undergone several changes, opening new venues. A change of behavioral patterns and the formation of new models in the relationship between a saint and his followers now characterize this ritual. In Morocco, the saint veneration was limited to the boundaries of the traditional ritual, as opposed, for example, to their Muslim neighbors. In Israel, the command of large communities of saint followers is sometimes translated to a demonstration and accumulation of power and political strength. The 1980s and 1990s were, from this point of view, a turning point. Numerous saint courts were established in various locations. The popularity of saints from Moroccan lineage increased and with it rivalries and tensions, creating a competition among courts, a phenomenon unheard of in Morocco.

The Pinto family has adapted to the new reality and is leading the way to the creation of international courts and to the expansion of the number of its followers. It can do so because of the participation of the family's youngest generation. Helping to achieve this goal is Rabbi Yoshiyahu, a modest and ascetic man with exceptional skills who lives isolated from the material world. Despite his young age, he has proved himself to be well versed on any subject of interest to his followers. He has acquired a large group of followers in New York, including some of the most prominent Jewish businessmen in the city. Manhattan has the first Moroccan court of its kind in the Americas; it serves as a pilgrimage destination. Yoshiyahu and his brother Rabbi Shlomo, a great scholar and a sharp *Talmid ḥakham* (Torah scholar), visit Israel as well as other centers in the Diaspora once a month to teach the Torah and bless the followers. Their father, Rabbi Ḥaim Pinto of Ashdod, directs the international activities of the family and contributes to it significantly. He says that "the family, the entire family, is only an envoy of the community and its only purpose is to assist and to help the believers."

Issachar Ben-Ami

See also: North Africa, Jews of.

Bibliography

Ben-Ami, Issachar. "Folklore Research in Israel." *Ariel* 35 (1974): 32–47.

———. "In Praise of Rabbi Ḥaim Pinto." In *Moroccan Jewry: Ethno-Cultural Studies,* by I. Ben-Ami. Jerusalem: Mass, 1975 (in Hebrew and French).

———. *Saint Veneration Among the Jews in Morocco.* Detroit: Wayne State University Press: 1989.

———. "Saints juifs marocains en Israel: continuité et changements." In *Saints et héros du Moyen-Orient contemporain,* ed. Catherine Mayeur-Jaouen, pp. 229–245. Paris : Maisonneuve et Larose, 2000.

Pinto, Ḥaim, and David Pinto. *And the Man Moshe, (R. Moshe Aharon Pinto).* Ashdod: n.p., n.d. (in Hebrew).

Tarim, Mazal-Makhlouf. *Book in Praise of Rabbi Ḥaim Pinto.* Casablanca: n.p, 1939 (in Judeo-Arabic).

Pipe, Shmuel Zanvel

See: Anthologies

Plants

Numerous cultures' plants, in general, and trees, in particular, are an inseparable part of their religious rituals, way of life, and folklore, and Jewish folklore is no exception. Many customs and views about nature are common to the people of the ancient Middle East. The contribution of Jewish folklore with respect to botany finds expression in the use of plants in Jewish ritual and in idioms and parables related to the natural world that remain current in the Hebrew language.

The relationship between the life cycle of plants and that of humans is widely expressed in the Bible. Jeremiah and the Psalms both compare man to a tree: "Blessed is the man that trusteth in the Lord, and whose trust the Lord is: For he shall be as a tree planted by the water, and that spreadeth out its roots by the river" (Jer. 17:7–8; Ps. 1:3). When a successful family is described, it is said: "Thy wife shall be as a fruitful vine, in the innermost parts of thy house; Thy children like olive plants, round about thy table" (Ps. 128:3). Biblical images based on vegetation are taken from the agricultural environment and the flora of Israel and reflect a close relationship to nature.

The Bible and talmudic literature are not scientific books or chapters of a "Natural History." The usage of the natural world comes from religious, ethical, and historical notions or as literary devices. The deep relation to plants is evident from their use and their descriptions.

Trees and the Ashera Cult

As in other ancient societies, that of the Semitic Middle East developed a veneration for trees, even a cult. According to Frese and Gray: "Trees are a form of nature that represent life and the continuity of spiritual, cosmic and physical worlds. A tree is often used to symbolize a deity or other being or it may stand for what is sacred in general" (1995, 26).

In Canaan, the cult of trees was expressed in the veneration not just of trees but of the deity that represented them. In the Middle East and in the Bible, the cult is characterized by the following themes:

1. Venerated trees are old giant oaks and terebinths (Ezek. 6:13), which are trees located on hilltops (Hos. 4:130; Deut. 12:2).
2. There was a conflict between Jewish monotheism and the Ashera cult (biblical heathen tree worship), which was mentioned by many prophets.
3. Sacred trees were centers of active worship to local deities, especially Astrate-Ashera (1 Kgs. 14:23; 2 Kgs. 16:4).
4. Sacred trees were used as foci for socially important activities such as a place of Judgment (Judg. 4:5) and burial sites of important figures (Gen. 35:8).
5. El was an important deity in pre-Judaic history. Its name remained in Hebrew in the plural form: Elohim. There is a close similarity between the Hebrew word for oak (*alon*) and terebinth (*ela*) (both are the most prevalent sacred trees in Israel), oath (*alla*) and El, which is no coincidence. Oaks and terebinths were and remain the place for taking oaths and votive offerings and are highly venerated and protected (mostly by the Druze and Arab Muslim but also by Jews).

Medicinal Plants, Perfumes, and Incense

In spite of the rich floral abundance in Israel, many medicinal plants mentioned in the Bible lack a direct connection to any practical use. Jeremiah (8:22, 46:11, 51:8) mentioned balm as a remedy in a symbolic sense; although there is a general agreement that balm is a medicinal plant, its botanical species is not clearly spelled out. Many medicinal plants are mentioned in the Bible (wormwood—*Artemisia* spp.; cumin—*Cuminum cyminum;* Nigella—*Nigella arvensis;* gourd—*Citrullus colocynthis;* hemlock—*Conium maculatum*), and it is logical to assume that due to extensive cultural relations between the various Middle Eastern countries, they would be expected to have similar uses of medicinal plants. According to this view, Judaism did not contribute knowledge of the use of medicinal plants. The use of mandrake (*Mandragora officinarum*) as an aphrodisiac (Gen. 30:14–17) was very common and is still used for this purpose in the Middle East as well as in Egypt. The use of marjoram (*Majorana syriaca*) for purification (Num. 19:18) reflects the common use of a decoction of the plant for disinfecting babies in Arab villages. The plant contains a high concentration of terpenes (thymol and carvacrol), which were experimentally tested as effective bactericides and fungicides. The same idea recurs in Psalms 51:9, in which the cleaning practice was accepted as mental purification of sins.

Most of the difficulties raised in identifying biblical plants are related to plants used for incense, for instance, balm frankincense. The use of incense for purification and in religious ceremonies (storax, ladanum, frankincense, myrrh, galbanum) was common in ancient Middle Eastern cultures, and the Israelites were no exception. The large number of references (Exod. 30:1–8, 34–38; Lev. 16:12; 2 Chr. 26:19; Isa. 1:13; Ezek. 16:19) shows the importance of perfumes, incense, and odiferous resins in daily practice in the holy Temple. Palestine was a central crossroads in the ancient perfume and spice trade routes between Asia and neighboring countries. Spices and medicinal plants such as saffron, cinnamon, spikenard, balm, cassia, and aloe were in use (Songs 4:13–14; Esther 2:12) and no doubt were expensive commodities used by the upper classes.

Plants in Jewish Rituals and Symbolism

The Land of Israel is blessed with seven plant species: "a land of wheat and barley, and vines and fig-trees and pomegranates; a land of olive-trees and dates" (Deut. 8:8). These species are the most important plants in the economy of the inhabitants and represent staple foods (wheat and barley), main fruits (fig and pomegranate), wine (vine), oil (olive) and sweetener (date honey). All these species were the spine of all the agricultural crops in the various areas of the Land of Israel.

In order to perform the ritual of Sukkot, myrtle, dates, willow and etrog are required: "And ye shall take you on the first day the fruit of goodly trees, branches of palm-trees, and boughs of thick trees, and willows of the brook, and ye shall rejoice before the Lord your God seven days" (Lev. 23:40). Myrtle and dates have wide folkloric use in the ancient Middle East, while the willow, the etrog, and the specific binding of these four species (*arba'at ha'minim*) seem to be an original Jewish contribution.

Talmudic literature enlarged the commentaries on why these species were chosen along with their symbolism, which is among others:

1. Etrog—the symbol of fertility
2. Lulav—symbolizes rejoice and victory over other nations (it is no coincidence that on the coin Judea capta, the Jewish figure seats under a palm tree)
3. Myrtle—the symbol of success and matrimonial sanctification, and prosperity
4. Willow—symbolizes the dependence on water for agriculture and the salvation from drought.

During sacrifices, bundles of *Majorana syriaca* were used (Num. 19:18), in belief that it prevents blood coagulation. This custom was kept among the Samaritans during Passover, and thanks to it we have a precise identification of the biblical plant, although it has been proved that the various oils included in this plant do not influence coagulation. A common usage of this plant is not known across the ancient and modern Middle East. It is a symbol of modesty (1 Kgs. 5:13). The oak and the cedar are symbols of strength (Amos 2:9; Zech. 11:2).

Plants and Human Life Cycle

Trees live much longer than humans. Job compares the tree life span to the short human life (Job 14:7–10). Among others, he uses the expression (verse 7): "For there is hope of a tree, If it be cut down, that it will sprout again, And that the tender branch thereof will not cease." Isaiah mentioned the eternity of David's dynasty: "And there shall come forth a shoot out of the stock of Jesse, and a twig shall grow forth out of his roots" (Isa. 11:1). In both cases, there is an accurate botanical description of scerophyll evergreen trees in Israel, currently the main landscape's components, which like the common oak, renew themselves from a root stock after being cut. The tree is a symbol of longevity: "For as the days of a tree shall be the days of My people" (Isa. 65:22), while the wicked are compared to annual plants, which disappear in the dry season: "When the wicked spring up as the grass" (Ps. 92:8).

The four species (*arba'at ha'minim*) used in the ritual of Sukkot, from *Sefer Minghagim*, Venice 1593.

Plants, Fables, and Proverbs

The "Plant" parable best known in the Bible is Yotam parable (Judg. 9:8–15). It uses the properties of the olive, fig, vine, bramble, and cedar. Besides the bramble whose identification is not agreed upon (some identify it as *Rhamnus palaestina* or *Lycium europaeum*), the connection to the plants' properties is clear: The olive tree is the source for oil by which "they honor God and man" (Judg. 9:9). The fig's characteristic is its "sweetness" (Judg. 9:11). The grapevine provides "wine which cheereth God and man" (Judg. 9:13). The bramble is a plant of no benefit but can cause disaster (Judg. 9:15). The cedar is the glory of the plants: "He shall grow like a cedar in Lebanon" (Ps. 92:13). The moral of this parable is that the most useless and despicable of all is the one ready to rule and destroy the others.

A well-known agriculture parable is the vineyard parable (Isa. 5:1–6), in which the prophet complains that after nurturing the vine plants (the People of Israel), God expected "forth grapes" and instead he got "putrid grapes." The moral is the unfaithfulness of the People of Israel to their God.

Amots Dafni

See also: Charms, Books of; Folk Medicine.

Bibliography

Dafni, Amots. "Why Are Rags Tied to the Sacred Trees of the Holy Land?" *Economic Botany* 56 (2002): 315–327.

Frese, Pamela R., and S.J.M. Gray. "Trees." In *The Encyclopedia of Religion,* vol. 15, ed. M. Eliade, pp. 26–33. New York: Macmillan, 1995.

Harrison, Roland Kenneth. *Healing Herbs of the Bible.* Leiden: E.J. Brill, 1966.

Zohary, Michael. *Plants of the Bible.* Cambridge, UK: Cambridge University Press, 1982.

POLAND, JEWS OF

The earliest history of the Jews in Poland is shrouded in legend. According to legendary chronicles, Jews arrived in Poland as early as the tenth and eleventh centuries, perhaps even the ninth century.

The folk tradition of Polish Jews includes many legends that relate to the first arrival of Jews in Poland and their reception there. The most popular legend is the Polin legend, which expounds the Hebrew name for Poland and translates it as "lodge here." This legend, like many local legends, turns Poland into a Jewish country. Other legends relate to the Jews' initial reception and deal with relations between Jews and Poles (Bar-Itzhak 2001).

One famous legend concerns Abraham Prochownik, the Jew who became a king of Poland and was instrumental in the coronation of Piast Kołodziej (Piast the Wheelwright), who founded Poland's first historical ruling dynasty.

The legends about Esther (or Estherka) and Kazimierz (or Casimir) III, called the Great, who fell in love with her, are used to explain his grant of settlement rights and the expansion of the privileges for the Jews of Poland.

These legends preserve in the collective memory central incidents in the history of Polish Jewry. They give symbolic and metaphoric expression to the problems that preoccupied the Jewish communities of Poland. They teach the various ways in which a society finds creative solutions to its most pressing existential and spiritual problems. For example, in the legends about the arrival of the Jews in Poland, Jews adopted a foreign country as their own and Judaized an alien space by using well-known methods of Jewish classical literature—expounding the signification of names and ancient symbols such as pages of the Talmud. In this way the geography of the non-Jewish world was Judaized and drafted into the service of Jewish history.

The legends pose the desire for a long-term and tranquil domicile in Poland and creation of substantial Jewish spiritual life there, against the myth of the ultimate redemption, according to which a full spiritual life is possible only in the Land of Israel. The legends find solutions that make it possible to overcome the dilemma by turning the Land of Israel into the eternal sanctified space of the Jews spiritual longings, from which a degree of sanctity emanates to the present domicile. Poland is thus associated with repose and the continuation of the ancient Jewish tradition of learning; but it is also associated with night, darkness, and transience. The legends propose, by way of resolution, that when the messianic redemption comes, this earthly Poland, with its synagogues and houses of study, will be bodily transferred to the Land of Israel. Such solutions to the dilemmas and the dissonance they raise made life in the Polish Diaspora possible, while preserving the ancient Jewish myths.

The question of relations between Jews and Poles arises in many of these legends, and with particular poignancy in the legends of acceptance. In these, told and written down during various periods of Jewish life in Poland, we are able to see the dialogic narration between the folk legends and the changing sociohistorical reality. As a function of the age from which they date, various legends build different models of desired relations between Jews and Poles, ranging from total separation and estrangement to a model of cooperation based on compassion and later on cooperation based on equality, in the spirit of liberalism and the Jewish demands for emancipation. These models express the changing cultural consciousness of Polish Jewry and the various ideological currents that flowed within it.

Medieval Jewish merchants traveled across Eastern Europe, establishing temporary merchant colonies, but the first privilege permitting permanent Jewish settlement was granted by Bolesław the Pious of Kalisz in 1264. This privilege was confirmed and expanded by subsequent monarchs, particularly Kazimierz the Great in 1348. Although tradition holds that this was the result of Kazimierz's love for his Jewish mistress, Esterka, in fact Jewish settlement was encouraged as part of a general move to create an urban network in Poland. The scholarly level of medieval Polish Jewry was not high, though some students of Judah the Pious did settle there. Jewish economic activity centered on money lending at all levels, including to the royal court.

Sixteenth and Seventeenth Centuries

Polish Jewry entered a period of rapid social, economic, and cultural growth in the sixteenth century. As Jewish

"The Kalisz Statutes," an illustrated text, by Arthur Szyk, one of the first privileges Bołeslaw of Kalisz granted the Jews in 1264. *(The Jewish Museum, New York/ Art Resource, NY)*

numbers increased, more communities were founded in different regions, basing their existence on community privileges rather than national grants of rights. The Jewish communities acted as agents of the Polish economic authorities in collecting taxes from the Jews. In the course of the sixteenth century, the communities in different regions banded together to deal with regional tax issues, and in 1580–1581, representatives of the four Polish regions (Great Poland, Little Poland, Red Ruthenia, and Volhynia) banded together to farm the Jewish poll tax directly from the treasury. On the basis of this role, the Council of the Four Lands was formed, which not only dealt with Jewish tax issues but also issued legislation on matters of importance to Polish Jewry as a whole, including responses to periodic anti-Jewish attacks and blood libels.

As the power of the Polish nobility grew, many Jews decided to move to the private towns, where they could negotiate for themselves a wide range of economic opportunities. After the Union of Lublin was formed in 1569, an even larger number of Jews moved to the huge magnate latifundia in the eastern parts of the Polish-Lithuanian Commonwealth. Their role as moneylenders was transformed into that of leaseholders (*arendarze*) of estates that they ran on behalf of the absentee owners. Poorer Jews leased parts of estates and even individual taverns from the great Jewish *arendarze*, so the Jews became an integral part of Poland's agricultural economy. Nonetheless they retained their social and cultural distinctiveness, continuing to organize their life in separate communities and to speak Yiddish among themselves.

This was also a period of cultural growth. The Polish yeshivas became the most important in Europe, with the new curriculum of Pilpul extremely popular. The spread of printing led to the acceptance of the *Shulḥan arukh* as the normative codex of Jewish law with the addition of the glosses by Rabbi Moses ben Israel Isserles (called the Rema) of Kraków, which allowed Ashkenazi Jews to follow their own customs rather than those of the Sephardic Joseph ben Ephraim Karo.

A popular legend about a historical figure of the sixteenth and seventeenth centuries is the legend of Saul Wahl. According to the legend he became king of Poland for a short time (see: Wahl, Saul).

The mid-seventeenth century saw a period of war in the Polish-Lithuanian Commonwealth, which, though not aimed directly against the Jews, led to widespread attacks on them. In 1648, the Cossack hetman, Bogdan Chmielnicki, led a revolt against the Polish government, which was soon joined by a mass of Ukrainian peasants, motivated by economic and religious hostility against both the Catholic nobility and their local Jewish representatives. Between 30 percent and 50 percent of the Jews in the Ukraine lost their lives.

There are many legends set during the period of the 1648–1649 pogroms. The most famous are about a woman who confronts a gentile (who is always a Jew hater) and has to defend herself against his lust. The seventeenth-century work *Yeven mezulah* (Abyss of Despair), by Nathan Neta Hannover (d. 1683), which commemorates those slaughtered in the pogroms of 1648 and 1649, tells of the two virgins of Nemirov (Niemirów); one of them tricked the Cossacks into shooting her, while the second threw herself into the river during her own bridal procession. These legends became part of Jewish collective memory through generations (An-Ski 1920), and some were recorded from oral tradition in the 1950s and are stored in the Israel Folktale Archives (Bar-Itzhak 2008, 64–70). Afterward, in the mid-1650s, Poland was invaded first by Sweden and then by Muscovy. Jews suffered much destruction and loss of life from the attacks of the Polish resistance led by Stefan Czarniecki.

Eighteenth and Nineteenth Centuries

The small group of the wealthiest magnates was the most active in reconstructing the Polish economy in the late seventeenth and the eighteenth century (following the Northern War of 1702–1720), making significant use of the Jewish population in this process. More Jews were invited to settle in the small towns on their estates, until they sometimes made up a majority of the population, giving the towns a Jewish character—they were known in Yiddish as shtetls. As the number of Jews grew (reaching about 1 million by 1800), they began to search for new forms of income: Many moved to the countryside to lease taverns, while in the towns, they became the leading merchants, settling around the market square, and also broke into a wide range of crafts, even forming their own guilds. The support of the nobility was important, as the Jews faced much hostility (including sporadic violence and accusations of ritual murder) from the non-Jewish townspeople and the local clergy.

In the folk tradition of Polish Jews there are various blood libel legends. Thirteen such legends are stored in the Israel Folktale Archives, all of them recorded from Polish Jews in Israel. The Jewish blood libel legend is a reaction to the Christian blood libel legends and the attack on Jews that followed. Most of these legends are sacred legends about a Jewish community that is saved from the accusation of ritual murder thanks to God's intervention. God's help is usually expressed by sending Elijah the prophet, who appears in Jewish legends as a savior in times of persecution, and is also connected to the coming of the messiah. These legends that end with the saving of the individual or the entire Jewish community and punishment of the wicked character are an expression of fear caused by blood libels and the yearning for divine help that will save the Jewish people, especially in the Jewish sacred time of Passover.

Nonetheless, there are also historical legends that end with the death of the Jewish protagonist. The protagonist is usually the leader of the community, a rabbi or a Torah scholar who is accused of ritual murder. He prefers to die in order to save the entire community and dies a martyr death, refusing to convert to Christianity. Among these legends in the folk literature of Polish Jews are the legends about the Raices brothers. There are also legends about Adil, the daughter of Moses Kikinish of Drohobycz, who chooses to die a horrible death to save the Jewish community.

In cultural terms, the late seventeenth century was a quiet period. Following the Sabbattean heresy, there seems to have been a growth in interest in mysticism, which led to various forms of religious revivalism in the eighteenth century. The most prominent of these was the Hasidic movement, popularly believed to have been founded by Israel Ba'al Shem Tov of Międzybórz (d. 1760) and his pupil, Dov Ber, the Maggid (preacher) of Mezritch (d. 1772). This movement prized spiritual experience over study and taught that religious experience could be achieved not just in prayer but in daily life. A central tenet of Hasidism was the spiritual role of the leader, or *tzaddik*, who acted as a conduit between God and the individual Ḥasid. The *tzaddik* also began to play a social role as the ultimate source of authority in Jewish daily life. By the nineteenth century, the number of *tzaddikim*, each maintaining his own court, had proliferated greatly, emphasizing the movement's essential decentralized structure. The *shevaḥ* (praise) became the most popular folk narrative told by the Hassidim about their Rebbe.

The partitions of Poland (1772, 1793, and 1795) saw the Jews divided among the centralistic and authoritarian regimes of Prussia, Russia, and Austria. Some Jews supported the Poles' military struggle against partition, with Berek Joselewicz even establishing a Jewish legion, though many simply accepted the change of regime. The Jews of the Posen region in the Prussian partition underwent a relatively rapid process of Germanization, with many migrating westward during the nineteenth century. Posen itself became a bastion of Jewish orthodoxy under Rabbi Akiva Eger (1761–1838). The Jews of southern Poland, renamed Galicia, were under Austrian rule. There, too, the authorities were interested in forcing the Jews into acculturation in terms of education, use of language, and economic structure. The enlightened Jews (*maskilim*) supported this policy on the part of the authorities, while the conservative Ḥasidim were highly opposed. This led to a cultural battle between the two groups. The Austrian cultural policy was not backed up by serious social and economic incentives, so most of Galician Jewry remained economically backward, dependent on the largely stagnant agricultural economy. Over the nineteenth century, however, the Jews of Galicia (particularly in the larger towns) did undergo a process of gradual acculturation. Emancipation, granted in 1867, allowed the Jews to begin organizing as a religious and national minority in Galicia, in parallel to the Poles and the Ukrainians. This tended to exacerbate economic, social, and religious tensions in the region.

After passing from Prussian to French rule, central Poland, with its capital in Warsaw, became a semi-independent kingdom under tsarist rule following the Congress of Vienna in 1815. Many Jewish rights of previous decades and centuries were restricted, though Jewish economic activity remained crucial to the economy as a whole. As the industrialization of this region developed, the Jews underwent a process of urbanization, concentrating in urban centers such as Łódz and Warsaw. Though they did not form a classic industrial proletariat, the numbers of Jewish poor grew rapidly; however, a Jewish bourgeoisie also developed, with a small number of Jews beginning to assimilate to Polish culture. Over the nineteenth century, some members of the Jewish plutocracy even converted to Christianity. By mid-century, Hasidism had made significant inroads in this region of Poland, too, providing all levels of Polish-Jewish society, from the poorest to the most wealthy, with a conservative Jewish orientation and an alternative to drawing closer to Polish culture. In later years, with the intensification of Russification, and the migration to Poland of Jews from Lithuania (Litvaks), some Jews in Poland developed a Russian cultural orientation.

In the Polish uprisings of 1830 and 1863, much anti-Jewish sentiment was expressed and many Jews remained indifferent or even hostile to the Polish cause. However, there were also important centers of Jewish support for the Poles' struggle, particularly in Warsaw, where the city's chief rabbi, Dov Ber(ush) Meisels (1798–1870), openly identified with the Polish side in the early 1860s. Previously, the Polish national poet, Adam Mickiewicz, had expressed his feelings of brotherhood with Polish Jewry, calling for their support in the Poles' national cause and supporting their emancipation. With the failure of the 1863 uprising, the structure and functioning of Polish society began to be reconsidered and the Jews' role within it brought into question. While the positivists supported Jewish integration, the growth of nationalist sentiment in the last decades of the century led to increased anti-Jewish hostility, which came to a head in the years before World War I.

Jewish legends about the 1863 uprising were transcribed and published by A. Almi (see below, pg 421). The legends first appeared in the Jewish newspaper in Warsaw, *Moment,* in 1910–1911 and were later republished in volumes in Yiddish (1927) and Polish (1929).

In Jewish folklore we may see diverse manifestations of intercultural communication between Jews and Poles: the use of Slavic words and even the interpretation of parts of non-Jewish songs (An-Ski 1925, 171–194); the use and Judaization of Slavic place names; the use of iconographic symbols like the Polish eagle on books and ritual objects and the influence of local architecture on Jewish synagogue buildings; and the documentation of folk narratives by Poles and the incorporation of non-Jewish historical figures in Jewish folklore. These figures occupy two contrasting niches—avatars of the wicked Haman in Polish Jewry history such as Bogdan Chmielnicki in legends about the pogroms of 1648–1649 and great benefactors of the Polish Jews, such as King Casimir the Great, King Jan III Sobieski, Count Lubomirski, and Count Potocki, among others.

Twentieth Century

Following the war, Poland was re-established as a nation-state, even though within its final borders about 30 percent of the population were not ethnically Polish. Some 3 million Jews were Polish citizens, making up almost 10 percent of the total population. Though the victorious powers insisted that Poland (and the other new nation-states in east-central Europe) sign a special treaty to secure the rights of national and religious minorities, its terms were largely honored in the breach. There were widespread attacks on Jews in the early years of independent Poland. Jewish cultural, religious, and educational institutions did not enjoy state support and there was much economic and religious discrimination against Polish Jews, openly supported by the Church. This situation grew considerably worse in the 1930s, when Poland's poor economic situation together with government policy brought Jewish poverty to unheard-of levels. A wave of extreme nationalism led to the outbreak of a series of pogroms in central Poland in 1935 and 1936.

Polish Jewish society in the interwar period organized not only to secure its place in independent Poland but to create a range of social and cultural institutions for Jewish society. Zionists formed the leading political party, but the orthodox Agudat Yisrael and the socialist Bund also were popular. Each orientation not only was a political party, with representatives in the Sejm, local councils, and Jewish communities, but also established its own school system, youth groups, newspapers and cultural institutions. As a result, Jewish society became highly politicized. In cultural terms, interwar Polish Jewry has been characterized as a cultural and linguistic polysystem, with creative branches in the Yiddish, Polish, and Hebrew languages. These acted independently but also interacted (often with much tension) to create Polish Jewry's complex cultural milieu. These years saw important achievements for Polish Jews in both high and popular culture, literature and theater (there was also the beginnings of a Jewish film industry in Poland), and academic research and Torah study. Thus, despite the discrimination and harsh conditions, this was a period of great cultural activity for Polish Jews, which was brought to an end by the outbreak of war and the German invasion of 1939.

The Study of Jewish Folklore

Since the nineteenth century, Jewish society in Poland was influenced by the prevailing ideologies in the countries where the Jews lived. Romanticism and resurgent nationalism affected the Jewish intelligentsia, too, and awakened an interest in Jewish folklore. But contemporary ideologies took on a unique guise in Jewish society, a direct consequence of the Jews' social and political situation during this period of change, upheaval, and revolutionary ferment. The efforts of Jewish thinkers and activists focused on achieving emancipation, of the sort the Jews had received in Western Europe, alongside an unremitting struggle against anti-Semitism. The campaign for emancipation was accompanied by constant attempts to prove the Jews' loyalty to and integration with non-Jewish society and to demonstrate patriotic feelings for the country in which they lived. Most of them did not believe, however, that this entailed turning their backs on Judaism and its spiritual treasures. These circles included a handful of pioneering folklorists who published in Polish; notable among them were Benjamin Wolf Segel, Henryk Lew, and Regina Lilienthal.

An interest in traditional Jewish culture first emerged among major Polish writers of the nineteenth century, notably Eliza Orzeszkowa and Bolesław Prus, who wrote on Jewish topics. Polish literary and artistic circles were fascinated by the individuality, complexity, and exoticism they attributed to Jewish culture. Interest in Jewish ethnography emerged before World War I in the circles affiliated with two Polish ethnographic journals, *Wisła* and *Lud.*

As for the works of the pioneering Jewish folklorists who wrote in Polish, special note attaches to the Polish-language weekly *Izraelita,* which represented the Polonizing Jews. Its editor starting in 1897, Naḥum Sokolow, opened its pages to folklore materials. He believed that the Jewish intelligentsia had to renew its acquaintance with the masses and urged abandonment of the *maskilic* strategy of keeping the people at arm's length. Sokolow, not yet a Zionist, wanted to rescue folk traditions; he called for organic change in Jewish life, in a manner that would not infringe the people's sensitivities. Sokolow's approach led to the drafting of a program for Jewish folklore studies, published in *Izraelita* in 1901 by Henryk Lucjan Kohn.

The journalist Henryk Lew was the moving spirit of *Wisła, Lud,* and *Izraelita.* He launched his project to collect folklore materials by publishing a questionnaire, first in *Izraelita* (*Izraelita* 32 [1897], 1) and later in *Wisła.* The questionnaire covered the following areas: beliefs and stories, folksongs and poetry, customs and traditions, folk medicine and superstitions, and folk notions and ideas.

Segel, Lew, and Lilienthal published in all three venues. Segel and Lilienthal also contributed to the publications of the Anthropological Commission of the Academy of Arts in Kraków. In addition to collecting and discussing folklore materials, these three pioneering folklorists helped spur widespread interest in Jewish ethnography among Jewish and Polish intellectuals.

Several different streams of nationalism spread in Eastern European Jewish society during the course of the nineteenth century. The Zionists advocated the Jews' return to Eretz Israel and the establishment of a national home there. Other movements championed solutions that involved Jewish autonomy in their countries of residence. The ideological preferences of the various movements influenced their attitude toward Jewish ethnography and folklore as well.

For the Zionists, Jewish folklore, which circulated in Yiddish and was an expression of Jewish life in the Diaspora, could not serve the ideological goal of rejecting Diaspora traditions in favor of a revival of the ancient national culture in Eretz Israel. The Jews did not need to prove that they had a national culture, since its greatest treasures had been written down for centuries. Nevertheless, some of the pioneers of Jewish ethnography and folklore in Eastern Europe were fervent Zionists who, no less than their colleagues from other ideologies, felt a great love for Jewish folk culture. But their Zionism affected their work in that it led them to publish folklore materials, both new anthologies of ancient folklore and collections of the folklore of Polish Jews, originally in Yiddish, in Hebrew.

The most important contribution to folklore studies was made by the "national poet," Haim Nachman Bialik (1873–1934). Bialik's link to Jewish folklore was manifested on three levels: (1) his use of Jewish folklore in his poetry and narrative fiction; (2) his program to collect and preserve the outstanding exemplars of Jewish literature (including folklore) over the generations; and (3) his co-editorship of the journal *Reshumot,* an anthology of Jewish memoirs, ethnography, and folklore.

It is important to mention the contribution of Micha Josef Berdyczewski (Bin-Gorion) to the study of Jewish folklore. Bin-Gorion published several anthologies of Jewish folktales in Hebrew that were translated by his wife, Rachel Bin-Gorion Ramberg, to German and published in Germany. Another pioneer of Jewish folklore studies in Eastern Europe and after that in Eretz Israel, a Zionist through and through, was Alter (Asher Abraham Abba) Druyanow (1870–1938).

It should be noted, however, that some Zionist folklorists published their collections in Yiddish. Pinḥas Graubard (1892–1952), one of the Warsaw circle that gathered around Noyekh Prilutski (Noah Prylucki; 1882–1941), published songs of thieves, prisoners, and prostitutes in the most important collection produced by the Warsaw folklorists, *Bay Undz Yidn,* edited by M. Vanvild (pen name of Moses Joseph Dickstein, who also used the pseudonym Leib Kave; 1889–1942). He also edited an anthology of literature and folklore (1914) and, along with Shmuel Lehman, published Yiddish folksongs in the Frischmann jubilee volume (1914).

We must not omit folklorists who were affiliated with the religious Zionist party Mizraḥi. Rabbi Yehuda Leib Avidah (pen name: Judah Elzet; 1887–1962) was active in Poland in 1910–1920, and after that in Canada and South Africa, and, after 1949, in Israel. He published in Yiddish (on prayers, 1918; on the human body, 1920; proverbs, sayings, and anecdotes, 1918–1920; on trades and tradesmen, 1920; and on food, 1920) as well as in Hebrew (on customs, in the journal *Reshumot,* 1918).

Rabbi Yeshayahu Zlotnick (1892–1943) published a three-volume *Folklore Ḥumash* (1937–38), a lexicon of Jewish wisdom (1930), and festival folklore (1930).

As mentioned, the Zionist vision was not the only expression of the Jewish national awakening in Europe. There were other Jewish national movements, including Folkism, Bundism, and Territorialism, which had in common a fondness for the Yiddish language and a romantic view of it as embodying the ethos of the Jewish people.

Yiddish folklorists believed that its language is the supreme achievement of every nation and that the most important thing a people creates in this language is its folklore, which expresses its pristine spirit. For the Yiddishists, philological and folklore studies were a means to bond with the masses.

Even before World War I, Yiddish folklorists rang up impressive achievements. But their most intensive activity took place between the two world wars. Their crowning achievement was the work of the Ethnographic Committee set up by YIVO (the Jewish Scientific Institute).

The most important activities and publications of Yiddish folklore studies before World War I were:

In 1895, *Der Hoyzfroynd* published the impressive list of 2,000 proverbs collected by Ignatz Bernstein. Ignatz Bernstein published an expanded version of his anthology of Yiddish proverbs in 1908. The introduction, which explains his method of classification, is in a foreign language (German). Bernstein intimates that by collecting the proverbs he viewed himself as helping in the birth of the national consciousness of the Jewish people.

In 1890 Isaac Leib Peretz, renowned as the greatest Yiddish author and a key figure in Jewish Warsaw, anchored folklore firmly at the center of the national movement when he began collecting Yiddish songs in 1890 and urged his friends to do likewise.

In 1901, the historians Saul Ginsburg (Ginzburg) and Pesaḥ Marek published their important anthology, *Evreiskiie narodnye pesny.* This is a scholarly work with the text of the songs in Yiddish transcription, although the annotations are in Russian.

In 1908, at the Czernowitz conference, I.L. Peretz maintained that the Hasidic story marked the beginning of modern literature in Yiddish (see: Peretz I.L.).

In 1912, Yehudah Leib Cahan (1881–1937) published a collection of Yiddish folk songs with their melodies.

In 1913, Shmuel Niger (pseudonym of Shmuel Tsharny; 1883–1955) edited and published *Der Pinkes,* the first collection of scholarly essays and articles devoted to Yiddish philology. Yiddish folklore occupied a prominent place in it, with three essays on the subject. In 1912–1914 the ethnographic expedition headed by S. An-Ski and funded by Baron Günzburg took place. Its members traveled through small towns in the Ukraine and collected a vast quantity of folklore materials.

The activity of Yiddish-oriented folklorists between the two world wars was diverse. Their activity was focused in Warsaw and Vilna (then part of Poland).

The Warsaw group centered around the philologist, attorney, politician, and folklorist Noyekh Prilutski (1882–1941), who published the *zamelbikher* (collections) of folklore material collected by himself and his associates (Prilutski 1912). He also coedited the *Arkhiv* of ethnographic materials with Shmuel Lehman (Prilutski and Lehman 1924–1933) and published folk songs in Yiddish (Prilutski 1911, 1913).

The most productive collector in Prilutski's circle was Shmuel Lehman (1886–1941), whose work was published by Prilutski, Graubard, and Vanvild. In 1921 he published the collection *Arbayt un Frayhat* (Labor and Freedom), edited by M. Vanvild. In 1923 he put out collections of Purimshpils, children's folklore, and thieves songs in the most important collection produced by the Warsaw folklorists, *Bay Undz Yidn,* edited by M. Vanvild. In 1922 he published folklore related to the World War in the Vilna-based *Lebn,* edited by Moshe Shalit. In 1928 he published thieves' songs, with melodies, edited and published by Pinḥas Graubard. In 1926 he published thieves' love songs in *Landoy bukh*. Lehman continued to collect folklore even in the Warsaw ghetto.

Another member of Prilutski's circle, between 1909 and 1912 (when he emigrated to New York) was A. Almi (Elia Chaim Scheps; 1892–1963), who was considered the biographer of the group's activity. His most important contribution consisted of stories about the Polish rebellion of 1863.

Another collector was the "people's poet," Hershl Danilevich (1882–1941), who published soldiers' songs, riddles, and anecdotes in *Bay Undz Yidn* (mentioned above). He also published seven songs of *cheder* boys in *Reshumot* (1930).

The Historical Ethnographic Society was established in Vilna in February 1919 by An-Ski; after his death, on November 8, 1920, the group took his name. This society made a major contribution to the study of Jewish folklore and ethnography in Eastern Europe. The most productive folklore collector was Shloyme Bastomski (1891–1941), who constantly emphasized the link between folklore and education.

The institution that achieved the most impressive results, despite the constraints that accompanied its work, was YIVO. The establishment of YIVO was a natural and inevitable part of the activities in interwar Jewish Poland. That country had become the center of autonomous Jewish culture.

The goal of the YIVO Institute, established in 1925, was to organize learned research into various areas of Jewish culture while providing an appropriate setting for research and publication and setting uniform standards for scholarly work. Folklore received prominent attention at YIVO. In keeping with the Yiddishist ideology that folklore was in the service of the language, the Ethnographic Committee was set up as part of the philological section on October 27, 1925, shortly after YIVO itself was founded. The committee's main goal was to organize the collection of Jewish folklore "wherever the Yiddish language is alive."

The committee decided to set up a network of volunteer collectors *(zamlers)* throughout Poland and, if possible, other countries, affiliated with Yiddish cultural institutions, mainly schools. Announcements about the collectors' network were made in meetings, periodicals, and Institute bulletins.

The committee's work was marked by a personal relationship with the collectors. It maintained a lively correspondence with them, was attentive to their needs, and did everything possible to assist them. This treatment increased their motivation; so did the fact that the collectors' names were published in the YIVO bulletin. The committee organized competitions for the best shipments of folklore materials. Later some of the collections were published by YIVO.

In 1929, the Ethnographic Committee convened a conference of fourteen leading collectors. Responding to an explicit request made at that meeting, it organized a special course for collectors the next year, with Y.L. Cahan of New York as the principal lecturer.

YIVO provided a mantle of scholarly respectability to folklore studies in its series *Filologishe Shriftn,* which included work on folklore starting with its very first volume, a festschrift for Dr. Alfred Landau. The Ethnographic Committee's end product was the anthology *Yidishe Folklor,* published in 1938, and edited by Cahan (who had died the previous year).

The collection of Yiddish folklore is usually noted as the YIVO Ethnographic Committee's most important accomplishment. There is no doubt that it was an impressive achievement realized in a very short period.

World War II—The Holocaust

On September 1, 1939, Germany invaded Poland and on September 17 the Soviet Union attacked from the east. About half of Poland's territories were annexed by the Soviet Union. The rest of Poland fell under German occupation. Part of the northern and western regions was incorporated directly into Germany. Warsaw, Kraków, Lublin, Kielce, and Radom and most of their provinces were constituted as the Government General administered by German civilian bureaucracy. On June 22, 1941, Germany invaded the Soviet Union and within a month German forces occupied all of the former Polish territories that had been taken in 1939 by the Soviet Union. Beginning in October 1939 increasing numbers of Jews were forced to live in ghettos.

After the German invasion of the former Polish territories occupied by the Soviet Union, the Germans started mass killings as part of the Nazi plan to annihilate all of the European Jewry. More than half the Jews who were killed by the Nazis as part of the Final Solution—the code name for the destruction of European Jewry—were exterminated in death camps. Six death camps ware established on Polish territory. Four of them were extermination camps—Chełmno, Bełżec, Sobibor, and Treblinka. The other two, Auschwitz-Birkenau and Majdanek, were both concentration camps and death camps. The majority of Polish Jews were annihilated in World War II. Although there were still Jews in post-Holocaust Poland, one can no longer speak of Jewish communities.

Folklore's treatment of the Holocaust raises several problems. The general public tends to identify folklore with amusement and aesthetics, and therefore to associate folklore with the Holocaust was problematic, although Jewish folklorists like Shmuel Lehman even collected folklore in the ghettos. Another problem with folkloric treatment of folk narratives set during the Holocaust was the genre classification of folklore studies such as legends with its vernacular connotations that may be understood as casting doubts on the veracity of the survivors' reports. This may be the reason for the preference to study personal narratives of Holocaust survivors rather than stories that can be identified as legends.

Many folk narratives of Polish Jews are still told by Holocaust survivors. The Israel Folktale Archives (IFA) at the University of Haifa holds some 2,800 tales recorded from Polish Jews in Israel since 1955. Many of these stories underwent transformation and are being recounted through the lens of the Holocaust. Thus, for example, legends about the origins of Jewish synagogues in Poland became legends of destruction and construct the myth of the Jews of Poland, which includes their origins on Polish soil and their catastrophe in the Holocaust.

Haya Bar-Itzhak and Adam Teller

See also: An-Ski, S.; Bar-Itzhak, Haya; Berdyczewski (Bin-Gorion), Micha Josef; Bialik, Haim Nachman; Blood Libel; Cahan, Y.L.; Druyanow, Alter; Estherke; Holocaust Folklore; Languages, Jewish; Lilienthal, Regina; Peretz, Isaac Leib; Prochownik, Abraham; *Reshumot;* Segel, Benjamin Wolf; Wahl, Saul.

Bibliography

An-Ski, S., "Folk Legends about 1648/49 Persecutions." *Ha'Olam* 27:5 (1920): 12–14.

An-Ski, S. (Shlomo Zanvil Rappoport). *Gezamelte Shriften* (Collected Works), vol. 15. Vilna, Warsaw, and New York: Ferlag An-Ski, 1925.

Bałaban, Meir. *The House of Israel in Poland: From the Beginning Until the Destruction*, ed. Y. Halperin. Jerusalem: World Zionist Organization, 1948 (in Hebrew).

Bar-Itzhak, Haya. "The Cossack and the Maiden." In *The Power of a Tale—The Jubilee Book of IFA*, ed. Haya Bar-Itzhak and Idit Pintel-Ginsberg. Haifa: Israel Folktale Archives, University of Haifa, 2008 (in Hebrew).

———. "Folklore as an Expression of Inter-Cultural Communication Between Jews and Poles." *Studia Mythologica Slavica* 7 (2004): 91–106.

———. *Jewish Poland, Legends of Origin: Ethnopoetics and Legendary Chronicles.* Detroit: Wayne State University Press, 2001.

———. *Pioneers of Jewish Ethnography and Folkloristics in Eastern Europe.* Studia Mythologica Slavica–Supplementa, Scientific Research Center of the Academy of Science and Arts, 2010.

———. "Women in Blood Libel Legends of Polish Jews: The Legend About Adil the Daughter of Moses Kikinish from Drochobych." *Chuliyot* 11 (2008): 227–235 (in Hebrew).

Bartal, Israel, and Israel Gutman, ed. *The Jews of Poland Throughout Generations.* Jerusalem: Zalman Shazar Center, 1997–2001 (in Hebrew).

Colman, Arthur P. "Language as a Factor in Polish Nationalism." *Slavonic Review* 13 (1934): 155–172.

Goldberg, Jacob. *Jewish Privileges in the Polish Commonwealth.* Jerusalem: Israel Academy of Sciences and Humanities, 1985–2001.

Gottesman, Itzik Nachmen. *Defining the Yiddish Nation: The Jewish Folklorists of Poland.* Detroit: Wayne State University Press, 2003.

Gutman, Israel, and Shmuel Krakowski. *Unequal Victims: Poles and Jews During World War II.* New York: Holocaust Library, 1986.

Hundret, Gershon David. *Jews in Poland-Lithuania in the Eighteenth Century.* Berkeley: University of California Press, 2004.

Kraushar, Alexander. *Historya Żydów w Polsce* (The Jewish History in Poland). Warsaw, 1865.

Lelewel, Joachim. *Polska wiekow srednich* (Poland in the Middle Ages). Poznań: Nakł. J.K. Źupań skiego, 1851–1856.

Mendelson, Ezra. *The Jews of East Central Europe Between the World Wars.* Bloomington: Indiana University Press, 1983.

Piechotka, Maria, and Kazimierz Piechotka. *Bóżnice Drewniane, Budownictwo I Architektura* (Wooden Synagogues, Construction and Architecture). Warsaw: Arkady, 1959.

Prilutski, Noyekh. *Yidishe folkslider* (Yiddish Folk Songs). 2 vols. Warsaw: Nayer, 1911, 1913.

Prilutski, Noyekh, and Shmuel Lehman. *Arkhiv far yiddisher shprakhvisnashaft, literaturforshung un etnologye* (Archive of Yiddish Language and Ethnology). Warsaw: Nayer farlag, 1926–1933.

Rosman, Moshe. "Innovative Tradition: Jewish Culture in the Polish-Lithuanian Commonwealth." In *Cultures of the Jews,* ed. David Biale, pp. 517–570. New York: Schocken, 2002.

Schipper, Yitzhak. *Di virtshaftsgeshikhte fun di yidn in Poiln beetan mitelalter* (Economic History of the Jews of Poland in the Middle Ages). Warsaw: Brzoza, 1926.

Sternberg, Herman. *Geschichte der Juden in Polen unter dem Piasten und Jagellonen.* Leipzig: Dunder & Humblot, 1878.

Weinryb, Bernard Dov. *The Jews of Poland: A Social and Economic History of the Jewish Community in Poland from 1100 to 1800.* Philadelphia: Jewish Publication Society of America, 1973.

Pope, Jewish

The story about a pope of Jewish origins came from a narrative cycle that circulated among the medieval Donau and Rhine communities. According to this tradition, Elḥanan, the son of Rabbi Simeon the Great of Mainz, was kidnapped from his father's house by his Christian nurse, was raised by gentiles, and on account of his erudition became a pope, and as such he was widely known for his great wisdom. One day, he wanted to trace back his family roots so as to find out the source of his wisdom. When his entourage told him that he had been stolen from the Jews, he demanded that Rabbi Simeon the Great be brought before him. According to earlier versions, the father recognized his son by certain marks on his body, while according to later versions (from the *Mayse Bukh* [Story Book] onward), the son's identity was revealed to his father in the course of a chess game they played together.

The father persuaded his son to return to the fold and sanctify the name of God. So the son summoned a group of kings, dukes, and cardinals and in their presence, while standing at the top of a high tower, he proclaimed his Jewish faith, denied Christianity, jumped off the tower, and died instantly. When Rabbi Simeon the Great heard that his son had sanctified the name of the Lord, he inserted his name in a *yozer* (hymn) in praise of the Creator, which he composed for the second day of the New Year, by adding the verse "God has shown grace [= El Ḥanan] to his heritage to improve it in sweetness."

The earliest version of this medieval legend is found in the Hebrew-written MS Cambridge, Add. 858, fol. 46–47 (Ashkenaz, fifteenth century). This version was copied several times and went through a number of adaptations until it finally found its way into the *Mayse Bukh* (Basle, 1602), which was written in Old Yiddish. There it appears in the section of medieval narratives as story No. 187, on pages 126–128, and it is this printed version that possibly made the story known. In the versions originating in sixteenth-century manuscripts, beginning with MS Moscow-Günzberg 256, fols. 108a–109a (Italy, the mid-sixteenth century) onward, the story is attributed to the son of Rabbi Solomon (or Shlomo) ben Aderet of Barcelona (Rashba). The story received special attention in modern Jewish literature, in Marcus (or Meyer) Lehmann's German-written novel (Rabbi Elḥanan, *Der Israelit,* 1867–69), Yudel Mark's Yiddish-written novel *Der Yidisher Poips* (New York, 1947), and Isaac Bashevis-Singer's short story "Zeidlus der ershter," published in Yiddish in 1943 and, in English, as "Zeidlus the Pope," in 1964.

According to scholars, this story originates in the character of Pope Anacletus II (who officiated in this capacity between 1130 and 1138), who was a descendant of the Pierleoni family of Roman nobility, whose progenitor was a Jew who converted to Christianity. This conjecture was raised by such scholars as Adolf (Aaron) Jellinek in his *Beit ha'Midrash* (Frankfurt, 1873) and Moritz Güdemann in his *Sefer ha'Torah ve'ha'Ḥayyim* (*Geschichte des Erziehungswesens und der Cultur der abendländischen Juden, während des Mittelalters und der neueren Zeit,* Vienna, 1880–1888).

The Jewish story of a boy who became a pope has parallels in European folklore. This is a folkloric type that is labeled in Aarne-Thompson's Index as "The Three Languages" (AT 671) and also appears in a related type (AT 517). This narrative type recounts the story of a child who mastered the language of animals. His father deems him a fool and orders that he be killed, but the child is saved because of his special knowledge; he arrives in Rome and becomes the pope. Subsequently the son summons his father to Rome for the purpose of absolution and the washing of his feet. This type became known particularly in its later rendition, Version No. 33, as adapted in the brothers Grimm's "Die drei Sprachen."

Avidov Lipsker

See also: *Ma'aseh Book* (*Mayse Bukh*).

Bibliography

Bamberger, Joseph. *The Jewish Pope: A Thematological Study of a Medieval Legend.* Ramat Gan: Bar Ilan University Press, 2005 (in Hebrew).

David, Abraham. "Tales Concerning Persecutions in Medieval Germany." In *Papers on Medieval Hebrew Literature Presented to A.M. Habermann,* ed. Zvi Malachi, pp. 69–83. Jerusalem: Rubin Mass, 1977 (in Hebrew).

Grabois, Aryeh. "From a 'Theological' to a 'Racial' Anti-

Semitism: The Controversy of the Jewish Pope in the Twelfth Century." *Zion* 47:1 (1982): 1–17 (in Hebrew).

Lipsker, Avidov. "The Mirror in Which Rabbi Simon the Great of Mainz Did Not See Clearly." *Chuliyot* 3 (1969): 33–57 (in Hebrew).

Prinz, Joachim. *Popes from the Ghetto: A View of Medieval Christendom.* New York: Horizon, 1968.

Sherman, Joseph. *The Jewish Pope: Myth, Diaspora, and Yiddish Literature.* Oxford, UK: Legenda, 2003.

PRAYER

Although the *siddur,* the compilation of Hebrew prayers, is second only to the Bible in terms of its importance in Jewish culture and history, the beginnings of Jewish prayer are one of the highly obscure issues and unsolvable riddles in Jewish cultural history. Actually, the *siddur* is a credible and reliable reflection of Jewish history throughout all generations since the last years of the Second Commonwealth.

Origins of the *Siddur*

Recent studies of the Hebrew prayer and the literary yield of the Dead Sea sect reveal a close relationship between the two. It might be declared quite confidently that Jewish prayer as a regular and fixed text and custom originated with the Dead Sea sect. Of no lesser importance is the fact that the texts included in the prayers of this sect were partly in prose and partly in rhythmic poetry. At the same time, worship of God in the Temple, originally consisting of animal sacrifices, was now accompanied by a text uttered by the high priest. Some of the liturgical texts and customs of the Dead Sea sect were documented in the scrolls discovered in Qumran, while those of the mainstream were documented in the Mishnah. The latter betray greater affinity to the corpus of prayers as established in Yavneh in the first years after the destruction of the Second Temple in 70 C.E.

The main figure in the establishment of the fixed text of the prayers was Rabbi Yoḥanan ben Zakkai, who settled in Yavneh with his pupils to build an alternative to Jerusalem as the spiritual center of the Jewish nation. Although rabbinic sources are nearly silent on this issue or offer late etiological explanations about the establishment of the obligatory acts and the texts of the prayer, scholars can deduce from these acts and texts the principles followed by the rabbis: (a) establishing a fixed and simple Hebrew text, yet with much attention to its linguistic and literary correctness, based on the Bible and written in prose, thus eliminating all other texts, in prose as well as in poetry, which were used by different groups or individuals for prayer; and (b) establishing a comprehensive obligatory etiquette for liturgical services. All this was intended to provide a substitute for the worship at the destroyed Temple, the loss of which was strongly felt at that time among Jews in the Land of Israel, and also to create a way to unite Jews and to remove the danger of the disintegration of their national identity.

The new liturgical text was clearly considered a creation of the rabbis, in sharp distinction to the divine Bible. They forbade anyone to write it down, which explains the need to perform the services in public and the very limited number of individuals who could serve as *sheliaḥ tzibbur* (emissary of the congregation). Only a small amount of liturgical texts was documented in the rabbinic literature, from which historians cannot construct any comprehensive depiction of the prayers. This also explains why there were different versions of the same parts in the prayer, thus violating the stability and consistency by which the first rabbis wished to characterize the Jewish liturgy. Moreover, violating other wishes of the first rabbis, popular tendencies caused the insertion of mystical elements, like the *Qedusha,* and poetic texts (*piyyutim*) into the prayers. The *piyyutim* in particular presented problems with respect to Halakhah, as they violated the idea of a fixed text. The rabbis' efforts to suppress them were in vain.

The Written Compilation of Prayers

The first written compilation of the prayers appeared in the mid-ninth century, when Rabbi Natronai Gaon in Iraq was asked by a Spanish-Jewish community to commit them to paper for them. Still, the term "*siddur*" was used to note the compilation of prayers, but the expression "*me'ah berakhot*" (one hundred blessings) was employed after the sages' verdict that each of the Jews has to say 100 benedictions every day. Although the term "*maḥzor*" was already in use, it denoted the collection of *piyyutim* written by one *paytan* for an annual cycle or the like. A later compilation of prayers was the one edited by Rabbi Amram Gaon, also in Iraq.

But the first *siddur*, which was a perfect compilation according to a very strict order and based on clear and solid rules, was that of Rabbi Sa'adiah Gaon (882–942). By and large this *siddur* served as a model for almost all later *siddurim* edited in the next generations. It was accepted in Jewish communities throughout the Muslim world, while in Western Europe (northern France, Germany, and Italy) the *siddur* of Rabbi Amram Gaon was considered a halakhic and liturgical authority.

Until the tenth century two main versions of the prayers were used; both originated in the Land of Israel but they respectively came to known as *nusaḥ bavel* and *nusaḥ Eretz Israel,* indicating the place of their use. The growing prestige of the Babylonian center eventually

Prayer book. Venice, 1772. *(Réunion des Musées Nationaux/ Art Resource, NY)*

caused the disappearance of *minchag Eretz Israel.* Thus, the wording of the permanent prayers (*nusaḥ ha'qeva'*) was consolidated and became common to all Jewish communities, except for some very small variations. But the selection of the *piyyutim* inserted in the permanent prayers showed large differences. These differences are the main factors in the formation of the four major *minhagim* (customs): (a) the Middle Eastern (Yemen and Persia); (b) Sephardic (North Africa and the Balkans; (c) Ashkenazi (North France and Germany); and (d) Italian. The strengthening of the Kabbalah in Jewish life and thought in the pre-exilic prestigious spiritual center in Safed in the sixteenth century greatly affected some of these *minhagim* and produced some hybrid *nusaḥim* based on the old version but including many kabbalistic additions and alternatives: (a) the later *nusaḥ* of the Sephardim; (b) the Ashkenazi *nusaḥ* Sefarad; and (c) the *baladi* in Yemen.

The core of the Hebrew prayer is the Amidah, which is obligatory for each adult Jewish male to recite three times a day: morning (Šaḥrit), afternoon (Minḥa), and evening (Arvit). On Saturdays, on the first day of the month, and during festivals there is an additional Amidah (*musaf*), and on Yom Kippur, the Day of Atonement, another additional Amidah (*ne'ilah*). All these prayers are said in silence (*laḥaš*) while standing and are then repeated by the *sheliaḥ tzibbur,* originally for those who did not know them by heart, when it was forbidden to write down the prayers. In Šaḥrit and Arvit three short passages of the Pentateuch (*Qeri'at Shema*) with two benedictions before them and one (Šaḥrit) or two (Arvit) after them are said before the Amidah. It is strongly recommended that a minyan, that is, a quorum of ten, be present to say both Amidah and *Qeri'at Shema* in the synagogue.

This combination of prayers is common to Jewish communities all over the world, and in this respect any Jew can participate in the prayers of any community. Yet, because of other aspects that are not essential for satisfaction of the religious obligation of prayer—the pronunciation of Hebrew wording, the music, and the like—it is somewhat unusual and sometimes impossible for a person who is an outsider to take part in the joint, public performance of a prayer. However, in modern congregations in the State of Israel, as a result of the great variety in the origins of their members, there is a tendency to be more tolerant of variations in *minhagim* and *nusaḥim.*

Yosef Tobi

See also: Blessing God.

Bibliography

Elbogen, Ismar. *Jewish Liturgy, a Comprehensive History.* Philadelphia: Jewish Publication Society, 1993.

Heinemann, Joseph. *Prayers in the Talmud: Forms and Patterns.* Berlin: de Gruyter, 1977.

Heinemann, Joseph, ed. *Literature of the Synagogue.* New York: Gorgias, 1975.

Hoffman, Lawrence A. *Beyond the Text: A Holistic Approach to Liturgy.* Bloomington: Indiana University Press, 1987.

Nitzan, Bilhah. *Qumran Prayer and Religious Poetry.* Leiden: E.J. Brill, 1994.

Reif, Stefan. *Judaism and Hebrew Prayer: New Perspectives on Jewish Liturgy.* Cambridge, UK: Cambridge University Press, 1993.

Vana, Liliane. "*La birkat ha'minim* est-elle une prière contre les judéo-chrétiene?" In *Les communautés religieuses dans le monde Gréco-Romain: essays de definitions,* ed. Nicole Belayche and Simon C. Mimouni, pp. 201–241. Turnhout: Brepols, 2003.

PROCHOWNIK, ABRAHAM

Abraham Prochownik, a legendary figure, was, according to a Polish-Jewish folk legend, a Jewish king of Poland. He was called "Prochownik" because of his occupation as a merchant in gunpowder *(proch).* The legend, which relates to the accession of the legendary King Piast (ca. 860), the founder of the glorious Piast dynasty that ruled Poland until 1370, has been incorporated into histories of Polish Jewry. In the absence of written documentation of the beginning of Jewish settlement in Poland, historians picked up and recorded the legend, which they usually gloss over briefly. There are very few folkloristic transcriptions that can be used for documentation and research.

Historians believe that the legend does not predate the thirteenth or fourteenth century, when gunpowder reached Europe. Some believe that it was created only in the eighteenth or nineteenth century, to serve apologetic needs. The legend implies that the Jews are essential to Polish society. Weinryb notes that in 1868, Smołka, a member of the Polish Sejm, used the story to defend the Jews of Galicia and demand equal rights for them (Weinryb 1973, 336; Bar-Itzhak 2001, 91). Although some historians believe that the first Jews reached Poland in the ninth century, most of them agree that the legend cannot be relied on to establish the date of Jewish settlement there.

The most extensive version of the legend, provided by Herman Sternberg in 1860, can be summarized as follows: The death of Popiel left the royal family of Poland without an heir. The nobles, assembled in conclave in Kruszwica, were unable to agree on a candidate. They accepted the proposal by the eldest elector that they crown the first man who entered the city after daybreak the next morning. Guards were posted to intercept him. That first arrival turned out to be Abraham Prochownik, who had come to town to sell gunpowder, and he was duly proclaimed king. However, he refused to accept the crown. Pressed on the matter, he asked to be left alone to think the matter over and pray to his god. He issued strict instructions that no one disturb him. After three days had elapsed and he failed to reappear, Piast declared that the country could not remain without a ruler and burst into his house. Abraham, addressing the assembled Poles, told them that Piast was the best candidate for the throne because he was intelligent and understood that the country could not exist without a ruler, as well as being courageous and unafraid of disobeying the king. So Piast became king of Poland.

This is an etiological legend to bolster the Jews' right of residence in Poland: If Jews were already living and accepted in the country at the very dawn of the Polish state, in its pre-Christian period, their right to live there could not be challenged. The legend legitimizes the Jews' main vocation, commerce, by showing that they had been engaged in it for centuries. Most of all, though, it presents their major contribution to Polish society and to the establishment of the glorious Piast dynasty, whose most esteemed member, Casimir (Kazimierz) the Great, expanded the Jews' rights of settlement in Poland and, so legend had it, was linked to the Jews through his mistress Estherke. The legend also refers to the Jews' crucial role in Polish society: It was a Jew's acumen that brought the Poles to select the person most suited to be their ruler, a man blessed with intelligence and courage, and to the establishment of the celebrated Piast dynasty.

Another important message, intended for both internal and external consumption, is that the Jews of Poland have no interest in exercising power that is not legitimately theirs. This is intended to assuage the fears of the host nation, but it also serves to preserve the myth of Jewish redemption, inasmuch as a Jewish kingdom can exist only in the Land of Israel.

There are several extended versions of this legend. The first transcription from the oral tradition is that by the Polish folklorist Roman Zmorski, who recorded it in Polish from Jewish informants in 1855. Another version of the story was printed in Hebrew in 1861 in *Ha'nesher,* the supplement of the periodical *Ha'mevaser*, and in Yiddish by Wiernik in 1901.

The legend of Abraham Prochownik no longer circulates. Not a single version is found among the 2,800 folktales collected from Polish Jews, starting in 1955, held by the Israel Folklore Archives (IFA) at the University of Haifa. Several Prochownik families in Israel report that they know they are descended from a king of Poland but cannot recount the legend itself.

S.Y. Agnon turned the folk legend into a literary legend as "Mi'shomerim laboker" (Watchers for the Morning), included in his collection *Poland: Legendary Tales* (first published in 1925). The legend also makes an appearance in a novel by the Russian-Jewish author Grigory Isaakovich Bogrov (Baharav), *Evreiskii manuskript* (A Hebrew Manuscript), published in 1878 and translated into Hebrew in 1900.

Haya Bar-Itzhak

See also: Estherke; Wahl, Saul.

Bibliography

Bałaban, Meir. *The Jews in Poland: From the Earliest Days Until the Destruction,* ed. Y. Halperin. Jerusalem: World Zionist Organization, 1948 (in Hebrew).

Bar-Itzhak, Haya. *Jewish Poland: Legends of Origin.* Detroit: Wayne State University Press, 2001.

Kraushar, Alexander. *Historya Żydów w Polsce* (The History of the Jew in Poland). Warsaw: n.p., 1865.

Lelewel, Joachim. *Polska wiekow srednich* (Poland Middle Ages). Poznań: Nakł. J.K. Żupańskiego, 1851–1856.

Schipper, Yitzhak. *Di virtshaftsgeshikhte fun di yidn in Poiln be-etan mitelalter* (Economic History of the Jews of Poland in the Middle Ages), Warsaw: Brzoza, 1926.

Sternberg, Herman. *Geschichte der Juden in Polen unter dem Piasten und Jagellonen.* Leipzig: Dunder & Humblot, 1878.

———. *Versuch einer Geschichte der Juden in Polen, seit deren Einwanderung in dieses Land (um das IX Jahrh.) bis zum Jahre 1848.* Vienna: n.p., 1860.

Weinryb, Bernard D. "The Beginnings of East-European Jewry

in Legend and Historiography." In *Studies and Essays in Honor of Abraham A. Newman.* Leiden: Brill, 1962.

———. *The Jews of Poland: A Social and Economic History of the Jewish Community in Poland from 1100 to 1800.* Philadelphia: Jewish Publication Society of America, 1973.

Wiernik, Peter. *Di yidishe geshikhte fun Avraham Avinu biz di yetztige zayt* (Jewish History from the Patriarch Abraham to the Present). New York: Hebrew Publishing Company, 1901.

Zamarski, Roman. *Domowe wspomnienia i powiastki* (Home Memories and Tales). Warsaw: n.p., 1854.

———. *Pisma orginalne i tlumaczone* (Original and Translated Writings). Warsaw: S. Lewentala, 1900.

Proverb

The proverb is a verbal genre known in almost every tradition in the world. It usually constitutes one sentence—less often a string of sentences—that conveys a message formulated as a collectively experienced wisdom. The proverb is often marked as separate from the verbal sequence in which it appears either by an introductory formula ("The proverb says," "My mother used to say," etc.) or by its characteristically poetic language, or both. Proverbs are effective tools for expressing group identity because of their great mobility from one context to another and because they can relatively easily be transposed from one linguistic environment to another. The Jewish tradition of proverbs has a long and complex multilingual history, including usage of proverbs in Hebrew, Aramaic, or Jewish languages such as Yiddish, Judeo-Arabic, or Judeo-Spanish (Ladino) interlacing the speech in other languages spoken in non-Jewish environments.

The Hebrew Bible contains two books devoted to the genre: Proverbs (*mishle,* pl. of *mashal,* which in biblical Hebrew means "proverb"), which excels in practical and socially applicable wisdom, rhetorically often formulated as the words of an older person, such as a father, to a younger person of high birth, possibly a future ruler; and Ecclesiastes, whose proverbs express a more philosophical, meditative, and skeptical mode of thought. Perhaps surprisingly, it is the latter whose verses are more likely to remain extant as spoken and written proverbs in contemporary Hebrew, possibly due to the wider knowledge of Ecclesiastes, which is read in the synagogues on the Sabbath that occurs during Sukkot and to the language of the book that resembles modern Hebrew more than the language of Proverbs. In addition, several proverbs in the Bible are inserted in the language of the narrators, the prophets and the poets, as well as in the mouths of biblical personae. Some quotations from the Hebrew Bible may not initially have been proverbs but have been adopted as proverbs in later speech and writing. Today one might encounter the use of biblical verses as proverbs in spoken Hebrew without the user's necessarily knowing the source. The apocryphal book of Ben Sira also belongs to the so-called wisdom literature, in which proverbs abound.

In rabbinic texts of late antiquity, the talmudic-midrashic literature, Hebrew and even more often Aramaic proverbs are a major rhetorical, didactic, and philosophical medium. A text from the earliest stratum of the corpus, tannaitic literature, known as the Wisdom of the Fathers, *Pirqe Avot,* or simply the *Mishnah Avot,* is a compilation of proverbs and proverbial sayings about the learning and teaching practices of the sages themselves, demonstrating the adequacy of the genre in the service of didactic and philosophical teaching, such as "The wise person learns from everyone" (IV, 1 in Hebrew) or "Speak little; do much" (I, 15, in Hebrew). The texts of *Pirqe Avot* are often applied as proverbs in contemporary Hebrew speech. Proverbs abound in other works of the period as well and proliferate even more in the later rabbinic period, in amoraic literature, and in the Palestinian Talmud (Yerushalmi) as well as the Babylonian Talmud (Bavli). The scholarly usage of proverbs in the internal discourse of the sages is sometimes interlaced with more popularly conceived proverbs, often but not always introduced with the formula "This is what people say" (*haynu de-amrei inashe*) (e.g., *b. Bava Qamma* 92a–93a): "This is what people say: 'Don't throw a stone in the well from which you drank water'" (92b, in Aramaic). The Hebrew and Aramaic proverbs are often paralleled by proverbs in other languages of the area and the period, mainly Greek but also Latin and Persian. Since the medieval period, Jews have lived in linguistically divergent environments and their use of Hebrew and Aramaic proverbs frequently incorporated proverbs from the languages of their new environments, especially in the developing Jewish languages characteristic of each region, such as the Yiddish of Central and East European Jews, Judeo-Arabic of the Middle Eastern Jews, Judeo-Spanish (Ladino) of the Jews of the Ottoman Empire, and Judeo-Persian of Iran and its environs.

New proverbs emerge in contemporary Hebrew, especially in the context of mass media; the subculture of the Israeli army ("Hard is only in bread," Israeli Proverb Index, Folklore Research Center, Hebrew University of Jerusalem); and various modes of advertisement. Jewish proverbs continue to constitute markers of group identity in varying language environments, easily communicable, and replete with meanings and associations due to their textual and contextual histories.

Galit Hasan-Rokem

See also: Dundes, Alan; Hasan-Rokem, Galit.

Bibliography

Alexander, Tamar. *Words Are Better than Bread.* Jerusalem: Ben Zvi Institute, 2004 (in Hebrew).

Alexander, Tamar, and Ya'akov Ben-Toulila. *La Palabra en su Hora es Oro: El Refrán Judeo-Español del Norte de Marruecos.* Jerusalem: Ben-Zvi Institute, 2008 (in Hebrew).

Bernstein, Ignaz. *Yiddishe sprikhverter un redensarten* (Proverbs and Sayings in Yiddish). Warsaw: In Kommission bei J. Kauffmann in Frankfurt a. m, 1908. Reprint. New York: Brider Kaminski, 1948.

Dahan, Hananyah. *Proverbs of Moroccan Jews.* Tel Aviv: Stavit, 1982 (in Hebrew).

Fontaine, Carole R. *Traditional Sayings in the Old Testament: A Contextual Study.* Sheffield, UK: Almond, 1982.

Hasan-Rokem, Galit. *Adam le Adam Gesher {Man Is a Bridge to Man}: The Proverbs of Georgian Jews in Israel.* Jerusalem: Ben Zvi Institute, 1993 (in Hebrew).

———. *Proverbs in Israeli Folk Narratives: A Structural Semantic Analysis.* Helsinki: Academia Scientiarum Fennica, 1982.

Meiri, Yehoshua. *On the Rivers of Babylon: Proverbs of the Iraqi Jews.* Jerusalem: Reuven Mass, 1996 (in Hebrew).

Silvermann-Weinreich, Beatrice (Bina). "Formale problemen baim forshen des yiddisher sprikhvort" (Formal Problems in the Study of Yiddish Proverbs). In *For Max Weinreich,* pp. 383–394. The Hague: Mouton, 1996.

Yitzhar, Mordechay. *Yemenite Parables and Proverbs.* Rosh Ha-Ayin: privately published, 1993 (in Hebrew).

Prylucki Noah (Noyekh Prilutski)

See: Poland, Jews of

Psalms

The first and most prominent book in the third division of the Bible (the Hagiographa), the Book of Psalms is a collection of 150 chapters, each a separate poem of praise. The word "psalm" derives from the Greek word "*psallo*," meaning "to play a stringed instrument," and ultimately "to sing to the accompaniment of a harp," and is akin to the Hebrew *mizmor,* which is also used as an appellation for the individual poems. The Hebrew name used from rabbinic times to the present to denote the book is *Sefer tehillim* (Book of Praises, often abbreviated to *tillim*), connected to the Hebrew root *hll* (praise), which is conspicuous in the oft-repeated cry found in many psalms, "hallelujah" (praise God).

These names indicate the original nature of the poems as hymns of praise to God, undoubtedly sung in unison or in antiphony to the accompaniment of stringed instruments, although the praise may be in the context of laments over personal or national misfortune or connected with didactic teachings. While not directly connected in form or content to the Temple cult, there is no doubt that already in the time of the first Temple the use of songs set to music formed an integral part of the worship service, providing an outlet for personal and group creativity as well as for religious sentiment. Indeed, many of the superscriptions of the individual psalms refer to musical instruments or to what must have been guilds of professional singers and musicians connected to the Temple service.

The content of the psalms is relatively devoid of specific historical details, except for occasional references to major events in ancient Israelite history, such as the promise to Abraham of land and progeny, the exodus from Egypt, and the splitting of the Red Sea and the wandering in the desert; other historical references include the Davidic monarchy, the centrality of Jerusalem and the Temple, and the exile. Even in those psalms for which a superscription provides a particular historical event as the reason for its composition (see below), the content of the psalm may not be directly related to the stated event. The most prominent type of psalm celebrates the majesty, goodness, and providence of God, evidenced through natural, personal, and historical events. Others contain laments of either personal or national misfortune; these are often accompanied by an expression of confidence that God will hear the psalmist's petition and respond. In the event that the psalmist believes that God has responded favorably in a time of his misfortune, the psalm may be a song of thanksgiving for deliverance. In all these, the psalmist makes frequent use of the first person and addresses God directly in prayer. Many psalms contain didactic teachings especially in relation to righteous living and to the proper education in God's teaching and His Torah.

The poetic language of the Psalms, which makes use of the common biblical literary forms of parallelism and repetition, is rich in metaphor, with abundant reference to nature and its wonders, the beasts of the fields, appeals to agricultural life (both horticultural and pastoral), and description of kings and their glory and of varied occupations of man and woman such as the warrior, the builder, and the nursing mother. Mount Zion, the abode of the earthly Temple in Jerusalem, is the subject of several psalms; a specific collection (Psalm 121, "Shir hama'alot," chapters 120 through 134) may be associated with pilgrimages to the Temple. Some mythological motifs common to other ancient Near Eastern cultures are also found in the psalms, such as the conquest of the primeval waters and the heavenly court. A number of psalms are arranged in an alphabetic acrostic according to the letters of the Hebrew alphabet, which may have been used as an aid to memory.

The composition of the Book of Psalms has traditionally been ascribed to King David, known to be a musician (1 Sam. 18:10) trained especially on the harp (1 Sam. 16:16–23), a singer (2 Sam. 23:1), and a composer (2 Sam. 23:1). Individual psalms are also ascribed by the rabbis to earlier authors, among them Adam, Melchizedek, Abraham, Moses, Asaph, and the sons of Koraḥ. Some of these figures, primary among them David, are represented as the authors of individual psalms already in some of the superscriptions (*le'David, Le'Moshe, le'Asaph, li'Shelomo*). Some of these titles point to an early attempt to relate the general hymns and laments to specific historical events especially in the life of David, an attempt that continued in rabbinic times. The five-part division of the Book of Psalms (already evident in the canonical arrangement) is related to the five-part division of the Torah: "Moses gave the five books of the Torah to Israel, and correspondingly David gave the five books of the Psalms to Israel" (Midrash to Psalms 1:2). The divine inspiration came to David through music: "A harp was suspended above the bed of David. At midnight the north wind blew on it and it produced its own music. Immediately David arose and occupied himself with Torah. . . . Until midnight he occupied himself with Torah; from midnight on with songs and praises" (*b. Berakhot* 3b).

The centrality of the Book of Psalms in Jewish family and societal life was already evident during the Second Temple period, as is attested by descriptions of the singing of psalms in the home (4 Macc. 18:15), by the large number of fragments of psalms (including a number of noncanonical psalms) found among the Dead Sea Scrolls (more than that of any other biblical book), as well as by the overwhelming use of verses from psalms in rabbinic literature, especially in homiletic contexts. The liturgical use of psalms was prescribed for Temple worship, in which a specific chapter was sung by the Levites on each day of the week during the daily sacrifice. In addition, psalms 113 through 118, known collectively as the *Hallel* (the Praise *par excellence,* also known as the Egyptian *Hallel*), were sung at the Temple by the Levites during the paschal sacrifice (and, according to one opinion, were recited by the Israelites at the Red Sea), and the Songs of Ascent (psalms 120 through 134) were sung during the water libation ceremony in the festival of Tabernacles. No doubt the cultic use influenced later synagogue liturgy. Thus the *Hallel* psalms were prescribed for recitation in the synagogue on the three Pilgrim festivals and during Ḥanukkah; later custom ordained the recital of a particular psalm for each day of the week, as was done in the Temple (*Masekhet Soferim* 18:1), the inclusion of six daily psalms (145 through 150, known as the *Pesukei de'zimra,* the verses of song) in the morning service, and numerous other psalms and verses of psalms during other parts of the liturgy. The *Hallel* psalms were recited at other times as well, notably during the recital of the Haggadah on Passover eve, both in the synagogue and during the Seder service at home. Many of these were sung antiphonally, with a leader singing each verse and the listeners responding by repeating the verse or by reciting a standard refrain. Throughout the development of liturgical prayer, individual psalms continued to be assigned to synagogue use; special mention should be made of psalms 95 through 99 and psalm 29, which were instituted by the sixteenth-century Kabbalists of Safed as an introductory service on the eve of the Sabbath (*Kabbalat Shabbat*). In the custom of Yemenite Jews, groups of psalms are sung artistically in predawn Sabbath prayer meetings (*ashmorot*), and verses from psalms are used as introductory material to the similar *bakashot* hymns of the Syrian Jews.

The particularly religious and didactic nature of the Psalms invited the widespread use of the recital of psalms for almost any occasion when prayer was called for, especially life-threatening experiences such as going on a journey, prayers for the dangerously ill, during the night vigil preceding circumcision, at a burial service, and in a house of mourning. In addition, it became customary to recite large portions of the Book of Psalms, or even the entire book, on specific occasions such as on the eve of the Day of Atonement. For these purposes "societies of psalm-sayers" (*ḥevrat tehillim*) were instituted for the regular recital of psalms, especially in Eastern Europe. These societies (celebrated by the Yiddish writer Sholem Asch in *Der tillim yid* [*Salvation*] [Warsaw, 1934]) included men and women of different backgrounds and classes, although they were generally shunned by the more learned classes of Jews. Hasidic masters especially encouraged the regular recital of psalms, and certain individuals were known to be experts in the knowledge of the recital of psalms.

The recital of a particular psalm at times of distress was at first naturally connected to the content of the psalm, and certain psalms, especially those including phrases of comfort in the face of adversity or calamity, by talmudic times were already considered particularly efficacious. As Jewish society, during talmudic times and throughout the medieval period, shared the common fear of demons (*maziqim*) and other malevolent forces, psalms were recited as protection against them. Thus psalm 3, and psalm 91 (known as *shir shel pega'im* [songs (against) demons]) are indicated in the Talmud as useful to ward off an attack by demons and are included in liturgical practices during subsequent ages, especially useful during those times when the demons might be particularly active, such as during illness, at funerals, or before going to bed. However, there is also evidence from the early Byzantine period of the recitation of particular psalms, or verses of psalms, as part of a magic praxis in a wide variety of everyday situations without regard to the specific content of the psalm. These magical uses—sometimes entailing the incantation of a psalm a number of times at propitious moments or the writing of specific verses for use as an amulet—are listed, along with appropriate instructions, in a book entitled *Shimush tehillim* (The Magical Praxis of Psalms). The book first appears in Palestinian Aramaic texts of the Byzantine period but became widespread in Jewish and Christian circles during the medieval period, in both the East and the West. In this work, psalms are prescribed for remedying such situations as bodily ills, miscarriage, a crying baby, a troubling spouse, demons, storms at sea, wild animals, judicial favor, success in business, and the discovery of the identity of a thief. The work was later expanded to include mention of mystical divine names embedded in the text and prayers including these names. These lists circulated widely, and to this day many editions of Psalms are printed that include introductory comments stating the efficacious use of each psalm. Verses of psalms, as incantations or as prayers, are also found regularly, along with other biblical verses, as part of inscriptions on amulets.

Paul Mandel

See also: Amulets; Magic; Prayer.

Bibliography

Berlin, Adele, and Marc Zvi Brettler. "Psalms: Introduction." In *The Jewish Study Bible,* pp. 1280–1284. Oxford, UK: Oxford University Press, 1999.

Childs, Brevard S. "Psalm Titles and Midrashic Exegesis." *Journal of Semitic Studies* 16 (1971): 137–150.

Gerstenberger, Erhard S. *Psalms: Part I, with an Introduction to Cultic Poetry.* Grand Rapids, MI: William B. Eerdmans, 1988.

Grünwald, Max. "Bibliomancy." In *The Jewish Encyclopedia,* vol. 3, pp. 202–205. New York and London: Funk and Wagnalls, 1905.

Sarna, Nahum M. "Psalms, Book of." *Encyclopedia Judaica* 13, 1303–1322. Jerusalem: Keter, 1971.

Purim

The holiday of Purim is based on the account in the Book of Esther about the attempt by Haman, the counselor to King Ahasuerus, to annihilate the Jews in the Persian Empire and how they were saved by the intervention of Mordechai and his niece Esther, who was married to the king. To commemorate the event and the defeat of the wicked Haman, the fourteenth day of the Hebrew month of Adar, the day when the Jews rested after their victory, was enshrined as the feast of Purim; the next day was called Shushan Purim, because the fighting continued in the capital of Susa for another day. (To commemorate the fast and prayer by Esther, her handmaids, and all the Jews in Shushan before the queen went to the king to beg for his mercy, the thirteenth of Adar is observed as the Fast of Esther.) According to the Book of Esther, the name Purim is derived from the Hebrew word "*pur*" (lot, as in a lottery), because Haman cast lots to select the most propitious day for his murderous onslaught against the Jews.

The Book of Esther recounts that Mordechai and Esther sent letters to all the Jewish communities in the Persian Empire, calling for them to observe these days as a festival. Purim is unique in that it was created in the Diaspora (the Persian Empire) and reflects the lives of Diaspora Jews who must rely on the mercies of a non-Jewish ruler to escape a bitter fate. His clemency is won by the efforts of learned Jewish intercessors, who know how to persuade the monarch to show favor to the Jews. This seems to be why the holiday was accepted in all Jewish communities, even though at first it does not seem to have been approved by the leaders in Eretz Israel (see *b. Megillah* 7a).

Ancient Sources

Purim is the Jewish version of carnival. Many scholars have pointed out that there are carnivalesque elements in the original biblical account, which stands out from other scriptural narratives for its epic scope and includes elements of feasting, drinking, merrymaking, and sex. Some trace the story to an ancient myth about the wars of the gods of Babylonia (Mardukh, Ishtar) against the deities of Elam (Homan).

Religious and Social Elements

The main religious precept associated with the holiday is the public reading of the Scroll of Esther (the Megillah) in the synagogue, in the evening and again the following morning. This precept is incumbent on all, including women and children. In cities that were walled in the days of Joshua, the Megillah is read on the fifteenth of Adar. The reading in the synagogue takes on a carnival air as children, and sometimes adults, attend in costume, often as characters related to the Purim story. In addition, whenever readers come to Haman's name in the text, they make a racket with noisemakers of various kinds.

The social element is manifested in mutual gifts of food (called "*mishloaḥ manot*") and charity to the poor. Both are mentioned in the Book of Esther. According to the Talmud (*b. Megillah* 7a), each person must send gifts to at least two people. The custom is to send various kinds of foods—the more the better. Charity to the poor also includes money and clothing. In mishnaic times, there was a "Purim Collection" (*b. Bava Metzia* 78b) to provide the poor with what they needed to celebrate the holiday.

Purim celebration in Tel Aviv, 1928, by S.I. Schweig. *(Courtesy of the photo archive of the Jewish National Fund, Jerusalem)*

Carnival Elements in Purim Customs

Ever since the beginning of observance of the festival, many Purim customs have carnival elements intended to engage participants in play and to release tension. Often they represent a breach of prohibitions that are stringently enforced the rest of the year.

Drinking wine: In the words of the Talmud, on Purim a person should drink "until he cannot distinguish between 'curse Haman' and 'bless Mordechai' " (*b. Megillah* 7b)—that is, until he has lost the capacity for moral judgment, an excess that is otherwise utterly forbidden. This precept has given rise to parodic songs in praise of wine.

Purim games: Among the games played on Purim is one that dates back to the time of the Amoraim (third to fifth centuries) and called *mashvarta De'Purya* (*b. Sanhedrin* 64b). The Geonim (eighth to tenth centuries) explain this as burning Haman in effigy. The medieval scholar Rashi (Solomon ben Isaac of Troyes) associates it with boys jumping over bonfires. The custom is associated with other forms of symbolic attacks on the wicked Haman, including writing his name on a stone and then obliterating it by banging one stone on another or making noise to drown out his name during the reading of the Megillah, as a way of hurting him or chasing him away. Another jest involves the selection of a special Purim rabbi or king. This was common in the yeshivas of Eastern Europe. The student chosen for the role would expound the law in a flippant and parodic fashion.

Disguises: Costumes and disguises became a central custom of the holiday and have become especially beloved by children. In Eastern Europe, yeshiva students (who were all male) would dress up as women (such cross-dressing is strictly forbidden the rest of the year). There is no end to the variety of costumes, which are no longer associated only with characters from the Megillah or Jewish history.

The Purimshpil (Purim play): Another expression of the lightheartedness of the holiday was the staging of plays, especially by yeshiva students in Central and Eastern Europe, but elsewhere, too. The first Purimshpil known to scholars, titled *Esther,* is based on the account in the Book of Esther and was composed by Solomon Osko and Eliezer Graziano in Ladino in 1567. The earliest extant Yiddish Purimshpil, the Akhashveyresh-shpil, was written in 1708 and printed in Frankfurt. In addition to stories based on the Book of Esther, there are also Purim plays that enact other biblical stories, such as the sale of Joseph, David and Goliath, and the binding of Isaac.

Purim in Israel

The residents of Tel Aviv were in the forefront of the celebrations of Purim by rebuilding the Jewish community in Eretz Israel. In 1912, Avraham Aldema, a teacher at the Herzliyya Gymnasium (high school), organized a Purim parade through the streets of Tel Aviv. The costumes expressed the holiday tradition, the biblical era, and current events. With the encouragement of the then-mayor, Meir Dizengoff, Aldema continued to organize similar events on Purim. In 1914 Tel Aviv held a so-called Hebrew carnival, a colorful procession through the streets of the town. This tradition expanded in subsequent years.

In 1932, taking up a suggestion by the author Y.D. Berkovitch, the organizers decided to rename the parade the Adloyada (lit., "until he can no longer distinguish"). The grand marshal and organizer of the proceedings was Moshe Halevy, the founder of the Ohel Theater. Four of the early parades had themes: "Immigration to the Land of Israel" (1932), "Songs in Israel" (1933), "The Tribes of Israel, in Ancient Times and Today" (1934), and "From Slavery to Freedom" (1935). Other street festivals took place as well: an Esther's Palace, erected in downtown Tel Aviv every year, hosted plays, dance performances, and vocal concerts. During the 1920s and 1930s, these performances attracted many visitors from elsewhere in the country and even from abroad.

There was also a public ball. The most famous of these were organized by the dancer and painter Baruch Agadati between 1920 and 1933. In 1926, a Queen Esther was chosen at the ball. Over the years, several theatrical troupes, including the Trask Club, the Ohel Theater, and the satiric Matate Theater, organized their own Purim balls in Tel Aviv.

In 1936, the Adloyada was canceled because of unrest in the country. The custom was revived in Tel Aviv in the 1950s and subsequently spread to other towns. The most important event, a student Purim parade known as the Archiparchitura, was held in Haifa for many years, at the initiative of students of architecture at the Technion.

Nili Aryeh-Sapir

See also: Esther; Esther Scroll; Papercut; Purimshpil.

Further Reading

Aryeh-Sapir, Nili. "Purim." In *The Formation of Urban Culture and Education: Stories of and About Ceremonies and Celebrations in Tel Aviv in Its First Years.* Dor Ledor 36. Tel Aviv: Tel Aviv University, (2006): 99–130 (in Hebrew).

Ben Ezra, Akiva. "Purim." In *Celebrations' Customs.* Jerusalem: M. Neuman, 1963 (in Hebrew).

Berlovitz, Yaffa. "New Festivals." *Et-mol* 14:4 (83), 5 (1989) (in Hebrew).

Carmiel, Batia. *Tel Aviv in Costume and Crown—Purim Celebrations in Tel Aviv,* 1912–1935. Tel Aviv: Eretz Israel Museum, 1999 (in Hebrew).

Gaster, Theodor Herzl. "Purim." In *Festivals of the Jewish Year.* New York: W. Sloane, 1952–1953.

Hasan-Rokem, Galit. "Purim." In *Les fêtes du soleil: Celebrations of the Mediterranean Regions,* ed. Alessandro Falassi. Sienna: Betti Editrie, 2001.

Levinski, Yom Tov, ed. "Purim." In *The Book of Holidays*, vol. 6. Tel Aviv: Oneg Shabbat, 1959 (in Hebrew).

Rappel, Yoel, and Aliza Shenhar. "Purim." In *Encyclopaedia of Jewish Holidays,* ed. Yoel Rappel, pp. 289–301. Tel Aviv: D.O.D. Press, 2000 (in Hebrew).

Waharmann, Nahum. "Purim." In *The Holidays and Festivals of the Jewish People (Their Customs and Symbols).* Tel Aviv: Ahiasaf, 1970 (in Hebrew).

Zeira, Moti. *Rural Collective Settlement and Jewish Culture in Eretz Israel During the 1920s.* Jerusalem: Ben-Zvi Institute, 2002 (in Hebrew).

Purimshpil

The Purimshpil, the Jewish folk theater enacted in Yiddish during the holiday of Purim, developed in early modern Europe into an ongoing folk tradition among the Jewish communities. The players, themes, motifs, and style are all in accordance with the definition of a folk genre: a traditional show based upon a well-known myth, put on at holiday time by small communities whose members were also the performers. Like similar phenomena in pre-industrial societies, the Jewish festive folk theater was characterized by rituals involving dance, feasting, masquerades, mock weddings, mock fights, impersonation, masks, and men wearing women's clothing. The popular customs manifested in the folk play include reference to the spirit of an upside-down world, anarchy, and rebellion. In the mode of the farce and the parody, the players evoke a world of chaos and the breaking of taboos.

The earliest known mention of the term "Purimshpil" is found in a "Poem on the Book of Esther" (dated 1555), composed by Gumprecht von Szczebrzeszyn, a Polish Jew working as a *melamed* (teacher of young children) in Venice. The term does not necessarily indicate a dramatic play and has been used to describe different types of performances and merriment, monologues, and parodies that were performed at the festive table.

Students from a Tarbut Hebrew-language school perform a Purimshpil. Podbrodzie, Poland (now Pabradė, Lith.), 1939. *(YIVO Institute, New York)*

The first complete extant dramatic text is dated to the seventeenth century. However, iconographic testimony suggests a tradition of such Jewish clownish merriment back to the fifteenth century.

The Purimshpil, as a liminoid manifestation—to use anthropologist Victor Turner's term for creative, reflective leisure activity—has preserved as conspicuously as any other folk drama the dynamic liminal symbols of the ritual.

The Play

The anonymous writers and performers—actors for the occasion—the craftsmen, *badchanim* (jesters), *klezmorim* (musicians), yeshiva *bokhers* (students) who produced the shows would parade through the streets in the play's costumes and masks, stopping at the wealthier Jewish households to demand food and money, for their own needs or for charity, in exchange for entertainment. The family with their invited guests around the festive table did not leave much room for a big-cast spectacle. The players had to wait outside, at the door, first for permission to enter, and then often for their turn to enter and play their parts. The invading players turned the provisional space of the private homes into an intimate theatrical space by incorporating the existing state of an ongoing Purim feast. Household objects were used on occasion, as characteristic of folk play transformation of any accessory on hand, to serve as iconic and symbolic stage signs: benches, chairs, and coat hangers, rustled up in the room where the show was to take place, transported the audience to the throne room, the royal banquet, or the gallows.

The plays, like other genres of Jewish folk culture, derive to a large extent from the existing "higher culture," perhaps more so than any other folk tradition. The elements of these folk plays betray their closeness to a literary origin and are manifested in a rather unusual relationship between high culture and folk culture. Even the least pretentious versions of the Purimshpil clearly reveal this reliance on elements from the learned Jewish sources: the scriptures, midrashim, *Targum sheni*, Aggadah, liturgy, and other "high" genres, including misogynist poetry. However, the Purimshpil reveals signs of oral transmission, too. Throughout the generations, the plays were transmitted either in writing or more often by word of mouth, together with their special melodies and traditional costumes. In many places, a Purimshpil remained in the domain of one family, which produced it by concessional right.

Themes

Biblical themes are central, the most common offering being the Akhashveyresh-shpil, an enactment of the Book of Esther, since the book tells of the origin of the Purim feast itself. Other popular themes such as the sale of Joseph (*Mekhires Yosef*), David and Goliath the Philistine (*Dovid un Goliyes haplishti*), the sacrifice of Isaac (*Akeydes Yitskhok*), and the Book of Daniel, where the weak overcome the mighty, are reflected in the social import or message. As happens frequently in folk plays that appropriate elements wherever they can find them, outright anachronisms appear. Random elements from beyond the world of the biblical myth were used to expand the tale. With the narrative continuity supplied by the myth, the play could distance itself from the original narrative and elaborate on the core story through use of extras, comic fragments, contemporary and comic characters and local allusions, jokes, liturgical parody, songs, and a medley of gibberish, as well as sketches on locally known rabbis, doctors, and cantors. The plays seem to be unstructured: Many of the monologues do not belong to the main plot, the entrances are not motivated, the mythical characters have been made into fools, and there are the abrupt changes in atmosphere, from laughter to tears and from pathos to low farce.

Purimshpil and the Rabbinical Establishment

Absorbed into popular humor, the language became totally unrestricted, containing obscenities, insults, curses, and blasphemies. The authorities were subverted and ridiculed by the players, who descended in numerous instances into scatological humor, from comic gesticulations and sexual allusions to blunt talk of sex and genitalia. These drew the wrath of the community elders. The strong objections that the rabbinical establishment had always felt vis-à-vis the very institution of the theater was now vindicated by this challenge to Jewish asceticism. And after the improvised text of the play was documented in writing, and thus subject to more sober scrutiny, it was doomed. Johann Jacob Schudt, who published the 1708 edition of Akhashveyresh-shpil in 1714, records that the Jews themselves were ashamed of what they had written, and, indeed, the elders of Frankfurt burned the entire edition at the stake. Nevertheless, the well-rooted tradition of the Purimshpil in Eastern Europe did not cease. There are hardly any memoires or stories from the shtetls (small towns) in East Europe that do not contain a Purimshpil experience. However, after the genre had crystallized into the definitive pattern of a play, its development stopped and it began to rely on tradition. This tradition of the Purimshpil lasted as long as it continued to reflect a life that had remained unchanged for hundreds of years. It constituted not only a means of provision and charity but also a vehicle for social comment and protest, expressing resistance by the weak against the strong on two levels: by asserting the identity of an oppressed Jewish minority culture within a dominant gentile culture and by registering the perspectives of the poorest and least-powerful members of the Jewish community within that community itself.

The Purimshpil, the only authentic Jewish folk theater, which had existed from early modern Europe for hundreds of years, began to decay in the late nineteenth and the early twentieth century with the waves of immigration to the big cities and out of Europe; and it came almost to its end with the extinction of European Jewry in the Holocaust. The Purimshpil still survives, however, in a few yeshivas in the United States and Israel.

Ahuva Belkin

See also: Purim.

Bibliography

Eyn sheyn purimshpil (A Nice Purimshpil). 1697. Leipzig, Municipal Library, no. 35.

Belkin, Ahuva. "Citing Scripture for a Purpose: The Jewish "Purimspiel" as a Parody." *Assaph* 3:12 (1997): 45–59 (in Hebrew).

———. "'Habit de Fou' in Purim Spiel?" *Assaph* 3:2 (1985): 40–55 (in Hebrew).

Chemerinsky, Mordechai."My Town Motili." *Reshumot* 2 (1947): 74–76 (in Hebrew).

Epstein, Shifra. *The Daniel-shpil.* Jerusalem: Magnes Press, 1998 (in Hebrew).

Kapper, Sigfried. "Ahasverus—Ein Judisches Fastnachtspiel." In *Deutsches Museum—Zeitschrift fur Literatur, Kunst und Offentliches Leben*, vol. 4. Leipzig, 1854.

Prilutski, Noah. *Zamlbikher far yidishn folklor, filologye un kulturgeshikhte* (Collection Book of Yiddish Folklore, Philology, and Culture History). Warsaw: Noyer Farlag, 1912 (in Yiddish).

Schudt, Johann Jacob. *Judische Merckwurdigkeiten*, vol. 2. Frankfurt and Leipzig, 1714.

Shmeruk, Chone. *Mahazot Mikraim b'Yiddish 1697–1750* (Yiddish Biblical Plays 1697–1750). Jerusalem: Israel Academy of Sciences and Humanities, 1979.

Stern, Moritz. *Lieder des Venezianischen Lehrers Gumprecht von Szczebrzeszyn.* Berlin: Hausfreund, 1922.

Turner, Victor. *From Ritual to Theatre: The Human Seriousness of Play.* New York: Performing Arts Journal, 1982.

Weinryb, Dov. "Economics and Social Factors in the Jewish Enlightenment in Germany." In *Compilation in Memory of Haim Nachman Bialik.* Tel Aviv: Dvir, 1938 (in Hebrew).

Weisenberg, Samuel. "Dus Pirimspiel: Du Spielt die Rolle Humen und Mordche." *Mitteilungen der Gesellschaft fur judiche Volkskunde* 13:1 (1904): 1–27.

Q

QINAH (LAMENT)

The Hebrew word *"qinah"* designates a lament. In Jewish folklore, the word has two distinct meanings: (1) a lament for the dead, on a private level; and (2) a lament for the destruction of the Temple of Jerusalem in the first century C.E., as recited on the legendary day of the event, Ninth of Av (Heb. Tisha Be'Av), on a collective level. Whereas the private laments for the dead are almost always, since antiquity and in various groups and regions, performed by women, the collective laments for the destruction of the Temple are often performed by men.

Laments for the dead are recognized as a literary genre in the Hebrew Bible, for example, David's poetically elaborate lament for Saul and Jonathan (2 Sam 1:17–27). The Hebrew Bible also mentions the social institution of lamenters, according to the grammatical form identified as lamenting women: "call for the lamenting women" (Jer. 9:16). Private lamenting with a strong national tone occurs in the case of the matriarch "Rachel weeping for her children" (Jer. 31:14).

The Talmud also retains at least one lament assigned to women—in this case the women of Shkanziv, a distant city in northern Babylonia—opening with the words: "Woe for his leaving, woe for our grieving" (*b. Mo'ed Qatan* 28b).

In various Jewish traditions more or less institutionalized forms of lamenting occur often with strong connections to local non-Jewish lamenting traditions. Although lamenting exists in different cultures (Karelia, Greek islands), in Israel lamenting traditions have persisted in many communities that emigrated from Muslim and Near Eastern countries as well as from Africa (Ethiopia). Kurdish Jewish women's lamenting in neo-Aramaic was a living tradition until about the 1970s, and some Yemeni Jewish women in Israel still perform laments in Judeo-Arabic, for dead relatives and deceased community members.

The performance of laments involves knowledge of the verbal repertoire of the genre, including a high level of individual variation and improvisation, similar to what is known of lamenting traditions from the Mediterranean region as well as around the world. Likewise the vocabulary and poetics of Jewish laments resemble those of other traditions: questioning the harshness of fate, wailing over the young age of the deceased, and describing the wonderful qualities of the lamented dead. The stylized use of body gestures also is part of the genre.

The other major designation of the term relates to the national and religious laments addressing the destruction of Jerusalem and its temple. The Hebrew Bible's book of Lamentations (Eikha) not only anthologizes a five-chapter selection of such poems from antiquity but also to this day constitutes the main repertoire read in the synagogue on the day commemorating the lamented events. In some Judeo-Arabic dialects the day itself is called "Eikha." The title of the book is actually the first Hebrew word of the text, also in accordance with the poetics of laments a question: "How [does the city sit solitary]?" The book is however also called "the scroll of laments," in Hebrew, *Megillat Qinnot,* and the recitation of the text is accordingly called the reading of *Qinnot.* Hebrew poets from late antiquity onward have added to the repertoire of readings on Tisha Be'Av. A prose work midrash, the Lamentations Rabbah, was originally composed in the late fifth century in Palestine in Hebrew and Aramaic, and it has become an additional text for mainly individual reading on Tisha Be'Av, which also is a day of fasting.

Some historical events, such as the mass murder of Jews in the Rhine valley in the eleventh century, accompanying the Crusades, and the Holocaust of the mid-twentieth century, have given rise to new poems of lamentation.

Galit Hasan-Rokem

See also: Death.

Bibliography

Alexiou, Margaret. *The Ritual Lament in Greek Tradition.* Cambridge: Cambridge University Press, 1974.

Einbinder, Susan L. *Beautiful Death: Jewish Poetry and Martyrdom in Medieval France.* Princeton, NJ: Princeton University Press, 2002.

Halevi, Leor. "Wailing for the Dead: The Role of Women in Early Islamic Funerals." *Past & Present* 183 (2004): 3–39.

Hasan-Rokem, Galit. *Web of Life: Folklore and Midrash in Rabbinic Literature.* Stanford, CA: Stanford University Press, 2000.

Madar, Vered. "Lamentations of Women from Yemen: Text Between Voice and Movement." *Jerusalem Studies of Jewish Folklore* 23 (2005): 89–119 (in Hebrew).

———. "The Story of the Exodus and the Story of Hannah and Her Seven Sons: A Gendered Reading of Two Stories in the Culture of Yemenite Jewish Women." *Nashim* 11 (2006): 84–105 (in Hebrew).

———. "What Did Death Tell You When It Came? Lamentations of Women from Yemen in Their Cultural Context." *Pa'amim* 103 (2005): 5–55 (in Hebrew).

Rosenblatt, G.C.P., R.P. Walsh, and D.A. Jackson. *Grief and Mourning in Cross-Cultural Perspective.* New Haven, CT: Human Relations Area File Press, 1976.

Suliteanu, Gisela. "The Traditional System of Melopeic Prose of the Funeral Songs Recited by the Jewish Women of the Socialist Republic of Romania." *Folklore Research Center Studies* 3 (1972): 291–349.

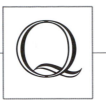

R

Rabbah bar bar Ḥannah

Rabbah bar bar Ḥannah (RBBH) was a third-century rabbi of Palestinian origin to whom a variety of legal and aggadic sayings are attributed in the rabbinic corpus. The sources (mainly *b. Berakhot* 53b, *Ḥullin* 55b, *Yebamot* 120a) suggest that his literary character was that of a traveler especially acquainted with the desert landscape and its inhabitants.

Specifically, RBBH recounted tall tales and mini-travelogues, genres with which his character has been identified in later generations. In his stories (*b. Bava Batra* 73b–74a) RBBH tells of fantastic phenomena that he had witnessed; for example, a gigantic frog was swallowed by a snake that was in turn swallowed by a bird or a huge bird whose head reached the sky. A few of his tall tales—all of which take place in the desert—address pivotal cultural symbols. In one, he is led by an Arab to the looming gigantic figures of the generation of Israelites condemned to die in the desert. There he witnesses their periodic awakening from a coma. In another, he is led to Mount Sinai, where he hears a heavenly voice asking to be freed. Both stories end with RBBH reporting his experience at the *beit ha'midrash* (house of study), only to be rebuked by the sages for what they perceive as his inappropriate response. According to them, he should have counted the threads on the tzitzit (fringes) of the dead of the desert and he should have released the heavenly voice, which he had failed to recognize as the *shekhina* lamenting her exile. In another tale, RBBH is led to the simmering crack through which he hears the Koraḥ family—doomed to eternal interrogation—admit their guilt. He also witnesses waddling geese that owe their obesity to the prolongation of the redemptive era in which they will serve as food for the righteous.

Entertaining and humorous as these stories may be, they also carry deep cultural meaning. Leading their traveler—and his audience—to transgress familiar geographic boundaries, the stories introduce him to temporal dimensions other than the present, namely, the primordial and the eschatological. It is in the framework of the premonotheistic primordial elements of chaos and the anxiety over the eschatological future that RBBH's encounter with figures such as the generation of the desert and the Koraḥ family presents a subversive narrative; RBBH's tall tales point at the inadequacy of the formal institutional discourse, confined by accepted geographic and temporal boundaries.

Dina Stein

See also: Agnon, S.Y.

Bibliography

Ben Amos, Dan. "Talmudic Tall Tales." In *Folklore Today: A Festschrift for Richard Dorson,* ed. Linda Degh, Henry Glassie, and Felix J. Oinas, pp. 25–43. Bloomington: Research Center for Language and Semiotic Studies, 1976.

Yassif, Eli. *The Hebrew Folktale: History, Genre, Meanings*, trans. J.S. Teitelbaum. Bloomington: Indiana University Press, 1999.

Rabbinic Literature

The term "rabbinic literature," also known as the "literature of the sages (of blessed memory)" (*sifrut ḥazal*), designates a corpus of texts, or rather, corpora of texts, redacted in the first centuries of the common era, containing records of traditions transmitted both orally and in written form by a diverse group of learned men. These sages (rabbis; lit., "masters") are generally considered the successors to the Pharisees of the Second Temple period, and flourished from the end of that period (commonly designated by the destruction of the Temple in 70 C.E.) until approximately the fifth century C.E., in the Jewish centers of Palestine and Babylonia. They were at the same time students of tradition and teachers of the people, whose self-proclaimed task was to preserve and interpret the traditions of law and lore of earlier generations and to direct the people in the proper conduct of their lives according to the precepts and teachings of those traditions.

The sages were not a homogeneous group; among them were political and religious leaders, judges and teachers, although the majority earned their livelihood from other activities as artisans, landowners, farmers, merchants, and day laborers. They came from diverse backgrounds, both rich and poor, and while there was often conflict between sages and even, at times, personal animosity, the attitude of those "sitting in the house of study" was in general one of mutual respect, with special honor shown teachers by their pupils. Yet there are indications of an aristocracy of the learned among the sages, with evidence of hereditary privileges accorded at times to the sons of scholars; there are also expressions of impatience and distrust among the sages toward those in the general population who were either unlearned or disdainful of observance of the commandments.

The Literary Production of the Sages: Halakhah and Haggadah

The literary production of this scholarly class of leaders and teachers, while not a direct expression of folk literature, incorporates elements characteristic of such literature. It originated in circumstances of oral transmission and often preserves the rhetoric and style typical of folktales and sayings. The result of collective traditions, it includes many parallel versions of the same story or parabolic saying. Dealing as it does with everyday life and with the need for instruction of the people at large, it reflects and refracts popular beliefs, customs, and means of expression. Thus, alongside intricate legal discussions concerning the many obligations incumbent upon a Jew as embodied in the concept of mitzvot (commandments), one also finds in this literature parables, folk medicine, astrological considerations, fantastic tales, hagiographies, legends, dream interpretations, descriptions of folk beliefs and practices, and humorous anecdotes. These elements are not found in separate works, but are integrated into the web of textual commentary and exposition characteristic of the literature.

A salient feature of the works comprising rabbinic literature is the anonymity of their final editors. Although some books are attributed to a particular sage (*Mekhilta de'Rabbi Ishmael, Avot de'Rabbi Nathan, Midrash de'Rabbi Tanhuma, Pesiqta de'Rabbi Kahana, Pirqe de'Rabbi Eliezer*), these attributions are, on the whole, of later origin. However, the named attributions of the individual traditions within each work are generally considered authentic, although the actual verbal formulation of the traditions may be due to later transmitters. Each individual unit of tradition is usually brief, from a few words to a few lines, thus facilitating the memorization of the unit. Because of the compilatory nature of the works, many units are found repeated, either identically or with variation, in several works. The individual work of the rabbinic corpus, then, may be seen as an ordered collection of earlier transmitted traditions edited by an anonymous editor or group of editors, for the purpose of transmitting these traditions to future generations for further study and reference. Although the editor/redactor may be responsible for the order of materials and even their specific formulation, it may be assumed that the individual units in any one work reflect comments from different periods and circumstances.

The content of rabbinic literature may conveniently be divided into two major areas: Halakhah (law) and Haggadah (lore). Halakhah (from the root *h-l-kh,* "to go, to walk") governs the obligations of Jewish life in every sphere, both public and private, and is rooted in the idea of the divine commandments as embedded in the Torah held to have been revealed by God to Moses at Mount Sinai. This Torah (lit., "instruction") is thought of as encompassing both the written word of God, as set forth in the five books of Moses, and the oral Torah ("Torah she'be'alpeh"), which comprises the orally transmitted laws and explanations that accompanied the written Torah and were revealed alongside it at Mount Sinai and further elaborated upon and augmented by interpretations and additional enactments of subsequent generations. Haggadah (from the root *h-g-d,* "to relate"), more commonly called "Aggadah," is more difficult to delineate and is often defined negatively as everything that is not Halakhah. Indeed, while Halakhah is limited to specific forms, Haggadah encompasses a rich assortment of literary genres, including exegesis, parable, metaphor, aphorism, folktale, historical legend, and hagiography.

The Works of Rabbinic Literature

Halakhah and Haggadah are convenient ways of classifying the contents of rabbinic literature, but these terms do not adequately define the nature of the individual works. A more accurate description divides the works by their method of exposition and arrangement, whether topically or as a sort of commentary or gloss to the biblical text.

The first method is embodied in the Mishnah (from the root *sh-n-h,* "to repeat," indicating the oral nature of its transmission), which is a vast ordered compilation, mostly of laws, arranged in tractates—separate compilations of the laws, divided into chapters—and individual *mishnayot,* each tractate dedicated to a particular area of law or subject. A supplemental work, the Tosefta (lit., "supplement"), ordered like the Mishnah, contains additional material, some of which predates the editing of the Mishnah. The second method of arrangement of the traditional material is exemplified by the midrashim (from *d-r-sh,* "to search," "to expound"; specifically, to search out meanings in a biblical text), which are a collection of expositions on biblical verses, usually arranged in the order of the verses of a biblical book. The earliest midrashim are the so-called halakhic midrashim, which relate laws to biblical verses; there exist whole or fragmentary midrashim to the five official books of the Pentateuch, from Exodus to Deuteronomy.

While Halakhah predominates in both Mishnah and halakhic Midrash, there is a considerable amount of unofficial material included in works of both genres. Several tractates of the Mishnah deal with descriptions of activity by the people in the Temple during festival occasions, or include unofficial, didactic lessons; there is, as well, an entire tractate (*Avot*) consisting of aphorisms of individual sages. The halakhic midrashim, too, contain much material related to unofficial as well as official sections of the biblical books, including legend, exegesis, and homily.

All the materials included in the above-mentioned works are in Hebrew and are culled from the first period of rabbinic literature, that of the so-called *tannaim,* from the end of the Second Temple period until around 220 C.E., the approximate year of the death of Rabbi Judah the Patriarch, who was responsible for the final redaction of the Mishnah. This event marks a watershed in the activity of the sages, for from this time on the Mishnah becomes a central, canonical work, laying the foundation for future exegetical and compilatory activity. In the next period, that of the Amoraim (third to fifth centuries C.E.), study in the academies focused on exposition of the Mishnah. The discussions of the sages and their decisions were mostly in Aramaic, the spoken language at the time; these became organized as commentary and elaboration of the Mishnah and were finally edited as the work known as the Talmud (lit., "study," "teaching"). Because there were major centers of activity in Palestine and in Babylonia, there arose two edited collections, the "Jerusalem" or Palestinian Talmud (actually produced in the Galilee) and the Babylonian Talmud. The Babylonian Talmud, whose final redaction at the end of the fifth century C.E. postdates the redaction of the Palestinian Talmud by more than a century, is by far the longer of the two and achieved a greater level of literary refinement.

Here, too, the redaction of materials was done anonymously. The "commentary" of the Talmud on the Mishnah is vast and varied, not limited to the issue at hand. It includes not only a dialectic discussion of the laws of the Mishnah and the juristic principles underlying the laws, but also a collection of case decisions, legends, hagiographies, biblical exegeses, homilies, and aphorisms, often arranged in an associative manner. As in the earlier works, both Halakhah and Haggadah feature prominently in the Talmuds and are interwoven. The Babylonian Talmud in particular contains vast amounts of Haggadah; there is hardly a tractate without significant amounts of haggadic discourse. Both Talmuds, but especially the Babylonian Talmud, which attained hegemony over the Palestinian Talmud during the last centuries of the first millennium (the Geonic period), became the centerpiece and basis for all subsequent Jewish law and practice, as well as the main object of advanced study.

Shortly after the redaction of the Palestinian Talmud near the end of the fourth century C.E., a series of midrashic works were redacted, almost all in Palestine, from the transmitted haggadic material of the Amoraic period. These are generally called haggadic midrashim, to distinguish them from the earlier halakhic midrashim. The earliest redacted work, and one of the most important, is the Midrash to Genesis, called Genesis Rabbah; shortly thereafter appeared midrashim to Leviticus (Leviticus Rabbah), and to those books of the Hagiographa that were used liturgically in synagogue service at specific times during the year, known collectively as the Five Scrolls (Song of Songs, Ruth, Esther, Lamentations, and Ecclesiastes). In time these were copied and printed together, along with other midrashim, in one collection that came to be called Midrash Rabbah (to the five books of Moses and the five scrolls). Another significant series of midrashim, of somewhat later date, were again compiled to the five books of the Torah, called Midrash Tanḥuma; other midrashim include collections ordered according to other books of the Bible (Samuel, Psalms, Proverbs), in addition to collections unconnected to a biblical book (e.g., Tanna devei Eliyahu, *Pirqe de'Rabbi Eliezer*), as well as numerous smaller works that include the word "midrash" in their title, many of them compiled only in the medieval period, and thus not considered part of the corpus of rabbinic literature.

It is common in scholarly circles to classify the haggadic midrashim as either "exegetical" or "homiletical" midrash, according to the method of exposition of the verses of the biblical book upon which the midrashic work is based: The exegetical midrashim (such as Genesis Rabbah and Lamentations Rabbah) attach midrashim to almost every verse of the book, appearing as a sort of running commentary, while the homiletical midrashim (Leviticus Rabbah, Midrash Tanḥuma) choose specific verses of the book (in order), around which are woven compilations of midrashic traditions loosely comparable to a homily, with the constituent elements organized around a common theme and with introductory passages, and often a concluding passage of a messianic or consolatory nature. However, these terms are somewhat misleading, since there is neither true exegesis nor homily in either type of midrash.

Origins and Folk Content

The origin of much of the material embedded in the rabbinic corpus, whether of the halakhic or haggadic form, derives from discourses and study sessions that were given regularly during the Tannaitic and Amoraic periods, especially on the Sabbath and holidays, in the synagogues (where the Torah and Prophets were publicly recited, translated, and commented upon) and in study circles (later, houses of study [*batei midrash*]), which provided the mainstay of communal activity. An additional source of material included life-cycle events (births, deaths, weddings) and public events (public fasts, funerals of leaders), during which homiletic expositions were commonly delivered. It should not be assumed, however, that the written traditions accurately reflect these discourses; they are, rather, carefully reformulated encapsulations of the oral presentations of sayings, stories, parables, and exegeses by scholars and others. Their main characteristic is an extreme brevity and condensation of expression and a precision and sophistication of language and form. Arising as they do from an intimate connection with the people at large, they contain a wealth of folkloristic material, including common beliefs about nature, flora and fauna, astronomy and astrology, demons, the efficacy of magic and magical practices, folk medicine, customs and practices relating to the life cycle (in particular, birth, marriage, divorce, and death), dreams, and the human body. Some of these practices are mentioned by the sages only to be criticized or condemned; others are naturally part of the beliefs and customs of the sages.

One of the most ubiquitous forms in rabbinic literature, especially in the Haggadah, is that of the brief narrative tale. The tale is employed in the retelling and expansion of biblical narratives and events, in biographical legend, whether of biblical characters or of contemporary sages and holy men, in historical legend, in exemplum, in parable and fable, in magic tales and comic tales. These tales, while exhibiting sophisticated narrative techniques, also utilize many forms of folk literature, embedding parables, folk legends, proverbs, and fables in new literary forms. The appearance of parallel versions of these tales in separate rabbinic works (and, indeed, at times in several places within one work) provides a fascinating opportunity to observe the ways in which the tales were retold in different circumstances and periods. At times it is possible to discern in these narratives and their parallel versions rhetorical devices, transformations of themes and motifs, and other aspects common to the transmission of folk literature, as well as influences from the folk literature of other peoples with whom the Jews had contact, especially folktales and motifs of Babylonian, Persian, and Hellenistic origins.

Later Influence of Rabbinic Literature

Rabbinic literature in all its forms became the source of study and inspiration to Jews in subsequent generations. It is impossible to overestimate the influence that the corpora of this literature in all its forms exerted on the philosophy, mores, customs, exegesis, and literature of Jewish societies in all parts of the world ever since the rabbinic period. The laws and customs presented in this literature served as the basis of Jewish private and communal life and were codified, epitomized, and commented on in the voluminous halakhic literature based mostly on exposition of the Babylonian Talmud (and, to a lesser extent, the Palestinian talmudic and midrashic literature). The synagogue liturgy was founded on the directives contained therein and incorporated numerous prayers found in these corpora; the comments on biblical passages and personages provided the foundation for Jewish biblical exegetical and homiletic activity throughout the medieval period (exemplified in the grand oeuvre of the medieval biblical commentator *par excellence,* Rashi), as well as a wellspring of sources for the Byzantine and medieval *payytan* (liturgical poet); the numerous tales and biblical comments were retold, compiled, and recombined in anthologies, compendia, and literary works (some of which came to be considered part and parcel of the rabbinic corpus despite their derivative status). During the Middle Ages, rabbinic tales, biblical retellings, and aphoristic comments were woven into homilies and assembled into compilations of didactic tales, while undergoing transformations through repeated alterations and by the incorporation of foreign elements from the ambient cultures in which the Jews found themselves. To a lesser extent, the rabbinic sources had an effect on medieval philosophy and mystical movements and texts, and the language and idioms of the Talmud and midrashim became incorporated in the popular and scholarly idiom, as well as in the local dialects, of Jews in all lands of the Diaspora. The rabbinic lore was translated and incorporated into popular works written in the vernacular for the unlearned, such as the sixteenth-century Yiddish work *Tzenah u'renah,* and the eighteenth-century Ladino compilation *Me'am lo'ez.* In the modern period, as Jews of many lands became increasingly divorced from the study of the rabbinic sources, many elements of rabbinic lore continued to be transmitted through popular discourses as well as through new literary avenues, such as the tales written by Yiddish writers from the period of the Enlightenment (Haskalah).

Scholarship

Modern scholarly research into the folklore of the rabbinic corpus has focused on two main areas: the compilation and comparative analysis of the wealth of biblical midrashic comment and aggadic supplement (as in Louis Ginzberg's monumental oeuvre, *Legends of the Jews* [1909–1938]; and, with a view to the later development of rabbinic legend, the work of Micha Josef Berdyczewski [called Bin-Gorion], *Mimekor Yisrael: Classical Jewish Folktales* [1939–1945; which originally appeared in German as *Der Born Judas,* 1916–1923]; compare also Haim Nachman Bialik and Yehoshua Hana Ravnitzky's *Sefer ha'aggadah* [1908–1911]), and the modern analyses of the folkloristic elements in the rabbinic narrative (Eli Yassif, *The Hebrew Folktale: History, Genre, Meaning* [1999]; Galit Hasan-Rokem, *Web of Life: Folklore and Midrash in Rabbinic Literature* [2000]). Individual studies have also explored the origins and development of laws and customs found in the rabbinic corpus, often with a comparison to contemporary non-Jewish custom. Recent studies have treated the rabbinic material along with the later manifestations of the rabbinic tale in a more general analysis of the development of the themes within Jewish culture ("thematology," developed by Yoav Elstein and Avidov Lipsker ([1995]).

While scholars at the beginning of the twentieth century tended to see the rabbinic corpus, specifically the Haggadah, as a refraction and refinement of a more basic folk element current among the people in rabbinic times (Ginzberg, Bialik), more recent scholarship has viewed the rabbinic corpus as part of general Jewish cultural development, incorporating both folkloric and learned-elitist elements. However, a more critical position has also been posited, in which the rabbinic corpus is seen purely as a literary (although oral) phenomenon of the learned elite, even if it makes use of folkloric elements (Fraenkel 2001).

Paul Mandel

See also: Folk Narratives in Rabbinic Literature; Midrash.

Bibliography

Bialik, Hayim N., and Yehoshua H. Ravnitzky. *The Book of Legends (Sefer ha-Aggadah)*, trans. William G. Braude. New York: Schocken Books, 1992.

Bin Gorion, Micha Joseph. *Mimekor Yisrael: Classical Jewish Folktales*. Bloomington and Indianapolis: Indiana University Press, 1990.

Elstein, Yoav, and Avidov Lipsker. "The Homogeneous Series in the Literature of the Jewish People: A Thematological Methodology." In *Thematics Reconsidered: Essays in Honor of Horst S. Dämmrich,* ed. Frank Trommler. Amsterdam: Rodopi, 1995.

Fraenkel, Jonah. "The Aggadic Story Compared with the Folktale." In *The Aggadic Narrative: Harmony of Form and Content,* ed. Frank Trommler, pp. 236–260. Tel Aviv: Ha'kibbutz Ha'meuḥad, 2001 (in Hebrew).

Ginzberg, Louis. "Jewish Folklore: East and West." In Ginzberg, *On Jewish Law and Lore.* Philadelphia: Jewish Publication Society of America, 1955.

———. *The Legends of the Jews.* 7 vols. Philadelphia: Jewish Publication Society of America, 1909–1938.

Hasan-Rokem, Galit. "Jewish Folklore and Ethnography." In *The Oxford Handbook of Jewish Studies,* ed. Martin Goodman, pp. 960–963. Oxford: Oxford University Press, 2002.

———. *Web of Life: Folklore and Midrash in Rabbinic Literature,* trans. Batya Stein. Stanford: Stanford University Press, 2000.

Heinemann, Joseph. "The Nature of the Aggadah," trans. Marc Bregman. In *Midrash and Literature,* ed. Geoffrey H. Hartman and Sanford Budick, pp. 41–55. New Haven: Yale University Press, 1986.

Lieberman, Saul. *Greek in Jewish Palestine.* New York: Jewish Theological Seminary of America, 1942.

———. *Hellenism in Jewish Palestine.* New York: Jewish Theological Seminary of America, 1950.

Neuman (Noy), Dov. *Motif-Index of Talmudic-Midrashic Literature.* Bloomington: Indiana University Press, 1954.

Rappoport, Angelo S. *The Folklore of the Jews.* London: Soncino Press, 1937.

Safrai, Shmuel, ed. *The Literature of the Sages. First Part: Oral Torah, Halakha, Mishna, Tosefta, Talmud, External Tractates.* Philadelphia: Fortress, 1987.

Strack, Hermann L., and Günter Stemberger. *Introduction to the Talmud and Midrash,* trans. Markus Bockmühl. Edinburgh: T & T Clark, 1991.

Theodor, Judah. "Midrash Haggadah." In *Jewish Encyclopedia,* vol. 8. New York: Funk and Wagnalls, 1904.

Urbach, Ephraim E. *The Sages: Their Concepts and Beliefs,* trans. Israel Abrahams. Jerusalem: Magnes Press, 1975.

Yassif, Eli. *The Hebrew Folktale: History, Genre, Meaning,* trans. Jacqueline S. Teitelbaum. Bloomington and Indianapolis: Indiana University Press, 1999.

Zlotnick, Dov. *The Iron Pillar—Mishnah: Redaction, Forms, and Intent.* Jerusalem: Bialik Institute, 1988 (in Hebrew).

Rachel

Rachel (from the Hebrew Rahel, meaning "ewe-lamb") is the daughter of Laban, the younger sister of Leah, Jacob's wife, and the mother of Joseph and Benjamin. Rachel is a symbol of tragic sacrifice in Jewish tradition. Due to her father's cunning, she is forced to wait many years before she can become Jacob's wife. Jacob is forced by Laban to work for seven years before he can marry Leah, Rachel's older sister, and then Jacob must work for another seven years in order to become engaged to Rachel. Rachel watches as her sister and Jacob have several sons; her prayers for a child of her own are answered, and Rachel gives birth to Joseph, and then to Benjamin, but she dies while giving birth. After her tragic death, Rachel's fortitude and faithfulness are honored.

Rachel holds a vital place in Jewish history and folklore. Her importance in Jewish tradition derives from her status as the mother of sons who were models for the tribes of Israel, as reflected in the language of the prayer: "May the Lord make the woman who is coming into your house like Rachel and Leah, who together built up the house of Israel" (Ruth 4:11). Popular Jewish belief that Rachel continues to care for her sons, and even laments and weeps for them at times of ruin (Jer. 31:15), stems from this view of her as a mother of sons.

In the Midrash Aicha Rabbah (opening section), Rachel acknowledges her bitter fate. She laments the years she spent waiting for Jacob and the sacrifices she made to preserve Leah's dignity, and asks for God's mercy; she is answered: "For Rachel I restore Israel to its place."

Scholars argue that stories in Genesis about the birth of Jacob's sons crystallized among tribes that traced their lines of descent to Rachel. This hypothesis can be strengthened in light of the fact that Rachel's character is emphasized and preferred to Leah's, both in explicit and cryptic references to her.

Rachel and Jacob meet for the first time near a well (Gen. 29:2–13). Before she reaches the well, she is called by name by shepherds and identified as Laban's daughter. In an emotional passage, Jacob kisses Rachel and weeps aloud while he reveals their family connections. Rachel wants to tell her father about Jacob's arrival. Rachel's beauty is described as a causal factor in the special, emotional attraction felt by Jacob; this attraction becomes entangled in relations between the sisters and the competition between them for Jacob. The difference in the daughters' appearances is implied in the negotiations between Laban and Jacob over the terms of work: "I will serve you seven years for your younger daughter Rachel," says Jacob (Gen. 29:18).

After the act of trickery (conferral of Leah in Rachel's stead), Jacob does not hesitate to work another seven years to win Rachel, who is to receive, after marriage, as her sister does, a maidservant.

Rachel's infertility is another obstacle in Jacob's path and explains why Rachel gave him her maidservant, Bilhah. There are hints of her infertility, such as the fact that she resorts to eating mandrakes in order to become pregnant. The mandrake image also foreshadows Joseph's heroic status in the biblical narrative, since mandrakes frequently figure in ancient folktales about the birth of cultural heroes.

In postbiblical literature, there is a debate as to whether Rachel ate the *madragora afficianrum* or its crushed root. Shevet Yissachar tends to believe the first possibility. Rachel's heart-wrenching request that she be given the roots, and her comment that she will never be blessed with children, recalls a Teutonic ritual in which the roots were used to fashion small statues of fortune tellers, which were called golden statuettes or gallows statuettes.

During the argument between Laban and Jacob, Rachel and Leah support their husband, not their father. They even complain about their father: "Are we not regarded by him as foreigners? For he has sold us, and he has been using up the money given for us" (Gen. 31:15). Out of a sense of having been discriminated against, and a determination to protect the sons' inheritance, Rachel steals her father's household gods (Gen. 31:19). The household gods were considered the most precious asset owned by the family.

In the Midrash, Rachel is said to have stolen the household gods not only as a way to cover Jacob's escape but also to purge her father's home of idols. Yet the curse that Jacob imposed on the head of the anonymous thief caused (according to the Midrash) Rachel's death a short time later, when she gave birth to Benjamin. And Rachel lied to her father when she said that she was unable to act because she was menstruating (*Pirqe de'Rabbi Eliezer* 39, *Tanḥuma v'yetze* 40, *Sefer ha'yashar* 103). But the Bible contains no denunciation of Rachel regarding her claim to the household gods. In the Zohar, Rachel is shown to have caused sorrow to her father by the theft of the gods, despite her good intentions; and so she is punished by not surviving to raise Benjamin.

Two traditions relate to Rachel's burial place. One version holds that she is buried north of Bethlehem, in Judea; the other places her in the land of Benjamin (Binyamin). Genesis (35:16–19) says: "And when they were still some distance from Ephrath . . . Rachel died, and she was buried on the way to Ephrath (that is, Bethlehem)."

But the tradition arose in the time of Saul that Rachel was buried in the territory of Benjamin: "When you depart from me today you will meet two men by Rachel's Tomb in the territory of Benjamin at Zelzah" (1 Sam. 10:2). The tradition placing Rachel's tomb near Bethlehem is accepted by Christianity and has taken precedence over the one involving Benjamin's tribes.

Jewish collective memory reserves a special place for Rachel, due to two prominent topics in the Book of Genesis: Jacob's deep love for her, as a result of which he was willing to toil seven years, and then another seven years, for Laban; and her desperate yearning for, and love for, her children.

The biblical story accentuates both these aspects, the feminine and the maternal sides, of Rachel's character. Both are engraved in the collective memory, after having been relayed from generation to generation from the Bible's pronounced patriarchal standpoint. Jacob's love for Rachel is described; her love and expectations are neglected. In addition, the story of her infertility and overcoming it (the birth of Joseph and, later, Benjamin) is depicted along patriarchal lines. Rachel is described as being impatient and as lacking faith. She knows that her status depends entirely upon her fertility ("She said to Jacob: 'Give me children, or I shall die!'" [Gen. 30:1]). At the same time, the male viewpoint, which is based on solid faith, is stressed ("Am I in the place of God?" [Gen. 30:2]). Moreover, the biblical narrator hints at an ironic side of Rachel's situation: While she says she will die if she does not have children, her unwillingness to be satisfied with one attests to greed. This greed is viewed, elliptically, as the cause of her premature death.

In Jewish Folklore

In Jewish folktales, which continue to be relayed orally, Rachel's status is complex and sometimes fluctuates: She is sometimes seen as the defender of the Jewish people in times of distress. For example, in one tale, when the Temple is destroyed, the people cry to Elijah the Prophet, calling on him to pray for it. Elijah turns to the patriarchs, who refer the prophet to Rachel.

Rachel asks God to hear her plea, since she was not jealous of her sister, whereas he envies his people and has thus burned the temple. God gives Rachel a sign that the people will return to their land. Since then the people call on Rachel for help (Israel Folktale Archives, IFA 9960–Israel, Sefardi).

Rachel provides care to orphans (IFA 5377–Israel, Ashkenazi) and creates miracles; when Arabs attacked a guard (from the Burla family) at Rachel's Tomb, he hid in the tomb for three days. Every day, he found a jug of milk, which he drank; eventually he heard a voice telling him to return home. Since then, Arabs have not attacked the site, and barren women have gone there to pray (IFA 9940–Israel, Sefardi).

In addition to being sought by childless women (IFA 15.766 Israel–Ashkenazi), Rachel is connected in Jewish folklore to humorous anecdotes (IFA 18.299–Yemen, 16.068–Poland, 18.121–ibid.). Rachel's import in the collective memory inspired a number of modern poets to evoke her image in their works.

Aliza Shenhar

See also: Jacob (Ya'acov); Leah.

Bibliography

Bright, John. *Early Israel in Recent History.* London: SCM, 1956.

Fuchs, Esther. "For I Have the Way of Women: Deception, Gender and Ideology in Biblical Narrative." *Semeia* 42 (1988): 68–83.

Graves, Robert, and Raphael Patai. *Hebrew Myths.* London: Cassell, 1963.

Greenberg, M. "Another Look at Rachel's Theft of the Teraphim." *Journal of Biblical Literature* 81 (1962): 239–248.

Lapsley, J.E. "The Voice of Rachel: Resistance and Polyphony in Genesis 31.14–35." In *Genesis: A Feminist Companion to the Bible,* ed. Athalya Brenner, pp. 233–248. Sheffield, UK: Sheffield Academic Press, 1998.

Niditch, Susan. "Genesis." In *The Women's Bible Commentary,* ed. Carol A. Newsom and Sharon H. Ringe, pp. 10–25. Louisville, KY: Westminster/John Knox, 1992.

Sarna, M. Nahum. "Rachel." In *Encyclopedia Judaica,* vol. 13. Jerusalem: Keter, 1973.

RAMBAM (MAIMONIDES) (1138–1204)

Moses ben Maimon (known to English-speaking audiences as Maimonides and Hebrew-speaking audiences as Rambam) has held a key place in the history of Jewish thought, culture, and folklore. He was a rationalist, a man of Halakhah, a philosopher and leader, a chief authority on religious matters, an active participant in Jewish community institutions, and royal physician.

The *Mishneh Torah,* his fourteen-volume compendium of Jewish law, established him as the leading rabbinical authority of his time and quite possibly of all time. His philosophical masterpiece, the *Guide for the Perplexed,* is a sustained treatment of Jewish thought and practice that seeks to resolve the conflict between religious knowledge and secular. He also wrote medical treatises on a number of diseases and their cures.

The figure of Maimonides and his pivotal place in the history of the Jewish people are what invited so many stories about his ability and greatness. These stories demonstrate no uniformity of time source or compiler, are scattered in written sources, and continue to be recounted even now. The Israel Folktale Archives (IFA) at the University of Haifa contains 145 stories about Maimonides.

These stories have little to do with the content of his ideological and philosophical teaching. At best, the tales touch on the writing of his books by coloring the act with a mystical hue. For example, according to the stories, Maimonides wrote his *Guide for the Perplexed* after being kissed by the angel Gabriel and the *Mishneh Torah* while in seclusion in the cave of Rabbi Shimeon Bar Yoḥai, where he hid from medical colleagues who were jealous of his success. From time to time, Moses visited to check on his progress and assist him (IFA 198, 754).

However, for the most part the stories have no connection to reality or to the character of the historical figure of Maimonides. Interreligious conflict is pivotal to the stories about him, manifested in the professional confrontation in which Maimonides represents a figure of authority who wields practical power and can stand up to kings and enemies. Maimonides acted in the stories and in the reality of the Diaspora, in the framework of a persecuted minority's struggle with foreign rule.

Maimonides is indeed a legendary hero, but one who is specifically Jewish. As such, he deals not with wars or marriage to a princess; rather, he shields his community from the authorities and, owing to his status, has the king's ear.

Through the folktale, the image of Maimonides underwent an unexpected process of sanctification. Many stories glorify his image as a maker of miracles and a magician who possesses a marvelous knowledge. He saves himself from his pursuers and brings salvation to individuals and to the community, accomplishes a miraculous shortening of a journey by uttering the Tetragrammaton (four Hebrew letters for God), sketches a ship on the wall of his prison and disappears into it, burns enemies chasing him at the gates of Fez, turns himself into a lion and tears his foes apart, turns a cow into a slaughtered woman borne on the back of a butcher who had done the Jews harm, and revives a murdered boy and saves the Jewish community from a blood libel (IFA 991, 5663, 6128, 13453, 13951, 13953).

The peak of this process of sanctification is reached in the tale that brings together Rabbi Isaac Luria (Ha'Ari), founder of the Lurianic Kabbalah, and Maimonides and attributes to the latter kabbalistic and mystical wisdom. Although the dominant theme of the stories about him is his mystical wisdom, he also used rationality to solve problems.

But on the whole, in the shaping of the folktale the legend is stronger than the biographical facts. The model of the life of the hero that lies in the cultural consciousness imposes itself on such figures and transfers dominant traditional motifs from one cultural hero to another.

As far as historians know, there were no stories about Maimonides during his lifetime or shortly thereafter. The tales are mostly of later provenance, and any connection between them and his biography is exceedingly tenuous. The multiplicity of tales praising Maimonides attests to their centrality in the spiritual-cultural consciousness of Jewish society through the ages. From the stories developed folk beliefs and customs that continue to function.

Maimonides's grave in Tiberias served as a pilgrimage site. Worshippers went there to pray and make requests in the belief that the holiness of the man passes to his grave. Nonetheless, it bears note that today there is no massive pilgrimage to Maimonides's grave, nor is there a commemoration to mark the anniversary of his death, as is the case at the graves of other saints. Nor are there many stories of healing and miracles taking place at his grave. Today, at least in Israel, the image of Maimonides as scholar, rather than saint, is dominant.

In Cairo, however, faith in the restorative powers of the Rambam Synagogue has not waned. Until the 1950s, the synagogue had special rooms where childless couples could spend a night in the hope of gaining Maimonides's blessing. Some stories that are still told describe how people were cured at the well of Cairo's Rambam Synagogue (IFA 4104). Thus, Maimonides continues his work of healing even after death.

Maimonides's books (mainly his medical treatises) are considered sacred to this day, and folk belief maintains that they have the power to heal their owners and make them financially successful (IFA 9103).

Tamar Alexander

See also: Magic.

Bibliography

Alexander-Frizer, Tamar. *The Heart Is a Mirror: The Sephardic Folktale.* Detroit: Wayne State University Press, 2008.

Alexander, Tamar, and E. Romero, ed. *Erase una vez Maimonides: Cuentos tradicionales hébréos.* Cordova: Ediciones el Alemandro, 1988.

Avishur, Yitshak, ed. and trans. *In Praise of Maimonides: Folktales in Judeo-Arabic and Hebrew from the Near East and North Africa.* Jerusalem: Magnes, 1998 (in Hebrew).

Scholem, Gershom. "From Philosopher to Kabbalist (A Legend of the Kabbalist on Maimonides)." *Tarbitz* 6:3 (1935): 90–98 (in Hebrew).

Rappoport, Angelo Salomon (1871–1950)

Angelo Salomon Rappoport was a prolific scholar of European history, religion, and philosophy, who culminated his career with the publication of *Folklore of the Jews* (1937). Nine years earlier he produced the three-volume *Myth and Legend of Ancient Israel,* which gained new life in 1966, when eminent folklorist Raphael Patai annotated and introduced a new edition. Relating to his Jewish heritage, Rappoport also produced *Psalms in Life, Legend, and Literature* (1935) and translated many Yiddish, German, French, and Russian texts into English. Rappoport tied his study of Jewish folklore to his interest in Christian legends and theology and showed the interrelations of these traditions in books such as *Mediaeval Legends of Christ* (1934). Rappoport also believed that an appreciation of the richness of Jewish folklore by non-Jews will help combat anti-Semitism. In his folklore studies, Rappoport used ideas from the British "survival" school of cultural evolutionary theory as well as diffusionist thinking relating to the influence of Jewish migration on many cultures to answer questions regarding the origin and spread of Jewish folklore. Following the method of comparing international versions of folklore, he argued against an innate "psychic unity of civilization" by making a case for the distinctiveness of the folklore of the Jews among other cultures, while showing that this lore informed the heritage of many nations.

Early Life and Scholarship

Rappoport was born in Baturin, Ukraine, in 1871. He studied in Russia, Paris, and Berlin, receiving his Ph.D. He settled in England, where he became a naturalized British subject in 1898. He was commissioned by the Alliance Israélite Universelle to study the group following Jewish traditions called the Falashas in what was then Egypt and Abyssinia. Beginning in 1901, he held an academic post in modern languages and literatures at Birkbeck College in London before undertaking the co-editing of the twenty-five-volume *Historians' History of the World.* Although ranging widely in world history, his areas of specialty were modern Russia and France as well as ancient Israel and Egypt. He had other major editorial posts, including work on the *New Gresham Encyclopaedia,*

British Encyclopaedia, Twentieth-Century Russia, and *Illustrated Palestine.* He was active in the Zionist movement and was a delegate to several Zionist congresses.

Contributions to Folklore Studies

Following cultural evolutionary theory, Rappoport held that folklore expresses the "psychology of early man," which persists in contemporary civilization "by force of habit and tradition" and typically loses its original meaning in modern use (1937, 2). He applied this idea in his study of the superstitions of sailors (1928) in which he claimed that modern sailors have retained beliefs dating to pagan antiquity and Christian medievalism but are not aware of their origins. He hypothesized that the beliefs remained to warn sailors of danger or augur success. Rappoport included Jewish legends in this work regarding sea voyages and origin narratives on the sea. The evolutionary idea also appears in *Myth and Legend of Ancient Israel,* in which he claimed that "myths, legends and hero-tales, folktales or *Märchen*" are stories told for amusement or instruction in modern life, whereas they held ritual purposes in ancient times. It is a view that Patai hotly disputed in his introduction to an edition published in 1966. Folklore does not, in Patai's view, degenerate over time, and in the modern world it retains significant social and psychological functions.

In looking for a source of folklore among the Jews, Rappoport traced the development of Jewish folklore to ancient Israel at the time of the end of Jewish national life. This assertion is also disputed by Patai, who took Rappoport to task for excluding biblical sources and not fully appreciating the epochs of oral circulation of lore before it appears in written sources in the fourth century B.C.E. After Rappoport established the golden era of Jewish folklore, he posited its diffusion as Jews moved out of ancient Israel and influenced the lore and literature of other countries where they settled. He took special pains to show the Jewish influence upon Christian legends and the influence of rabbinic myths and legends on Muslim literature. As a result of this thesis that Jews contributed their lore to host countries as they moved, he had to deal with the evolutionary implication that they therefore would lose their distinctiveness in the process. Rappoport went against the cultural evolutionary claims of Victorian anthropologists such as John Sterling Kingsley that Jews represented a "backward race" because of their lack of development by pointing out modern ethical values developed by Jews. The most important one, Rappoport claimed, is their belief in one God. In an apparent answer to critics and anti-Semites who decried the superstitious character of Jews, Rappoport blamed "foreign influence since the Middle Ages . . . which in spite of ghetto walls penetrated into the Jewish communities" (1937, 4).

Rappoport extolled the pure strains of Jewish folklore in ancient Israel and their influence on great literature as well as on the lore of modern civilization while bemoaning the anti-modernism that could be discerned from the increasing "store of popular beliefs which that conservative race had been dragging along on its shoulders for centuries." He angrily bemoaned instances when "Slavonic and Teutonic pagan superstitions" force their way into "the Folklore of the Jews and are now being styled Jewish survivals of primitive Judaism" (1937, 4). Thus Rappoport's Zionist sentiment may be apparent before the establishment of the modern State of Israel when he stated in the introduction to *Folklore of the Jews,* "The Jews have been a wandering race and—alas—are still condemned to wander from clime to clime and from country to country, in spite of the trumpet-call of a return to their own which has resounded in recent times."

In his works, Rappoport resisted the evolutionary temptation to view New Testament Christianity as a replacement for the older Judaism. He used a relativistic argument to show their differences rather than view them in a single developmental line. Indeed, he pointed out the pagan sources of Christian belief, which distinguish Judaism from Christianity. Later scholars such as Patai were skeptical of this generalization. Their criticisms represent late twentieth-century folkloric concerns for ascertaining the function and performance of folklore in social and historical context rather than assuming that ancient uses of lore dictated later meanings.

Other contrasts can be made between Rappoport's survivalist approach to a common folklore of the Jews and the nationalistic belief in a Jewish cultural unity espoused by Nathan Ausubel or the functionalism of Jewish folklore in Judaism presented by Joshua Trachtenberg in *Jewish Magic and Superstition* (1939) around the same time that *Folklore of the Jews* appeared. The irony of Rappoport's work is that while applying evolutionary theory to Jewish folklore, he helped undermine its basic doctrines and opened inquiry into the structure, function, and performance of heavy influence of the folklore of the Jews on modern civilization.

Final Years

The outbreak of World War II disrupted Rappoport's prolific writings on history and culture. Working in France as the Nazis occupied the country in 1940, he joined the French resistance movement to produce anti-Nazi literature, but the Gestapo arrested him in December 1940. Weakened from prolonged imprisonment, Rappoport did not resume his scholarship after liberation. He spent the last years of his life in Paris before dying on June 2, 1950.

Simon J. Bronner

Bibliography

Rappoport, Angelo S. *The Folklore of the Jews.* London: Soncino, 1937.

———. *Medieval Legends of Christ.* London: Ivor Nicholson and Watson, 1934.

———. *Myth and Legend of Ancient Israel.* 3 vols. New York: Ktav, 1966.

———. *Psalms in Life, Legend, and Literature.* London: Centenary, 1935.

———. *Superstitions of Sailors.* London: Stanley Paul, 1928.

Utley, Francis Lee. "Review of *Myth and Legend of Ancient Israel* by Angelo S. Rappoport." *Journal of American Folklore* 80 (1967): 403–406.

Trachtenberg, Joshua. *Jewish Magic and Superstition.* New York: Behrman's Jewish Book House, 1939.

Rebekah

Rebekah (Heb. Rivka; the root meaning "cart" or "soft and pliant") is the daughter of Bethuel (Gen. 24:15), the sister of Laban (Gen. 24:29), the wife of Isaac (Gen. 24:67), and Abraham's niece (Gen. 24:15). She is described in the Bible as an ideal woman. "The maiden was very fair to look upon," Genesis states (Gen. 24:16) and alludes to her kind-heartedness and hospitable bearing (Gen. 24:18–19, 25). Scholars have noted that the story that relates how she became Isaac's wife (Gen. 24) underscores the vital importance of marriage within the family unit.

Folklore traditions before the Bible feature courting-engagement motifs near wells. In them, the future groom (or his representative) travels to a foreign land, which is apparently a metaphor symbolizing the emotional journey he will make in relations with his future bride. The man meets a woman or women around the well, which is a feminine symbol of fertility. Drawing water from the well symbolizes male-female relations, as well as host-guest contact. After the newcomer's arrival is known, he is invited to the woman's house until terms of the betrothal are arranged.

The most elaborate presentation of this motif arises in the meeting between Rebekah and Abraham's servant (Gen. 24:10–61), yet the well theme can also be found in a scene between Jacob and Rachel (Gen. 29: 1–20) and Moses and Zipporah (Exod. 2:15–21).

The archetypal well scene between Rebekah and Abraham's servant features many of the key components of the oral story-telling tradition. First there is a trio—three men, two of them elderly and one young man—who understand that a mate must be found for the young man (Isaac) before his mother, Sarah, passes away. Also, the repetition of various water-drinking and washing rituals in this passage is consistent with oral story traditions. However, the scene is atypical in that it is Rebekah, and not the newcomer male, who draws water from the well; and she does so not for her intended fiancé but, rather, for his delegate. The groom, who is absent during the scene, is indeed the most passive of the patriarchs. In contrast, Rebekah, the designated fiancée, is distinctive for her intense, vigorous, and purposeful character. In four short passages (Gen. 24:16, 18–20) she is credited with eleven actions (she fills the jar, lets down the jar, gives a drink, draws water for camels, and so on). She effectively dominates the scene of her engagement.

The scene describing Rebekah's conferral to Isaac as a wife in the presence of Abraham's emissary makes prominent mention of her brother Laban and her mother. Missing, however, is her father Bethuel. Traditional commentators speculated that in local custom, the father ended his daughter's virginity before her betrothal. On this theory, after giving his consent to Rebekah's engagement to Isaac, Bethuel would have created a scandal, had he not died suddenly. Some wrote that Bethuel, as king of Haran, would have insisted on his right "to the first night" with every bride. When Rebekah reached the age of marriage, all rulers of the land gathered together and decided that if Bethuel did not act toward his daughter as the rulers behaved toward their own daughters, they planned to slay both father and daughter (*Masechet Sofrim* 21, 9; *Masekhet Nida* 5:4, *Yalqut Bereshit* 109).

The Midrash relates that Isaac was on his way home from heaven when a convoy arrived from Hebron. Rebekah saw him walking alongside it and was stunned; she fell off a camel and onto a fallen tree. Abraham counseled Isaac to verify whether she was a virgin, after having made such a long journey with his servant Eliezar. Isaac discovered that she was not a virgin, but Rebekah insisted that her state resulted from her fall upon the tree. She even showed Isaac the blood of her deflowering upon the tree, which had been watched by birds (*Yalqut Bereshit* 109, *Midr. Hagadol Bereshit* 366, 369–379; *Midr. Aggadah Bereshit* 59–60; *Hadar Zkenim* 9–11).

Genesis 26 describes Isaac's relations with Abimelech, king of the Philistines, and the danger posed to Rebekah before she disguises herself as her husband's brother. This story resembles that of Sarah and the Egyptian pharaoh, and Sarah and Abimelech. Isaac relates to Rebekah as though she were his "sister," as happened in the case of Abraham and Sarah in the presence of the same king, Abimelech, in the same location. The reason: Isaac worries that people in the area will take note of Rebekah's beauty. Abimelech looks out a window and sees "Isaac caressing his wife Rebekah" (Gen. 26:8). The king realizes he has been fooled and complains to Isaac: "What is this you have done to us? One of the men might well have slept with your wife, and you would have brought guilt upon us" (Gen. 26:10).

As in the experiences of Sarah and Rachel, Rebekah is described as infertile for a prolonged period. After twenty years of marriage she is blessed by God (Gen. 25:21) and gives birth to twins (Gen. 25:26). Like the other two women, she gives birth only to sons.

Legends hold that during her pregnancy, while Rebekah was passing by a Canaanite religious site, Esau tried to leave her womb. When she passed by a place of worship of true believers of God, Jacob tried to leave the womb. During birth, Esau ripped her womb, and so Rebekah was no longer able to have children (*Ber. Rab.* 110; *Seder Eliyahu Zuta* 26–27; *Tanḥuma ki tetze* 4). These tales continue to be told orally by Jews (see, e.g., Israel Folktale Archives [IFA 18.976 Poland]).

The image of conflict in the womb between sons also reoccurs. In this connection, there is the question of why in the Torah it is written: "The children struggled together within her" (Gen. 25:22). It has been said that Jacob studied all of the Torah while still in his mother's womb. But if he was so virtuous, why did he "struggle"? One answer is that the Torah is indeed good for Jacob, but so long as Esau is by his side it has no beneficial effect (IFA 20.054 Israel, Ashkenazi).

Rebekah sides with her preferred son, Jacob, during his struggle with his twin brother after they reach maturity. She takes the initiative, urges Jacob to cunningly seize the father's blessing from Esau; thus, the mother plays an active part in deceiving the blind father, Jacob (Gen. 27:8–17). She also slyly helps Jacob flee to Haran, to escape Esau's wrath.

The Bible says nothing of Rebekah's death. In contrast, the death of Deborah, Rebekah's nurse, who arrived with her from Haran, is described (Gen. 35:8). According to Genesis 49:31, Rebekah is buried in the Cave of the Patriarchs (Machpelah).

Commentators lavishly praise Rebekah, particularly her righteousness. One source refers to her wondrous effects on a spring and on the women who visited it (*Ber. Rab.* 60:6). Isaac also acknowledges her righteousness: "All the days when Sarah was alive, a cloud graced her tent, and its doors were open to prosperity. . . . When she died, that ended; but when Rebekah arrived, everything returned (*Ber. Rab.* 60:16).

Aliza Shenhar

See also: Isaac.

Bibliography

Alter, Robert. *The Art of Biblical Narrative.* New York: Basic Books, 1981.
Freedman, David R. "A New Approach to the Nuzi Sistership Contract." *Journal of the Ancient Near Eastern Society of Columbia University* 2 (1970): 77–85.
Graves, Robert, and Raphael Patai. *Hebrew Myths.* London: Cassell, 1963.
Holt, John Marshall. *The Patriarchs of Israel.* Nashville: Vanderbilt University Press, 1964.
Niditch, Susan. "Genesis." In *The Women's Bible Commentary,* ed. Carol A. Newsome and Sharon H. Ringe, pp. 10–25. Louisville, KY: Westminster/John Knox, 1972.
Sandnel, Samuel. *The Enjoyment of Scripture.* New York: Oxford University Press, 1972.
Sarna, Nachum M. *Understanding Genesis.* New York: Schocken, 1966.
Tennbal, Savin. *Sarah the Priestess.* Athens, OH: Swallow Press, 1984.
Thompson, Thomas L. *The Historicity of the Patriarchal Narratives.* Berlin: Walter de Gruyter, 1974.

Reshumot

The periodical *Reshumot* (Chronicles) was established to collect and study Jewish folklore and folklife. The periodical experienced two life cycles. It was founded in 1918 in Odessa by Alter Druyanow, who was joined by Haim Nachman Bialik and Yeshoshua Ḥone Ravnitzky. The title pages of volumes 1–4 stated that the periodical was edited by Druyanow with the participation of Ravnitzky and Bialik. Only the first volume was published in Odessa, by the publisher Moriah; it was reprinted in Tel Aviv by Dvir. Five more volumes were published between 1918 and 1930 by Dvir. In the first life cycle, six volumes of *Reshumot* appeared. Druyanow retired from the journal's editorial board after the publication of volume 4. Volumes 5 and 6 were edited by Bialik and Ravnitzky.

The goal of *Reshumot* was clearly stated in the editors' preface to volume 1: It was to be an organ for research and study of the life of the Jewish people and its folklore and for the collection and assembly of such materials. The editors thereby hoped to involve the general public, from whom was required "not excessive expertise and no particular literary talent, but a measure of understanding of the subject, some warmth towards it, and a little good-will."

The editors appealed to anyone who held the people and its culture close to their hearts to send materials to *Reshumot.* The sentences opening volume 1 describe the trials and tribulations of publication and express the editors' commitment to carry on. The appeal to readers is emotional, ending with the declaration: "We must make haste to deliver from the teeth of annihilation everything that can be saved." The periodical was planned to contain six sections: Ways of Life, Faith and Religion, Language and Literature, Art and Poetry, Historic Documents, and Miscellaneous. Each section had its own subdivisions. For example, Ways of Life included accounts of remote communities, famous people, livelihood and crafts of Jews, special foods, and dress. The details of the sections and the areas of interest were printed at the beginning of every volume of *Reshumot.*

The structure of the volumes of this first series was consistent, including features on the Diaspora, memoirs, customs, texts, and letters. The slight differences arose from the nature of the subject-matter that was collected and assembled. Volume 3 is exceptional: It is devoted to the decimation of the Jews of Russia, principally Ukraine. Druyanow dedicated this volume to Bialik on his fiftieth birthday.

The second cycle of *Reshumot* (*Reshumot–New Series*) appeared from 1945 to 1953. The editors were Yom-Tov Lewinsky and Dov Shtok (Sadan), except for the sixth and final volume, which was edited by Lewinsky and Yoḥanan Tversky. The new series too was published by Dvir.

Influenced by their predecessors, the editors of the new series continued the work of collection, fully aware of the central place of folklore and ethnography in Jewish culture. In his Preface to volume 1 of the new series, "On the Renewal of *Reshumot,*" Shtok praises the three editors of the first series. Out of commitment to the founding trio and in recognition of the magnitude of the enterprise, he expresses his sense of "veneration of grandeur" in light of the new beginning of publication of the journal.

Shtok resolved that the new series, unlike the first one, would center on only three areas—memoirs, ethnography, and folklore—and would not continue to include subjects unrelated to these three domains, which by then had found their own forum.

The sections covered in the new series were: "chronicles of the remnant of Jewish communities at the time of the destruction of the European Exile; monographs of personalities and types in the life of various communities and groups; ethnography, customs and communities, folk proverbs and sayings of different tribes, in the various Jewish languages and in different dialects, folk poems and melodies, collections of tales that may shed light on the nooks and crannies of the life of the people or of persons that were an expression of the life and spirit of the people; collection of ethnographies and folklore scattered in books and published collections, bibliography of what has been published in the field of this forum, chronicles," as stated in the opening sentence of the first issue in the new series.

The practical structure of the volumes consisted of generally permanent sections, according to the plan devised by Shtok. Among others, the section headings were: "From the Turmoil" (accounts of the destruction of communities), "Characters and Recollections," "Passages on Way of Life," "Documents and Notebooks," "Folk Proverbs," and "Folksongs."

Although Dov Shtok resolved that the focal point of the periodical was to be the Diaspora, "the continued extension of the threads of folklore" through "the existence and the life of the Settlement" in the Land of Israel would also be reflected in the new series. *Reshumot* can be seen to a large extent as the realization of Bialik's project for cultural revival in Eretz Israel, a compilation program (*Tokhnit Ha'Kinus*) to collect and preserve the cultural production of past generations in Hebrew translation. The compilation project was also to include folklore. *Reshumot,* as a periodical dedicated to folklore and published in Hebrew, was the expression of Zionist folklorists to collect and publish folklore materials in Hebrew for the future generations.

Haya Bar-Itzhak

See also: Bialik, Haim Nachman; Druyanow, Alter; Lewinski, Yom-Tov; Sadan, Dov.

Bibliography

Bar-Itzhak, Haya. *Pioneers of Jewish Ethnography and Folkloristics in Eastern Europe.* Ljubljana: Studia Mythologica Slavica–Supplementa, Scientific Research Center of the Academy of Science and Arts, 2010.

Resurrection

See: Afterlife; Angel of Death

Riddles

Riddles are one of the oldest genres in Jewish folklore, beginning with the Bible. The riddle is a gnomic, playful genre, consisting of a witty question (e.g., in the form of an image) and a suitable solution. In a true riddle, the clues for the solution are contained within the question itself, whereas the solution in "neck riddles" relies on extratextual information, to which the solver has no initial access. Riddling games involve two parties—one that poses the question, and the other that solves it.

Riddles in the Bible

Wisdom literature in the Bible (Psalms, Proverbs) may contain remnants of riddles (*ḥidot*), and riddles are also mentioned in relation to parables (Habakkuk 2:6) and divine revelation (Num. 12:8). However, the riddle as an explicit genre appears only twice in the biblical texts.

Samson, at the wedding banquet, presents the guests with a neck riddle (i.e., a riddle to which only the person posing the riddle knows the answer since it is based on his/her private experience; such riddles are typical of stories in which solving a riddle is a matter of life and death). "Out of the eater came something to eat, out of the strong came something sweet" (Judg. 14:14). And it is to his persistent wife that Samson finally divulges the answer "What is sweeter than honey, and what is stronger than a lion?" (ibid., 18). Here, the riddle plays a key role in the unfolding of the plot, as do the riddles that are mentioned as the core of the meeting between King Solomon and the Queen of Sheba (1 Kgs. 10:1–13).

In both instances, the riddle figures in an encounter in which cultural and sexual boundaries are at stake:

In the Samson tale, it is clearly a matrimonial setting whereas the erotic character of the meeting between Solomon and the foreign queen who comes to "test him with riddles" is only alluded to.

Riddles in Midrash

In the case of the riddles of the queen of Sheba, Scripture does not mention the content of the riddles themselves. The Midrash takes it upon itself to fill in the scriptural gaps by specifying the riddles and by intensifying the erotic aspect of the encounter. The second Aramaic translation to the Book of Esther (ch. 3) lists three of the riddles, and the Midrash on Proverbs (1:1) contains an elaborate riddling tale consisting of four consecutive riddles. In the first riddle, the queen asks: "Seven exit and nine enter, two pour and one drinks," to which the king replies: "Surely, seven days of menstruation exit and nine months of pregnancy enter, two breasts pour and the baby drinks." The riddling tale then progresses from issues pertaining to the identity of the fetus/baby to sexual and gendered identities culminating in the national identity when Solomon distinguishes between Israelites and gentiles.

Eleven riddles appear in an earlier midrashic work (*Lam. Rab.* 1) prompted by the first verse in Lamentations, "How does the city sit solitary, that was full of people (*rabbati am*). . . . She that was great among the nations (*rabbati bagoyim*)." The repetition of the word *rabbati* is understood by the rabbis to refer to the wisdom of the Jerusalemites vis-à-vis the Athenians. This wisdom is in turn expressed in the series of riddles, or riddle-related anecdotes, in which the superiority of the now desolate people is played out.

In the first riddling tale, a Jerusalemite arrives in Athens in order to claim an inheritance that his father had entrusted to a local man. After pulling off some tricks, the son succeeds in locating that person and after dishing out the five young birds that were served for dinner in an enigmatic manner—which he explains—he is allowed to return home with his father's belongings. The second tale tells of four men of Jerusalem who went to Athens and stayed with a certain man who, having heard of the great wisdom of the Jerusalemites, decides to eavesdrop while the men are in their room. The first man is not deceived and recognizes that the bed that he was given is damaged; the second notes that the meat they had eaten tasted like dog meat; the third that the wine they had drunk had the taste of a grave. The fourth man exclaims: "Is it any wonder? The man himself, the proprietor, is not the son of his father." Upon hearing this, the host investigates their assertions, only to learn that they were indeed right on all counts. Thus this story establishes the superiority of the Jerusalemites while casting doubt on the very premise of the Athenian's identity.

Humor, playfulness, and wit—coupled with morbid themes—characterize the string of eleven tales, rendering them an especially powerful cultural tool in the face of the puzzling theological and political crisis following the destruction of the Second Temple. It is in the riddle that calls for a (temporary) mixing of categories, for a chaotic disruption of a structured universe, with its appeasing and fleeting solution, that the sense of loss can both be expressed and as if overcome. And it is by telling these riddles that the fantasized world where the historically vanquished Jews overshadow their Hellenistic oppressors comes into being.

Riddles in Later Periods

An entirely different cultural and intellectual milieu gave rise to emblem riddles (named after the enigmatic picture to which they refer), a subgenre of the literary riddle that enjoyed great popularity in Italy and the Netherlands of the seventeenth century. Serving at different festivities, this literary genre—albeit distinct from "folk" riddles—bears similarities to the latter, namely in its social function in riddling contests at weddings.

Modern Hebrew folktales contain numerous riddling-tales with varying degrees of culturally specific markers. One such tale is of Moroccan origin, about the medieval Torah commentator Abraham ibn Ezra, who, disguised as a bishop, provides the king with satisfactory answers to the questions he poses. To the king's second question "How much am I worth?" he answers "ten pounds," explaining that it is more than he had paid for a crucifix. After disclosing his true identity—as an answer to the third question—Abraham ibn Ezra not only earns a handsome reward but also the king's esteem for the greater Jewish community (an oicotype of AT 922 *The Shepherd Substituting for the Priest Answers the King's Questions*).

Dina Stein

Bibliography

Camp, Claudia V., and Carole R. Fontaine. "The Words of the Wise and Their Riddles." In *Text and Tradition: The Hebrew Bible and Folklore,* ed. Susan Niditch, pp. 127–151. Atlanta: Society of Biblical Literature, 1990.

Hasan-Rokem, Galit. *Web of Life: Folklore and Midrash in Rabbinic Literature.* Stanford: Stanford University Press, 2000.

Noy, Dov. *A Tale For Each Month* (English summary, 272–273). Jerusalem: Hebrew University, 1976–77 (in Hebrew).

Pagis, Dan. *A Secret Sealed: Hebrew Baroque Emblem-Riddles from Italy and Holland* (English summary, pp. v–xvii). Jerusalem: Magnes, 1986 (in Hebrew).

———. "Towards a Theory of the Literary Riddle." In *Untying the Knot: On Riddles and Other Enigmatic Modes,* ed. Galit Hasan-Rokem and David Shulman, pp. 81–108. New York and Oxford: Oxford University Press, 1996.

Stein, Dina. "A King, a Queen and the Riddle Between." In *Untying the Knot: On Riddles and Other Enigmatic Modes,* ed. Galit Hasan-Rokem and David Shulman, pp. 125–147. New York and Oxford: Oxford University Press, 1996.

ROMANIA, JEWS OF

The Jewish population in Romania according to the 1930 census was 759,000. In 1940, Romania was forced to yield northern Transylvania, where 150,000 Jews lived, to Hungary. As of 2010, there were between 7,000 and 8,000 Jews living in Romania; the majority of Jews of Romanian descent (approximately 400,000) live in Israel. Thus, the Jewish folk traditions of Romania are preserved mostly among the elderly immigrants to Israel, where those traditions underwent changes in their new context.

Origin of the Romanian Jews

The majority of the Romanian Jews were part of the community of East European Ashkenazim. But unlike the rest of Eastern Europe, Romania was under Ottoman rule until the 1870s. In addition, the southern Romanian province of Muntenia was home not only to Ashkenazi Jews but to a small community of Sephardim (descendants of Jews expelled earlier from Spain and Portugal).

Romanian Jews, as a distinct community, emerged relatively recently, in line with the history of Romania as a political entity. Muntenia (or Walachia, a denomination sometimes applied to both Romanian duchies) and Moldavia, which had been separate countries, were united as one state in 1859. After World War I, other regions—Transylvania, Bukovina, and Bessarabia, which had a population that was mainly Romanian—joined them to become part of what historians call "Greater Romania." Of these, Moldavia was the great reservoir of Romanian-Jewish folk traditions.

Jews began to settle in the Romanian duchies in the sixteenth century, most of them coming from Poland and Russia; Muntenia became home to Sephardic Jews migrating from the Ottoman Empire and Ashkenazi Jews from the outskirts of Hungary as well as from Poland and Russia via the neighboring countries, especially the then-independent Moldavia. Successive waves of religiously observant settlers from Poland and Russia, who had come at the request of Moldavian landowners and princes who wanted to increase the number of taxpayers and thereby improve the economic fortunes of the area, led to a strengthening in religious faith among Moldavian Jews during the eighteenth century and the first decades of the nineteenth century. Each group of these immigrants, called "Hrisoveliţi" Jews, settled on the basis of a contract called a *hrisov*, which stipulated the right of the newcomers to build a house of prayer, a ritual bath (*mikveh*), and a cemetery for the community.

Not only did the newcomers initiate and develop commercial activity in certain towns, but they helped spur urbanization. They opened markets on the land they rented from boyars (upper nobility), and those markets soon attracted people from surrounding areas, turning villages into small towns. For more than a century, such towns, the local version of the East European shtetl, developed a dense Jewish population, becoming a stronghold of *Yiddishkeit*. The Jewish population of Moldavia increased suddenly during the first half of the nineteenth century, mainly due to those fleeing Russia not only to escape forced conscription into the tsarist army but also to improve their economic circumstances. Among the materials held by the Israel Folktale Archives (IFA 8915) is a tale of the humble odyssey of a five-year-old boy during the reign of Nicholas I, when even small Jewish children were taken by force into the army, in order to estrange them from their people and creed. Most of these immigrants were poor, and many arrived in Moldavia crossing the border illegally.

By contrast, such small towns with a dense Jewish population did not exist in Muntenia. Jews there were integrated into the surrounding non-Jewish population. In large towns, they lived near the synagogues, but amid the secular mentality of the city.

The Influence of Hasidism

The Hasidic movement began in Eastern Europe as a Jewish sect focused around Israel ben Eliezer, called the Ba'al Shem Tov (1700–1760). Romanian Jews and non-Jews alike believe that he lived in northern Romania, in Maramureş, though there are some who believe it was Podolia. The present oral tradition of Romanian Jews retains few legends traceable to the first stage of Hasidism. One of these legends points to the period of seclusion of the founder of Hasidism in the Carpathian mountains. A peasant who had followed the Ba'al Shem Tov approaches him and says:

> "I know you are a man sent by God. I pray you, bless me."
> "What blessing do you want me to bestow on you?"
> "I would like to have children." . . .
> "I'll grant your request."

In another legend, relevant for what may be called the ideology of early Hasidism, the Ba'al Shem Tov displays the faculty of floating on water. This miraculous faculty is bestowed by God not only on the Ba'al Shem Tov but

Talmud Torah school in Siget-Maramureş, Romania, ca. 1930. *(YIVO Institute, New York)*

also on an ignorant Jew (who cannot even pronounce correctly the creed of Judaism, the "Shema") as a reward for his unadulterated faith. Both of them, the Ba'al Shem Tov and the ignoramus, comfortably seated on pieces of cloth, slide on the surface of a river, as if they were being carried in boats. This legend is part of a series of legends expressing the hostility of the poor and half-literate Jews toward the oligarchy of the rich and the rabbis.

In its first stage, the movement opposed rabbinic authority in many ways; singing and dancing, disapproved by rabbis, were encouraged by early Hasidism and were regarded as a means of worshipping God. In the first half of the nineteenth century, the legends about the Ba'al Shem Tov were gradually replaced by narratives corresponding to a radical shift in Hasidism. From a persecuted sect, Hasidism had turned into a widespread current, shaping the pattern of community life and the style of leadership in large segments of East European Jewry. The movement branched into local centers, each center having its own leader, the *tzaddik*, who in time founded a dynasty, maintained a large household (a so-called court), and exerted his influence over a geographic area. The fact that, in the first half of the nineteenth century, part of the Moldavian-Jewish community came under the sway of Rabbi Yisruel fun Rizhyn (Russia) is substantiated by testimony included in the diary of two missionaries.

In the second half of the nineteenth century, the descendants of Rabbi Yisruel, known by the family name Friedman, founded Hasidic courts in Moldavia. Among these courts, those of Stefăneşti and Buhuşi attracted not only crowds of Moldavian Jews but also less observant Ashkenazi Jews from Muntenia. Even a significant number of non-Jewish Romanians were among the visitors to the Stefăneşti and Buhuşi courts. The legends about the Stefăneşti and Buhuşi courts relate to what was called Hasidic hagiography, produced during the dynastic stage of the movement. Some Moldavian-Jewish legends acquired local color by referring to historic events and their echoes among the surrounding Jewish and non-Jewish population, for example, the 1877 War of Independence against the Turks or the two world wars. The dignified and lenient approach of the Friedmans to their visitors explains in part why in Romania Hasidism remained influential beyond 1870, the year Simon Dubnow considers the beginning of the decline of tzaddikism.

The Emergence of Romanian Jewry

In the first half of the nineteenth century, while in Muntenia the acculturation of the Jews was well advanced, in Moldavia only the Jews who had immigrated long since and those who had settled on the basis of a contract blended into the local population. By contrast, those who had come more recently from Russia knew little Romanian and remained more culturally distinct. The first mark of acculturation was that the Yiddish spoken in both Romanian duchies replaces certain words of German or Slavic origin with Romanian words. After the two Romanian duchies joined in 1859, especially toward the end of the century, Jews in Moldavia increasingly migrated to Muntenia and melted into the Ashkenazi Jewish community there, adopted its ways of thinking, became fluent in Romanian, and became acculturated, because of contact with their co-religionists and the surrounding non-Jewish townspeople. In the last two decades of the nineteenth century, the variegated

Jewish community of both duchies began to merge into a relatively distinct Romanian Jewish community.

Soon this incipient community produced a distinguished elite. Some of these intellectuals devoted their energies to the study of the history and traditions of Romanian Jews and to the fight for their emancipation, while scholars like Moses Gaster and L. Şăineanu, during their stay in Romania, contributed to Jewish studies but mainly to Romanian philology and folklore. Polish and Lithuanian Jews looked on Romanian Jews as a peripheral community, with no pedigree and no long-standing centers of Jewish studies. With certain exceptions, until the final decades of the nineteenth century, Romanian Jews could not claim a noticeable contribution to scholarly Judaism. Their praiseworthy qualities lay elsewhere.

Romanian Jews had a taste for music and art that became well developed. Through their professions (innkeepers, grain and wine merchants, etc.), Moldavian Jews became well acquainted with the music of the peasantry. Romanian folk music inspired the type of Yiddish song called "*vulebel*" and left an imprint on the Hasidic repertoire that incorporated motifs of the Romanian *doina*. Romanian Jews also contributed to the development of Yiddish folk genres and Yiddish literature, frowned on as secular and impious by religious circles in many East European Jewish communities (e.g., Benjamin Wolf Ehrenkrantz's parodies of rabbis). Playwright Abraham Goldfaden (1840–1908) was received with enthusiasm by Romanian Jews, prompting him to expand his theatrical sketches into full-length comedies and in 1876 to found, in Iaşi (Jassy), the first Yiddish theater. Although Romanian Jews increasingly expressed themselves in Romanian, they continued to use Yiddish. A revival of Yiddish literature took place in Iaşi, on the eve of World War I and especially between the two world wars (when Bessarabia and Bukovina were reintegrated into Greater Romania).

Romanian Jews During World War II

Embittered by their forced retreat from Bessarabia and Bukovina (annexed by the Soviet Union in the Molotov-Ribbentrop pact) and instigated by rumors that the Jews were working hand in glove with the Soviet invasion force, Romanians took their revenge on their Jews and allied with the Nazis. The few Jews serving in the Romanian army were shot in the summer of 1940 at Dorohoi in Moldavia. These killings were the prelude to two cruel barbaric crimes against the Jews. At Iaşi, on June 29, 1941, a pogrom was perpetrated in the court (yard) of the police by Romanians and Germans, in which some 8,000 were killed initially; on July 2, 1941 in Iaşi, thousands of Jews were locked by the Romanians in the death trains, in which most of them died of thirst, starvation, and suffocation. The total number of victims in Iaşi has been variously estimated by the Romanian government and the Jewish community, the latter of which believes the toll was some 15,000. The few survivors were saved by a courageous Romanian woman, Viorica Agarici, chair of the local Red Cross, who became a legendary character for Moldavian Jews. At Bucharest on January 21–23, 1941, a densely populated Jewish district was plundered and devastated. The synagogue was set on fire, and 120 Jews were tortured and killed by the Iron Guard, a fascist terrorist organization. In 1941 began the deportation of categories of Jews from different towns and certain regions to Transnistria. It is difficult to estimate exactly how many Romanian Jews were killed at Transnistria.

In Transnistria proper, the deaths of Jews were mainly caused by typhus, cold, and hunger. Despite the miserable conditions of life imposed upon them, more than anything the Romanian Jews from Transnistria feared being sent to the area on the other side of the Bug river, which was under Nazi administration, where deportees were immediately killed. At least some of the Romanian deportees survived and returned to Romania. In Romania, more than half the Jews survived World War II.

Monica Bratulescu

See also: Languages, Jewish.

Bibliography

Ancel, Jean. "The Jassy Syndrome." *Romanian Jewish Studies* 1:1 and 2 (Winter 1987: 36–38).

———. *Transnistria: The Romanian Mass-Murder Campaigns.* Tel Aviv: Goren-Goldstein Research Center, Tel Aviv University, 2003.

Bonar, Andrew A., and Rob M. M'Cheyne. *Narrative of a Mission of Inquiry to the Jews from the Church of Scotland in 1839.* Edinburgh: Presbyterian Board of Publication, 1844.

Dubnow, Simon. *Geschichte des Chassidismus.* 2 vols. Reprint, Jerusalem: Jewish Publishing House, 1969.

Eskenazy, Victor. *Izvoare si marturii referitoare la evreii din România I* (Sources and Testimonies Concerning the Jews in Romania I). Bucharest: Federatia Comunitatilor Evreesti din Republica Socialista Romană, 1986.

Gries, Zeev. "Hasidism: The Present State of Research and Some Desirable Priorities." *Numen* 34:1 (1987): 96–108.

Ioanid, Radu. "The Fate of the Romanian Jews Under the Antonescu Regime: Statistical Data, Preliminary Conclusions." In *The Jews in the Romanian History,* vol. 1, pp. 201–203. Silex, Bucharest: Institute of History N. Iorga and the Goren-Goldstein Research Center Diaspora Institute, Tel Aviv University, 1999.

Liptzin, Sol. "Yiddish Literature in Rumania." *Jewish Book Annual* 27 (1969): 13–19.

Platon, Gh. "Populatia evreiasca din targurile si orasele

Moldovei la mijlocul secolului XIXIea" (Jewish population of Moldavian villages and towns in the mid XIX century). *Studia et Acta Judeorum Historiae, Romanii.* 1998.

Saineanu, L. *Studiu Dialectologic asupra graiului evreo-german* (Study of German-Jewish dialects). Bucharest: Wiegrand, 1889.

Schwarzfeld, E. *Din istoria Evreilor Impopularea, reimpopularea şi intemeierea tîrgusoarelor in Moldova* (A history of Jewish settlement, re-settlement and beginnings of small merchant towns in Moldova). Bucharest: Editura Evreilor Pamînteni, 1914.

Tufescu, Victor. *Iasii şi oraşele din Nordul Moldovei* (Iasii and other towns of Northern Moldavia). Chişinău: Cartea Româna, 1932.

ROSH ḤODESH

See: Month

ROSH HA'SHANA

Rosh Ha'Shana (ראש השנה, New Year) is the name of the festival that celebrates the Jewish New Year and a tractate in the Mishnah dealing with this festival. In biblical times, Rosh Ha'Shana was observed for only one day, but in modern times it is observed for two days, both in the Diaspora and in the Land of Israel. However, in some Reform congregations only one day is observed.

It is a day of prayer, supplication, and atonement, and together with Yom Kippur is celebrated by the vast majority of Jews. Even secular Jews are encouraged to participate in some kind of ritual service.

According to the Midrash Rosh Ha'Shana 1:1, four days of the year are regarded as New Year's days for different purposes. The first of the month of Nisan marks the New Year's days for dating the reigns of Jewish kings and the order of the months for religious purposes. In the time of the Temple, the first of Elul was the New Year for cattle tithes, for cattle born in the preceding year. The first of Tishrei is the New Year for the civil calendar, and for the sabbatical and jubilee years. The fifteenth of Shevat (or, according to the Beit Shammai school of thought, the first of Shevat) is the New Year for trees (the holiday is called Tu Be'Shevat, Tu being Hebrew for "fifteen"). However of these four dates, only the first of Tishrei is mentioned in the Bible as a festival: "A Sabbath, a memorial of the sounding of the shofar" (Lev. 23:23–24) and "A day of sounding the shofar" (Num. 29:1–6), although no mention is made of its being a New Year's day. It is also the only one celebrated as a religious festival, since rabbinical tradition has it that on that day "All who have entered into the world pass before Him [in judgment] like a flock of sheep (or a troop of soldiers sneak *numeron*)."

The most distinctive feature of the festival is the sounding of the shofar (ram's horn) during the *musaf* service. Symbolically, it serves to awaken the slumbering to ameliorate their ways (Maimonides, Teshuvah 3.4). The form of the ram's horn is bent to indicate to humans that they should bend their will to that of God (*b. Rosh Ha'Shana* 16a). It is held in the right hand and blown out of the right side of the mouth, as Gideon's rams' horns were held by his soldiers in their right hand in their battle against the Midianites (Judg. 7:20). Hence, the shofar also symbolizes a weapon used to combat the forces of evil. And, indeed, many strategies were utilized to neutralize Satan, who always wishes to sabotage the blowing of the shofar. It is for this reason that the shofar is blown in two sets of soundings, one when the congregation may be seated (*Tekiyot de'meyushav*) before *musaf*, which serve only to confuse Satan (*Levalbel et hasatan*) because they are not the real sounding, followed later by those during the *musaf* service, when the congregation stands (*Tekiyot de'me'umad*).

During this service three groups of prayers are included, each consisting of ten scriptural verses selected from the three sections of the Bible, each introduced with a passage compiled by Rav in the early third century C.E. The first, Malchuyot, describes the sovereignty of God. The second, Zichronot, speaks of God's remembering all His creatures and their deeds, good or otherwise, and the third, Shofarot, relates to the sounding of the shofar. After each section the shofar is sounded according to a fixed pattern (varying slightly according to the different rites). In all, 100 "soundings" (*kolot*) occur throughout the service.

In medieval times, the person who blew the shofar (*ba'al tekiyah*), according to Ashkenazi illuminated manuscripts, would place one foot upon a small footstall as he did so. This has been interpreted by scholars variously as a means of protecting him from the machination of Satan or as a way to cause the sounds to ascend the throne of glory more quickly.

In the Ashkenazi rite, worshippers wear white during the service as a symbol of the purity that they wish to attain. Additional customs are connected with this festival, such as eating apples dipped in honey on the first night, while a prayer is recited for a good and sweet year. In addition, the head of a sheep was placed on the table to be eaten, so that "we be as a head and not a tail" (*Shulḥan arukh, Oraḥ Ḥayyim* 583:2). Of special note is a custom that takes place in the afternoon of the first day of Rosh Ha'Shana (or, on the second, if the first falls on a Sabbath). In this custom, called Tashlikh, people go down to a river, seashore, or well, and while reciting a series of biblical verses, including Micah 7:19, "He will again have compassion upon us; He will subdue our iniquities; and you will cast all their sins in the depth of the sea," empty out their pockets, casting crumbs—

symbolizing sins—into the water. The custom in its present form first appears in the late Middle Ages in Germany, but has its origin in the Geonic period, and most likely has pagan antecedents. But mainly these were days of self-examination in preparation for the divine judgment of all mankind, for this day marks the beginning of the ten days of repentance culminating in Yom Kippur.

Daniel Sperber

See also: Food and Foodways; New Year Cards; Shofar.

Bibliography

Goodman, Philip, ed. *The Rosh Hashana Anthology.* Philadelphia: Jewish Publication Society of America, 1992.

Hakohen, Dvora, and Menachem Hakohen. *Haggim and Moadim: Rosh Ha-Shanah.* Jerusalem: Keter, 1978 (in Hebrew).

Lauterbach, Jacob Zallel. "Tashlich: A Study in Jewish Ceremonies." *Hebrew Union College Annual* 11 (1936): 207–340.

Sperber, Daniel. *Customs of Israel,* vol. 3. Jerusalem: Mossad Ha-Rav Kook, 1994 (in Hebrew).

———. *Customs of Israel,* vol. 7. Jerusalem: Mossad Ha-Rav Kook, 2003 (in Hebrew).

Russia, Jews of

The earliest Jewish settlements in Russia were in the region of the Caucasus Mountains and date as far back as 721 B.C.E. During the first half of the eighth century, the powerful Khazar kingdom adopted Judaism as its state religion. Jews have lived in Kiev and other areas of contemporary Ukraine since the ninth century. When the Lithuanians gained control over western areas of Russia in the fourteenth century, Jews were given economic privileges. Documentary evidence of the presence of Jews in Muscovite Russia is first found in the chronicles of 1471. During the 1470s, a religious sect known as "Judaizers" gained popularity among peasants in the Novgorod region. Some scholars suggest that the sect was called "Judaizers" in order to scare off potential members. Others suppose that the Jews had an influence on the sect doctrine. Repressions and restrictions against Jews followed. For example, Tsar Ivan IV ("the Terrible") ordered the drowning of all Jews who did not convert to Christianity in the sixteenth century. In 1648, anti-Jewish riots led by Bogdan Chmielnicki had a devastating effect on the Ukrainian-Jewish community. The memory of the Chmielnicki massacre remained an important part of Yiddish folk songs, legends, and stories.

The largest Jewish population came to live under the rule of the Russian Empire in the late eighteenth century, when partitions of Poland in 1772, 1793, and 1795 left areas of dense Jewish population under Russian jurisdiction. It is estimated that by the end of the eighteenth century, the Russian-Jewish population totaled around 1 million. In order to contain and manage the Jewish population, Tsarina Catherine II introduced the "Pale of Settlement," where the Jews were allowed to live in 1791. The borders of the Pale expanded in 1795 with the last partition of Poland and then were revised slightly several times in the nineteenth century. The majority of Russian Jews lived in the Pale at the outset of World War I, when it was abolished de facto, and then in 1917 it was abolished de jure by the provisional government.

During the nineteenth century, the Jewish population experienced unprecedented growth. In 1850, the Jews numbered over 2,350,000 and reached 5 million at the close of the nineteenth century. The economic position of Jews in the Pale was complicated. Jews were involved in industry, alcohol sales, and money-lending. In the 1860s, Jews were active in the emerging financial industry of the Russian Empire. Educational quotas enabled members of the Jewish bourgeoisie to enter Russian institutions of higher education and to gradually obtain permits to settle outside the Pale of Settlement. It is estimated that by the end of the nineteenth century, approximately 100,000 Jews lived in St. Petersburg and Moscow, Russia's largest cities.

In the first half of the nineteenth century, Russia annexed parts of contemporary Azerbaijan, Dagestan, and Chechnya, which were home to Mountain Jews, a non-Ashkenazi Jewish group. Their vernacular was Judeo-Tat, but they also had some knowledge of Hebrew, used in reading holy texts and religious services. By the mid-twentieth century, they numbered around 70,000. Gradually, Russian replaced Judeo-Tat in daily use. The most important literary heritage of the Mountain Jews is the national epic in Judeo-Tat, the *Shiraha* (the name probably is derived from the Hebrew *shirah* [poem]), which abounds in biblical associations and figures. No systematic work on collecting folklore among Mountain Jews was done until the late twentieth century.

Tsars of the nineteenth century had an ambivalent attitude toward the Jews. Nicholas I introduced the draft of Jews into the Russian army. While contemporary historians speak of the ambivalence of this legislation, pointing out that through service in the army, many Jews received opportunities to settle outside the Pale, to become better integrated into Russian politics and culture, and even to help other Jews in the Pale, yet Yiddish popular culture and memory display extremely negative attitudes toward the draft: The majority of the Yiddish folk materials, such as songs, short stories, and legends, portray despair, disappointment, and fear associated with conscription.

Culture

Jewish culture in the Pale was influenced largely by religious movements, such as Hasidism (especially popular in Ukraine) and mitnagdism (in Byelorussia and Lithuania). In the mid-nineteenth century, the forces of Jewish enlightenment (Haskalah) reached Russian Jews as well. As a result, a vibrant Yiddish, Hebrew, and Russian Jewish literary culture began to appear in the Russian Empire, written by the most important Jewish writers.

In 1881, after the assassination of Alexander II, government policies toward Jews became more restrictive. Quotas at institutions of higher education were reduced; laws that restricted Jewish economic activities, known as May Laws (1882), were introduced by his successor, Alexander III. Anti-Jewish riots (pogroms) that swept the country at the end of the nineteenth century, combined with the difficult economic position of the Jewry in the Pale, catalyzed the emigration of Jews from Russia to North America and other destinations as well as increased Jewish involvement in socialist, Zionist, and other political movements. During the reign of the last tsar, Nicholas II (1894–1917), the process of radicalization of the Jewish population in the Pale intensified, Jewish emigration increased, and the number of Jews living outside the Pale reached its highest level, reaching 300,000 by the eve of World War II.

The Study of Jewish Folklore

The economic, social, and even religious divisions between the Jews who remained in the Pale and those who lived in large urban centers became the most important factor in how the studies of Jewish folklore developed in the Russian Empire. All scientific endeavors of collecting and preserving Jewish folklore were sponsored solely by Russian-Jewish businessmen and philanthropists who lived outside the Pale, and all the work on collecting the folklore was conducted inside the Pale.

In the late nineteenth century, Russian-Jewish intellectuals became increasingly interested in studying Jewish folk culture. Influenced by German romantic scholarship, West European Jewish intellectuals, such as Moritz Steinschneider (1816–1907) and Moritz Godeman (1835–1918), encouraged studying Jewish folklore in Yiddish, Ladino, and Judeo-Arabic, because legends, family genealogies, and memorial books could become a valuable historical source. These German-Jewish scholars advocated a "literary" approach to folklore. In addition, Jewish ethnographic museums began to appear in Western Europe at the end of the nineteenth century. Rabbi Dr. Max (Meir) Grünwald (1871–1953) was the first to study the folklore of East European Jews. In fact, he is credited with founding the discipline of Jewish folkloristics—the study of Jewish folklore. He compiled a six-part questionnaire, including "Jewish Names," "People's Poetry," "Superstitions," "Rituals," "Folk Medicine," and "Household and Dress Code."

Enlighteners (*maskilim*) had an ambivalent attitude toward folklore. Some believed that these folk beliefs and rituals stood in the way of modernization of the Jewish community and its emancipation into the Russian society. Others, like Alexander Cederbaum (1816–1893), adopted the German-Jewish attitude toward folklore as a literary source and published some Jewish folktales in *Kol Mevaser,* the first Russian-Jewish journal.

At the end of the nineteenth century, Julius Engel (1867–1927), Shlomo Zanvil Rappoport (S. An-Ski) (1863–1920), Saul Ginsburg (Ginzburg), and Pesaḥ Marek began to systematically collect Jewish folktales and music. In 1901, the first collection of Yiddish folk songs was published in St. Petersburg, edited by Marek and Ginsburg.

In 1892, the Society for the Spread of Enlightenment among the Jews of Russia was established in St. Petersburg. In 1908, it was reorganized into the Jewish Historic-Ethnographic Society. In 1912–1914, the society funded a series of ethnographic expeditions to sixty-six regions of the Pale by S. An-Ski, J. Engel, and Zalman Kisselgof (1876–1939). During the expeditions, Jewish folk legends, fairy tales, songs, customs, rituals, and beliefs were recorded, and handmade artifacts and synagogues were photographed. Many of the synagogues were later destroyed during World War I and World War II. For this expedition, ethnologist Lev Shternberg (1861–1927) designed the questionnaire, which consisted of over 2,000 questions, and it remains a standard in Jewish ethnography.

In 1916, a Jewish historic-ethnographic museum was created in St. Petersburg. It functioned until 1930 (with a break between 1917 and 1920). Expeditions also collected a tremendous amount of Hasidic and *misnagdic* folklore. In the aftermath of the destruction of European Jewry during the two world wars, these collections contained the only records of these cultural products.

Important works in Jewish folklore studies were conducted by I. Tavayev, the author of *Otzar ha'meshalim ve'hapitgamim* (Treasure of Jewish Proverbs and Tales), published in 1919. In 1911–1917, Noyekh Prilutski (Noah Prylucki), an important philologer, published collections of Yiddish folklore in Warsaw. He and his colleagues believed that the existence of a rich folklore in Yiddish signifies the existence of the true Jewish culture and to some extent justifies Jewish national movements.

Jewish Life Under Soviet Rule

In 1917, the February Revolution abolished the monarchy and invested the provisional government with political power. One of its first official decrees officially abolished the Pale of Settlement and granted equal rights to Jews, which began a new chapter in Russian-Jewish history. In October 1917, the provisional government was overthrown by the Bolshevik Revolution. Vladimir Lenin became the head of the state, now renamed a Soviet republic.

Scholars characterized Jewish life under Soviet rule as essentially ambivalent. On the one hand, many Jews suffered from Soviet economic policies, which engaged in nationalization of businesses and collectivization of agriculture; thus small businesses lost their property to larger urban industries, while small farmers lost their land to large collective farms. The state sought to reduce all variety of religious observance, both Christian and Jewish. Important rabbinical dynasties felt compelled to leave the country. Many religious and political Jewish activists were arrested in the 1920s and even more were arrested and killed in the 1930s in purges.

At the same time, compared to the situation under the tsars, Jews had greater educational and professional opportunity. This attracted younger Jews in Ukraine and Byelorussia to migrate to larger cities in Russia, especially Moscow and Leningrad (formerly St. Petersburg). For the predominantly Yiddish-speaking Jews who stayed in the former Pale of Settlement, the government designed programs of *korenizatsiia* (nativization), which were designed to transmit knowledge about the new Soviet system in Yiddish. Thus Yiddish-language party cells, trade unions, schools, theaters, and other political and cultural institutions were created. Jewish sections of the Communist Party were established in 1918 and functioned until 1930. While the major role of most of these institutions was for the government to spread propaganda among Jews, some Yiddish activists and scholars took advantage of government policies to conduct serious academic research in all aspects of Jewish culture, especially folklore.

In the late 1920s and early 1930s, Kiev became the center of Jewish folklore studies in the Soviet Union. Folklorist Moshe Beregovski (1892–1961) established a phono-archive of Jewish music in Kiev. Beregovski and his colleagues collected Yiddish folklore in large centers of Jewish culture (Kiev, Odessa); in small cities and boroughs in Volhynia and Podolia; in Galicia; and in ancient Jewish agricultural settlements in southern Ukraine (Dnepropetrovsk, Kherson, Zaporozhye, the Nikolaev region, Crimea).

In 1922–1929, Zalman Kisselgof conducted a Yiddish folklore collecting expedition in Byelorussia, the results of which were stored in part at the Leningrad Jewish Ethnographic Museum. Kisselgof managed to record a few Purimshpils (Purim folk performances). This work was later continued by Beregovski, who collected thousands of Purim plays in the 1930s.

In 1936, Beregovski expanded the areas where folklore was collected. Now researchers went to places where the Soviet government supported Jewish agricultural colonies in the Nikolaev region, such as Kalinindorf, Sterndorf, Lvovo, Bobrovyy Kut, Sholom Aleichem, and Freilebn. This was the first and the last Soviet expedition to record the Yiddish folk songs and stories. Some of this work was published as late as 1938, long after all other Yiddish cultural institutions had been ended in the Soviet Union. An important collection of Soviet-Yiddish folklore was published in 1938, *Yiddish Folk Songs of the Soviet Union*, edited by Beregovski and Itsik Fefer, the Soviet-Yiddish poet. Another collection, edited by Y. Dobrushin and A. Yuditski, came out in 1940 in Moscow.

Like their prerevolutionary colleagues, Soviet scholars had an agenda (which was partially suggested to them by state ideology). Scholars believed that one could find the roots of socialism in prerevolutionary Jewish folk culture and therefore prove that the Jewish people fully supported the revolution. In addition, folklorists had the task of reinterpreting the folk heritage in order to minimize the influence of religion on folk songs, stories, and riddles. Therefore, Soviet folklorists paid special attention to the creations that ridiculed tsarist governments, rabbis, and Hasidic leaders, as well as middle- and upper-class members of Jewish society. Consequently, serious attention was paid to collecting Yiddish folklore during the 1920s and 1930s. Kiev collections, recorded in 1929, contain love songs and family lyrics in Yiddish, as well as music of artisans, revolutionary workers' songs, and songs of the "underworld," including beggars and thieves. Some Hasidic music was recorded as well and published as instrumental pieces.

Soviet Jewish folklorists were equipped with institutional financial support and professional equipment to conduct their work. Most of them were professionally trained specialists. Yet ideological constraints inevitably affected the quality and the content of their work. First, all the songs and stories that they were able to record were extremely supportive of the Soviet regime and its policies toward Jews. All Yiddish songs encouraged Soviet policies such as the military draft, work in collective farms, and even resettlement to Birobidzhan. No critical materials were recorded, partly because the informants were afraid to volunteer such materials and partly because the researchers were not willing to give incriminating pieces. As a result, we can rely only on personal family and oral histories to recover such critical materials. Second, not all efforts of Jewish folklore collectors were directed at Yiddish culture. During the Soviet period, Yiddish was only one of the languages spoken by Soviet Jews. Russian was becoming an increasingly popular vernacular. However, according to government ideology, Jews were defined as a people based only on their language, so by acquiring

Russian, Jews lost their status as a separate "nation." Therefore, Russian-Jewish folklore was not recorded. Neither was folklore in Hebrew, as it was assumed that the Hebrew language was the language of religion and the bourgeoisie.

During World War II, the Kiev Institute and its workers were evacuated to Ufa. After their return in 1944, they resumed their work and collected unique post-Holocaust testimonies, especially from survivors in Transnistria. In 1945, Beregovski launched a new project, which aimed to record Yiddish folklore from the war years. The following year, in Chernivtsi (Ukraine), folklore was not recorded in the Zhitomir region. In 1948, the institute was closed, and that marked the end of professional studies of Yiddish folklore during the Soviet period.

Nonetheless, Jewish folklore continued to thrive, though predominantly expressed in Russian. The main genre became the joke (*anekdot*), in which Soviet institutions, bureaucracy, and anti-Semitism were ridiculed, particularly the ability to identify and discriminate against Jews as their ethnicity was recorded in their internal passports. Because Soviet cultural policies toward Jews aimed to eliminate the meaningful connections between Jewish ethnic identity and Judaism, jokes expressed anxieties associated with being Jewish. For example:

> A Jew fills an [application] form: Were you a member of other political parties? No. Were you in the occupied territories [during World War II]? No. Were you ever convicted of a crime? No. Your nationality? Yes.

During the late 1960s and early 1970s, when the Soviet government allowed limited emigration of Jews from the Soviet Union, the jokes began to reflect how having Jewish status suddenly became advantageous. In the late 1990s, the joke "a Jewish wife is not a luxury, but a mean of transportation" (a word play on a Soviet slogan about cars) became one of the most popular Soviet jokes of the late Soviet era.

The studies of Russian-Jewish folklore were rudimentary during the Soviet era, yet developed very quickly in the 1990s. Jewish studies in academic institutions in St. Petersburg, Dnepropetrovsk, and Moscow included courses on Jewish life. Centers of Jewish education in St. Petersburg and Kiev launched projects to collect the remains of Yiddish and Russian-Jewish oral histories in the former Pale of Settlement. Similar studies are being conducted by researchers from England, the United States, Israel, and Canada, who record the folklore in the former Soviet Union and in the destinations of Jews who fled the Soviet Union upon its collapse in 1991. It is estimated that about 1.8 million Jews left the Soviet Union and post-Soviet states to settle in Israel, the United States, Germany, Australia, and Canada. About 500,000 remained in the former Soviet Union. Their culture and their folklore are being transformed in the new environment, yet often retain remnants of the unique Soviet-Jewish culture and identity. Oral folklore is one of the few areas of daily culture where this identity survives. Pioneering works by Fialkova and Yelenevskaya are devoted to the study of folklore of Russian immigrants in Israel.

Anna Shternshis

See also: An-Ski, S.; Grünwald, Max; Languages, Jewish; Poland, Jews of.

Bibliography

An-Ski, S. *The Enemy at His Pleasure: A Journey Through the Jewish Pale of Settlement During World War I.* New York: Metropolitan, 2003.

Beukers, Mariella, and Renee Waale, eds. *Tracing An-Sky: Jewish Collections from the State Ethnographic Museum in St. Petersburg.* Amsterdam: Joods Historisch Museum, 1992.

Fialkova, Larisa, and Maia N. Yelenevskaya. *Ex-Soviets in Israel: From Personal Narratives to a Group Portrait.* Detroit: Wayne State University Press, 2007.

Goluboff, Sascha L. *Jewish Russians: Upheavals in a Moscow Synagogue.* Philadelphia: University of Pennsylvania Press, 2003.

Gonen, Rivka, ed. *Back to the Shtetl: An-Ski and the Jewish Ethnographic Expedition 1912–1914.* Jerusalem: Israel Museum, 1994.

Gottesman, Itzik Nakhmen. *Defining the Yiddish Nation: The Jewish Folklorists of Poland.* Detroit: Wayne State University Press, 2003.

Kantsedikas, A.S. *Albom evreiskoi khudozhestvennoi stariny semena an-skogo,* ed. I. Sergeeva. Moscow: Mosty kultury, 2001.

Klier, John. *Imperial Russia's Jewish Question, 1855–1881.* New York: Cambridge University Press, 1995.

———. *Russia Gathers Her Jews: The Origins of the "Jewish Question" in Russia, 1772–1825.* DeKalb: Northern Illinois University Press, 1986.

Levin, Meyer, compiler. *Classic Hassidic Tales: Marvellous Tales of Rabbi Israel Baal Shem and of His Great-Grandson, Rabbi Nachman, Retold from Hebrew, Yiddish, and German Sources.* New York: Dorset, 1985.

Litvak, Olga. *Conscription and the Search for Modern Russian Jewry.* Bloomington: Indiana University Press, 2006.

Nathans, Benjamin. *Beyond the Pale: The Jewish Encounter with Late Imperial Russia.* Berkeley: University of California Press, 2002.

Nemtsov, Jascha, ed. *Judische Kunstmusik im 20. Jahrhundert: Quellenlage, Entstehungsgeschichte, Stilanalysen.* Wiesbaden: Harrassowitz, 2006.

Raize, E.S. *Evreiskie narodnye skazki, predaniia, bylichki, rasskazy, anekdoty,* ed. V.A. Dymshits. St. Petersburg: Simpozium, 1999.

Sholokhova, Lyudmila. *The Phonoarchive of Jewish Folklore at the Vernadsky National Library of Ukraine.* 2001. www.archives.gov.ua/Eng/NB/Phonoarchive.php.

Shternshis, Anna. *Soviet and Kosher: Jewish Popular Culture in the Soviet Union, 1923–1939.* Bloomington: Indiana University Press, 2006.

Stolovich, L.N., ed. *Evrei shutiat: Evreiskie anekdoty, ostroty i aforizmy o evreyakh.* Tallinn: Evreiskaia obshchina Estonii, 1996.

Zhovtis, Aleksandr. *Nepridumannye anekdoty: Iz sovetskogo proshlogo.* Moscow: ITS-Garant, 1995.

RUTH

Ruth, heroine of the Book of Ruth, one of the five scrolls, is a Moabite woman who married one of the sons of Elimelech and Naomi, who left Moab due to famine toward the end of the era of the Judges.

Ruth's importance and virtues have been assessed in various ways. Many traditional Jewish interpreters identified her identification with the Jewish people as the key element in her dramatic story (*m. Ruth Rab.* 2, 22; *Yevamot* 47b). Other commentators praise Ruth's modesty and righteousness (*Yevamot* 63a). Probably the most extensive commentary deals with the meeting between Ruth and Boaz at the threshing floor (see, e.g., *Ruth Rab.* 5–7); Ruth's behavior in this encounter is seen as a tribute to feminine wile and persistence and as a parable about overcoming various obstacles.

The Book of Ruth is relatively short, with a simple summary of its main plot lines: After Elimelech dies, Naomi returns with her daughter-in-law, Ruth,to her homeland, the land of Judah. Her second daughter-in-law, Orpah, remains in her homeland. Ruth goes to glean in the fields of Bethlehem at the beginning of the barley harvest and encounters Boaz, a relative of Elimelech. Taking advice from her mother-in-law, Ruth goes to the threshing floor, where Boaz sleeps at night, and asks him to marry her. Ruth and Boaz have a son, Obed, who himself becomes the father of Jesse (father of King David).

In this plot sequence, Ruth plays a role reinforced in familiar folk narratives devoted to the birth of a hero. Her interaction with Naomi features contrasts and qualities that are commonly associated with women. The two women share a destiny and their well-being depends upon cooperation. Their social status differs: Naomi hails from an established family and is the older, superior figure. Ruth is of lower status in terms of her foreign, Moabite origins and her status as the young daughter-in-law. After the departure from Moab, both lack children, need to find a source of income, and yearn for a son (Ruth desires a biological son; Naomi seeks a legal, male heir).

Ruth is presented as an enticing woman who uses unacceptable sexual attractions to attain her legitimate goal of perpetuating her line. She loyally fulfills her social obligation of heeding Naomi's demands; she follows Naomi, finds income for her, agrees to her request to tempt Boaz, uses feminine wiles to get him to marry her, and conceives a son whose birth brings the trials and tribulations she shares with her mother-in-law to an end. The happy resolution of the story comes when both women obtain what they lack: income and an heir.

In personal and collective senses, this satisfactory ending reinforces the existing desired social hierarchy that is based on patriarchy and family norms. The moral, which appears repeatedly in narratives about women in a variety of cultural contexts, is clear: a woman who clings to a positive social goal (marriage, the birth of an heir to preserve the memory of a family and retain a claim to an estate) and who operates on the basis of feminine wiles and wisdom to reach this goal will succeed in the end, no matter how daunting the challenges she faces appear to be at the start of her journey.

Ruth attains her goal partly because she symbolizes unconditional love and boundless fidelity. Sages interpreted her name as *reut* (love and friendship). But her name can also be interpreted in terms of the Hebrew root ר ו ה connoting a source of water.

If the symbol of water is joined to the barley harvest, then it seems that Ruth embodies from the start of the story hopes of a bountiful future that are destined to be redeemed.

Naomi and Ruth can be viewed as two sides of one female experience: a symbol of young, hopeful womanhood joined to an emblem of aging womanhood. On a mythological-psychological level, which arguably serves

Detail from "Naomi and Her Two Daughters-in-Law" (Łódź, 1935), from the Szyk Haggadah. *(The Robbins Family Collection. Reproduced with the cooperation of The Arthur Szyk Society, Burlingame, CA. www.szyk.org)*

as the deep structure for the story of Ruth and Naomi, the two faces of female personality cannot be separated.

The same is true of the Greek legend of Demeter and Persephone—a tale that, in some ways, parallels that of Ruth and Naomi. Demeter and her daughter, Persephone, are goddesses connected to harvest seasons; in a harvest season, they are associated with passages that move from death (winter) to life (growth and the reaping of the harvest), and these themes are found in the Book of Ruth.

Some suggest that the source of the Book of Ruth is oral tradition narrative formulated as poetry. The Book as it is written indeed contains verses that substantiate this thesis about poetic origins: "Entreat me not to leave you or to return from following you; for where you go I will go, and where you lodge I will lodge; your people shall be my people, and your God my God" (Ruth 1:16).

In the Aggaddah, Ruth was a daughter of the king of Moab, who was the grandson of Balak (*Ruth Rab.* 2:9). When the events of the book transpired, she was forty years old (*Ruth Rab.* 4:4), and Boaz's wife is said to have passed away on the day she arrived in Eretz Israel (*b. Bava Batra* 91a). Ruth is also said to have seen the grandchildren of her grandchild and to have lived until the days of King Solomon (*Bava Batra,* 91b).

Aliza Shenhar

See also: David, King.

Bibliography

Brenner, Athalya. *The Israelite Woman: Social Role and Literary Type in Biblical Narrative.* Sheffield, UK: JSOT, 1985.

———. *Ruth and Naomi.* Tel Aviv: Afik, 1988 (in Hebrew).

Cambell, Edward F. "Ruth." In *The Anchor Bible*, vol. 7. New York: Doubleday, 1975.

Fisch, Harold. "Ruth and the Structure of Covenant History." *Vetus Testamentum* 32:4 (1982): 425–437.

Ozick, Cynthia. "Ruth." In *Congregation: Contemporary Writers Read the Jewish Bible,* ed. David Rosenberg, pp. 361–382. New York: Harcourt, Brace, and Jovanovich, 1987.

Pardes, Ilana. *Counter Traditions in the Bible: A Feminist Approach.* Tel Aviv: Ha'kibbutz Ha'meuḥad, 1996 (in Hebrew).

Sasson, Jack M. *Ruth.* Baltimore: Johns Hopkins University Press, 1979.

Trible, Phyllis. "A Human Comedy." In *God and the Rhetoric of Sexuality.* Philadelphia: Fortress, 1978.

Weinfeld, Moshe. "Ruth." In *Encyclopedia Judaica,* vol. 14. Jerusalem: Keter, 1971.

Ashrei, the first word in Psalms 1:1, Italy, fifteenth century. *(© The Israel Museum, Jerusalem by Ardon Bar-Hama)*

Painted papercut, by Moshe ben Aharon. Poland, ca. 1875. *(Gross Family Collection, Tel Aviv)*

Embroidered Sabbath tablecloth showing the Western Wall. Jerusalem, 1928. *(Gross Family Collection, Tel Aviv)*

F. KAXELINE
לשנה טובה תכתבו

New Year card with a Taslich scene. Likely Polish, 1910s. *(Shalom Sabar Collection, Jerusalem)*

Adar poster. Paper cutout from Germany. Juedisches Museum der Schweiz, Basel, Switzerland. *(Erich Lessing/Art Resource, NY)*

Farewells of Abou Zayd and Al Harith before the return to Mecca. Illustration by Al-Wasiti, from al-Hariri's *Māqāmat* (Assemblies or Entertaining Dialogues), Baghdad, ca. 1240. Bibliotheque Nationale, Paris, France. *(Erich Lessing/Art Resource, NY)*

"Moses Receives the Torah from Sinai." Illustration to the first chapter of "Avot," Italy. *(Courtesy of the Library of the Jewish Theological Seminary)*

Ornamental plate showing Samson tearing down the pillars of the Temple. Ceramics painted with gold rim, Hebrew inscription, from Bohemia. Judaica Collection. Max Berger, Vienna, Austria. *(Erich Lessing/Art Resource, NY)*

זה שלמה המלך העושה משפט משתי נשים
BRITISH
MUSEUM

King Solomon judges two harlots who claim the same child. From The North French Hebrew Miscellany (folio 518a), written and illustrated in northern France, ca. 1278. The British Library (Ms. 11639). *(HIP/Art Resource, NY)*

S

Sabar, Shalom (b. 1951)

Shalom Sabar is a professor of Jewish art and folklore at the Hebrew University of Jerusalem. He joins together the disciplines of art history and folklore, highlighting issues such as the folk nature of Jewish art and Jewish material culture; visual materials and objects associated with life-cycle and annual rituals; and the evidence that these materials provide about Jewish daily life and the relationships between the Jewish minorities and the societies that hosted them in Christian Europe and the Muslim Middle East.

Shalom Sabar was born March 3, 1951. He was the last Jewish child born in the age-old neo-Aramaic-speaking Kurdish-Jewish community of Zakho, Iraq, before its emigration to Israel.

Sabar studied art history and related fields at the Hebrew University (1974–1976) and the University of California at Los Angeles (1977–1987), where he earned his Ph.D., with his dissertation on the illustrated *ketubbah* (marriage contract) used by Italian Jews during the seventeenth and eighteenth centuries.

His books include *Ketubbah: Jewish Marriage Contracts of the Hebrew Union College Skirball Museum and Klau Library* (1990); *Mazal Tov: Illuminated Jewish Marriage Contracts from the Israel Museum Collection, Jerusalem* (1994); *Jerusalem—Stone and Spirit: 3000 Years of History and Art* (with Dan Bahat; 1997); *The Life Cycle of the Jews in Islamic Lands* (2006).

In addition, he has published numerous essays on various topics pertaining to Jewish folklore, including Hebrew amulets and magic, the *ḥamsa*, New Year cards and postcards, illustrated Passover *Haggadot*, the Bible and Midrash in folk art, traditional images of Jerusalem and the Temple, and folk art and artists of the Old Yishuv.

He has contributed to folklore research as editor of *Rimonim* (a Hebrew periodical on Jewish art), coeditor of *Jerusalem Studies in Jewish Folklore*, and as a member of the editorial board of the periodical *Pe'amim* and a twenty-volume series, both dedicated to the Jewish communities in the lands of Islam (both published by Ben-Zvi Institute).

Sabar has been a visiting professor and has lectured widely at numerous universities and public institutions in Israel and abroad and leads tours to Jewish sites in selected countries in Europe and North Africa.

Haya Bar-Itzhak

See also: Folk Art; Jerusalem and the Temple; *Ketubbah*; New Year Cards.

Bibliography

Bahat, Dan, and Shalom Sabar. *Jerusalem—Stone and Spirit: 3000 Years of History and Art.* Tel Aviv: Matan Arts, 1997 (in Hebrew).

Sabar, Shalom. *Ketubbah: Jewish Marriage Contracts of the Hebrew Union College Skirball Museum and Klau Library.* Philadelphia: Jewish Publication Society of America, 1990.

———. *Mazal Tov: Illuminated Jewish Marriage Contracts from the Israel Museum Collection, Jerusalem.* Jerusalem: Israel Museum, 1994.

Sabar, Shalom, et al. *The Life Cycle of the Jews in Islamic Lands.* Jerusalem: Ben-Zvi Institute, 2006 (in Hebrew).

Sadan, Dov (1902–1989)

Dov Sadan (Shtok) was born on February 21, 1902, in Brody, Eastern Galicia. During World War I his family moved to Lvov (Lviv today), where he was active in the Zionist He'Halutz movement and became one of its leading spokesmen.

In 1925, Sadan immigrated to Israel. He joined the editorial board of the *Davar* newspaper and served as editor of its literary supplement. Sadan was an active member on many boards of cultural institutions. He co-edited the folklore journal *Reshumot—New Series* from 1945 to 1953. In 1950, he joined the faculty of the Hebrew University and two years later became chair of Yiddish Studies. In 1962, he became a member of the Israeli National Academy of Sciences, and in 1968 he won the prestigious Israel Prize. He was elected to the Knesset (the Israeli Parliament) in 1965 as a member of Mapai Party, but resigned before the end of his term.

Sadan was first and foremost a scholar of Jewish literature and folklore. He believed that modern Jewish literature was a reaction to the crisis in traditional Jewish culture in the eighteenth century and that it developed in three directions: the new Rabbinic movement, the mystic-Hasidic trend, and the Haskalah (Enlightment) trend. Sadan viewed this complex as one Jewish literature, a literature written by Jews for Jewish readership.

In Jewish folklore, his accomplishments were outstanding. He studied various genres of folklore, including folk narratives, folk songs, proverbs, beliefs, and customs, as well as life and the year cycle. He was most fascinated by the neglected aspects of Jewish folklore, and he worked in areas considered by many scholars in Jewish studies to be unimportant. His findings and scholarship gave legitimacy to these subjects and conferred academic legitimacy to Jewish folklore studies.

Sadan adopted a pluralistic, multilayered approach to folklore studies while maintaining a geographic-historical focus. In his studies he identified the period, background dissemination, and function of each folklore item under study. He saw Jewish folkloric creation as organic in that it is an integral part of a culture and must be studied in its cultural and social context. But he also viewed folklore genres and items as transorganic in that after their creation the original context is no longer needed for the continued existence of the phenomenon. Folklore items are mobile, transcending linguistic borders and migrating from one culture to another, where they are re-told and take new forms.

Sadan's trend toward incorporating past and current realities while deploying a historical-functional approach is exemplified in his article "The Blasphemer from Hamlin," in which he presents an array of approaches and interpretations before drawing the conclusion that a mouse-trapper is actually a prototypical Jew, one who is foreign in Central Europe and saves himself from various dangers, even though he becomes a victimized citizen. The article was written in 1940, on the eve of the Holocaust.

Sadan concentrated on the compilation of folklore materials. He set new standards in the deployment of his dynamic approach and became a pioneering figure in folklore research. He believed that the modern "secular" Jewish culture that broke away from traditional Judaism is only an episodic stage in the history of Jewish culture.

Sadan died October 14, 1989. Following his death, Dov Noy edited a volume of Sadan's articles titled *Dov Sadan: Twelve Studies in Folklore* (1990).

Aliza Shenhar

See also: *Reshumot.*

Bibliography

Galron-Goldschalger,Yosef. "Bibliography of Dov Sadan's Writings, and a Sample of Works About Him and His Work." In *Sadan: Studies in Hebrew Literature*, vol. 1, pp. 265–296. Tel Aviv: Ha'kibbutz Ha'meuḥad, 1994 (in Hebrew).

Ganuz, Yitzhak. "Dov Sadan's Contribution to the Study of Jewish Proverbs." *Ha'uma* 21 (1983): 72 (in Hebrew).

Govrin, Nurit. "Dov Sadan's Serious Amusements." In *Reading the Generations*, vol. 2, pp. 369–370. Tel Aviv: Gvanim, 2002 (in Hebrew).

Halperin, Sara. "The Autobiography of Abundance." *Moznayim* 34 (1982): 23–25 (in Hebrew).

Laor, Dan. "Dov Sadan: The Struggle for Jewish Memory." In *The Struggle for Memory*, pp. 327–333. Tel Aviv: Am Oved, 2009 (in Hebrew).

Miron, Dan, "From the Sides to the Center: On Dov Sadan's Work." *Hadoar* 37 (1990): 13–15, 38 (in Hebrew).

———. "Sadan, Dov." *Encyclopedia Judaica*, vol. 14, pp. 618–620. Jerusalem: Keter, 1971.

Noy, Dov. "Final Words: Dov Sadan's Path in the World of Jewish Folklore." *Dov Sadan: Twelve Studies in Folklore*, pp. 187–194. Jerusalem: Magnes, 1990 (in Hebrew).

Sadan, Dov. *A Bowl of Nuts: A Humor Anthology.* Tel Aviv: M. Newman, 1952 (in Hebrew).

———. *A Bowl of Raisins: A Humor Anthology.* Tel Aviv: M. Newman, 1950 (in Hebrew).

———. *Stones of Memory.* Tel Aviv: Am Oved, 1954 (in Hebrew).

———. *Stones of Threshold: Essays on Yiddish Writers.* Tel Aviv: I.L. Peretz, 1957 (in Hebrew).

———. *Trees and Stones: To the History of One Figure of Speech.* Jerusalem: Committee for Hebrew Language and Bialik Institute, 1954 (in Hebrew).

———. *Twelve Studies in Folklore.* Jerusalem: Magnes, 1990 (in Hebrew).

Shamir, Ziva. "Dov Sadan Exposes Gemstones." *Language and Hebrew* 7 (1991): 71–75.

Shenhar, Aliza. "Dov Sadan's Contribution to Folklore Research." *Al Ha'mishmar* 16:9 (1977): 6–7.

Yasif, Eli. "Dov Sadan as a Jewish Folklore Scholar." *Jewish Sciences* 30 (1990): 97–100.

SAFED, LEGENDS OF

The proliferation of legends about the town of Safed in the Upper Galilee region coincided with its economic, social, and spiritual flowering in the second half of the sixteenth century. In the relatively short span of slightly more than fifty years, this previously unknown place, with almost no ancient historical significance, experienced an economic boom, social diversity and wealth, and vigorous intellectual activity relating to Halakhah, Kabbalah, moral philosophy, exegesis, and homiletics that made it, for a brief while, the spiritual capital of the Jewish people.

During the town's heyday, from the 1530s until approximately 1600, the Jewish community of Safed knew both relative security, thanks to the consolidation of the new Ottoman regime in the country, and economic prosperity, based on the local textiles industry. Safed attracted exiles from Spain and many merchants and intellectuals from all over the Diaspora, who noted that the town had an appropriate Jewish spirit and economic basis.

One key aspect of this cultural development includes the legends that developed and spread in and around Safed during this period, which have rarely been studied. This is somewhat surprising, given that so much of what we know about life in Safed, especially its image in the Jewish consciousness over the generations, derives from these legends. When they have attracted attention, it has been chiefly from the historical and philological perspectives. Some scholars assumed that the legends were reliable historical testimony and made use of them; others have dismissed them as worthless fictions and ignored them. The important philological work done on these legends, Meir Benayahu's 1967 edition of *Toledot Ha'Ari* (Praise of the Ari), focuses on the manuscripts and textual variants in pursuit of the authentic version and tries to use

Jewish men pray and lay their hands on the grave of Rabbi Isaac Luria, a sixteenth-century Jewish mystic and Kabbalah scholar. *(David Silverman/Getty Images)*

them to identify particulars of the lives of the circle that gathered around the Rabbi Isaac Luria (Ha'Ari). Scholars of Hebrew literature and Jewish folklore, notably Joseph Dan and Tamar Alexander, have discerned the importance of the legends about Luria and assigned them to the genre of the *shevaḥ* (saints' legend)—the earliest Jewish examples thereof—like the hagiographies of medieval Christianity.

Documentation of the Safed legends begins slightly later, in 1602 or 1607. In 1602 (thirty years after Luria died in a cholera epidemic that swept the town), a Moravian Jew by the name of Solomon (Shlumel) Dresnitz liquidated his property, divorced his wife, and moved to Safed, the focus of his dreams, in order to study the Lurianic Kabbalah in its place of origin. The four letters that he wrote to his teachers and relatives back in Moravia, starting in 1607, include many details about economic and intellectual life in Safed. He writes of his great desire to meet Luria's disciples, the members of the intimate circle that had gathered around the sage, in order to learn the Lurianic Kabbalah from them, as well as of his equal avidity to hear the stories of the wonders Luria performed. With this in mind, according to his own testimony, Shlumel Dresnitz accosted men and women in the study halls and synagogues, in the marketplace and the street, who knew of Luria's deeds at first hand or by report.

All the narratives that Shlumel included in his letters are legends in the classical sense of the term. They are anchored in the real world of Safed, were recounted by informants who fully believed them to be true, and were accepted as such by their faithful transcriber as well as by subsequent generations. From this perspective one must see him as the first Jewish ethnographer and folklorist whose name and biography are known today. It is true, however, that documenting folklore was not his goal. Rather, as he writes to his correspondents, his intention was to spread knowledge of Rabbi Luria's wondrous deeds and sanctity to Jewish communities that were unaware of them and thereby use these legends to establish the sacred nature of the Lurianic Kabbalah.

The scholarly literature has tended to view the Safed legends, especially those about Luria, as the work of a small group of his disciples and followers during his life and in the first years after his death. If these legends were indeed produced in this circle, they would be sectarian rather than folk legends. Consequently, one must emphasize that folk literature is not "folk" by virtue of those who create the myth, legend, or tale but because of its acceptance by society. The person who uncovered and documented the Safed legends in their earliest versions was Shlumel Dresnitz, who arrived in Safed more than thirty years after Luria's death. By his own account he collected the legends from those of Luria's disciples who were still living in Safed, but also and principally from men and women in the marketplace, the streets, the synagogue, and the house of study (*beit ha'midrash*). Scholars have demonstrated, too, that there were almost no legends circulating about Luria right after his death and that those that did exist were known only within the immediate circle of his disciples. Taken together, these two items mean that the bulk of the legends developed and circulated outside that circle during the three decades between his death and Shlumel Dresnitz's arrival in Safed. During those years, even those legends that did originate among his closest disciples metamorphosed from sectarian legends into folk legends. Others, evidently the vast majority, were created during this period or shortly after.

The biographical facts about Luria, abstracted from the dozens of legends included in Shlumel's letters, arranged in chronological order and published as *Shivḥei Ha'Ari*, date to the first edition of Dresnitz's letters, published in 1629 as part of *Ta'alumot Ḥokhmah* (Mysteries of Wisdom) by Joseph Solomon Delmedigo (Yashar mi-Qandia). *Shivḥei Ha'Ari* is in fact the earliest work of Jewish folklore and anthology of stories about a venerated figure that can be assigned to the genre of the saints' legend. It was the forerunner of dozens of later compositions that imitated it in various ways.

Although the Safed legends are usually and rightly classed as saints' legends, given their focus on Luria, two other aspects must be emphasized. First, many focus not on Luria but on other prominent sages with whom he came into contact, including Shlomo Alkabetz, Moses ben Jacob Cordovero, Joseph ben Ephraim Karo, Moses Alsheikh, Abraham ben Eliezar Halevi Berukhim, Eleazar Azikri, Joseph Ashkenazi, and, of course, Luria's closest disciple, Ḥaim ben Joseph Vital. While each of these personages is the subject of only a few legends, rather than a full corpus of tales such as that surrounding Luria, it is plausible that many oral traditions about them were never documented. The second point is that the essence of the Safed legends is not their hagiographic character but their local color. Even a quick glance at these tales, in the various formats in which they have been preserved, reveals the centrality of the spatial element: hills and orchards, caves, springs, tombs, roads, and fields, and especially the streets and houses of the town of Safed. Therefore, fundamentally the Safed legends are both hagiographic saints' legends and local legends.

The Israel Folktale Archives (IFA) in Haifa contains more than a hundred texts about Safed. Some of them celebrate Safed's zenith in the sixteenth century and feature heroes such as Luria, Joseph Karo, and Eleazar Azikri. Others exemplify narrative traditions relating to later periods, through the very recent past—Israel's War of Independence (1948) and later events, for example. Of special interest are those narratives of sixteenth-century Safed that are not incorporated into *Shivḥei Ha'Ari* or other documents of that age. It is possible that at least some of them are contemporary traditions that were not transcribed by Shlumel Dresnitz but were passed down orally by the Safed community until modern times.

Eli Yassif

See also: Yassif, Eli.

Bibliography

Alexander, Tamar. "Saint and Sage: Isaac Luria and Maimonides in Folktales." *Jerusalem Studies in Hebrew Literature* 13 (1991/2): 29–64 (in Hebrew).

Bar-Itzhak, Haya. "The 'Saints' Legend' as a Genre in Jewish Folk Literature." Ph.D. dissertation, Hebrew University of Jerusalem, 1987 (in Hebrew).

Benayahu, Meir. *Sefer toledot ha'Ari: The History of the Text and Its Value as an Historical Source.* Jerusalem: Ben-Zvi Institute, 1967 (in Hebrew).

Ben-Zvi, Izhak. "The Golden Age of Safed." In *Eretz-Israel Under Ottoman Rule.* Jerusalem: Yad Ben-Zvi, 1975/76 (in Hebrew).

Dan, Joseph. "Hagiographic Literature: East and West." *Pe'amim* 26 (1986): 77–86 (in Hebrew).

———. *The Hebrew Story in the Middle Ages.* Jerusalem: Keter, 1974 (in Hebrew).

Hacker, Joseph. "The Intellectual Activity of the Jews of the Ottoman Empire During the Sixteenth and Seventeenth Centuries." In *Jewish Thought in the Seventeenth Century,* ed. Isadore Twersky and Bernard Septimus, pp. 95–136. Cambridge: Harvard University Center for Jewish Studies, 1987.

Kna'ani, Ya'akov. "Economic Life in Safed and Its Environs in the Sixteenth Century and First Half of the Seventeenth Century." *Me'assef Ziyon* 6 (1934): 172–217 (in Hebrew).

Meri, Josef W. *The Cult of Saints Among Muslims and Jews in Medieval Syria.* Oxford: Oxford University Press, 2002.

Schechter, Solomon. "Safed in the Sixteenth Century: A City of Legists and Mystics." In *Studies in Judaism,* ed. Solomon Schechter, pp. 202–308. Philadelphia: Jewish Publication Society, 1908.

Yassif, Eli. *Safed Legends: Life and Fantasy in the City of the Kabbalists.* Haifa: University of Haifa Press, 2011 (in Hebrew).

Samael

Samael is one of the major characters in Jewish demonology, even though he is not mentioned in the Bible and no major text summarizes his characteristics and roles. The etymology of the name has two versions: the Blind Angel (Suma-El), and the Poisoning Angel (Angel of Death; Sama-El). These two interpretations reverberate in the Jewish tradition.

Samael's character appears sporadically, in a discontinuous manner in the textual tradition that is thousands of years old, dispersed in dozens of texts from various periods and different regions.

In the Apocrypha and Pseudoepigraphy, Samael is mentioned in three different texts, each of which emphasizes a different trait of his character. In the text "The Ethiopian Enoch" (second to first century B.C.E.) he is described as one of the rebel angels, though not their leader, who descended to Earth to fornicate with human daughters.

In the text "Slavic Baruch's Vision" (first century C.E.), Samael the angel is described as having been present in Paradise at the time of the original sin. He was the one who planted the tree of knowledge, according to this source. That was the reason for God's wrath. Since then, Samael envied Adam and wanted to corrupt him. Samael is also mentioned as having disguised himself as the snake that tempted Eve.

In the text "The Ascension of Isaiah" (first to second century C.E.) Samael is the embodiment of evil, overpowering man and acting through him. Alternatively named Samael, Belial, and Satan, he is the leader of evil forces. Samael gains control over King Menashe and, through him, takes revenge on the prophet Isaiah and kills him.

These three elements in Samael's character—its heavenly source, his involvement in the original sin, and his evil nature—persisted in later Jewish traditions.

In the Midrash, Samael's traits are various and diverse. The Midrash *Pirqe de'Rabbi Eliezer* (Eretz Israel, seventh to eighth century B.C.E.) retains ancient traditions about Samael. These were preserved in later sources:

- He is the high angel, leader of the rebellious group of angels. He opposed the creation of Adam, envied him, and therefore descended from Heaven to tempt him. In Paradise, he tempted Eve to eat the forbidden fruit, while riding on the snake (*Pirqe de'Rabbi Eliezer*, ch. 13).
- He impregnated Eve, and he is the father of Cain (*Pirqe de'Rabbi Eliezer*, ch. 21).
- He is the opponent of the Archangel Michael (*Pirqe de'Rabbi Eliezer*, ch. 27; Shmot Raba 18:5; *Yalqut Shimoni* Gen. Leh Leha 68).
- He serves as the People of Israel's prosecutor (*Pirqe de'Rabbi Eliezer*, ch. 21).
- On Yom Kippur, the Scapegoat is offered to him (*Pirqe de'Rabbi Eliezer*, ch. 46).
- He is often identified with Satan (Pintel 1981, pp. 76–77).
- He is the guardian of Esau, Edom, and Rome (*Tanḥuma Vayishlah* 8; *Bereshit Rabati*).
- He is the Angel of Death (*Devarim Raba* 11).
- In some of the midrashic sources, Samael is part of elaborated stories, involving major biblical figures.

One of these stories involves the confrontation between him and Abraham, on the way to Isaac's sacrifice. In this Midrash (*Bereshit Raba* 56) Samael has no demonic characteristics. His function is to raise doubts about Abraham's faith. Samael approaches Abraham with a sequence of painful questions about the validity of God's promises and about humanity's ability to withstand divine, demanding trials. Abraham overcomes all these doubts, and the immensity of his faith is proved once more. Samael approaches Isaac as well, but is able to reveal the breaches of his faith.

The other elaborated story in the Midrash concerns Moses's death (*Avot de'Rabbi Nathan*; *Devarim Rabbah* 11:10; *Yalqut Shimoni*, *Vayelekh* 940). Samael in this context takes the role of the Angel of Death. His duty is to take the souls of all living creatures. His traits here are the traditional ones associated with death: He wears a sword, and he is cruel and full of wrath.

The focus in the Midrash is on Moses's difficulty in accepting his own death. This problem is represented in other forms as well, such as in a verbal and physical struggle with the Angel of Death.

Samael is pictured as wicked and is called Head of all Satans. He is described as waiting impatiently to take Moses's soul. During the physical struggle between the two, Moses attacks Samael with his staff, on which the holy name of God is engraved. Samael flees while Moses chases him and blinds him with the beam of glory he has between his eyes.

In early Kabbalah, in the "Treatise on the left emanation" (thirteenth century C.E.) Samael is mentioned as the great prince and great king of all the demons, and as Lilith's spouse. In the Zohar, he is described as the leader of the "Sitra Aḥra," the evil side of the divine forces of destruction.

He appears also in the Lurianic Kabbalah story of Rabbi Yosef dela Reina, who seeks in vain to bring final redemption by chaining Samael and Lilith. Their appearance in this story is as two large black dogs.

The custom, derived from the sixteenth-century Isaac Luria's practice, is to abstain from using in any way the full name of Satan. The abbreviation "Sameh Mem" and hints of Samael's name are used instead.

Idit Pintel-Ginsberg

See also: Demon; Lilith.

Bibliography

Dan, Joseph. "The Story of Joseph della Reina." In *The Book of Zefat I.* Jerusalem: Ben-Zvi Institute, 1962 (in Hebrew).

———. "Treatise on the Left Emanation." In *The Early Kabbalah.* New York: Paulist Press, 1986.

Martin, François. *Le livre d'Henoch traduit sur le texte ethiopien.* Paris: Letouzey et Ane, 1906.

Pintel, Idit. "The Development of Lilith Ashmedai and Samael in Judaism, from the Bible to the Geonic Period." M.A. thesis, Hebrew University, 1981 (in Hebrew).

Pintel-Ginsberg, Idit. "Michael and Samael, Reflecting Jewish Ethos Through Demonology." In *Between Two Worlds: Concepts of Demons in the Slavic and Jewish Cultural Traditions.* Moscow: Sefer, 2002.

Scholem, Gershom. "Samael." In *Kabbalah.* Jerusalem: Keter, 1974.

Trachtenberg, Joshua. *Jewish Magic and Superstition.* New York: Atheneum, 1939.

SAMARITANS

The Samaritans, an ethnoreligious group that follows Samaritanism, an Abrahamic religion similar to Judaism, trace their origins to the biblical northern tribes of Israel. They do not conceive of themselves as Jews but, rather, as an independent and more true form of the Israelite religion. In fact, Samaritans interpret their name not as a locative that refers to Samaria but as "those who keep the Torah," the *Shamerim.* Today Samaritans often refer to themselves as Samaritan Israelites.

Samaritan religious principles may be summarized as:

1. There is one God, YHWH (referred to as *Shema,* "the Name").
2. The Torah in the Samaritan version was given by God to Moses and is the only divinely sanctioned biblical book.
3. Moses was God's only prophet.
4. Mount Gerizim, near Nablus, is the *axis mundi,* chosen by God as his dwelling place from time immemorial (as expressed in the Samaritan version of the Ten Commandments).
5. The Aaronite priests, primarily the oldest Levite, who serves as the high priest, are the legitimate interpreters of the law and the keepers of tradition (since the demise of the Aaronite priesthood in 1624).
6. Reward and punishment await after death.
7. Moses will return as the *Taheb,* who will end the period of divine "disfavor" initiated with the hiding of the Tabernacle at the time that the Judeans sinned and split with the Gerizim temple.

In terms of ritual, public Sabbath rites take place within synagogues, where Torah scrolls are housed within shrines (the Holy Ark) that are covered with decorated veils (*parokhet*), and the podium upon which the shrine stands is named after the sacrificial altar of the Tabernacle, the *mizbe'aḥ.* Public prayer consists of florilegia of Torah verses and liturgical poetry in Aramaic and Hebrew. Torah scrolls are not read from but venerated and displayed iconically. Scriptural performance and study is carried out from codices, and it is expected that boys and girls memorize the entire Torah. Samaritans celebrate seven holy-day periods, which include ritual processions to the top of Mount Gerizim. These periods are divided into festivals (*moadim*): Passover, the Festival of the Seventh Month, the Day of Atonement, and Shemini Atzeret (the day following the week of Sukkot [Tabernacles]), and pilgrimage holidays (*ḥagim*): the Festival of Unleavened Bread (*matzot*), which follows Passover, Shavuot (Pentecost), and Sukkot. On Passover, Samaritans perform the paschal sacrifice, a high point of their liturgical year that has long fascinated Westerners. On Sukkot, they build tabernacles within their homes, rather than outdoors, a practice that they attribute to persecution. The ceilings of Samaritan tabernacles are decorated with an array of fruit arranged in geometric patterns. All members of the community, including pregnant women, children, and the sick, fast on the Day of Atonement. Like Karaites, and unlike the less literally minded Rabbinites, Samaritans do not eat heated food on the Sabbath. Similarly, they do not make use of air conditioners on the Sabbath and festivals. The Samaritans maintain a solar/lunar calendar, which, because of differing systems of intercalation, does not necessarily coincide with that of the Jews.

Enactment of biblical purity laws is particularly significant within this community. Samaritans are punctilious in their response to seminal and menstrual emissions, with husbands and wives avoiding all physical contact, including sharing living space, food, and household items, for the week that the wife is in menses. Although ritual baths (*mikveh*; pl. *mikvaot*) have been discovered in late antiquity Samaritan contexts (including a synagogue), today ritual immersion is performed in bathtubs. Circumcision is practiced strictly and, in keeping with the Samaritan version of the Pentateuch, must be carried out on the eighth day after birth with no exceptions. The high priest is the ultimate legal decision maker in all areas of ritual law. Deeply conservative at its core, Samaritan law and custom are dynamic and develop in response to internal as well as external stimuli.

The liminal boundary separating and connecting Jews and Samaritans, which can be seen as early as biblical literature and traced archaeologically from the Persian period onward, reflects a unique element in both Jewish and Samaritan thought. Samaritans were numerous during the early centuries of the Common Era, and archaeological

Samaritans sit under a sukkah made of fruits inside their house during the holiday of Sukkot on Mount Gerizim near the northern West Bank city of Nablus. *(Menahem Kahana/AFP/Getty Images)*

evidence for Samaritan settlements in Samaria and adjacent areas as well as in cities of the eastern Mediterranean has been discovered. Samaritan communities are known to have existed in medieval Egypt, Syria, and a number of locations within and outside of Palestine. Only a small remnant survived Christian and Muslim persecutions and proselytism into the twentieth century. In 1901 the community comprised 152 individuals, all of whom resided in Nablus.

During the latter nineteenth and early twentieth centuries, American Protestants and then early Zionists provided considerable aid to the Samaritans and nurtured the community. Most significantly, Zionist scholar Yitzhak (Isaac) Ben-Zvi, later president of Israel, convinced some single Samaritan men in Jaffa to marry Jewish women, a practice that was previously forbidden. A small colony settled in Tel Aviv during the 1930s. Today, the community numbers approximately 740, 350 in Nablus/Mount Gerizim and 390 in the Samaritan neighborhood of Neve Marqeh, in the Tel Aviv suburb of Holon. Israeli Samaritans are regarded by the State of Israel as Jews, and their priests are compensated by the state as clergy. They serve in the Israel Defense Forces and speak Hebrew at home, while their brethren in Nablus primarily speak Arabic and attend Palestinian schools.

Scholarship

Western interest in the Samaritans has its origins in European biblical scholarship of the early modern period. Although European scholars showed considerable interest in Samaritan customs, their most sustained concern was the Samaritan Pentateuch and its significance for the history of the text of the Hebrew Bible. Correspondence between Samaritan leaders and mainly Western scholars—often on the false pretense of representing European Samaritans—began in the sixteenth century and continued on less-colonial terms into the twentieth century; in its later phase, it focused on Samaritan customs and concentrated on ethnography. These documents are particularly significant in assessing diachronic changes in ritual or interpretation in recent centuries. Only in the early twentieth century did scholarship that might be considered folklore studies develop, first in Europe and in British Mandate Palestine. The work of the London-based Moses Gaster is particularly significant for folklore studies, as it focused on custom and magic, as well as comparison of homiletical texts with Second Temple and rabbinic biblical interpretation. Ben-Zvi carried out significant local fieldwork and surveyed archaeological discoveries. Samaritan oral traditions were collected by Dov Noy during the 1950s, and forty-seven stories are held by the Israel Folklore Archives (IFA) at the University of Haifa. Beginning in the late 1930s, historical linguist Ze'ev Ben-Hayyim and his students set about publishing critical editions of the most important Samaritan writings and their oral traditions of recitation, together with Hebrew translations.

After 1970 a broad flowering of Samaritan studies of all periods took place, carried out by an international group of scholars organized as the Société d'Etudes Samaritaines (Society for the Study of the Samaritans) in 1985. The broad range of Samaritan studies was united under the rubric of the society and its quadrennial congresses and their proceedings. This diverse community was brought together by Alan D. Crown of the University of Sydney in a series of compilations, most prominently a handbook called *The Samaritans* (1989). This volume was followed in 2002 with a parallel Hebrew publication edited by Ephraim Stern and Hanan Eshel, which updates Crown's handbook and integrates recent archaeological discoveries. Reinhard Pummer of the University of Ottawa has been the most prolific modern scholar focusing on folklore-related issues, ranging from his corpora of texts relating to Samaritans in Josephus and the Church fathers to the publication of Samaritan marriage contracts (with Abraham Tal), folk art, and fieldwork relating to Samaritan rituals and customs. Among the Samaritans themselves, a member of the Holon community, Benyamim Tsedaka, the son of Noy's original informant, Ratson Tsedaka, has published a series of academic and semiacademic articles and collections in English and modern Hebrew relating to Samaritan history, customs, biblical interpretation, foodways, and contemporary life. As the centerpiece of his project, Tsedaka has published a biweekly newspaper that reports on academic and community developments and has become an important source for the study of contemporary Samaritanism.

Literary and Oral Traditions

Samaritan literature is rich in literary sources that are of significance to folklorists. The most important Samaritan collection is *Tibat Marqe* (lit., the "[Book] Chest of Marqe"), an anthology of midrashic interpretations centered on the Five Books of Moses. Composed in a late antiquity Aramaic that is akin to Jewish Palestinian Aramaic, the earliest sections of *Tibat Marqe* (books 1 and 2) date to the fourth to fifth century, while the later sections, dating to the eleventh to twelfth century, are composed in medieval Samaritan literary Aramaic with numerous Arabic influences and biblicizing forms (which Ben-Hayyim calls "Samaritan"). As a diachronic anthology of biblical reflections (midrash), *Tibat Marqe* parallels the great early modern rabbinic anthology known as *Midrash Rabba,* which similarly preserves biblical interpretation compiled over a thousand-year period. *Piyyutim* (liturgical poetry), which date from late antiquity and continue to be produced for wedding feasts and other significant occasions to this day, are a major branch of Samaritan literature. The most significant late antiquity poets were Amram Dare, Marqa, and Ninna (son of Marqa), whose works were edited by Ze'ev Ben-Hayyim. These poems are replete with biblical interpretation.

Finally, a broad literature of Chronicles in Hebrew, Aramaic, and Arabic was produced by the Samaritans into modern times. The earliest of these is the *Tulidah,* which in its oldest part dates to the twelfth century; the monumental Arabic chronicle attributed to Abu'l Fath dates from the fourteenth century. The chronological structure of the Chronicles provided frameworks for the preservation of folk memory relating to the heroes of previous generations, particularly the priestly genealogy, and shows numerous points of contact with Jewish, Arabic, and general folklore literature and motifs. Noy was well aware of the importance of Samaritan literary tradition in the formation of the oral traditions that he collected from Tsedaka. This intermingling of literary and oral elements is evident throughout the Chronicles literature and is not only a modern phenomenon. Samaritan musical tradition is essentially liturgical, and early recordings of Torah readings are preserved in a number of libraries (including the Jewish Theological Seminary in New York). In recent years Benyamim Tsedaka has organized a choral group, not all of whose members are Samaritan.

Visual Culture

Evidence of Samaritan visual culture has survived from the Persian and Greco-Roman periods and from the early modern and modern periods. Fragments of Samaritan manuscripts were discovered in the Cairo Geniza, and a number of medieval codices are extant. All codices on parchment predate the fifteenth century, as scrolls were written on the hides of sacrificial animals, which required a state of purity that was unavailable when Samaritans lost access to the ashes of the red heifer, apparently in the seventeenth century. Late twentieth-century excavation on Mount Gerizim, carried out under the direction of the archaeologist Yitzhak Magen, has uncovered extensive remains of the Samaritan temple precinct, dating as early as the sixth century B.C.E., which was destroyed by the Hasmonean John Hyrcanos II in ca. 110 B.C.E. Significantly, the existence of this temple is not recalled in Samaritan tradition, though Josephus and rabbinic sources mark its destruction. Extensive remains of Aramaic dedicatory inscriptions have been uncovered, written both in the Samaritan script and what later came to be called Jewish square script. Synagogue remains from late antiquity have been uncovered across Samaria and in adjacent regions, as well as on the island of Delos in Greece.

In the Palestinian examples, images of Torah shrines and menorahs appear in mosaics and bas-relief. Even at this early date, Samaritan strictness in regard to forbidden imagery, based in the second commandment of the Ten Commandments, is a hallmark of late antiquity Samaritan visual culture. Although no medieval ritual objects or architecture are extant, bronze containers for Torah scrolls similar in design to Jewish Torah cases created in the Middle East (*tiqim*) and ultimately derived from Qur'an cases are extant from as early as the sixteenth century, as is an embroidered Torah ark curtain dated 1509/1510. These are decorated with Torah verses, and one case is decorated with schematic drawings of the tabernacle.

In the nineteenth and early twentieth centuries, polychrome tabernacle drawings based upon the Torah curtain image—together with a large quantity of handwritten books—were prepared and sold to visiting collectors. Samaritans interpret Deuteronomy 6:9—"and you shall write them upon the doorpost of your house and upon your gates"—literally, inscribing biblical verses in Samaritan script on or near the doorpost of their homes. This practice is known from late antiquity and continues to the present. *Mezuzot,* as they are called, are sometimes used to decorate the interiors of Samaritan homes. A wide variety of biblical verses has been used, both in the past and present. Some contemporary *mezuzot* have verses formed into a variety of shapes, including doves, flames, and the menorah. Samaritan homes in Holon as well as official documents such as calendars are sometimes decorated with *mezuzot* in the form of the seal of the State of Israel, with the word "Israel" written beneath the menorah. This image in particular reflects the depths of Samaritan participation in modern Israeli life. The most significant Samaritan religious icon is the Samaritan script itself, a writing system that dates to biblical times and is distinct from the script used for Jewish Hebrew and Aramaic. Both in Neve Marqeh and on Mount Gerizim the ubiquitous use of Samaritan script defines Samaritan public and private space.

Samaritan amulets in bronze that are extant from late antiquity have been discovered in both Palestine and Corinth in Greece. Modern amulets are known to have been written on wood, paper, and leather. The texts consist of biblical verses written in Samaritan script. Today, Samaritan amulets are sold to Jews, Christians, and Muslims, and Samaritan amulet writers are regarded by their clients as magical experts.

Steven Fine

Bibliography

Ben-Zvi, Izthak. *Sefer ha'Shomronim.* 2d ed. Jerusalem: Ben-Zvi Institute, 1970 (in Hebrew).

Crown, Alan David, ed. *The Samaritans.* Tubingen: Mohr Siebeck, 1989.

Pummer, Reinhard. *The Samaritans.* Leiden: E.J. Brill, 1987.

Stern, Ephraim, and Hanan Eshel, eds. *Sefer ha'Shomronim.* Jerusalem: Yad Ben Zvi, 2002 (in Hebrew).

Tsedaka, Benyamim, Ayala Lowenstamm, and Haim Z. Hirschberg. "Samaritans." In *Encyclopedia Judaica,* vol. 14. New York: Macmillan, 1971.

Tsedaka, Ratson. *Samaritan Legends: Twelve Legends from the Oral Tradition,* ed. D. Noy. Haifa: Haifa Municipality, Ethnographic Museum and Archives, Israel Folktale Archives, 1965 (in Hebrew).

SAMBATION

Sambation (Sabbation, Sanbation, Sabatino, Sambatya, Sabbath River) is a legendary river beyond which the Ten Lost Tribes of Israel were exiled in 721 B.C.E. by Shalmaneser V, king of Assyria. Legends describe it as a roaring torrent (often not of water but of stones), the turbulence of which ceases only on the Sabbath, when Jews are not allowed to travel.

Sambation is mentioned for the first time in the Yerushalmi Talmud: "Rabbi Brachia and Rabbi Chalbo say in the name of Rabbi Shmuel bar Nachman: (the tribes of) Israel exiled to three exiles, one behind the river Sanbation and one to Daphneh of Antiochia and one that the cloud descended on them and covered them" (*y. Sanhedrin,* 10).

Sambation is also mentioned in the Babylonian Talmud in a legend about Rabbi Akiva: "Rabbi Akiva was questioned by Turnusrupus, the wicked: Why is this day (of Sabbath) distinguished from all other days? To which Akiva answered: Why is this man (Turnusrupus) distinguished from all other men? And he answered: Because it is the will of my master (the king). Rejoined Rabbi Akiva: Sabbath is also distinguished because it is the will of the Lord of the Universe. Said Turnusrupus: You misunderstand me. My question is: Whence do you know that this day is Sabbath? And he answered: From the river of Sabbation (which rests on this day)" (*b. Sanhedrin* 65b).

Rabbi Akiva does not explain how the river distinguishes the Sabbath from all other days of the week, but Rashi (Rabbi Solomon ben Isaac of Troyes, 1040–1105 C.E.) says in his interpretation of this text: "A river of stones, and all days of the week it goes and flaws, and in the day of Sabbath it keeps still and rests." Rashi relies on other midrashim that enlarge the story. For example, in Midrash Bereshit Rabba, it was said: "River Sambation will prove—that it drags stones all the days of the week and on Shabbath it rests" (*Bereshit Rab.* 11:5).

Both legends, the legend about Rabbi Akiva and Turnusrupus and the legend about the river Sambation as the place of exile for the ten tribes of Israel, are mentioned many times in the Midrash (*Bereshit Rab.* 73:5; *Bam. Rab.* 16:5; *Eicha Rab.* 2:5; Midrash *Zuta Shir Ha'Shirim* 1, 5 (16); *Psiqta Rabbati*, 23:5, 31:5; Midrash *Tanḥuma*, Mikets, 17).

The name Sambation is mentioned in the Targum of pseudo-Jonathan to Exodus: "I will remove them from there and place them beyond the River Sambation" (Exod. 34:10).

Nachmanides (Moshe ben Nachman, 1194–c. 1270), in his comment to Deuteronomy (32:26), explains that the name Sambation derived from the root S.B.T., which means "cease working" and the suffix *-yon* is the Arabic form of the adjective, like ezov–ezovion. Nachmanides identifies the river Sambation as the river Gozan, to which the tribes of Israel were exiled: "And the king of Assyria carried Israel away unto Assyria, and put them in Halah, and in Habor, on the river of Gozan, and in the cities of the Medes" (2 Kgs. 18:11).

Josephus Flavius, in his book, *The Wars of the Jews,* describes a river that runs every seventh day and rests on six:

> Now Titus Caesar tarried some time at Berytus, as we told you before. He thence removed, and exhibited magnificent shows in all those cities of Syria through which he went, and made use of the captive Jews as public instances of the destruction of that nation. He then saw a river as he went along, of such a nature as deserves to be recorded in history; it runs in the middle between Arcea, belonging to Agrippa's kingdom, and Raphanea. It hath somewhat very peculiar in it; for when it runs, its current is strong, and has plenty of water; after which its springs fail for six days together, and leave its channel dry, as any one may see; after which days it runs on the seventh day as it did before, and as though it had undergone no change at all; it hath also been observed to keep this order perpetually and exactly; whence it is that they call it the Sabbatic River that name being taken from the sacred seventh day among the Jews. (*J.W.* Book 7, 5:1)

Pliny the Elder (Gaius or Caius Plinius Secundus, 23–79 C.E.), in his book *Naturalis Historia* (Natural History), tells about a river that runs on six days and rests every seventh, though it in no way appears by his account that the seventh day of this river was the Jewish Sabbath (*Nat. Hist.* 31).

The first to disseminate the legends was Eldad Ha'dani. According to his narrative, the Sambation surrounds the land not of the ten tribes, but of the children of Moses, who have there a powerful kingdom in Africa. Eldad represents the Sambation as consisting entirely of sand and stones (Julius [Judah David] Eisenstein, *Otzar Midrashim*, 1915; Eldad Ha'dani, 19:5).

As a result of Eldad Ha'dani's stories, the legends about the ten lost tribes of Israel who live beyond the Sambation River spread among Jewish communities all over the world. The Israel Folktale Archives (IFA) at the University of Haifa holds many stories about the lost tribes of Israel, and some among them mention the Sambation. Many of these stories are confrontation stories, in which a Jewish community is in danger and receives help from a Jewish hero who comes from beyond the Sambation River.

A Yemenite-Jewish story that is found in three different versions at the IFA (IFA 943, 4311, and 11289) describes the rescue of a Jewish community by a Jewish maiden from beyond the Sambation, who is brought by a messenger of the community.

A confrontation story of Polish-Jewish origin that is found in two versions (IFA 206 and 2208) tells about confrontation between a Christian minister and Rabbi Meir ben Isaac Nahorai, cantor of the Vermaiza and Magentsa communities. The minister asks the cantor to demonstrate a miracle; and Rabbi Meir enters the raging Sambation and immediately the river calms down. According to the legend, after this miracle, Rabbi Meir writes a *piyyut* of "Akdamot" to the day of Pentecost.

A confrontation story from Morocco that is found in the IFA in two versions (IFA 11248 and IFA 13947) makes the connection between the Jewish hero who comes from beyond the Sambation and the building of a mosque by the name "Mulay ha'Shabbat" (the Master of Sabbath).

Yoel Perez

See also: Tribes, Ten Lost.

Bibliography

Davidy, Yair. *"Ephraim, The Gentile Children of Israel": The Location of Lost Israelite Tribes in the West According to the Bible, Jewish, and Non-Jewish Tradition, and General Fact.* Jerusalem: Russell-Davis, 1995.

Flavius, Josephus. *The Wars of the Jews.* Book 7, trans. William Whiston. Grand Rapids, MI: Christian Classics Ethereal Library, 2000.

Parfitt, Tudor. *The Lost Tribes of Israel: The History of a Myth.* London: Weidenfeld & Nicolson, 2002.

Pliny, the Elder (C. Plini). *Secundi naturalis historiae.* libri XXXVII/Post Ludovici IAni obitum recognovit et Scripturae Discrepantia adiecta edidit Carolus Mayhoff, Lipsiae, Teubner, 1892 (1970).

Schloessinger, Max. *The Ritual of Eldad Ha-Dani Reconstructed and Edited from Manuscripts and a Genizah Fragment.* Leipzig: Rudolf Haupt, 1908.

Samson and Delilah

Samson is the last of the judges in the Book of Judges. In the Jewish folkloric tradition, the story of Samson, like the story of Hercules and other ancient heroes, such as Perseus, Cadmus, and Bellerophon, expresses the folk wish for a strong hero who can bring salvation to his people. His lover, Delilah, the only woman in the tales of Samson whose name is cited, betrays him and brings about his downfall. According to some scholarly interpretations, her name stems from a Hebrew acronym that refers to the loom of the web in Judges 16:13–14.

The history of Samson's life in the Bible is divided into three parts:

1. The dedication of Samson to God before his birth. The story is connected to the motif found around the world of a baby born by supernatural powers to a barren woman. An angel of God appears before the woman alone (Judg. 13:3) and informs her of the expected birth of a Nazarite, who will save Israel from the Philistines. The angel also mentions the law relating to the rules of the boy: A razor shall not touch his head. Later the angel appears before the woman and her husband (13:11).

The story of the birth of Samson has gone through a process of demythologization. Unlike the stories of coupling between gods or angels of God and human women, which were known in different versions throughout many cultures, in the story of Samson, the angel of God is only the messenger. Some scholars maintain it is likely that the biblical storyteller wanted to avoid the mythical tradition of sexual coupling between Samson's mother and a heavenly creature, as a result of which a giant was born.

2. The first actions of Samson (14–15)—a series of outstanding deeds. On his way to his Philistine fiancée he kills a lion (14–16); on the way to the second visit, he removes honey from a beehive in the carcass of the lion (14:8–9). These events enable him to ask several riddles at his wedding banquet (14:12–14). His Philistine friends force his wife to tell them the answer to the riddle. Samson gives them thirty changes of garments as he had promised, but in order to do this, he kills thirty men in Ashkelon (14:19). The marriage to a Philistine woman is not viewed favorably by Samson's parents and brings about a violent disagreement. After his wife's father gives her to his friend, Samson catches 300 foxes, attaches torches to their tails, and sets fire to the fields of the Philistines.

Scholars have found a similar connection to dispatching of the foxes in the story of Obidius in the Roman ritual of the holiday in honor of the goddess of grain: At the circus in Rome, they raced foxes with burning torches attached to their tails. Perhaps in this tale of Samson there is a provocation to Dagon, the Philistine god of grain. In Aesop's fables, there is also a similarity: A man hated a fox who caused him damages. He soaked linen in oil, tied it to the fox's tail, and lit it, but the fox arrived during the harvesting of the man's fields and burned them.

Inspired by the spirit of God, Samson killed 1,000 men with a donkey's jawbone (15:15–16). At the same time, he became thirsty, a miracle occurred, and a well was created (14:15–19). These two stories offer an etiological explanation of names of places: Ramat Lehi (cheek's heights) and Ein-Hakoreh (the caller's spring).

3. The last deeds of Samson and his death. The reason for Samson's failure is connected to his love of women. He is nearly captured in Gaza when he visits a prostitute. He escapes at night after tearing off the doors of the gates of Gaza (16:1–3). After that he falls in love with Delilah, who manages to extract from him the secret of his strength (16:17). She shaves his head (16:19), and, after he loses his strength, she delivers him into the hands of the Philistines (16:18–20). The Philistines gouge out his eyes and tie him up. In the meantime, his hair begins to grow. The Philistines gather in the temple of their god Dagon in order to mock his downfall. Samson prays to God and requests vengeance. After that, he destroys the temple and dies in the destruction. More people are killed at this event than Samson has killed in his lifetime (16:29–30). His death represents his special character, and at this event it transpires that his exceptional strength came to him directly from God.

Three stories are interwoven in this part:

1. the removal of the gates of Gaza (16:1–3)
2. Delilah (16:4–20)
3. the death of Samson (16:30).

The motif of Samson's hair is similar to that in the story of Nisus, king of Megara. At first, the story of Samson was told independently and was passed down orally from generation to generation.

Only later was it adapted to a successive poem like the story of Gilgamesh, who excelled in physical strength, and Gretir, the hero from Iceland.

In contrast to other judges, Samson fought the Philistines alone, and his battles were due to his personal conflicts. His assistance to his people is through weakening his enemies, but his activities are not of political importance.

The Book of Judges relates the tale of Samson's love for Delilah, a woman from the Valley of Sorek (Judg. 16:4). Five Philistine leaders each offer her eleven hundred pieces of silver, should she agree to turn Samson over to them, so that he could be bound and tortured. Delilah assents to their bribes—not for ideological reasons but, rather, out of greed. She unsuccessfully tries three times to tempt Samson into revealing the source of his strength to her.

The First Attempt to Entice Samson (Judges 16:6–9)

The manipulative Delilah asks Samson to prove his love for her. The biblical account (Judg. 16:6–9) describes the first attempt to entice Samson: Delilah said to Samson, "Tell me, please, wherein lies the secret of your great strength, and how you can be bound to render you helpless." Samson replied, "If they bind me with seven fresh, wood fiber cords not yet dried, then I shall become weak and be like any other man." The princes then brought her seven fiber cords that had not dried, and she bound him with them. Having men hidden in her room, she said to him, "The Philistines are upon you, Samson!" But he snapped the cords as a strand of rope snaps when it is exposed to fire. So they did not discover the secret of his strength.

The Second Attempt to Entice Samson (Judges 16:10–12)

Delilah said to Samson, "You have deceived me: you have lied to me: but tell me now, please, with what you can be bound." He said to her, "If they bind me tightly with new ropes that have never been used, then I shall become weak and be as any other man." So Delilah took new ropes, bound him with them, and said, "The Philistines are upon you, Samson!" Men were waiting in an inside room. But he snapped the ropes from his arms like a thread.

The Third Attempt to Entice Samson (Judges 16:13–14)

Then Delilah said to Samson, "Until now you have fooled me and told me lies: Do tell me wherewith you can be bound." He said to her, "If you weave the seven locks of my head with the web." So she fastened it with a pin and said to him, "The Philistines are upon you, Samson." He awakened from his sleep and tore away the pin of the loom with the web.

Delilah finally succeeds in her fourth attempt to entice Samson: "And so, when she had nagged him with her words day after day and pressured him, he was exasperated to the point of death" (16:16). At last, Samson reveals his secret to her. Delilah has Samson fall asleep with his head on her lap, asks a Philistine for a razor, and then snips off the braids of Samson's head. The erotic overtones of this specific passage are self-evident.

In the original oral tradition, the tale of Samson and Delilah is an erotic story in which the woman overpowers the man in the act of intercourse; this fact is blurred in subsequent renderings. One reads that "She [Delilah] made him sleep upon her knees" (19) and about Yael and Sisera "He was fast asleep" (Judg. 4:21). The author's idea was to protect the image of the biblical heroes. "At her feet he bowed, he fell, he lay down; at her feet he bowed, he fell" (Judg. 5:27).

The motif of the invincible male hero who is tempted by his beloved to reveal the secret of his strength to her is well known in folktales. The treacherous woman delivers her lover to the enemies in the ancient Gilgamesh tales, which refer to a hero who loses his supernatural strength due to the betrayal of a prostitute.

The story of Samson and Delilah is unlike biblical tales, such as those of Yael and Sisera and Esther and Haman, in which the reader is meant to revere the heroine, who saves her people from a hostile enemy. In the biblical account of Delilah, readers identify with the male hero, whereas Delilah is represented as a negative character. Samson is a towering figure capable of all acts of heroism; but he is unable to withstand the seductive powers of Delilah, a foreign woman, and finally reveals his great secret to her.

The biblical text reports that Samson loved Delilah (16:4), but not that she loved him—a hint, perhaps, that she does not love him and will have no qualms about betraying him.

Folklore scholars hypothesize that the tale originally was told by the Philistines, who admired Delilah's actions and rejoiced at Samson's demise. When the story was transposed in the Hebrew narrative, Delilah's character changed: In the biblical version, she carries out her act not for patriotic motives but, rather, out of greed.There is some similarity between the tale of Samson and the life of Hercules. As with Samson, Hercules' death is caused by a woman he loves.

In Hebrew, the name Samson (Shimshon) conspicuously includes the root for "sun" (*shemesh*), whereas the name Delilah includes the letters for "night." Folklore scholars have thus interpreted the tale of Samson and Delilah as an example of the eternal mythological struggle between the day (sun) and night. The name Delilah is connected by the rabbis with *delal* (to enfeeble), because she "enfeebled Samson's strength, she enfeebled his actions, and she enfeebled his determination" (*Midr. Num. Rab.* 9:24).

Aliza Shenhar

Bibliography

Ben-Gurion, Emanuel. *The Aggadah Paths.* Jerusalem: Bialik Institute, 1970 (in Hebrew).

Exum, Cheryl J. *Fragmented Women: Feminist (sub)Versions of Biblical Narratives.* Sheffield, UK: JSOT Press, 1993.

Fishelov, David. *Samson's Locks.* Haifa: Haifa University Press, 2000 (in Hebrew).

Fox, Everett. "The Samson Cycle in an Oral Setting." *Alcheringa: Ethnopoetics* 4 (1978): 51–53, 63–68.

Meyers, Carol L., ed. *Women in Scripture.* Grand Rapids, MI: William B. Eerdmans, 2000.
Sasson, Jack M. "Who Cut Samson's Hair (and Other Trifling Issues Raised by Judges 16)." *Proof Texts* 81 (1988): 333–339.
Simon, Uriel. *Seek Peace and Pursue It.* Tel Aviv: Yediot Ahronot, 2002 (in Hebrew).
Webb, Barry G. *The Book of the Judges: An Integrated Reading.* Sheffield, UK: Sheffield Academic Press, 1987.
Zakovitch, Yair. *The Life of Samson (Judges 13–16)*. Jerusalem: Magnes, 1982 (in Hebrew).

Sarah

Sarah (Sarai), Abraham's wife (Gen. 11:29) and Isaac's mother (Gen. 17:19), is the first of the four Jewish matriarchs. According to Abraham (Gen. 20:12), Sarah was also his half-sister, the daughter of his father but not of his mother.

The usual interpretation of the name Sarah is "princess" or "chieftain[ness]," though it may also be connected with the Akkadian S'arrat, one of the designations of the mother-goddess Ishtar.

Sarah was infertile, and in biblical times infertility was considered a disgrace and a curse for a woman. The folkloric motif about the infertility of a beautiful, beloved wife characterizes biblical myths of the mothers Rebekah and Rachel as well as the theme of deliverance from infertility with God's help.

The use of the infertility motif serves as a bridge connecting the recognition that birth expresses God's will and his power to control fertility and the need to cast light upon his intervention in special circumstances. Hence the infant (Isaac), whose birth is announced by three angels, is perceived as the product of the connection between God and a mortal woman. In a demythologizing process, the biblical story emphasizes the results of this connection not in terms of mythic concepts of children of the gods but, rather, as regular mortals.

The announcement of Isaac's birth is connected to a passage that relates to Abimelech, king of Gerar (Gen. 1–18), which makes clear that Sarah returned to her days of youthful beauty before the birth. In Egypt Abraham tells the pharaoh that his wife is his sister to save him from being killed out of jealousy (Gen. 12:11–14). The pharaoh takes the beautiful Sarah from him; after God afflicts the pharaoh with the ten plagues, the Egyptian ruler returns Sarah with gifts ("all that he had" [Gen. 12:20]). In the Midrash, Sarah prayed to God to deliver her from the pharoah, and an angel was sent to whip the king at her command (*Bereshit Rab.* 45:1).

It can be hypothesized that this folkloric motif derives from the Egyptian legend of two brothers. The Midrash relates that Sarah was concealed in a box so that she could be smuggled from Canaan across the border into Egypt—the account resembles the first story in the tales of the Arabian nights.

The fact that the story is repeated three times in the Book of Genesis (Sarah and the pharaoh, Sarah and Abimelech of Gerar, and Rebekah and Abimelech) might reflect various folk traditions passed among the people orally and incorporated into the biblical text. The repetition is characteristic of narrative traditions. In addition to the repetition, processes by which the story is told in gradual stages and intensifies from version to version are evident.

After the birth of Ishmael, Sarah struggles with Hagar, her Egyptian maid whom she offered to her husband so that she could give birth to a child. She changes her name from Sarai to Sarah only after Isaac's birth; similarly, Abram becomes Abraham after the birth (Gen. 17:5), in accordance with the popular belief that a change in a person's name changes his or her fortune.

The promise of offspring was repeated when the angels visited the tent of Abraham and Sarah. Sarah laughed when she heard the news, thus providing the basis for the name of the son, Isaac: The Hebrew for Isaac, Yitzhak, is based on the Hebrew root for "laughter" (*tazḥak*).

The midrashic literature provides effusive descriptions of Sarah's beauty; for example, during the ninety years in which Sarah did not give birth, she had the appearance of a "bride at the wedding canopy" (*Midr. Bereshit Rab.* 45:4). This motif is familiar in story-telling that emphasizes that a hero's qualities are unaffected by time. There are also legends that stress her righteousness and the miracles that occurred to her. In one legend, villagers gossip about the old man and old woman who are said to have brought a street urchin from the market (the boy is said to be their son). A miracle occurs, and her breasts open as two fountains, and she nurses all infants of women who were there (*Midr. Bamidbar Rab.*). In addition, during her lifetime, the doors of her house were always hospitably open; her dough miraculously increased in volume; a light burned from Friday evening to Friday evening, and a pillar of the divine cloud rested above her tent (*Midr. Bereshit Rab.* 60:16).

According to the Midrash, after Abraham offered Isaac in sacrifice, Satan related to Sarah that Abraham had slaughtered their son. She fainted, lost her mind, and died of grief (*Targum* Jonathan, Gen. 22:20; *Sefer ha'yashar,* based on ancient sources). Beauty was extinguished when she died, and everything was thrown into confusion (*Midr. Ha'gadol Bereshit*).

Sarah passed away at the age of 127, in Kiryat Arba. Abraham purchased the Cave of the Patriarchs (Machpelah) to bury her.

Sarah should have reached Abraham's lifespan of 175, but forty-eight years were taken away because of her readiness to argue with Abraham over Hagar's misdeeds (*Bereshit Rab.,* 45:5). Sarah's behavior toward Ishmael, whom she drove away from Abraham's tent, is justified on the grounds that she saw him commit idolatry, rape, and murder (Tosfata Sota 6, 6; *Bereshit Rab.* 53:11).

Sarah appears in fifteen stories registered in the Israel Folklore Archives (IFA), only a few of which are continuations of midrashic tales, including Sarah's response after she heard of Isaac's sacrifice (Morocco, IFA 10.022).

In folktales that are still transmitted orally, Sarah figures as a righteous woman who lived a long life with Abraham because she seldom spoke. This point is made by a sage in Jerusalem who wants women to keep quiet in their portion of the synagogue (Sephardi, Eretz Israel, IFA 622). She can play a starring role in legends—an elderly woman who brings cures for a mortally ill child is said to be Sarah (Ashkenazi, Eretz Israel, IFA 5194).

Humorous formulas based on word play in Yiddish and Hebrew were common to Jews in Eastern Europe. For example, Sarah, the daughter of a rabbi from Kraków, asked for a bone (Yidd., *bayin*). During a Sabbath meal, her brother believes that she has acted impolitely and slaps her. After she starts to cry, he justifies his action by saying that he had to recite the passage that begins "and Sarah's son (*ben*)" (Poland, IFA 14463).

The Arab-Israeli conflict also finds expression in these tales. In one tale from Tunisia, a Jewish boy who is struck by an Arab boy claims that he appealed to Sarah, who complained that she allowed Abraham to wed Hagar, thereby giving rise to a loathed nation. The qadi (Muslim religious judge) revokes the rite of striking Jews due to this boy's deed (IFA 9670).

Aliza Shenhar

See also: Abraham.

Bibliography

Dennis, Trevor. *Sarah Laughed: Women's Voices in the Old Testament.* Nashville: Abingdon Press, 1994.

Jeansonne, Sharon Pace. *The Women of Genesis: From Sarah to Potiphar's Wife.* Minneapolis: Fortress, 1990.

Otwell, John. *And Sarah Laughed: The Status of Women in the Old Testament.* Philadelphia: Westminster, 1977.

Rothkoff, Aaron. "Sarah." In *Encyclopaedia Judaica,* vol. 14. Jerusalem: Keter, 1973.

Sandnel, Samuel. *The Enjoyment of Scripture.* New York: Oxford University Press, 1972.

Speiser, Ephraim A. "The Wife-Sister Motif in the Patriarchal Narratives." In *Biblical and Other Studies,* ed. A. Altmann. Cambridge: Harvard University Press, 1963.

Teubal, Savina J. *Sarah the Priestess.* Athens, OH: Swallow, 1984.

Trible, Phyllis. "Genesis 22: The Sacrifice of Sarah." In *Not in Heaven: Coherence and Complexity in Biblical Narrative,* ed. Jason P. Rosenblatt and Joseph C. Sitterson, Jr. Bloomington: Indiana University Press, 1991.

Satan

In the Bible, the early etymology of the name Satan means "opponent" or "enemy" and is used in the context of human relations (e.g., Num. 22:22, 32; 1 Sam. 29:4; 2 Sam. 19:23; 1 Kgs. 5:18; Ps. 109:6). But in the books of Zechariah and Job, the name refers to a separate entity, who lacks any detailed physical aspect. He is a heavenly being and serves as the celestial prosecutor (Zech. 3:1–2), challenging Job's faith and moral integrity (Job 1:6–12; 2:1–7).

This trait of the heavenly prosecutor was adopted and further developed in rabbinical sources and midrashic literature. Satan became the dreadful denunciator of any private or collective wrongdoing by a person or by Israel (*Avot de'Rabbi Nathan,* [addition 2 to version 1], ch. 9; *Gen. Rab.* 57:4; *Exod. Rab.* 31:2; *Lamentations Rabba* Buber 2). This characteristic of Satan has predominated in Jewish culture as well as in folktales (e.g., IFA 2015; IFA 3162; IFA 15277; IFA 6791).

Various customs are explained as being designed to prevent Satan from denouncing individuals or Israel as a whole, such as the fast on the Day of Atonement (Yom Kippur) (*Psiqta Rabbati* 45:185b) or a blessing immediately following ritual hand washing (*netilat yadaim*) (*Deut. Rab.* 2:10; *Makhzor Vitri* 17).

His name is often replaced by other terms, such as Samael (*Exod. Rab.* 18:5; *Lev. Rab.* 21:4), the Angel of Death, or the evil inclination (*b. Bava Batra* 16a).

One of Satan's major cultural functions is to act as an arbiter of moral issues. He is described as rejoicing and dancing while a person sins (*Num. Rab.* 20:11) and is eager to punish evildoers. Assisting Noah in the planting of the vine, he caused the appalling aspects of drunkenness (*Tanḥuma Noah* 13:13). He controls the four matters viewed as provoking sins: wealth, women, evil inclination, and feuds (*Kallah Rabbati* 6:1). In this context, he is represented as connected to women: the creation of Eve generated his existence (*Gen. Rab.* 17:6; *Yalqut Shimoni* Gen. 23). Some actions involving women are regarded as bringing him into one's home, such as a father envying a beautiful woman (Num. 218:18) or marrying two women (*Tanaim* Deut. 21:22). According to medieval Judah the Pious, he provokes men into adultery (e.g., *Sefer ḥasidim* Wistinetzki 361). He causes quarrels among couples (IFA 4016). The custom that at the conclusion of funerals women should leave the cemetery first is explained by the belief that Satan and the Angel of Death are dancing before them (*Yalqut Shimoni* Zech. 570:3; *Tashbetz Qatan* 447). A humorous element in folktales is his request from God to experience marriage with a human wife. After his request is granted, Satan unhappily married, flees to avoid his wicked wife (e.g., IFA 14104; IFA 14894; IFA 14969).

Satan is a vehicle through which critical doubts about divine justice can be approached. For example, Isaac's sacrifice is explained as being initiated by Satan (*b. Sanhedrin* 89b). He is described as obstructing the journey of Abraham and Isaac to the site of the sacrifice, while questioning the strength of human faith and the justification of divine commands (*Gen. Rab.* 56:22; *Tanḥuma Vayar* Buber 261:114; *Yalqut Shimoni* Vayar 22:98; IFA 10022).

National disasters and suffering are explained as a result of his insistence that harsh sentences be imposed for collective sins, such as the making of the Golden Calf (*Exod. Rab.* 43:1; *Tanḥuma Ki Tisa* 19) or the decadent behavior of Persian Jewry (*Esth. Rab.* 7:13).

He is also described as disrupting righteous activities and behaviors (*mitzvot*) such as Moses's reception of the tables of law (*Exod. Rab.* 41:7; *Maḥzor Vitri* 508), blowing the horn on Rosh Ha'Shana (IFA 1609; IFA 1645), and carrying out the ritual of the Sabbath ending (IFA 2007); he is said to be annoyed by Torah study sessions (*Gen. Rab.* 38:7; 84:3). These events end with the righteous overcoming Satan, and as a result the sacred and normative ethos is strengthened.

Some of the views concerning him seem to reflect human fears of dangerous situations: He is active during periods dangerous to people (such as giving birth or engaging in battle) (*y. Shabbat* 1:1, 2:6; *Gen. Rab.* 91:9). Some people are subjected to his threats: the lonely traveler, the person who sleeps alone in a dark house, and the one who sails upon the open sea (*y. Shabbat* 2:6; *Eccl. Rab.* 3:2).

Paradoxically, some beliefs about Satan also reflect human apprehension about happy events: He is believed to be present wherever there is calm, food, and drinks (*Gen. Rab.* 38:7, 84:3). The ancient proverb "Man should never open his mouth to Satan" (*b. Ber.* 19a, 60a), is an excellent example of this tendency.

Various customs were viewed as reducing Satan's malefic actions, and these change according to time and space. For example, in tannaitic sources a person intending to travel was advised to refrain from leaving on the same day as the wicked, because he would be accompanied by Satanic angels (*t. Avoda Zarah,* Liberman 17:3). The scapegoat on Yom Kippur was considered a bribe to him to deflect his denunciations (*Sifrei* Shemini 1:3). Yet Satan is powerless while peace dwells among the people of Israel, even if they worship idolatry (Num. 42; *Num. Rab.* 11:7). In the Midrash, observing a righteous way of life according to the Torah and giving charity prevent his actions and prosecution (*Deut. Rab.* 2:10). The different ways of blowing the shofar are supposed to confuse him (*b. Rosh Hashanah* 16b; *Sekhel Tov* Buber Gen. 22). On the Day of Atonement, he does not prosecute (*Lev. Rab.* 21:4).

In the Middle Ages, reading the Torah continuously (*Maḥzor Vitri* 426) and putting salt on a table before the meal starts were supposed to prevent Satan from acting (*Hagahot Ashrey* on Berakhot ch. 6, 22:1; Trachtenberg 1977, 155, 160). The use of amulets carrying the expression "Krah Satan" (lit., "rend Satan") is supposed to cure a person who has been attacked by an evil spirit (Trachtenberg 1977, 95).

Idit Pintel-Ginsberg

See also: Demon.

Bibliography

Day, Peggy Lynne. *An Adversary in Heaven: Satan in the Hebrew Bible.* Atlanta: Scholar, 1988.

Gershenson, Daniel E. "The Name Satan." *Zeitschrift für die Alttestamentliche Wissenschaft* 114:3 (2002): 443–445.

Goldberg, Sylvie-Anne. "Satan et Samael, le double visage de la mort juive." *La mort et ses representations dans le judaïsme,* pp. 109–121. Paris: Champion, 2000.

Jacobs, Joseph, and Ludwig Blau. "Satan." In *Encyclopeadia Judaica,* vol. 14. Jerusalem: Keter, 1996.

Kluger, Rivkah Scharf. *Satan in the Old Testament.* Evanston: Northwestern University Press, 1967.

Pagels, Elaine H. *The Origin of Satan.* New York: Vintage, 1996.

Trachtenberg, Joshua. *Jewish Magic and Superstition.* New York: Atheneum, 1977.

Urbach, Efraim Elimelech. *The Sages: Their Concepts and Beliefs.* Jerusalem: Magnes, 1975 (in Hebrew).

Yassif, Eli. *The Hebrew Folktale.* Bloomington: Indiana University Press, 1999.

Schwarzbaum, Haim (1911–1983)

Haim Schwarzbaum's mastery of ancient and modern languages, as well as his unlimited interest in world cultures, positioned him as one of the last great comparative folklorists of the twentieth century. Schwarzbaum brought to folklore studies his background in European, ethnographic-Orientalist learning and the school of Jewish studies at the Hebrew University in the first half of the twentieth century. The combination of the two formed the basis of his folkloristic achievements, which included a lifetime of scholarship and the authorship of five books.

Schwarzbaum was born on September 24, 1911, in Warsaw, Poland. He began his academic studies in his hometown, where he remained until his immigration to Palestine in 1937. He continued his studies in Arabic and Muslim culture at the Hebrew University in Jerusalem.

Haim Schwarzbaum. *(Courtesy of Moshe Schwarzbaum)*

Schwarzbaum's folklore publications began in 1938 with short articles in daily newspapers in Hebrew and English, then developed into articles in professional Israeli and international journals in the 1960s and 1970s, and culminated in his great research books. Schwarzbaum's scholarly achievements can be categorized in three large-scale fields.

First, the postbiblical traditions in Judaism and Islam. His first scholarly article, "The Denier and the Loaves of Bread" (*Edot* 1946), clearly belongs in this category. Here Schwarzbaum revealed his preference for the comparative discipline, his immense mastery of sources in a great number of languages, and his keen attention to the cultural diversity of tales. Schwarzbaum continued his extensive publication in international folklore journals as *Fabula,* but his main achievement in this category was the last book published in his lifetime, *Biblical and Extra-Biblical Legends in Islamic Folk Literature* (1982). Here he explored the traces of biblical traditions in the main literary genres of Arab folk literature. His findings about the cultural interchange between Jewish and Muslim cultures in the domain of oral, folkloric traditions are of first-rate importance for understanding both cultures.

Second, Jewish folk narratives of the Middle Ages. Schwarzbaum was one of the first scholars in Jewish studies to understand the importance of the narrative traditions of the Middle Ages to the study of European folklore. He studied the sources and analogues of major folklore works such as Joseph ben Meir ibn Zabara's *Book of Delight,* Moses Gaster's edition of *Sefer ha'Ma'asiyot* (The Exempla of the Rabbis), Rabbi Nissim ben Jacob ibn Shāhīn's *An Elegant Composition Concerning Relief After Adversity* and the *Chronicles of Yerahmeel.* However, his most important publication in this area, which also brought him international recognition, was his book-length study of Petrus Alfonsi's *Disciplina Clericalis,* published in *Sefarad* (1961–1963). In it, Schwarzbaum studied one of the most influential exempla books of medieval Europe, revealing the Arab and Jewish sources of the stories as well as their influence on European folklore. The most comprehensive of Schwarzbaum's publications is *The Mishle Shu'alim* (Fox Fables) *of Rabbi Berechiah ha'Nakdan: A Study in Comparative Folklore and Fable Lore* (1979). The study is dedicated to the thirteenth-century Hebrew collection of fables by the French Rabbi Berechiah ben Natronai ha'Nakdan—one of the most important medieval books of fables. This is a comprehensive study of fable theory in general and of each of the fables included in the Berechiah collection.

Third, the study of Jewish folk literature. Throughout Schwarzbaum's scholarly publications, he expressed important observations and findings on the history and development of Jewish folkloristics. In 1961, in one of his early articles, he presented an authoritative examination of recent studies in the field. So did his "The Contribution of the Jewish Scholars in England to Jewish and General Folklore"—a fundamental and comprehensive survey of the works of two of the most influential British folklorists: Joseph Jacobs and Moses Gaster. However, his main achievement in this field is *Studies in Jewish and World Folklore* (1968), in which he devoted special attention to the study of Jewish folk narrative, folk song, dance, proverbs, folk beliefs, and customs and material culture. This book is still considered one of the basic tools for understanding the history and methods of Jewish folkloristics.

A selection of the most notable of Schwarzbaum's articles was published after his death by the archive of Jewish and Muslim Folklore bearing his name at Ben-Gurion University of the Negev in Israel. His articles in English were published as *Jewish Folklore Between East and West: Collected Papers,* edited and introduced by Eli Yassif (1989), and articles in Hebrew in *Roots and Landscapes: Collected Studies in Folklore,* edited by Eli Yassif (1993).

From 1939 to 1948 Schwarzbaum served as librarian and archivist of British Mandate Palestine, and from 1948, when the State of Israel was founded, to 1977, he worked as archivist of the Israel Defense Forces. He died on November 11, 1983.

Eli Yassif

See also: Yassif, Eli.

Bibliography

Ganuz, Itzhak. "A Bibliography of Haim Schwarzbaum's Essays and Books in the Realm of Jewish and Arabic Folklore." *Yeda Am* 22 (1984): 10–19 (in Hebrew).

Yassif, Eli. *Jewish Folklore: An Annotated Bibliography.* New York: Garland, 1986.

Sea

The admiration aroused by mankind's first encounter with the sea gave birth to many myths, including the biblical myth of creation. Comparing this myth to myths from the ancient Middle East reveals that the act of creation had always involved the surrender of the sea as a threat over civilization and its submission to the will of God. The divine act of separation of the upper waters from the lower ones (Gen. 1:6–7), as well as the struggle between God and the whale, the Great Dragon or *Rahab* in biblical sources (Isa. 27:1; Ps. 74:13–14, 89:11) developed into a moral conflict in latter rabbinic literature, reflecting the evil nature of the sea and its destructive force restrained only by the unlimited powers of God (*b. Bava Batra* 74b). The rebellious nature of water reflected in the story of the flood (Gen. 7) and the crossing of the Red Sea (Exod. 14) also demonstrate the possibility of using the great powers of the sea in order to regain God's sovereignty or prove his supremacy. Later sources show as well how the sea punished Rabban Gamliel for confiscating Rabbi Eliezer (*b. Bava Metzi'a* 59b) and how it carried Rabbi Akiva and Rabbi Meir safely upon its waves to the shore (*b. Yebamot* 121a).

The great distance from home as part of the seamen's lives evoked its own apprehensions. As representatives of the social order, the sages warned the seamen that the sea is one of the three places where Satan takes up his prosecution and might harm them (*Yalqut Shimoni* Gen. 31) and that "money that came from overseas countries . . . never contains a sign of blessing" (*b. Pesaḥim* 50b). Such sayings were meant to protect travelers not only from the risks involved in sailing but also from the risks of crossing cultural borders and being exposed to foreign values.

The fear of the sea, its dangers and uncontrollable conduct, was also reflected through the description of the extreme dimensions and imaginative characteristics attributed to it. The depth of the sea, for example, was so great that Adrianus, having spent three and a half years dropping ropes to the bottom of the sea, stopped only when a divine voice intervened (*Shoḥer Tob* 93). Ancient maps often reflected the common conception according to which the sea surrounded the entire world, and sailings were likely to involve extreme weather or an unpleasant encounter with mythological monsters, such as the animals Rabbah bar bar Ḥannah saw while traveling with seamen (*b. Bava Batra* 73b). Animals and sometimes even human characters that dwelt underwater maintained social order, such as the reign of the whale in the story "The Heart of the Fox" (*Alphabet of Ben Sira,* question 21). The creatures living underwater in this story enjoy eternal life, but when they try to convince the fox to join them, he realizes he will not be able to come back. In this way, the sea becomes a symbol of both life and death, fertility and barrenness, the predictable and the unknown.

According to folk traditions, overseas one could find imaginary places such as Paradise or the country of demons, which the hero of "The Story of the Jerusalemite" visited. These places were described not in accordance with actual maritime experience but often as a projection of people's fears and desires. That is why such places were characterized in familiar terms relating to reward and punishment. The Jerusalemite arrived in the country of demons by flying on a miraculous owl and could not leave without the help of a crippled demon and an oath that he would return. Thus, even when the sea is described as a dangerous place, its random actions could be explained by means of a familiar cultural rationale and thus could be controlled.

"Miracles on the Sea," as Isaac Leib Peretz shows in his literary tale, might turn the wild environment of the sea into a religious site, but this will occur mostly for the righteous and on Jewish religious festivals or other holy occasions. The sea turned into a space of distinct boundaries upon which God's spirit dwelt also in S.Y. Agnon's book *In the Heart of the Seas* (1956), based on Jewish traditions. Ḥanania, the hero, crossed the sea and reached the land of Israel traveling on top of a handkerchief. Folk stories dealing with the swift crossing of the sea on horseback, by means of an eagle, giant hand, handkerchief, or mat, are held in the Israel Folktale Archives (IFA) at the University of Haifa as well (5507, 3615, and others), reflecting the attempt to control the incomprehensible dimensions of the sea.

Through the mediation of prayers and vows, such as reading *Shirat hayam* (Song of the Sea) in times of danger at sea (IFA 4094, and in Agnon's aforementioned story [pp. 60–61]), dealing with the sea inspired Jewish cultural patronage. In light of this patronage, even the image of seamen was associated with a positive description of people of the wider world, and despite their reservation about seafaring, *Ḥazal* (sages) consulted seamen more than once concerning general knowledge on materials with which they were not familiar (*b. Shabbat* 90a).

The attitude toward the sea often found in Jewish folk tradition therefore remains dualistic. It has been considered frightening, on the one hand, while challenging, on the other hand, and endangering as well as enlightening and broadening the mind, as is said: "There are two who draw in abundance and give forth in abundance: And these are they: the sea and the government" (*Sifre* to Deut. 354).

Alongside Jewish sea traditions, universal traditions were also common among Jews. One example of this was the custom of throwing a person or an object into the sea in order to pacify it or to make the wind blow. This custom, popular among other peoples in ancient times, has its sources in the animistic perception that the sea has a will of its own and can be appeased when offered a sacrifice. Evidence of this can be found as early as in the story of Jonah (Jonah 1:12–15) or in the talmudic story of Nikanor, who called upon seamen to throw him into the water together with the temple door in order to appease the sea (*b. Yoma* 38a). Traditions and customs of this kind exist to this day as a means of mediation between the unpredictable sea and the human consciousness wishing to control it. Such is the story of the *Dakar,* the submarine that submerged and disappeared underwater on its very first journey at 1968 because it lacked its Indian totem, considered by folk belief to be its protector.

The return to Israel with the rise of Zionism and the naval reality along its seashores raised new cultural opportunities. These were expressed through personal sea stories reconstructing the immigration to Israel as an experience of revelation and refoundation of Zionist values and symbols. Through this cultural filter, life at sea has become a national and social challenge more than a physical one, aiming to grasp the frequently changing substance of the sea and thereby to turn exile into a home.

Tsafi Sebba-Elran

See also: Patai, Raphael; Seamen Tales and Traditions.

Bibliography

Agnon, Shmuel Yosef. *In the Heart of the Seas.* Tel Aviv: Schocken, 1956 (in Hebrew).

Almog, Yosef, and Shmuel Yanai, eds. *Gates Are Open.* Tel Aviv: Pal-Yam Foundation, 2001 (in Hebrew).

Ginzberg, Louis. *The Legends of the Jews.* Philadelphia: Jewish Publication Society of America, 1937.

Graves, Robert, and Raphael Patai. *Hebrew Myths: The Book of Genesis.* New York: Doubleday, 1963.

Patai, Raphael. *The Children of Noah: Jewish Seafaring in Ancient Times.* Princeton: Princeton University Press, 1998.

———. *Jewish Seafaring in Ancient Times.* Jerusalem: Bialik and Jewish Palestine Exploration Society, 1938 (in Hebrew).

Pinto, D. "Tfu, Tfu, Tfu." *Bamahane* 51 (2001): 24–27 (in Hebrew).

Sebba, Tsafi. "Like a Tree Planted on Sea Waves: The Personal Narrative as a Door to the Seaman's World." M.A. thesis, Tel Aviv University, 2002 (in Hebrew).

Shenhar, Aliza. "Folk Sea Stories." M.A. thesis, Hebrew University, 1970 (in Hebrew).

Sobel, Samual, ed. *A Treasury of Jewish Sea Stories.* New York: Jonathan David, 1965.

Yassif, Eli. "Discovering the Other Israel: The Journalist as Ethnographer and Literary Critic." *Alpayim* 11 (1995): 185–209 (in Hebrew).

Seamen Tales and Traditions

Water motions and wave voices occupied the human imagination and invoked an animistic perception of the sea. Stories about mythological sea animals of monstrous dimensions, such as the great whales, appeared as part of the Jewish myth of creation (Gen. 1:21). Only the divine powers of God could master the outburst of the sea as demonstrated by the story of the flood (Gen. 7) or that of Jonah. The prophet who ran away from God into the sea had to be thrown from the ship to the water at the time of a storm in order to appease the sea and thereby to control God's anger (Jonah 1).

Later encounters with the sea, as seen through Rabbah bar bar Ḥannah's corpus of sea tales in the Talmud, also involve gigantic waves surging up to the stars or a monstrous fish that took the ship three days and three nights to surround (*Bava Batra* 73a). Here as well as in other traditional contexts, the mighty forces of nature surrender to God, using a biblical verse or other magic means such as Rabbah bar bar Ḥannah's club with the biblical verse engraved on it. Prayers, vows, and other traditional practices assigned to control the sea were often connected to Passover, when, according to Jewish beliefs, the miracle of crossing the Red Sea took place. Throwing the unleavened bread (*matzah shmura*), the *afikoman,* or the Omer salt into the sea, for example, could calm the water and appease a storm (Israel Folk Archives {IFA} 6628; Sholem Aleichem's "Home for Passover").

Among sea stories reflecting the unique difficulties and challenges of Jewish travelers, there are stories about the Sabbath at sea. As sailing at sea made it necessary to violate the Sabbath rest, many rabbis made use of supernatural forces to delay the ship from sailing on the Sabbath, as did Rabbi Ya'akov Abuḥatsera (IFA 12339) and Rabbi Shmuel (IFA 13809). Through the mediation of God or his messenger, the threatening boundless sea turned not only into a familiar place but into a religious experience of miracles. According to this view, the sea became a place of refuge. Jewish heroes such as Maimonides (known as the Rambam) escaped foreign leaders into the sea and crossed it swiftly through the use of the divine name, put on a piece of paper and cast into the sea. The miraculous experience is also expressed through the Jewish tale type "cast thy bread upon waters" (AT 670*b), according to which a son casting bread into the sea to obey his father gained the ability to comprehend the language of animals and found a treasure.

As a mediator between the familiar social order and the unknown borders of the sea, the fish has become a Jewish symbol of good luck. In addition to being able to fulfill wishes (AT 555), it has also the power to enrich the poor and to compensate the righteous. Thus, for instance, a fish that the fisherman's son put back into the water helped him and enriched him in exchange, at AT 506 tale type. According to the Jewish tale type A*980, either the Rambam or a different hero in the story miraculously found the king's ring inside a fish and thus restored his status as leader of the Jewish community. Likewise, a flock of fish built a "bridge" so that the hero could reach his kidnapped wife (IFA 14389), as in another story, in which crossing the Red Sea took place on back of a giant fish (IFA 4954).

The sea was also considered a dubious and dangerous environment because it was out of reach for the Jewish congregation. Those Jews who did sail were mostly a minority, being exposed to foreign values without the protection and the supervision of the community. Jewish travel diaries dating from the Middle Ages and later reflect this social and cultural seclusion, as one can read in Judah Halevi's poem "At Sea, 16," in Rabbi Moshe Bassola's Diary, or in the travel story of Rabbi Nachman of Bratslav, all based on Jewish folk traditions as well as on personal testimonies.

Social life on board a ship has always been an issue to be dealt with for the seamen. The intercultural meeting point between strangers on a ship aroused the fear of mutiny or scheming, as recounted in the Midrash of the man who drilled a hole in the ship and threatened to drown all its passengers (*Yalqut Shimoni* Jer. 324). These fears stemmed from the negative image attributed to seamen in most texts. Although seamen enjoyed a certain religious halo, being so close to wild nature and depending on the grace of God (*b. Nida* 14a), they were presented as greedy womanizers, especially in modern folktales. The tale type AT 938, which describes a washerwoman snatched by a captain on shore, has a multitude of parallel versions in the IFA and perpetuates the image of the seaman as a rootless person exploiting each port to have a good time with women of all kinds. Hence, going to sea has often been associated with disobeying social conventions, the results of which would be devastating. One example of this is the medieval story "The Story of the Jerusalemite," in which the son breaks an oath he gave to his father by going to sea. Overseas he marries Ashmedai's daughter who kills him for not being loyal to her.

After the development of oceanography, technology, and shipping, perception of the sea was less affected by religious traditions. Stories related to the revival of Israel, such as immigration under British Mandate Palestine and the establishment of the Israeli navy and the fishing industry, evoked mainly social and ideological issues, such as the implications of life away from home, the social equality at sea under the influence of kibbutz values, and the formation of an Israeli identity in the cosmopolitan context of the sea. All can be seen in personal sea stories from the late twentieth century.

Tsafi Sebba-Elran

See also: Sea.

Bibliography

Almog, Yosef, and Shmuel Yanai, eds. *Gates Are Open.* Tel Aviv: Pal-Yam Foundation, 2001 (in Hebrew).

Bin Gorion, Micha Joseph. *Mimekor Yisrael,* vols. 2 and 5. Tel Aviv: Bialik Foundation and Dvir, 1945, 1952 (in Hebrew).

Lewinski, Yom Tov. "For the Knowledge of the Mediterranean Seamen." *Yeda Am* 2–3:2 (1954): 209–212 (in Hebrew).

Patai, Raphael. *The Children of Noah: Jewish Seafaring in Ancient Times.* Princeton: Princeton University Press, 1999.

Sebba, Tsafi. "Like a Tree Planted on Sea Waves: The Personal Narrative as a Door to the Seaman's World." M.A. thesis, Tel Aviv University, 2002 (in Hebrew).

Shenhar, Aliza. "Folk Sea Stories." M.A. thesis, Hebrew University, 1970 (in Hebrew).

Sobel, Samuel, ed. *A Treasury of Jewish Sea Stories.* New York: Jonathan David, 1965.

Ya'ari, Avraham. *Journeys to Israel.* Tel Aviv: Gazit, 1946 (in Hebrew).

Seder Plate

The central object on the table in many Jewish homes on the first and second nights of Passover is a large plate, the Seder plate, known in Hebrew as *ke'arat le'il haseder.* The plate and the different articles placed or, rather, displayed on it serve to recount the story of Passover in a symbolic way. Thus each of the foods on the plate is understood and interpreted in the context of the slavery in Egypt, the Exodus and freedom, and the celebration of Passover in the era of the Temple.

The selected foods and their traditional symbols are as follows: Three *matzot*—the unleavened bread or *matzah* generally symbolizes the haste in which the Jews left Egypt—however, the three *matzot* gained additional meaning, especially in the Lurianic Kabbalah (see below); *zroa,* grilled shank bone of a lamb—symbol of the ancient ceremonial meal of the roasted paschal sacrifice (*korban Pesaḥ); beitzah,* hardboiled egg—symbol of the festival offering (*korban beitzah*); *maror,* bitter herbs—symbol of the embittered lives and difficult labor of the Israelites under the yoke of their Egyptian taskmasters; *haroset,* a mixture of minced apples, nuts, and wine—symbol of the mortar and bricks used by the Israelite slaves during their bondage in Egypt; *karpas,* any green leafy vegetable eaten during the meal (lettuce, celery, parsley, etc.)—originally it stood for the hors d'oeuvres eaten in the meals of the upper class in antiquity and thus served as a symbol of freedom and nobility at the Seder. The custom of dipping the *karpas* in saltwater, however, has been interpreted by some scholars as a reminder of the tears the Israelites shed in Egypt, among other explanations.

The manner in which the different foods are arranged on the plate differs from one community to another. Efforts to standardize the order have been offered by the followers of Rabbi Isaac Luria (Ha'Ari) and Rabbi Elijah, the Gaon of Vilna. In the Lurianic Kabbalah, Passover foods acquired additional meaning connected to the ideas of the school. Thus the plate and its foods have been associated with the ten *sefirot,* or divine emanations, in Lurianic Kabbalah, and the three *matzot*—representing the three "classes" of Jews: Cohen, Levi, and Israel—parallel the upper *sefirot: Keter, Ḥokhmah,* and *Binah.* According to this tradition, *maror,* the bitter herb, is placed in the center of the round plate, while the shank bone (right) and egg (left) are above, and the *ḥaroset* (right) and the *karpas* (left) below. In the tradition of the Vilna Gaon only two *matzot* are placed at the center of the plate—representing the two loaves of bread (*leḥem mishneh*) used on the Sabbath or holiday. Above the *matzot* are the *maror* (right) and *ḥaroset* (left), and below are the bone (right) and egg (left). It should be noted that the Lurianic custom is much more widespread and most extant plates from the past follow this practice.

While the symbolic foods are mentioned in the early sources, a Seder plate is not described in the talmudic or geonic literature. Medieval authorities, such as the twelfth-century Rabbi Abraham ben Nathan ha-Yarhi (i.e., of Lunel, Provence; ca. 1155–1215), mention "a basket in the center of the Passover table" (in his book of customs *Sefer hamanhig,* Istanbul, 1519). Wicker baskets to hold the three *matzot* were also used by the Jews of medieval Spain, as seen in the illuminations of some Sephardic *Haggadot* (e.g., the Barcelona Haggadah, London, British Lib. Ms. Add. 14761, fol. 28v). The miniature shows the young son carrying the covered basket on his head—re-enacting the Exodus from Egypt. This custom was preserved after the expulsion from Spain and is known to this day among descendants of the Sephardim from Morocco and Tunisia. From Spain also comes the earliest extant Seder plate, which is preserved at the Israel Museum, Jerusalem. Judging from its style, decoration, and similarity to Spanish lusterware, this attractive glazed ceramic plate (d. 57 cm), characteristic of Hispano Moresque pottery, is apparently from Manisas in Spain (late fifteenth century). However, the poorly written Hebrew on the plate and uncertainty of its use have led some scholars to doubt its Jewish origin.

By the time the *Shulḥan arukh* was composed, the Seder plate is mentioned in several rabbinic sources, and Rabbi Joseph ben Ephraim Karo himself refers in his code to "a vessel or dish brought to the Seder table" and recommends that the table be "set with beautiful vessels . . . in the manner of freedom" (*Oraḥ ḥayyim* 472:2). Other authorities expanded this idea and emphasized the importance of elaborate ware on the Seder table: "Although during the rest of the year it is best not to display too many beautiful dishes, so that we may keep in mind the destruction of the Temple, yet on the night of Passover, it is good to display as many fine dishes as possible" (Ganzfried, *Kitzur Shulḥan Arukh* 118:7).

During the Renaissance, Italian ceramic masters developed and perfected the production of colorfully painted pottery in a technique known as majolica. Some twenty-eight Italian majolica Seder plates, tentatively dated to the sixteenth to the eighteenth century, have survived. On the rims of these plates appear in bright colors biblical and ceremonial scenes and figures related to the Passover story. However, as the images on these plates are clearly inspired by printed *Haggadot*, one of which was printed only in the nineteenth century (Trieste, 1864), it is now assumed that these are not genuine Renaissance plates but were made in Italy in the late nineteenth century.

The eighteenth century, in which Jewish communities in Europe grew and prospered, witnessed creativity and growth as well in the production of ceremonial art. Many of the extant Seder plates in museums and private collections were made in this period, emanating from Germany, Austria, Bohemia, Moravia, and the Netherlands. Common were shallow plates made of pewter and engraved with Jewish symbols, scenes related to Passover, and Hebrew inscriptions taken from the Haggadah. The pictorial motifs were often inspired by popular illustrated printed *Haggadot*, such as the Venice Haggadah of 1609 or the Amsterdam Haggadah of 1695 and 1712. Similar scenes also appear on ceramic plates of the eighteenth and nineteenth centuries, which were produced in countries such as England, France, and Hungary. At times the Passover episodes are phototransferred—mechanically copied and printed from the *Haggadot* in black and white, while some colorful porcelain plates, chiefly from Herend, Hungary, employed images based on contemporary popular paintings such as those by Moritz Daniel Oppenheim.

A new type of Seder plate, fitted for both the three *matzot* and the symbolic foods, came into use among wealthy Jewish families in Germany, Austria, and Poland toward the end of the eighteenth century and was still popular in the 1930s. This is a large three-tiered cylindrical plate, made mostly of silver or brass, and at times also of wood. The bottom three levels of the plate, often surrounded by a metal grill and silk curtains, are used for separating the three *matzot* (replacing the cloth pockets customarily used for this purpose), while the symbolic foods are placed on top. The makers of these plates developed toylike silver vessels for the ceremonial foods, at times held by complete (that is full, whole, three-dimensional figures) Jewish figurines. Thus, for example, an elderly Jew holds the *ḥaroset* container in the shape of a wheelbarrow—reminiscent of the hard labor in brick and mortar. At the center of some of these plates is a holder for the Elijah's Cup.

In Muslim lands, no such intricate Seder plates were created. Some communities, where Jewish artisans excelled in the craft of brass, large brass plates were used as

Seder plates. Such plates, engraved with lengthy Hebrew inscriptions, the names of the foods, and ornamental and symbolic designs, such as a wine bottle and cups, emanate in particular from Morocco. Simpler plates, made also of wood, are known from Eretz Israel under the Ottoman Empire. In other communities, for example, Kurdistan, simple but large plates are used, and the foods on them are more abundant, including as many *matzot* as needed for all the participants. Among Yemeni Jews, the entire round Seder table, filled with plenty of green vegetables, actually turns into a "Seder plate."

In the twentieth century the art of the Seder plate was revived by Judaica artists, particularly of German origin. The aforementioned three-tiered plate was designed in a modern style by artists such as Friedrich Adler and Ludwig Wolpert, whose work is influenced by design concepts of the noted Bauhaus school. The Zionist movement and the establishment of Israel influenced the commercial or souvenir brass plates produced in large quantities, mainly in the 1950 and 1960s, when the symbols of the freedom festival found new outlets. In the final decades of the twentieth century, many new innovative plates were created by young artists, and international competitions for designing Seder plates were held in the United States and Israel.

Shalom Sabar

See also: Haggadah of Passover; Passover.

Bibliography

Avrin, Leila. "The Spanish Passover Plate in the Israel Museum." *Sefarad* 39 (1979): 1–19.

Davidovotch, David. "Ceramic Seder Plates from Non-Jewish Workshops." *Journal of Jewish Art* 2 (1975): 50–61.

Ganzfried, Shlomo. *Code of Jewish Law.* Brooklyn, NY: Kehot, 1992 (in Hebrew).

Gomberg, Betsy, and Susan Schaalman Youdovin, eds. *The Seder Plate: The 1996 Philip and Sylvia Spertus Judaica Prize.* Chicago: Spertus Museum, 1996.

Mann, Vivian B. "Forging Judaica: The Case of the Italian Majolica Seder Plates." In *Art and Its Uses: The Visual Image and Modern Jewish Society. Studies in Contemporary Jewry,* ed. E. Mendelson, pp. 201–226. New York: Oxford University Press, 1990.

Muller-Lancet, Aviva, and Dominique Champault, eds. *La vie juive au Maroc.* Jerusalem: Israel Museum, 1986 (in Hebrew).

Roth, Cecil. "Majolica Passover Plates of the Sixteenth to Eighteenth Centuries." *Eretz Israel* 7 (1964): 106–111.

Sabar, Shalom, ed. *And I Crowned You with Wreaths . . . : The International Judaica Design Competition.* Jerusalem, 1996 (in Hebrew and English).

Shachar, Isaiah. *Jewish Tradition in Art: The Feuchtwanger Collection of Judaica.* Jerusalem: Israel Museum, 1981 (in Hebrew).

SEGEL, BENJAMIN WOLF (1866–1931)

Benjamin Wolf Segel contributed to the study of Jewish folklore as collector of East European Jewish folklore in general and Galician-Jewish folklore in particular. He also made a meaningful contribution to the analysis of various genres.

Segel was born in Rohatyn in 1866 and grew up in Lwów in Western Galicia (now Ukraine); not much is known of his childhood. In his publicistic writings he fought strenuously on two fronts: defending his community, the Jews of Poland and Galicia, against anti-Semitism, while battling supporters of Jewish nationalist ideologies within that community, whether Zionist or Yiddishist. Emancipation was his heart's desire; he fervently believed that a Jew could be at home in Poland and its culture. For Segel, emancipation did not mean assimilation. Eliminating the barriers between Poles and Jews did not have to lead the latter to surrender their identity as Jews.

Segel's worldview shaped his work in Jewish folklore. He was a fervent admirer of Jewish folk culture and an energetic collector: His writings reflect the broad interests of someone who deals with many folklore genres, including folktales, folk songs, proverbs, belief and customs, and folk medicine. As someone who believed in emancipation he published in Polish and German. Because much of his work appeared under pseudonyms, including Bar-Ami (son of my people), B. Safra, Dr. Zeev, and B. Rohatyn, his vast contribution to the study of Jewish folklore has not yet been recognized. Few know that Segel collected and interpreted parts of the famous anthology of proverbs published by Ignatz Bernstein. On several occasions, he served as guest editor and wrote a large part of the content of the monthly *Ost und West,* edited by Leo Wintz.

Segel's work appeared in a number of periodicals—*Urquell, Ost und West, Globus, Mitteilungen zur Jüdischen Volkskunde, Wisła, Lud,* and *Izraelita*—as well as in the publications of the Anthropological Commission of the Academy of Arts in Kraków. In this last publication, he published a fascinating anthology of Galician Jewish folktales and folk songs, all of them in Polish translation except one tale, which was printed in Yiddish transcribed in the Latin alphabet.

Haya Bar-Itzhak

See also: Poland, Jews of.

Bibliography

Bar-Ami. "Z ludoznawstwa" (Ethnography). *Izraelita* 37 (1902): 10–36.

———. "Der Todesengel und die böse Frau." *Ost und West* 5 (1905): 42–44.

Bar-Itzhak, Haya. "Folklore as an Expression of Inter-Cultural Communication Between Jews and Poles." *Studia Mythologica Slavica* 7 (2004): 91–106.
———. *Pioneers of Jewish Ethnography and Folkloristics in Eastern Europe.* Ljubljana: Scientific Research Center of the Academy of Science and Arts, 2010.
Schwarzbaum, Haim. *Studies in Jewish and World Folklore.* Berlin: Walter de Gruyter, 1968.
Segel, Benjamin Wolf. "Legendy i opowiescie ludowe" (Legends and Folk Narratives). *Izraelita* 34 (1899): 20–26.
———. "Materiały do etnografii Żydów wschodnio–galicyiskich" (Materials on the Ethnography of Jews in Eastern Galicia). In *Zbiór Wiadomości do Antropologii Krajowej* 8 (1893): 261–331. Kraków: Komisja Antropologiczna Akademii Umiętności.
———. "O chasydoch i chasydyzmie" (On Hasidim and Hasidism). *Wisła* 8 (1893).
———. "Śmierć i obrzędy pogrzebowe u Żydów–Polemika" (Death and Funeral Ceremonies Among Jews: A Polemic). *Izraelita* 34 (1899): 25–29.
———. "Wierzenia i lecznictwo ludowe Żydów" (Jewish Beliefs and Their Folk Medicine). *Lud* 3 (1897): 49–69.
———. "Z ludoznawstwa Żydowskigo: Eliash Prorok" (From Jewish Folklore: The Prophet Elijah). *Izraelita* 32 (1897): 21–22.
Shazar, Zalman. "Benjamin Segel." In *Or Ishim*, p. 129. Tel Aviv: Am-Oved, 1955 (in Hebrew).

SEHRANE

Sehrane is a traditional festival celebrated by the Jews of Kurdistan on the ninth day of the spring, immediately after the end of Passover. Sehrane (alternately, Serane) is derived from the Arabic *sayaran* (to walk, to stroll) and from the Kurdish *sayaran* (I look, I see). The central Sehrane celebrations mark the changing seasons and people's rejoicing at the end of winter and the transition to spring, when members of the Kurdish community could put behind them the limitations imposed by winter and go outside to spend some time in nature. Additional, secondary ceremonies were celebrated out in the fields to mark specific occasions, such as pupils going out for a picnic to mark the completion of reading the Pentateuch or an outing by pupils and youngsters on Shabbat Nahamu (the Sabbath immediately after the Ninth of Av [Tisha Be'Av]), on which the weekly Portion of the Law "Comfort ye, comfort ye, My people" is read).

History of the Festival

The Sehrane festival has no religious or historical significance of its own. For centuries before arriving in Israel, some communities in Kurdistan celebrated the Sehrane in the fall, during the intermediate days of the holiday of Sukkot (that is, not the first two or last two), but most of them did so after Passover, a holiday with historical significance, being the festival of national liberation. The Sehrane celebrations also reflect geographic conditions in Kurdistan, the character and values of its population, and the customs and relations between Kurdistani Jews and their non-Jewish neighbors.

Kurdistan is a mountainous region whose harsh and snowy winters present an obstacle to travel. The populace used to store food for the winter months, during which they would hardly leave their homes. With the coming of spring, as the snow melted and everything began to bloom again, the people would return to work their fields, and these celebrations expressed the joy of rejuvenation. One can identify in the Sehrane the archaic and universal element of springtime rejuvenation and resurrection that was expressed, in one way or another, by both pagan and Christian societies.

One aspect of the celebrations was a heightened sense of social cohesion and equality. Sometime before the holiday, the communal leaders would assemble to discuss the rituals and would then set tasks for each household to fulfill, according to its capabilities, such as provision of foodstuffs, costumes, and hospitality tents; help for the underprivileged; and assuring the presence of singers and musicians, including some who would play the *dola*—a large wooden cylinder-shaped drum on which one beat with a thick wooden stick on its front and a thin one on its back surface—and musicians to play the *zirne,* a wooden reed flute or mountain oboe. On the day after the end of Passover, members of the community would go out into the countryside to a pleasant site that was far from their permanent place of residence and blessed with flowing water, abundant vegetation, and fresh air. There they would pitch their tents and spend five to seven days.

The Sehrane also played a role in interreligious relations. Muslims were involved in the preparations for the festival and its implementation, as a sign of goodwill and cooperation. The area in which the celebrations were held was generally put at the Jews' disposal by the local tribal leader, who also saw to the security of the celebrants, guarded their vacant homes, and even provided foodstuffs whenever this was necessary. The Jews would repay his kindness by naming the Sehrane after him. Muslim Kurds would bring their Jewish neighbors bread and milk products.

The women would cook over open fires, preparing and serving characteristic dishes such as flat bread, pastry stuffed with meat, stuffed grape leaves, and alcoholic beverages. The well-to-do hosted the poorer members of the community. The men would congregate at a special meetingplace where they recounted folktales, legends, and fables that had been transmitted from generation to generation within the community. During the holiday

A Jewish Kurdish dance with traditional costumes. *(Courtesy of Haya Gavish)*

celebrations, public prayers were conducted three times a day.

Members of the community donned their finest traditional costumes; the women wore their jewelry and lent some to those who had none. They engaged in folk dancing and sang songs of love and of yearning for Zion and Jerusalem, in addition to traditional Kurdish songs in the Kurmanji dialect. Many engagement ceremonies were held during the Sehrane, more liberal behavior among individuals was condoned, and social customs relating to social standing, age, and sex were not rigidly observed. This happy frame of mind continued among the community members long after the festivities and instilled a hope for a better future.

Modern-Day Celebrations

In 1971, the Association of Kurdistani Jews in Israel decided to revive the traditional Sehrane festivities with the objective of preserving the Kurdish community's unique culture, of enhancing pride in their cultural heritage, and of expressing their successful integration into Israeli society. The first celebrations, held in 1975 in the cooperative agricultural settlements of Beit Yosef and Yardena, both in the Jordan Valley, were attended by 20,000 members of the Kurdish community in Israel. So as not to compete with the Moroccan-Jewish festival of the Mimuna, which that community celebrated on the day after the conclusion of Passover, the date of the Sehrane was moved to the day after the end of Sukkot.

There are some striking differences between the festivities in Kurdistan and the manner in which the Sehrane is celebrated in Israel. In Kurdistan each community organized its own celebrations. But in Israel the event is centrally organized and held at one site in the country, after the end of Sukkot. Jews who hail from Persian Kurdistan, however, decided not to deviate from their traditional custom and, since 1987, have held their own, separate celebration—which they call Sayaran—on the day after the end of Passover.

Despite these changes, Kurdish Jews in Israel have successfully maintained the spirit of popular, joyful spontaneity that characterized the Sehrane in Kurdistan over the years.

Haya Gavish

See also: Kurdistan, Jews of.

Bibliography

Alper, Jeff, and H. Abramovich. "Sehrane Celebrations in Kurdistan and Israel." In *Jews of the Middle East,* ed. Sh. Deshen and M. Shokeid, pp. 260–270. Jerusalem and Tel Aviv: Schocken, 1984 (in Hebrew).

Brauer, Erich, and Raphael Patai. *The Jews of Kurdistan.* Detroit: Wayne State University Press, 1993.

Huja, Nehemyah. "The Sehrane." *Hithadshut: Journal of the Kurdish Community in Israel* 1 (1972): 100–101 (in Hebrew).

Kleinberg, Aviad. "Islands in the Ocean of Routine." In *Carnivals: Islands in the Ocean of Routine,* ed. Ronit Yoeli Tlalim, pp. 8–13. Tel Aviv: Masa Aher, 1995 (in Hebrew).

Shimoni, Habib. "The Sehrane, Traditional Celebrations of the Jews of Kurdistan." In *The Jews of Kurdistan: Bulletin in the Framework of Events Commemorating 170 Years of Immigration to and Settlement in Eretz Israel.* Jerusalem: n.p., 1983 (in Hebrew).

Smith, Robert Jerome. "Festivals and Celebrations." In *Folklore and Folklife,* ed. R. Dorson, pp. 159–172. Chicago: University of Chicago Press, 1972.

Turner, Victor, ed. *Celebration: Studies in Festivity and Ritual.* Washington, DC: Smithsonian Institution Press, 1982.

Yaakov, Yaakov. "The Sehrane." *Hithadshut* 7 (2000): 299–301 (in Hebrew).

Yoeli-Tlalim, Ronit. "Death and Rebirth." In *Carnivals: Islands in the Ocean of Routine,* ed. Ronit Yoeli-Tlalim, pp. 130–132. Tel Aviv: Masa Aher, 1995 (in Hebrew).

Serpent

See: Animals; Birth; Cain and Abel; Eve

Seven Benedictions (*Sheva Berakhot*)

See: Marriage

SEVEN SPECIES (*SHIV'AT HA'MINIM*)

See: Plants

SHABAZI, SHALOM (1619–CA. 1680)

Shalom Shabazi was a poet and Torah scholar who contributed to the consolidation and finalization of Yemeni-Jewish poetry. He was the most significant Jewish poet in Yemen and can be viewed not only as the greatest poet of Yemenite Jewry but of Jewish and Hebrew literature through generations.

Yemeni-Jewish poetry can be traced back at least to the mid-twelfth century. At that time it was already influenced by the Hebrew poetry of Spain, but retained some of its affinity for the ancient Eastern paytanic school (a school of liturgical religious poetry) of the Land of Israel. During the following generations it was gradually shaped, almost completely, in accordance with the qualities of the Hebrew poetry of Spain. A crucial change took place in the sixteenth century, when the influence of the new pre-exilic school of Safed, mainly embodied in the poetry of Israel Najjārah, was brought to Yemen by one of its distinguished creators, the poet and the *māqāmist* (an Arabic and Hebrew literary genre of rhymed prose), Zekharyah al-Dāhiri, who visited Safed, where he met prominent Jewish scholars. This influence, in terms of form and contents, became a basic element of Yemeni-Jewish poetry, as is shown in al-Dāhiri's work as well as in that of his younger contemporary, Yosef ben Israel. Another significant feature of Yemeni-Jewish poetry, already known from the works of Zekharyah Ha-Rofe and Sa'adyah ben David in the fifteenth century, is that it was written not only in Hebrew but in Judeo-Arabic as well. The second half of the sixteenth century, then, is when Yemeni-Jewish poetry began to develop as a singular poetic school, although it did not abandon its strong affinity for Spanish-Hebrew poetry.

Living in the seventeenth century, Shabazi witnessed the tragic events from which Yemenite Jews suffered. He was one of the social and spiritual leaders of his community and adhered to the messianic movement centered on Shabbatai Zvi, the Jewish false messiah from the 1660s.

As the most admired historical figure among Yemeni Jews, Shabazi is the most popular protagonist of Yemeni-Jewish folktales. Many of those folktales present him as the national Jewish hero who fought to abolish the evil anti-Jewish deeds of the mythical Muslim wizard Ibn 'Alwān, although the latter lived some hundreds of years before him (d. 1267). No wonder, then, that his tomb was the destination of thousands of pilgrims, Jews as well as Muslims, men and women, who came seeking remedies for their ills—sickness, sterility, poverty, and the like.

Shabazi's prominence as a poet is due to various aspects of his poetry: (a) its sheer quantity; (b) the variety of poetical genres in which he wrote, covering all Jewish life within the yearly circle and the life circle; (c) his mastery of the three languages used in Yemeni-Jewish poetry: Hebrew, Arabic, and Aramaic; (d) his linguistic originality and ability to invent new words; (e) his erudition in terms of Jewish and Arab sources, including Arab poetry; (f) his development of the *muwašša* (a special kind of Arabic and Hebrew poem known by that name but also called a "girdle poem") construction to an unprecedented extent; (h) his treatment of the sufferings of Jews under Muslim rule during his lifetime, such that his poems constitute substantive documentation of the contemporary history of the Yemeni Jews. But beyond all that, his contemporaries as well as his successors considered his poetry the best expression of their hard life, while advancing the messianic aspirations that would be redeemed in the Land of Israel. No wonder, then, that his poems were recited by Yemeni Jews when they returned to their ancestors' homeland. Shabazi, whose poetry overshadowed not only that of all his Yemenite or Spanish antecedants but that of those who succeeded him, was the only Yemeni-Jewish historical figure about whom a huge amount of folktales developed. This is also why almost every Yemenite *dīwān* (a book of poems), in manuscript or in print, is attributed to Shabazi, while all other poets represented in it are completely ignored.

According to popular tradition, Shabazi wrote fifteen hundred poems. But leaving that tradition aside, more than 750 poems of his are listed by scholars of Yemeni-Jewish poetry. Few, if any, other figures in the long history of Jewish literature can boast of such a literary yield. Furthermore, many of his poems are very long, frequently more than 150 lines.

In spite of his popularity, the number of his poems printed in traditional *dīwāns* or in other kinds of liturgical anthologies of poetry is relatively limited, as the repertoire used by the community was very selective and assigned for special occasions. The majority of his poetic writings remained in manuscripts. Through the efforts of modern Israeli scholars, many of Shabazi's poems were published for the first time. Unfortunately, however, no comprehensive scholarly edition of Shabazi's poetry has appeared.

The date of his death is unknown, but scholars have evidence that he was still alive in 1680.

Yosef Tobi

See also: Yemen, Jews of.

Bibliography

Bar-Itzhak, Haya. "'And We Came to the Land of Our Forefathers . . .': The Folk Legend of Yemenite Jews in Israel." *Jewish Folklore and Ethnology Review* 14:1–2 (1992): 44–54.

Noy, Dov. "Rabbi Shalom Shabazi in the Folk Legend of Yemenite Jews." In *Boi Teyman,* ed. Razhabi Yehuda, pp. 106–133. Tel Aviv: Afikim, 1967 (in Hebrew).

Seri, Shalom, and Yosef Tobi. "New Songs by Rabbi Shalom Shabazi." *Sefunot* 9 (1965): 133–166 (in Hebrew).

———. *The Songs of Rabbi Shalom Shabazi: Bibliography.* Tel Aviv: n.p., 2003 (in Hebrew).

Tobi, Yosef. *Studies of Yemenite Scroll.* Jerusalem: Magnes Press, 1986 (in Hebrew).

———. "To the Identification of the Yemenite Midrash Hemdat Yamim." *Tagim* 3–4 (1972): 63–72 (in Hebrew).

———. "Two Songs About Shabtaic Events in Yemen." *Peamim* 44 (1990): 53–63 (in Hebrew).

Tobi, Yosef, ed. *Shalom ben Yoseph Shabazi.* Jerusalem: The General Committee of the Jewish Yemenite Community, 1972 (in Hebrew).

Tobi, Yosef, and Shalom Seri, ed. *Amalel Shir: A Collection of Yemenite Poetry.* Tel Aviv: A'ale Ba'tamar, 1988 (in Hebrew).

SHABBAT

In Jewish tradition, the Sabbath (Heb., Shabbat) is the seventh day of the week. It is a day of rest, on which labor is forbidden, after the six workdays. According to various biblical passages, the primary meaning of the word *shabbat* is "stop," "suspend," or "refrain from acting," and not just "rest." The talmudic sages accordingly applied the term "sabbath" to all the holidays mentioned in the Torah, even those that do not fall on the seventh day of the week.

Biblical Roots of the Sabbath

The Sabbath, as distinguished from and different from the other days, is an original Jewish concept. Its observance proclaims that the Sabbath was created along with the universe and is an essential part of its structure, just like the moon and the stars, the sun and the heavens, the sea and the dry land. The Sabbath is the only holiday established during the seven days of creation and the only one mentioned in the Ten Commandments (Exod. 20:8–11; Deut. 5:12–15). This repeated reference attests to the great importance attached to the Sabbath in biblical thought and in Judaism. The Sabbath is one of the topics addressed most frequently in the Hebrew Bible, especially in the Torah. The Sabbath is not a human product but a divine creation, sanctified by God's actions, which appointed it as a day of rest for the entire universe. It exemplifies the principle of social justice in that all human beings are equal—"so that your male and female slave may rest as you do" (Deut. 5:14) and that all creatures, even animals, have a right to rest: "you shall not do any work—you, your son or your daughter, your male or female slave, your ox or your ass, or any of your cattle, or the stranger in your settlements" (ibid.; cf. Exod. 20:10).

The Sabbath was given to the people of Israel as a sign of the Lord's covenant with them and as a remembrance of the creation (Exod. 31:16–17), but also as a remembrance of the exodus from Egypt and the Lord's deliverance of the Israelites (Deut. 5:15). Consequently their observance of the Sabbath is proof that Israel is the favored nation of the Creator, that He sanctifies them and that they are faithful to the covenant with Him. The prophets linked the destinies of the people, of Jerusalem, and of the Davidic monarchy, as well as the people's visions, aspirations, desires, and dreams, with their observance of the Sabbath (Isa. 56:2–6, 58:13–14; Jer. 17:21–27; Ezek. 20:12–24; Neh. 9:14). In the well-known formulation of the Jewish thinker and essayist Ahad Ha'am (pseudonym of Asher Ginsberg, 1856–1927), "more than the Jews have kept the Sabbath, the Sabbath has kept the Jews." That is, their meticulous observance of the Sabbath as described in the Bible was crucial to the national survival of the Jewish people over the generations, in all their diasporas, despite the unremitting pressure of assimilation, massacres, pogroms, blood libels, persecution, and even the genocide of the first half of the twentieth century.

The Sabbath is a holy day. The Torah prescribes severe penalties for its desecration: "Anyone who profanes it shall be put to death: whoever does work on it, that person shall be cut off from among his people" (Exod. 31:14). To remove any doubt, the Torah reports the stoning of a man who was found gathering wood on the Sabbath (Num. 15:32–36).

The customs and ordinances of the Sabbath, including permitted and forbidden labors, are not enumerated in the Torah or counted individually among the positive and negative precepts. It was the sages of the Mishnah, especially its redactor, Rabbi Yehuda ha'Nasi, who first introduced order and logic to the Sabbath regulations. Drawing on a tradition that traced back to the days at Mount Sinai, the sages defined thirty-nine categories of labor that are prohibited on the Sabbath—those that were required for construction of the sanctuary in the wilderness.

From these thirty-nine primary categories (Heb., *avot melakhah*) of prohibited labors, many secondary categories (Heb., *toladot*) are derived. The observance of the Sabbath, with meticulous attention to its special character, has a strong mark on Jewish life. Despite the immense difficulties, the Jewish people held observance of the Sabbath to be equal in weight to all the other precepts in the Torah. Jewish life in the Land of Israel or the Diaspora has always been conducted from Sabbath to Sabbath—emotionally,

A cup and a plate for *Kiddush* and *Havdalah* at beginning and conclusion of Shabbat. Silver. Inscription: Glass of Elijah. 20th century, Morocco. *(© The Israel Museum, Jerusalem)*

spiritually, and physically. In the Bible and Talmud, *shabbat,* as its focal point and terminus, sometimes has the sense of "week."

The mishnaic sages stipulated that one must give the Sabbath feasts a special and festive air, to further distinguish them from weekday meals. Accordingly, starting in the middle of the week Jews would set aside the finest foods and delicacies they found in the market, so that they could experience the "delight of the Sabbath" and the "honor of the Sabbath," making their Sabbath repasts the best of the entire week.

The Jewish concept of the Sabbath has influenced the entire world. One reflection of this is that the weekly day of rest is referred to as "Sabbath" by many peoples in many languages. According to Josephus Flavius, the first-century Jewish historian, "there is not any city of the Grecians, nor any of the barbarians, nor any nation whatsoever, whither our custom of resting on the seventh day hath not come" (*Against Apion* 2.40, trans. Whiston). The Roman philosopher Seneca censured Romans who observed the Sabbath, carping that "the vanquished [the Jews] have given laws to their victors [the Romans]" (*De superstitione,* quoted by Augustine, *City of God* VI 11). Evidence of the infiltration of Jewish customs into Roman life is also provided by the poet Persius (*Satires* 5:179–1984), who mocks Romans who mark Friday night by lighting candles, drinking wine, and eating fish and derides his fellow citizens who go to the synagogue to hear the sermon.

The two younger monotheistic religions accepted the principle of the Sabbath but modified its date, with the Christians moving it to Sunday and the Muslims to Friday.

The Start of the Sabbath

The Sabbath arrives in a gradual process lasting for several hours, which includes emotional, spiritual, and logistical preparations. Because an excessively rapid transition from the profane to the sacred would detract from the special atmosphere of the Sabbath, one stops work early on Fridays in order to have sufficient time to complete these preparations. (In modern Israel Friday is a day off, in addition to the Sabbath [Saturday], but Sunday is a regular workday, unlike in Europe, North America, and elsewhere.) The Talmud reports a tradition of blowing the shofar on Friday afternoons to alert the people to the approach of the Sabbath: "Six blasts were blown on the eve of the Sabbath" (*b. Shabbat* 35a). This tradition is still followed in some orthodox Jewish communities in the Diaspora and Israel (Jerusalem, Bene Berak, Betar Illit, and elsewhere). Another custom is to bathe before the start of the Sabbath; the especially pious immerse themselves in a *mikveh* (ritual bath). This is the first step in readying the soul for the Sabbath.

Jewish traditions emphasize the special garments reserved for the Sabbath. "If you honor it [the Sabbath] and go not your ways" (Isa. 58:13) is expounded by the Talmud to mean that "your Sabbath garments should not be like your weekday garments" (*b. Shabbat* 113a). The sages took this seriously and prescribed that every person own two suits of clothing, one for weekdays and the other for the Sabbath.

On Friday afternoon, the table is set for the Sabbath meal. In this task the mistress of the house is joined by other members of the family; traditionally each of them has a fixed assignment. The Sabbath eve meal is the most important family gathering of the week as well as an occasion for hosting guests. The table is set with a white tablecloth, two or more candlesticks with lit candles, a wine goblet for the *Kiddush* (blessing over wine), two *challot,* and, of course, the dishes and utensils for all the diners. A perusal of Jewish literature over the generations reveals that the Sabbath table, which creates a feeling of the special and different nature of the day, is one of the strongest memories of home that Jews carry with them.

The actual onset of the Sabbath is marked by the lighting of candles. According to tradition, the Sabbath enters with the lighting of candles and wine (the Friday night *Kiddush*) and exits with a candle and wine (the *Havdalah* rite). The laws of candle-lighting are summarized by Maimonides (*Mishneh Torah,* Laws of the Sabbath). Having a Sabbath candle burning in the house is mandatory for both men and women, as part of the special "delight of the Sabbath." A blessing is recited when the candles are lit, while it is still daytime (eighteen minutes before sunset). This precept applies more particularly to women than to men. This priority has been explained in several ways. Some say that women are generally at home during the week and tend to the house; thus the burning candles express the family's gratitude to the mistress of the house. Another reason, proposed by Rashi (Solomon ben Isaac of Troyes) in his commentary, is that "there is no serenity in a house where there is no candle [light], because people are apt to bump into things in the dark."

The Friday afternoon prayer begins with a special service, *Kabbalat Shabbat* (Greeting the Sabbath). To the three prayer services recited every day—the evening service, after sunset at the start of the new day; the morning service; and the afternoon service (from shortly after noon until sunset)—two additional services are added on the Sabbath: *Kabbalat Shabbat,* which precedes the Friday evening service, and the *musaf* (additional) service, in commemoration of the additional sacrifice offered in the Temple, which follows the reading of the Torah on Saturday morning.

According to ancient traditions dating to talmudic times, on Friday afternoon people would go into the fields outside their towns and villages to greet the Sabbath in nature. This is recounted of Rabbi Ḥanina ben Dosa or Rabbi Yannai (*b. Bava Qama* 32b). The sixteenth-century Safed kabbalist Rabbi Isaac Luria (Ha'Ari) and his disciples used to stroll outside the town to greet the Sabbath with joyful song. According to a legend, one Sabbath eve when they were carried away in their spiritual ecstasy Rabbi Luria turned to his disciples: "Would you like to go to Jerusalem before the Sabbath and spend the Sabbath there?" "First, we have to go tell our wives," some of them replied. Rabbi Luria was shattered by their hesitation. "Alas, we did not have the merit to be redeemed! Had you all said that you wanted to go to Jerusalem, redemption would have come for all Israel." Safed in the sixteenth century is also where kabbalists devised the *Kabbalat Shabbat* service as it is known today, based on six Psalms and the liturgical poem "Lekha Dodi" ("Come, my friend, to greet the Sabbath bride") by Rabbi Solomon ben Moses Alkabetz.

Friday Night

It is customary for a father to bless his children on Friday night, in the synagogue or after returning home—even if they are already parents themselves. The blessing for sons repeats Jacob's blessing of Joseph's sons, "May God make you like Ephraim and Manasseh" (Gen. 48:20); for daughters it is "may God make you like Sarah, Rebecca, Rachel, and Leah."

After the children have been blessed, the assembled company sing the hymn "Shalom Aleikhem" (Peace Upon You), which is based on a legend recounted in the Talmud (*b. Shabbat* 119b):

> Rabbi Jose Judah said: "Two ministering angels accompany a man home from the synagogue on Sabbath eve, one good and one evil. If he arrives home and finds the lamp burning, the table set, and his couch covered with a spread, the good angel exclaims, 'May it be this way next Sabbath,' and the evil angel responds, unwillingly, 'amen.' But if not, the evil angel exclaims, 'May it be this way next Sabbath,' and the good angel responds, unwillingly, 'amen.'"

Scholars do not know who wrote this hymn or when, only that it was made part of the Sabbath opening ritual by the kabbalists of Safed. The melodies to which it is sung have made it extremely popular and turned it into one of the most prominent manifestations of the Sabbath.

After he has sent his angelic escort on its way, the husband surveys the house, all decked out in honor of the Sabbath, and praises and thanks his wife by reciting Proverbs 31:10–31 ("Who can find a good wife!"), which extols the virtues of the diligent wife and good mother.

The Sabbath eve and Sabbath noon meals both begin with the *Kiddush* (sanctification) over the wine, recited in the place where one eats. Highlighting the sanctity of the day, it is based on the biblical injunction to "Remember the Sabbath day to keep it holy" (Exod. 20:8).

The members of the household fulfill the obligation of *Kiddush* by hearing it recited, but then each tastes the consecrated wine. During the *Kiddush* the special Sabbath loaves, or *challot,* are on the table, but covered with a special embroidered cloth. They are covered, we are told, to spare them embarrassment. Usually the blessing over bread marks the start of the meal. On Sabbath eve, however, the bread has to wait until after the *Kiddush.* Solicitous for the bread and its honor, one places it on the table but covers it until its own moment arrives.

The word *challot* derives from the loaf or cake (Heb., *challah*) set aside for the priest from each batch of dough (Num. 15:20). Because the dough for the Sabbath meals and the rest of the week was prepared on Friday, the special Sabbath bread came to be called *challah.* Although the usage originated in the European diaspora, it spread throughout the Jewish world. Some refer to the Sabbath bread as *leḥem mishneh* (double bread), in reference to the biblical account that the Israelites in the wilderness received a double portion of manna on Fridays (Exod. 16:22).

The Sabbath foods of the different Jewish communities are a central part of the "delight of the Sabbath" (*oneg Shabbat*). The sages derived this obligation from Isaiah's plea that the people "call the Sabbath 'delight' [and] the Lord's holy day 'honored'" (Isa. 58:13). This delight was conceived of in several ways: an especially fine main course, a fine wine, physical pleasure, spiritual delight, and so on. Part of the Sabbath delight is the obligation to eat three full meals: one on Friday night and two more during the course of the next day. This custom is learned from Exodus 16:25, which refers to the manna and repeats the word "today" three times: "Moses said, 'Eat it *today,* for *today* is the Sabbath of the Lord; you will not find it outside *today.*'" To emphasize the importance of this precept, the sages said that "even a poor man who is dependent on charity is obligated to eat three Sabbath meals"; and "everyone who observes the precept of three Sabbath meals will be delivered from three evils: the travails of the messiah, the punishment of *Gehinnom*, and the war of Gog and Magog" (*b. Shabbat* 118a).

Because of the obligation to eat well on the Sabbath, special recipes were devised for this day. Some of them are common to all or most Jewish communities throughout the world. Two foods are an integral part of every Sabbath table—fish and a pudding or stew that is kept warm in the oven from Friday afternoon until the Sabbath noonday meal. This could be *cholent* or *kugel* (Eastern Europe), *tabit* (Iraq), *arissa* (Djerba, Tunisia), *mebosa* (Kurdistan), or *skhina* (Morocco).

All communities sing special hymns *(zemirot)* at the Sabbath table, during and after the meal. Their lyrics are based on Sabbath customs, legends, and praise of the Lord. The Talmud explains why they are sung: "When the Temple was standing the altar atoned for human beings; now a person's table atones for him" (*b. Ḥagigah* 27a). The analogy has another aspect: Because the festive meal represents the sacrificial ritual in the Temple, during which the Levites sang Psalms, our own feast should be accompanied by songs and hymns. Some of these *zemirot* are known in all Jewish communities (*Tzur mishelo akhalnu, Yah ribbon, Deror yiqra*), while others are sung by only one or two of them.

Another special Sabbath precept is hospitality. Jewish and Hebrew literature features extensive accounts of Jewish householders' efforts to have guests in their homes on the Sabbath. This custom, too, can be traced to a talmudic dictum: "Hospitality is greater than welcoming the Divine Presence" (*b. Shabbat* 127a). It was the custom to invite travelers from out of town to dine with a prominent householder on the Sabbath. Anyone who had not yet arranged his meals would come to the synagogue, where the heads of the congregation would make sure to find him a place for the Sabbath, a practice that remains to this day.

The Sabbath is held to radiate a light to which the Jew is attracted during the six workdays. When the Sabbath arrives, Jews enter the domain of spirit and soul and endeavor to hold fast to its sanctity, so that it will accompany them throughout life's profane endeavors during the following week. The Sabbath is not just a day of rest for the body; it is, even more so, a day for the "extra soul" that is hidden away during the week.

Joel Rappel

See also: Food and Foodways; Lamps and Candles.

Bibliography

Ariel, Shlomo Zalman. *The Book of Holidays.* Tel Aviv: Dvir, 1975 (in Hebrew).

Baruch, Ytzhak L., ed. *Shabbat Book.* Tel Aviv: Oneg Shabbat–Dvir, 1965 (in Hebrew).

Ha'Cohen, Dvora, and Menachem Ha'Cohen, eds. *Holidays and Festivals: Shabbat and Rosh Hodesh.* Jerusalem: Keter, 1979 (in Hebrew).

Leshem, Haim. *Shabbat and Jewish Holidays.* Tel Aviv: Niv, 1965–1969 (in Hebrew).

Lewinski, Yom Tov. *Encyclopedia of Folklore, Customs, and Tradition in Judaism.* Tel Aviv: Dvir, 1970 (in Hebrew).

Noibirt, Joshua I. *Shabbat Keeping.* Jerusalem: Feldheim, 1989 (in Hebrew).

Rappel, Joel. *Jewish Holidays: Encyclopedia of Shabbat and Holiday.* Tel Aviv: IDF Press, 1990 (in Hebrew).

Shoa, Zvi, and Arie Ben-Gurion. *Shabbat Collection.* Tel Aviv: Brith Hatnua Hakibbutzit, 2000 (in Hebrew).

Wassertiel, Asher, ed. *The Anthology of Customs.* Jerusalem: Ministry of Education, 1977 (in Hebrew).

SHABBAT ḤATAN

See: Marriage

Shalit, Moshe

See: Poland, Jews of

Shavuot (The Feast of Weeks)

Shavuot is one of the three festivals, along with Passover and Sukkot, on which the Israelites were commanded to go on a pilgrimage to the Temple in Jerusalem. Shavuot differs from the other festivals in one respect. Whereas the Bible specifies the dates of the other festivals according to the Hebrew calendar, it does not give the date for Shavuot. Instead, it is set by counting seven weeks from the day following the first full day of Passover, the day on which the first sheaf of barley (*omer*) was harvested for an offering in the Temple.

> You shall count off seven weeks; begin counting the seven weeks when the sickle is first put to the standing grain. (Deut. 16:9)

Names of the Festival

Shavuot is a one-day festival, but it has many names, reflecting the complex essence of the festival and its multiple aspects, which were emphasized during different periods in history.

The Feast of Weeks: This is the most common and widely used name for the festival. It expresses the way its date is determined: seven weeks, that is, forty-nine days, are counted from the day that the *omer*—the first sheaf of barley—is harvested, on the day after the first day of Passover, and the festival is observed on the fiftieth day.

The Festival of the Harvest, the Festival of the First Fruits: These names express the agricultural nature of the festival—the grain harvest and the offering of the first fruits in Jerusalem:

> Three times a year, all your males shall appear before the Lord God. (Exod. 23:17)

> You shall observe the Feast of Weeks, of the first fruits of the wheat harvest; and the Feast of Ingathering at the turn of the year. (Exod. 34:22)

The Bible links the pilgrimage to Jerusalem with the bringing of the first fruits to the Temple:

> You shall bring the best of the first fruits of your land to the house of the Lord your God. (Exod. 23:19)

A more detailed description of the bringing of the first fruits to the Temple appears in Deuteronomy:

> When you enter the land that the Lord your God is giving for an inheritance, and take possession and settle in it, you shall take some of every first fruit of the soil, which you harvest from the land that the Lord your God is giving you, put it in a basket, and go to the place that the Lord your God chooses to establish His name there. You shall go to the priest who is in office at that time and say to him, "Today, I affirm before the Lord your God that I have entered the land that the Lord swore to our fathers to give us." The priest shall take the basket from your hand and set it down in front of the altar of the Lord your God. (Deut. 26:1–4)

The Mishnah describes the folk festivities associated with the bringing of the first fruits:

> How were the first fruits brought to Jerusalem? All of [the inhabitants of] the smaller towns in the *ma'amad* [groups of laymen who performed certain liturgical functions in regular rotation, one *ma'amad* after another, through the course of the year] gathered in the central town of the *ma'amad* and slept in the city square, but they did not enter the homes. In the morning, the leader called out, "Arise and let us ascend to Zion, to the House of the Lord our God." Those [who lived] close by brought fresh figs and grapes, and those [who lived] far away brought dried figs and raisins.
>
> An ox with gilded horns led the procession, with a wreath of olive leaves on its head. A flute was played before them until they neared Jerusalem. When they neared Jerusalem, they sent messengers ahead and decorated their first fruits. The prefects and the deputies and the Temple treasurers went out to greet them. [The dignity of the welcoming party] was proportional to the dignity of those who were coming. All of the artisans in Jerusalem would stand and greet them: "Our brothers, the inhabitants of such-and-such a place, welcome!" [They proceeded through Jerusalem] while the flute was played until they reached the Temple Mount. When they reached the Temple Mount, even King Agrippas would carry the basket [of first fruits] on his shoulders and enter the Temple Courtyard. When they reached the Temple Courtyard, the Levites opened with the song (Ps. 30:2): "I will exalt You, O Lord, for You have drawn me up and You have not allowed my enemies to rejoice." (*m. Bikkurim* 3:2–5)

The Festival of the Giving of Our Torah: This name derives from the tradition that associates the giving of the Torah with Shavuot.

When the Jews lived in the Land of Israel and were able to make the pilgrimage to Jerusalem and bring the first fruits to the Temple, the religious-agricultural aspect of the festival was emphasized. After the Temple was destroyed and the Jews went into exile, it was the giving of the Torah that was emphasized. Many customs developed around this facet.

Other names for the festival are the Day of Assembly (Yom Ha'Khel) (Deut. 9:10, 10:4, 18:6) and Atzeret (which also means "assembly") in rabbinical literature (e.g., *b. Bava Batra* 147b).

Festival Customs

The various customs of Shavuot are associated with the several elements that give it its names. One of the customs tied to the holiday as the Festival of the Giving of the Torah is known as *Tiqqun Leil Shavuot:* men stay up all Shavuot night and engage in Torah study, reading passages relating to the 613 precepts, taken from the Bible, Mishnah, Talmud, Zohar, and liturgical poetry.

The custom of the Shavuot *ketubbah* (marriage contract) is also related to this. The Shavuot *ketubbah* symbolizes the bond established between the Jewish people and God on the day of the giving of the Torah. There are also special liturgical poems that relate to Shavuot as the Festival of the Giving of the Torah. The most famous, "Aqdamot," was written in the eleventh century by Rabbi Meir ben Isaac Nehorai of Worms. The poem is a ninety-line rhymed acrostic in Aramaic, with every line ending in the letters *taf* and *aleph* (תא), the last and first in the Hebrew alphabet. The poem extols God as creator of the world and the Jews as the chosen people, and describes the days of messiah. In many congregations, the cantor's repetition of the "Musaf Amida" service includes "Azharot," liturgical poems that enumerate the 613 precepts.

Although the importance of the elements related to nature and agriculture diminished after the Jews went into exile, even in the Diaspora they would customarily decorate their homes and synagogues with greenery and flowers for the festival. In Central and Eastern Europe, they would decorate their windows with papercut rosettes (Yidd., *reyzeleh*). The custom of spilling water on the ground on Shavuot, found among North African Jews, is also connected with the natural aspect of the festival and symbolizes fertility.

According to Jewish tradition, King David was born and died on Shavuot. In his memory, it is customary to read the Book of Ruth, which ends with his genealogy, during the festival. In Jerusalem, it is customary to visit his reputed grave on Mt. Zion. Jews of Asian and North African descent bring food there, light 150 candles (one for each chapter in the Book of Psalms), and recite psalms.

Eating dairy foods at the festival meal, such as cheese blintzes in Ashkenazi communities (which also are said to resemble the tablets of the Ten Commandments), is a widespread custom. Various explanations have been offered for this custom. Some link it to nature, as milk symbolizes fertility. Others relate it to the giving of the Torah, because the Torah is compared to milk and honey.

There is also a custom of eating filled pastries, another symbol of fertility. Tradition explains this custom, too, in various ways. Triangular pastries, for example, were seen as representing the three sections of the Hebrew Bible—the Torah, the Prophets, and the Writings. It is customary to bake cakes and cookies whose ingredients include cheese, honey, and raisins and give them to children, so that learning Torah will be sweet for them, just like these sweet foods.

Shavuot in Israel

In the twentieth century, the festival took on a new character in Israel, one that expresses the Zionist ideology and ethos.

The agricultural settlements (kibbutzim and moshavim) developed a secular version of the offering of the first fruits. This began with Ein Ḥarod, Geva, and Kefar Yeḥezkel in the Jezreel Valley in 1924. The ceremony of bringing the first fruits became the core of the Shavuot celebrations in the agricultural settlements. A procession of agricultural machinery, decked out with the recently harvested produce, made its way to a central stage. The procession was accompanied by readings, singing, and dancing by members of the kibbutz or moshav. The first fruits were dedicated to the Jewish National Fund. When kibbutzim started to build factories, industrial goods were also included in the ceremony of the first fruits.

In 1944, at Kibbutz Dalyah, the folk-dance pioneer Gurit Kadman (see: Kadman, Gurit) introduced a special dance based on the Book of Ruth. The Dalyah dance tradition later emerged from this ceremony.

At the end of the 1960s, a trend of returning to Jewish traditional practices began in the kibbutzim. On Shavuot, this was manifested by communal readings of a *Tiqqun Leil Shavuot* adapted to their ethos.

In cities as well, new ceremonies and customs were introduced in the period before 1948. In Tel Aviv, Shavuot became the Festival of Flowers as children bedecked in flowers paraded through the streets of the city. In Haifa, too, there were first-fruit celebrations (1932–1935). Instead of dedicating the first fruits to the Temple as was done in ancient times, the Zionist-Socialist movement dedicated the first fruits to the Jewish National Fund.

Today, Israel has a multicultural society and therefore various expressions of celebration of Shavuot can be found in various communities.

Nili Aryeh-Sapir

See also: Papercut.

Bibliography

Aaronson, Ran. "Stages in the Development of the Settlement of the First Aliyah." In *The First Aliyah,* ed. Mordechai Eliav, pp. 25–84. Jerusalem: Ben-Zvi Institute, 1981 (in Hebrew).

Aryeh-Sapir, Nili. "Shavuoth." In *The Formation of Urban Culture and Education: Stories of and About Ceremonies and Celebrations in Tel Aviv in Its First Years. Dor Ledor* 36. Tel Aviv: Tel Aviv University, 2006 (in Hebrew).

Ben Yehuda, Baruch. *The Educating Keren: The Teachers' Movement for Zion and Its Salvation on Its Twenty-Five Years of Activity.* Jerusalem: K.K.L., 1952 (in Hebrew).

Gaster, Theodor H. *Festivals of the Jewish Year*. New York: W. Sloane, 1953.

Goren, Zcharia. "The Celebrations and Holidays of the Secular Jew." In *Regard and Revere: Renew Without Fear. The Secular Jew and His Heritage,* ed. Yehoshua Rash, pp. 255–276. Tel Aviv: Sifriat Poalim, 1987 (in Hebrew).

Hasan-Rokem, Galit. "Shavuoth." *Les fêtes du soleil: Celebrations of the Mediterranean Regions,* ed. Alessandro Falassi, pp. 106–107. Sienna: Betti Editrie, 2001.

Levinski, Yom Tov, ed. "Shavuoth." In *The Book of Holidays,* vol. 3. Tel Aviv: Oneg Shabat, 1956 (in Hebrew).

Rappel, Yoel. "Shavuoth." In *Encyclopaedia of Jewish Holidays.* Tel Aviv: Department of Defense Press, 2000 (in Hebrew).

Sitton, Shoshana. "The Contribution of the Teachers' Council for the Keren Ha'Kayemet le'Yisrael to the Formation of the Zionistic Ceremonies and Celebrations." In *Proceedings of the Eleventh World Congress of Jewish Studies,* Division B, II, pp. 235–242 (in Hebrew).

Tur Sinai, Naftali Hertz. "A First Flower Day in Jerusalem." *Folklore Research Center Studies* 1 (1970): 153–154 (in Hebrew).

Waharmann, Nahum. "Shavuoth." In *The Holidays and Festivals of the Jewish People (Their Customs and Symbols).* Tel Aviv: Ahiasaf, 1970 (in Hebrew).

Zeira, Moti. *Rural Collective Settlement and Jewish Culture in Eretz Israel During the 1920s.* Jerusalem: Ben-Zvi Institute, 2002 (in Hebrew).

SHENHAR, ALIZA (1943–)

The scholar Aliza Shenhar's contributions to the study of Jewish folklore include an analysis of the relationship between international tale types and Jewish folktales; the relationship between children's literature and folk literature; discussion and analysis of contemporary Israeli folklore, including urban legends and kibbutz folklore; the substructure of folk narrative in the works of Jewish authors; and a feminist reading of tales about biblical heroines.

Born in Tiberias on July 1, 1943, Aliza Shenhar was educated at the Hebrew University of Jerusalem, where she wrote her dissertation, "Family Confrontation and Conflicts in Jewish Folktales," under the supervision of Dov Noy.

Shenhar published extensively in Hebrew, English, and German. Among her books are *From Folk Literature to Children's Literature* (1982), *The Jewish Folktale* (1982), *Stories of Yore: Children's Folktales* (1986), *Jewish and Israeli Folklore* (1986), *Folkloristic Sub-Structures in Agnon's Stories* (1989), *Jewish Moroccan Folk Narratives from Israel* (with Haya Bar-Itzhak) (1993), and *The Story Teller, the Story and the Audience* (1994).

Her articles deal with topics such as images of the Jewish sage and *tanna*, Rabbi Meir, Yemenite folktales, Libyan-Jewish folktales, Iraqi-Jewish versions of midrashic legends, animal tales, teaching folk literature, folktales about adolescents, Eretz Israel pilgrimage tales, and Jewish and Druze folktales.

Organizationally, she contributed to the study of folklore as head of the Folklore Studies Program at the University of Haifa (1975–1980), as head of the Israel Folktale Archives, and in a number of other senior administrative posts before becoming rector of the University of Haifa (1991–1994).

Shenhar was a visiting professor and research fellow at the University of California at Los Angeles (1979, 1984) and the University of Göttingen (1987). In the 1990s she headed a national commission on Jewish studies in Israeli schools. She also served as Israel's ambassador to Russia (1994–1997). Since 1997 she has been the president of Max Stern Academic College of Emek Yezreel.

Haya Bar-Itzhak

See also: Folk Narratives in Israel.

Bibliography

Bar-Itzhak, Haya, and Aliza Shenhar. *Jewish Moroccan Folk Narratives from Israel.* Detroit: Wayne State University Press, 1993.

Shenhar, Aliza. *From Folk Literature to Children's Literature.* Haifa: University of Haifa, 1982 (in Hebrew).

———. *The Jewish Folktale.* Tel Aviv: Cherikover, 1982 (in Hebrew).

Shenhar-Alroy, Aliza. *Jewish and Israeli Folklore.* New Delhi: South Asian Publishers, 1986.

———. *Loved and Hated.* Haifa: Pardes, 2010.

———. *Stories of Yore: Children's Folktales.* Haifa: Haifa University, 1986 (in Hebrew).

———. *The Story Teller, the Story, and the Audience.* Tel Aviv: Ha'kibbutz Ha'meuḥad, 1994 (in Hebrew).

———. *Women's Time.* Tel Aviv: Kineret, Zmora-Bitan, 2008 (in Hebrew).

SHEOL

See: Afterlife

SHEVA BERAKHOT (SEVEN BENEDICTIONS)

See: Marriage

SHIMEON BAR YOḤAI

Shimeon Bar Yoḥai was a *tanna* who lived in the middle of the second century around the years 140–170 C.E. and was active mainly in Upper Galilee. Legends portray him as a fascinating and charismatic figure, holding not only halakhic wisdom but also characteristics of a miracle worker. The writings ascribed to him emphasize the supreme importance of Torah study; some display a lack of tolerance for human weakness. The sources indicate that he studied for thirteen years with Rabbi Akiva, one of the greatest sages of all times, in Bene Berak. Bar Yoḥai was among his greatest disciples, and even continued to study with him after Rabbi Akiva was imprisoned by the Romans. Bar Yoḥai was ordained by Rabbi Akiva, but later he was also ordained by Judah ben Bava. Rabbi Akiva held Shimeon Bar Yoḥai in high esteem (*y. Sanhedrin* 1:3, 19a). His best-known disciples were Eliezer, his son-in-law, Pinhas ben Yair, and Rabbi Yehuda ha'Nasi. Tradition crowns Rabbi Shimeon with a mystical aura, mainly because of his role in the Kabbalah, as represented in the Zohar.

Life Told Through Legend

The main legend, delineating the historical portrayal of his personality and life story, occurs in the Yerushalmi Talmud (*Shevi'it* 89:1), and in the Babylonian Talmud (*Shabbat* 33b, 34a).

The Yerushalmi Talmud reveals that Rabbi Shimeon Bar Yoḥai lived in a cave for thirteen years, eating nothing but carobs, until it adversely affected his health. However, the story does not focus on his life in the cave, but on the change he underwent upon leaving it. At the moment of leaving, he saw a hunter trying to catch birds, and he heard a divine voice that determined whether the birds would be caught or would escape the hunter's trap. From this experience, he understood that everything taking place on earth is determined from above. From this point on, his deeds are explained as stemming from the insight gained on leaving the cave. In its version of the story of his life in the cave, the Babylonian Talmud portrays Shimeon Bar Yoḥai as a person who railed against Roman rule after the failure of Bar Kochba's revolt (the Jewish revolt against Rome in 132–135 C.E.). On account of his widely publicized censure, he was condemned to death. He escaped together with his son, and after hiding for a short time in a seminary for religious studies (*beit ha-midrash*), he hid in a cave and stayed there with his son for twelve years, in total isolation. A miracle took place in the cave, providing them with water and carobs.

While in hiding, Shimeon Bar Yoḥai and his son studied the Torah and prayed, experiencing spiritual exultation through Torah study. They continued their study until the prophet Elijah announced to them that the death sentence was no longer in effect. Shimeon Bar Yoḥai and his son then left the cave. As they were on their way, they saw a man plowing and sowing, and they exclaimed: "They forsake eternal life and engage in temporal life!" Whatever they cast their eyes upon was immediately incinerated. As punishment for destroying God's creation, Shimeon Bar Yoḥai and his son were confined to the cave for one more year by a divine voice. On leaving the cave for the second time, his son Eliezer continued to act with fanatic fervor, but Shimeon Bar Yoḥai restored what he had destroyed. The story then describes the way Shimeon Bar Yoḥai's attitude changed, for he had learned his lesson about the danger of extremism and the need to combine and compromise this world with study and devotion to the Torah.

Various researchers have attempted to clarify which parts of the legends about Shimeon Bar Yoḥai were literary fictions, taken from legends transmitted orally or collected from sources unavailable to the contemporary reader, and which could be considered historical details, enabling students to learn about events and figures during that period. The story of Shimeon Bar Yoḥai's purification of Tiberias after he had left the cave has aroused special interest.

Magical Powers, Esoteric Wisdom, and the Power to Redeem

The stories about Shimeon Bar Yoḥai—his fanatic rebellion against Roman rule, his opinions against gentiles, the miracle in the cave, Elijah's coming to tell him that the danger had passed, and the encounter with the divine voice that taught him that all is in God's hands—endowed him with a mystical aura. He was also perceived as a hermit, with unusual powers, a person able to protect and redeem those of his generation. (*Gen. Rab.* 35b; *y. Ber.* 89:2). Hence, later writings were also ascribed to him, containing apocalyptic themes, such as *Nistarot de Rabbi Shimeon bar Yoḥai* and *Tefilat Rabbi Shimeon bar Yoḥai;* some researchers also ascribe *Mekhilta de Rabbi Shimeon bar Yoḥai* to him. Moreover, the kabbalists perceived him as the author of the Zohar, published in the thirteenth century. According to the Zohar, he and the nine sages, his friends, used to meet in various circumstances during their journeys all over the Land of Israel:

in the Tiberias district, in Tzipori, Ushah, Kisarin, and so on. The Zohar considers Tiberias Shimeon Bar Yoḥai's main place of residence. He was the sage at the center of the group and the one who answered all the difficult questions and solved all the problems disturbing them, inspiring them with the divine spirit through his words and deeds. The publication of the Zohar made Shimeon Bar Yoḥai the main mystical figure of the Kabbalah.

An ancient tradition locates the graves of Shimeon Bar Yoḥai and his son on Mount Miron, and since the sixteenth century Lag Ba'Omer (thirty-third day of Counting the Omer) has been determined as the day of his death; masses of people go on a yearly pilgrimage to his grave celebrating and praying (*Hillula of Rabbi Shimeon Bar Yoḥai*). Later traditions suggested that the cave where he had been hiding was in Peki' in the northern district of Israel.

The Zionist movement, which aspired to found a Jewish state in the Land of Israel, adopted the figure of Shimeon Bar Yoḥai, perceiving him as a brave man who clung to his teachings and rebelled against the Roman conquerors, even at the risk to his own life. The custom of playing with bows and arrows on Lag Ba'Omer, introduced by Jewish communities in the Diaspora, has been explained as Shimeon Bar Yoḥai's efforts to teach the Torah, which was forbidden by the Roman authorities, under the guise of such games.

The hymn "Bar Yoḥai, nimshaḥta, Ashrekha," composed by the kabbalist Rabbi Simon Lavie and sung at the celebration on Mount Miron, also presents him as a hero who risked his life for the sake of the Torah and also knew how to combine physical stamina and violent struggle with the study and glorification of the Torah. The hymn pays tribute to the wisdom of Shimeon Bar Yoḥai, who, according to the tradition, wrote the Zohar while in the cave.

Yael Poyas

See also: Kabbalah; Lag Ba'Omer.

Bibliography

Becher, Benjamin-Zeev. *Agadot ha'Tannaim.* Jerusalem: Dvir, 1920–1923 (in Hebrew).

Binyamini, Yafa. "The Myth of Rabbi Shimeon Bar Yoḥai." *Mehkarei Hag* 12 (2001): 87–102 (in Hebrew).

Libes, Yhuda. "The Messiah of the Zohar: The Messianic Figure of Shimeon Bar Yoḥai." In *The Messianic Idea in Israel: Study Day in Honor of Gershon Shalom's Eightieth Anniversary.* Jerusalem: Israeli National Academy of Sciences, 1982 (in Hebrew).

Meir, Ofra. "The Story of Rabbi Shimeon Bar Yoḥai in the Cave." *Aley Siah* 26 (1989): 145–160 (in Hebrew).

Rosenfeld, Ben-Zion. "R. Simeon b. Yoḥai—Wonder Worker and Magician: Scholar, *Saddiq* and *Hasid.*" *Revue des études juives* 158 (1999): 349–384.

Shiviti-Menorah

The Hebrew word "*shiviti*" is the first word of Psalm 16, verse 8, "I have set the Lord always before me" (alternately translated as "I am ever mindful of the Lord's presence"). It is also the name of a devotional mnemonic, a mystic, amuletic page or meditative plaque inscribed with two core components: the *shiviti* verse (Ps. 16:8) and the seven-branched temple menorah inscribed with the words of Psalm 67.

In many variations, with additional texts and decorations, it is prevalent in many Jewish communities. It is traditionally called a *shiviti* by Ashkenazi Jews and a menorah by Sephardi (descendants of the Jews expelled from Spain as well as Jews from Arab/Muslim countries or Middle Eastern countries), referring to its two major components.

The *shiviti*-menorah functions as a reminder of the divine presence and as an aid to concentration in prayer. It is believed that the inscribed menorah and the *shiviti* verse are endowed with protective amuletic powers. In addition, it usually contains various other amuletic formulas, especially names of God (one of the recurring names of God is the 42 letters; a name that is believed to derive from acronyms of the prayer "Ana bekhoaḥ" attributed to Rabbi Nehunia ben ha'Kana, known for its magical powers), blessings such as the Priestly Benediction (Num. 6:22–26), combinations and abbreviations of biblical verses, and psalms.

The *shiviti*-menorah is found in synagogues as well as in private homes, in the *siddur* (prayerbook), and as personal amulets. It displays a rich variety of technique, shape, and decoration. It is preferably handwritten on parchment by a scribe (*sofer stam*), but it can also be printed on paper or cut in paper, chiseled in wood or stone, painted on glass, or embroidered on textiles.

In Ashkenazi synagogues, one *shiviti* is placed in front of the reader's desk. It is meant to help the reader set aside or drive away inappropriate thoughts and concentrate on prayer. In Sephardi and Middle Eastern synagogues many *menorot* are hung: flanking the Torah Ark and above it, and on the synagogue walls.

In *siddurim,* especially in those incorporating kabbalistic customs or rituals, the *shiviti*-menorah page is found mainly in two contexts: in the morning prayers close to the Psalms *pesukei de zimra* or in the counting of the Omer prayers; in other cases the *shiviti*-menorah is a separate leaf kept inside the *siddur*.

The *shiviti*-menorah is hung in the home as a protective amulet. In Ashkenazi communities, it is commonly combined with the *mizraḥ* plaque indicating the direction of prayer toward Jerusalem. It exists also as a personal amulet hung as a pendant.

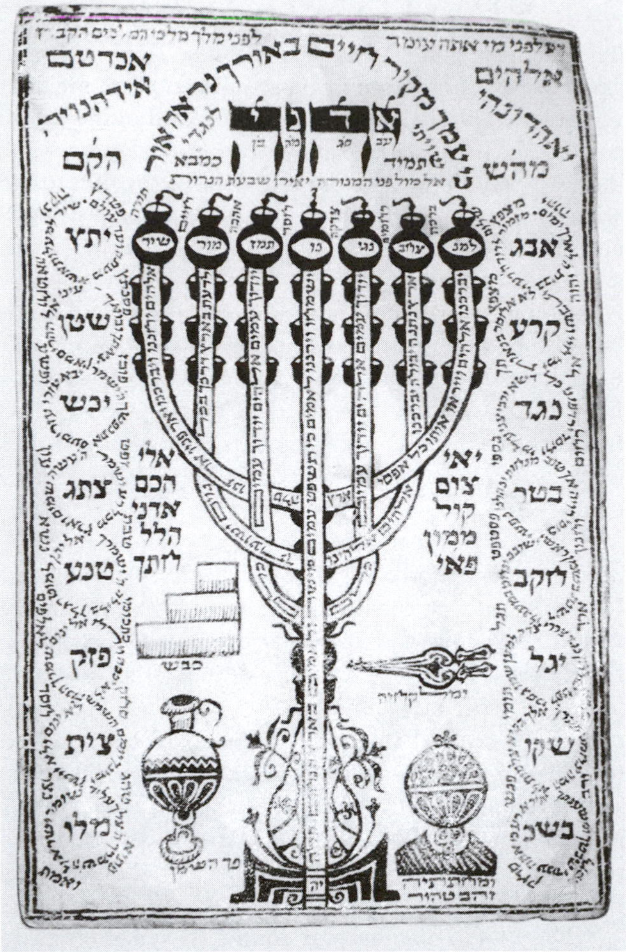

A handwritten parchment *shiviti*, kept between the pages of a prayerbook. Morocco, ca. 1945. *(Gross Family Collection, Tel Aviv)*

Historically, the menorah page incorporating Psalm 67 in the shape of the menorah is known from the fourteenth century, and joined with the *shiviti* verse it appears during the eighteenth century or even in the late seventeenth century. Since the nineteenth century, they have been strongly associated with each other, rendering them interchangeable.

The combination of Psalm 67 and the menorah is a visual-textual symbol heavily imbued with mystic magic meanings. The association of Psalm 67 and the menorah is based on the number seven: the psalm has seven verses (not counting the first introductory verse) corresponding to the seven branches of the menorah. The parallel between the structure of the menorah and that of the psalm has been seen as a mystical substructure, on which further cosmic temporal and other connections were based, such as the analogy with the seven planets, the seven days of the week, and the forty-nine days (seven times seven) of the counting of the Omer. The tradition linking the menorah and Psalm 67 and its amuletic protective potential goes back to the fourteenth century where it is mentioned in *Sefer Abudraham* (a compilation of prayers and customs by Rabbi David ben Josef ben David Abudraham dating from Seville in 1340).

The *shiviti* verse expresses a fundamental desire of the devout Jew to feel the encompassing presence of God at all times. The English translation of the verse does not convey the nuance of the verb in Hebrew לשוות. The alternate translation ("I keep The Lord ever in my sight") conveys an additional meaning of the word that involves mental visualization. This understanding of the verse generated a tradition of mystical exegesis involving mystic, magic techniques of visualizing the letters of God's ineffable name as it appears in the verse and, via this contemplation, cleaving to God, as is recommended in the *shiviti* verse.

This visualization is believed to help keep people from doing evil and to lead to righteous behavior and thereby to protect them.

The *shiviti* plaque is not rooted in any halakhic precepts. It is a compilation of religious magical traditions embodied in a devotional object.

Esther Juhasz

See also: Jerusalem and the Temple; Mizraḥ; Papercut.

Bibliography

Juhasz, Esther. "The Making of a Jewish Votive Object: Between Text and Image, Spirit and Matter: The Example of the *Shiviti-Menorah* Plaque." *Jerusalem Studies in Jewish Folklore* 14–15 (2006–2007): 349–382 (in Hebrew).

Nosek, Bedřich. "Synagogical Tablets from the Collections of the State Jewish Museum (Textual Analysis)." *Judaica Bohemiae* 18:2 (1982): 88–106.

Schrire, Theodore. *Hebrew Amulets: Their Decipherment and Interpretation.* London: Routledge & K. Paul, 1966.

SHOFAR

The shofar, created from the horn of a ram or other kosher animal, was used in ancient Israel to announce the new moon as well as to call people together for communal meetings. It was sounded on Rosh Ha'Shana to mark the beginning of the Jewish New Year and to signal a call to repentance. The shofar has played a central role in Jewish practice over the years. In modern times, the shofar continues to be sounded during the month of Iyar, in spiritual preparation for the approaching New Year, and Jews gather to hear it blown during Rosh Ha'Shana and at the end of Yom Kippur. It is considered a commandment (mitzvah) to hear the shofar blown on this High Holy Day.

The shofar is one of the most significant ritual objects in Judaism. Its unique sound was acknowledged throughout Jewish history as it was used to represent and objectify holiness and evoke spiritual elevation. The appearance of the shofar in folklore also recognizes its unique standing both as a musical instrument and ritualistic object or tool.

In the case of the shofar an amazing relation between the instrument's musical characteristics and its spiritual and ritualistic function can be easily drawn:

1. The shofar is a valveless wind instrument with a basic system of sound production and projection. It functions as an extension of the human mouth, empowering or amplifying the act of exhaling. In this way, the shofar sound symbolizes the essentiality and the emotional potential of human respiration.
2. The production of the normative shofar sound creates the musical impression of an unanswered question. The blower can produce an upward melodic gesture but not a downward gesture: There is no way of returning to the exact departing musical point. As a result, the shofar cry remains edgy, plaintive, and "unresolved" in traditional musical terminology. The sound imparts a feeling of instability and the only way to tame its wild effect is by repeating the musical gesture a few times until one gets used to the repeated cry.
3. Another expressive aspect of shofar tone results from the fact that the shofar cry is endless and unpredictable in nature. The musical tone lasts as long as the shofar blower has air and is not divided into traditional subdivisions or musical "beats." In this regard, the tension prior to the moment the tone sounds (the uncertainty as of the very moment of its beginning), the tone's unpredictable length, and the lack of ability to anticipate its length or subdivisions add to its unusual and holy effect.

The shofar's folklore representations are characterized by reflection on the instrument's piercing sound, historical and mythical symbolic connotations (e.g., the association with Isaac's sacrifice or Joshua's Battle of Jericho), and its theological function as a mediator between heaven and earth (as symbolized by the instrument's vessel-like open, ascending physical shape).

The Shofar in the Aggadah

Reviewing the *Aggadot* (legends) regarding the shofar indicates a common reference to this instrument as an object that is both earthly and divine, a ritualistic object used in high holy rites, a constant reminder of the sacrifice of Isaac, and as an instrument that is used for national or festive declarations about the sacrifice of Isaac.

The most significant Aggadah is attributed by Rabbi Yossi ben Zimra to Rabbi Yoḥanan and depicts a harsh dialogue between God and Abraham.

As in good philosophical dialogues, the rhetoric intensifies in dramatic pitch: The angel cries desperately to prevent Abraham from slaughtering his son; Abraham demands to speak to God directly. God asks Abraham to spare the young boy. Abraham insists on remaining committed to his own oath and argues with the Almighty that he (the Lord) has to commit himself to be merciful to the seed of Abraham: "Just as I [Abraham] fought my parental instincts and was ready to honor my oath and sacrifice my son, I insist that you will remember your commitment and testament to me and my seed, and when my children and all their seed will sin against you, You will have mercy on them and imagine that the ashes of my Isaac are present on this altar." God replies: "Your seed will sin and I will judge them unless they ask my forgiveness and I will remember the sacrifice of Isaac and they shall sound the shofar made of the horn of this ram." God directs Abraham's attention to a wild ram whose horns are caught in the brambles: "So will Israel get caught up in troubles among themselves and their enemies, and their salvation will come from the ram's horn."

This legend presents two parallel emotional perspectives: the divine and the human. Abraham is elevated to the role of an almost super-being, able to argue with God, while God gets a human touch, which makes him more emotionally accessible to the reader. At this same symbolic level, the victim of divine pride (the sacrificial innocent ram) is meant to remind God of his own anger (through the sound produced by blowing through the animal's horn) and thus evokes God's mercy. The human cry that morphs into a superhuman statement is manifested and formed in this Aggadah through the symbolism of the shofar.

The Aggadah regarding King David's humbleness makes interesting use of the difference between trumpets and shofars. In this legend, the Israelites blow shofars and trumpets while King David dances in front of the Holy Ark. Trumpets and shofars are earthly musical instruments alongside the ark (a divine, holy instrument), contrasting sacred and profane sounds against a secular background.

It is clear from the way the story is told that the human king wanted to draw God's attention to his act, and as the story unfolds King David provides the following explanation: I am dancing around the ark (and the shofar), so that it will be clear to everyone that Israel's salvation did not come from a human like me but, rather, by the hands of the Almighty, who is the only one that can save his people (*Bamidbar Rabba* 4).

Jewish men blow the shofar during the ritual of the Cohanim at the Western Wall during the celebration of the Jewish festival of Sukkot in Jerusalem, Israel, 2003. *(Marco Di Lauro/Getty Images)*

The shofar is also mentioned as the instrument used in excommunication ceremonies. In this context, the cry of the shofar functioned as a signal for communal gatherings as well as the sound that can shatter walls, binding the community during the excommunication of one of its members.

The shofar call is believed to signal the gathering of the Israelites in exile. The basic assumption that there is an element in the genome of the people of Israel that will allow them to sense this signal, no matter where they are, implies that Abraham's seed are bound together by their ability to notice such a great moment. This sound, which rings throughout the universe, is more important than the *mezuzah*, circumcision, or any other physical sign. The belief that a "right" sound exists, which only the "right" people can understand and decode, is a universal concept that is utilized in a Jewish context due to the holiness of the shofar (*Mekhilta* 24).

The Aggadah discusses the holy status of the ram from whose horn the shofar is made. The various body parts of the ram are believed to have become holy in several ways; thus, the "breaking" of the whole into its parts can be regarded as an analogy of the nation of Israel, whose people are separated and scattered among nations (*Pirqe de'Rabbi Eliezer* 31).

The shofar, as an aesthetic object, is well represented in the Aggadah. It has its place on the list of significant Jewish ritual objects, which also includes sukkah, *lulav,* tzitzit, and *sefer Torah*. Here the shofar occupies an intermediary spot between two different groups; one group of concrete objects (sukkah) and symbolic representations of nature (*lulav*) and another group of spiritual, abstract objects (tzitzit) and divine representation (*sefer Torah*), which serves to emphasize the shofar's transitional function between the concrete and spiritual. The modulation or transition from *lulav* to shofar is fascinating as well: Both are natural products (vegetation and a ram's horn), but while the *lulav* functions as an exhibition or representation, the shofar is used to evoke a deep spiritual feeling. On a different level, the transition in this sequence of objects between shofar and tzitzit is notable because the focus shifts from the human mouth to man's clothing (and hence to the body). This Aggadah also displays theories on the concept of infinity; by reading these *Aggadot*, one can explore an interesting process of iconization. Some important historical events (such as Isaac's sacrifice or the Exodus from Egypt) were commemorated by symbolic objects (such as shofar and *lulav*); at times, the very physical beauty of these objects becomes a desired merit by itself. Remembering and reliving history through objects of beauty is an interesting addition of these *Aggadot* to the shofar legend.

In a similar tale dealing with the duty to respect one's parents, Rabbi Shimeon Bar Yoḥai discusses the meaning of the verse כבד את ה מהונך in which a list of good deeds showing respect for the Lord is enumerated. It starts with the command to give away a portion of one's harvest and proceeds with the recommendation to obtain a beautiful sukkah, *lulav*, and shofar. This sequence starts with the idea of giving away (or giving back) to God what he created in acknowledgment of his generosity, and the remainder resembles the previous Aggadah. Yet in this Aggadah there is special meaning ascribed to natural elements. The earth (land) whose fruits we consume allows us also to understand the power of God, who created us; the sukkah's leaves and branches transform into a small temple or shelter, and the ram's horn turns into an element of worship and holiness.

In the writings of the disciples of the Ba'al Shem Tov, the founder of Hasidism, there is a legend the great rabbi used to recite just before the sounding of the shofar during the New Year's evening prayer:

A mighty and wise monarch created an illusion that made his people believe that there were walls and watchtowers (barriers) between themselves and him. He also commanded his people to approach him only through these gates, where some of the state's treasures were supposed to be hidden. Various people were able to make different progress on the path through the gates toward the monarch, each according to his skill, motivation, and determination. One day the monarch's own son had a great desire to see him. As the son started on his way, he suddenly realized that nothing separated him and his father. The moral of this fable is obvious: God's holiness fills the earth and no barriers exist between Him and humankind.

In his book *Das Ritual* (1928), psychoanalyst Theodor Reik explained that the Ba'al Shem Tov would relate this legend at this particular hour to indicate that the shofar's tone does not shake the gates of heaven; rather, the tone is intended to shake man and make him realize the presence of the divine all around him. From a musical viewpoint, one might say that the shofar stirs holy overtones around the people who are willing or motivated or determined to hear them.

Shofar in *Piyyutim* (Religious Chanting)

A *piyyut* (pl. *piyyutim*) is a liturgical poem. The shofar is frequently presented in traditional *piyyutim,* especially those sung on High Holy Days. A closer look at some of the more significant *piyyutim* can indicate the importance of the shofar regarding both its traditional functions and poetic expansions of its representation. After a consideration of the sound of well-known traditional *piyyutim,* it should be noted that none have tried to musically imitate the melodic characteristics of the shofar cry. Furthermore, a large number of the melodies of the shofar *piyyutim* are characterized by descending, melismatic melodic lines. It can be assumed that there is no match for the real effect of the shofar's sound.

In the *piyyut* "Yom Yom Ode" (To Thee I Will Give Daily Thanks), the Iraqi-Jewish melody of the final line of each verse is emphasized by repetition. Each of these lines is repeated twice. An accumulation of these final lines gives us the following combination:

עשרת דברות קדשו השמיענו
בקול שופר חזק מאד יעננו
ושם עין בעין ראתה עיננו
ועינינו יראו וישמח לבבנו

The ten holy commandments we have heard
With a very loud shofar cry we will be answered
And thus we saw things eye to eye
And with our eyes we saw, and in our hearts rejoiced

The spiritual progression described in this *piyyut* is clear: We take part in a human-divine dialogue consisting of three elements: the ears, eyes, and heart. Even in the section describing what the people of Israel heard, there is a clear differentiation between content (the commandments) and rhetoric (the sound of the shofar); the commandments are unquestionably and a priori holy, while the shofar is strong and powerful. Holiness is eternal and unquestionable, but the sound effect of the shofar is amazing, effective, and earthshaking and yet can be conceived through our human ears. To Western listeners, the sung version of this *piyyut* (especially in the Iraqi-Jewish tradition) with its prolonged instrumental intervals resembles, in some ways, the form of the Christian nativity acts (with a crucial difference resulting from interchanging the birth of Jesus with the revelation of the Jewish God).

In the *piyyut* "The Lord Is Our God," by Moshe ben Natan for the holiday Shavuot, in a version sung by Turkish Jews, the word "shofar" appears not only in its literary and spiritual context but also in its phonetic and alphabetic order. An acrostic including the words שופר

(shofar) and תורה (Torah) is created, leading to the next key word in the following line: the word אל, which starts with the next letter in the alphabetic sequence, א.

וקול שופר השמיענו
ותורה הנחילנו
ופתח אל באנוכי

In the *piyyut* "Yona ma Tehegi," by Rabbi Judah Halevi, the relevant verses describe a shofar that is brought to the mouth of a yearning dove (which symbolizes the nation of Israel), in order for it to declare salvation. There is an almost erotic element in the description of the shofar presented to the lips of the loved one (symbolically, the entire scene takes place between God and the nation of Israel), but at the same time there is a very strong sense of empowerment. The actual signal of redemption comes from the mouth of Israel, which has the power to initiate and execute. The erotic, almost sexual, symbolism that enables such a responsibility is envisioned through the metaphorical talent of the poet and at the same time indicates the importance of the shofar in Jewish spirituality. Some of the textual melodies attached require an unusually large vocal range, which hints at the important solo vocal roles in such passages.

In conclusion, one of the most musical *piyyutim*, "Halelu Halelu El" (Glory, Rejoice the Lord), lists a number of musically instrumental ways of glorifying God.

Glorify him with a shofar blow
Glorify him with harp and violin
Glorify him with a drum and with dance
Glorify him with wind instruments and organ
Glorify him with (audible) bells
Glorify him with brass instruments
Thy soul will glorify the Lord

Granted that the biblical musical instruments in this *piyyut* are different from the equivalent modern instruments, one can recognize here an attempt to reflect on the means of giving praise to the glory of the Lord. The shofar is placed on the top of the list as an obvious "gate opener": "Blow the shofar that both people and heavens will attend to everything that follows." Even more so, the opening statement (the shofar call) includes all the elements in its very sound. After this opening statement, all one needs to do is to elaborate or specify the instruments related to the shofar (the way different kinds of humans are related to the Almighty) and to note that the other instruments are the "seeds" or parts of the holy shofar call.

The shofar is one of the rare ways that an abstract monotheistic religion such as Judaism manifests holiness in a natural object. God, who has no shape and no time, can be manifested through the shofar call. Theodor Reik, a follower of Austrian psychoanalyst Sigmund Freud, dedicated an entire book to the issue of the manifestation of holiness though the shofar. Jewish folklorists have reached similar conclusions.

Oded Zehavi

See also: Rosh Ha'Shana.

Bibliography

Bialik, H.N., and Y.H. Ravnitzky. *The Book of Legends.* Tel Aviv: Dvir, 1948 (in Hebrew).
"Shofar." *Encyclopaedia Hebraica.* Tel Aviv: Sifriat Poalim, 1988 (in Hebrew).
Reik, Theodor. *Das Ritual: Psychoanalytische Studien.* Leipzig: Internationaler Psychoanalytischer Verlag, 1928.

Sholem Aleichem (1859–1916)

This popular modern author, whose given name is Solomon Rabinovich, has published under many names, corresponding to the multilingual and multicultural environment of his birth, as well as a tradition prevalent among Jewish writers at the end of the nineteenth century of using pseudonyms, often ones that testify to the affinity of the writer with common and unsophisticated parts of the population. In this case, "*Sholem* (variously spelled *Sholom* or *Shalom*) *Aleichem*" is a common greeting in Yiddish, essential to the initiation of almost any pedestrian conversation. The various pronunciations and spellings of Rabinovich's name also testify to the beginning of his writing in Russian, Ukrainian, Hebrew, and Yiddish. It is difficult to overestimate his importance as a writer, journalist, and activist, as Rabinovich greatly influenced twentieth-century Yiddish and Jewish literature. He is popularly considered the third in a trilogy of Yiddish authors who are respectively viewed as the representatives of three generations of Jewish writers, often referred to as the "grandfather," "son," and "grandson" of Yiddish literature: Shalom Jacob Abramovitsh (Abramovich) (better known as Mendele Moykher Sforim; 1835–1917), Isaac Leib Peretz (1852–1915), and Sholem Rabinovich. In addition, Rabinovich is often referred to as a "Jewish Mark Twain," recalling the two writers' common use of pseudonyms, their descriptions of common life, and their association with the inception of a literary tradition of national folklore.

Life Story

The only son of Menachem-Nukhem and Chaye-Esther Rabinovich, Sholem Rabinovich was born on March 2, 1859, in Pereyaslav and grew up in nearby Voronko, in the area of Kiev (capital of present-day Ukraine), then part of the Russian Empire. Rabinovich attended a non-Jewish school at Pereyaslav and graduated with excellent grades in 1876. After graduation, Rabinovich worked as a Hebrew teacher and married his student, Olga (Golde) Love on May 12, 1883. Olga came from a wealthy family, and Rabinovich's marriage marked a period of affluence in his life. In addition, he and his wife had six children. He lost most of his money in 1890 in the stock market and worked very hard to replenish his income by writing for the press in Russian and Hebrew (in addition to his writing in Yiddish) and going on reading tours. At the same time, his health deteriorated, and he contracted tuberculosis.

After a series of anti-Semitic attacks in Kiev in 1905, Rabinovich's family resettled in Geneva, and he was forced to commute between Geneva, New York, and various reading tours across Eastern Europe. In 1908, during a reading tour in Russia, Rabinovich collapsed and was forced to spend two months recovering at the local hospital of Baranowicze (in present-day Belarus). For some time after this incident, Rabinovich had to curtail his activities, and his family was supported by donations from friends and admirers until he was able to regain his strength.

Rabinovich's family immigrated to the United States in 1914 and settled on the Lower East Side of Manhattan. However, his son Misha, who was ill with tuberculosis, was not allowed to enter the United States. Misha stayed in Switzerland with his sister Emma and died in 1915.

Rabinovich died in New York City in 1916, and his funeral, attended by about 100,000 mourners, was a monumental event in modern Jewish history. Among Rabinovich's children were painter Norman Raeben and Yiddish writer Lyalya Kaufman, whose daughter, Bel Kaufman, wrote the novel *Up the Down Staircase* (1965), which was made into a popular film in 1967.

Rabinovich's Work

Writing in Russian for the Odessa newspaper *Voskhod* and in Hebrew for the Odessa newspaper *Hamelitz,* as well as for Yehoshua Hana Ravnitzky's Hebrew anthology, was only a part of Rabinovich's journalistic work and of his work in Hebrew and in Russian. But the main crux of his work, for which he is best known, was written in Yiddish. Rabinovich was an extremely proficient writer; before 1890 he had already produced more than forty volumes of fiction. A contemporary search will yield hundreds of titles—well over a thousand titles if translations of his work and collections of his short stories in various languages are included. Widely read and popular during his lifetime, Rabinovich's work encompasses many aspects of Jewish life during his time, including life in small towns, as in his work (not to be confused with Shalom Jacob Abramovich's) *The Little People* (Berlin: Menorah, 1948); city life and commerce, as in *The Adventures of Menachem-Mendl* (1969) (and *The Further Adventures of Menachem-Mendl* [2001]) and *The Railroad Stories* (New York: Schocken, 1987); and immigration and life in the United States as in his unfinished novel, *Motl, the Cantor's Son* (New Haven: Yale University Press, 2002), with which he was preoccupied at the time of his death. Rabinovich is probably best known for his novel *Tevye the Dairyman* (1987), which served as the basis for the 1964 musical *Fiddler on the Roof.*

In addition to his literary work, Rabinovich was an important activist for the cause of Yiddish literature, supporting other writers and inspiring the creation of a national Yiddish literature through his essays, journalistic writing, and reading tours, all of which drew many admirers and supporters. During the years in which he was well off, Rabinovich funded *The Yiddish Library,* an almanac of Yiddish writers featuring various new works. The third volume of this almanac was not published, as it was completed in 1890, the year in which Rabinovich lost most of his money. His generosity during good times was repaid after 1908, when Rabinovich's health did not allow him to work, and his family was supported for a while by his many admirers and sponsors. For a while, he was the beggar king of a beggar's nation, a public figure who symbolized a newly acquired legitimacy for Yiddish language, culture, and literature. Rabinovich also embraced the cause of Zionism, both in his work *Why Do the Jews Need a Land of Their Own?* (1984), and as a delegate to the Eighth Zionist Congress held in The Hague in 1907. In 1908 he was prevented from attending the First Conference for the Yiddish Language in Czernowitz for health reasons. Rabinovich also wrote an autobiography, *From the Fair* (1916; English trans., 1986).

Folklore

Rabinovich's very first literary work was a lexicon of epithets used by his stepmother. It foretells his great interest in documenting the language, customs, and lifestyles of East European Jews. Most Jewish intellectuals at the end of the nineteenth and the beginning of the twentieth century were educated according to the values of the Enlightenment (Haskalah): a scholarly, anticlerical tradition, which took a didactic approach in trying to improve the language, beliefs, and lifestyles of common readers. Later, romantic literature, and the interest in folklore that developed in the second half of the nineteenth century, inspired Jewish writers as well. Influenced by theories such as that of British writer William John Thoms and projects such as the collection of folk stories by the famous Grimm brothers, Jewish intellectuals also began to document Jewish life and culture. Among the best known of those documents is the collection *Yiddish Folksongs in Russia,* by Saul Gins-

Sholem Aleichem. *(Courtesy of the Library of the Jewish Theological Seminary)*

burg (Ginzburg) and Pesaḥ Marek (1991), comprising folk songs and melodies from various Jewish towns in imperial Russia. Rabinovich was no exception, and his education in the spirit of enlightenment was soon supplemented by the desire to document and describe authentic Jewish culture.

Rabinovich's folklore tendency was also motivated by the economic and political situation of East European Jews and the realities of war, poverty, immigration, and the destruction of the Jewish family wrought by economic necessity, immigration, and loss of traditional life. While nineteenth-century writers like Shalom Jacob Abramovich and Solomon Ettinger could envision the Jewish town, a rabbinical elite, and a class of rich Jewish merchants as worthy adversaries whose authority should be dismantled, for writers of Rabinovich's generation, the Jewish town (shtetl) was already an object of nostalgia and of pity, as well as a site of old traditions that might be lost forever if not saved by more affluent and well educated Jews. The trilogy of major Yiddish writers—Abramovich, Peretz, and Rabinovich—all arrived at some affinity to Jewish tradition, though they did so in different ways. Isaac Leib Peretz is best remembered for his documentation of Hasidic legends and traditions. And the comparison between *The Little People,* roughly similar titles of novels by Abramovich and Rabinovich (Abramovich's more accurately translated as *The Little Person* [1924] and Rabinovich's better remembered for the name of his imaginary town, Kasrilivke), reveals a marked difference: Despite Abramovich's empathy for poor Jews and his philological interest in Yiddish, he uses his story as a pedagogical tool for sharp criticism of the social and economic structure of East European Jewish society. Rabinovich also uses a fair amount of irony in his work, but his irony is less systematic and is by far less judgmental of the circumstances of Jewish poverty and provincialism. As Miriam Roshwald argues in *Ghetto, Shtetl, or Polis,* Rabinovich does not use his imaginary city of Kasrilivke for "patronizing the shtetl or branding it a ghetto" but, rather, is "identified with his material . . . [and] can imbue the setting with the spirit of his characters" (2007: 50–51). Moreover, Rabinovich documents all walks of Jewish life during his time, treating with equal ridicule urban and rural, rich and poor, East and West European Jews as well as Jewish immigrants to the United States, and even his own fans and sponsors. He creates a "comedy of manners," drawing types rather than espousing a particular political agenda.

However, Rabinovich's authored folk literature, as well as that of other Yiddish writers of his time, was also criticized as unauthentic and distortive of real Jewish tradition. In *A Bridge of Longing,* David Roskies (1995) argues that the documentation of East European Jewish life by Yiddish authors, dramaturges, poets, songwriters, and researchers was skewed by the secular tendencies of such intellectuals and their education in the spirit of the Enlightenment. Such writers, Roskies argues, were motivated not only by a secularist agenda but also by their lack of knowledge of Jewish tradition. Roskies recalls Rabinovich's defense of Mark Warshavsky's songs in a debate with music critic Joel Engel about the nature of folk songs. Rabinovich claimed that "folk songs" are songs written in the language of "the folk" and for their benefit (1995, 13). This argument was probably meant to extend to Rabinovich's work itself. His work is, for better or worse, a popular depiction of East European Jewish life that has been adopted by many factions and contingents of world Jewry. In fact, a significant feature of Rabinovich's work is that during a time of sharp ideological disputes, political rifts, and sometimes even a lack of communication between Jewish communities around the world, it was accepted by very distant and extreme components of the Jewish world. Immensely popular among Yiddish readers in the United States and Western Europe, Rabinovich's work was also widely translated into Hebrew, to the extent that Rabinovich has been virtually accepted as a major original Hebrew writer. And even the heavily censored publications of Soviet-Yiddish literature include many volumes that transcribe Rabinovich's work in the special orthography of Soviet Yiddish, abandoning the original spelling and orthography of Hebrew words. Consequently, if Rabinovich's work does not fit a certain strict definition of folk literature, it must at least be admitted that "the folk" never cared.

Autobiographical Approach

In *Author as Character in the Works of Sholom Aleichem* (1985), Victoria Aarons suggests an additional reading of Rabinovich's work. According to Aarons, Rabinovich's use of fictitious narrators allows for dramatic monologues, such as those of characters Menachem-Mendl and Motl, the cantor's Son, in which the author indirectly addresses the more sophisticated reader, inserting his own comments about social customs and political developments. In this light, Rabinovich is no longer a mere "documenter" of Jewish life but an engaged participant who is partially depicted and partially disguised in the characters of his fictitious narrators. Aarons provides even greater room for the reading of contemporary context and the representation of historical development in Rabinovich's work.

Dror Abend-David

See also: Shtetl.

Bibliography

Aarons, Victoria. *Author as Character in the Works of Sholom Aleichem.* Lewiston, NY: Edwin Mellen, 1985.

Abramovich, S.Y. (Mendele Moykher Sforim). *Dos Kleyne Menshele* (The Little Person). Warsaw: Mendele, 1924.

Friden, Ken. *Classic Yiddish Fiction: Abramovitsh, Sholem Aleichem, and Peretz.* Albany: State University of New York Press, 1995.

Ginzburg, Saul M., and Pesach S. Marek. *Yiddish Folksongs in Russia [Yidishe Folkslider in Rusland]: Photo Reproduction of the 1901 St. Petersburg Edition,* ed. Dov Noy. Ramat Gan: Bar Ilan University Press, 1991.

Miron, Dan. *The Image of the Shtetl and Other Studies of Modern Jewish Literary Imagination.* Syracuse: Syracuse University Press, 2000.

Rabinovich, Solomon N. (Sholem Aleichem). *The Adventures of Menahem-Mendl.* New York: Putnam, 1969.

———. *From the Fair: The Autobiography of Sholom Aleichem,* trans. Curt Leviant. New York: Penguin, 1986. New York: Varhayt, 1916.

———. *Fun'm yarid: Lebensbeshraybungen* (At the Fair: Memoirs). New York: Varhayt, 1916.

———. *The Further Adventures of Menachem-Mendl: New York—Warsaw—Vienna—Yehupetz,* trans. Aliza Shevrin. Syracuse: Syracuse University Press, 2001.

———. *Ḳleyne Mentshelekh mit Ḳleyne Hasoges* (Little People with Little Thoughts). Berlin: Menorah, 1948.

———. *The Letters of Menakhem-Mendl and Sheyne-Sheyndl; And, Motl, The Cantor's Son,* trans. Hillel Halkin. New Haven, CT: Schocken, 2002.

———. *Tevye the Dairyman and the Railroad Stories,* trans. Hillel Halkin. New York: Schocken, 1987.

———. *Why Do the Jews Need a Land of Their Own?* New York: Cornwall, 1984.

Roshwald, Miriam. *Ghetto, Shtetl, or Polis? The Jewish Community in the Writings of Karl Emil Franzos, Sholom Aleichem, and Shmuel Yosef Agnon.* San Bernardino, CA: Borgo, 2007.

Roskies, David G. *A Bridge of Longing: The Lost Art of Yiddish Storytelling.* Cambridge: Harvard University Press, 1995.

Samuel, Maurice. *The World of Sholom Aleichem.* London: Vallentine-Mitchell, 1973.

Waife-Goldberg, Marie. *My Father, Sholom Aleichem.* New York: Simon and Schuster, 1968.

Wisse, Ruth R. *The Modern Jewish Canon: A Journey Through Language and Culture.* New York: Free Press, 2000.

SHTETL

The word "shtetl" (Yid., town; pl. *shtetlekh*) refers to what was the archetypal East European Jewish place of residence from the sixteenth century until World War II. Since the time of East European Jews' encounters with the Haskalah (Jewish Enlightenment), the West European movement to offer a philosophical defense of Jewish modernity), in the late 1800s, the shtetl has assumed a symbolic value as the quintessential locus of Jewish folkways, articulated in a wide array of cultural practices, including ethnographic and folkloristic studies, as well as works of literature, music, visual art, theater, and film that are informed by folk idioms. The attention to the shtetl as a cultural fountainhead of Jewish folkways has continued after the Holocaust, taking on new significance in connection with remembering Jewish victims of the Nazi genocide.

Origins of Shtetl Folklore

As early as the thirteenth century, Jews began to settle in cities and towns in the kingdom of Poland. During the sixteenth century, Jewish settlement under Polish rule expanded significantly, especially in newly established towns in what is now Ukraine. As part of this expansion, Jews came to play a central role in the regional economy, in which these towns served as vital nodes of trade and commerce. Eventually, Jews became a sizable presence in towns throughout Eastern Europe, where the Jewish population began to surge during the eighteenth century. By the nineteenth century, the majority of the world's Jews lived in these towns.

As a consequence of the Haskalah, the shtetl became an object of self-scrutiny for Jews as they began leaving these towns behind—whether physically, as immigrants, or intellectually, as *maskilim* (advocates of the Haskalah). For these Jews in particular, the shtetl came to exemplify a parochial, premodern way of life. During the twentieth century the symbolic value of the shtetl expanded, emerging both as a fount of Jewish folk creativity for an array of writers, composers, artists, performers, and folklorists and as a social paradigm of Jewish communal life for anthropologists and sociologists. In the wake of the Holocaust, the shtetl came to serve not only as the point of entry par excellence into pre–World War II European Jewish life but also as a model for characterizing Jewish life elsewhere, including American small towns and suburbs.

Shtetl lore informed the literary efforts of *maskilim,* writing in Yiddish and Hebrew, beginning in the late eighteenth century, usually within satires that assailed shtetl traditions as exemplary of all that hindered Jewish progress. These early efforts constitute what literary scholar Dan Miron termed an "anti-folklore" that both documented and derided shtetl mores. The shtetl figured centrally in seminal works of modern Yiddish and, to a lesser extent, Hebrew literature—including in the prose of Isaac Mayer Dik, S.J. Abramovitch, and, most famously, Sholem Aleichem—who, following the pattern established by *maskilim*, offered astute critiques of traditional Jewish mores and provincial society through satire. Other writers, including I.L. Peretz and S. An-Ski, transformed traditional Yiddish folklore, especially Hasidic storytelling, into works of modern Jewish literature set in *shtetlekh*.

The early twentieth century witnessed a new interest in traditional East European Jewish life among modernizing Jews, prompting early ethnographic efforts to collect folklore in these towns and in rural villages. Among the first of these efforts was that spearheaded by political activist and philologist Noyekh Prilutski (Noah Prylucki), who helped organize a circle of Jewish folklorists in Warsaw at the beginning of the twentieth century. Their collections of folklore materials appeared in Jewish newspapers and in books, such as the anthology *Bay undz yidn* (Among Us Jews), edited by M. Vanvild, published in 1923. Though Jewish folklorists tended to be based in major cities (such as Vilna and St. Petersburg), the target of their collecting efforts was the *folksmentsh*—the "ordinary" person, whose life was relatively unaffected by modern education, politics, or culture—whose archetypal setting was the shtetl.

The most famous organized effort to collect Jewish folklore in East European towns and villages was the 1912–1914 expedition in Ukraine led by An-Ski. His expedition amassed thousands of folktales, proverbs, folk songs, objects, photographs, and sound recordings. An-Ski's collecting efforts were interrupted by the outbreak of World War I. Even as he devoted his energies to relief work, An-Ski also documented the lore of Jewish communities experiencing unprecedented violence. An-Ski subsequently drew on his folklore collection to write *The Dybbuk,* the best-known Yiddish play.

During the interwar years, scholarly efforts to study East European Jewish folkways were organized by the Ethnographic Committee of the YIVO Institute for Jewish Research in Vilna and by researchers in state-supported institutes in the Soviet Union. These undertakings included grass-roots projects, such as a pamphlet published in Minsk in 1928, which exhorted amateur folklorists, "Forsht ayer shtetl" (Research your town). Individual ethnographies, memoirs, literary works, and journalistic accounts of shtetl life also appeared during this period in Yiddish, Hebrew, Polish, Russian, German, and other languages.

For Jewish immigrants to North America, Old World *shtetlekh* remained important symbolic resources, especially as realized in the activities of hundreds of *landsmanshaftn,* mutual aid societies whose members were *landslayt* (immigrants from the same hometown). American Yiddish popular culture in the interwar years spawned an extensive number of songs, plays, and films that celebrated the shtetl in nostalgic terms as the embodiment of a traditional past left behind by immigrants. By contrast, Soviet film and theater portrayed shtetl life from a Marxist perspective that situated these towns as the locus of an obsolescent Jewish life to be transformed by Soviet society.

The Shtetl After the Holocaust

During World War II, the majority of Jews who had lived in these towns were murdered; those who survived seldom returned to their former homes, and Jewish community life in most of these towns came to an end. In the wake of the Holocaust, many former residents of these towns initiated efforts to memorialize their local histories, customs, and murdered townsfolk, most notably by compiling *yisker-bikher* (communal memorial books). At the same time, American anthropologists undertook a major project to write a composite study of prewar East European Jewish life, based on research from a pioneering wartime "anthropology-at-a-distance" project overseen by Margaret Mead and Ruth Benedict. The resulting book, *Life Is with People: The Jewish Little-Town of Eastern Europe* (1952), quickly became the standard work in English on shtetl life. As folklorist Barbara Kirshenblatt-Gimblett has observed, this book's approach offers an idealized, paradigmatic vision of the shtetl—timeless, uniform, insular—that is as intellectually problematic as it was affectively appealing in the aftermath of the Holocaust. The impact of *Life Is with People* has been extensive, influencing, among other works, *Number Our Days* (1978), anthropologist Barbara Myerhoff's study of storytelling among elderly American Jewish immigrants from Eastern Europe. Having become in the post–World War II era the metonymy of prewar East European Jewish life generally—even as this population had been urbanizing and immigrating—the shtetl serves as a paradigm for conceptualizing and presenting

East European Jewish history, Yiddish songs, and works of fiction in a number of anthologies.

At the same time, the growing interest in documenting the life stories of Holocaust survivors has generated an extensive body of individual recollections of prewar life in former hometowns, both in written memoirs and in audio- and videotaped interviews. The postwar era is also witness to a distinctive Hasidic remembrance of particular towns; memorialized in religious storytelling and in the preservation of local religious customs, the names of these towns mark the original of Hasidic communities that now thrive in an international diaspora.

Shtetl memory practices have increasingly expanded beyond literary efforts to other activities. A number of memory artists—including Mayer Kirshenblatt, whose memoir of his childhood in Apt (Pol., Opatów) interrelates narrative with works of visual art—have documented their recollections of prewar life in these towns in paintings and drawings. Prewar shtetl life has been realized in several feature films, including *Moi Ivan, toi Abraham,* directed by Yolande Zauberman (1993), and *Train de Vie,* directed by Radu Mihaielanu (1999). Travel back to *shtetlekh* is the subject of a number of documentary films, such as Willy Lindwer's *Return to My Shtetl Delatyn* (1992) and Marian Marzynski's *Shtetl* (1996). The desire to visit these towns has engendered new tourist practices in the years since the collapse of communist rule in Eastern Europe; among these efforts is ShtetlSchleppers, a tourist service run by genealogists at Jewishgen.org. Descendants of East European Jews, such as Theo Richmond (author of *Konin: One Man's Quest for a Vanquished Jewish Community,* 1996), have written about their return journeys to their forebears' *shtetlekh.*

In some instances, recalling one's shtetl has engendered multiple undertakings. Aaron Ziegelman, for example, has underwritten the creation of a documentary film, a traveling exhibition, an archival project, and a Web site dedicated to his native town of Libivne (Ukr., Liuboml). Similarly, Yaffa Eliach's desire to commemorate Jewish life in prewar Eishyshok (Pol., Ejszyszki; Lith., Eisiskes) has inspired her to collect hundreds of photographs of the town's Jews (many of which are installed in a monumental display, the Tower of Faces, in the United States Holocaust Memorial Museum in Washington, DC), to write an extensive history of the town, and to participate in the production of radio and film documentaries on returning to Eishyshok. Her culminating effort—a plan to create a living history shtetl museum that replicates Jewish life in prewar Eishyshok on a plot of land in Rishon Le'Zion, Israel—is perhaps the most ambitious postwar undertaking to engage the shtetl as a fountainhead of bygone Jewish folkways.

Jeffrey Shandler

See also: An-Ski, S.; Poland, Jews of; Russia, Jews of; Sholem Aleichem.

Bibliography

Gottesman, Itzik Nakhmen. *Defining the Yiddish Nation: The Jewish Folklorists of Poland.* Detroit: Wayne State University Press, 2003.

Kirshenblatt, Mayer, and Barbara Kirshenblatt-Gimblett. *They Called Me Mayer July: Painted Memories of a Jewish Childhood in Poland Before the Holocaust.* Berkeley: University of California Press, 2007.

Kugelmass, Jack, and Jonathan Boyarin, ed. *From a Ruined Garden: The Memorial Books of Polish Jewry.* 2d ed. Bloomington: Indiana University Press, 1998.

Miron, Dan. *The Image of the Shtetl and Other Studies of Modern Jewish Literary Imagination.* Syracuse: Syracuse University Press, 2000.

Myerhoff, Barbara. *Number Our Days.* New York: Touchstone, 1978.

Shandler, Jeffrey. "The Shtetl Subjunctive: Yaffa Eliach's Living History Museum." In *Culture Front: Representing Jews in Eastern Europe,* ed. Benjamin Nathans and Gabriella Safran. Philadelphia: University of Pennsylvania Press, 2008.

Zborowski, Mark, and Elizabeth Herzog. *Life Is with People: The Culture of the Shtetl.* New York: Schocken, 1995. Introduction by Barbara Kirshenblatt-Gimblett. Originally published as *Life Is with People: The Jewish Little-Town of Eastern Europe.* New York: International Universities Press, 1952.

Shtyyah Stone

The Shtyyah stone is the name given to the large rock embedded in the floor of the Temple's holiest place, the Holy of Holies (Dvir). It is identified by scholars as the rock situated in the center of Jerusalem's Dome of the Rock Mosque. The Shtyyah stone was first mentioned in tannaic sources (*m. Yoma* 5:2, *t. Moed Kippurim* 2). The oldest etymology of the Hebrew word *"shtyyah"* gives its definition as "foundation" (*t. Moed Kippurim* 2). Later in the Talmud, it was related to the word *"shti,"* meaning "crisscross weaving" (*y. Pesaḥim* 4:1), and in the Midrash to the root word *"shata,"* meaning "to drink" (*Torah Shlema Bereshit* 28).

The rabbinical and midrashic sources related to it can be divided in two, based on their emphasis. The first refers to this rock as an omphalos, the center and navel of the earth (*Tanḥuma Qedoshim* 10; *Yalqut Shimoni*, Vayetze 120; *Midr. Tehilim Buber* 91:7), from which the world was created (*Num. Rab.* 12:4; *Tanḥuma* Piqudei 3; *Midr. Tehilim Buber* 11:2). It restrained the expanding world (*b. Ḥagigah* 12a); it sits on primordial waters and seals the primordial void (Tehom) (*Yalqut Shimoni* Yona 550; *Midr. Tehilim Buber* 91:7; *Pirqe de'Rabbi Eliezer* 9). The world could be destroyed if this rock were to be removed (*Yalqut Shimoni* Vayeshev 145).

The second focus is on the Axis Mundi: the site on earth where one has the most direct route to communicate with Heaven. It is identified by the Midrash as the sacred center where the Temple was erected (*Sehel Tov Buber Gen.* 30; *Midr. Tehilim Buber* 91:7); it is the site of the Altar (*Otzar Midrashim* 104). It is believed to be

Mount Moriah, on which some of the major events in Jewish history occurred, such as Abraham's sacrifice of Isaac. Jacob prostrated himself on it, praying for God's assistance, and took an oath on it, according to the narrative in Genesis 28:22 (*Midr. Tehilim Buber* 91:7). The stone on which Jacob slept and dreamed (Gen. 28:18) is identified by the Midrash as the Shtyyah, the emplacement of both Beth El and Jerusalem (*Pirqe de'Rabbi Eliezer*, end of ch. 35).

In the Temple in Jerusalem, on the Day of Atonement, since the tabernacle was no longer there, the ritual of purifying the Dvir was performed on this rock (*m. Yoma* 5:2; *t. Moed Kippurim* 2).

Interesting resonances of the Shtyyah etymology are preserved in folk customs. Based on the etymology of the word "*shti,*" meaning "crisscross weaving," an Eretz Israel amoraic source mentioned that at the beginning of the month of Av, when the Temple was destroyed and the Shtyyah stone ceased to be used, women abstained from weaving (*y. Ta'anit* 1:6; *y. Pesaḥim* 4:1). This custom prevailed in the sixteenth century (*Kitzur Shulḥan arukh* 126:11).

Idit Pintel-Ginsberg

See also: Stones.

Bibliography

Eliade, Mircea. "Sacred Architecture and Symbolism." In *Symbolism, the Sacred and the Arts,* ed. Diane Apostolos-Cappadona, pp. 105–129. New York: Crossroad, 1985.

———. "Symbolisme du centre." In *Images et symboles.* Paris: Gallimard, 1952, pp. 33–65.

Graves, Robert, and Raphael Patai. *Hebrew Myths.* New York: Doubleday, 1964.

Kaufman, Asher. "The Emplacement of the Shtya Stone and the Temple." *Ariel* 11 (1989): 64–65, 179–181 (in Hebrew).

Lieberman, Saul. *Tosefta k'pshuta moed, kippurim.* Jerusalem: Beit Hamidrash LeRabanim BeAmerica, 1993 (in Hebrew).

Noy, Dov. "The Shtyyah Stone and the Creation." In *Veleyerushalim,* pp. 360–394. Jerusalem: Yahdav, 1968 (in Hebrew).

Padya, Haviva. "Changes in the Holy of Holies: From Edge to Center." *Jewish Studies* 37 (1997): 53–110 (in Hebrew).

Patai, Raphael. *Man and Temple in Ancient Jewish Myth and Ritual.* London: Thomas Nelson & Sons, 1967.

Shiler, Eli. "The Shtyyah Stone." *Ariel* 11 (1989): 63–72 (in Hebrew).

SHVAT, FIFTEENTH OF (TU BE'SHVAT)

Tu Be'Shvat (the fifteenth of Shvat) is a minor festival on the Jewish calendar, celebrated on the fifteenth of Shvat. It is also called the Festival of Trees or Jewish Arbor Day.

History and Interpretations

Unknown in the Bible, the first phases in the festival's development are mentioned in the Mishnah (*m. Rosh Ha'shanah* 1:1), specifically in a list of dates on which different new years start. There, Tu Be'Shvat is the date of the "New Year for Trees." This date was set for taxation purposes.

Beit Hillel and Beit Shammai (the two schools of Jewish legal thought active in Jerusalem in the first century C.E.) argued about the exact date on which it should occur. Beit Shammai determined that it should start the first day of the month of Shvat. Beit Hillel, however, ruled a two-week delay, for meteorological reasons, letting the weather warm up so that the first signs of vegetative revival would be visible all over the country. The Halakhah adopted Beit Hillel's ruling. No celebration or rituals are connected to this date in the Mishnah or either of the Talmuds.

Liturgical poems dating from the tenth and eleventh centuries praising the Land of Israel and its fruits were found in the Cairo Geniza. Scholars interpreted them as dedicated to Tu Be'Shvat.

The medieval Ashkenaz introduced several customs to Tu Be'Shvat. By the ruling of Rabeinu Gershom Maor Hagola (tenth to eleventh century), communal fasts (Ta'anit Tzibur) were not allowed. The recitation of Repentance Prayers (Tahanun) was forbidden as well.

According to testimony by Rabbi Issachar ben Mordecai ibn Susan (1510–1580), during Tu Be'Shvat in sixteenth-century Zefat, the custom was to abstain from fasting or to prostrate during the Tahanun. Ashkenazis (descendants of western and Eastern Europe Jewry) commonly eat numerous types of fruits on this day, but this custom was unknown to Sephardim (descendants of Jews who lived on the Iberian Peninsula, before their expulsion in the late fifteenth century).

Major changes occurred in Tu Be'Shevat celebrations after the sixteenth century, when the ritual called a Tu Be'Shvat Seder was introduced. It is described for the first time in the book *Ḥemdat Yamim*, written by an unknown author and published in 1731–1732 in Izmir, Turkey.

Chapter 3 of this book has a detailed description of the Tu Be'Shvat Seder. This chapter is still currently in print, as a separate pamphlet titled "Pri etz hadar" (the citrus fruit, lit., "fruit of the tree of splendor"). The Seder includes the consumption of twenty-one different fruits (six of them from the seven species mentioned in the Bible as crops of the Land of Israel: wheat, barley, grapes, figs, pomegranates, olives, and dates) and four cups of wine (the first white, the second mostly white mixed with a small amount of red wine, the third half white and half red, and the last cup mostly red with a little bit of white wine). Eating and drinking are combined with spiritual reflections on the various pronunciations of the explicit

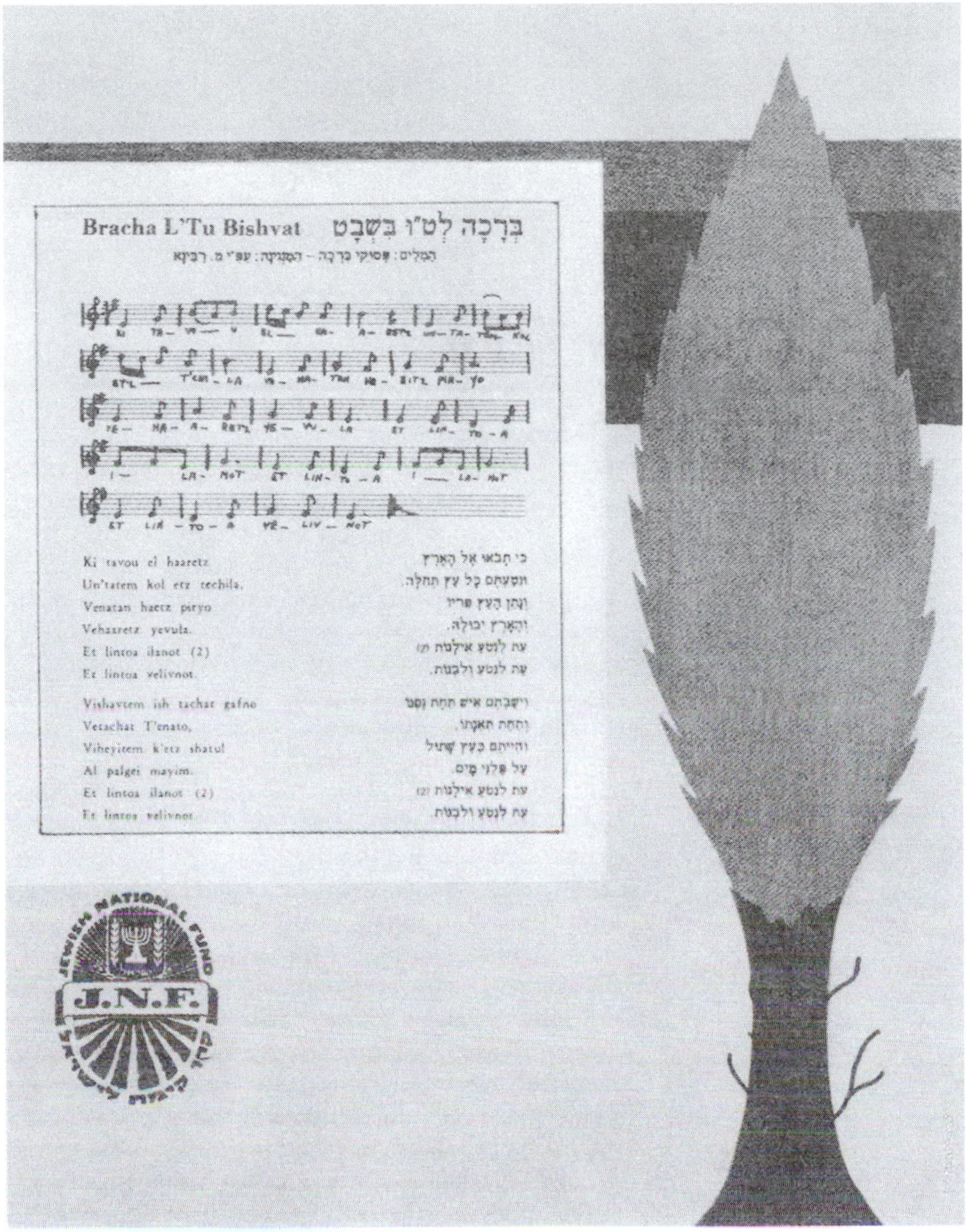

A poster for Tu Be'Shvat issued by the Jewish National Fund. *(Jewish National Fund)*

name of God, according to the Lurianic Kabbalah's (the kabbalistic doctrines of Isaac Luria, Zefat, sixteenth century), and readings mainly taken from the Zohar (lit. "Book of Splendor," the major text of Kabbalah, written in Spain in the thirteenth century) with some additions from the Mishnah (canonic text of the Jewish Law, redacted in the second century).

The identity of this ritual's initiator is unknown and disagreed upon by scholars. Some attribute its origin to kabbalist Lurianic disciples from seventeenth-century Zefat. Others agree upon the period but attribute it to a Shabtaic (followers of Shabbati Zvi, who led a Jewish messianic movement in the seventeenth century) source. Finally some researchers agree on the Shabtaic source but postpone the time of its writing to the eighteenth century, around the time *Ḥemdat Yamim* was published. The author of *Ḥemdat Yamim* claims that he invented this ritual. But scholars have raised doubt over the credibility of his statements.

Tu Be'Shvat Seder, according to the *Ḥemdat Yamim* tradition, is held to this day by Balkan, east Mediterranean, and North African Jewish religious communities. Ashkenazi communities, strongly opposed to even the slightest Shabtaic influence, have rejected this ritual and do not perform it. Among religious communities that do not hold Seders for Tu Be'Shvat, the prevalent ritual is eating different kinds of fruit.

Contemporary Celebrations

Another turning point in Tu Be'Shvat's development occurred with the modern return to the Land of Israel. At the beginning of the twentieth century, the Zionist movement transformed it into a tree-planting holiday. In 1908, the Teacher's Union in Tel Aviv declared this day a planting festival for students. This remains the major secular custom associated with this festival.

Songs were specially written in its honor: "So Walk the Tree Planters" (written in 1926, with lyrics by Isaac Shenhar/Sheinberg and music by Yedidia Admon/Gorohov), "The Almond Tree Blossoms" (written in the 1930s, with lyrics by Israel Dushman and music by Menashe Rabinah/Rabinowitz). Even in the 1940s these songs were considered folk songs. Today, they are taught to toddlers and in kindergartens as part of the preparations for the festival.

Government agencies and national groups, mainly the Jewish National Fund (JNF, a not-for-profit organization founded in 1901 to purchase and develop land for the Jewish state), usually organize formal planting activities. Lack of suitable planting spaces, a more professional approach to tree planting, and disagreements over where to plant the trees, together with inclement weather and perhaps an insufficient ritual framework to the celebration, have made these planting ceremonies more and more problematic (Pintel-Ginsberg 2006). At the beginning of the twenty-first century, even virtual plantings have been proposed through JNF Web site.

In Israel, since the beginning of the 1970s, along with the custom of planting trees, Tu Be'Shvat Seders were introduced to secular Jews. Inspired by the *Ḥemdat Yamim*, the late Amnon Yadin first celebrated a Seder at the Oranim Teachers' Seminary. This Seder differs from the traditional one, mainly in its textual content and the abandonment of mystical reflection. The structured framework was kept; the first twelve of the twenty-one fruit species are used, and four cups of wine are drunk in the same order and mixture as the traditional cups with one slight difference: the last cup is completely red.

New texts were introduced from various sources, some traditional and some secular: midrashic and Hasidic sayings and tales, modern Israeli poetry and prose. Their content is related to the festival, to the Land of Israel's nature and love for it. Songs are incorporated into the Seder. The different wine combinations and colors are explained as symbolizing various aspects of nature during the four seasons.

Another type of secular Seder was introduced by Noga Hareuveni, one of the founders of Neot Kedumim (Biblical Landscape Reserve in Israel, which aims to recreate the physical setting of the Bible). These Seders do not resemble the traditional Tu Be'Shvat Seder. Their ritual structure is mainly influenced by the Passover Seder. The textual emphasis of these Seders is learning about Tu Be'Shvat sources and its development.

Since the 1970s, the practice of celebrating Tu Be'Shvat Seders has been adopted by kibbutzim, educational establishments, and Zionist youth movements in Israel and abroad. It is celebrated on Tu Be'Shvat eve, but often, when the weather or other reasons make the planting ceremony impossible, it is celebrated on Tu Be'Shvat. The structure of the ritual and the texts are usually printed in a Haggadah, the same term as used for Passover. Dozens of different versions of these Tu Be'Shvat Hagaddot are found in the Kibbutz Festival's Archives, in Kibbutz Beit Ha'Shita. The ritual structure is more or less stable, as the quantities of fruit vary, but the texts and the songs are often changed. More traditional texts, such as blessings and prayers, are sometimes included. Songs are constantly updated to fit current trends.

Since the late 1990s, several editions of Tu Be'Shvat's *Haggadot* were written by Yoel Rapel and distributed to Israeli schools before the holiday. The ritual described in them is a combination between Amnon Yadin's and Noga Hareuveni's Seders.

Along with the deepening of the Seder ritual on Tu Be'Shvat, an invented tradition is emphasized among the secular Jews: It claims that this ritual's source is Isaac Luria, who invented and practiced it. This tradition has no historical basis and lacks Lurianic ritual logic. Nevertheless, it is used to intensify ideals and promote the love of Israel, the land and people, and the ideas of returning to Zion and celebrating its natural heritage.

This festival has been the subject of different studies. Yom-Tov Lewinsky, in his 1954 broad survey of Jewish festivals, devoted an entire chapter to it. Avraham Ya'ari thoroughly researched its development and presented his findings in several articles during the 1950s and early 1960s. Sharing the same views on the early stages of Tu Be'Shvat development, these two scholars are divided on the causes and the exact period when major changes occurred to the festival since the sixteenth century. Although often using the same sources, they interpret them differently. More recent reviews on Tu Be'Shvat (such as Hacohen 1969; Hacohen and Hacohen 1980; Goldberger 1994) are based mostly on Levinsky's conclusions and tend to repeat them.

Idit-Pintel Ginsberg

Bibliography

Ben Susa, Isashar. *Leap of the Years*. Jerusalem: Bezalel Landoy, 1988 (in Hebrew).

Benyau, Meir, ed. "The Shabtaic Movement in Greece." *Sfunot 14, Sefer Yavan* 4. Jerusalem: Yad Ben Zvi Institute, 1978 (in Hebrew).

Goetschel, Roland. "La célébration du nouvel an de l'arbre: Analyse d'un rituel kabbalistique du XVIIIe siecle." *Daat* 10 (1983): 39–43.

Goldberger, Dov, ed. "Winter." *Haf'alopedia*, vol. 3. Tel Aviv: Sifrey Hemed, 1994 (in Hebrew).

Hacohen, Deborah, and Menahem Hacohen, eds. *Festivals and Solemn Days: Ḥanukkah, Tu Be'Shvat, Purim.* Jerusalem: Keter, 1980 (in Hebrew).

Hacohen, Menahem, ed. *Tu Be'Shvat. Arahim* 8. Tel Aviv: Moshvei Ovdim Beisraeli, 1969 (in Hebrew).

Hareuveni, Noga. *The New Year of the Trees.* Kiryat Ono: Neot Kedumim, 1979 (in Hebrew).

———. *Tu Be'Shvat Eve Seder.* Neot Kedumim: Keren Kayemet LeIsrael, 1998 (in Hebrew).

Ḥemdat Yamim. Kushta, 1735. Reprint: Jerusalem: Makor, 1970 (in Hebrew).

Lewinsky, Yom Tov. *The Book of Festivals,* vol. 5. Tel Aviv: Agudat Oneg Shabbat, 1954 (in Hebrew).

Pintel-Ginsberg, Idit. "Narrating the Past: 'New Year of the Trees' Celebrations in Modern Israel." *Israel Studies* 11:1 (Spring 2006): 174–193.

Scholem, Gershom. "And the Enigma Is Still Standing." *Shabtaic Studies*, pp. 250–288. Tel Aviv: Am Oved, 1991 (in Hebrew).

Tishby, Isaiah. "Studies in Ḥemdat Yamim Sources." In *Paths of Faith and Heresy*, pp. 108–142. Jerusalem: Magnes, 1982 (in Hebrew).

Yadin, Amnon. *Seder Tu Be'Shvat.* Geva: Shkedia, 1982 (in Hebrew).

Ya'ari, Avraham. *A Book Enigma: Ḥemdat Yamim, Its Author and Its Influence.* Jerusalem: Mosad Harav Kook, 1954 (in Hebrew).

———. "The History of Tu Be'Shvat." *The Book of Festivals and Solemn Days,* ed. Z. Ariel, pp. 168–174. Tel Aviv: Am Oved, 1962 (in Hebrew).

———. "The History of Tu Be'Shvat." *Maḥanaim* 42 (1960): 15–24 (in Hebrew).

———. "Tikkunim and Prayer Books According to Ḥemdat Yamim." *Kiriat Sefer* 38 (1963): 97–400 (in Hebrew).

Silverman Weinreich, Beatrice

See: Anthologies

Simchat Torah Flags

In the folklore of Simchat Torah—a rabbinical festival marking the completion and the beginning of the annual reading of the Torah—the object associated most with the holiday, at least in the world of children, is undoubtedly the small ornamental flag (Heb., *degel simchat Torah*) made for children out of paper or cardboard and printed with rich and colorful designs pertaining to the holiday and its meaning. Until a few years ago, most flags were customarily attached to wooden sticks topped with apples, which were hollowed out and filled with a burning candle.

While it is not known when and where this custom originated, it is certainly an Ashkenazi tradition, which in the past was especially popular in Eastern Europe. The earliest known source that mentions a flag for Simchat Torah is found in the enactments (*Takkanot*) issued in 1672 by Polish Jews who settled in Amsterdam. The leaders of the community feared that the candle atop the flag might cause a fire in the synagogue and therefore limited its usage. It is evident from this document that the custom existed much earlier and most likely was brought to the Netherlands from Poland.

A few other sources mention the flag in the eighteenth and nineteenth centuries. The German Hebraist Johann Bodenschatz describes the custom in *Kirchliche Verfassung der heutigen Jüden* (Erlang, 1748): "On the night of Simchat Torah . . . when the children leave the synagogue, they hold onto their flags upon which is inscribed 'standard of the camp' and the names of the tribes. They march as if they were soldiers." In southern Germany the children were rewarded with sweets and cookies, while in Hungary the *shammash* (a synagogue's beadle and caretaker) would provide each child with a candle before marching.

Some rabbinical authorities attempted to explain the symbols behind the flag and its features. Thus, the children marching with the flags have been compared to military units: While the latter march with fluttering banners to battles in which people are killed, the Jewish banners of war and war tactics are tantamount to the Torah. In the words of one rabbi: "And the reason for the flags is to show that as in tactics of war, the [children] carry flags as a sign of war . . . and we show in this way that our flags and our tactics are the Torah, and [that we are] students of the war of Torah." Lighting a candle atop the flag carries a parallel association, which is based on the verse "For the commandment is a light and Torah is light" (Prov. 6:23). Evoking the love of Torah in the children by lighted candles is also implied by the words of Isaiah: "Therefore glorify you the Lord in the regions of light" (Isa. 24:15).

The earliest extant Torah flags date to the last quarter of the nineteenth century and come from Eastern Europe. They are printed in black from woodcuts on oblong light-colored paper, depicting Hasidim rejoicing with Torah scrolls, lions of Judah holding flags and "guarding" an open scroll, a deer, and a lion, accompanied by the saying "Be fleeting as a deer and mighty as a lion [to do the will of your father in Heaven]" (*Pirqe Avot* 5:20), building a sukkah, and biblical scenes and figures (e.g., the Binding of Isaac, Moses and Aaron, David and Solomon). Toward the end of the century colored flags, printed (mainly in Warsaw) in the technique of lithograph, appeared. These are swallow-tailed in shape, resembling medieval European knights' banners or town flags. Several common motifs are repeated in these flags: the lawgiver

Zionist Simchat Torah flag featuring Zionist leaders Theodor Herzl and Max Nordau. Belarus, 1902. *(Gross Family Collection, Tel Aviv)*

Moses with horns and his brother, Aaron, dressed as the high priest, flank a Torah ark topped by heraldic lions, flanking the tablets of the Ten Commandments. Flags were also prepared at home by the family members and were hand-painted or cut out (no old cut-out flags have survived, however).

With the mass immigration to the United States in the early twentieth century, the swallow-tailed flags with their popular designs at the time reached the United States and later also the Land of Israel. The majority of the flags produced in Israel repeat the typical Polish prototypes, but gradually new motifs were added, reflecting Zionist sentiments and the new realities of life. The depicted children are *sabras* (native-born Israelis) or newly arrived immigrants. One flag has a Boy Scout, standing next to a Yemenite boy. New national buildings, such as that of the Jewish Agency or the Hebrew University in Jerusalem, appear on some flags as well.

In the 1950s and 1960s national symbols (menorah, flag of Israel) appeared side by side with farmers toiling on the land. The desired holy sites, in particular the Western Wall and the Tomb of Rachel, became more and more dominant. After the Six Day War, soldiers carrying Torah scrolls and war heroes (e.g., Yitzhak Rabin and Moshe Dayan) became favorite themes. These themes disappeared following the Yom Kippur War and the traditional motifs were revived.

In the 1980s and 1990s the production of flags was no longer limited to commercial manufacturers and organizations. Yeshivas, banks, and even religious political parties started to produce their own flags. Rabbis and religious political leaders of the various sects in Israeli society appear on these flags as well. Today, cheaper, plastic flags (some manufactured in Asia) often replace the paper flags. Little creativity can be seen in the flags used in the Diaspora communities in the past several decades; they mostly either perpetuate earlier traditional designs or use Israeli models.

Shalom Sabar

Bibliography

Arbel, Rachel, ed. *Blue and White in Color: Visual Images of Zionism, 1897–1947.* Tel Aviv: Beth Hatefutsoth, 1997 (in Hebrew).

Behroozi Baroz, Nitza (exhibition curator). *The Flags of Simchat Torah from Popular Jewish Art to Hebrew-Israeli Culture.* Exhibition catalog. Tel Aviv: Eretz Israel Museum, 2012 (in Hebrew and English).

Goodman, Philip, ed. *The Sukkot and Simhat Torah Anthology.* Philadelphia: Jewish Publication Society of America, 1973.

Liptez, Isaac. *Sefer Mat'amin* (Book of Reasons), sec. 142, pp. 65–66. Warsaw, 1890.

Sabar, Shalom. "The History of the Simchat Torah Flag: From Ritual Object to National Symbol and Back." In *The Flags of Simchat Torah from Popular Jewish Art to Hebrew-Israeli Culture.* Exhibition catalog by Nitza Behroozi Baroz, pp. 8e–24e.
Wischnitzer-Bernstein, Rahel. *Gestalten und Symbole der jüdischen Kunst.* Berlin: Siegfried Scholem, 1935.
Ya'ari, Avraham. *The History of the Simchat Torah Holiday: The Development of Its Customs in Jewish Communities over the Ages.* Jerusalem: Mosad Harav Kook, 1964 (in Hebrew).

SINGER, ISAAC BASHEVIS

See: Bashevis-Singer, Isaac

SIPORIN, STEVE (1947–)

Steve Siporin is a prominent American folklorist distinguished by his research and publication on Italian Jewry. Born Stephen Charles Siporin in Omaha, Nebraska, on February 3, 1947, he graduated from Stanford University in 1969 and then spent a year working on a farm in Italy followed by a kibbutz experience in Israel for another year. He returned to the United States to pursue graduate studies in English at the University of Oregon, where he had his first folklore classes from Barre Toelken, who encouraged Siporin's Jewish folklore work. After receiving the M.A. in English from Oregon in 1974, Siporin entered the doctoral program in folklore at Indiana University and became a lecturer there in Jewish folklore in 1976. In 1978, he undertook fieldwork in Venice that led to his dissertation, completed in 1982, "Continuity and Innovation in the Jewish Festivals of Venice, Italy." In the dissertation and a number of articles that grew from it, he interpreted the declining community's broad tolerance for creative innovation so as to suggest the possibility of revitalization.

Siporin extended his work on the issue of Italian-Jewish identity in the midst of a majority Catholic culture and later expanded this kind of research on American-Jewish identity, in contrast to predominant trends in Jewish studies concentrated in metropolitan areas of the East and West coasts, to examine Jews as a small minority in the American West, and in particular in the Mormon cultural region, where Jews are colloquially called "gentiles."

Siporin worked as a folk arts coordinator for the Oregon Arts Commission (1980–1981) and the Idaho Commission on the Arts (1982–1986) before being hired in 1986 as an assistant professor in the folklore program at Utah State University (USU). At USU he built upon his experience in public folklore, folk art, and ethnic and religious folklore to teach general courses on folklore, Jewish folklore, and ritual and festival. In 1992–1993 he received a Fulbright grant to teach at the Universidade Nova in Lisbon, Portugal, and in 2010, he was a Lady Davis Fellow at the Hebrew University of Jerusalem, where, in 1985, he had been a research fellow at the Folklore Research Center, recording narratives of Italian immigrants to Israel. In 2008, he became director of the folklore program.

In addition to making contributions to research on Jewish festival, Siporin developed specialties in Italian-Jewish foodways, legendry, and cultural tourism. Foodways in the modern Italian context, he has argued, symbolically ease a tension caused by the ambiguous nature of Italian-Jewish identity. In his influential article "From Kashrut to Cucina Ebraica" for the *Journal of American Folklore*, he interpreted the integration of food for Jewish festivals within the traditional structure of an Italian meal. His structural analysis was that this combination in cookbooks and practice provided a model for Italian-Jewish identity in modern Italian society. As part of the concern for the tensions on Italian-Jewish identity, Siporin continued this query with studies of the cultural perception by Italian non-Jews of Jews in places such as Pitigliano, where tourists flock to Jewish-themed attractions although Jews no longer live in the town.

Siporin was active as a translator from the Italian into English of Augusto Segre's twentieth-century memoirs of Jewish life in Rome and Jerusalem, and chronicles of the Jews of Pitigliano, Italy. He participated in several important global publication projects in Jewish folklore studies, including serving as associate editor for the *Jewish Folklore and Ethnology Review* from 1985 to 2000 and as an inaugural editorial board member of the Jewish Cultural Studies series for the Littman Library of Jewish Civilization established in 2008.

Simon J. Bronner

Bibliography

Biondi, Angelo, and Carlo Fê. *The Jews of Pitigliano*, trans. Steve Siporin. Grotte di Castro, Italy: Ceccarelli, 2009.
Fê, Carlo. *Pitigliano: Water, Green, and Tufa*, trans. Steve Siporin. Montefiascone, Italy: Grafico Livio Marsili, 2006.
Rogers, Ty. "Bus Driver Job Led Steve Siporin to a Career in Folklore." *Hard News Café*, December 12, 2010. http://hardnewscafe.usu.edu/?p=3490.
Segre, Augusto. *Memories of Jewish Life: Casale Monterrato-Rome-Jerusalem, 1918–1960,* trans. Steve Siporin. Lincoln: University of Nebraska Press, 2008.
Siporin, Steve. *American Folk Masters: The National Heritage Fellows.* New York: Harry N. Abrams, 1992.
———. "From Kashrut to Cucina Ebraica: The Recasting of Italian Jewish Foodways." *Journal of American Folklore* 107 (1994): 268–281.
———. "A Jew Among Mormons." *Dialogue: A Journal of Mormon Thought* 24 (1991): 113–122.
———. "The Survival of 'the Most Ancient of Minorities.'" In *The Most Ancient of Minorities: History and Culture of the Jews of Italy*, ed. Stanislao Pugliese, pp. 316–368. Westport, CT: Greenwood, 2002.

———. "'The Table of the Angel' and Two Other Jewish-Venetian Food Customs." *Lares* 50 (1984): 357–365.
———. "'To Hold High Their Glorious Origins': The Jewish Festivals in Venice." *Shofar* 8 (1989): 30–46.
Siporin, Steve, Polly Stewart, and C.W. Sullivan III, eds. *Worldviews and the American West: The Life of the Place Itself.* Logan: Utah State University Press, 2000.

Slobin, Mark

See: Anthologies

Sodom

See: Abraham

Solomon, King

King Solomon, the son and successor of King David, ruled over the united kingdom of Judah (Judea) and Israel between 970 and 930 B.C.E. He is a key part of Jewish folklore and the subject of hundreds of folk narratives. Most of the folk narratives portray him as a wise ruler who knows how to solve enigmatic cases as well as a riddler and one who solves riddles; this is the main reason many of the folk stories about him are novellas of wisdom.

Folk Elements in the Bible

The portrayal of King Solomon in the Book of Kings reflects the historiographers' conflict: On the one hand, they wished to enhance Solomon's name and perpetuate him as both the builder of the Temple and as living evidence of the fulfillment of the divine promise to establish the House of David (2 Sam. 7). But, on the other hand, they needed to provide a theological justification for the tragic division of the monarchy, which occurred immediately after Solomon's death and which, in the end, led to the fall of the Northern Kingdom (722 B.C.E.) and, finally, to the destruction and exile of Judah (586 B.C.E.) (Walsh 1995).

According to their view, the biblical historiographers related the reason for the chain of developments to Solomon's sins: His foreign women "turned away Solomon's heart after other gods, and he was not as wholeheartedly devoted to the Lord his God as his father has been" (1 Kgs. 11:4).

However, all throughout the biblical narratives, the first trend overshadows the second one, thus imprinting the apparent image of Solomon as a legendary paragon. Unlike King David, there are no biographical stories about Solomon. The bulk of the literary material consists of elaborate reports of his glorious reign. As part of this, the narrators indulge in lengthy descriptions of Solomon's riches as well as of the expanded borders of his kingdom, his wide-ranging international relations, and his success in ensuring his kingdom's peace and security.

The historiographers' evaluation of all these events is indicated by their descriptions such as "Judah and Israel were as numerous as the sands of the sea; they ate and drank and were content" (1 Kgs. 4:20) and "All the days of Solomon, Judah and Israel from Dan to Beer-Sheba dwelt in safety, everyone under his own vine and under his own fig tree" (1 Kgs. 5:5). Since this positive judgment of Solomon's reign contrasts with the negative one, scholars relate these two attitudes to two different literary levels. However, it is within the positive stratum that three prominent folktale motifs are interspersed: The first is the story of Solomon's dream at Gibeon (1 Kgs. 3:4–15), which is mainly based on the universal motif of "three wishes." The second is the story of the two harlots (prostitutes), which demonstrates the characteristic of the king as a wise judge (1 Kgs. 3:16–28), and the third is the story of the visit of the queen of Sheba, which is actually based on the genre of "riddles" (1 Kgs. 10:1–13). All three could be gathered under the heading of "wisdom," since they mainly illustrate the various aspects of Solomon's wisdom. Yet it is noteworthy that these folklore examples also imply a most significant contribution to the historiographers' ideology: The motif of the divine gifts and Solomon's wish could be interpreted as a counter-balance of David's tragic choice between three possibilities of divine punishment, in the story of the Census and the Pestilence (2 Sam. 24), thus achieving an image of Solomon not only as David's successor, but also as the compensatory and complementary half of David's enterprise.

The story of the two harlots is a familiar one in folktales. Yet the plot itself is quite problematic: There is no agreement among commentators about the identity of the real mother. Some maintain that the real mother was the shy one, not the talkative one. Others even question the cleverness of Solomon's first decree: "Cut the live child in two, and give half to one and half to the other" (1 Kgs. 3:25). Therefore, rather than a story about the king's wisdom, this appears to be a story about real motherhood. Accordingly, we can interpret it as an allegorical protest against the division of the monarchy by Jeroboam—the "false mother" being the monarch who prefers a torn kingdom, which in the end means that "it shall be neither yours nor mine," for it was the division that led to the final destruction of both kingdoms. Solomon's ability to preserve the united monarchy, even though it had the high costs (heavy taxes, compulsory labor), is therefore regarded as an incomparable achievement.

Another folk element, which includes the riddles, is mainly meant to glorify Solomon's international relations. This becomes apparent by the fact that the narrative, while consisting of an elaborate description of the grandeur and the rich presents, tells nothing about the topics of the riddles themselves.

Much like in other cases, here, too, the folk motifs are interwoven in order to illustrate the historiographers' trends and their ideology. Their main effort seems to be meant to advocate all of Solomon's political initiatives. The nature of this justification is most apparent in this concluding paragraph: "The Lord endowed Solomon with wisdom and discernment in great measure, with understanding as vast as the sands on the seashore. Solomon's wisdom was greater than the wisdom of all Kedemites and than all the wisdom of the Egyptians. . . . His fame spread among all the surrounding nations. He composed three thousand proverbs, and his songs numbered one thousand and five. He discoursed about trees . . . and discoursed about beasts, birds, creeping things and fishes. Men of all peoples came to hear Solomon's wisdom" (1 Kgs. 5:9–14).

Because Solomon's enterprises could thus be summarized as manifestations of his wisdom, it is no wonder that this characteristic became the most prominent factor in all further presentations of Solomon. This is why later biblical sources ascribed to Solomon the authorship of the books of the Song of Songs, the Book of Proverbs, and the Book of Ecclesiastes (Songs 1:1; Prov. 1:1; Eccl. 1:1,12), although all three of them are relatively late compositions, and even the talmudic sages subtly intimated their doubts on this matter (*Shir Ha'Shirim Rabba*, A, a:10). The same is true about ex-biblical composition, such as The Book of Solomon's Wisdom (= Sapienta, Σοφια Σαλωμωνος), the origin of which is uncertain, but which had become part of the Christian holy scriptures, and the book of Solomon's Psalms (Ψαλμοι Σαλομωντος), which consists of eighteen hymns in Greek, of various sources, all of them translated from the Hebrew.

Solomon in Postbiblical Literature

The postbiblical literature, mainly the Talmud and midrashim, includes a large number of legends that present a variety of attitudes toward Solomon. Some of them recount miraculous events, and in many of them Solomon's image is expanded far beyond historical and earthly limits. He is endowed with prophetic visions (*Bam. Rab.* 19), and, in the scene of the trial of the two harlots, the Holy Spirit is present (*b. Makoth* 3, 23 b). The visit of the queen of Sheba is described in detail, including the riddles (*Targum Sheni*, Esther A, 3; cf. *Midrash Mishle*). He composed three thousand proverbs on each single issue of the Torah (*b. Eruvim* 2:21b), and before his time the Torah was like a vessel without handles, but Solomon came and provided it with handles (*b. Jebamoth* 2:27a). He who sees Solomon in his dream should expect wisdom (*b. Berakhot* 9:57b). Yet other sayings intimate a critical attitude, such as "even in the days of Solomon wisdom and greatness never dwelt under the same roof" (*b. Gitin* 8:59a; *Sanhedrin* 4:36a), and in some legends Solomon was punished for his pride and greed. He was deprived of his kingdom and was cast away to live as a beggar, in order to learn the ways of humility (*b. Gitin* 68ab; cf. *y. Sanhedrin* 2:20, 3; Midrash Tanḥuma Leviticus). Moreover, for a while Solomon was even accompanied, guided, and dominated by Ashmedai, the king of demons (*y.* 2 *Sanhedrin* 20:3). Yet in other legends he was even ruling over the demons, guiding them to be useful to humankind. Some of these themes also became prevalent motifs in medieval mysticism.

The most varicolored image of Solomon has been the source of inspiration for many literary works. In the Israel Folktale Archives at the University of Haifa, 204 folk narratives were recorded from oral tradition.

Shamai Gelander

See also: David, King; Folk Narratives in the Bible; Magic.

Bibliography

Auld, A. Graeme. "Salomo und die Deuteronomisten–eine Zukunktvision?" *Theologische Zeitsschrift* 48:3–4 (1992): 343–355.

Beuken, W.A.M. "No Wise King Without a Wise Woman (I Kings 3:16–28)." In *New Avenues in the Study of the Old Testament*, ed. A.S. Van Der Woude, pp. 1–10. Leiden: Brill Academic, 1989.

Bloch-Smith, E.M. "Who Is King of Glory? Solomon's Temple and Its Symbolism." In *Scripture and Other Artifacts*, ed. Michael D. Coogan et al., pp. 18–31. Louisville, KY: Westminster John Knox, 1994.

Cohen, S.J.D. "Solomon and the Daughter of Pharaoh: Intermarriage, Conversion, and the Impurity of Women." *JANES* 16/17 (1987): 23–37.

Deurloo, K.A. "The King's Wisdom in Judgement." In *New Avenues in the Study of the Old Testament,* ed. A.S. Van Der Woude, pp. 11–21. Leiden: Brill Academic, 1989.

Fidler, Ruth. "Problems of Propaganda: On King Solomon's Visit to Gibeon." In *Proceedings of the Eleventh World Congress of Jewish Studies,* Division A: The Bible and Its World. Jerusalem: Hebrew University Magnes Press, 1994.

Gray, John. *I & II Kings*. London: Westminster, 1964.

Knoppers, Gary N. "Prayer and Propaganda: Solomon's Dedication of the Temple and the Deuteronomist's Plan." *Catholic Biblical Quarterly* 57:2 (1995): 229–254.

Koerner, R. "Maerchenmotive bei Koenig Salomo (I Koen. 1–11)." *Biblische Notizen* 62 (1992): 25–31.

Lasine, Stuart. "Jehoram and the Cannibal Mothers (2 Kings 6:24–33): Solomon's Judgement in an Inverted World." *Journal for the Study of the Old Testament* 50 (1991): 27–53.

———. "The Riddle of Solomon's Judgement and the Riddle of Human Nature in the Hebrew Bible." *Journal for the Study of the Old Testament* 45 (1989): 61–86.
Leibovitz, E., and G. Leibovitz. "The Trial of Solomon." *Beit Mikra* (1990): 122, 242–244.
Lemaire, André. "Wisdom in Solomonic Historiography." *Wisdom in Ancient Israel* (1995): 106–118.
Luke, K. "The Queen of Sheba (I Kings 10:1–13)." *Indian Theological Studies* 23 (1986): 248–272.
Nelson, Richard D. "The Anatomy of the Book of Kings." *Journal for the Study of the Old Testament* 40 (1988): 39–48.
Ogden Bellis, Alice. "The Queen of Sheba: A Gender-Sensitive Reading." *Journal of Religious Thought* 51 (1994–1995): 2, 17–28.
Parker, Kim I. "Solomon as Philosopher King? The Nexus of Law and Wisdom in I Kings 1–11." *Journal for the Study of the Old Testament* 53 (1992): 75–91.
Rachman, G., and J. Rachman. "Solomon's Trial." *Beit Mikra* 132 (1993): 91–94.
Tomes, Roger. "'Our Holy and Beautiful House': When and Why Was I Kings 6–8 Written?" *Journal for the Study of the Old Testament* 70 (1996): 33–50.
Walsh, Jerome T. "The Characterization of Solomon in First Kings 1–5." *Catholic Biblical Quarterly* 57:3 (1995): 471–493.
Zalevski, Sha'ul. *Solomon's Ascension to the Throne: Studies in the Books of Kings and Chronicles.* Jerusalem: Markus, 1981.

SOUL

See: Afterlife

SPAIN, JEWS OF

The Jews of Spain produced a glorious chapter of Jewish history from the tenth through the thirteenth century, a period that scholars and historians have called a "Golden Age." This chapter's uniqueness derives from the impact on Jewish history and culture of (1) a wide-ranging cultural burgeoning in different fields over a long period; (2) acquisition of high social status; (3) solid economic standing; and (4) Jewish religious autonomy that included religious courts with the authority to adjudicate and to impose sanctions.

During this period, Spain took over from Babylonia as the center of the Jewish world. Works in different areas, such as philosophy, mysticism, grammar, astronomy, rabbinic literature, and belle lettres shaped Jewish culture for generations.

According to ancient traditions handed down through the generations, Jewish settlement in Spain originated in the early Second Temple period. References in midrashic and talmudic literature (in which Spain is called Ispamya), however, mention that the start of the Jewish settlement predates the destruction of the Second Temple (*m. Bava Batra* 3:2; *b. Yevamot* 63a; *Niddah* 30a; *Lev. Rab.* 3:6; 29:3). The same information is found in Josephus Flavius (*J.W.* 7.3.3) and in the New Testament (Epistle to the Romans 15:24, 28).

Yet the initial blossoming of Jewish culture and creativity began only a few centuries later with the Islamic conquest (710) and reached its zenith in the eleventh and twelfth centuries. During those centuries, Jews functioned as neutral bearers of religion between Muslims and Christians, which enabled productive cultural contact and reinforcement of the Jews' economic and social status. A number of Jews held high positions at the royal court and were among the country's elite. As early as the tenth century, Hisdai ibn Shaprut served at the caliph's court in Córdoba, and Samuel Hanagid was appointed vizier of Grenada in the eleventh century.

During these centuries, Jews produced works in Hebrew, Spanish, and Arabic in all fields: religious and secular poetry; halakhic, ethical, and homiletic literature; grammar, philosophy, and mysticism. They demonstrated expertise in the hard sciences and were at the forefront of projects translating Greek and Latin texts into Arabic. Almost all these areas are also reflected in folklore.

Hebrew Poets as Legendary Figures

The greatest poets writing in Hebrew, such as Solomon Ibn Gabirol (1021–1058), Judah Halevi (1075–1141), and especially Abraham Ibn Ezra (c. 1092–1167), became the heroes of cycles of legends in oral folk tradition.

The most widely disseminated legends are the story of Ibn Gabirol's murder under a fig tree, in which after the figs ripened, they revealed the identity of the murderer; the story of the marriage of Judah Halevi's daughter to Abraham Ibn Ezra; and the death of Judah Halevi at the Western Wall. More than a hundred stories are about Ibn Ezra, who is presented as an eternal wanderer, the Other who is disguised as a pauper, rejected by the community, but ultimately revealed to be a greatly learned Jew and a miracle worker who saves the community.

Folktales in Books of *Māqāma*

Folk motifs and folktales incorporated in their entirety in literary writing are found in particular in the genre called *māqāma,* which is a narrative in rhymed prose.

This is the case with *Minhat Yehudah sone nashim* (The Tribute of Judah the Misogynist), by Judah ibn Shabbethai, *Sefer Taḥkemoni* (The Wise One), by Judah al-Harizi (d. before 1235), and especially in *Sefer Sha'ashuim* (Book of Delights), by Joseph ibn Zabara (b. 1140), who interpolates into *māqāma* fables, animal tales, and ethical tales taken from both Jewish and non-Jewish sources. So it is with the stories about the fox, which successfully used his wiles to kill the lion even though the latter was his friend and loved him, and with Aesop's fable about the thin, hungry fox that entered the vineyard through a hole but could not leave, having become too fat from overeating. An example of an ethical tale is the story that is usually told about King Solomon, who proved the treacherousness of a woman. In the book of *māqāma,* it is related to one of the kings of Arabia who tested the nature of a man and a woman. The woman was ready to kill her husband in order to be free to marry the king, but her husband relinquished the prize to marry a princess since he took pity on his wife and refused to kill her. This story functions as an illustration of the biblical verse: "I found only one human being in a thousand, and the one I found among so many was never a woman" (Eccl. 7:28).

In the same misogynist vein, the *māqāma* goes on to tell about a widow from Ephesus, a story taken from Petronius. The widow, while mourning her husband at the cemetery, made love to a guard who was watching over the remains of a robber who had been hanged. When they realized that the robber's body had been stolen while the guard's attention was diverted, the widow hanged her husband's body to put in its place in order to save the guard.

From an Arab source comes the tale of a king who dreams about a monkey jumping on his wives' necks. From the dream, he understood that the women were hiding a man in the palace and being unfaithful to him. From a Hebrew source comes a story of a test for a true son, who was unwilling to mutilate his father's corpse, in contrast to a servant who was pretending to be a son.

Center of Jewish Learning

Halakha (Jewish Law)

The center of Jewish learning that developed in Spain severed its links with the Babylonian gaonate and became an independent center considered supreme in the Jewish world of its time and henceforth for hundreds of years. This process, which reached its zenith in the eleventh century with the arrival in Spain of Rabbi Isaac Alfasi, called the Rif (the acronym in Hebrew for his name), had begun during the tenth century with the arrival of Rabbi Moses and his son Hanokh to Córdoba, where they founded a yeshiva, which became the highest Jewish religious and halakhic authority in Spain. A description of Rabbi Moshe's arrival had appeared in a legendary story in Abraham Ibn Daud's *Sefer ha'Kabbalah* (written after 1161).

The story, called "Legend of the Four Captives," tells about four captives who were redeemed, one in Alexandria, the second in Kairouan, the third in Córdoba (and the fourth not discussed). Each of them founded a yeshiva in his new location. But the main story and most of the details are about Rabbi Moshe, who founded a center of learning in Córdoba.

Kabbalah

Most of the rabbinic written works in Spain until the time of Nachmanides (Moshe ben Nachman) dealt with making practical decisions in Jewish law or with interpretations of Hebrew canonic sources for the same purpose. Nachmanides was the father of a new Spanish school of talmudic exegesis that remains influential to this day. He worked in Gerona in the thirteenth century until he emigrated to the Holy Land in 1263. Also active there in the same period was Rabbi Jonah Gerondi. Both of them were esteemed scholars of Jewish law who commanded great authority as well as being kabbalists.

At this time, at the beginning of the thirteenth century, kabbalistic teachings began to flower in Spain, apparently under the influence of proponents of the Kabbalah in Provence. A group of kabbalists formed in Gerona, disciples of Rabbi Isaac Sagi Nahor (1160–1235), who, like their teacher, advocated putting Kabbalah into writing and disseminating it. Nachmanides opposed spreading it to the masses and instead established his own kabbalistic school of thought, which viewed Kabbalah as a hidden, esoteric system orally passed down from teacher to disciple. Most of Nachmanides's mystical conceptions are interwoven in his highly influential commentary on the Torah.

Nachmanides himself became the hero of a cycle of legends that establish his practical mystical ability through the working of miracles and the display of wondrous characteristics such as moving from place to place instantly by means of magic (*kfitzat ha'derekh*), passing through walls, changing into the shape of another person, and possessing knowledge of hidden things. Legends like these appeared in writing in the mid-sixteenth century in Gedaliah ibn Yahya's *Shalshelet ha'kabbalah* (The Chain of Tradition).

The main trend in Kabbalah, however, was the theurgic theosophical one that developed in Castile. This strain of Kabbalah gave rise to an extensive literature, a great deal of which became the masterpieces of Kabbalah. The main figures in this group were Rabbi Moses de Leon, Rabbi Joseph Gekatilla, and Rabbi Joseph of Hamadan. Through their writings, Kabbalah established itself as a central literary, experiential, and intellectual phenomenon in Judaism. The most important achievement of this trend is the Zohar (end of the thirteenth century), attributed to Rabbi Shimeon Bar Yoḥai (Rashbi) of the second century.

The pseudoepigraphic framework of the work creates the legend upon which the book is based: how Rabbi Shimeon Bar Yoḥai received the Zohar from the supernal worlds and how he wrote it down while hiding in a cave. Attributing the Zohar to Rashbi in the second century (according to the legend intentionally created by those who produced the book in the thirteenth century) also required adapting the work to the ancient format of midrashic literature, including the interpolation of tales, fables, and folklore elements.

To make the *tanna* Rabbi Shimeon Bar Yoḥai an exceptionally holy figure, the authors of the Zohar created the hagiographic legend, which describes the lives of Rashbi and the members of his group as a sequence of astonishing, miraculous events replete with linkages between this world and the supernal worlds. An additional factor emphasizing the narrative element in Kabbalah literature is the mythic perception of the worlds, the way the divine world is understood, and the description of the system of the spheres and the relations between them using the symbolic dynamics of relationships: familial, sexual, between good and evil, between God and Satan. There is a mythological dimension in the description of the world and man aimed at the creation of narrative, to the handing down of a chain of events. Many sections in the Zohar are written as mythic stories.

Philosophical and Ethical Literature

More surprising is the interpolation of literary and folk genres into philosophical literature in Spain, mainly in ethical literature, since, according to the philosophers' way of thinking, only people incapable of high, abstract thought need stories to understand abstract ideas. Obviously, following this notion, it is clear that the most fitting genre for this purpose is the parable. Even in decidedly philosophical works, including Maimonides's *Guide to the Perplexed,* there are parables—for example, the parable of the Heikhal (*Guide for the Perplexed,* chap. 51, part 2), in which Maimonides reveals his idea of the ways of serving God and indicates the superior status of the philosophers in contrast to all others. But greater use is made of parables and proverbs in the ethical literature, which is intended from the outset for the general public. The assumption was that the use of stories promised popularization. So the collection *Musarei hapilosofim u'mivhar peninim* (The Teachings of the Philosophers and Selection of Pearls) attributed to Solomon Ibn Gabirol comprises, for the most part, proverbs and literary parables; the same is true of Ibn Gabirol's ethical work *Tikkun middot hanefesh* (The Improvement of the Moral Qualities), and it is particularly true of Bahya Ibn Paquda's *Hovot halevavot* (Duties of the Hearts), written in Arabic. The sources of the parables are varied and mixed. Some of them are known from Persian and Indian literature and reached Spain through the intermediary of Arab culture; others are based on rabbinic literature, in which one commonly finds parables with formulaic openings such as "a parable of the kings" or "a tale about a sage"; still others are parables whose authors produced them to elucidate their aims. For example, in "Sha'ar habehinah" (Gate of Reflection) in *Ḥovot ha'levavot,* there is a parable about a group of blind people brought to a house in which everything is arranged to accommodate them, including a physician who can cure them. They do not listen to his advice, and so they bump into furniture, stumble, fall, get hurt, and vilify the owner of the house. Bahya tries to refute those who complain about the rules of nature and the reality created by God and to reinforce the traditional philosophical argument that the Lord created the world in his goodness to bring loving kindness to his creatures. Whoever does not discern this suffers from moral blindness: A person who refuses to be cured prefers in his foolishness to fall and be injured.

The uniqueness of the genre of the parable is that at times there is more to the parable than to the moral drawn from it. The use of a plot, figures, and poetic means occasionally makes the parable more extreme in relation to the moral, as in the comparison between the nonphilosopher and a stubborn, stupid blind man. The genre of the parable helps to reveal ideas not formulated or explicitly expressed in the ongoing discussion.

Even though Maimonides despised stories as suited only to simple people incapable of abstract thinking, folk stories needed to attribute legendary characteristics to such a central figure. Thus, even close to his own lifetime, legends began to develop depicting him as a miracle worker, rescuer of the Jewish community, punisher of its enemies, and curer of its members in wondrous ways, including revival of the dead. The need to tell praise legends predominated the historical biography of the man, who was a strict rationalist. The image of him was linked to reality by only a few isolated facts, such as the family's journey from Córdoba to Morocco, Maimonides's escape from Morocco to Egypt, his appointment as court physician, and the writing of the *Guide for the Perplexed.* Maimonides remains one of the most popular figures in Jewish folk narrative.

Decline of Jewish Predominance

The flourishing of culture in Spain continued until the middle of the thirteenth century, when signs began to appear of a decline in the status of the Jews (mainly in Aragon) under the influence of the Catholic Church and as a result of decisions made by the Fourth Lateran Council in 1215. In Saragossa in 1250, for the first time in Spain, a blood libel was spread through a rumor about the killing of a Christian child by Jews and about the miracles that the child experienced. This marked a turning point in the standing of the Jews in Spain.

Thereafter followed the extensive code promulgated by King Alfonso X called "La Siete Partidas," named for its seven divisions. The code ratified the laws of the Church regarding Jews and established a special legal procedure for blood libels, which the king and his advisers considered trustworthy accounts. The prohibition against charging Christians interest began to be enforced, and from that time on Jews were targeted as usurers, in line with a repeated motif in Spanish anti-Semitic narrative, both written and oral, that describes the Jews as avaricious, money-chasing, exploiters of the poor. Limitations were increasingly imposed on the Jews' living conditions. In the 1260s King Enrique I coined the phrase "freeing the country from the burden of the Jews."

Riots that broke out in Seville in June 1391 ushered in a period of increasing violence against the Jews in Spain as well as Portugal. About a third of Spanish Jews died, about a third converted to Christianity (some of them as crypto-Jews), and about a third survived, some fleeing to North Africa and others to countries of the Ottoman Empire.

During this period of sweeping anti-Semitic decrees, great homiletical activity developed that left its mark in a plethora of written works that were useful as springboards for sermons (*derashot*) as well as for debates on them. This may have resulted from the influence of Christian society, which during this period developed an interest in the art of preaching and tried to establish norms and methods for it; alternatively, it may have come out of the harsh, increasingly bitter reality itself, which led to the development of this genre, whose aim was to moralize and to teach the proper way to conduct one's life.

In 1432 the leaders of the Jewish communities of Castile assembled in Valladolid to discuss the establishment of new regulations for the renewal of community life, with a guiding principle of modest behavior. At around the same time, the first third of the fourteenth century, Rabbi Joshua Ibn Shueib, one of the great preachers of that period, wrote his *Derashot al ha'Torah* (Sermons on the Pentateuch), a comprehensive book with sermons for every public Torah reading: the weekly portions and those read on holidays. The work contains a rich treasure of midrashim (rabbinic interpretations), and in many instances, Ibn Shueib used legends as the basis for his ideas. He demonstrates great ability as an interpreter of legends, through an allegorical-philosophical lens as well as using kabbalistic concepts. All of these sermons are accompanied by images, parables, and short stories.

At the end of the fifteenth century, Rabbi Isaac Arama wrote *Akedat Yitzhak* (The Sacrifice of Isaac), which is a homiletical, philosophical exegesis of the Pentateuch that deals with the question of the relationship between the written and oral homily—two different methods that he believes should remain distinct. The oral sermon is much more folk-oriented and rhetorical.

The genre of preaching about morality had appeared about a hundred years earlier in *Proverbios Morales* (Moral Proverbs) by Santob de Carrion (d. 1360). Composed of proverbs and short poems written in Spanish, the book was also aimed at the Christian audience. The author himself used the term *derashah* (sermon) in defining his writing: "The Lord the King the sublime emanation / hear this Sermon / that will be given by Santob / a Jew from Karyon."

In 1474 Ferdinand and Isabella, called the "Catholic monarchs," ascended the throne and initiated the unification of Castile and Aragon as a single monarchy under one faith. This policy enabled broad expansion of the application of Tomas de Torquemada's concept that proposed a three-stage program: the expulsion of Jews who maintained their faith, the solution of the problem of the *anusim* (the Hebrew term for forced converts who maintained Judaism secretly), and the conquest of Granada, which was the last Muslim city. Now Spain was entirely Christian, and the kings could turn to the problem of the Jews. The Inquisition was founded and Torquemada was appointed to lead it. One of the first acts of the Inquisition was to accuse a number of Jews and *anusim* of murdering a Christian child and using his blood for magical purposes that would lead to the destruction of Christianity and its institutions (the trial of the Holy Child of La Guardia, 1490–1491). In 1492 Granada was captured and the edict of expulsion was signed.

One of the most important historical sources for the history of the expulsion from Spain is the historiographic work *Shevet Yehudah* (The Tribe of Judah) by Rabbi Solomon ibn Verga. The book's value derives not only from its importance as a historical source but also from its literary quality and its place in Jewish culture. Written in Italy during the 1530s, a generation after the expulsion, the book uses a pseudoepigraphic technique. It continues to serve as a source for tales told orally about the tribulations of the Spanish Jews before the expulsion and about the vicissitudes of the expulsion itself. Rabbi Solomon attributes the book to a relative in the generation before his own, Rabbi Judah ibn Verga, one of the leaders of Spanish Jews who had been deported to Portugal, converted, and ultimately died a martyr.

The narrative traditions included in *Shevet Yehudah* move between stories whose plots remain realistic and faithful to historical events and those that exceed reality and glide into the supernatural. These variations stand out, for example, in the blood libel story type, all four of whose subtypes appear in *Shevet Yehudah* and are described as events that took place in Spain. Yet in the folktale, as opposed to reality, a miracle occurs and the dead child is resurrected and reveals who murdered him.

In July 1492 the last Jews left Spain and scattered, mainly to the lands of the Ottoman Empire, North Africa, and Italy (except Sicily, from which the Jews had been expelled as well). The oral narrative tradition says of this day that the expellees took with them the keys to their homes so that they could reclaim their property when they returned one day. A contrasting literary tradition is manifested, for example, in a tale that explains the source of the family name Toledano, still common among Jews with origins in Spain: According to the sound of the name, the meaning is Toledo-No, that is, "we will never return to the land that spewed us out."

Some of the Jews who remained in Spain converted outwardly but remained crypto-Jews. All the anti-Semitic stereotypes that had gained strength as the expulsion approached were then transferred to them, now called New Christians.

During the period called the "Golden Age" in the arts and literature of Spain, from the mid-sixteenth century to the end of the seventeenth, anti-Semitic expression in Spanish society became more pronounced, as seen in the works of the most prominent Spanish authors, such as Lope Felix de Vega, Francisco de Quevedo, and Tirso de Molina. The negative attitude toward Jews stands out even more sharply in folk literature, in stories, and in proverbs. A typical proverb epitomizes the lack of faith in Jews and converts, as seen in this one from a comprehensive collection of Spanish proverbs edited by Louis Martínez Kleiser that includes collections from the fifteenth century:

> *No fíes del judío converso ni de su híjo ni de su nieto*
>
> Do not trust a converted Jew, not his son nor
> his grandson
> (Martínez-Kleiser proverb no. 34,775)

The Jews responded in the same vein in Ladino (Judeo-Spanish), as seen in this verse taken from a poetic work by Abraham Toledo.

> *No ay emuna en goy ni afilu en la fuesa*
>
> There is no trust in a non-Jew even in the grave.
> (*Coplas de Yoçef hazaddik* [1732], ll. 1820–1821)

Other oral versions of this verse are still commonly heard among Jews of Spanish origin.

The *anusim* were cruelly persecuted by the Inquisition to make them confess their heresy, that is, that they maintained their Jewish faith. Members of the Inquisition kept close watch over the lives of the New Christians and their habits to discover whether they were practicing Jewish customs or whether there was pork in their homes. Did they begin observance of the Sabbath on Friday night? Did they go outside on Saturday night and point heavenward to see whether three stars were visible, indicating the end of the Sabbath? This custom developed into the popular belief, still commonly found among Jews of Spanish origin, that one should not point at stars lest warts grow on one's fingers, an explanation that began during the Inquisition to frighten the children and prevent them from engaging in this dangerous custom.

Many converted Jews fled Spain, leading to an unceasing stream of refugees throughout the sixteenth century who migrated to other lands in order to practice Judaism. In this way, large Jewish centers came into being in Amsterdam, England, southern France, Mexico, and Peru.

Those who remained in Spain tried to assimilate into Christian society and wrote in Spanish in an attempt to blur their Jewish origin. Today various scholars are grappling with traditions, and literary works attempt to determine their historical origin. For example, was Columbus or Cervantes, the author of *Don Quixote*, of Jewish origin?

The Sephardic Traditon

The Jews who left took with them not only written works but also the oral heritage that was handed down to them from previous generations, largely in the language they had used even before the expulsion, Judeo-Spanish (Ladino). This language is still employed for telling stories, reciting proverbs, and singing *romancas* (ballads) *coplas* (actual songs), and *canciones* (lyric songs) that originated in Spain. In this way Jewish oral tradition has preserved songs that Hispanist scholars thought were lost.

The study of Sephardic culture (the culture of the decendants of the Jews expelled from Spain) and their folklore flourishes today in different universities and research centers in Israel and all over the world. Ladino language and culture are taught at all Israeli universities. Important research centers were established in Israel: Moshe David Gaon Center at Ben Gurion University and the Yehoshua Salti center at Bar Ilan University. Research centers operate in Europe and the United States, such as the Higher Scientific Council of Spain (CSIC) in Madrid, and other centers in Berlin, Basel, Paris, Istanbul, and Stanford. International conferences are held every year all over the world.

Sephardic folklore is gaining more and more research attention (see bibliography below). Three books were published by Tamar Alexander on folktales and proverbs. Samuel Armistead published his groundbreaking work on the study of ballads, Elena Romero on *coplas* and Ladino folk plays, Shmuel Refael on ballads and *coplas*, Shoshana Weich-Shahak on folk music, and many others. Dozens of collections of folk stories have been published by researchers and people in the community. For example, Matilda Koén-Sarano alone has published nearly twenty-five collections of folktales in Ladino and Hebrew. Hundreds of proverb collections have been published since the nineteenth century for almost every community: For instance, those by Enrique Saporta y Beja (Greece, 1978), Yitzhak Moscona (Bulgaria, 1981), Jamila Kolonomos (Macedonia and Bosnia, 1978), Yosef Gabai (Tetuan, 1990), and Klara Perhaya (Turkey, 1994).

There are still approximately 300,000 speakers of Ladino (mostly in Israel and Turkey), although it is no longer a living language used by the present generation of children and young adults.

Tamar Alexander

See also: Bulgaria, Jews of; Folk Narratives, Sephardi; Folk Songs and Poetry, Judeo-Spanish (Ladino); Greece, Jews of; Illuminated Manuscripts; Kabbalah; Languages, Jewish; North Africa, Jews of; Turkey, Jews of.

Bibliography

Alexander, Tamar. The *Heart Is a Mirror: The Sephardic Folktale.* Detroit: Wayne State University Press, 2008.

———. *"Words Are Better Than Bread": The Judeo-Spanish Proverb.* Jerusalem: Ben-Zvi Institute; Beer-Sheva: Ben-Gurion University Press, 2004 (in Hebrew).

Alexander, Tamar, and Bentulila Yaakov. *La palabra en su hora es oro: The Judeo-Spanish Proverb from Northern Morocco.* Jerusalem: Ben-Zvi Institute, 2008 (in Hebrew and Spanish).

Armistead, Samuel G. *El Romancero judeo-espanol en el Archivo Menendez Pidal.* 3 vols. Madrid: Catedra-Seminario Menendez Pidal, 1978.

Baer, Yitzhak. *A History of the Jews in Christian Spain.* 2 vols. Philadelphia: Jewish Publication Society, 1966.

Beinart, Haim, ed. *Moreshet Sepharad: The Legacy of Spain.* Jerusalem: Magnes, 1992.

Dan, Joseph. *The Hebrew Story in the Middle Ages.* Jerusalem: Keter, 1974 (in Hebrew).

Horowitz, Carmi. *The Jewish Sermon in Fourteenth-Century Spain: The Derashot of R. Joshua Ibn Shu'eib.* Cambridge: Harvard University, Center for Jewish Studies, 1989.

Idel, Moshe. *Kabbalah: New Perspectives.* New Haven: Yale University Press, 1988.

Koen-Sarano, Mathilda. *Kuentos del Folklore de la Famiya Djudeo-Espanyola.* Jerusalem: Kana, 1986.

Landa, Louis. *Cervantes and the Jews.* Beer-Sheva: Ben-Gurion University Press, 2002 (in Hebrew).

Martinez Kleiser, Luis. *Refranero general ideologico español.* Madrid: Real Academia Española, 1953.

Refael, Shmuel. *I Will Tell a Poem: A Study of the Judeo-Spanish (Ladino) Coplas.* Jerusalem: Keter, 2004 (in Hebrew).

———. *The Knight and the Captive Lady: A Study of the Judeo Spanish (Ladino) Romance.* Ramat Gan: Bar Ilan, 1998.

Romero, Elena. "Las coplas sefardíes: Categorías y estado de la cuestión." *Actas de las Jornadas de Estudios Sefadíes* (1980): 69–98.

———. *El teatro de los sefardies orientales.* Madrid: CSIC, Instituto Arias Montanto, 1979.

Schirmann, Haim. *The Hebrew Poetry in Spain and Provence.* Jerusalem: Bialik Institute and Dvir, 1961 (in Hebrew).

Scholem, Gershom. *Major Trends in Jewish Mysticism.* New York: Schocken, 1941.

Weich-Shahak, Shoshana. *Musica y tradiciones sefardies.* Salamanca: Centro de Cultura Tradicionale Diputacion de Salamanca, 1992.

Zfatman, Sara. *The Jewish Tale in the Middle Ages Between Ashkenaz and Sefarad.* Jerusalem: Magnes, 1993 (in Hebrew).

STAR (SHIELD) OF DAVID

See: Kurdistan, Jews of; Symbols; Tombstones

STEINSCHNEIDER, MORITZ

See: Russia, Jews of

STERNBERG (SHTERNBERG), LEV

See: An-Ski, S.; Russia, Jews of

STONES

Throughout history, stones have been intertwined in different aspects of Jewish life, culture, and folklore. Whether used to construct buildings and altars, to mark sacred grounds, or to carve sarcophagi, stones provided a practical material for daily life while symbolizing eternity, permanence, firmness, solidity, and hardness.

Ancient Daily Life and Culture

In daily life, stone, being a natural structure of the geological layers of the soil, was the major construction material of ancient Israel. Stones were commonly used in agriculture as borders, terraces, fences, and fill for ditches. In trade, they were used as weights. Various biblical verses refer to the commandment that only "just stones," meaning accurate stone weights, should be used in commerce (Lev. 19:35–36; Deut. 25:13; Mic. 6:11; Prov. 20:10, 23). In the Midrash, this biblical term is viewed as representing one of the principles of divine justice (*Pesiqta de'Rav Kahana* 3:4; *Esth. Rab.* 1:3).

During the Second Temple period (2 B.C.E.–1 C.E.) stone was considered one of the main materials which remained clean and pure, even after it was touched by an impure person or object (*m. Ohalot* 5:5; *m. Kelim* 5:11). A soft type of limestone was used to manufacture furniture, such as tables, chairs and benches, as well as utensils—vases and vessels. The remains of a high priest's house in Jerusalem with its stone interior, dating from the first century B.C.E., are a good example of this trend. A rather negative meaning related to stones is their ability to be used to inflict lethal injury. Mentioned in the Bible as a weapon in feuds, the stone could be used to kill (Exod. 21:18; Num. 35:16–18). Capital punishment in the Bible was death by stoning, performed by the whole community (Deut. 17:5; 22:21, 24). Hail was regarded as stones falling from heaven and as a divine lapidation specially targeting Israel's enemies (Joshua 10:11). The Midrash developed this concept further (*Sifrey Zuta* 6:26; *Mekhilta de'Rabbi Shimon bar Yoḥai*, Exod. 20:5; *Song Rab.* 1:10). Yet another negative aspect connected to stones is their relation to idolatry. In the Bible, the "Other" is identified as a stones and trees worshipper (Deut. 4:28; 28:36, 64; 2 Kgs. 19:18; Isa. 37:19). This view has been adopted by later generations (*Eccl. Rab.* 3:8; *Pesiqta de'Rav Kahana* I 16:1).

The symbolism of stones as the embodiment of strength and endurance is manifested in the fact that it was the main construction material of the Temple and other holy sites in ancient Israel. It included the Temple Mount in Jerusalem, the walls surrounding it, the First and Second Temples, and their altars (e.g., 1 Kgs. 6:2, 7, 36; 7:12; *m. Tamid* 1:1; *m. Midot* 2:3, 7). In particular, the Shtyyah stone, the name given to the rocky floor of the holiest part of the Temple, was considered the holiest site in the world. The same symbolic context may also explain the fact that in some instances God is called a "rock" (e.g., 2 Sam. 22:2–3, 47; Ps. 18:3, 31:4, 71:3).

In the Bible, stones were mounted in heaps or erected as pillars (Gen. 31:45–6), to attest a meaningful event, as remembrance (Gen. 31:48; Joshua 7:26), and to mark sacred grounds (Gen. 28:18). Certain stones were related to major figures and hence received attention in later generations. For example, the stone on which Moses sat during the war against the Amalekites (Exod. 17:12) was referred to in talmudic sources (*b. Berakhot* 54a; *b. Ta'anit* 11a). Midrashic tradition considers the stone on which Jacob slept and dreamed at Beth El (Gen. 28:11–21) the location of Mount Moriah, the Temple in Jerusalem, and the Shtyyah stone (*Pirqe de'Rabbi Eliezer*, 35).

Stones are intertwined with the Jewish life cycle. In the Bible, women gave birth on a special stool, whose name in Hebrew can be read as either "a stool" (*ovnaim*) or "stones" (*avanim*). Some Midrash prefer the latter version (*Mekhilta de'Rabbi Yishmael*, Bashelah: 5; *Mekhilta de'Rabbi Shimon bar Yoḥai*, Exod. 15:5).

Pregnant women, in order to prevent miscarriages, used to wear an amulet called a Tkumah stone, a small stone encased in another one (*t. Moed Shabbat* 4:12; *b. Shabbat* 66b) (see also the medieval dictionary: *Aruch*: "Even Tkumah").

Stone is one of the materials used in burial. Coffins, sarcophagi, and ossuaries made of stones were commonly in use during the Second Temple period. Burial caves were sealed with a large stone. Tombstones were used by Jews throughout the Diaspora, and some remnants can be dated to the early Middle Ages. A characteristic custom among Jews is to place a small stone on the tombstone when visiting the grave, a symbolic silent greeting or a token of honoring the deceased. This custom may have universal echoes of ancient nomads' burial practices: Graves were marked by a pile of stones and restructured when revisited. In the Bible, marking graves with stones indicates the site of outcast people's graves (Josh. 7:25–26; 8:29; 2 Sam. 18:17). In rabbinical sources, putting a stone on one bier had a context of abomination; it signified that the deceased deserved lapidation (*m. Eduyot* 5:6; *b. Moed Qatan* 15a). Among the Ashkenazi communities in the Middle Ages, putting a stone on a grave was considered to counteract the ill effect of reading the inscriptions on tombstones, which caused forgetfulness of acquired Torah knowledge.

Numerous parables, idioms, and proverbs refer to stones (Exod. 15:16; Ezek. 11:19, 36:26; Ps. 118:22; Job 14:19; Eccl. 3:5; *b. Sanhedrin* 14a; *Exod. Rab.* 22:4). Jewish folktales (IFA 502, IFA 553) tell of stones flying to Jerusalem in order to assist in building the Temple (*Song Rab.* 1:4) or stones brought from Jerusalem to the Diaspora to build new synagogues.

Stones Today

In modern times, stones remain important in Jewish culture, such as the placing of a small stone on a tombstone of the deceased during a cemetery visit. Large rocks are left to mark the site of violent deaths along roads, on battlegrounds, and at the location of a terrorist attack. Stones and rocks are used in Holocaust memorials, such as the Treblinka Memorial, which integrates 17,000 stones, each representing a perished Jewish community, and the "Valley of the Communities" at Yad Vashem in Jerusalem, carved in rock. The stones of the Western Wall in Jerusalem are the center of renewed veneration: prostrated to, caressed, and kissed, visited on Jewish holidays and on private family celebrations. Small scraps of paper with wishes written on them are tucked between these stones in the belief that they will thus be fulfilled. These stones are also a common topic in songs and in poems. They are considered "stones with a human heart" (after the song "Ha'Kotel," written in 1967, with lyrics by Yossi Gamzo and music by Dubi Zeltser), symbolizing the yearning of the Jewish people for a physical sacred center.

Idit Pintel-Ginsberg

See also: Shtyyah Stone.

Bibliography

Almog, Oz. "War Casualties' Memorials in Israel: A Semiotic Analysis." *Megamot* 34:2 (1991): 179–201.

Bar-Ilan, Meir. "A Rock, a Stone and a Seat That Moses Sat On." *Sidra* 2 (1986): 15–23 (in Hebrew).

Bar-Itzhak, Haya. *Jewish Poland: Legends of Origin.* Detroit: Wayne State University Press, 2001.

Levinger, Esther. *War Memorials in Israel.* Tel Aviv: Ha'kibbutz Ha'meuḥad, 1993 (in Hebrew).

Magen, Yitzhak. *"Stone Vessels in the Late Second Temple Period.* Haifa: Hecht Museum, 1994.

Patai, Raphael. *Man and Earth,* vol. 2. Jerusalem: Hebrew University Press, 1943.

Pintel-Ginsberg, Idit. "The Phenomenology of a Cultural Symbol in Judaism: The Stone as a Case Study in Rabbinic and Midrashic Literature." Ph.D. dissertation, Haifa University, 2000 (in Hebrew).

———. "'Throwing a Stone to Merculis': Symbolizing the 'Other' Within Jewish Cultural Context." *Jerusalem Studies in Jewish Thought* 21:2 (2007): 455–468 (in Hebrew).

Schwarzbaum, Haim. "The Synagogue in Folktales." In *Roots and Landscapes.* Beer Sheva: Ben Gurion University, 1993: 137–149 (in Hebrew).

Trachtenberg, Joshua. *Jewish Magic and Superstition.* New York: Atheneum, 1977.

SUKKAH

See: Sukkot

SUKKOT

Sukkot is one of the three pilgrimage festivals, along with Passover and Shavuot (Exod. 23:14). Sukkot begins on the fifteenth of the month of Tishrei and lasts for seven days (Lev. 23:39, 42). The name "Sukkot" (Tabernacles) derives from the principal religious object associated with it, the sukkah (booth). The holiday is also referred to as the Feast of Ingathering (Exod. 34:22), as "the season of our rejoicing" (in the liturgy), and, throughout the Talmud, as simply "the Festival" (the last two are oblique references to Deut. 16:14, "You shall rejoice on your festival").

The talmudic designation reflects the holiday's primacy during the Second Temple period, when it was considered the most important festival. (After the destruction of the Temple, that role was taken over by Passover.) There were several reasons for the centrality of Sukkot. First, it is a harvest festival—and in those days the vast majority of the Jewish residents of the land of Israel, as well as the community in the Babylonian Diaspora, were farmers and agricultural laborers. Further, harvest festivals are not celebrated until the harvest has been completed, when farmers no longer have any work to do in the fields. This makes it an appropriate season for a pilgrimage to Jerusalem to give thanks for the bounteous harvest. Another reason is simply that in autumn the journey on foot to Jerusalem was easier.

All work is forbidden on the first day of the festival (the first two days in the Diaspora). The next six days (five in the Diaspora) are *ḥol ha'mo'ed* (intermediate days), when most work is permitted. The eighth and concluding day, when all work is again forbidden, is a separate holiday (Shmini Atzeret), with its own rituals and customs.

Reasons for the Festival

The Torah provides two totally different reasons for Sukkot. The first is historical: "That your generations may know that I housed the Israelites in booths when I brought them out of the land of Egypt" (Lev. 23:43). The second is contemporary: to thank the God of Israel for the harvest (Lev. 23:39; Deut. 16:13). The Midrash adds another reason: "Why does Israel build a sukkah? [To remember] the miracles that the Holy One Blessed be He worked for them when they left Egypt, when clouds of glory surrounded and covered them" (*Pesiqta de'Rav Kahana* 169a).

According to Philo of Alexandria, the sukkah is intended to remind the Jews of their ancestors' years of wandering in the wilderness. Another reason is to spur human beings to recognize that one must not take pride in material wealth or be ashamed of poverty. For an entire week, all are commanded to leave their homes—whether lavish or ramshackle—to live and sleep in the sukkah. Rashbam (Shmuel ben Meir), the biblical commentator and grandson of Rashi (Solomon ben Isaac of Troyes), takes a similar approach. He says that the festival was set in the season when farmers gather the harvest from the threshing floor and winepress to keep them from excessive pride and to remind them that in the wilderness no one had a house or field. This recognition will lead them to praise the Lord for what they have received from him.

According to the *Shulḥan arukh,* the sukkah is a symbol and reminder of the clouds of glory that accompanied the Israelites in their wanderings in the wilderness. The talmudic sages saw the sukkah as a symbol of the messianic renewal of the Israelite kingdom. The grace after meals recited on Sukkot includes an extra petition: "May the Merciful One rebuild the booth of David that is fallen" (after Amos 9:11). The sages also said that those who are meticulous in their observance of the precept of the sukkah will merit being seated among the righteous in the World to Come, in the "booth made of the skin of the leviathan" (based on the legend in *b. Bava Batra* 75a).

בא׳ אמה אקב
וצונו
לישב בסכה

A decorative sukkah plaque, featuring a verse from the Scripture. Italy, 1800. *(Gross Family Collection, Tel Aviv)*

The Four Species

The Torah enjoins the enjoyment of the four species (*arba'at ha'minim*) on this holiday: "You shall take on the first day the fruit of the *hadar* tree, branches of palm trees, and boughs of leafy trees, and willows of the brook" (Lev. 23:40). The Talmud rules that the fruit in question is the *etrog* (citron).

The four species are interpreted as symbolizing four types of Jew. Those who have both flavor (the Torah) and fragrance (good deeds) are represented by the *etrog*, which has both of these. Those with savor but no fragrance are represented by the palm branch, which has a flavor but no aroma. Those who have a scent but are tasteless are represented by the myrtle, and those who have neither, by the willow.

Alternatively, some of the four species bear fruit (the palm and the *etrog*), while others do not (the myrtle and the willow); the same is true for the Jews.To fulfill the precept of the four species, all of them must be present and held together. This symbolizes the unity of the Jewish people.

Halakhah goes into great detail about the four species. The most important stipulation is that the *etrog* be whole and shaped somewhat like a tower, that is, broad at the bottom and narrower toward the top. For the past 400 years some *etrogim* have been produced by grafting an *etrog* branch onto the stock of a lemon tree, to make it hardier. Because rabbinic authorities disagree as to whether a grafted *etrog* is fit for performing the precept, many people insist on buying one that is certified as not having been grafted.

There is also disagreement about the size of the *etrog*. Some hold that the minimum size is that of a walnut. Others speak of a maximum size. The Talmud reports that Rabbi Akiva came to the synagogue with an *etrog* so large that he had to carry it on his shoulder. Very large *etrogim* are customary in some Jewish communities today, notably among the Yemenites.

The *lulav* is the frond at the apex of the palm tree, whose leaves are still unopened and flush against the central spine. The *lulav* must be moist, green, closed, and perfectly straight. Moroccan Jews tie colored strings around the *lulav* to reinforce and decorate it; other communities tie up the *lulav* with its own leaves, so as not to add another species to the four ordained by the Torah.

The myrtle must be moist, green, and "threefold," meaning that the leaves are arranged in groups of three, with each set of three leaves attached at a single point on the branch. The willow must be moist and green and often has a reddish stalk. Because the willow dries out quickly, the custom is to replace it at least once during the course of the festival. Three myrtles are bundled on the right side of the *lulav* (with the spine facing the person holding it) and two willows on the left side.

The Torah ordains that the four species be assembled only on the first day of the festival. In the Temple (according to Maimonides, throughout Jerusalem as well) the custom was to do so all seven days. After the destruction of the Temple, Rabbi Yoḥanan ben Zakkai decreed that they be gathered on all seven days of the festival (except for the Sabbath) everywhere, in commemoration of the Temple.

The blessing over the four species mentions only the largest of them—the *lulav*. They are held during the recitation of the Hallel psalms in the morning service and again in a procession around the synagogue during the recitation of the *hoshanot* supplications (see below).

The Sukkah

The sukkah (booth) is the main manifestation of the festival. Although the Bible is silent as to its construction and use (except for a list of the types of branches employed [Neh. 8]), the talmudic tractate *Sukkah* enumerates the halakhic provisions in great detail.

Those most meticulous in the observance of the commandments start work on the sukkah as soon as they return from the synagogue at the end of the Day of Atonement, to go straight from one observance to another or in order to begin the new year by fulfilling a commandment, in keeping with the homiletic understanding of the verse "they go from strength to strength" (Ps. 84:8). The walls are erected first, followed by the roof (*skhakh*). The roof must be made of materials that cannot acquire ritual impurity—vegetation that is no longer connected to the ground and has not been used for some other purpose. The original idea was to use the scraps of the threshing floor and winepress, abundant in the autumn, for this purpose. The *skhakh* must be dense enough that the shaded area within the sukkah exceeds the unshaded area, but not so thick that the stars cannot be seen through it at night.

Because the "splendor of the precept" is particularly important on this festival, the custom is to use one's finest utensils in the sukkah and to decorate it lavishly. There may be brightly colored paper ornaments, fresh fruits, and pictures of the Western Wall, ancient Jerusalem, and important rabbis. The minimum height of a sukkah is 10 spans (about 90 centimeters); the maximum, 20 cubits (about 10 meters). The length and width must be at least 7 spans each (60 centimeters). There is no maximum size, however; the sages said, "would that all Israel would sit in a single sukkah."The sukkah may not be built under a tree or solid roof; nothing can encroach between a kosher sukkah and the sky.

The talmudic sages interpreted the injunction to "dwell in booths for seven days" to mean that one must "dwell as you normally dwell" in your house all year long (*b. Sukkah* 26a). Consequently one may not eat a regular meal outside the sukkah, and the most meticulous even sleep in the sukkah throughout the festival. On the first night, all must eat in the sukkah (regardless of whether they are hungry); but for the rest of the festival, although meals must be served there, there is no obligation to eat. Women are exempt from the sukkah because it is a time-dependent positive precept.

Another ritual associated with the sukkah is that of the *Ushpizin,* an Aramaic word derived from the Latin *hospes* (guest). The Ushpizin are the ancestors of the nation—Abraham, Isaac, Jacob, Joseph, Moses, Aaron, and David—who are invited to visit the sukkah. Many Jews also invite human guests—the poor—hosting them lavishly as the representatives of the spiritual guests.

Sukkot in the Temple

In the Temple ritual for Sukkot, special burnt offerings were made each day, in diminishing numbers: thirteen bullocks on the first day, twelve on the second day, eleven on the third day, and so on, winding up with seven bullocks on the seventh and last day. This brought the total to seventy, corresponding to the seventy nations of the world. They were offered on the altar in order to atone for the transgressions of the nations and to pray that peace reign among them. According to Rabbi Joshua ben Levi, "had the nations of the world realized what a benefit the Temple gave them, they would have surrounded it with fortifications to protect it" (*Num. Rab.* 1).

The Jewish pilgrims were required to bring the festal sacrifice—"every one according to this capacity" (Deut. 16:17). There were other precepts as well. One of the most important of these was the "water libation." Throughout the year, every sacrifice had its accompanying libation of wine; during Sukkot, the morning sacrifice was also accompanied by a libation of water.

Hoshana Rabbah

Another feature of the Sukkot ritual is the worshippers' procession, the four species in hand, around the altar (when the Temple stood) or around the central lectern of the synagogue (in modern times), while the congregation recites the supplications called *hoshanot.* On the seventh day of Sukkot, which has its own name—Hoshana Rabbah or "the great *hoshana*"—the worshippers make seven circuits. After the last one, they beat a special bunch of willows on the ground. (In Tunisia and Morocco it was customary to strike the members of one's household with the willows on their hand, to wish them well in the year to come.)

Why seven circuits? "Rav Aha said, in commemoration of Jericho" (*y. Sukkah* 19a), whose wall fell on the seventh day, when the Israelites circled it seven times. Why should Jericho be remembered precisely then? Because "on Rosh Ha'Shana all pass in front of God to be counted, including Israel. . . . The tutelary angels of the nations say, 'we have triumphed and won our case.' But no one knows who has triumphed—Israel or the nations. . . . But when Hoshana Rabbah comes, they take the willows and make seven circuits, and the prayer leader stands like an angel of god with the Torah scroll in his arm and the people circle him as if he were the altar. . . . At once the ministering angels rejoice and say, 'Israel has triumphed, Israel has triumphed!'" (*m. Tehillim* 17:5).

The judgment rendered on the High Holy Days is given its final ratification on Hoshana Rabbah. The kabbalists of Safed initiated the custom of staying awake the entire night to study, with a fixed order of texts from the Bible, Mishnah, and the Zohar. Some recite special penitential prayers.

According to the Mishnah, the amount of rainfall for the coming year is set on Sukkot: "The world is judged concerning water on the festival" (*m. Rosh Hashanah* 1:2). This, according to Rabbi Akiva, is why Temple ritual for Sukkot included the special water libations: "The Holy One, blessed be He, said: 'Pour out water before Me on Sukkot, so that your rains this year may be blessed'" (*b. Rosh Hashanah* 16a). Today, in addition to the special prayer for rain that is recited on the eighth day of the festival, the festival liturgy contains many references to rain.

Hakhel

The Torah prescribes a ceremonial reading of the Torah (or sections thereof) at a public assembly (Heb., *hakhel*) of all of Israel, on the first intermediate day of Sukkot at the conclusion of each sabbatical year (Deut. 31:10–13). Although it is not clear from this passage whether the reading was to take place in the Temple only or in each city, the sages of the Second Temple period understood it to mean the former. The talmudic literature, which refers to the ceremony as the "chapter of the king" (*m. Sotah* 7:8), prescribes that the king himself conduct the reading, in a festive celebration attended by many of the pilgrims.There is documentary evidence on several of these observances from the last years of the Second Temple. In modern Israel the custom has been revived to some extent.

Ecclesiastes

Ecclesiastes (Kohelet) is one of the Five Scrolls. In Ashkenazi communities, it is read on the intermediate Sabbath of Sukkot. Some read it from a parchment scroll and recite the corresponding benediction as well as the "Sheheheyanu" blessing ("who has kept us alive and preserved us and enabled us to reach this season"). Several reasons have been given for this custom, which dates to the period of the Geonim (seventh to eleventh centuries). The true reason seems to be the desire that all five of the scrolls be read in the synagogue during the course of the year. Another explanation links the book of Kohelet to the *hakhel* ceremony (the words derive from the same Hebrew root): King Solomon, the author of Ecclesiastes, is supposed to have read it during the *hakhel* ceremony.

Customs of the Various Communities

Ashkenazi Jews hang colorful fabrics in the sukkah; some also hang small containers of flour, wine, oil, and honey, along with strings of dried figs, a fresh branch of dates, and a pomegranate, representing the seven characteristic species of the Land of Israel. They supplement them with colorful paper lanterns and birds made of dyed eggshells. Rosettes of colored paper are hung from the walls, along with small baskets containing a pebble. Imaginary portraits of Moses and Aaron and important sages, along with signs welcoming the Ushpizin, may also adorn the walls. A plan of the Third Temple is often hung at the center of the eastern wall.

Jews in Kurdistan lay precisely seven beams across the walls of the sukkah, one for each of the Ushpizin, to support the *skhakh.* In one corner they place a chair covered with a colorful cushion, to serve as the throne of the patriarchs, meaning the seven Ushpizin (like the chair of the prophet Elijah at circumcisions).

Moroccan Jews hang a small stool, which they call "the chair of the prophet Elijah," on the wall of the sukkah and decorate it with colorful fabrics. They use it to hold books used during the festival, such as prayerbooks.

Jews in Tunisia use palm fronds to cover the sukkah. If this is not possible, they try to stand at least one palm frond in each corner of the sukkah.

In Persia, Jews would build large *sukkot* to be shared by several families. The children built smaller ones nearby and decorated them lavishly. They referred to the festival as *Muddeh Sukkah,* a corruption of the Hebrew *Moed sukkah* (Sukkah festival), and this was sometimes corrupted further to *Madda Sukkah.* People left their shoes by the door when they entered the sukkah; otherwise it was thought to be invalid. When the men returned from the synagogue, they stood at the door. One of them, usually a scholar, would read various prayers and invite the seven "sustainers of the covenant" to enter, each on his own evening, following the sequence of the Ushpizin.

Joel Rappel

See also: Jerusalem and the Temple; Papercut.

Bibliography

Ariel, Shlomo Zalman. *The Book of Holidays and Festivals.* Tel Aviv: Dvir, 1975 (in Hebrew).

Ha'Cohen, Devora, and Menahem Ha'Cohen, eds. *Holidays and Festivals: Rosh Hashanah, Day of Atonement, Sukkot.* Jerusalem: Keter, 1978 (in Hebrew).

Lau, Israel Meir. *Practical Judaism.* Jerusalem and New York: Feldheim, 1997.

Lewinsky, Yom-Tov. *Encyclopedia of Folklore, Customs and Tradition in Judaism.* Tel Aviv: Dvir, 1970 (in Hebrew).

Lewinsky, Yom-Tov, ed. *The Book of the Festivals: Sukkot.* Tel Aviv: Oneg Shabbat, 1951 (in Hebrew).

Rappel, Joel. *Jewish Holidays: Encyclopedia of Sabbath and Holidays.* Tel Aviv: MOD, 1990 (in Hebrew).

Tabory, Yosef. *Jewish Festivals in the Time of the Mishnah and Talmud.* Jerusalem: Magnes, 1995 (in Hebrew).

Wasserteil, Asher, ed. *Anthology of Customs.* Jerusalem: Ministry of Education and Culture, 1977 (in Hebrew).

Symbols

In a cultural context, symbols are vehicles that convey the worldview and ethos of a society. They have two parts: One is the physical aspect that can be captured objectively by the senses (the symbolizer), such as a word, an image, or an object; the other (the symbolized) is its significance, the sum of all the various meanings derived from the first part. These meanings require a constant process of interpretation by both the user and the receiver of the symbol. Some scholars differentiate between types of cultural symbols according to their meaning. A symbol conveying one clear and defined meaning is called a "referential" or "instrumental" symbol, while a symbol conveying several meanings, often unclear or contradictory, is called a "condensed" symbol.

Jewish symbols in general are condensed. They are the corollary of Jewish culture's singular characteristic: its substantial bonds to traditional Holy Scriptures.

Every generation carries out a continuous creative dialogue with the previous generations' texts and commentaries. The meanings of Jewish cultural symbols are composed of various layers, including a layer of universal or archetypical meanings and a body of meanings that derive from cultural contexts. This cultural entity comprises different types of meanings. The first is the layer of instrumental meanings, derived from the daily usage of the symbolizers. The second has actual and current meanings which originate in a specific period by the latest generation. Some groups in different periods extensively contributed new meanings to Jewish symbols: the rabbinical and midrashic literature, the Spanish and Lurianic Kabbalah, Hasidism, and the Zionist movement. These new meanings were added to the immense pool of all the former meanings of the same symbol and became for latter generations a part of the symbol's density. The third layer is made up of the cumulative meanings existing in Jewish culture since the Bible, adopted by further generations through an interactive process of commentaries.

In Jewish culture, there is an extensive pool of symbolizers. It is partially composed of universal archetypes shared by mythologies and religions around the world. They reflect humanity's close acquaintance with heavenly bodies, still-life, fauna and flora, family, the human body, and geometrical symmetric shapes (such as the Star of David). However, the main body of symbolizers in Judaism is derived from a cultural context.

Major landmarks in Jewish history such as divine revelations to the patriarchs, the Exodus from Egypt, the wandering in the wilderness, the building and destruction of the Temple, conflicts with conquering empires and the diasporas have all been used as symbolizers throughout the generations. Unique biblical references, such as the patriarchs, the well and the pillars of cloud and fire accompanying Israel in the wilderness, Jacob's ladder, Beth El, the Tabernacle, the Temples, the menorah, kings and heroes, just to name a few, became major symbolizers over time. Subjects borrowed from the immediate surroundings and daily life, such as construction features, local distinctive trading habits, agriculture, arts and crafts, domestic animals, typical Israeli landscapes, fauna and flora, social establishments and relationships, also provided symbolizers.

Symbols have been used since the Bible to express major issues relevant to the Jewish discourse. Among them: the affinity between God and the people of Israel, the rhythmic patterns of Jewish history viewed as a sequence of destruction/exile/redemption, God's essence, the people of Israel, their essence and nature, and human faith and existence.

Various symbolizers were used to discuss common issues, each of them emphasizing a slightly different aspect of these issues. For example, the nature of Israel is symbolized by numerous symbolizers, some taken from Israel's fauna and flora, such as the dove (*Song of Songs Rab.* 2:2; 4:2), the vine (*Lev. Rab.* 36:2–3), the palm tree (*Gen. Rab.* 40:1), the olive (*Exod. Rab.* 36:1), and the lily (*Lev. Rab.* 23:5). The stormy relationships between God and Israel are symbolized through family ties—for example, a loving father and his beautiful daughter (*Song of Songs Rab.* 1:5; 3:2), an enraged father and his rebellious son (*Eccl. Rab.* 4:14), a moody king and his weary mistress (*Song of Songs Rab.* 5:1), a vanished husband and his faithful wife (*Pesiqta de'Rav Kahana* on Jesaiah 51:12). Humanity's ephemeral existence is symbolized by diverse objects, such as an oil lamp and a plucked fig (*Gen. Rab.* 62:5), a passing shadow (*Gen. Rab.* 96:1), and a stone (*Gen. Rab.* 100:7).

Jewish cultural symbols are expressed verbally in the cultural literary corpus, beginning with the Bible and its commentaries, and are integrated into parables, proverbs, Midrash, and tales. They are also present in material culture, as meaningful objects integrated into customs and rituals connected to daily life and the Jewish calendar and life cycle.

Idit Pintel-Ginsberg

See also: Animals; Jerusalem and the Temple; Menorah; Papercut.

Bibliography

Bar-Itzhak, Haya. "'The Unknown Variable Hidden Underground' and the Zionist Idea." *Journal of American Folklore* 112:446 (1999): 479–496.

Bialer, Yehuda L. "Symbols in Jewish Art and Tradition." *Ariel* 20 (1966–1968): 5–16; 21:5–22 (in Hebrew).

Frankel, Ellen, and Betsy Platkin Teutsch. *The Encyclopedia of Jewish Symbols.* Northvale, NJ: Jason Aronson, 1992.

Geertz, Clifford. *The Interpretation of Cultures.* New York: Basic Books, 1973.

Goodenough, Erwin. *Jewish Symbols in the Greco-Roman Period.* 12 vols. New York: Pantheon, 1954–1965.

Mishory, Alec. *Lo and Behold: Zionist Icons and Visual Symbols in Israeli Culture.* Tel Aviv: Am Oved, 2000 (in Hebrew).

Ortner, Sherry. "On Key Symbols." *American Anthropologist* 75/4 (1973): 1338–1346.

Pintel-Ginsberg, Idit. "The Phenomenology of a Cultural Symbol in Judaism: The Stone as a Case Study in Rabbinic and Midrashic Literature." Ph.D. dissertation, Haifa University, 2000 (in Hebrew).

Sapir, Edward. *Anthropologie,* vol. 1. Paris: Les Editions de Minuit, 1967.

Stern, David. *Parables in Midrash.* Cambridge: Harvard University Press, 1991.

Turner, Victor. "Symbols in Ndembu Ritual." In *The Forest of Symbols: Aspects of Ndembu Ritual.* Ithaca: Cornell University Press, 1967.

T

Tamar

In Jewish and world folklore, Tamar represents the lethal woman, a familiar motif since biblical times. A lethal woman is one who has become a widow twice and who, according to custom, is not to be married again. She has no male counterpart; there is no such example of a lethal man, no matter how many times a man becomes a widower.

According to Genesis 38, Judah betroths Tamar to his oldest son Er; and after Er dies childless, Judah gives Tamar to Onan, to raise offspring for his brother. Onan, who knows that children born to him and Tamar will not be his, spills his semen on the ground, and the Lord slays him in punishment. Judah sends his daughter-in-law to her father's home as a widow; she is to wait there until his son Shelah grows old enough to wed her. But Judah delays this marriage, fearing that his young son will also be struck down.

Tamar hears that Judah (after the death of his wife) is headed to Timnah to shear his sheep, and from this moment on, she no longer plays the role of the passive object, whose fate is shaped by Judah and his sons. She appears in the guise of a determined, forceful woman, who acts quickly and decisively: She takes off her widow's clothes, wraps herself in a scarf, sits in a conspicuous place by the road, consents to the proposal of Judah (who does not recognize her), and receives meaningful gifts and guarantees from Judah in support of her agreement to marry into his family—Judah's signet and cord and staff, and a kid from his flock. After three months, Judah discovers that his daughter-in-law has become pregnant, and he declares that the "harlot" should be brought out and burned. Before this punishment is carried out, she shows her father-in-law the signet, cord, and staff, and he acknowledges her propriety.

This sequence is familiar in folklore: A man who condemns someone to death recognizes a sign (a ring) given at a time of sexual relations, and the execution order is overturned after this discovery.

The "happy ending" comes when Tamar gives birth to twins, and her desire to have sons is fulfilled twice over.

When Tamar is in labor, one of the infants extends a hand, and the midwife wraps a scarlet thread around it; but his brother comes out first. Tamar exclaims: "What a breach you have made for yourself" and names the boy Perez, after the Hebrew word for "breach." Then the infant with the scarlet threat comes out, "glowing" (*zoreah*, which has the same Hebrew root as "scarlet"), and is called Zerah.

Tamar thus emerges as a determined woman who is unconcerned about the means and is not afraid of taking risks in order to secure her rights and fulfill her destiny by conceiving with the seed of the family to which she was betrothed. She transgresses the limits and rules of the framework in which she is confined.

Some have speculated that Tamar was holy in the original story (as a sacred harlot)—the scarlet thread, a symbol of prostitution (Joshua 2:18), is used as evidence of her connection to the profession. Midrashic literature holds that Tamar, like all matriarchal figures, was blessed by a prophetic spirit. She anticipated that a messiah would be born to her descendants; this prophetic knowledge compelled her to comply with the local law that required a young woman to wait by the gate of a city for seven days before her wedding and offer herself to strangers.

Some scholars have claimed that Judah, a righteous man, should have continued on his way without stopping for Tamar. She, however, prayed to God, who sent an angel to stir lust within Judah (*Bereshit Rab.* peh 8, *Tanḥuma Buber Hakdama*, *Shevet Yehuda* 11, 14:3–5).

The Midrash relates that the guarantee provided by Judah to Tamar was lost. Only her pleading, and promise that her survival would bring three holy figures who would sanctify God, saved her (*Tirgum Yonatan Bereshit* 38:25).

The Midrash compares Tamar's acts with Ruth's—both tempted Jewish men. In other words, there is no denunciation of the bold act carried out by the women, because their intentions are worthy. The dynasty of Solomon and David was thus conceived out of acts involving incest and mixed marriage.

Regarding Tamar's overall moral status, the judgment of traditional commentators can be misleading. The phrase "she is more righteous than I" suggests that Tamar is holier than Judah, a male head of a family in a patriarchal society. Yet subsequent Aramaic translations of the Bible, and Jonathan Ben Uzziel's translation, obscure this suggestion of Tamar's superiority; their formulations, "Tamar was right, she has conceived by me," appear to conceal the moral superiority of the woman figure.

Aliza Shenhar

Bibliography

Emerton, John A. "Judah and Tamar." *Vetus Testamentum* 29 (1979): 403–415.

Kirsch, Jonathan. *The Harlot by the Side of the Road.* New York: Ballantine, 1997.

Speiser, Ephraim A. *Genesis.* Garden City, NY: Doubleday, 1964, 1994.

Van Dijk-Hemmes, Fokkelein. "Tamar and the Limits of Patriarchy: Between Rape and Seduction." In *Anti-Covenant: Counter Reading Women's Lives in the Hebrew Bible,* ed. Mieke Bal, pp. 135–156. Sheffield, UK: Almond, 1989.

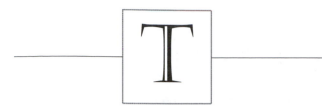

Tavayev, I.

See: Russia, Jews of

Tobit, The Book of

The Book of Tobit (*Sefer Tuvya*) is a Jewish composition from the Second Temple period, dated no later than the beginning of the second century B.C.E. In its Greek translation, it was included in the Septuagint and preserved in Christian writings in two principal versions (short and long) and was also translated into Latin, Syriac (a dialect of Aramaic), and Ge'ez. The work was translated back into Hebrew and Aramaic from these languages in the course of the Middle Ages.

Textual History

Its place of composition is unknown. A theory of Egyptian origin has never been substantiated, and despite the evidence of influence of the Persian religion, it would appear that the author's lack of familiarity with Babylonian geography—the plot takes place there between Media (in modern-day Iran) and Nineveh (in modern-day Iraq) in the reign of "Shalmaneser, the king of Assyria," immediately following the exile of the Ten Tribes—disproves the theory that the story originated in this region. It is possible, therefore, that it originated in Palestine or its vicinity, although this view, too, lacks solid proof. Hebrew and Aramaic fragments of the work, found in the caves of Qumran, confirm scholars' speculations, based on internal textual evidence, that the work was originally composed in Hebrew, and from this language it was then translated into Aramaic and Greek. However, it would appear that its versions in Semitic languages, which preceded the Greek version, were already lost to the Jews in ancient times, and at the same time all recollection of the work was lost, too. It is not mentioned at all by the ancient Jewish writers Philo and Josephus, or even in the rabbinic literature.

The Story

The story opens with a description of the life of Tobit, who was exiled to Nineveh, where his only son, Tobias, was born. Tobit, meticulous in the observance of the divine commandments in his homeland, amassed wealth in the service of Shalmaneser, and persevered in his benevolent ways for both the living and the deceased. Once, on the night following the festival of Shavuot, having contravened the express order of the king and buried a corpse that had been cast into the street, Tobit slept in the courtyard of his house on account of his ritual impurity (resulting from handling the deceased). Birds that hovered overhead released their droppings into his eyes, which blinded him. This initial loss, which is the turn of events that sets the development of the plot in motion, is magnified when he also becomes impoverished. In his sorrow, Tobit turns to God in prayer. At this point in the story, a second front is created in the plot, which is later woven together with the first. At that very moment Sarah, the daughter of Raguel, a relative of Tobit, prays to the Lord in Ecbatana to deliver her from her bitter fate. She had wedded seven husbands, but the demon Asmodeus had slain them all on her wedding night before the consummation of the marriage, and now she was despised and humiliated by her family. The two prayers are heard in the heavens, and God sends Raphael, the angel charged with healing, to alleviate their pain by means of Tobias, the son of Tobit, and Sarah's future groom, who is the main hero of the narrative. Raphael reveals himself to Tobias in the form of a man named Azariah, when Tobias sets off on a journey to Rages, accompanied by his dog, in order to redeem money that Tobit had left with his relative. Raphael directs him and helps him at the only event mentioned in the story that visits them along the way.

While Tobias is washing in the Tigris River, a fish comes out of the water and attempts to swallow him up. Upon the instructions of the angel, Tobias throws the fish onto dry land, pulls out its gall, heart, and liver, and puts them away for safekeeping. Tobias and the angel then make a detour to Ecbatana, to the house of Raguel, in order to meet Sarah. Tobias wishes to marry her, but he fears the demon who is enamored of her and murders her grooms. Her relatives and family members also warn him against the marriage. The angel, however, instructs him to smoke the fish's heart and liver on coals in the bridal chamber and to expel the demon in this way. By following his instructions, Tobias forces the demon to flee, which it does to the furthermost extremes of Upper Egypt, where it is bound by Raphael.

Now that this thread of the story has been resolved, the narrator resumes the former part (Tobias's original mission). Tobias sends Raphael to Rages and when he returns with the bags of money, Tobias, Sarah, the angel, and the dog all return to Nineveh. Following the angel's instructions, Tobias smears the fish's gall over the blind eyes of his father, who regains his sight. When they desire to thank him and to share with him their fortune equally, Azariah's true identity is revealed to them, and he declares his divine mission to heal Tobit and Sarah, his intended daughter-in-law, as a reward for Tobit's exemplary righteousness, especially toward the deceased. The story concludes with Tobit's song of praise to God and with his bidding his son to remove himself to Media on account of the prophecy on Nineveh's approaching fall. With the death of his parents, Tobias buries them beside each other, in accordance with his father's wishes, and moves to Media where he learns, at the end of his days, of the destruction of Nineveh.

Folkloristic Elements

The folkloristic elements of the Book of Tobit, both the motifs woven into a narrative type and the customs and beliefs reflected therein, are most conspicuous. Scholars, at the same time, are divided over the question of whether it is a novella, in the composition of which the author made use of folkloristic elements, or a written and reworked version of a Jewish oral popular story. Regarding the narrative type, the plot of the Book of Tobit combines two elements: the grateful dead and the intended bride (scholars are divided, as well, on which element is at the core of the plot and which is added to it). As for the first element, the story is the earliest known version of this folktale type (AT 505–508; cf. Stith Thompson's *Motif-Index of Folk-Literature*, E341, E341.1). The basic theme of the grateful dead tales involves a corpse lying unburied because the creditors of the deceased will not allow its burial until the dead man's debts are paid. A stranger who passes through has compassion upon him, pays his debts, and buries him. The deceased, for his part, recompenses the favor sevenfold. He returns in the form of a mysterious personage (an old man, a manservant, an animal, an angel), accompanies the stranger on his travels, saves him from dangers that await him, and leads him to success and riches. Finally, he also helps his benefactor to attain the wife he desires by showing him how to deliver her from the monster that has taken hold of her. In some versions, the deceased promises his help in return for an equal division of the gains attained by the hero with his help. All these motifs are indeed woven into the version of the narrative type that is laid before us in the Book of Tobit. Its uniqueness, being a Jewish oicotype, is in the absence of any appearance of the deceased person himself, as the mysterious personage. In place of this, our version offers the appearance of an actual angel, sent by God, to bestow kindness on the righteous man who buries the dead.

The intended bride folktale type (AT 930A), or the match made in heaven, originates in the notion that the match between two people is preordained and may not be changed. In stories of this type, this motif develops in two main directions based on the principle guiding the chief protagonist: knowledge of his fate, and his opposition to it, or lack of knowledge, and acting innocently. However, whether they relate the hero's attempts to harm the intended bride and to remove her from his path, or they envelop his life with wanderings and dangers that end in revelation and, on occasion, even saving the intended bride, who is controlled or imprisoned by a monster or other evil powers, all these plots lead to the recognition that the intended fate will be realized. Every attempt by one of the couple to escape it and to link his or her life with someone else is doomed to failure. In the Book of Tobit, the entire plot is arranged around the motif of the intended bride, as it becomes apparent that Tobit's illness, the appearance of the helpful angel, and Asmodeus's love for Sarah and his slaying of the prospective husbands contribute jointly in the plot to the purpose of the intended unification of Tobias and Sarah. Nevertheless, the explanation provided by Raphael for the virtue of Tobias's marriage with Sarah provides this story with a Jewish foundation, while revealing to us the custom of the marriage of relatives that was apparently widespread among the Jews at that time. The *ketubbah* (marriage contract) is mentioned in the story for the first time in Jewish literature (long before it became explicit law adopted by the rabbis), as are some other marriage customs. Pieces of information on Jewish customs in the areas of ritual purity, prayer, festival, and burial are revealed, too, in the story, here and there.

Two additional foundations are added to this combination of two folktale types in the Book of Tobit. The first is the legend, known throughout the ancient Middle East, of the Babylonian sage and teller of parables and morals, Ahiqar, the adviser to King Sennacherib. This serves the author of the Book of Tobit in two ways: (a) regarding the narrative, the very adoption of the figure of Ahiqar, and his assimilation into the story as the Jewish nephew of Tobit who supports him in time of need and rejoices with him when his fortunes take a turn for the better; (b) from the structural perspective, the incorporation into the plot of two moral sermons by Tobit. The second essential foundation of the story is the demonological side. The narrative function of Asmodeus is as the bride's protector for her intended husband, while he makes her into what the rabbis later termed "a murderous woman," whose husbands die one after the other (in this aspect the story is also tied to the popular motif of the hero predestined to die on his wedding day. Cf. AT 934b). In rabbinical law, such a woman was limited to no more than three husbands (*b. Yevamot* 64b; *Niddah* 62a). The story of Tobit indicates that this law was not yet in practice at the time of its composition, even in the form of a custom. The system of beliefs and the popular praxis related to demons, as revealed in the story, is broad.

The Book of Tobit provides the earliest evidence in Jewish literature of the notion of an emotional connection between a demonic creature and a human being. The actions of Asmodeus, on the one hand, and the accusations against Sarah by her family members as a result of the death of her husbands, on the other, reveal the perception of the demon as evasive, invisible, and possessing great destructive power. Alongside this, the story provides the first testimony of the magical practice of the exorcism of demons. The angel's instructions to Tobias (6:8)—"With regard to the heart and the liver, make a smoke in front of a man or a woman whom a demon or evil spirit has attacked; and they will no longer be harmed"—seem to be an exorcistic, magical recipe. The way it continues—"And as for the gall, anoint a man's eyes, over which white films have crept, and they will become well"—tells us something of contemporary popular medicine (one should note that at the time of the Talmud a cataract was viewed as a case of demonic possession and its cure was, therefore, achieved through exorcism).

It may be that the surprising occurrence of the dog in this cultural context, as Tobias's companion on his journey, is also related to this matter. A number of scholars hold that the inclusion of the dog within the story originates in the belief and practice of the Persians, who associated the dog with the expulsion of demons. From this perspective, it was for the express purpose of struggling with Asmodeus that the dog came along on the journey. Others hold that it is no more than a decorative narrative motif, concerned with reflecting the brotherhood and partnership between man and dog that was retained in the Jewish version of the story. Either way, it would seem that the dog testifies to the foreign origins (Hellenistic, Babylonian, or Persian) of the Book of Tobit. At the same time, scholars have argued that the appearance of the dog in the Jewish oicotype (twice, and with no function apart from accompanying Tobias on the road) challenges the common view of sweeping antagonism to dogs in Jewish culture in ancient times. In this case one might be able to derive information on the custom of Jews to strike up a friendly relationship with this animal at the time and place of the author of the work, or even in the time and place of the oral version of Tobit, if such existed before being put into writing.

Yuval Harari

See also: Asmodeus; Demon; Magic.

Bibliography

Bow, Beverly, and George W.E. Nickelsburg. "Patriarchy with a Twist: Men and Women in Tobit." In *Women Like This: New Perspectives on Jewish Women in the Greco-Roman World*, ed. Ami-Jill Levine, pp. 127–143. Atlanta: ACLS Humanities E-book, 1991.

Charles Robert H., et al. *The Apocrypha and Pseudepigrapha of the Old Testament*, vol. 1. Oxford: Clarendon Press, 1913.

Deselaers, Paul. *Das Buch Tobit: Studien zu seiner Entstehung, Komposition und Theologie*. Göttingen: Vandenhoeck & Ruprecht, 1982.

Fitzmyer, Joseph A. "The Aramaic and Hebrew Fragments of Tobit from Qumran Cave 4." *Catholic Biblical Quarterly* 57 (1995): 655–675.

———. *Tobit*. Berlin: W. de Gruyter, 2003.

———. "Tobit." In *Qumran Cave 4: XIV: Parabiblical Texts, Part 2*, ed. M. Broshi et al., pp. 1–76. Oxford: Clarendon Press, 1995.

Flusser, David. "Tobit, The Book of Tobit." In *Encyclopedia Biblica,* vol. 3, pp. 367–375. Jerusalem: Mossad Bialik, 1958 (in Hebrew).

Greenfield, Jonas C. "Ahiqar in the Book of Tobit." In *De la Tôrah au Messie*, ed. M. Carrez, J. Doré, and P. Grelot, pp. 329–336. Paris: Desclée, 1981.

Grintz, Yehoshua M. *Chapters in the History of the Second Temple Times.* Jerusalem: Marcus, 1969 (in Hebrew).

Heller, D. "The Book of Tobit." In *The Apocryphal Books*, vol. 2, ed. A. Kahana, pp. 291–347. Jerusalem: Makor, 1936 (in Hebrew).

Liljeblad, Sven S. *Die Tobiasgeschichte und andere Märchen mit toten Helfern*. Lund: P. Lindstedts Univ.-Bokhandel, 1927.

Moore, Carey A. *Tobit: A New Translation with Introduction and Commentary*. New York: Doubleday, 1996.

Pfeiffer, Robert H. *History of New Testament Times.* New York: Harper, 1949.

Rabenau, Merten. *Studien zum Buch Tobit.* Berlin: W. de Gruyter, 1994.

Schüngel-Straumann, Helen. *Tobit.* Freiburg: Herder, 2000.

Soll, William M. "Misfortune and Exile in Tobit: The Juncture of a Fairy Tale Source and Deuteronomic Theology." *Catholic Biblical Quarterly* 51 (1989): 209–231.

Wills, Lawrence M. *The Jewish Novel in the Ancient World*. Ithaca: Cornell University Press, 1995.

Yassif, Eli. *The Hebrew Folktale: History, Genre, Meaning,* trans. J.S. Teitelbaum. Bloomington: Indiana University Press, 1999.

TOMBSTONES

Throughout Jewish history, tombstones have marked the burial places of Jews, evolving over history. Their shapes, decorations, rich symbolic motifs, and inscriptions provide one of the best-documented and most elaborate cases of development of Jewish folk traditions and forms of material culture. Millions of tombstones known to us, either preserved or at least documented, constitute undoubtedly the richest and most available repository of Jewish material culture.

Early History

Ritual burials and graves were known in Palestine as early as the Neolithic period. The earliest evidence of the settlement of Judaic tribes in the land of Canaan in patriarchal times unequivocally connects this settlement to the establishment of ancestral burial places (see Genesis 23:17 regarding the purchase of the cave of Machpelah by Abraham), both materially and symbolically. The custom of marking places of burial certainly already existed at this time, as references in the Bible to Jacob's placing of a monument (*tsiyun*) at the grave of

Rachel (Gen. 35:20) attest; this custom was continued later (see, e.g., 2 Kgs. 23:17 and Ez. 39:15). The marking of graves at that time could already be tied to the goal of preserving the ritual purity of the *Cohanim* (Jewish priests); placing heavy stones on graves was meant to prevent them from being dug up by wild animals.

The first known burial structures of the Jews date from a significantly later period. In addition to the so-called monolith from Siloam and several other simple sepulchral structures (e.g., Jerusalem tombs located in the area of the so-called tomb in the garden) possibly from the period before the Babylonian exile, the earliest known and preserved burial structures date to the period of the Second Temple: the supposed tomb of Jason to the west of ancient Jerusalem, the so-called tomb of Herod, and in the valley of Kidron the greatest concentration of such tombs, such as the so-called tomb of Absalom, the tomb of Zacharias, and the tomb of the sons of Hezir. Without exception, these were monumental family vaults (similar to the description in 1 Macc. 13:27–29 and Josephus, *Ant.* 13:211, the grave of the Hasmoneans), with an architectural character making them difficult to recognize as the equivalents of typical gravestones. These monumental architectural graves were apparently the subject of critique by Simeon ben Gamliel and the Talmudic dictum that "the just do not need a tombstone" (*y.* Shekalim 2:7, 47a). Though this critique continued within rabbinical circles (and was also made by Maimonides), later halakhic tradition sanctioned the custom of placing tombstones (not ostentatiously large ones) as a sign of honor for the dead.

At least from the second century B.C.E. ossuaries and sarcophagi, common under the influence of Greek culture, were known in Palestine and sometimes decorated with typical later motifs of rosettas, heraldic arrangements of animals, or floral, geometric, or architectural motifs. The largest and most valuable necropolis of this type is located in Beit She'arim, where in the period from 200 C.E. to 351–352 C.E. was found the central place of burial of Jews living in Palestine. Catacomb burials were also practiced in the Diaspora, especially in Italy, at least beginning in the first century C.E. The greatest concentration of Jewish catacombs is found in Rome (Monteverde, Vigna Randanini, Vigna Cimarra, Via Labicana, Via Appia Pignatelli, Villa Torlonia). The epitaph tablets found there were inside closed, isolated burial alcoves and the sporadic sarcophagi were, as a rule, decorated with figurative representations and an epitaph most often in Greek. Of 191 inscriptions found in Monteverde, 130 were written in Greek, twenty-nine in Latin, and five in Hebrew. This proportion is common for all Jewish epitaphs of the ancient period. Of approximately 1,600 known burial inscriptions from that period, 68 percent were in Greek, 18 percent in Hebrew or in one of the Aramaic dialects, 12 percent in Latin, and 2 percent were bilingual. Figurative representation, frequently developed into a rich iconographic program, drew on Greco-Roman mythological motifs, Jewish symbolism, and universal decorative motifs. Among the ostentatious elements related to Greco-Roman mythology are found Fortuna with a horn of plenty, Pegasus, Nike, and winged geniuses (mythological protective semigodly creatures). The most common Jewish symbol is the menorah, but representations of *etrogs* (citrons), *lulavs* (palm leaves), shofars (ram's horns), and cabinets with Torah scrolls also appear. Also popular were images of animals, especially birds, and plant motifs that can be connected to the symbolism of the tree of life.

Middle Ages

The epitaph tablets found in the later ancient catacombs of Italy, in Rome and Venosa, can be seen as a transition between the ancient burial markings and the tombstones created in the early medieval period. Archaeological finds in Venosa suggest the following evolution there: The period of the catacombs was from the third to around the sixth centuries, during which were preserved fifty-four epitaph tablets; twenty-three tombstones found in a cemetery operating from the fourth century to 1241 and similar to those known from later Jewish cemeteries in medieval Europe continued the form of the fifty-four epitaph tablets. A similar evolution can be seen in the case of Jewish tombstones from the Iberian Peninsula.

The basic features characteristic of Jewish medieval tombstones differ fundamentally from later ancient epitaph tablets in the lack of ornamental motifs and the dominance of the Hebrew language, which is virtually the only language of Jewish burial inscription from the earliest known medieval tombstones beginning in the tenth century (epitaphs of the elite include Aramaic barbarisms, though this does not usually go beyond standard religious vocabulary, only sometimes playing a bit with references to the religious literature). The Hebrew alphabet was written in block script, though in its different types (cursive and semicursive script appeared sporadically only in the sixteenth and seventeenth centuries in the writing of final letters or parts of letters). These features are common on tombstones from the areas of Ashkenazi and Sephardic culture and also from the independently developing Middle Eastern traditions, for example, tombstones from Yemen and Afghanistan (though frequently inscriptions in Judeo-Persian also appear there), and even for Karaim tombstones from the Crimean Peninsula.

In Europe, the fundamental feature distinguishing tombstones of the Sephardic and Ashkenazi areas, the placement of the tombstone, appeared probably somewhat later, perhaps in the twelfth century. While in the Ashkenazi tradition the tombstone as a rule is placed vertically, in the earlier Sephardic tradition, the stone may also be horizontal. In the period after the expulsion of Jews from Spain in 1492, horizontal tombstones were becoming the dominant form in Sephardic Jewish cemeteries through other areas of settlement of the Sephardic Jews in the Mediterranean, the Netherlands, England, and elsewhere. Medieval tombstones from Spain were also often larger than Ashkenazi tombstones, and their epitaphs longer and stylistically richer. The oldest dated medieval inscription found on the Iberian Peninsula comes from Calatayud in 919; in addition to this inscription, numerous tombstones or their fragments from Toledo, Barcelona, Gerona, and individual tombstones in many other locations (e.g., in Puento Castro from 1026) have been preserved. Unfortunately, the poor state of their preservation and the lack of continuity after the 1492 expulsion prevents us from seeing their evolution in Christian Europe. Sephardic Jews who settled in the Ottoman Empire continued the form of the horizontal tombstone, as a simple stone or conical pseudo sarcophagus, initially richly decorated, but introducing in the eighteenth century an increasingly rich arabesque, plant, or, less frequently, architectural decoration. Under the influence of Islamic culture, these tombstones were usually devoid of animal or anthropomorphic motifs, even in places where the Sephardic and Ashkenazi traditions overlapped (the Hasköy cemetery in Stambul is an interesting example).

The tombstones of Sephardic Jews in Northern Europe and the Americas in the seventeenth century recall medieval Sephardic tombstones in their horizontal placement. However, given that, culturally, the community was dominated by Marranos returning to Judaism, the art of tombstones and the language of inscription refer directly to the sepulchral art of Christian Europe. An excellent example of this is the best-known cemetery of Sephardic Jews in Ouderkerk in the Netherlands, active since 1614. Until the end of the eighteenth century, almost all tombstones there include an epitaph in Portuguese (sometimes supplemented with a short Hebrew formula), and the rich ornamentation and symbolism refers directly to Christian art. Especially well represented there are full figured anthropomorphic biblical representations (Abraham in Mamre, the sacrifice of Isaac, Rebekah at the well, Jacob's ladder, the death of Rachel, Joseph's dream, David playing the harp, Daniel in the lion's den), usually referring to the name of the dead person, but also Christian sepulchral motifs (hourglasses, crying angels, skulls and crossbones) and motifs of mythological provenance (cherubim, Chronos). An extreme case is the scene of Samuel's dream in the temple in Shiloh (1 Sam. 3: 1–14), depicted by an anthropomorphic figure of God rising from the clouds and speaking to Samuel. After the eighteenth century, this type of representation foreign to the Jewish halakhic tradition disappears, Portuguese is supplanted by Hebrew, and ornamentation becomes somewhat limited. Similar, though not so spectacular, are features from seventeenth- to eighteenth-century graves in Sephardic Jewish cemeteries in Curaçao in the Caribbean (from 1656), Emden (from 1705), and Hamburg-Altona (from 1611). There one can find shocking *danse macabre* images and a portrait of a scholar in a monastic cassock.

More than in the Sephardic tradition, the condition of preservation of tombstones from the Ashkenazi areas allows us to see the continuity in the development of burial forms from the early medieval tombstones from the eleventh century to contemporary times. The oldest tombstones from the Ashkenazi region were preserved in cemeteries in Mainz (1064), Worms (1077), and Speyer (1112), in Worms in situ with the continuity of tombstones preserved from the eleventh to the twentieth centuries. Numerous tombstones appear in other German cities from the thirteenth century on, as well as in France (Paris, 1230–1235), England (after 1259), Poland (1203), Moravia (1269), and Hungary (1278). Tombstones from the eleventh, twelfth, and the beginning of the thirteenth centuries (individual tombstones outside the Rhineland, e.g., from 1130 in Völkermarkt in Carinthia and from 1203 in Wrocław in Silesia) carry numerous archaic features and differ from the type dominating from the thirteenth to fifteenth centuries. These earlier tombstones were small, topped flat or with a full arch, devoid of decoration, with short very formulaic inscriptions in a broad, indented band encircling the stone and engraved with script of a pre-Ashkenazi type (with Middle Eastern influences) with equal thickness of vertical and horizontal lines.

From the thirteenth century on, tombstones in all of Northern Europe from France to Silesia and Hungary became significantly larger, and the length of the inscription increased as well. Indeed, until the end of the Middle Ages, simple architectural motifs remained the single decorative element, primarily simple lines encircling a shallow inscription with figurative motifs appearing sporadically (e.g., the tombstone of Bluma in Speyer from 1365 ornamented with a large decorative flower and the fourteenth-century tombstone from Prague decorated with images of the sun and moon); the introduction of script of the Ashkenazi type, with a significant difference in the thickness of vertical and horizontal lines as well as numerous fractures of the lines, increases the artistic value of the tombstones from this period. Epitaphs from the same period contain the basic elements of the formulas that characterized later inscriptions, although individual elements of the epitaph (the opening formula, closing formula, and information block) had at this point not yet been entirely differentiated. The inscription is always engraved.

Expulsions of Jews from England (1290), France (1395), and the majority of Germany meant that the Ashkenazi type of medieval tombstone continued in only a few German cities (the most important cemeteries from this period are in Frankfurt am Main and Worms) and, above all, in the Czech lands, in Moravia, and in Poland. From the period before 1500, these include more than twenty examples in Bohemia (Prague, from 1439; Cheb [Eger], 1242–1385; also, though the documentation there is lacking), sixty-one in Moravia (Olomouc, 1269–1338/39; Znojmo, 1306–1430; Brno, 1349–1443), twenty-nine in Silesia (Wrocław, 1203–1345; Świdnica 1289–1383; Brzeg 1348; Nysa 1350), and thirty in Hungary (Buda, 1278–1431, 1492?; Trnava, 1340–1396; Skalica, 1398; Sopron, 1411/12). Only in Prague and Kolín, however, have the tombstones survived in situ, and the use of the cemeteries continued without interruption into the early modern era. In Germany, numerous medieval tombstones have been recorded in the Jewish cemeteries of Worms, Frankfurt am Main, Spandau, Vienna, Rothenburg ob der Tauber, Regensburg, and Ulm, while individual tombstones have been preserved in many other communities. In Poland, aside from Silesia, which Poland lost to Bohemia in the mid-fourteenth century, the oldest surviving Jewish tombstones date from the mid-sixteenth century, but the medieval type of tombstone predominated in all of Eastern Europe until the second half of the sixteenth century, and in more remote localities until the beginning of the seventeenth. The most interesting and largest groups of gravestones of this type, dating from the second half of the sixteenth and the beginning of the seventeenth centuries, are preserved in Busk near Lwów (from 1520), Lublin (1541), Szczebrzeszyn (1545), Lesko (1548), and Buczacz (1587).

Modern Times

A new type of gravestone appeared in the mid-sixteenth century in cemeteries of the large Jewish communities of Central and Eastern Europe, for example, Kraków (where the oldest-known tombstone dates from about 1549), Przemyśl (1574), Frankfurt, and, above all, Prague, where the sixteenth century saw the development of a school of sepulchral stonemasonry of high artistic value and very particular local traits. For instance, Prague's tombstones used figurative anthropomorphic motifs, family symbols, and the Star of David, rarely encountered elsewhere. Sixteenth-century tombstones from Prague, as is the case with those found in large Jewish communities in Germany and Poland or even in provincial centers such as Chęciny or Pińczów that had a highly developed artistic culture, embodied a Renaissance (and later Baroque) aesthetic, incorporating classical architectural motifs to enrich the composition of the face of the tombstone. Locally, for example, in Prague and Kraków, tombstones in the shape of pseudo sarcophagi became very widespread.

By the mid-seventeenth century, this type of tombstone spread throughout the region, at the same time undergoing significant simplification and a rapid evolution toward folk art forms. The folk version of this type of gravestone, sometimes referred to as Jewish Baroque, became the best-known type among East European Jewish communities; it predominated until the mid-nineteenth century and, in many localities in Ukraine, eastern Poland, and Belorussia, as late as the Holocaust. The inscription field continued to be the most prominent element in a tombstone of this style, but the composition of the front of the stela changed under the influence of contemporary architectural models, as seen, for instance, in the motif of the arcade, the aedicula (decorative niche), and, beginning in the early seventeenth century, a notable tendency toward dividing the front of the stela into clearly differentiated parts: a pediment, a framed inscription field, and a base. Initially, the pediment contained the opening formula of the inscription (or at least part of it), but beginning in the late seventeenth century, it was more frequently filled with ornamental and symbolic images; at the same time, the pediment itself grew larger. An extreme example of this tendency can be seen in the gravestones of eighteenth- and early nineteenth-century southeastern Poland, Ukraine, and Moldavia, where the pediment, richly ornamented and filled with symbolic motifs, constituted almost half the tombstone, and the main principle of its composition seems to have been horror vacui.

The repertoire of motifs employed to decorate tombstones included ornamental architectural elements as well as about 100 symbolic, figurative motifs, often tied together in stylized, complex, and very specialized compositions. Examples of these specialized hieratic schemes include crowns flanked by heraldic lions or deer, the pitcher and bowl of Levite tombstones, professional symbols (such as the caduceus often seen on physicians' graves), and family symbols (e.g., a goose seen on the tombstones of the Gans family in Prague). The inscription field was often filled with ornamented epitaphs done in relief script, with much variation in the height and style of the letters, and flanked by various sorts of ornamental fringe, pilaster strips, pilasters, or demicolumns. The epitaph formula was also elaborated, with laudatory and elegaic sections enriched by poetic elements, frequently with rhyming verse (initially monorhymes, then geminate, cruciform, and encircling in form), acrostics, or chronograms. Stylistically, folk literature with its bead-string structure predominated as a model, in the elite version suggestive of biblical figures of speech and employing citations from and allusions to the Bible. More commonly, however, the epitaphs were quite simple, often with spelling and grammar mistakes, with very simple forms and a limited repertoire of formulas. The largest and most remarkable collections of tombstones of this sort are preserved in Satanów, Międzyboż, Sienawa, and Lesko. Traditional tombstones were often covered

Tombstone of Zeev ben Abraham Landau (1813–1899), from Warsaw. *(Courtesy of Marcin Wodzinski)*

with paintings, scarcely preserved to this day (one might conclude that this feature was common for all medieval and early modern Jewish tombstones, but this is not certain). The *ohel*, that is, simple architectural constructions protecting the graves of famous scholars, rabbis, and *tzaddikim*, was also a characteristic sepulchral form in the cemeteries of Eastern Europe; they appeared at the end of the eighteenth and beginning of the nineteenth centuries and quickly became important pilgrimage centers, especially in the Hasidic movement.

The development of this style of tombstones in eastern Poland, Ukraine, Moldavia, and Belorussia in the eighteenth century resulted in a growing divergence between the eastern and western parts of Europe. In German lands, Bohemia, western Poland, and the reemerging Jewish settlements in France, tombstones continued to resemble and imitate Christian sepulchral art, and in some areas (including small provincial towns such as Lesko, Krotoszyn, and Dobruška) the influence of high-art styles such as Baroque, rococo, and, later, classicism, was notable. In the nineteenth and twentieth centuries, however, Eastern and Western traditions again began to resemble each other, as Jewish burial art in all areas of Europe evolved quickly in the direction of traditional Christian art. In Western regions, alongside the German language (initially written in Hebrew letters), obelisks, columns, full relief sculpture, and greater architectural foundations became a popular, broadly applied historical style; traditional Jewish symbolism almost disappeared. There also appeared symbolic tombstones and collective graves (e.g., war graves), and even monuments placed on burial urns. In the nineteenth century, a style of more traditional East European sepulchral art also evolved. Beginning in the nineteenth century, symbolic elements of non-Jewish origin (e.g., hourglasses, butterflies, pommels, or poppies) became increasingly common. Inscriptions grew increasingly formulaic, stiff, and segmented. The number of available symbolic motifs gradually decreased. At the same time, however, there was a loosening of hieratic symbolic compositions, as a result of which symbols were composed more freely and new compositions of a narrative character began to appear.

Decline

Toward the end of the nineteenth century, just as the influence of Christian sepulchral art intensified, there followed the mass production of tombstones and further standardization. One can safely assume that the most common material for tombstones, also before the nineteenth century, was wood. Grave markers were simple planks with painted inscriptions or images of full-size gravestones carved into the wood. Given the material's lack of permanence, very few of these have survived (a few are in Belarus; others are preserved in museums in, e.g., Bucharest and Helsinki), and, to be sure, their lives were quite short. Until the end of the eighteenth century, only elite members of society were able to afford stone tombstones, while the more popular burial signs were made of wood. The former, because of their durability, have been preserved in relatively large numbers; the latter, because of their impermanence, were very quickly ruined. Material preserved from medieval and early modern cemeteries, then, is not representative of all Jewish burial art; rather, this material represents only the graves of the wealthiest. In the later nineteenth century, alongside the universalization of the mechanical production of stone, there appeared mass engraved, inexpensive, and at the same time relatively durable stone tombstones; similarly, *matzevot* (tombstones) of cast iron were mass produced, though only locally. In areas where stone suitable for production was difficult to find, inscriptions were engraved in small boulders (glacial erratic) or made by breaking off stone from rocks of a layered structure. The proliferation of prefabricated tombstones reached the most traditional centers of Europe in the nineteenth and twentieth centuries and caused an evident regression in Jewish sepulchral art and the further disappearance of traditional iconography. Ornamental plane lettering was replaced by typographic styles, while relief inscriptions gave way to sunken lettering. This type of a tombstone was also reproduced in the twentieth century in Palestine and even now dominates among the Orthodox. There was no revival of the earlier style of sepulchral art after the Holocaust.

In the twenty-first century, Jewish tombstones in Europe are made according to generic stone-working models, with Jewish symbolism principally restricted to a Star of David, while Hebrew is generally used only for the closing formula of the epitaph.

Marcin Wodziński

See also: Cemetery; Death.

Bibliography

Brocke, Michael, and Christiane E. Müller. *Haus des Lebens: Jüdische Friedhöfe in Deutschland.* Leipzig: Reclam, 2001.

Castro, David Henriques. *Keur van grafstenen op de Portugees-Isräelietische begraafplaats te Ouderkerk aan de Amstel, met beschrijving en biografische aantekeningen* (Selected Gravestones from the Dutch Portuguese Jewish Cemetery at Ouderkerk aan de Amstel, with Descriptions and Biographical Notes). Ouderkerk aan de Amstel: Foundation for the Preservation and Maintenance of Historic Jewish Cemeteries in the Netherlands, 1999.

Goodenough, Erwin. *Jewish Symbols in the Greco-Roman Period.* 13 vols. New York: Pantheon Books, 1953–1968.

Horst, Pieter Willem van der. *Ancient Jewish Epitaphs: An Introductory Survey of a Millennium of Jewish Funerary Epigraphy (300 B.C.E.–700 C.E.).* Kampen: Kok Pharos, 1991.

Krajewska, Monika. *A Tribe of Stones: Jewish Cemeteries in Poland.* Warsaw: Polish Scientific, 1993.

Künzl, Hennelore. *Jüdische Grabkunst von der Antike bis heute.* Darmstadt: Wissenschaftliche Buchgesellschaft, 1999.

Millás, José Maria, and Francisco Cantera. *Las inscripciones hebraicas de España.* Madrid: Consejo Superior de Investigaciones Científicas, 1956.

Muneles, Otto, and Milada Vilimková. Starý židovský hřbitov *v Praze* (Old Jewish cemetery in Prague). Prague: Státni pedogogické nakl, 1955.

Scheiber, Alexander. *Jewish Inscriptions in Hungary, From the 3rd Century to 1686.* Budapest: Akademiai Kiado, 1983.

Wiesemann, Falk. *Sepulcra judaica: Bibliographie zu jüdischen Friedhöfen und zu Sterben, Begräbnis und Trauer bei den Juden von der Zeit des Hellenismus bis zur Gegenwart.* Essen: Klartext, 2005.

Torah Ark

The Torah ark, called *aron* or *aron kodesh* (Holy Ark) in Ashkenazi communities and *hekhal* in Italian, Middle Eastern, and Sephardic communities, is the receptacle in which the Torah scroll and its accessories are kept. Therefore, it is one of the two focuses of the sacred service in the synagogue, the other being the *bimah* (platform) or (in Italy, the Sephardic Diaspora, and Middle Eastern communities) the *tevah.* The ark is always located on the wall facing the direction of prayer; in most communities it is covered by a curtain.

Early Representations

The earliest representations of receptacles in which Torah scrolls are kept appear in the burial art of the fourth century C.E. in the Land of Israel and in Rome (drawings and engravings found in Beit She'arim and in the catacombs of Rome). These representations, along with remains of niches (Dura-Europos, Susiya) or installations built into ancient synagogues, indicate that when the practice of keeping the Torah scrolls in a permanent place developed in antiquity, two types of ark took shape in the Land of Israel, Babylonia, and the territories of the Roman Empire: a freestanding wooden cabinet and a niche embedded in the synagogue wall, or in an adjacent room, in the wall facing the direction of prayer.

Arks of this type were used in the Middle Ages throughout the Diaspora. Over time, the niche, sometimes without doors, became the accepted form of the ark in Muslim countries. In these communities, the ark ultimately became a niche with wooden doors. Open niches were used in Iran and Bukhara (in present-day Uzbekistan) until the beginning of the twentieth century; in Afghanistan, the ark was a room with niches in the walls for Torah scrolls. In a few Middle Eastern communities, as well as North Africa, synagogues sometimes had more than one ark, sometimes in the form of an ark with multiple doors, spanning the entire width of the synagogue. In European synagogues, two main forms may be distinguished from the Middle Ages on: a niche with wooden doors, which evolved into a wooden cabinet with its back embedded in the niche and its front protruding from the wall; and a freestanding wooden cabinet standing against the wall. In many cases, the freestanding arks were simply ordinary storage cabinets, used as they were without change or converted for use as Torah arks by the addition of a Hebrew text. In most communities, however, Torah arks were designed for that purpose from the outset and are therefore characterized by well-defined Jewish content.

That content derives primarily from the perception of the synagogue as a "lesser sanctuary" (Ezek. 11:16), in consequence of which the Torah ark is seen as a representation of the Ark of the Covenant. Accordingly, in Central and Eastern Europe, the upper part of the ark represents the *kapporet,* the golden cover of the Ark of the Covenant (Exod. 25:17, 21). It hence became customary to place on the ark reliefs, or even statuettes, of the two cherubim that, in the Tabernacle, were mounted on the Ark of the Covenant (Exod. 26:31–35). In keeping with traditional interpretation, these cherubim were made in the shape of a pair of lions, eagles, or an imaginary combination of these creatures—griffins. In time, a short curtain or valance, with depictions of the cherubim, was added to the upper part of the ark. The identification of the ark with the Ark of the Covenant was the source of inspiration for depiction of the Tabernacle utensils on the doors of the ark, mainly on their inner sides. This design is typical of Italian synagogues, as well as those in Central and Eastern Europe. When the doors of these arks are opened, one sees the seven-branched candelabrum on the right-hand door, that is, to the south, in accordance with its position in the Temple; similarly, the Showbread Table is seen on the left-hand door, that is, to the north (Exod. 26:35). The Torah scroll kept in the ark was also a source of inspiration for two of the most common symbols of the Torah: the Torah crown, which appeared simultaneously on Italian and Polish arks in the mid-sixteenth century, and the Tablets of the Law, first found on the ark of the Portuguese Synagogue in Amsterdam (1675).

The perception of the synagogue as a "lesser sanctuary" is also the root of the comparison of the ark with the gate of heaven. This metaphor is frequently used in the liturgy, and it explains the custom of opening the doors of the ark for especially important prayers. The inscription "Our Father, our King, open the gates of heaven to our prayers," often seen on the doors, is an obvious expression of this idea. The architectural depiction of the ark as a gate—a physical expression of the metaphor—was common in many European communities and later also outside Europe.

A unique phenomenon in Eastern Europe in the eighteenth century was the construction of tall arks in two or three tiers, which offered considerable scope for the introduction of new, complex motifs against a background of decorative floral and faunal patterns. These arks, especially those carved in wood and painted in a profusion of colors, were a major outlet for Jewish folk art. They influenced the design of ceremonial objects in the synagogue in general, in particular that of the *shiviti* plaques mounted on the cantor's desk; their influence is also manifest in the popular genre of *mizraḥ* papercuts sometimes hung on the eastern wall of the home.

In the nineteenth century, when the Moorish style of synagogue architecture came to the fore in Europe and the United States, arks in the form of large niches appeared, often with sliding doors and stiff curtains. In the twentieth century, in particular, after World War II and the establishment of the State of Israel, new motifs were incorporated in the design of Torah arks, many of which, especially in wealthy communities, have been designed by famous artists.

Torah Ark Curtain (*Parokhet*)

The Torah ark curtain is a screen hanging over the Torah ark that serves as a partition between the ark and the prayer hall. The Hebrew word "*parokhet*" is based on its identification with the curtain, which separated the holy section of the Tabernacle and the Temple from the Holy of Holies (Exod. 26:31–35; 40:21). This identification is based on the concept of the synagogue as a "lesser sanctuary" (Ezek. 11:16). According to the available literary and visual sources, the curtain became a fixture in Ashkenazi and Italian synagogues during the Middle Ages. Scholars have no information about the existence of Torah ark curtains in communities outside Europe until the twentieth century. According to the literary and visual material from Spain, it seems that the outer curtain was not customary in Spanish communities. However, they did apparently use an inner curtain, as evidenced by the presence of an inner curtain in all Sephardic diasporic communities. In Italy, all arks have inner curtains, whereas an outer curtain is present only in some communities—perhaps out of reluctance to hide the ornate doors. Because the curtain serves as a cover for the ark, its position within the hierarchy of ceremonial objects is that of a "secondary" ceremonial object. Only when the need arises to use it as a covering for the *bimah,*

"Making a request in front of the open Torah Ark." From the Sarajevo Haggadah, fol. 34r. Spain, ca. 1350. *(National Museum of Bosnia and Herzegovina, Sarajevo)*

that is, as the cloth on which the Torah itself is rested, does it become a primary ceremonial object.

Like other ceremonial objects in the synagogue, the Torah ark curtain is usually donated by individual members of the congregation, to commemorate life-cycle events, such as the birth of a son or a marriage, or as a memorial to a deceased family member. This has engendered the custom of embroidering the name of the donor and the occasion of the donation directly on the curtain or on an attached piece of cloth. In the twentieth century, dedicatory plaques of beaten silver appeared in Iraq.

The traditional design of the Torah ark curtain varies from community to community. In most, the curtain was made of a choice fabric according to the local cultural conception. In most communities, a luxurious fabric, which had previously been in the family's possession, was used, and a common practice was specifically to use a costly piece of woman's clothing. The typical curtain in Iraq was made from the *izar,* a woman's upper veil that she wears when leaving the house. This veil, a rectangular piece of brocade, was donated by women in memory of their husbands or, upon their death, by relatives in their memory. It was the embroidered dedicatory inscription that transformed the piece of clothing into a ceremonial object. There was a similar custom among the Cochinese Jews in India, who covered the coffin of a deceased man with a wraparound skirt, which was made of especially costly material. After the funeral, the skirt was used to make a Torah ark curtain dedicated to the memory of the deceased person. Torah ark curtains in the communities of Iran and Afghanistan were principally made of *suzani* embroidered sheets, and in Iran a tradition also developed of using paisley-printed cotton material with Hebrew inscriptions.

Yemeni Torah ark curtains were designed, as were covers for the *tevah* and for Torah scroll cases, in the form of a large sheet in the center surrounded by a broad patchwork frame with a chessboard pattern. In the Sephardic communities of the Ottoman Empire, it became customary to make Torah ark curtains from silk velvet with gold embroidery or from women's dresses, also of embroidered velvet with silk embroidery. In such cases, the different parts of the dress were ripped and resewn to create a rectangle.

It appears that neither in the Middle Eastern communities nor in the Sephardic Diaspora did this custom arouse opposition on the part of the rabbis. European rabbis, however, differed regarding the fashioning of Torah ark curtains from used material, especially from clothing in general and from women's clothing in particular. The circumstances under which pieces of clothing were used generally involved vows taken by women in times of stress or used elegant clothing purchased for reuse of the cloth. Rabbinical objections to the practice abound in the responsa literature, where we find repeated questions on this subject. Those objecting to the reuse of fabrics relied on the law that the Temple utensils must be made of new material, which was not previously used (*b. Menachot* 22a). The more permissive rabbis, who were willing to take popular feeling into consideration, cited midrashic commentaries on the episode of the copper mirrors donated by the women of Israel for the Tabernacle (*Midr. Tanḥuma Pequdei* 9). According to this interpretation, it is permitted to use a piece of clothing, provided that its form is changed. The many examples of secondary use of clothing, both in rabbinical literature and in actual Torah ark curtains, indicate the popularity of this practice in Europe beginning in the Middle Ages.

Alongside curtains of costly materials, European communities began to use embroidered Torah ark curtains. In Italy, a center of the art of embroidery, many communities traditionally embroidered curtains using the Florentine stitch technique, which is particularly conducive to the execution of detailed and precise patterns. Women used it to embroider a variety of Jewish motifs, including biblical themes, such as the Giving of the Torah, and scenes from festivals and life-cycle events.

An entirely different embroidery tradition developed in the communities of Central and Western Europe, where there were professional embroiderers who specialized in gold embroidery on a silk velvet background. The most outstanding motif of the eighteenth-century Torah ark curtain in these communities is that of a pair of columns, topped by a pair of lions flanking a Torah crown. Between the two columns is an ornate sewn or embroidered rectangular sheet. This motif dates back to the earlier architectonic motif of an actual gate, above which is the verse that identifies it as the gateway to heaven: "This is the gateway to the Lord—the righteous shall enter through it" (Ps. 118:20). Underlying the depiction of this motif on Torah ark curtains is the identification of the Torah ark with the "gateway to heaven." Originally found in Italy, the motif spread eastward to Turkey, northward to Bohemia and Moravia, and westward to Germany.

Turkish Jews carefully preserved the architectonic form of the gateway and the verse woven or embroidered above it. The presence of the verse was essential, because Jews not infrequently converted Muslim prayer rugs, which typically featured the shape of a gate, into Torah ark curtains. It was the addition of the biblical verse that achieved the conversion. In all other communities, however, the architectonic form of the gateway was corrupted by the addition of a dedicatory inscription in place of the gate's arch or gable. After the original motif had been corrupted, a pair of lions was added above the columns on each side of the Torah crown, reminiscent of the cherubim mounted on the Ark of the Covenant. The components of this motif—columns, lions, and Torah crown—may still be found today on Torah ark curtains embroidered in Israel. A new generation of artisans has emerged in the modern era, who have transformed the traditional Torah ark curtain by the use of new techniques and motifs.

Torah Ark Valance (*Kapporet*)

The *kapporet* is a short curtain hung on the Torah ark, above the *parokhet*. This ceremonial object, which first appeared in Eastern Europe at the end of the seventeenth century, evolved in connection with the identification of the upper part of the Torah ark in the synagogue with the *kapporet* on the Ark of the Covenant in the Tabernacle (Exod. 25:21). This identification was one manifestation of the concept of the synagogue as a "lesser sanctuary" (Ezek. 11:16). On that basis, the Torah ark in the synagogue is identified with the Ark of the Covenant, and its upper part with the *kapporet,* the cover of the Ark of the Covenant. Accordingly, it was customary in Eastern Europe to inscribe the verse "He made a cover of pure gold" (Exod. 37:6) on the upper part of the ark. The identification then came to be applied to the short curtain hung over the upper part of the ark to conceal the rod on which the main curtain was mounted. Indeed, we find the verse "Place the cover [*kapporet*] upon the Ark of the Covenant" (Exod. 26:34) embroidered on early Torah ark valances. As part of the synagogue furnishings, the valance was most likely introduced under the influence of seventeenth-century interior decoration in Europe, where such valances were integral parts of curtains in general. Further influence of the cultural environment is evident in the scalloped lower edge of the valance.

The identification of the valance hung on the Torah ark with the gold cover on the Ark of the Covenant is also evident in the motifs used in its decoration. Thus, most early valances employ the motif of a pair of cherubim flanking a Torah crown, as per the biblical description of two golden cherubs with outspread wings mounted on the ends of the cover (Exod. 37:7–9). The depiction of the cherubim as a pair of eagles, lions, or griffins is based on the traditional interpretation of the creatures figuring in Ezekiel's Vision of the Chariot (Ezek. 1:5; 10:14–15). Another characteristic motif of the valance is the Tabernacle utensils embroidered on the scalloped edges. The Ark of the Covenant is embroidered on the central scallop below the Torah crown; the Showbread Table and the menorah are generally embroidered on matching scallops on either side of the central one, as are the golden altar and sacrificial altar on another pair of matching scallops. Eventually, the two motifs—the cherubim and the Tabernacle utensils—developed and changed, the most significant change being the appearance of the motif of three crowns (*Pirqe Avot* 4:13) in the upper part of the Torah ark valance.

The Torah ark valance spread from Eastern Europe to Central Europe and Western Europe (but not to the Italian communities), and by the beginning of the eighteenth century it had already become a regular iconographic feature. In most instances, valances were donated separately from the Torah ark curtain, most of them being embroidered by professionals. During the eighteenth century, a workshop in Prague specialized in the embroidery of Torah ark valances, and thus many of the valances produced in that city during this period show remarkable similarities. A unique feature of the Prague valances is the addition of a pair of freestanding wings attached to the upper part of the Torah ark on either side of the valance. These wings were fashioned from rigid materials and covered with an embroidered cloth. In southern Germany, however, Jewish embroiderers worked separately; German valances are therefore less similar to one another, displaying a richer vocabulary of iconographic motifs.

In Eastern Europe, where Torah arks typically show greater iconographic variety, the two motifs on the valance disappeared in the course of the eighteenth century, most of the valances known from this area being made of patterned fabrics without embroidered motifs or inscriptions. In contrast, in Central and Western Europe, velvet valances with motifs and dedicatory inscriptions in rich gold embroidery continued to be fashioned until the twentieth century. The existence of valances in distant communities at the beginning of the twentieth century, and even into the twenty-first, is evidence of the influence of the European valances.

Bracha Yaniv

See also: Torah Ceremonial Objects; Torah Ornaments.

Bibliography

Cassuto, David. "A Venetion *Parokhet* and Its Design Origins." *Jewish Art* 14 (1988): 35–43.

Gutmann, Joseph. "An Eighteen-Century Prague Jewish Workshop of Kapporot." *Visible Religion* 6 (1988): 180–190.

Landsberger, Franz. "Old-Time Torah Curtains." In *Beauty in Holiness: Studies in Jewish Customs and Ceremonial Art,* ed. J. Gutmann, pp. 125–163. New York: Ktav, 1970.

Mann, Vivian B. "Jewish-Muslim Acculturation in the Ottoman Empire: The Evidence of Ceremonial Art." In *The Jews of the Ottoman Empire,* ed. A. Levy. Princeton, NJ: Darwin, 1994.

———. "The Recovery of a Known Work." *Jewish Art* 12–13 (1986/87): 269–278.

Narkiss, Bezalel. "The Heikhal, Bimah, and Teivah in Sephardi Synagogues." *Jewish Art* 18 (1992): 30–47.

Piechotka, Maria, and Kazimierz Piechotka. "Aron ha-kodesz w bóżnicach polskich: Ewolucja między XVI i początkiem XIX wieku" (The Holy Ark in Polish Synagoues: Evolution Between the Sixteenth Century and the Begining the Nineteenth Century). In *The Jews in Poland,* vol. 1, ed. A. Pałuch, pp. 475–481. Kraków: Jagiellonian University, 1992.

Putík, Alexander. "Before the Curtain, Behind the Curtain: Parokhot of Prague Synagogues and Their Donors, 1648–1744." In *Textiles from Bohemian and Moravian Synagogues from the Collections of the Jewish Museum in Prague,* ed. L. Kybalová, E. Kosáková, and A. Putík, pp. 73–91. Prague: Zidovske Muzeum Praha, 2003.

Veselská, Dana. "Special Features of Moravian Synagogue Textiles: Material, Influences, Ornamentation and Symbols." In *Textiles from Bohemian and Moravian Synagogues from the Collections of the Jewish Museum in Prague,* ed. L. Kybalová, E. Kosáková, and A. Putík, pp. 31–45. Prague: Zidovske Muzeum Praha, 2003.

Veselská, Dana, and Michaela Scheibová. "The Kapporet as a Synagogue Item: Its Origin and Development." In *Textiles from Bohemian and Moravian Synagogues from the Collections of the Jewish Museum in Prague,* ed. L. Kybalová, E. Kosáková, and A. Putík, pp. 47–60. Prague: Zidovske Muzeum Praha, 2003.

Weber, Annette. "Ark and Curtain: Monuments for a Jewish Nation in Exile." *Jewish Art: The Real and Ideal Jerusalem in Jewish, Christian and Islamic Art* 23–24 (1997–98): 89–99.

Wischnitzer, Rachel. "Ark." In *Encyclopaeidia Judaica,* vol. 3, pp. 450–458. Jerusalem: Keter, 1973.

Yaniv, Bracha. "The Cherubim on Torah Ark Valances." *Assaph* 4 (1999): 155–170.

———. *Ma'ase Rokem: Textile Ceremonial Objects in the Ashkenazi, Sephardic and Italian Synagogue.* Jerusalem: Ben-Zvi Institute, 2009 (in Hebrew).

———. "The Origin of 'The Two-Column Motif' in European Parokhot." *Jewish Art* 15 (1989): 26–43.

———. "The Three Crowns Motif in Eastern European Torah Arks." *Knishta* 2 (2003): 67–88 (in Hebrew).

TORAH CEREMONIAL OBJECTS

The sacred and ceremonial objects in the synagogue revolve around the Torah scroll: the case and the mantle in which it is kept; the cloth cover (*mitpaḥat*); the binder and wrapper that hold it closed when not in use; the Torah crown and finials for decoration. The breastplate designates the scroll to be used for the Torah reading, and the pointer is used during the reading to keep the place. In addition, there is a Torah ark in which ceremonial objects are kept. The curtain hides the ark and the valance is hung above it. These objects differ from one place to another and not every object exists in every community.

The earliest of these artifacts are the objects used to store or wrap the Torah: the cloth cover and the case. These two items are mentioned in the list of sacred objects in the Babylonian Talmud (*Megillah* 26b) and are still used today. Over the course of the centuries, they have assumed a variety of forms, according to the needs and customs of the community, as well as the material culture of the host society. The other objects evolved in the Middle Ages, and their design differs from one community to another, in light of the differing artistic traditions of the localities where they were made.

There is a hierarchical relationship among ceremonial objects, depending on their physical proximity to the Torah. For instance, the mantle, which actually touches the parchment, is considered holier than the curtain hung on the ark. The latter is defined as a secondary object, since it serves the ark and not the Torah scroll. Popular tradition attributes to ceremonial objects the capacity to heal, protect, or confer blessing, through direct or indirect contact with the object. This belief resulted in the development of certain customs, such as the European custom of wrapping a Torah binder around a woman's body to prevent miscarriage, or the custom of Jews in Afghanistan, who drink water in which a Torah finial is dipped as a guarantee of a successful marriage.

Torah *Mitpaḥat* and Case

The length of cloth known in Hebrew as the *mitpaḥat* is the earliest known item used in storage of the Torah scroll. The *mitpaḥat* (pl. *mitpaḥot*), also known as

Torah case. Jerusalem, 1914. *(Gross Family Collection, Tel Aviv)*

mappah, is mentioned in the Mishnah and in the Tosefta and later in the Jerusalem and Babylonian Talmuds (*m. Kelim* 28:4, *Megillah* 4:1, *Kil'ayim* 9:3; *t. y. Berakhot* 6:4; *b. Megillah* 26b, etc.). These sources state that in ancient times woolen or linen *mitpaḥot* were used, sometimes with colorful stripes woven in; some were provided with bells. Greek and Latin literature describes ancient Middle Eastern scrolls of importance regularly wrapped in cloth. In time, the Jewish communities of the East Mediterranean Basin, as well as Eastern communities, began to keep their Torah scrolls in special cases. Such cases were common in the classical world; they are referred to as *theca* in Greek or *capsa* in Latin. Archaeological finds from all parts of the Roman Empire attest to the shape of the case: a cylindrical or prism-shaped container used to carry various objects, including scrolls. Used in the Jewish world to carry Torah scrolls, such cases were eventually used as the main permanent receptacle for Torah scrolls in the communities of the East and the East Mediterranean Basin. In European communities, several textile objects ultimately evolved from the *mitpaḥat* in which the Torah scroll was originally kept.

The case is a small wooden cabinet, either cylindrical or prism-shaped with eight, ten, or twelve faces, in two parts, which open lengthwise. It may be adorned with colorful drawings or covered with leather, a rich fabric, or beaten silver plates. In some communities, such as in Yemen, Tunisia, and Libya, the case is usually wrapped in a rich fabric. There are three main types of case: the flat-topped case used in Yemen, Cochin (India), eastern Iran, and Afghanistan; the case with a circular or onion-shaped crown used in the Babylonian communities, that is, Iraq and western Iran; and the case with a coronet used in Libya, Tunisia, and the Greek Romaniote communities.

The Torah cases generally have inscriptions around the edges, on the front or inside. In Eastern cases, in which the crown is divided into two, the inner sides serve as dedicatory plaques. In the Mediterranean Basin, a silver inscription plaque is attached to the front of the case. Two types of inscription are characteristic: biblical verses extolling the Torah, mainly from the books of Proverbs and Psalms, and personal information about the donor. The personal information is generally concerned with commemorating a deceased relative, but one also finds prayers for healing or for the birth of a son or inscriptions giving thanks for salvation from danger. Inscriptions in eastern Iran frequently pronounce a curse on whoever would harm the Torah scroll.

Because historians' knowledge of Torah cases and *mitpaḥot* in premodern times is meager, the process of the evolution from a mere receptacle for carrying the Torah into a sacred artifact can only be conjectured. It can be assumed that in the first stage, when the case was used only for storage, the scroll was wrapped in a *mitpaḥat* when placed in the case, as is still done in the Yemenite community. However, it was difficult to handle the Torah scroll wrapped in the *mitpaḥat* in its case, and most communities therefore removed it from the case. Only in Yemen did the Jews continue to wrap the Torah in two or three *mitpaḥot,* and until they immigrated to Israel they used colorful, cotton prints with a geometric pattern of Indian manufacture. Among the Yemenite Jews, the *mitpaḥat* has an important function during the Torah reading: It is used to cover the text adjacent to the text being read, thus preventing its unnecessary exposure. In other communities, the *mitpaḥat* is used only to cover the scroll during pauses in the reading, when it is placed on the case and not on the Torah scroll itself. In Eastern communities, the *mitpaḥat* is usually tied to the poles of the finials when not in use; in Tunisia and Libya, it is placed on the top of the case, in the Torah ark, or hung on the platform (*bimah* or, in Italy, among the Sephardim, and in Middle Eastern communities, *tevah*). The *mitpaḥat* became a very popular dedicatory item, as it enabled even congregants who could not afford to donate a whole Torah scroll to contribute an inexpensive ceremonial object to the synagogue.

The Torah case is customarily used in all Middle Eastern and eastern Mediterranean communities. The westernmost communities using Torah cases were those of Tunisia, while the northernmost recorded use in the Mediterranean Basin was in the Romaniote communities of Asia Minor. Cases were still being used in Greece and the Levantine Synagogue in Venice as late as the twentieth century. In Israel in the twentieth century, Torah cases were introduced in Sephardic synagogues, which originally kept their Torah scrolls in the same way as other European communities, that is, in textile wrappers, a practice that continues to the present.

Torah mantle. Prague, 1879. *(Réunion des Musées Nationaux/Art Resource, NY)*

Torah Wrapper, Binder, and Mantle

The Torah wrapper and binder are two textile objects developed from the *mitpaḥat* in European communities. The wrapper (*yeriah*), found only in Italy and in communities of the Sephardic Diaspora, is of a height equal to that of the parchment sheets from which the Torah scroll is made and rolled up together with the scroll. Sephardic communities in Israel have not consistently preserved the use of these wrappers, which are gradually disappearing. The binder, wound around the Torah scroll in Ashkenazi communities, in Italy, and in the Sephardic Diaspora, is a long narrow strip of cloth with which the Torah is bound, either on top of the wrapper or directly on the parchment. Its purpose is to keep the scroll securely bound when not in use. Both wrapper and binder are referred to in rabbinic literature as *mappah* (the same term used occasionally in the Talmud for the *mitpaḥat*).

There are also various terms for the binder in the local vernacular. In Italy and in the Sephardic communities, for example, the term used is *fascia;* it is made of a costly material or of linen embroidered in silk thread. In the sixteenth century, it became customary in northern Italy to embroider binders with biblical verses or personal dedicatory inscriptions. Such binders, embroidered by girls and young women, were often dedicated to life-cycle events. The decorative patterns in these binders resemble those of contemporary Venetian embroidery, but the variety of inscriptions is original, personal, and rich in content and design. In Germany, it became customary in the second half of the sixteenth century to prepare a binder for the

Torah scroll on the occasion of the birth of a son. This binder was fashioned from a piece of square linen cloth, which was placed near the infant during the circumcision ceremony. After the circumcision, the cloth was cut into four narrow strips, which were sewn together to form a long strip on which the infant's name, his father's name, and his date of birth were embroidered or written, as well as the blessing recited during the ceremony: "May he enter into the Torah, the marriage canopy, and into good deeds." Binders from the sixteenth century feature only the inscription, with the letters themselves the only means of ornamentation. In the seventeenth century, however, binders could also have drawings illustrating the three elements of "Torah, the marriage canopy, and good deeds." These embroidered or painted depictions, executed by members of the infant's family, exhibit a great variety of decorative patterns, representations of everyday life, and visual imagery. The binder was donated to the synagogue on the occasion of the child's first visit to the synagogue and wound around the Torah scroll for the first time in a special ceremony. This custom spread to Northern and Central Europe as German Jews emigrated there; it is still in practice today, mainly in Alsace and in communities of German origin in Israel and the United States.

The Torah mantle is the clothing of the Torah scroll. In Sephardic communities, Italy, and Germany, and in halakhic literature, it was occasionally known as *beged* (garment) or *mappah,* but later the term *me'il* became standard in most communities. The earliest attestation to the shape of the mantle appears in the fourteenth-century Sarajevo Haggadah, created in Spain. The mantles shown there are made of a costly material, probably not embroidered. This tradition of using a costly, unembroidered material is still common in Sephardic communities, with the exception of Morocco and Algeria, where Torah mantles are made of velvet with elaborately embroidered patterns and dedicatory inscriptions. Common motifs on these mantles are the Tree of Life (in Morocco) and a gate (in Algeria). The Torah mantle in Italy and the Spanish Diaspora is wide and open in the front; it consists of a rigid top with a trapezoid robe sown around it. In Italy and in the Portuguese Diaspora in the Netherlands and in England one finds mantles predating the seventeenth century on which there is a kind of cape above the robe. In Algeria another type of Torah mantle took shape, comprising a rectangular length of material gathered at its upper borders.

In other European communities, that is, those following Ashkenazi tradition, the Torah mantle is generally narrower and smaller than the Sephardic mantle, with the robelike part made of two rectangular lengths of material sewn together. Two openings at the upper end of the mantle enable the staves to protrude. The earliest German mantles are described in fifteenth-century manuscripts. Even at this early stage, it is already possible to distinguish two types of mantle. One was made of costly patterned material, depending on the donor's economic situation; if there was a dedicatory inscription, it was embroidered on a piece of plain material attached to the front. The second type was made of a single-colored material, usually velvet, on which motifs and dedicatory inscriptions were embroidered. The designs on Torah mantles in Germany and Central Europe are influenced by the ornamentation of the Torah ark curtain, with such motifs as a pair of columns, lions, and the Torah crown most frequent.

"Tablets of the Law" Plaque

A unique object, the "Tablets of the Law" plaque, was used in Iraqi Kurdistan to call congregants up for the Torah reading. The silver plaque was engraved with the Tablets of the Law and kept in the Torah ark in an embroidered cloth purse. Before the beginning of the Torah reading, the synagogue official responsible for distributing the honors (the *gabbai*) approached each man to be called up and offered him the plaque. A man who wished to accept the honor would take the plaque, kiss it, and return it to the *gabbai;* otherwise he would motion rejection with his hand (as direct refusal to perform a mitzvah would be considered improper).

Ceremonial objects in the synagogue are donated by individuals or social groups and are considered the property of the congregation, unless otherwise indicated. Generally speaking, the donors specify their names, the occasion of the gift, and the date on the object, in a dedicatory inscription. The occasions differ for different objects. In most communities, it is customary to commemorate the departed by the dedication of sacred objects, in particular, Torah scrolls and their mantles or cases. In Europe, it was customary for wealthy members of the congregation to dedicate sacred objects in their lifetime, mainly sumptuous Torah ark curtains, often to commemorate a life-cycle event, such as a marriage or the birth of a son. Life-cycle events often inspired women to embroider dedicatory inscriptions on sacred objects, such as the linen wrappers wound around Torah scrolls in Italy and the linen binders embroidered in Germany to commemorate the birth of a son. In addition, ceremonial objects were often donated to fulfill vows, especially those taken by women.

Bracha Yaniv

See also: Torah Ornaments.

Bibliography

Abbink van der Zwan, P.J. "Ornamentation on Eighteenth-Century Torah Binders." *Israel Museum News* (1978): 64–73.

Boll, Günter. "The Jewish Community of Mackenheim" In *Mappot . . . Blessed Be Who Comes: The Band of Jewish Tradition,* ed. A. Weber, E. Friedlander, and F. Armbruster, pp. 22–27. Osnabrück: Secolo Verlag, 1997.

Davidovitch, David. "Die Tora Wimpel im Braunschweigischen Landesmuseum." In *Tora Wimpel: Zeugniss jüdischer Volkskunst aus dem Braunschweigisches Landesmuseum,* ed. R. Hagen, pp. 12–27. Braunschweig: Braunschweigisches Landesmuseum, 1978.

Dolezelova, Jana. "Binders and Festive Covers from the Collections of the State Jewish Museum in Prague." *Judaica Bohemiae* 10:2 (1974): 91–104.

———. "Die Sammlung der Thorawickel." *Judaica Bohemiae* 16:1 (1980): 60–63.

———. "Torah Binders from Four Centuries at the State Jewish Museum in Prague." *Judaica Bohemiae* 9:2 (1973): 55–71.

———. "Torah Binders in the Czech Republic." In *Mappot . . . Blessed Be Who Comes: The Band of Jewish Tradition,* ed. A. Weber, E. Friedlander, and F. Armbruster, pp. 99–103. Osnabrück: Secolo Verlag, 1997.

Eis, Ruth. *Torah Binders of the Judah L. Magnes Museum.* Berkeley, CA: Judah L. Magnes Memorial Museum, 1979.

Grossman, Cissy. "Italian Torah Binders." *Jewish Art* 7 (1980): 35–43.

Guggenheim-Grünberg, Florence. *Die Torawickelbänder von Lengnau Zeugnisse jüdischer Volkskunst.* Zürich: Verlag Jüdische Buchgemeinde, 1967.

Gutmann, Joseph."Die Mappe Schuletragen." In *Mappot . . . Blessed Be Who Comes: The Band of Jewish Tradition,* ed. A. Weber, E. Friedlander, and F. Armbruster, pp. 65–69. Osnabrück: Secolo Verlag, 1997.

———. "Torah Ornaments, Priestly Vestments, and the King James Bible." In *Beauty in Holiness: Studies in Jewish Customs and Ceremonial Art,* ed. J. Gutmann, pp. 122–124. New York: Ktav, 1970.

Kirshenblatt-Gimblett, Barbara. "The Cut That Binds: The Western Ashkenazic Torah Binder as Nexus Between Circumcision and Torah." In *Celebration: Studies in Festivity and Ritual,* ed. V. Turner, pp. 136–146. Washington, DC: Smithsonian Books, 1982.

Kybalová, Ludmila, Eva Kosáková, and Alexandr Putík, eds. *Textiles from Bohemian and Moravian Synagogues from the Collections of the Jewish Museum in Prague.* Prague: The Jewish Museum in Prague, 2003.

Landsberger, Franz. "A German Torah Ornamentation." In *Beauty in Holiness: Studies in Jewish Customs and Ceremonial Art,* ed. J. Gutmann, pp. 106–121. New York: Ktav, 1970.

———. "The Origin of European Torah Decorations." In *Beauty in Holiness: Studies in Jewish Customs and Ceremonial Art,* ed. J. Gutmann, pp. 87–105. New York: Ktav, 1970.

Raphaël, Freddy. "On Saturday My Grandson Will Bring the Mappah to the Synagogue." In *Mappot . . . Blessed Be Who Comes: The Band of Jewish Tradition,* ed. A. Weber, E. Friedlander, and F. Armbruster, pp. 73–79. Osnabrück: Secolo Verlag, 1997.

Sabar, Shalom. "'May He Grow Up to the Huppah': Representations of the Wedding on Ashkenazi Torah Binders." In *Romance & Ritual: Celebrating the Jewish Wedding,* ed. Grace Cohen Grossman, pp. 31–45. Los Angeles: Skirball Cultural Center, 2001.

Weber, Annette. "The Culture of Rural Jewry in Swabia and Franconia." In *Mappot . . . Blessed Be Who Comes: The Band of Jewish Tradition,* ed. A. Weber, E. Friedlander, and F. Armbruster, pp. 82–91. Osnabrück: Secolo Verlag, 1997.

———. "From Leo to Virgo: The Binders of the Synagogue at Ichenhausen." In *Mappot . . . Blessed Be Who Comes: The Band of Jewish Tradition,* ed. A. Weber, E. Friedlander, and F. Armbruster, 92–99. Osnabrück: Secolo Verlag, 1997.

Yaniv, Bracha. "Ceremonial Objects in the Synagogue." *Mahanaim* 11 (1995): 220–228 (in Hebrew).

———. *Ma'ase rokem: Textile Ceremonial Objects in the Ashkenazi, Sephardic and Italian Synagogue.* Jerusalem: Ben-Zvi Institute, 2009 (in Hebrew).

———. "Regional Variations of Torah Cases from the Islamic World." In *For Every Thing a Season: Proceedings of the Symposium on Jewish Ritual Art.* Cleveland: Cleveland State University, 2002.

———. "The Samaritan Torah Case." *Samaritan Researches* 5 (2000): 4.04–4.13.

———. *The Torah Case: Its History and Design.* Ramat-Gan: Bar Ilan University, 1997 (in Hebrew).

Torah Ornaments

The earliest Torah ornaments are the Torah crown and the finials mounted on the Torah case or on the staves of the Torah scroll. These two objects are interconnected and, historically speaking, appeared one after the other, first in the East, in Egypt, Spain, and Italy, and later also in Germany. From there they spread to Central and Eastern Europe. Another ornamental object that appeared later is the breastplate—a metal plate or shield hung in front of the Torah scroll in all European communities and in the Sephardic communities of the Balkans. It was known in Italy as the "crown" (*keter*), since its design was that of a flat crown; but in all other communities, including Turkey, it was called the "breastplate" (*tas*). These three objects—crown, finials, and breastplates—are usually richly ornamented and made of silver or silver-plated base metal. Many of them carry bells, whose tinkling announces that the Torah is being taken out of the ark or being returned there. Other objects, used during the Torah reading, are the pointer and small plaques used to call people up to the Torah reading. Like all ceremonial objects in the synagogue, these may be dedicated by congregants, social groups within the synagogue, or individuals in memory of deceased family members, or in honor of themselves or their family on important life-cycle events.

Torah Crown

The Torah crown was first mentioned in the eleventh century, in a responsum of Rav Hai Gaon, head of the Pumbedita Yeshiva in Babylonia, concerning the use of a crown for a Torah scroll on Simchat Torah. The use of the Torah crown is linked in this responsum to the custom of crowning the "Bridegrooms of the Law," that is, those called up on Simchat Torah to complete the annual cycle of the Torah reading and to initiate the new cycle. Another detail evident from the same event is that, at the time, the Torah crown was an ad hoc object made from various decorative items, such as plants and jewelry. About a hundred years later, fixed crowns, made of silver and used regularly to decorate Torah scrolls in the synagogue, are mentioned in a document from the Cairo Geniza. Later, in the fourteenth-century Spanish Sarajevo Haggadah, one illustration depicts Torah crowns on Torah scrolls. Over time, the Torah crown became a regular ornament mounted on the Torah scroll. In most communities where Torah cases are used, the crown is mounted on the upper part of the case; in European communities, it is removable and used either together with or separately from the finials, depending on its design.

Torah crowns are used in almost all communities (the exceptions are those in Morocco and Yemen), their design being influenced in each locality by local tradition. The shape of the spherical crown of the Iraqi-Persian Torah case follows the tradition of the crowns of the Sassanid kings, the last Persian dynasty prior to the Muslim conquest. Apparently the earliest of all Torah crowns, it is onion-shaped or conical. In Cochin, India, and in Aden, a tapering domelike crown developed, through which protrude finials mounted on the staves on which the Torah scroll is wound; the crown is not fixed to the case.

By the twentieth century, the Torah crown in Cochin showed distinct European features. In eastern Iran, where the Torah had a small crown, the outer sides of the crown lost their spherical shape and became flat dedicatory plaques. Today this crown looks like a pair of flat finials, and only their designation as "crowns" hints at their origin in the Torah crown. The circlet or coronet on the Mediterranean case, which became an integral part of the case, was based on a local medieval crown tradition typified by floral patterns. The European crown is shaped like a floral coronet with arms closing over it. In Eastern Europe, a two- or three-tiered crown developed, inspired by the crown motif on the Torah ark in this region. The closed structure of the European crown made it unsuitable for use together with the finials, and in Europe it therefore became customary to use the finials on weekdays and the crown on the Sabbath and festivals. In Italy, however, the Torah crown (Heb., *atarah*) was a coronet, which could be used together with the finials.

Torah Finials

The finials evolved from knobs at the upper end of the staves on which the Torah scroll is wound, possibly because of the appearance of the Torah crown, which could not be mounted stably on the Torah scroll unless the knobs were separated from the staves. The knobs were therefore mounted on two hollow shafts, thus becoming separate, independent objects. Because the shape of the spherical finial recalled that of a fruit, it was called a *tappuaḥ* (apple) among the Jews in Spain and in the Sephardic Diaspora, and a *rimmon* (pomegranate) in all other communities.

Torah crown. Ukraine, 1820. *(Gross Family Collection, Tel Aviv)*

The earliest-known reference to Torah finials occurs in a document from 1159, found in the Cairo Geniza, from which scholars have learned that by the twelfth century finials were already being made of silver and had bells. Around the same time, Maimonides mentioned finials in his great legal code *Mishneh Torah* (*Hilkhot Sefer Torah* 10:4). Despite the variations on the spherical shape that developed over the centuries and the addition of small bells around the main body of the finial, the spherical, fruitlike form remains the basic model for the design of finials in Middle Eastern communities. The spherical form was also preserved in Europe, but with some variations, of which the most obvious was the addition of a crown on top of the sphere.

A most significant variation appeared in fifteenth-century Spain, Italy, and Germany, where the shape of finials was influenced by that of various objects of church ritual, whose design often incorporated architectural motifs. Imitating Christian silverwork, a miniature tower was added on top of the spherical body of the finial and eventually merged with it. The resulting towerlike structure, which seems to have appeared around the same time in different parts of Europe, became the main type of finial in eighteenth-century Germany and Italy. The tower-shaped finial was also brought by the expelled Spanish Jews to their new countries of residence. In Morocco it became the dominant form of finial.

Breastplates and Metal Shields

Breastplates—ornamental metal plates or shields hung in front of the Torah scroll—are found in all Ashkenazi communities, as well as in Italy and Turkey, but designed differently in each community. In most cases the breastplate is made of silver or silver-plated base metal. In Italy the breastplate is shaped like a coronet and known as the *keter,* "crown," whereas the coronet atop the Torah scroll is known as the *atarah.*

In Turkey, the breastplate can assume a variety of different shapes—circular, triangular, oval, or even the Star of David. In Western, Central, and Eastern Europe the breastplate's function is not merely ornamental: It designates which Torah scroll is to be used for the Torah reading on any particular occasion. To that end, small interchangeable plaques are kept in a special holder fixed in the center of the breastplate, indicating that the scroll is to be used for the Sabbath or a specific festival, as the case may be. The most notable early breastplates, from seventeenth-century Germany and the Netherlands, were either square or rectangular. Later, in the eighteenth century, the border of the breastplate became rounded and decorative, and bells or small dedicatory plaques were suspended from its lower edge. During this period, the design of breastplates was influenced by that of the Torah ark and the *parokhet* (curtain) concealing it, featuring various architectural motifs, the menorah (the seven-branched candelabrum), Moses and Aaron, lions, or Torah crowns.

Beginning in the early twentieth century, some Ashkenazi communities that do not use breastplates hang small plaques on the Torah scroll to indicate which Torah scroll is to be read on a particular occasion.

Torah Pointer

The pointer used by the Torah reader to keep the place is known in European communities as the *yad* (hand) or the *etzba* (finger), and in Sephardic and Middle Eastern communities as the *moreh* (pointer) or *kulmus* (quill), the former because of its function and the latter because of its shape. Halakhic sources also use the terms *"moreh"* or *"kulmus."* The pointer was originally a narrow rod, tapered at the pointing end, usually with a hole at the other end through which a ring or chain could be passed to hang the pointer on the Torah scroll.

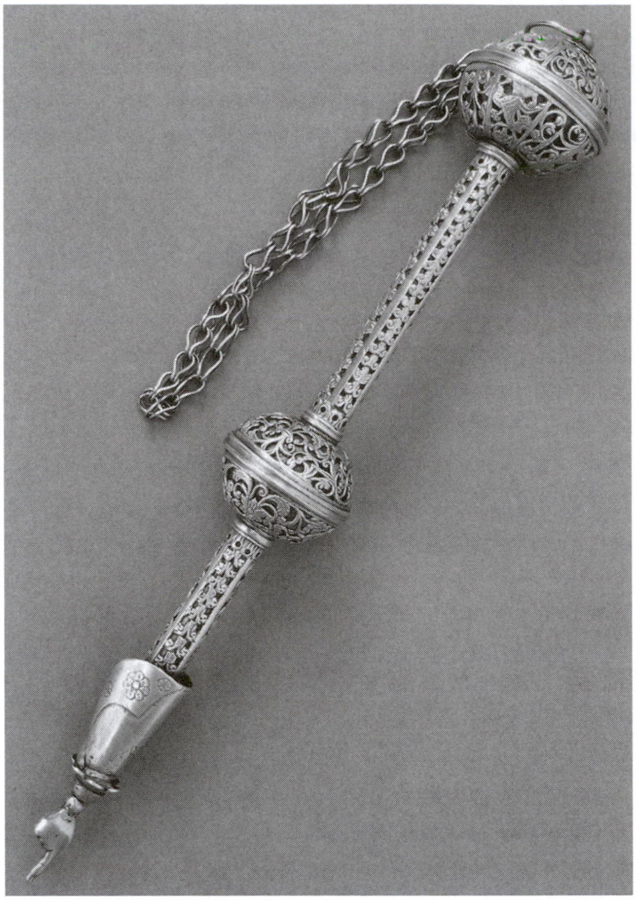

Torah pointer. Ukraine, 1850. *(Gross Family Collection, Tel Aviv)*

The original form of the pointer was preserved in Middle Eastern communities, the differences from one community to another being mainly in length and ornamentation. In Europe and North Africa, however, changes occurred in its design. In Libya and Tunisia, the pointing end took the form of an oval spatula, and in Europe certain parts were added to the rod. Thickened joints were added at the holding end and in the middle of the rod; at the other end a hand with a pointing finger was added. The "hand" model influenced the design of the pointer in Morocco, and local influence then transformed it into a *ḥamsa.* In most communities the pointer is suspended from a chain on the Torah scroll or the Torah case.

Pointers are made for the most part of metal, but in a few European communities they used to be made of wood. In such cases the "hands" were carved in the local folk-art style. In most Sephardic and Middle Eastern communities the pointer is made of silver, while in Europe, depending on the economic circumstances of the donor, it is made of silver or silver-plated brass.

Bracha Yaniv

See also: Torah Ceremonial Objects.

Bibliography

Cohen, Yerahmiel. "Torah Breastplates from Augsburg in the Israel Museum." *Israel Museum News,* 1978, 75–85.

Grafman, Rafi. *Crowning Glory: Silver Torah Ornaments.* New York: David R. Godine, 1996.

———. *50 Rimmonim: A Selection of Torah Finials from a European Family Collection.* Tel Aviv: Tel Aviv University, Jewish Museum, 1998.

Gutmann, Joseph. "Torah Ornaments, Priestly Vestments, and the King James Bible." In *Beauty in Holiness: Studies in Jewish Customs and Ceremonial Art,* ed. J. Gutmann, pp. 122–124. New York: Ktav, 1970.

Jacoby, Ruth. "The Torah Pointer in the Persian World." Ph.D. dissertation, Hebrew University of Jerusalem, 2004 (in Hebrew).

Landsberger, Franz. "A German Torah Ornamentation." In *Beauty in Holiness: Studies in Jewish Customs and Ceremonial Art,* ed. Joseph Gutmann, pp. 106–121. New York: Ktav, 1970.

———. "The Origin of European Torah Decorations." In *Beauty in Holiness: Studies in Jewish Customs and Ceremonial Art,* ed. Joseph. Gutmann, pp. 87–105. New York: Ktav, 1970.

Schoenberger, Guido. "The Ritual Silver Made by Myer Myers." In *Beauty in Holiness: Studies in Jewish Customs and Ceremonial Art,* ed. Joseph Gutmann, pp. 66–78. New York: Ktav, 1970.

Shaked, Shaul, and Ruth Jacoby. "An Early Torah Pointer from Afghanistan." *Ars Judaica* 1 (2005): 147–152.

Stown, J. "Silver English Rimmonim and Their Makers." *Quest,* September 23–30, 1965.

Tahon, D. "Refresh Me with Apples" *Rimmonim* 4 (1994): 20–27 (in Hebrew).

Yaniv, Bracha. "An Attempt to Reconstruct the Design of Tower-Shaped Rimmonim in Morocco According to Models from Spain." *Pe'amim* 50 (1992): 69–98 (in Hebrew).

———. "Ceremonial Objects in the Synagogue." *Mahanaim* 11 (1995): 220–228 (in Hebrew).

———. "The Mystery of the Flat Torah Finials from East Persia." In *Padyavand: Judeo-Iranian and Jewish Studies Series,* ed. A. Netzer, pp. 63–74. Costa Mesa: Mazda, 1996.

Trachtenberg, Joshua (1904–1959)

Joshua Trachtenberg is influential in Jewish folklore scholarship for locating medieval Central European sources of present-day Jewish customs and anti-Jewish beliefs held by non-Jews. He identified a "folk Judaism" that he defined as "the beliefs and practices that expressed most eloquently the folk psyche—of all the vagaries which, coupled with the historic program of the Jewish faith, made up the everyday religion of the Jewish people" (1979 [1939], viii). As his mention of "folk psyche" indicates, he posited psychological rationales for the persistence of customs in place of the view that Jews lived in ignorance or resisted progress. He explained the concentration of rituals around life-cycle events responding to anxiety and danger. He argued against the popular view that Jewish belief and magic were forms of witchcraft or idolatry. He hypothesized that the primary principle of Jewish magic was an implicit reliance upon benevolent powers associated often with attributes of God.

Unlike many rabbinical scholars who, prior to Trachtenberg's studies, had criticized or ignored folk Judaism as embarrassingly "unworthy of the Jew," Trachtenberg advocated for an objective understanding of Jewish folklore "if we are truly to learn what Judaism has been for its adherents" (1942, 174). He advocated for the study of Jewish practices in the historical and cultural context of the locations in which Jews lived. He proposed that much of present-day Jewish folklore arose from a syncretic process of Jewish customs' being affected by their non-Jewish surroundings and, in some cases, preserving in Ashkenazi folklore practices and beliefs of non-Jews that had disappeared from the Central European culture.

Trachtenberg was born in London on July 11, 1904, and moved to New York City at the age of three. He received a B.S. degree from City College of New York in 1926 and then was ordained a Reform rabbi at Hebrew Union College in 1930. Thereafter, he served Congregation Brith Shalom (now called Temple Covenant of Peace) in Easton, Pennsylvania. He completed his Ph.D. in history at Columbia University in 1939 and received a D.D. from Hebrew Union College in 1945.

Completed under the guidance of Jewish social historian Salo Baron, medievalist Lynn Thorndike, and Talmudist Louis Ginzberg, Trachtenberg's dissertation was published in 1939 as *Jewish Magic and Superstition: A Study in Folk Religion*. Trachtenberg drew attention for his thesis that Judaism evolved from, and owed its persistence to, the incorporation of folklore into the everyday religious practices of Jews. His provocative thesis was that Judaism became essentially a folk religion during the medieval period and owes its enduring flexibility to this transformation. A religious implication of his study related to his Reform background is that Judaism, if it is to survive, needs to respond to the communal needs of Jews in historic periods and the conditions of the surrounding community. The core of his study is in printed sources from medieval Germany, and modern scholars have raised questions about the representativeness of and tendency to generalize from these specific community experiences.

Trachtenberg developed the theme of the medieval folk roots of gentile anti-Semitism in *The Devil and the Jews: The Medieval Conception of the Jew and Its Relation to Modern Antisemitism* (1943), which has enjoyed several popular reprint editions. In the book, Trachtenberg expanded the first chapter of *Jewish Magic and Superstition* on Jewish magical practice into an extensive study of the gentile accusation that Jews practiced sorcery. Well aware of state policies demonizing Jews in Nazi Germany at the time of its writing (he cites Hitler in the preface), Trachtenberg editorialized: "If the Jew is today despised and feared and hated, it is because we are the heirs of the Middle Ages. If it is possible for demagogues to sow the seeds of disunion and discord, to stir fanatical emotions and set neighbor against neighbor, it is because the figure of the 'demonic' Jew, less than human, indeed, antihuman, the creation of the medieval mind, still dominates the folk imagination."

The Devil and the Jews is influential for developing the area of "exoteric folklore," or symbolic narratives about groups by outsiders to the group, and showing its impact upon visual as well as oral traditions. Trachtenberg connected, for example, exoteric Christian beliefs in the secret mystical knowledge possessed by Jews to images of Jews with horns and the blood libel legend. As with *Jewish Magic and Superstition*, which posited a medieval source for developments in Judaism, *The Devil and the Jews* had a religious implication, although more for Christian churches. He claimed that medieval folk narratives became institutionalized within Christian theology and were then used by modern anti-Semites as authentic Christian values. He noted the split between official Christian efforts to separate from the anti-Semitic medieval sources by stating, "The Christian religion is in disfavor today among certain leading anti-Semitic circles whose consuming aim it is to destroy all Christian values; among others hatred of the Jew is preached in the name of a hypocritical and false Christianity."

Inspired again by his mentor Salo Baron, in 1944 Trachtenberg turned to American-Jewish community history with the publication of *Consider the Years: The Story of the Jewish Community of Easton, Pennsylvania, 1752–1942*.

An ardent Labor Zionist using the community-bonding concepts of folklore to build a united foundation for a new Israel, he spent 1951 and 1952 on a survey sponsored by the Union of American Hebrew Congregations and the Central Conference of American Rabbis of religious conditions in Israel toward a campaign to further Reform Judaism there. Upon his return to the United States in 1952, he briefly served as chaplain of the United States Veterans Hospital in Northport, New York, before becoming rabbi at the Bergen County Reform Temple (now called Temple Emeth) in Teaneck, New Jersey.

Trachtenberg died of a heart attack at his temple office on September 14, 1959. His widow, Edna Suer Trachtenberg, donated his extensive rare book collection to the temple library as the core of the Rabbi Joshua Trachtenberg Memorial Library Center, and the temple sponsors an annual Rabbi Joshua Trachtenberg memorial lecture.

Simon J. Bronner

See also: Magic.

Bibliography

"Dr. Trachtenberg of Jersey Temple." *New York Times*. September 15, 1959, 39.

Noy, Dov. "Is There a Jewish Folk Religion?" In *Studies in Jewish Folklore*, ed. Frank Talmage, pp. 273–285. Cambridge, MA: Association for Jewish Studies, 1980.

Temkin, Sefton D. "Trachtenberg, Joshua." In *Encyclopedia Judaica*, 2nd ed., vol. 20. Detroit: Macmillan, 2007.

Trachtenberg, Joshua. *Consider the Years: The Story of the Jewish Community of Easton, Pennsylvania, 1752–1942*. Easton, PA: Temple Brith Sholom, 1944.

———. *The Devil and the Jews: The Medieval Conception of the Jew and Its Relation to Modern Antisemitism*. Philadelphia: Jewish Publication Society, 2002 [1943].

———. "The Folk Element in Judaism." *Journal of Religion* 22 (1942): 173–86.

———. *Jewish Magic and Superstition: A Study in Folk Religion*. New York: Atheneum, 1979 [1939].

Transmigration of the Soul (*Gilgul Neshamot*)

See: Afterlife

Tribes, Ten Lost

The claim of belonging to the Ten Lost Tribes of Israel (Reuben, Simeon, Issachar, Zebulun, Menasseh, Ephraim, Dan, Naphtali, Gad, and Asher) dates back to biblical times and is shared by hundreds, if not thousands, of groups throughout the world, from Africa to Asia to Australasia. Folk beliefs abound as to the Israeli or ancient Hebraic customs of these different groups.

According to the Bible, the northern Kingdom of Israel was conquered by the Assyrians in the eighth century B.C.E. and the ten tribes in the Kingdom were exiled "in Halah, and in Habor by the river of Gozan and in the cities of the Medes" (2 Kgs. 17:6). The fate of these Ten Lost Tribes has always been something of an enigma. Although it was generally assumed that the Israelites who were exiled eventually assimilated, particular biblical passages documenting their place of exile (1 Chr.

5:26) and prophetic proclamations (Isa. 11:11–12; Ezek. 37:21–23) suggested that they continued to live on and would be "ingathered" in latter days. Hopes of discovering the Ten Lost Tribes and belief in the possibility of their ultimate return were kept alive throughout the ages. The myth of the Ten Lost Tribes gained momentum in certain historical periods, particularly during periods associated with the rise of messianism or the growth of fundamentalism.

The Universal Legend

While particularly pervasive in the Jewish world, the legend has become universal. Numbering more than 15 million, the Pathans comprise the largest single tribe in the world, inhabiting an extensive area from Afghanistan through Pakistan to Kashmir in India. They are divided into distinct local tribes reminiscent of the Ten Lost Tribes: Rabbani may be Reuben; Shinwari may be Shimon; Daftani may be a corruption of Naphtali, Jajani of Gad, Afridi of Ephraim. Yusufzai, another tribe, means "the sons of Joseph."

The Ten Lost Tribes legend was also popular among various Christian denominations that sought out "Israelites," among both Jews and gentiles, whom they could convert to Christianity in order to hasten the arrival of the messiah. Thus, in the sixteenth century, the Spanish priest Bartolome de Las Casas attempted to "prove" that the Native Americans were lost Israelites in order to protect them from the Spanish colonizers. In the nineteenth century, Reverend Wolff, a missionary for the London Society for Promoting Christianity Among the Jews, believed that the Jews in Bukhara (in present-day Uzbekistan), as well as other non-Jewish tribes in the Hindu Kush area, were descendants of the tribes of Naphtali and Zebulun. In this vein, nineteenth-century missionary work among the Karen tribe of Burma (Myanmar) was inspired by the belief that they, too, were part of the Lost Tribes. Dr. Francis Mason, of the American Baptist Foreign Mission Society, arrived with his wife in Toungoo, Burma, in 1814. By the mid-nineteenth century, Mason became convinced that indigenous Karen worship and, in particular, their belief in a monotheistic eternal god called Y-wa, were similar to that of the ancient Israelites and that they were of the seed of Israel. In recent years, some groups, including the Shinlung of northeast India, desire to "return" to the people of Israel by adopting Judaism and immigrating to Israel.

Folk Beliefs

Examples abound from the world over, but this discussion is limited to two groups that claim or have others claim lost tribe status for them. According to the Shinlung (also called Bnei Menashe), their ancestors were Israelites exiled by Shalmaneser, the king of Assyria, in 722 B.C.E. They lived in Persia and Afghanistan and were then pushed eastward into northern India, through the Hindu Kush, and to Tibet. They migrated to China and settled in Yunnan province. From there, they moved to central China, where they came into contact with the now-extinct Jewish community in Kaifeng in around 240 B.C.E. During the reign of the emperor Qin Shihuangdi, who built the Great Wall of China, they were treated as slaves. They retained their own customs, but were persecuted by the Chinese, who killed all their priests and burned their holy books. In order to escape from the emperor's soldiers, some of the Shinlung escaped and took refuge in caves. They became known as "cave dwellers," a familiar motif in this part of the world. Emerging from the cave, the people established a separate village named Shinlung (hence, their collective appellation, Shinlung). In approximately 1300 C.E. they moved to Shan state in Burma and crossed the great river Irrawady and penetrated into the Aupalling hills. Here, they were mistreated by the king and again escaped. They reached their present location in India on the Burmese border in about 1600 C.E., and to this day, it is obvious that their origins are different from that of the rest of the local population.

In addition to a song in their repertoire about what seems to be the crossing of the Red Sea, several stories in their folklore seemed to be biblical in origin, such as one resembling the Joseph story, and another about the Noah's ark flood story. In a popular song, they recall "Manmaseh," and as a result, in the late twentieth century, they have been called the "Bnei Menashe" (Children of Menashe).

Pathan legend has it that King Saul bore a son by the name of Jeremy, whose birth is not recorded in Jewish texts. Jeremy fathered a royal prince called Afghana, whose descendants fled to Jat in Afghanistan. In 662 C.E. the descendants of Afghana were converted to Islam at the explicit request of Mohammed. The mission was accomplished by his emissary Khalid ibn al-Walid, who returned to his master with "proof" of his activities: seventy-six converts and seven leaders of the "Children of Israel."

Afghan and Western scholars alike who have made detailed investigations into the subject provide folk "proofs" of the Israelite origins of the Pathans. Some write that they "look" Jewish: They have sallow skin and dark hair and eyes, are of medium stature, wear beards and sidelocks, and have a typically "Jewish" profile. They also "act" Jewish: They perform circumcision on their boys on the eighth day or after; the women observe purification laws prescribed in the Torah; and they wear amulets, which may contain the words of the Shema, "Hear, O Israel . . ."

Shalva Weil

See also: Sambation.

Bibliography

Godbey, Allen. *The Lost Tribes: A Myth.* Durham: Duke University Press, 1930.

Mason, Francis. *The Karen Apostle: or Memoir of Ka Thah-Byu.* Boston: Drew Kendall and Longchamps, 1843.

Popkin, Richard, ed. *The Rise and Fall of the Jewish Indian Theory.* Leiden: E.J. Brill, 1989.

Weil, Shalva. *Beyond the Sambatyon: The Myth of the Ten Lost Tribes.* Tel Aviv: Beth Hatefusoth: Museum of the Jewish Diaspora, 1991.

———. "Lost Israelites from North-East India: Re-Traditionalisation and Conversion Among the Shinlung from the Indo-Burmese Borderlands." *Anthropologist* 6:3 (2004): 219–233.

———. "The Pathans of Afghanistan." In *Encyclopaedia of the Jewish Diaspora,* ed. M. Avrum Erlich, pp. 1230–1231. Santa Barbara, CA: ABC CLIO, 2008.

Wolff, Joseph. *Narrative of a Mission to Bokhara.* London: Parker, 1946.

TURKEY, JEWS OF

Within the geographic areas that form modern Turkey, permanent Jewish communities can be traced back to the third century B.C.E. Jews have lived there under the Seleucid, Roman, Byzantine, Seljuk, and Ottoman empires and still live there today, in the Republic of Turkey. Their history and folklore are rich and diverse.

History

From medieval times well into the twentieth century, Hebrew writers referred to the Turkish lands by the biblical name Togarmah. Togar and his brothers Ashkenaz and Riphat were sons of Gomer, grandsons of Japheth (Gen. 10:3). The people of Togarmah—Togar's descendants—were renowned horsemen and horse traders (Ezek. 27:14) and were associated with the Turks.

When the Ottomans captured the city of Bursa in 1324, Sultan Orhan granted the Jews of the city permission to build a new synagogue—the famous Etz Ha'Ḥaim (Tree of Life) synagogue, which was active in Bursa until the last quarter of the twentieth century. When Sultan Mehmet II took over Constantinople (Istanbul) in 1453, he transferred subjects from other areas of his kingdom to Constantinople, in order to populate the newly conquered city. Thus, the size of Jewish communities outside Constantinople was reduced, only to dramatically increase with the arrival of vast numbers of Jewish exiles from Spain. Constantinople, too, had a special name in Jewish writings: It was called Coshtandina, abbreviated as Coshta—the Aramaic word for "truth" and the name of a legendary city of truth-speakers (*b. Sanhedrin* 11a).

In the sixteenth century the Jewish population in the Ottoman Empire was divided among four major communities: the Romaniote Jews, who lived in Asia Minor beginning in the time of the Byzantine Empire; an Ashkenazi community of Jewish immigrants from Central Europe; *musta'rib* (arabicized) Jews who lived in the Arab lands conquered by the Ottomans; and Sephardic Jews, those expelled from *Sepharad* (Heb., Spain) and from Portugal. The Sephardic Jews were welcomed by Sultan Bayezid II, and their community soon became the largest and most dominant of the four Jewish groups in the empire.

The exiles from Spain founded large communities in Constantinople, Salonika, Edirne, Bursa, Izmir, and many other cities throughout the empire. Details about their legal, social, and economic life were recorded not only in official Ottoman documents but also in vast rabbinical responsa written over the centuries. The Sephardic community was at first divided within itself into many congregations, according to the various Spanish and Portuguese cities of origin: Toledo, Aragon, Lisbon, and so on. Over the centuries, the differences among those congregations faded, until only the synagogues' names echoed the exact Iberian places of origin.

The pluralistic character of Ottoman society, and the unprecedented measure of freedom that Jews enjoyed, made the Ottoman Empire an attractive home for them. Soon, that attraction was magnified: With the victory of Sultan Selim I (1465–1520) over the Mamluk sultanate, the Holy Land became part of the Ottoman Empire. A seventeenth-century Jewish legend tells how his son and successor, Suleiman I (1494–1566), discovered the location of the Western Wall, which was until then unknown: The location was found when the sultan's men saw a Christian woman from Bethlehem dropping garbage at a certain spot in Jerusalem. When asked why she brought garbage from afar specifically to that location, the woman explained that such was the tradition. The sultan then ordered the place to be dug up and cleared, and soon the Wall was fully revealed. Upon hearing of the rediscovery, the sultan ordered the Wall to be washed with rosewater.

Ottoman Jews, who now had the opportunity to go on pilgrimage to the Holy Land and even settle there, were also impressed by Suleiman's efforts toward rebuilding the city walls of Jerusalem. The sultan, who was called "Suleiman the Magnificent" in the West, was referred to in some Jewish writings as Shlomo ha'Melekh, an honorary comparison to the admired biblical king Solomon.

Language

The Sephardic Jews throughout the Ottoman Empire held on to elements of their Spanish culture, of which the most important was the language: Judeo-Spanish (known as Ladino) was their everyday language well into the twentieth century. They settled in neighborhoods

Tas (breastplate). Tukat, Turkey, 1844. *(Gross Family Collection, Tel Aviv)*

with a Jewish majority, but with Muslim and Christian neighbors. Jewish men spoke Turkish and worked with their neighbors in a variety of occupations. Jewish women, by contrast, hardly had any contact with non-Jews. Their lives were centered at home, and until the late nineteenth century most of them did not speak Turkish, did not attend school, and rarely worked outside the home. These conditions made them an important instrument through which the Judeo-Spanish language and folklore were preserved for centuries, orally transmitted from one generation to another.

Folk Songs, Customs, and Traditions

In the field of folk songs, Sephardic Jews have preserved the old Spanish genre of the *romanca,* which is, to this day, a source of great interest for scholars: *Romancas* passed on by Jews in Turkish communities are compared to those preserved by Spanish Jews in Morocco, and both these traditions are studied in light of the *romancas* of Christian medieval Spain. Alongside old *romancas,* Jews throughout the Ottoman Empire created new *romancas,* keeping the poetic and thematic old forms and at the same time reflecting the cultural changes: Turkish words appeared in the Judeo-Spanish text, joining the Hebrew words already present in the Judeo-Spanish language, and customs of the time were reflected within the medieval style.

In the mid-seventeenth century, Shabbatai Zvi, a native of Izmir, declared himself to be the messiah. He established circles of believers, causing turmoil in the Jewish world. Zvi was banished by the rabbis, arrested by the Turkish authorities, and in the end converted to Islam. At the time the singing of *romancas* was very popular, so it was only natural that this religious drama was expressed in song. Researcher Moshe Attias mentions two such songs: The *romanca* "Melizelda hija del emperante" (Melizelda, daughter of the Emperor"), which Zvi is believed to have sung in mystic conviction, and an original *romanca* written about Zvi by his followers, "Hakhamim van airando" (The rabbis are angry).

In the genre of the *canción,* also sung in Ladino, contemporary life in the Ottoman Empire was much more evident, and Turkish words or customs were common in folk love songs such as this one, documented in Moshe Attias's *Judeo-Spanish Cancionero* (1972):

Konca mia, konca mia,
Çiçek de mi cabeza
La luna me s'escuricio
La mar me se hizo preta

(My rosebud, my rosebud [*Konca* is Turkish for "rosebud"]
Flower of my head [*Çiçek* is Turkish for "flower"]
The moon has darkened upon me
The sea has turned black)

While some of the Judeo-Spanish folk genres were strongly connected to Spanish tradition, others were influenced by the local Turkish tradition. The humorous tales about Joha are such a case. Joha the fool, a well-known folk character throughout the Middle East, became a folk hero among Jews as well. In a multicultural manner characteristic of the Sephardic Turkish Jews, the "Jewish" Joha kept his cross-cultural image as a fool, remaining loyal to his local Turkish roots, occasionally facing specific Jewish circumstances, and always speaking Ladino.

An interesting cultural dialogue took place in the field of music, where melodies of Ladino folk songs and of Turkish songs were used for singing liturgical Hebrew poems, performed by Jewish men in the synagogue. In their religious singing, Turkish Jews have adopted elements from Turkish art music, such as vocal techniques, musical forms, and the *māqāma* modal system.

The Sephardic betrothal and marriage were celebrated in several events, each having special rituals, customs, and folk expressions, such as specific songs, food, and clothes. One of the events was the presentation of the bride's dowry to the groom's family. The dowry included many items—sewed, knitted, and embroidered by the bride, her mother, and other female relatives—accumulated over many years, starting in the girl's early childhood. The long preparation, trouble, and worry are reflected in many Judeo-Spanish wedding songs and in proverbs, such as these:

> *La hija en la faja, l'anjugar en la caja.*
> (The girl in her diaper, the dowry in the chest.)
> (Juhasz, 1999)

> *Hija de cazar—nave de encargar.*
> (To marry a daughter—to load a ship.)
> (Gaon, 1989)

The most elaborate embroidered objects—such as the bride's gown and the nuptial bed cover—were inspired by the Ottoman style, with gold braid embellishment that initially had been seen only in the sultans' courts and later became popular among the Turkish middle class. After being used in the Sephardic home, these embroidered objects were given as presents to the synagogue, where they enjoyed a new life as Torah ark curtains (*parokhet*) or Torah mantles.

A similar wealth of folk traditions was connected with *la parida*—the new mother—and her newborn baby, especially a baby boy. The new mother would stay in bed for eight days, covered by beautiful bedding, adorned with jewelry as well as with amulets to protect her and the baby from the female demon Lilith. Special protective herbs such as *ruda* (rue) were hidden in her clothes, in her bed, and in the newborn's clothes and cradle, in order to protect them from *mal ojo* (evil eye). Throughout these days, the mother and her baby were not left unattended. Female relatives would stay with her, visitors would come to congratulate her, and special songs were sung for her.

The Turkish art of paper cutting—used in the Ottoman Empire for decoration as well as for the *karagöz* shadow play—was adopted by the Sephardic Jews and used in religious contexts: Papercuts were popular decorations in the synagogue and in the sukkah and were used to decorate the *ketubbah* (marriage contract). The Judeo-Spanish art of illuminated *ketubbot* was popular in medieval Spain and characteristic of Sephardic Jews in Europe as well as in the Ottoman Empire. In Istanbul and in Izmir, this art was expressed in new styles, first hand-painted and then printed.

In the field of folk medicine, Sephardic women in Turkey, well into the second half of the twentieth century, maintained various domestic practices. Such practices included the recitation of blessings and charms; the making of ointments and medicines; the use of sugar and sugarwater against the evil eye, and against *espanto* (fright) caused by *los mijores de mozotros* (those better than us), as the demons were referred to. These practices were considered superstitious by the normative male religion represented by the rabbis, yet they were a vital part of everyday life.

Among the many important religious works created in Turkey by Sephardic sages, the one that should be mentioned in this discussion of folklore is the commentary on the Pentateuch "Me'Am lo'ez." Initiated by Rabbi Ya'akov Culi and completed by other scholars, it was published in Constantinople in 1733 and became one of the most popular volumes published among the Sephardic Jews. The commentary was written in Ladino, with materials from the Talmud, Midrash, Zohar, and rabbinic literature. These materials were woven together in a highly readable language, full of legends and tales, accessible to ordinary people. Indeed, this was the most popular Ladino book in Turkey.

In the eighteenth and nineteenth centuries, during the gradual decline of the Ottoman Empire, its large Jewish communities suffered economic hardship. Yet they continued to be intellectual centers, and in the nineteenth century they were also active in the field of secular literature and journalism. Jews, who in 1494 had established the first printing press in the empire—printing Jewish writings in Hebrew and Ladino—now published Ladino translations of European literature and had several Ladino newspapers. In the nineteenth century, the founding of branches of the international Jewish school system Alliance Israélite Universelle added the French language to the Sephardic Jews' multilayered cultural life. Newspapers and scholarly and literary works were written in French, and the Judeo-Spanish folk songs started to include French words.

The process of the Ottoman Empire's disintegration and the rise of nation-states in its territory came to its final stage in 1923 with the empire's fall and the establishment of the Republic of Turkey. To the vast reforms implemented in the empire during the nineteenth century were added new reforms by the republic's first president, Mustafa Kemal Ataturk. As part of these reforms, all children were required to attend school, including children of minority groups and girls. A mixture of influences—modernization, secular education, Zionism—changed the Sephardic folk traditions completely. Several traditions were abandoned, and others changed. The bride's dowry, for example, was still important, but instead of elaborate embroidered costumes, it now included modern objects, such as a sewing machine.

Beginning at the end of the nineteenth century, Sephardic Jews started emigrating from the Ottoman Empire, mainly to North and South America. After the State of Israel was founded in 1948, they immigrated there in massive numbers. In Israel, Turkish Jews integrated into society with relative ease, learning to speak Hebrew and leaving behind their Sephardic customs in favor of a modern Israeli identity. At the same time, Jews who remained in Turkey abandoned Ladino in favor of Turkish, as part of the process of assimilation in modern Turkey. At the beginning of the twentieth century, an estimated 450,000 Jews lived in the Ottoman Empire,

The Altalef family, Turkey, early twentieth century. *(Courtesy of the Altalef family Yehud. Photographic Archive of the Isidore and Anne Falk Information Center for Jewish Art and Life, Israel Museum, Jerusalem.)*

of which more than 200,000 lived in territories that later comprised modern Turkey. A hundred years later, the Jewish community in Turkey totals about 23,000, among which only the older generation still speaks Ladino. One Jewish weekly newspaper serves the community: *Salom* (Shalom), printed in Turkish with one page in Ladino.

For descendants of the Turkish Jews, the Sephardic folk tradition ceased to be a part of everyday life. Yet some of its treasures have gained new life, as in the case of the Ladino songs, which are enjoying a revival on concert stages. Web sites and Internet forums are dedicated to Judeo-Spanish language, folk songs, tales, proverbs, and food, as well as to documentation of personal stories told by Sephardic Turkish Jews—the parents and grandparents of the forums' members.

Etty Ben-Zaken

See also: Greece, Jews of; Illuminated Manuscripts; Joha; *Ketubbah*; Languages, Jewish; Lilith; Papercut; Spain, Jews of.

Bibliography

Alexander, Tamar. *The Beloved Friend and a Half: Studies in Sephardic Folk Literature.* Jerusalem: Magnes; Beer Sheva: Ben Gurion University Press, 1999 (in Hebrew).

Armisted, Samuel G., and Joseph H. Silverman. *Judeo-Spanish Ballads from Oral Tradition.* Berkeley: University of California Press, 1986.

Attias, Moshe. *Judeo-Spanish Cancionero.* Tel Aviv: Hamahon Leheker Yahadut Saloniki, 1972 (in Hebrew).

———. *Spanish Romancero.* Jerusalem: Kiryat Sefer, 1961 (in Hebrew).

Ben-Dov, Meir, Mordechai Naor, and Ze'ev Aner. *The Western Wall.* Jerusalem: Ministry of Defense Publishing House, 1983.

Culi, Rabbi Yaakov. *MeAm Lo'ez,* trans. Rabbi Aryeh Kaplan. New York, Jerusalem: Maznaim, [1733], 1969.

Gaon, Moshe D. *Spices from Spain.* Jerusalem: Keter, 1989 (in Hebrew).

Juhasz, Ester, ed. *Sephardi Jews in the Ottoman Empire: Aspects of Material Culture.* Jerusalem: Israel Museum, 1999 (in Hebrew).

Levy, Avigdor, ed. *The Jews of the Ottoman Empire.* Princeton, NJ: Darwin, 1994.

Levy, Isaac J., and Rosemary Levy Zumwalt. *Ritual Medical Lore of Sephardic Women.* Urbana and Chicago: University of Illinois Press, 2002.

Kohen, Elli. *History of the Turkish Jews and Sephardim.* Lanham, MD: University Press of America, 2007.

Seroussi, Edwin. *Mizimrat Qedem: The Life and Music of R. Isaac Algazi from Turkey.* Jerusalem: Renanot Institute for Jewish Music, 1989.

Shmuelevitz, Aryeh. *The Jews in Ottoman Empire in the Late Fifteenth and the Sixteenth Centuries.* Leiden: E.J. Brill, 1984.

Varol, Marie-Christine. "Recipes of Magic-Religious Medicine as Expressed Linguistically." In *Jews, Turks, Ottomans,* ed. Avigdor Levy, pp. 260–271. Syracuse: Syracuse University Press, 2002.

TZITZIT

Attaching *tzitziyot* (Heb., fringes or tassels) to one's clothes or outer garment is the only explicit biblical precept regarding Jewish dress; it applied traditionally exclusively to men, as women are exempted from this precept. In the modern age, it is fulfilled by two separate ritual garments: the prayer shawl (or *tallit*) and the poncho-like garment called "tzitzit" (lit., fringe), *tallit katan* (lit., "small *tallit*"), or *arba kanfot* (lit., "four corners").

According to the biblical commandment (Num. 15:37–41; Deut. 22:12), one should attach fringes or tassels to the four corners of one's dress. "You shall make yourself tassels [fringes] on the four corners of the garment with which you cover yourself" (Deut. 22:12). These fringes are intended to serve as constant reminders of faith and of the religious precepts a Jew must follow. "That shall be your fringes: look at it and recall all the commandments of the Lord and observe them" (Num. 15:39).

In biblical times, fringes were attached to the outer garment, which was probably a kind of sheet-like wrap with four corners. (Scholars do not know when the *tallit*, which was a garment regularly worn during the rabbinical period, became a ritual garment.) When dress styles changed, two separate ritual garments evolved to fulfill this precept. Only among Jews in Yemen did a variation of the biblical custom survive, until the twentieth century: *tzitziot* or tassels were attached to a shawl that was a regular part of the costume. The prayer shawl is a rectangular fringed shawl, worn for morning prayers every day of the year, all day on the Day of Atonement, and for important events in the Jewish lifecycle. It is used as a *ḥuppah* (wedding canopy). Traditionally in Ashkenazi communities, it is customary that a man dons the *tallit* only after marriage and the bride's family gives the groom a *tallit* as a wedding present. According to other customs, a boy dons the *tallit* when he becomes a bar mitzvah. A Jewish man is also buried wrapped in a *tallit,* and according to some traditions it is the custom to cut one of the fringes to render it ritually unfit. Prayer shawls are preferably made of sheep's wool, but they may also be made of silk or other fabrics. The tassels should not be made of a material contrary to the *sha'atnez* prohibition (in Deut. 22:11) on wearing a garment made of a mixture of wool and linen.

In some communities, mainly Sephardi, the four corners of the *tallit* are decorated. Among Ashkenazi Jews, a decorated neckband marks the top of the *tallit* called *atarah*. Today, the most common type of *tallit* is white with black stripes; others have blue stripes or are all white.

The *tallit katan*, which evolved probably in the twelfth century, was introduced in order to allow the fulfillment of the precept of wearing tzitzit all the time and not only while praying. A poncho-shaped garment, it is worn by men and boys mostly under their regular shirt all day.

According to the Torah, one tassel of the tzitzit should be blue (Num. 15:18), but since the process of production of the blue dye extracted from the *murex purpura* (a snail used to produce blue and purple dye in the Mediterranean) was lost, the fringes are usually white.

The fringes themselves consist of four cords that pass through holes at the four corners and are folded to produce eight strands, knotted and wound in differing numerical combinations that have various symbolic meanings. As each Hebrew letter has a numerical value, the number of loops and knots represents the numerical value of the letters (*gematria*) of the Names of God or the number of the mitzvoth. The religious, mystic-symbolic meaning attributed to these garments is believed to protect the wearer from immoral conduct and imbued them with protective and magical powers.

Esther Juhasz

See also: Costume.

U

Ukraine, Jews of

See: Poland, Jews of; Russia, Jews of

United States, Jews of

Folklore has been at the center of debates about the relation of Jewish identity to a gentile "host society" in the United States since 1654, when twenty-three Jews from Brazil established the first Jewish community in New Amsterdam (now New York City). Depending on the measure of population used, the United States has either the largest or second largest (after Israel) population of Jews among countries of the world (as of 2010, the U.S. figure was estimated between 5 million and 7 million, or 35 percent of all Jews in the world). Yet Jews compose a tiny proportion of the U.S. population, approximately 2 percent. The Jewish community ranges widely in terms of religious denomination, country of origin, and regional difference. Nonetheless, some general patterns—such as placing a greater importance on the observance of Ḥanukkah and the holding of the bar or bat mitzvah than Jews in other countries—can be discerned indicating the existence of a normative American tradition of Jewish folk practice. Although Jewish communities still predominantly are found in urban centers such as New York, Philadelphia, Chicago, and Los Angeles, according to surveys in 2010, American Jews have become increasingly intermarried with non-Jews, unaffiliated with a synagogue, secular, and spread out across the country. Against this tendency, at the same time growth is apparent in both the Reform and Orthodox denominations, revivals abound in Jewish arts and music, and tradition and continuity—hallmarks of folkloric concerns—are the keywords of public campaigns undertaken by Jewish organizations in order to reaffirm Jewish identity.

Because of the relationship between Jews and the wider American society, scholars have often made a distinction between *Jewish folklore*—that which Jews perpetuate within their own communities—and the *folklore of Jews*—transmitted by non-Jews about Jews, such as in ethnic jokes. The two areas converge in the discourse on identity—because the former is concerned with the public and private cultural displays of Jewishness and the latter refers to societal attitudes to which Jews respond. A historical review of the role of Jewish folklore in American culture reveals the changing character of Jewish identity in the United States and the role that folklore has played in its construction.

Early Settlements

A Jewish merchant class arose in important economic enclaves of New York, Philadelphia, Charleston (SC), Newport (RI), and Savannah (GA) along the Eastern seaboard, although the total population did not exceed 2,000 when the American Revolution erupted in 1776. Many were descendants of Dutch-Jewish refugees who were forced to leave the Recife region of northern Brazil after the Portuguese displaced the Dutch West India Company. Congregation Shearith Israel, comprising Spanish and Portuguese Jews, was organized in 1654, although it was not allowed to establish a synagogue until 1730. The conquest of New Amsterdam by the English in 1664 changed the pattern of immigration to the New World with more British Jews, including a number of merchant families from the British islands of Barbados and Jamaica who had been displaced by the changing economy of the large sugar plantations. Reflecting the national origins of many in this merchant class, Sephardic religious customs prevailed, and Jews who settled outside the main communities often made accommodations to gentile society.

After the first quarter of the eighteenth century, Ashkenazi Jews from Central Europe, many of whom were village Jews whose trades were displaced by the European Industrial Revolution and who sought religious or political autonomy, grew in numbers in the New World. By the mid-eighteenth century, most Jews lived on the East Coasts in northern British colonies in the three settlements of Newport, New York, and Philadelphia. In the South, Kahal Kadosh Mickva Israel, composed of Spanish and Portuguese Jews fleeing the Spanish Inquisition, was established in 1735 in Savannah, Georgia, and rented a building for use as a synagogue. As Jews from different backgrounds joined congregations in the early years of the republic, synagogues began to be formed to reflect their traditions, which varied from the Sephardic rites. In 1795, Dutch and German Jews, who were Ashkenazi, left the Sephardic Congregation Mikveh Israel in Philadelphia to organize a second congregation in the city. This first secession from a founding congregation in the United States signaled the first of a series of often heated discussions among American Jews about, first, establishing a normative tradition for the country's Jews and, second, the appropriate public forms of ethnic display by a minority culture. The first president of the new republic, George Washington, drew praise from American Jews when, in answer to concerns about anti-Semitism from the Jews of Newport, Rhode Island, he underscored the principle of religious freedom. When Washington's

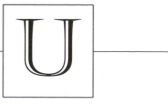

Dedication of the Kesher Israel Synagogue in Harrisburg, Pennsylvania, 1948. *(Photo courtesy of Simon Bronner)*

birthday in February became an official national holiday in 1800, Jewish congregations often celebrated it with events to commemorate his support of the principle of tolerance.

The early synagogues quickly established cemeteries, and many communities recorded the presence of a *shochet* (ritual slaughterer) to provide the community with kosher meat. Early records indicate that finding a qualified *mohel* for ritual circumcision was often more difficult. Shearith Israel, having erected a synagogue in 1730, later built a separate small stone building for a *mikveh* (ritual bathhouse). The synagogue exteriors built in the eighteenth century often reflected British Georgian and federal styles, but interiors were modeled after European precedents for Sephardic (with use of a *teba,* or platform "box") and Ashkenazi layouts (with a *bimah,* or platform, typically in the middle) and influences from American Protestant churches, such as lecterns and theater-style seating.

A narrative theme that emerged from the early republican period in the *folklore of Jews* was the humor, and sometimes ethnic slurs, in the comparison between the New World folk type of the pioneer Yankee and the Old World Jew transplanted to a new land. Both are attributed with entrepreneurship, deception, and mobility, but the Yankee typically prevails in tales in which the narrative frame involves a contest. As the motif of trickery by Jew and Yankee developed in American humor, the Jewish merchant replaced the Yankee peddler and the comparison extended to blacks, with the implication that Jews occupied a liminal racial category, as is evident in widely circulating stories that begin "There was a black man, a Jew, and a white man":

> A white man, a black, and a Jew die and go to heaven. When they get there, Saint Peter says to the white, "What do you want?" The white man answers, "Nice food, a nice pasture, and some nice sheep." Saint Peter then asks the black what he wants. He says, "A big flashy Cadillac, a million dollars, and a big white house." Saint Peter then asks the Jew what he wants and the Jew replies, "All you got to give me is a suitcase full of trinkets and the address of that black."
>
> (collected by Simon Bronner in the 1970s)

Another form of this comparison in jokes has a religious theme, involving a Protestant, a Catholic, and a Jew, but the Jew is separated from the other two in the derisive punchline:

> There was these fellas one time, were friends, and they all agreed that whichever one died first, the others

would each put $10 in his coffin. So the one died, and the Protestant came and put $10 in his coffin, and the Catholic came and he put $10 in the coffin, and the Jew, he wrote out a check for $30 and put that in, and took out the $20 change. (collected by Mac Barrick in 1968)

Other themes in American narrative folklore that emerge from the image of Jews in the early United States are more often focused on the exotic representation of the lone Jew rather than the folklife of Jews in a community. Indeed, the international legend of the "wandering Jew" was applied to many Jews who ventured out to the American frontier. The Jew with Yiddish-inflected English is not as evident in folk narratives during this period, when most Americans were foreign born, as it became in later periods, when Yiddish became attached to the American-Jewish persona. Much of the outgroup lore revolves around how peripatetic Jews were identified—their noses and eyes—or by their aversion to pork. Legends persist, however, about "lost" Jewish settlements during the early period, such as a mystery surrounding a cemetery with Hebrew inscriptions in rural Schaefferstown, Pennsylvania. Townspeople today credit the influence of this early group in the local custom of avoiding eating milk with meat.

The Wave of Central European Immigration

The American-Jewish population dramatically grew in the mid-nineteenth century as a result of a tide of immigrants from German-speaking countries. By 1880, the number of Jews in the United States swelled to 250,000, most of them German Jews from the Ashkenazi tradition who subsequently redefined American-Jewish folkways that they encountered. Many of these Jews settled inland in the rising industrial cities of Cincinnati, St. Louis, Chicago, Detroit, Milwaukee, and St. Louis. Many Irish also came in this wave of immigration, and they enter into an emerging ethnic lore in which Jews and Irish become joined as stereotyped folk types, sometimes appearing together in ethnic humor comparing comical immigrant behavior. There is some interchangeability with some of the motifs of misunderstanding "English" ways of Americans because the stereotyped immigrant characters of "Pat and Mike" are involved in humor similar to that of "Abe and Sol." Out of this period of Jewish mobility came the legends and anecdotes of the Jewish peddler selling wares to non-Jews as a new American folktype, as many German-born Jews established country peddling routes and opened general stores to serve the growing westward movement. A number of ghost stories circulating throughout the frontier featured Jews, with the commentary on the repercussions of attacking the lone vulnerable figure. Some ambivalence enters into many legends because the Jewish peddler is valued for bringing trade to the countryside, but suspicion lingers about his background. The following example is from a reminiscence documented in a local history:

> A German peddler was murdered. His body was found under a lone pine tree on the edge of the open [field], his pack rifled, all his valuables and some of his clothing removed. . . . The country people saw strange sights and one young man, returning home late at night, reported that he had seen the peddler, whom he had known well in life, running around the tree pursued by a man with an axe. So great was the dread of the spot, that no one ventured to pass the grave if they could avoid it, and there were rumors of moans and cries in that vicinity, heard from a distance. (collected by Ella Zerbey Elliott in Pottsville, Pennsylvania, 1906)

In *Jewish folklore,* German Jews actively engaged in folk art and craft, producing calligraphy, paper cutting, decoration, and needlework to be used for religious purposes. From this period date artifacts made by German Jews: elaborate decorations for eastern walls of synagogues, embroidered and appliquéd challah covers, micrographic portraits, illuminated *ketubbot* (marriage contracts), Torah binders (Ger., *wimpel*), embroidered prayer shawl bags, illuminated family registers, carved arks, and crafted metal Ḥanukkah lamps (*ḥanukkiyot*).

The East European Influx

By most estimates, more than 3.5 million Jews came to the United States from Eastern Europe between 1880 and 1920, increasing the American-Jewish population by a factor of fifteen. Driven to leave Russia, Poland, Romania, and the Austro-Hungarian Empire because of state-sanctioned anti-Semitism, which resulted in pogroms and severe legal and economic restrictions, they established in their new home a tradition of *Yiddishkeit*, or folkways brought from Yiddish-speaking areas of Eastern Europe. Many historical narratives recount conflicts between the new immigrants and assimilated German Jews, who apparently resented the purported superstitious and pietistic East European Yiddish speakers. There is evidence that many East European immigrants remained separated from gentiles and Americanized Jews by language (Yiddish), custom (in areas of dress, hair, and food), and location (establishing many dense urban "Jewish neighborhoods"). Social organizations that perpetuated homeland traditions were *landsmanschaften* (hometown benevolent associations), Yiddish-speaking union locals, and synagogues devoted to immigrants from the town of origin. They often sponsored cultural events featuring art and song and ensured that burial ceremonies and gravestones would follow that town's customs. The distinct Jewish urban settlements of the immigrants, such as the Lower East Side in Manhattan and Brownsville in Brooklyn entered into folk songs, dramas, and narratives as common settings for American-Jewish folk characters. Fusion of Old and New World traditions occurred on the American scene with new band music played for weddings (sometimes referred to as "klezmer"), labor and protest songs, legends of miracle-working rabbis, and tales of ghosts and demons in the new land. Immigration restrictions created by the U.S. government that essentially cut off the influx after 1924 also created an association of these traditions with a historic period (1880–1920) and place (New York City). In narrative folklore that entered Jewish folklore as well as folklore of Jews, a number of developments could be discerned: the folktype of the selfless, overprotective Jewish mother, the Yiddish dialect joke told by second-generation immigrants, and the figure of the assimilated Jew struggling with public assimilation and private ethnicity. Some examples of these developments illustrate the use of humor to redress the balance between Americanization as a sign of success and the emotional security of Jewish tradition.

> Sophie Goldberg was social climbing and had gone so far as to change her last name to Mont d'or [gold mountain, or a French translation of the literal meaning of Goldberg]. At a society dinner party, she asked, in her best upper-class accent: "I beg your pardon. Would you pass the butter?" But as the butter was passed, it fell into her lap. "Oy vey!" she yelled. Then, hastily composing herself, she added, "Whatever *that* means!"
>
> An old Jewish man was going to take a vacation in Hawaii, and he was worried about sounding too Jewish when he went there. So he asked his agent, "Excuse me, could you tell me again how to pronounce *Havaee*? The agent slowly pronounced it for him—H-a-w-a-ee. The man practiced and finally said "Hawaii" correctly. He came back to the agent all excited and thanked him for his help. "You're *velcome,*" the agent replied.
>
> (collected by Simon Bronner, 1970s)

In addition to narrative, an active Yiddish folk song tradition emerged in American-Jewish communities during this period. Many songs of uncertain origin using Old World tunes circulated with texts about the joys and frustrations of the American experience. In contrast to the out-group humor of the "rich Jew," in-group Yiddish folk songs about the United States often express emotional conflict. Folklorist Ruth Rubin identifies the American contribution to Yiddish folk song as theater songs based on folk tunes and songs written by poets working in a folk style.

The East European immigrants also brought other beliefs, foodways, and material culture that became integrated into American-Jewish culture. Bagels and lox (a ring-shaped bread associated with origins in Jewish Poland where the hole in the middle allowed for peddlers sticking a stick or string through it; it is commonly eaten with cream cheese and cured salmon fillet called *laks* in Yiddish) became standard American fare, for example (facilitated by the automated production and distribution of frozen bagels in the 1960s by the commercial enterprise Lender's Bagels, established by a Jewish immigrant from Poland, Harry Lender), but other foods such as *kishke* (stuffed derma) and blintzes (crêpes with a filling such as cheese or fruit) did not spread from immigrant Jewish communities to general American culture. In Jewish folklore, parents protected Jewish infants from the "evil eye" (*kein ayin hora*) by hanging *roytten bendele* (red bands) on doors and carriages and spitting three times.

Federal immigration restrictions, including the Emergency Quota Act of 1921 and the Immigration Act of 1924, limited the flow of Jews from Eastern Europe. With new immigrants lacking, this interwar period has often been characterized by historians such as Henry L. Feingold (1992) as a time for second-generation Jews to leave immigrant "ghettos" and work to enter the American cultural mainstream with organizational development and college attendance. Many of the organizations battled anti-Semitism and the imposition of quotas on Jews in higher education admissions. The groundbreaking Jewish organizations were Pi Lamda Phi, founded in 1895 at Yale, and Zeta Beta Tau, established in 1898 by students attending the Jewish Theological Seminary and New York colleges. The separation of Jews in these organizations followed the parallel development of Jewish and non-Jewish law firms, summer camps, sports leagues, and hospitals. The Jewish fraternity became an important social link to an ethnic professional network in a society through the twentieth century that restricted Jews' access to position and power. The rate of membership by Jewish college students was high up to World War II: As much as one-fourth to one-third of all young Jews from 1920 to 1940 attending universities outside New York City joined Jewish fraternities.

Post-Holocaust, Cold War, and Zionism

A surge of displaced persons, survivors of the Holocaust, as well as political refugees from communist regimes in Eastern Europe after World War II, added to *Yiddishkeit* in the United States, because many of them were

Yiddish speakers and joined existing urban communities where previous waves of Jewish immigrants had already settled. Indeed, the number of Yiddish speakers identified by the United States Census reached an all-time high in 1970 before rapidly declining thereafter. Vacation resort communities also featured Jewish folk entertainment appealing to these groups in the hotels and bungalow colonies of the Catskill Mountains in New York State during the summer and in Miami and other cities in southern Florida during the winter. The influence of the Holocaust survivor immigrants on the American experience is evident in traditional memorials filled with song and ritual on Yom Hashoah (Holocaust Remembrance Day) and in the frequent commemoration of Kristallnacht (Night of Broken Glass, which initiated Nazi violence against the Jews in Germany in 1938) in November.

The prevailing tendency among second- and third-generation immigrants was to leave the original ethnic neighborhoods in the city and move out to houses in the suburbs, following the trend of young families in postwar American society at large. Indeed, many commentators observed that the growth of Zionism in the postwar period informed a reorientation from European heritage to Israel, including adoption of Sephardic Hebrew used in Israel, increasing popularity of Middle Eastern foods and dance, crafts such as decorative *ḥamsa* making, and celebration of Israeli Independence Day. During this period, the celebrations of the bar mitzvah and weddings expanded in importance for most American Jews. Cultural historians such as Jenna Weissman Joselit (1994) have been influential in interpreting their functions changing from familial religious ceremonies to social occasions for drawing together an increasingly dispersed Jewish family unit and pronouncing economic arrival in the country to a wider community. In some areas of the American South, where Jewish social occasions required significant travel to draw a community, the rites of passage would often be planned to last several days. The egalitarian concern in many Reform and Conservative congregations influenced the American innovations of the bat mitzvah for girls and the naming ceremonies for newborn girls of the *simchat bat* or the older *zeved habat* (Sephardic).

In the *folklore of Jews,* the perception during the 1970s that Jewish daughters were given special consideration resulted in a derisive acronym—JAP—for Jewish American Princess. Building on the earlier stereotype of the selfless, overprotective Jewish mother, a JAP riddle-joke cycle spread widely in American society, usually ridiculing the selfishness of the daughter. The Jewish mother themes dwell on her providing food for the family to show love and silently accepting suffering so that the children could succeed.

What does a JAP make for dinner? Reservations.
What do you call 12 JAPs locked in the basement? A whine cellar.
How many Jewish mothers does it take to change a light bulb? None—I'll sit here in the dark.
How many Jewish princesses does it take to change a light bulb? What, and ruin my nail polish!

The joke cycle was interpreted variously as to whether it was anti-Semitic or, as told by Jews, self-deprecating. Folklorist Alan Dundes believed that Jewish women in the cycle had become symbolic in American society of *all* upwardly mobile American women who grew dissatisfied, during the period of the women's movement, with the traditional WASP (White Anglo Saxon Protestant) roles of submissive wife and mother, perceived to be normative in America. While Jewish men in humor appeared emasculated, Jewish women were conspicuously liberated. Replacing the racialized male Jew in humor, the Jewish woman as controlling and independent becomes symbolic of subtle but significant differences between assimilated Jews and the American society into which they integrated. Feminist literary critic Judith Stora-Sandor saw in the cycle an insidious extension of the "rich Jew" trope applied to the Jewish woman, with the implication that civil, and civic, values had been abandoned. In ethnographies of its exoteric performance on college campuses, the joke cycle also suggested baneful "Jew-baiting" in this period: forcing assimilated Jews to identify themselves by their reactions to the accusatory jokes. Another interpretation of the JAP and Jewish mother cycles when performed as esoteric lore by Jews is their similarity to the dialect joke in dealing with conflicts about the religious and social values lost from the older immigrant generation to the new Americanized, upwardly mobile, individualistic generation. The jokes often ask for a commentary on the differences between the immigrant generation of the sacrificing, socially concerned Jewish mother and the acquisitive, ungrateful Jewish daughter.

While such joke cycles circulating in the United States suggested secularization and assimilation by American Jews, Modern Orthodox as well as Hasidim and other ultra-Orthodox groups reasserted cultural separation and religious pietism. Strengthened by post-Holocaust immigration and a high birth rate, Hasidim grew from bases in Brooklyn, New York, to new localities such as Monsey and New Square (named for Skver, their town of origin in Ukraine), New York, where they could create homogeneous communities. Divided into separate movements such as Lubavitch, Bobover, and Satmar, according to their town of origin in Europe, they formed urban folklife enclaves revolving around charismatic rabbinical leaders such as Menachem Mendel Schneerson (Lubavitch), Shlomo Halberstamm (Bobover), Joel

Teitelbaum (Satmar), and Mordechai Shlomo Friedman (Boyaner). Massive gatherings where the rabbi speaks and *nigunim* (chanted melodies) are sung are distinguishing events. They reinforce separation from American society as well as identifying themselves to other Hasidic groups by donning prescribed clothing for everyday use (e.g., a *kapote,* or long black overcoat) and holidays (e.g., a *shtreimel*, fur hat made of sable). Non-Hasidic Jews thus often refer to the Hasidim as "black hatters." Hair customs also distinguish the groups, since the men wear untrimmed beards and *payes* (sidelocks) and married women don a *sheitel* (wig). Yiddish is still spoken in these communities, and ritual specialists including a *shochet*, *sofer* (scribe, who repairs Torahs and inscribes the text for *mezuzot*), and *mohel* are active. In addition to European-based legends of the founder of Hasidim, the Ba'al Shem Tov, new legends of miracle-working rabbis in America and of the Holocaust experience have entered into the rich oral tradition of Hasidim.

As congregations identified themselves as Orthodox, Conservative, Reform, or Reconstructionist in orientation, a folk humor arose to comment on diversity, and divisiveness, within American-Jewish religious identity. The common types include:

> A Jewish man who graduated from college wanted to know if there was a *bracha* (blessing) appropriate for the occasion. He first went to the Orthodox rabbi in town and asked him. His reply was, "I'll have to check the Talmud." He then went to a Conservative rabbi who said, "We can write one for the occasion based on tradition." He finally went to a Reform rabbi who said, "What's a *bracha?*"
>
> A shipwrecked Jewish man is rescued from a desert island, and the rescuers notice two imposing structures that he has built on the island. The rescuers ask him what they are, and he replies, "They're synagogues." "But why two?" they ask. He answers, "One is the one I pray in, and the other one is the one I'm mad at [or the one I wouldn't set foot in]."
>
> (collected by Simon Bronner, 1980s)

In response to a growing perception by Jews in the 1970s that they had become more assimilated and homogenized in the third and fourth generations after immigration, grassroots Jewish movements emerged, advocating for renewal, ethnic diversity, and, in many cases, innovation in the performance of religious customs. The Havurah (Fellowship) movement, for example, encouraged small groups to define traditions for themselves, create an intimate face-to-face folk experience, and adapt custom to their social needs as members of gay, deaf, feminist, and convert networks. Congregations such as the Yemenite Jewish Center of America in Brooklyn, New York, acted to preserve rites that were neither Sephardic nor Ashkenazi. Further adding to diversity, African-American congregations were established in Philadelphia and Baltimore and adapted African heritage to the practice of Judaism.

Interest in East European heritage was also informed by the new tide of Jewish immigration from the former Soviet Union. These immigrants spread into many urban areas, but Brighton Beach in Brooklyn became one particular focus and was dubbed "Little Odessa" in recognition of the special ethnic atmosphere of the neighborhood. While Russian Jews were not known for their religious pietism, they reinvigorated the foodways repertoire of breads, meats, and fish, and various folk arts, associated with *Yiddishkeit.* Yet folklorists noted the distinctive subcultures of the Soviet immigration that represented evolving forms of tradition, much of which was not in Yiddish, such as folk music and customs from Uzbekistan and Tajikistan. The Bukharan community from Uzbekistan in particular settled in towns in Queens, New York, where its Central Asian dress and music drew folkloristic interest. Fatima Kuinova, founding member and vocalist of the Bukharan Jewish Ensemble, received a National Heritage Award from the National Endowment of the Arts (NEA) in 1992 in recognition of masters of traditional arts.

In addition to this East European influx, a new wave of Sephardic immigration took place from the 1960s to the 1990s that helped form new folk communities. After the Six-Day War in 1967 and the spread of Islamic fundamentalism, among other factors, Jews who had long lived in Arabic-speaking countries began to depart in large numbers, migrating to the United States and other Western countries. Jews from Morocco, Syria, Yemen, Iran, and Iraq often settled in ethnic enclaves and established cultural institutions of music, food, and art. Much attention has been paid to Syrian Jews who settled in Brooklyn, many of whom came from Aleppo, Syria, and continued a repertory of folk song called *pizmonim* (lit., adoration or praise). These paraliturgical hymns consist primarily of Hebrew texts set to melodies borrowed from Middle Eastern Arab music. Other communities of Moroccan Jews settled in Los Angeles and Miami, and a new transnational identity—Israelis distinct from the previous immigrant waves in their back and forth migration—formed ethnic cultural zones in Los Angeles, Miami, and New York. Ladino, the ancient language of Sephardim that combined Spanish with Hebrew, experienced a revival as some immigrants recorded the legacy of Ladino song, narrative, and music. Flory Jagoda, who came from Bosnia and settled in the area of Washington, D.C., became revered as a prominent American Ladino performer; she recorded extensively, had a film made about her (*Key from Spain: The Songs and Stories of Flory Jagoda,* 2000), and received a National Heritage Award in 2002.

As the profile of American Jews diversified with varieties of religious expression, forms of community, and ethnic and national backgrounds, the ways in which Jewish identity is culturally expressed, and would be perpetuated, became a public issue of concern. Population surveys in the early twenty-first century showing high rates of intermarriage, assimilation, dispersal, and commercialization in the United States raised questions about the sustainability of Jewish communities and the role of holiday traditions, ritual observance, folk storytelling, and music making in perpetuating a singular Jewish culture.

Simon J. Bronner

See also: Dialect Stories, Jewish-American; Dundes, Alan.

Bibliography

Abramovitch, Ilana, and Sean Galvin, eds. *Jews of Brooklyn.* Hanover, NH: Brandeis University Press, 2002.

Bronner, Simon J. "Fathers and Sons: Rethinking the Bar Mitzvah as an American Rite of Passage." *Children's Folklore Review* 31 (2008–2009): 7–34.

———. "From *Landsmanshaften* to *Vinkln:* Mediating Community Among Yiddish Speakers in America." *Jewish History* 15 (2001): 131–48.

Bronner, Simon J., ed. *Revisioning Ritual: Jewish Traditions in Transition.* Oxford, UK: Littman, 2011.

Dundes, Alan. *Cracking Jokes: Studies of Sick Humor Cycles and Stereotypes.* Berkeley, CA: Ten Speed, 1987.

Feingold, Henry L. *A Time for Searching: Entering the Mainstream, 1920–1945.* Baltimore: Johns Hopkins University Press, 1992.

Glanz, Rudolf. *The Jew in the Old American Folklore.* New York: Waldon, 1961.

Joselit, Jenna Weissman. *The Wonders of America: Reinventing Jewish Culture, 1880–1950.* New York: Hill and Wang, 1994.

Kleebat, Norman L., and Gerard C. Wertkin. *The Jewish Heritage in American Folk Art.* New York: Universe Books, 1984.

Mintz, Jerome R. *Hasidic People: A Place in the New World.* Cambridge, MA: Harvard University Press, 1992.

———. *Legends of the Hasidim: An Introduction to Hasidic Culture and Oral Tradition in the New World.* Chicago: University of Chicago Press, 1968.

Ochs, Vanessa. *Inventing Jewish Ritual.* Philadelphia: Jewish Publication Society, 2007.

Peltz, Rakhmiel. *From Immigrant to Ethnic Culture: American Yiddish in South Philadelphia.* Stanford, CA: Stanford University Press, 1998.

Prell, Riv-Ellen. *Prayer and Community: The Havurah in American Judaism.* Detroit: Wayne State University Press, 1989.

Rubin, Ruth. *Voices of a People: The Story of Yiddish Folksong.* 2d ed. New York: McGraw-Hill, 1973.

Shelemay, Kay Kaufman. *Let Jasmine Rain Down: Song and Remembrance Among Syrian Jews.* Chicago: University of Chicago Press, 1998.

Sherman, Josepha. *A Sampler of Jewish American Folklore.* Little Rock, AR: August House, 1992.

Slobin, Mark, ed. *American Klezmer: Its Roots and Offshoots.* Berkeley: University of California Press, 2002.

Soyer, Daniel. *Jewish Immigrant Associations and American Identity in New York, 1880–1939.* Cambridge, CA: Harvard University Press, 1997.

Staub, Shalom. *Yemenis in New York City: The Folklore of Ethnicity.* Cranbury, NJ: Associated University Presses, 1989.

Stern, Gail F. *Traditions in Transition: Jewish Culture in Philadelphia, 1840–1940.* Philadelphia: Balch Institute for Ethnic Studies, 1989.

Stora-Sandor, Judith. "From Eve to the Jewish American Princess: The Comic Representation of Women in Jewish Literature." In *Semites and Stereotypes: Characteristics of Jewish Humor,* ed. Avner Ziv and Anat Azjdman, pp. 131–141. Westport, CT: Greenwood, 1993.

Wertheimer, Jack. *A People Divided: Judaism in Contemporary America.* Hanover, NH: Brandeis University Press, 1993.

USHPIZIN

See: Sukkot

W

Wahl, Saul (c. 1542–1622)

The legend about Saul Wahl is one of the most famous and popular legends in the folklore of Polish Jewry. It tells about a Jew who became the king of Poland for a short time.

Saul Wahl was a historical figure of the sixteenth and seventeenth centuries. According to Meir Bałaban, Wahl was a well-to-do merchant who dealt in lumber, salt, customs duties, highway tolls, and so on. His business interests included the famous salt works of Wieliczka, near Kraków. In 1588 King Sigismund III granted him a ten-year lease on the revenues of the fortress of Brisk. In a decree published on June 7, 1589, the king conferred on him the highest title that a Jew could attain, that of *servus regis* or "royal servant," which meant, among other things, that he could not be summoned before an ordinary court of law, only the royal tribunal, and had to report on his actions exclusively to the king. This dignity elevated Wahl's status among his fellow Jews, who were proud of the "royal servant" who could appear before kings and princes and need fear no one. Wahl was an important and honored member of his community and renowned throughout Lithuania. He was the head of the community in Brisk, saw to the welfare of the Jews of that town, and became a member of the Council of the Four Lands when it was founded in 1581. His son Meir, who became the rabbi of Brisk, was the first to bear the family name Wahl.

According to the legend, Saul Wahl had a very brief reign as king of Poland (twenty-four hours or even just one night). Another Jew said to have been king of Poland is Abraham Prochownik (see: Prochownik, Abraham). Several versions of the legend appear in *Gedulat Sha'ul: Memories, Stories, and Tales About the Rabbi and Sage Rabbi Saul Wahl,* by Hirsch Edelmann, printed in London in 1854 (and reprinted in Warsaw in 1925, with an introduction by Meir Bałaban). The book was commissioned by Wahl's descendants, who treated it as a sacred heritage. The legends about Wahl circulated orally, as Bałaban attests; they existed in slight variants in different places and in the accounts of different narrators. Common to all versions is that Wahl was briefly king of Poland. The legends are replete with etiological elements. In particular, they explain the hero's surname: Saul, the son of Rabbi Samuel Judah Katzenellenbogen, the head of the rabbinical court in Padua, received the surname Wahl because he was elected (Yid., *veyl'n*) king of Poland. According to Bałaban (ibid.), however, the name derives from Saul's birthplace, Italy. Italian Jews were known as *Vlokh* (Ger., *Wohl*), whence the surname Wahl. Saul's paternal grandfather was a German Jew from the town of Katzenellenbogen in Nassau who studied in Polish yeshivas in his youth and then moved to Italy, where he married the daughter of the rabbi of Padua and eventually inherited his father-in-law's post. His son Samuel Judah, Saul's father, served in the rabbinate there until his death in 1597. In a letter from Rabbi Leon (Judah Aryeh) de Modena to Rabbi Phineas Horowitz in Kraków, he is referred to as "the prince, our teacher Saul, son of our teacher the Gaon Samuel Judah [Katzenellenbogen] of Padua." In royal documents he is referred to as Saul Judycz (i.e., son of Judah).

The legend explains Wahl's unanimous acclamation as king of Poland by the fact that, after the death of the previous king, the assembled nobles failed to elect his successor within the period fixed by law. Consequently, they decided to enthrone Saul temporarily until they could agree on a permanent ruler. Historians dismiss this possibility outright. According to Bałaban, the folk imagination turned a leading figure of the Jewish community, who was "rich as a king," into a flesh-and-blood king of Poland. But, he adds, the narrators understood that a Jew could not be elected king in the normal fashion and consequently added the disagreement among the electors and his selection for a limited term.

The legend ascribes legislation favorable to the Jews and especially the establishment of synagogues to Saul Wahl's brief reign. After his enthronement, all the nobles and clergy proclaimed, "Long live the king!" Shortly thereafter, they brought forth the *Great Book of Privileges*, in which Saul proceeded to inscribe in his own hand various decrees to benefit the Jews. The holdings of the Israel Folktale Archives at the University of Haifa include a legend (IFA 5217) that ascribes the construction of the synagogue in *Szczebrzeszyn* to the Jewish king of Poland, Saul Wahl (Bar-Itzhak 2001, 155–158); Saul Wahl's name was in fact associated with the synagogue. In Lublin it was customary to distribute the various honors on Simchat Torah "with the permission of the prince Reb Saul Wahl." The Lublin synagogue, too, was known as the Saul Wahl Synagogue. Bałaban conjectures that Wahl was responsible for its construction and may even have prayed there when the Council of Four Lands was in session. Although documentary evidence is lacking, it is known that his descendants ran the synagogue for centuries. In his final years, he also seems to have sponsored the construction of a synagogue in Brisk. When it was torn down in 1840, on orders of the Russian tsar Nicholas I (r. 1825–1855), an inscription was found in the women's gallery: "The prince Reb Saul, son of the sage our teacher Samuel Judah of Padua, built the women's gallery for a sign and testimonial, in memory of his wife, Deborah, of blessed memory, the pious and righteous woman, daughter of [Reb David Dr]ucker, his memory for eternal life . . . [the month of] Tevet in the year . . . in her house."

Another point explained by the legend is Wahl's eminence. He is said to have traveled in many countries before he reached Lithuania and settled in Brisk. There he married the daughter of David Drucker and lived with his wife in extreme poverty. Around that time, the rich nobleman Prince Radziwiłł made a pilgrimage to the Holy Land. Returning home through Italy, he found himself short of funds. To avoid being humiliated among his peers, the prince turned to Rabbi Samuel Judah, who lent him a large sum of money. Before he resumed his journey, Prince Radziwiłł l asked the rabbi whether he had any relatives in Poland. When he reached Brisk, he gave orders to summon the rabbi's son and showered him with largesse. From then on, luck was with Saul, and he rose steadily in wealth and honor.

Bałaban reports that Prince Karol Mikolaj Radziwiłł (known as Sierotka, "the orphan") did make a pilgrimage to the Holy Land in 1582–1584. On his way home, he was robbed by highwaymen in Italy and forced to borrow money to cover his expenses. In his published account, Radziwiłł reported that he obtained the funds from a Venetian merchant named Quinctilius (thus not from a Jew), offering as collateral several small items he had brought back from Palestine.

Contrary to the legendary version that young Wahl was destitute until his encounter with Prince Radziwiłł, Bałaban cites historical documents to show that, as early as 1578, he was a well-to-do merchant, running important salt works. But the prince did not set out on his pilgrimage until 1582, was waylaid in 1584, and returned to his estate that same year.

Another legend concerns Saul's daughter Ḥannah. Saul's prominence had won him many enemies among the Jews of Brisk. When all their slanders had come to naught, they decided to tell the court officials, who were looking for a bride for their widowed monarch, about the beautiful young girl. Ḥannah delighted the courtiers and was a princess, besides; so they decided to abduct her from her father's house by night and smuggle her to the royal palace.

But one nobleman, Saul's friend, tipped him off, and he resolved to marry the girl off without delay and forestall the plot. Because of the difficulty of finding a suitable groom within a short time, his choice fell on the recently widowed rabbi of Brisk, the sixty-year-old Zalman Shor, author of the book *Tevuot Shor.* Their son became a great scholar in his own right.

This legend touched off friction within the Jewish community, including slander and attempts to harm Saul even if it meant violating a major Jewish taboo. The motif of marriage between an old rabbi and a young girl, whose offspring is a great sage, is found in many legends about women in troubled times, such as that about the sister of Rabbi Shabbetai ben Meir HaCohen (1621–1662), known as the Shakh (Ben-Yehezkiel 1961, vol. 3: 273–278).

According to tradition, Wahl died in 1617; the biographer Sergei Bershadski assigned his death as 1622. His tombstone has never been located.

Haya Bar-Itzhak

See also: Poland, Jews of; Prochownik, Abraham.

Bibliography

Bałaban, Meir. *Yidn in Poylen* (Jews in Poland). Vilna: Klatzkin, 1930 (in Yiddish).

Bar-Itzhak, Haya. *Jewish Poland: Legends of Origin.* Detroit: Wayne State University Press, 2001.

Ben-Yehezkiel, Mordechai. *Book of Folktales.* Tel Aviv: Dvir, 1961 (in Hebrew).

Bershadski, Sergei. "Yevrei korol polski" (Jew King of Poland). *Voskhod* 9 (1889): fasciles I–II, 3–37; III, 3–17; IV, 11–23; V, 101–115.

Bloch, Philip. "Die Sage von Saul Wahl, dem Einsags Koening von Polen." *Zeitschrift der Historischen Gessellschaft für die Provinz Posen* 4 (1889), 234–258.

Edelmann, Hirsch. *Gedulat Sha'ul.* London, 1854 (in Hebrew).

Karpeles, Gustav. "A Jewish King in Poland." In *Jewish Literature and Other Essays,* pp. 272–292. Philadelphia: Jewish Publication Society of America, 1895.

Wandering Jew

The Wandering Jew, also called "the Eternal Jew," is a legendary figure known especially from European Christian folklore. The tradition of the Wandering Jew is manifest in a number of major modes: (1) local legends announcing his arrival at a specific location usually close but not identical to the narrator's; (2) a religious legend narrating the etiology of his wandering in a meeting between the Wandering Jew and Jesus at the Crucifixion; (3) chapbooks including both aforementioned elements; (4) visual images of the figure in chapbooks and other media; (5) inclusion of the figure in works of art, literature, and drama.

The Plot

The religious legend that serves as the narrative core of the Wandering Jew tradition tells how Jesus, when he was carrying the cross on the Via Dolorosa toward Golgotha, asked to rest for a while against the wall of a

Postcard of "The Wandering Jew." Original artwork by Leonid Pasternak. *(Joseph and Margit Hoffman Judaica Postcard Collection, Folklore Research Center, Hebrew University of Jerusalem. Cat. no. hof9–0211)*

local Jerusalemite cobbler's house. The cobbler denied the request, and consequently Jesus cursed him, saying: "Also you shall not rest but wander until my return," or a similar phrase that constitutes in general the most stable element of the legend's tradition. Ever after the man is condemned to wander the world and is seen in various locations, especially in times of catastrophe and war.

In many versions, the man is called Ahasver, or Ahasverus, emulating somewhat mysteriously the name of the Persian king of the biblical Book of Esther. Because surely this name was never given to any Jewish person, the theories explaining its choice for this particular tradition range from a reference to the famous stupidity of the king in Jewish folklore, to his role in the Purimshpil performances that may have been known even among non-Jews in late medieval Central Europe, and to King Ahasverus's hanging of Haman in the Purim story, which had satirically been compared to the Crucifixion in some rabbinic traditions in late antiquity. Whereas English-language traditions prefer the Wandering Jew, as does the French "le juif errant," in Scandinavian oral traditions he is almost invariably known as "the Cobbler of Jerusalem," and the German language has favored the name "Ewige Jude"—the Eternal Jew—referring to his immortality, rather than to his wandering. The local legends that accompany the religious legend mention the curious imprints left by his feet and his strange apparel often replete with features such as a tiger-hide hat or a camel-hair coat. It is also made clear by the legends that he is now a repentant and believing Christian who is generous with alms, that he knows all languages wherever he goes, and, above all, that he cannot die.

Sources

The earliest-known version of the complete legend was published in German chapbooks more or less simultaneously in 1602 in a number of editions in various European cities, including Basel and Reval, bearing a long and detailed title: "The Short Description of a Jew Who etc." The frame narrative describes his meeting in a church in Hamburg in the mid-sixteenth century with the priest Paul von Eitzen, one of the students of Philip Melanchton who was also the teacher of Martin Luther and his main adviser in his translation project of the Bible into the German vernacular. The legend about the Crucifixion is told to von Eitzen by the Wandering Jew himself—here named Ahasverus for the first time—to explain his strange destiny.

Research, above all by George K. Anderson in a masterful comprehensive monograph (1965), has unearthed a great number of earlier sources that have been integrated in the legend's full-fledged form. Some eternal wanderers, such as the biblical Cain, on the one hand, and Elijah, on the other hand, are natural candidates; the Quranic Sameri, incessantly wandering after having been cursed by Moses, is another. In addition to Jesus's own promise to return (Matt. 16:28), the New Testament figures of Malchus, the Roman soldier who hurts Jesus's ear, another nameless one who slaps Jesus on one hand, and John the beloved disciple who immortally awaits his master's Second Coming (John 21:22 ff.) appear more plausibly linked to the legend. An early-thirteenth-century (1228) note in Roger de Wendover's chronicle *Flores Historiarum*—recounted in Matthew Paris's chronicle of St. Alban's Abbey in England (1252), and before that in a French-language text by Philippe Mouskes (1243)—mentions a visiting Armenian bishop who told about an immortal, cursed wanderer related to the Crucifixion story.

Thus the tradition seems to have circulated in southern Europe by the time of the late Middle Ages and the Renaissance, plausibly distributing traditions carried from the Holy Land by those returning from the Crusades and by the more and more frequent pilgrims. Learned texts, too, sometimes refer to an eternal wanderer, notably an astrological treatise from the fifteenth century reporting on the earliest visit of the figure in Europe, allegedly in the thirteenth century; however, no mention is made of his being a Jew. Some names from those traditions include the Italian Giovanni Buttadeo, referring to the slapping, and Juan Espera en Dios, he who awaits the coming of the Lord.

Context

The function of the legend in the context of Reformation theology seems obvious: an immediate eyewitness report of the life of Jesus and the Crucifixion as a worthier substitute for the mediated traditions in the Orthodox and Catholic traditions. It is thus no wonder that the legend was widely distributed, most typically in German but later in almost every European language. According to Leonhard Neubaur, who made the first full-length and thorough philological-historical study of the legend in the late nineteenth century (1884), the chapbook was one of the most popular German chapbooks of the seventeenth century, second only to the *Faustbuch*. The legend was also widely integrated in anti-Semitic rhetoric culminating in the Nazi propaganda film *Der ewige Jude* (1940). The visual representations of the Wandering Jew figure constitute a very important medium of transmitting the concrete elements of the image as well the beliefs associated with it and reflect its versatility in changing cultural environments.

Contrary to the general view, however, the Wandering Jew was not only an image projected by Christian Europeans on Jews, as there also exist intra-Jewish traditions about wanderers such as the early medieval travelers from Europe to the Holy Land (e.g., Benjamin of Tudela, Petaḥiah of Regensburg), but also typological wanderers, such as itinerant merchants or sages, and even restless souls wandering around in the universe. Naturally these did not traditionally apply the motifs and themes extant in the Christian legend that constitutes the major European tradition of the Wandering Jew. This is, however, true until modernity. From the early nineteenth century onward, the Wandering Jew was adapted from the until then predominantly folk and popular traditions into canonized literature and art. Famous adaptations are Eugene Sue's novel *Le juif errant* (1844) and Hans Christian Andersen's drama *Ahasverus* (1847). It is from canonical literature and art that Jewish authors, especially in German but later also in English, Hebrew, and many other languages, adapted the figure, combining the characterization of the wanderer as embodying modernity itself, its dynamism and changes, as well as a growing sense of estrangement, most famously and masterfully embodied in the Jew Leopold Bloom, the protagonist of James Joyce's *Ulysses* (1922).

Galit Hasan-Rokem

See also: Dundes, Alan; Hasan-Rokem, Galit.

Bibliography

Anderson, George K. *The Legend of the Wandering Jew.* Providence: Brown University Press, 1965.

Finzt Menascé, Esther, ed. *L'ebreo errante: Metamorfosi di un mito.* Milan: Cisalpino, 1993.

Hasan-Rokem, Galit, and Alan Dundes, eds. *The Wandering Jew: Essays in the Interpretation of a Christian Legend.* Bloomington: Indiana University Press, 1986.

Körte, Mona, and Robert Stockhammer. *Ahasvers Spur: Dichtungen und Dokumente vom "Ewigen Juden."* Leipzig: Reclam, 1995.

Millin, Gaël. *Le cordonnier de Jérusalem: La véritable histoire du juif errant.* Rennes: Presses Universitaires de Rennes, 1997.

Sigal-Klagsbald, Laurence, and Richard Cohen. *Le juif errant, un témoin du temps.* Paris: Adam Biro and Musée d'art et d'histoire du judaïsme, 2001.

WEDDING

See: Marriage

WESTERN WALL

Dating from the Second Temple period, the Western Wall commonly refers to an 187-foot (57-meter) exposed section of ancient wall situated on the western flank of the Temple Mount in the Old City of Jerusalem. The wall functioned as a retaining wall, built to support the extensive renovations that Herod the Great carried out around 19 C.E. It is a sacred Jewish religious site that has appeared in multiple folktales.

Over the centuries, land close to the Western Wall became built up. Following the Six-Day War (1967), a large plaza for prayer was created that stretched from the wall to the Jewish Quarter. Archaeological finds have revealed a much shorter section known as the Little Western Wall, which is located close to the Iron Gate.

The Western Wall is venerated by Jews as the sole remnant of the Temple. Since the seventeenth century, it has become a place of pilgrimage and prayer for Jews, as it is the closest accessible site to the "Holy of Holies," which lies on the Temple Mount, access to which was permitted to Jews by the Muslim authorities until 1917 and by the British authorities during the Mandate period (1917–1948). During the Jordanian occupation of the old

Silver tobacco box, engraved with the Western (Wailing) Wall. Jerusalem, late nineteenth century. *(Gross Family Collection, Tel Aviv)*

city of Jerusalem (1948–1967), Jews from Israel were not allowed to visit the site.

Every year on Tisha Be'Av large crowds congregate at the wall to commemorate the destruction of the Temple. The Western Wall Plaza is the site of worship and public gatherings, including bar mitzvah celebrations and swearing-in ceremonies of newly full-fledged soldiers in the Israel Defense Forces, following basic training.

The Western Wall is mentioned several times in the Midrash (*Shemot* [Exodus] *Rabba* 2:2; *Bamidbar* [Numbers] *Rabba* 11:2; *Shir Ha'Shirim Rabba* 2:4; *Eicha Rabba* 1:3; *Midr. Kohelet Zuta* 7:8; *Tanḥuma, Shemot* 10, and more). All these refer to the western wall of the temple and not to the present Western Wall. According to these midrashic sayings, God promised that the Western Wall would never be destroyed and the *Shekhinah* (The Divine Presence of God) never moved from the western wall of the temple. According to the Zohar, the word *kotel* (wall) is made up of two parts: *ko,* which has the numerical value of God's name, and *tel*, meaning "mount," which refers to the temple, that is, the Western Wall (Zohar, Vol. II [Shmot]; Mishpatim 116:1). These sayings were the basis for the sanctification of the Western Wall as a holy place.

According to Jewish custom, one is obligated to feel grief and rend one's garment upon visiting the Western Wall. This custom is based on the Babylonian Talmud (Mo'ed Katan 26:1).

There is a practice of placing slips of paper containing written prayers in the crevices of the wall. The earliest account of this custom is by Abraham Isaac Sperling in his book *Sefer ha'minhagim u'mekorei ha'dinim* (The Book of Customs and Origins of Laws) (1891). There is a legend about Rabbi Ḥaim ben Atar (1696–1743), who wrote an amulet on parchment and advised a poor man to place it between the stones of the wall in order to obtain help from God. Recently, the Israeli Telephone Company has actually established a fax service to the Western Wall, so that petitioners can send notes to be placed in the wall.

An old custom of removing one's shoes upon visiting the wall has faded over the years and is no longer observed. Other customs that no longer exist involve inserting one's finger into cracks in the wall to receive God's mercy, putting a palmprint with blue paint on the wall or inserting a nail into a crack in the wall before going on a journey. This last custom is based on the biblical verses: "And I will fasten him as a peg in a sure place" (Isa. 22:23); "and to give us a nail in His holy place" (Ezra 9:8). Another custom is measuring some stones with a woolen thread and putting the thread around the loin of pregnant women to relieve the pain associated with childbirth or to prevent a spontaneous miscarriage.

Some people rented houses with a window that faced the wall. This custom was based on a biblical verse about Daniel: "His windows were open in his upper chamber toward Jerusalem" (Dan. 6:11). There are many legends and traditions connected with the wall. A legend that was probably created in the fifteenth century recounts that on the night of Tisha Be'Av the candles in Mosque of Omar (Al-Aqsa Mosque), which is near the Western Wall, burn out. Another tradition states that when water starts trickling through the stones of the wall, it is a sign of the advent of the messiah.

The Israel Folktale Archives (IFA) at the University of Haifa holds about thirty folktales about the wall. Many legends concern miracles that occurred to worshipers who came to pray near the wall (IFA 1002, 3542, 10680, and 11827). A Yemenite-Jewish story that is found in the IFA in two versions (IFA 1026 and 3096) and appears also in other communities (IFA 10613, 12990, 13575, and 13848) tells of rioters who tried to hurt Rabbi Shalom Sharabi (1720–1777) when he came to pray near the wall, and their limbs were paralyzed as a punishment. An Iraqi-Jewish legend (IFA 489) tells about a stone used for the purpose of idolatry that is stuck in the wall and prevents salvation. There are also some modern jokes about the wall: A tourist is looking for the "Wailing Wall" and is directed to the office of the income tax (IFA 17712); a groom brings his bride to the wall to teach her about "speaking to a stone" (IFA 21590).

Yoel Perez

See also: Bar and Bat Mitzvah; Jerusalem and the Temple.

Bibliography

Ben-Dov, Meir, Mordechai Naor, and Zeev Aner. *The Western Wall.* Tel Aviv: Ministry of Defence Publishing House, 1983 (in Hebrew).

Chesler, Phyllis, and Rivka Haut, eds. *Women of the Wall: Claiming Sacred Ground at Judaism's Holy Site.* Woodstock, VT: Jewish Lights, 2003.

Schiler, Eli and Gabriel Barkay, eds. "The Western Wall." *Ariel* 181–182 (2007) (in Hebrew).

WOMEN IN RABBINIC LITERATURE

In rabbinic literature, folk motifs related to women can be found in two themes: (1) the cycle of life, including birth, childhood, marriage, the conceiving and bearing of children, and death; and (2) the contents of life, such as personality traits, activities, and physical appearance.

Life Cycle

The birth of a baby girl historically was seen as less desirable than the birth of a baby boy. Many sayings by different sages suggest methods for ensuring the birth of a son. For example: "He who sanctifies himself during cohabitation will have male children" (*b. Shevuot* 18b), "From the third to the fortieth day (after conceiving) he should pray that the child should be a male" (*b. Berakhot* 60a), and so on.

Other sayings present a clear distinction between the joy of fathering sons and the misery of fathering daughters. For example: "The rabbi said: . . . nor can the world exist without males and females, happy is he whose children are males, woe to him whose children are females" (*b. Pesaḥim* 65a).

In spite of the misery attributed to parenting girls, there are many stories in the Talmud that praise the wisdom, the grace, and the moral strength of daughters. These include the stories of Rabbi Joshua ben Ḥananiah's meeting with wise and brave girls (*b. Erubin* 53a; *Lam. Rab.* 1), the stories of arguments between Rabban Gamliel's wise daughter and the Roman governor (*b. Sanhedrin* 39a, 90b–91a), the stories of Rav Hisda's wise daughter (*b. Bava Batra* 12b, 141a), and many others.

The sages assumed that the mental development of girls is more rapid than that of boys. Therefore, according to their judgment, a girl becomes a woman when she reaches the age of twelve years and one day while a boy becomes a man only when he is thirteen years and one day.

The usual concept in the sages' world was that even though it is natural that a man pursues a woman, it is the woman who desires to marry. Perhaps this belief was prevalent because the bride, not the bridegroom, was the center of the marriage celebration.

The obligation of bringing joy to the bride was considered so important that the sages themselves used to dance in front of or even with brides and sing hymns of praise for them. "Our rabbis taught: How does one dance before the bride? Beit Shammai say, 'the bride as she is.' And Beit Hillel say, 'beautiful and graceful bride'" (*b. Ketubbot* 16b–17a). "When Rabbi Dimi came, he said: 'Thus they sing before the bride in the West: no powder and no paint and no waving (of the hair) and still a graceful gazelle'" (*b. Ketubbot* 17a). "They tell at Rabbi Judah ben Illai that he used to take a myrtle twig and dance before the bride and say beautiful and graceful bride. Rabbi Samuel, the son of Rabbi Isaac danced with three twigs. . . . Rabbi Aḥa took her on his shoulder and danced [with her]" (*b. Ketubbot* 17a–b).

Many folk motifs are connected to what was considered women's most important role: bearing children. Conception itself was viewed as a miracle that could not occur without the interference of God and angels.

"Our rabbis taught: There are three partners in man: the Holy one blessed be he, the father, and the mother" (*b. Qiddushin* 30b). "Rabbi Ḥanina ben Papa made the following exposition: The name of the angel who is in charge of conception is 'Night' and he takes up a drop and places it in the presence of the Holy One" (*b. Niddah* 16b).

There are numerous beliefs related to the right ways to conceive, proper behavior during pregnancy, appropriate foods for women to eat during pregnancy and while breast-feeding, and the changes a woman's body undergoes after having a baby. The difficulties with regard to conception and the pains women suffer during delivery are topics of many folk stories, words of advice, and idioms that appear in many places in the talmudic and midrashic literature.

Burial and mourning customs for men and women are almost equal. They differ in two ways: (1) in cases where the death occurs simultaneously, the woman is buried first; and (2) a woman's body should not be presented in public, unlike that of a man.

Women participated in funeral ceremonies just as men did, but not side by side with them. In the Galilee, women went in front of the deathbed and men behind it, and in Judea vice versa. Women had specific roles as mourners in the funeral and burial ceremonies.

Contents of Life

Many negative human qualities are attributed to women in the sages' sayings and in folk stories. They were accused of being: lazy, envious, talkative, overly curious, quick to anger, apt to speak too loudly, vain, and of a disposition to become prostitutes and thieves. Some of these bad qualities were in dispute, with certain sages disagreeing that women speak too loudly, are vain, and are disposed to become prostitutes. Ancient Jewish sources also attributed to women some positive qualities, such as a pleasant voice, beauty, sensitivity, and compassion.

Women were usually expected to stay in their homes and gain their satisfaction from caring for their husbands and children. The typical occupations of women, apart from housework, were sewing and knitting.

However, some professions were regarded as more suitable for women, even though historians do not know whether women received payment for their tasks. Women were known for being mourners, hairdressers, midwives, and the source of sustenance for their children.

Sorcery was also considered a woman's domain. The connection between women and magic is expressed in general sayings found in many sources such as *Mishnah Avot* 2 and *b. Soferim* 15. This connection is also expressed in many specific tales, such as the story of Yohani bat Retivi, who disturbed women during labor (*b. Sottah* 22a), the story about eighty witches who troubled the whole world from their cave in Ashkelon until Rabbi Simeon ben Shatach suppressed them (*y. Ḥagigah* 2,13), and many others.

Another field in which women were active was medicine. Numerous talmudic stories relate to the medical knowledge of a woman who was called "Em" (mother) by the Babylonian sage Abbaye. Women would gather at, for example, riverbanks, where they would fetch water and launder clothes, and where they used to discuss their problems.

Although the predominant view at the time of the Mishnah and the Talmud was that women should stay in their homes, there are many talmudic stories about women who were active in male domains. For example, despite laws that made women economically dependent and a world view that regarded negotiation with men and going to court as unworthy of women, both the Babylonian and Yerushalmi Talmuds give instances of women who were familiar with business practice and show independence and expertise in business transactions (an anonymous woman who had a quarrel with Bibi bar Abbaye in *b. Bava Batra* 137b; Rav Zutra's mother, Ramei bar Hama's mother, Rav Toovi bar Matanah's sister, and Rav Dimi bar Yosef's sister, *b. Bava Batra* 151a–b; Rabbi Honya's sister, *y. Bava Batra* 8:7; Rabbi Gurion's sister, *y.* Peah 3:7; a daughter of Rav Nahman's relative, *b. Ketubbot* 85b–86a, and many others). Moreover, many stories tell of women who were involved in the sages' world and were famous for their knowledge of the laws, language, and manners (a female guest, an anonymous little girl, a rabbi's handmaid, and Beruria, *b. Erubin* 53a–54a; a rabbi's handmaid, *b. Rosh Hashanah* 26b; *b. Megillah* 18a; *y. Megillah* 2:2; *y. Shevi'it* 9:1, and others).

There were no substantial differences between the clothing of women and men. A story about the sage Judah bar Illai states that he and his wife shared the same garment. Women were expected to cover their entire body, as the exposure of skin was believed to arouse men's sexual desires. It was also considered a good custom for women to cover their hair using either a veil or a wig. The Mishnah *Ketubbot* (5:8), which deals with a man's obligations to his wife, teaches that the regular clothes of women were: a small hat (*kippah*), a belt, shoes, and simple garments.

Other sources tell that women liked colorful clothes and that rich women used to wear silk clothes. During religious festivals, unmarried women wore white clothes. Use of perfume, makeup, and jewelry was considered a feminine act. Some sages believed that the ultimate desire of women is to own jewelry. One of the sages said that the sole purposes of women's existence are beauty and procreation.

Shulamit Valler

Bibliography

Baskin, Judith R. *Midrashic Women: Formations of the Feminine in Rabbinic Literature.* Hanover, NH: Brandeis University Press, 2002.

Biale David. *Eros and the Jews: From Biblical Israel to Contemporary America.* New York: Basic Books, 1992.

Boyarin, Daniel. *Reading Sex in Talmudic Culture.* Tel Aviv: Am-Oved, 1999 (in Hebrew).

Bronner, Leila Leah. *From Eve to Esther: Rabbinic Reconstructions of Biblical Women.* Louisville, KY: Westminster John Knox, 1994.

Gross, Moshe D. *Otzar Hagadah.* Jerusalem: Mossad Harav Kook, 1986 (in Hebrew).

Hauptman, Judith. *Rereading the Rabbis: A Women's Voice.* Boulder, CO: Westview, 1998.

Ilan, Tal. *Jewish Women in Greco-Roman Palestine.* Tubingen: J.C.B. Mohr, 1995.

Rubin, Nisan. *The End of Life-Burial and Mourning Ceremonies in Rabbinical Sources.* Tel Aviv: Ha'kibbutz Ha'meuḥad, 1997 (in Hebrew).

Valler, Shulamit. *Women in Jewish Society in the Talmudic Period.* Tel Aviv: Ha'kibbutz Ha'meuḥad, 2000 (in Hebrew).

Wegner, Judith R. *Chattel or Person? The Status of Women in the Mishnah.* New York: Oxford University Press, 1988.

WONDER TALE

The wonder tale, also called the "fairy tale" in modern vernacular, is a folktale that contains a supernatural, marvelous element and is a characteristically timeless and placeless tale. The wonder tale is prevalent in the Israeli folktale tradition. Because the genre is international, beyond boundaries of place and time, the distinction between the Jewish wonder tale and the international one is complex. This distinction has been analyzed over the past few decades by several scholars, most notably Dov Noy in 1971, Aliza Shenhar in 1982 and 1987, Tamar Alexander in 1984, Haya Bar-Itzhak in 1993, and Eli Yassif in 1992, all of whom described the ways in which Jewish versions differ from international ones and characterize the adjustments the international versions went through in order to fit into Jewish culture. Despite the important contribution of these studies, more research is needed to refine these distinctions.

Versions of the Jewish wonder tale can be found in print—with different versions for each ethnic community—and in documented narratives in the Israel Folktale Archives (IFA) at the University of Haifa. Most of the tales were told by women. According to the Aarne and Thompson classification index, many Jewish wonder tales belong to different international tale types. Among them are the tales "Beauty and the Beast" (AT 425), "Brother and Sister" (AT 450), "Midwife to Demons" (AT 476), "Cinderella" (AT 510), "Hero Fights Against His Father" (AT 519), "The Dumb Princess" (AT 559), "The Sun Rises in the West" (AT 570), "The Animal Languages" (AT 670), "The Slandered Maiden" (AT 706), "Snow White" (AT 709), and "King's Mother Persecutes Her Daughter-in-Law" (AT 712).

In many wonder tales in the IFA, specific Jewish characteristics can hardly be distinguished and the tales remain similar to their international counterparts. This fact coincides with Yassif's finding that Jewish oicotypes exist mainly in other genres of folk literature, such as the legend, while the wonder tale tends to retain its international character.

In other cases, Jewish characteristics infiltrated international tales but not in a way that changed the structure and plot of the tales, such that they require a special classification, deviating from the international one. Examples of such characteristics are Jewish customs, holidays, the existence of a synagogue, the Torah, biblical verses, and mentioning the fact that the hero is a Jew. Sometimes characters who tend to appear in other genres of Jewish folk literature can be found in Jewish wonder tales, such as the prophet Elijah, King Solomon, Moses, and Rabbi Akiva.

There are some Jewish versions that deviate from the international tale types in their structures and plots and present a repeating Jewish special pattern, so they could be described as Jewish oicotypes. Among them are the ethnic types "The Abducted Wife" (AT 300*B), "Miraculously Born Child, Studies with Saint" (AT 314*C), "Faithless Sister and Her Faithful Son" (AT 315*B), "The Blinded Queen" (AT 321*A), "Marvelous Being Woos Princess" (AT 425*Q), "The Fortune of the Greatest Fool" (AT 460*C), "Persecuted Stepdaughter" (AT 480*D), "Dead and Elijah the Prophet as Helpers" (AT 506*C), "The Maiden in the Chest" (AT 510*C), "Killing the Mother" (AT 510*D), "Prince Marries the Ogre's Sister, with the Help of His Friend" (AT 516*D), "The Child Who Rescues the Community" (AT 517*A), "The Princess Prefers the Poorest Suitor" (AT 653*C), "Woman Revives Decapitated Husband and Lover" (AT 653*D), "The Clever Advisor and the King's Reward" (AT 655*B), "Cast Thy Bread upon the Water" (AT 670*B), "The Miraculous Journey" (AT 681*A), "The Slandered Maiden" (AT 706*D), and "The Peak of Good Luck" (AT 736*B).

The Jewish character of the aforementioned oicotypes can be divided into two different groups. In the first one, a structure that appears exclusively in Jewish culture does not necessarily include overt Jewish features. Because all these cases refer to tales that deal with family relationships, this adjustment process, which might be called "neutral absorption" (Yassif 1992), touches upon the concept of the family in Jewish culture. Two typical examples of this kind of tale are the oicotypes "The Maiden in the Chest" (AT 510*C) and "Killing the Mother" (AT 510*D), which were subjected to a multidisciplinary examination by Bar-Itzhak, and "The Slandered Maiden" (AT 706*D), which was studied by Shenhar (1987). In cases like these, the deviations appear at the beginning of the story as well as at the end. In addition, they may appear in decorative elements and special remarks. Different ethnic communities provided distinct expressions to the Jewish versions. As an example, in the tale "Smeda Rmeda" (the Moroccan-Jewish version of "Cinderella"), the storytellers use expressions such as "God was everywhere" or "Nothing is great but God." Although these additions are indicative of the centrality of religion in the culture of the storytelling community (a phenomenon that deviates from the common characteristics of the wonder tale genre), the tale still maintains its generic appearance. It seems that the purpose of these cultural additions is to strengthen the bonds between the tellers and the audience and to enhance their sense of cultural affinity.

The second group includes those tales that went through oicotypification processes, altered to suit the particular Jewish culture, which resulted in the loss of their generic nature, so that they transmuted into local legend or moral tales. The pattern remained identical to that of the international tale-type, but the tale had changed its genre. This is the case of the type "The Fortune of the Greatest Fool" (AT 460*C), which, in contrast to the international type, has a happy ending and preaches the importance of following religious law. Other examples are the Jewish versions of the type "Beauty and the Beast" (AT 425), which when told in the Jewish culture changed their nature and became sacred legends (Shenhar 1982). The aim of the Jewish addition is to strengthen religious belief and to preach support for following religious law.

In some cases, the evil characters are punished and change their ways. The anonymous characters are replaced by specific common figures originating in the Jewish folktale tradition, such as the prophet Elijah, Moses, or Rabbi Akiva. In other cases, figures such as a saint or rabbi appear ("Miraculously Born Child, Studies with Saint," AT 314*C). Another motif repeated in the Jewish versions is the saving of the Jewish community ("The Child Who Rescues the Community," AT 517*A). Occasionally, such tales will include biblical verses and reminders from the Talmud and the Haggadah.

The adjustment that the international wonder tales went through in order to fit into Jewish culture can be divided into four different groups. Many wonder tales, which are common in the folktale tradition of Israeli ethnic communities, present a similar or even an identical pattern to those that appear in their international equivalents. Other tales contain Jewish characteristics, such as Jewish customs and figures, but these additions do not alter the structure of the narratives in a way that requires a special classification. Some other Jewish versions of wonder tales present a repeating special pattern; these could be described as Jewish oicotypes, but their special structure does not necessarily include overt Jewish characteristics. The last group includes tales that in their adjustment process to Jewish culture lost their universal nature and became sacred legends.

Ravit Raufman

See also: Israel Folktale Archives.

Bibliography

Alexander, Tamar. "The Judeo-Spanish Legend About Rabbi Kalonimous." *Jerusalem Studies in Jewish Folklore* 5–6 (1984): 85–123 (in Hebrew).

Bar-Itzhak, Haya. "The Jewish Moroccan Cinderella in Israeli Context." *Journal of Folklore Research* 30 (1993): 2–3, 93–125.

Noy, Dov. "Jewish Versions of the Animal Languages Folktale (AT 670)—A Typological-Structural Study." *Scripta Hierosolymitana* 22 (1971): 171–208.

Shenhar, Aliza. *The Folktale of Israeli Ethnic Communities.* Tel Aviv: Cherikover, 1982 (in Hebrew).

———. "'The Maiden Without Hands' Folktale." In *Jewish and Israeli Folklore*, pp. 47–68. New Delhi: South Asian Publishers, 1987.

Yassif, Eli. "Re-Evaluating the Ways in Which International Folktales Adjusted to the Jewish Folklore of Recent Generations." *Jerusalem Studies in Jewish Folklore* 13–14 (1992): 275–302 (in Hebrew).

World to Come (*Olam Ha'Ba*)

See: Afterlife

Writing

The alphabetic script of the Western world was born in Canaan (roughly corresponding to present-day Syria, Lebanon, part of Jordan, Palestine, and Israel) in the second millennium B.C.E. When it emerged, other scripts already existed: To the south, the Egyptians were using a hieroglyphic script, while to the north, the Sumerians in Mesopotamia used a cuneiform script. The pictographic script that was created at the crossroads between these two cultures is known as the Proto-Canaanite script. The famous Proto-Sinaitic inscriptions from ca. 1500 B.C.E. written by west Semitic workers or slaves, discovered in 1905 by the English Egyptologist Flinders Petrie in the turquoise mines of Serabit al-Khadim, also used a Proto-Canaanite script. Several alphabetic scripts split from the Proto-Canaanite script, among them the Phoenician script and its descendants, the Aramaic and ancient Hebrew scripts, the latter referred to in the Talmud (*Sanhedrin* 22a) as *Da'atz* or *Ra'atz* script.

The archaeological finds that are written in ancient Hebrew, although not numerous, provide information concerning the methods of writing that were employed during the period of the first Temple. *Ostraka*—pieces of broken pottery—were a common writing material, mainly for administrative documents. The text on the *ostraka* was sometimes engraved but was usually written with brush and ink. Dedication inscriptions were engraved on stones. Such is the inscription that describes the impressive water project of Hezekiah, the king of Judea, who prepared the city of Jerusalem in anticipation of a siege by the Assyrian king Sennacherib (2 Kgs. 20:20; 2 Chr. 32:2–4, 30). Inscriptions on papyrus or parchment did not survive, yet historians assume that they existed because inscriptions in other ancient Middle Eastern languages have been found. In 1979/1980, during archaeological excavations in Jerusalem, two small silver scrolls were discovered. Archaeologists believe that these silver objects served as amulets. Incised on each are the names of their owners and the priestly benediction. Monumental epigraphs on stone, written in ancient Hebrew, do not exist. Nevertheless the stela of Mesha, the Moabite king from the ninth century B.C.E., is written in a script identical to the ancient Hebrew, thus providing scholars with an example of engraved monumental script.

Jewish Script

Hebrew script developed in Judea and Israel without interruption until the destruction of the First Temple, in 587 B.C.E., and the exile of most of the literate class to Babylonia. In 539 B.C.E., the Babylonian Empire was conquered by Cyrus, the Persian king, and Aramaic became the official script of the Persian Empire, hence among the Jews.

With the fall of the Persian Empire and the Greek occupation of the region, Aramaic lost its power and the various nations in the region, among them the Jews, developed their own scripts based on the old. The new script of the Jews was named by the Talmudic sages "Assyrian," while the name "Hebrew" was assigned to the ancient script. But although this new script developed from Aramaic, it was quite distinct. For this reason, the

Fragments of the Temple Scroll (early Jewish script). The Israel Museum, Jerusalem, Israel. *(Shrine of the Book. Bridgeman Art Library)*

proposition of Frank Moore Cross to rename it "Jewish script," was accepted by the scholars. This new script, which has been in constant use since its creation, is known today as Hebrew script.

A large number of texts written in Jewish script were discovered in the late 1940s and the 1950s in the Judean desert—at Qumran, and Nahal Hever and Wadi Muraba'at—and in the Negev—at Masada. These discoveries included fragments of scrolls with biblical texts and fragments of phylacteries, apocryphal texts, various treatises, and several hundred *ostraka.* One of the more unusual texts, belonging to the Dead Sea sect, is an astrological-physiognomic treatise that analyzes the human character according to the form of a person's limbs and zodiac sign. The text is ciphered, written in Jewish script from left to right, with additional ancient Hebrew and Greek letters.

Writing Techniques

The early phase of Jewish script appears in diverse types of writing material: *ostraka,* engraved or written with ink; texts written on hide, parchment and papyrus with ink and a reed brush; and epigraphs engraved on stone, among them burial inscriptions on ossuaries and representative epigraphs, some of which are influenced by the elegant Greek and Roman epigraphs. Another type is the synagogue inscription. Apart from the engravings, some were written with *tesserae* (mosaic pieces), as part of the mosaic floors' decoration. Such is the inscription in the synagogue of Rehob, which deals with tithes, or another from the Ein-Gedi synagogue. The latter details the names of the thirteen patriarchs of the world (based on 1 Chr. 1:1–4), the signs of the zodiac, the Hebrew months of the year, the three patriarchs, the three Hebrews in the furnace (the book of Daniel [chapter 3] tells the story of the three Hebrews who were thrown into the furnace by order of Nebuchadnezzar, the Babylonian king, and were saved by God), and finally an oath, accompanied by a curse, directed at anyone who intends to harm members of the community. All these types of Jewish text were also discovered outside Israel, in the Middle East (Dura Europos, Babylonia, North Africa, and Egypt), in Europe (Greece, Italy), and elsewhere. Some of these inscriptions predate the revolt of Bar Kochba (132–136 C.E.); others belong to the Byzantine period.

The main source of texts from the Byzantine period is the Cairo Geniza (translated "hiding, concealing"; a room or a chest in the synagogue or outside in which worn-out sacred books or their fragments were hidden) in the Ben Ezra Synagogue of Fustat (old Cairo), where administrative and personal documents were found, in addition to biblical, liturgical, and literary texts. The Geniza also revealed a large number of amulets and magic and incantatory texts, which were very popular at the time. The incantation was a prayerful plea for help directed to the supernatural powers. Books of magic that were found in the Geniza provide instructions for writing amulets. One of these books suggests different writing media for the amulets according to their function: deer parchment for a barren woman; plates made of copper, gold, or lead to prevent miscarriage; eggs to enable sleeping; leaves to ensure love; and bones to protect against hatred. Incantations were also written on cloth and clay. Most of the surviving incantations are those written in Babylonia with ink on clay bowls, in Egypt on papyrus, and others, from the Land of Israel, incised on metal amulets.

While papyrus, *ostraka,* and stone served as main writing materials at the time of the First Temple, most of the surviving texts from the Second Temple period are written on parchment; only a few are written on papyrus. The common use of parchment for writing a sacred text led to the creation of a series of laws regarding the writing of scrolls of the Torah, phylacteries (*tefillin*), and *mezuzot* (pl. of *mezuzah*).

Although Mediterranean Christian society had already adopted the codex by the first century B.C.E., Jews substituted the scroll for the codex much later; the earliest manuscripts found in the Cairo Geniza date to the tenth century. These manuscripts were produced in the Middle East, either Syria, Israel, or Egypt.

The Hebrew script in the Middle East is called Oriental script. In the eleventh century it spread westward, via Byzantium and Italy to Ashkenaz (Germany, northern France, and England), and was called Ashkenazi script; it also spread via North Africa to Spain and was called Sephardi script. In all regions, Jewish script had three main forms: square (the representative type), semicursive, and cursive script. The Jewish scribes in the Diaspora used the local writing material—calamus, a pen made of reed, in Spain and the Orient, and a quill pen in Ashkenaz and Italy—and were influenced by the local script: The semicursive and the cursive Sephardi scripts were influenced by Arabic script; the semicursive Ashkenazi script was influenced by the Gothic style that took over in the thirteenth century. In addition to copies of the Bible and prayer books, medieval scribes wrote all sorts of halakhic books, philosophic and kabbalistic treatises, and medical treatises, many of which were translated from Arabic by Jewish scholars.

In the mid-fifteenth century, when Johannes Gutenberg invented movable type (the first dated mass-printed book is from 1460), the production of Hebrew manuscripts was quite intensive. Initially, the printed Hebrew books (the first was printed ca. 1470) did not replace those written by hand. Moreover, the early printed letters mimicked the various script styles of the manuscript. In the Hebrew incunabula (books printed before 1500) one can identify the Sephardi, Ashkenazi, and Italian square and semicursive script. The printed Hebrew letters began flourishing in the sixteenth century with the printing press established by Gershom Soncino. New letters were constantly designed in Italy, France, Flanders, and Germany. In the eighteenth century, the center of Hebrew printing, which moved to Eastern Europe, did not produce innovations. Following a stagnation in the development of the Hebrew letters in the nineteenth century, it was imbued with new life after World War II, first in Europe and then in Israel.

Yael Zirlin

Bibliography

Beit-Arié, Malachi. *Hebrew Manuscripts of East and West: Towards a Comparative Codicology*. London: British Library, 1993.

Cross, Frank Moore. "The Development of the Jewish Scripts." In *The Bible and the Ancient Near East, Essays in Honor of W. F. Albright.* Garden City, NY: Doubleday, 1955.

Habermann, Avraham M. *Studies in the History of Hebrew Printers and Books*. Jerusalem: Ruben Mass, 1978 (in Hebrew).

Naveh, Joseph. *Early History of the Alphabet: An Introduction to West Semitic Epigraphy and Palaeography*. Jerusalem: Magnes Press/Hebrew University, 1987.

———. *On Sherd and Papyrus. Aramaic and Hebrew Inscriptions from the Second Temple, Mishnaic and Talmudic Periods.* Jerusalem: Magnes Press/Hebrew University, 1992 (in Hebrew).

Naveh, Joseph, and Shaul Shaked. *Amulets and Magic Bowls: Aramaic Incantations of Late Antiquity*. Jerusalem: Magnes Press/Hebrew University, 1987.

Offenberg, Adri K. *Hebrew Incunabula in Public Collections: A First International Census.* Nieuwkoop: De Graaf, 1990.

Sirat, Colette. *Hebrew Manuscripts of the Middle Ages.* Cambridge, UK: Cambridge University Press, 2009.

Trachtenberg, Joshua. *Jewish Magic and Superstition: A Study in Folk Religion.* New York: Behrman's Jewish Book House, 1939.

Yardeni, Ada. *The Book of Hebrew Script.* Jerusalem: Carta, 1991 (in Hebrew).

Y

YASSIF, ELI

Eli Yassif contributed to the study of Jewish folklore in the area of medieval Hebrew storytelling, the history of folklore research, folk literary genres, anthologies, and written folk literature.

Yassif was born in Bucharest, Romania, on March 15, 1946. He studied Hebrew literature and Jewish folklore at the Hebrew University, where he received his Ph.D. in 1977 after completing his dissertation, "Pseudo Ben-Sira: The Texts, Its Literary Character, and Status in the Hebrew Literature of the Middle Ages." He completed his postdoctoral work in folklore at the University of California, Los Angeles.

The main areas of research Yassif worked in were the history of Jewish folkloristics and Jewish folk literature in the Middle Ages. Among his contributions to the first area was *Jewish Folklore: An Annotated Bibliography* (1986)—the first attempt in Jewish folkloristics to list research publications from the beginning of the study of Jewish folklore in mid-nineteenth century to the 1980s. This publication was not only a source for specific studies but also an overview of the major developments and trends in the study of Jewish folklore. On this was based the series of studies on the contribution of Jewish folkloristics to the various fields of Jewish studies, "Folklore Research and Jewish Studies: Directions and Goals" (1987). The editing and publication of the research papers of Haim Schwarzbaum (1990, 1994), the study of folklore in Israel (1990), and the work of one of the greatest scholars of Jewish studies, Moritz Steinschneider in the field of Jewish folklore (2011), are some of his contributions to the history of Jewish folkloristics.

Despite these accomplishments, Yassif's long-lasting contribution is not in the historiography of Jewish folkloristics but in the history of Jewish folk literature. His book *The Hebrew Folktale: History, Genre, Meaning* (1994; English translation, 1999) is a bold attempt to write the history of the Hebrew folktale from its sources in the biblical period through the Apocrypha and talmudic and midrashic literature to the Middle Ages and modern Jewish folklore. The folk literature of each major period of Jewish history is studied in its historical and cultural context, in an effort to understand its meaning and function in Jewish society of its time.

In the field of medieval studies, Yassif followed in the footsteps of the great scholars of the second half of the nineteenth century, Moses Gaster, Israel Lévi, and Louis Ginzberg, who considered the Hebrew folk narratives of the Middle Ages an essential component of Jewish culture of the time and a major factor in understanding the role of Jewish culture as mediating between the Muslim East and the Christian West. In this field, his contribution can be divided into three areas: the preparation and publication of critical editions of medieval narrative texts (*Tales of Ben-Sira in the Middle Ages,* 1984; *R. Yehuda Yudle Rosenberg: The Golem of Prague and Other Tales of Wonder,* 1991; texts from *Sefer ha'Ma'asim,* 1997; *Sefer ha'Zichronot,* 2001; and the *Collection of Tales in Jerusalem,* forthcoming). The second area in this field is folkloric and literary studies of books, collections, and narratives, and specific tales written down in medieval manuscripts. Some of these studies were published again in the book *The Beginning of Hebrew Prose Literature: The Hebrew Collection of Tales in the Middle Ages* (2004), and many others were published in scholarly journals. The third direction in Yassif's medieval studies is his ongoing theoretical attempt to understand the interrelationship between legend and history in Jewish culture of the Middle Ages. The major claim in these publications is that Jewish historiography of the Middle Ages did not understand and did not have the proper research tools in order to fully understand the importance of folk narratives for understanding Jewish culture of the Middle Ages.

Safed Legends: Life and Fantasy in the City of Kabbala (2011) is a research effort in the same direction. Sixteenth-century Safed was one of the most interesting cultural periods of Jewish culture. Typically, while its historical background, its halakhic achievements, its kabbalistic innovations, and its contribution to Jewish moral literature have been explored in depth, Safed legends—perhaps the most "authentic" expression of its society during that period—were almost neglected. This book is another attempt to expose the importance of folk narratives in Jewish culture of a historical period.

Yassif contributed to the study of Jewish folklore as one of the founders of the Department of Hebrew Literature and the Haim Schwarzbaum folklore archive at Ben-Gurion University in Beer-Sheva. He serves on the faculty of the Literature Department and as the head of the folklore program, which he founded in 1995 at Tel Aviv University.

Yassif has been a visiting professor of folklore and Jewish studies at numerous universities, including the University of California at Los Angeles, University of Oxford, University of California at Berkeley, University of Chicago, University of Michigan at Ann Arbor, and Institute of Advanced Studies at the Hebrew University, Jerusalem.

Haya Bar-Itzhak

See also: Folk Narratives in the Middle Ages; Safed, Legends of.

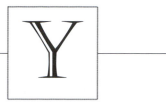

Bibliography

Schwarzbaum, Haim. *Jewish Folklore: Between East and West.* Edited with an introductory essay by Eli Yassif. Beer Sheva: Ben Gurion University Press, 1990 (in Hebrew).

Schwarzbaum, Haim. *Roots and Landscapes: Collected Studies in Folklore*, ed. Eli Yassif. Beer Sheva: Ben-Gurion University Press, 1994 (in Hebrew).

Yassif, Eli. *The Beginning of Hebrew Prose Literature: The Hebrew Collection of Tales in the Middle Ages.* Tel Aviv: Ha'kibbutz Ha'meuḥad, 2004 (in Hebrew).

———. *The Book of Memory That Is the Chronicle of Jerahme'el.* Tel Aviv: Tel Aviv University, Rosenberg Jewish Studies School, 2001 (in Hebrew).

———. "Folklore Research and Jewish Studies: Directions and Goals." *Newsletter of the International Association of Jewish Studies* 27 (1987): 3–27 (in Hebrew).

———. *The Golem of Prague and Other Tales of Wonder.* Jerusalem: Bialik Institute, 1991 (in Hebrew).

———. *The Hebrew Collection of Tales in the Middle Ages.* Tel Aviv: Ha'kibbutz Ha'meuḥad, 2004 (in Hebrew).

———. *The Hebrew Folktale: History, Genre, Meaning.* Bloomington: Indiana University Press, 1999.

———. *Jewish Folklore: An Annotated Bibliography.* New York: Garland, 1986.

———. *Safed Legends: Life and Fantasy in the City of Kabbala*, Haifa: University of Haifa Press, 2011 (in Hebrew).

———. *The Tales of Ben-Sira in the Middle Ages.* Jerusalem: Magnes, 1984 (in Hebrew).

Yeda Am

Yeda Am (Folklore) was the Hebrew name of both the Jewish Folklore Society and its periodical. The Jewish Folklore Society was founded in 1942 by Nahum Sluszec and Yom Tov Lewinski. According to the bylaws adopted at its founding meeting, its objectives were "to make contact with all ethnic communities in order to collect customs, lifestyles, beliefs and religion, foods and beverages, poetry and music, etc., to sponsor conferences for the study of folklore, and to publish books and periodicals."

The first issue of *Yeda Am,* a forum for Jewish folklore, appeared in 1948, under the editorship of Lewinsky and Getzel Kressel. It was intended to be a continuation of *Reshumot,* an anthology of memoirs, ethnography, and folklore in Israel. A letter that accompanied the first issue of *Yeda Am* emphasized the challenge that the mass immigration of Jewish communities to Israel posed for the Society, namely, collecting, preserving, and studying the folklore traditions that these communities were bringing with them: "The ingathering of the exiles in our land, dozens of communities with their customs, languages, and ways of life, will provide a firm foundation and inexhaustible source for our work. On the soil of the homeland, where brethren dwell together, new lifestyles become entrenched and cultural values mix and fuse. Much will be lost if we do not make the effort to rescue what can be saved from oblivion and the ravages of time."

For the more than fifty years, since its first issue, *Yeda Am* has published a wealth of material dealing with many areas of folklore (various genres of folk literature, realia, folk music, folk dance, and so on), presenting material collected and documented by veteran folklorists alongside studies by young scholars for whom it was the arena of their first publication. Both the veterans and the newcomers performed their labor with enthusiasm and boundless dedication to collecting and preserving the folk traditions of Jewish communities. The articles found in the volumes of *Yeda Am*—which, as stated, were written, edited, and organized with love and effort by a group of veteran writers and volunteers—constitute a vast treasure-house and inexhaustible source for future generations of scholars, teachers, and students. After the death of Lewinsky in 1973, the periodical was edited by Haim Schwarzbaum, Yitzhak Ganuz (Ganuzovitch), and S.Z. Kahane, and subsequently by Ganuz alone.

Over the years, the Society has sponsored many conferences, lectures, and symposia in various parts of Israel. The topics addressed have included the patriarchs and matriarchs in Jewish life; the legend of the Ten Lost Tribes and the Sambation in the rabbinic sources; the Prophet Elijah; Jerusalem in folklore; motifs in Aggadah; legends of saints (legenda); the relationship between stories and customs; magic and amulets in Jewish tradition; the longing for redemption in Jewish folklore; and Holocaust stories over the generations. Today the Jewish Folklore Society is not active, but the journal continues to be published.

Yitzhak Ganuz

See also: Lewinski, Yom-Tov.

Bibliography

Archive of the Israeli Folk-Lore Society (Yeda Am). The National Library, Jerusalem.

Yemen, Jews of

Jewish-Yemenite traditions date to the last years of the First Temple, when the first Jews left Jerusalem to settle in Yemen. Although these traditions cannot be considered a reliable source, there are some data and scholarly findings that support them. The earliest unequivocal proof for Jewish existence in Yemen is from the beginning of the third century C.E.: the burial inscriptions in Beit She'arim (near Haifa) of Himyarites, Jews whose corpses were brought for burial in the Land of Israel from the kingdom of Himyar, at that time the main kingdom in Yemen.

Historians have concluded that by the second half of the second century there already existed a flourishing Jewish community in Yemen. Jews who left Jerusalem as a consequence of the destruction of the First Temple appeared to settle in the northern part of Arabia (later known as Wādī al-Qurā). From there, some of them went farther south and settled in central Arabia (Khaybar) and western Arabia (Yathrib and its environs) and eventually reached the southwestern corner of the Arabian Peninsula: Yemen. From that time until the modern era, a Jewish community existed in Yemen, though it was decimated by immigration to the Land of Israel beginning in 1881. The most heaviest stream of immigration took place between 1949 and 1951, when about 55,000 of the Jews of Yemen made *aliyah,* leaving behind hundreds of their brethren who remained for economic reasons. Even before 1948, almost half of the community had already settled in the Land of Israel, where it stood out among all the other ethnicities.

Yemeni Jews are distinct in terms of their continuity and stability, having been in Yemen continuously for at least 1,800 years without being expelled or forced to relocate. That means that Yemeni Jews could preserve their original traditions; some of them, such as their pronunciation of Hebrew, date to the era of the First Temple. Nevertheless, Yemeni Jews have never been completely secluded, and nearly all trends and streams that developed in Jewish centers outside Yemen trace their roots to that community.

Yemeni Jews never attained prominence among all the Jewish communities; however, they have been highly appreciated by scholars of Judaic studies are who interested in the old Jewish traditions—which have been kept alive by Yemeni Jews even though they have been nearly or entirely forgotten by other Jewish groups.

From the very limited information scholars have about the Jews of Yemen in antiquity, they have determined that they appear to have made their living from agriculture, including the ownership of large palm plantations. Their social and political status and power were so high that they could eliminate the influence of the local Christians, backed by strong kingdoms such as Ethiopia and the Byzantine Empire, and bring the local Himyarite kingdom to Judaicize in the fourth century. Recent research, based on written Muslim sources and ancient inscriptions deciphered in Yemen since the mid-nineteenth century, reveals that perhaps the majority of the Yemeni population had converted to Judaism.

But after the fall of the Jewish Himyarite kingdom in 525, a consequence of the Christian invasion from Ethiopia, the Jews quickly lost their special status. It did not improve under the new Muslim regime after the country was invaded by the army sent by Muhammad in 628. In fact, the legal status, and consequently the social and economic status, of the Jews of Yemen diminished, as they became, religious-political "protégés" of the Muslim Empire who had to pay a poll tax and conduct themselves in accordance with many oppressive and discriminatory rules, such as the prohibition on wearing fancy cloths, building tall houses, or carrying weapons.

In the tenth century, when, as a result of the expansion of the vast Muslim empires from China to Spain, along with the Mediterranean, in the Middle Ages, the general population in the East changed the main source of its livelihood from agriculture to commerce; Jews of Yemen followed suit. Moreover, they successfully took advantage of their proximity to the area's most important port in Aden, on the main international maritime route from the Mediterranean to India. During those years, from the tenth to the thirteenth century, Yemeni Jews formed an integral part of the Jewish communities living in Muslim/Arab countries, a fact that is well documented in the high level of their literature, as evident in midrashic compilations, poetry, philosophy, and halakhic works. Of all should be noted their close ties with Maimonides, his understanding of Jewish tradition and his philosophy, and his decendants.

With the rise of a new Sunni dynasty in Yemen—the Rasulids, in 1225—Jews' social and economic status once again began to change. This tendency was strengthened under the rule of the Tahirids (1454). They gained some measure of relief after the Ottoman Turks took control of the country (1536), but after the Qāsimis expelled the Turks from Yemen and established a new Zaydi dynasty, conditions for the Jews deteriorated. The culmination of those conditions was in 1679, when the imam expelled them from Yemen, but only to Mawza, a locality in western Yemen, because the imam could not enforce his decree, even though it had the support of most of the religious Muslim authorities.

The Jews were permitted to return from their exile after about a year and a half, now deprived of their agrarian possessions and many of their civil rights. They were gradually pushed almost exclusively to the status of craftmen, with no access to the main sources of the local economy: land and trade.

Jewish-Yemenite culture of the past two centuries had only a few features of traditional Yemeni culture, loosely updated with post-Sabbatean cultural developments in Europe and North Africa. At the same time, it was sharply colored by the local Arab folklore, especially in the spoken language and the culture of women. In many aspects of life, the Jews retained their uniqueness amid the Muslim majority. Even the Jewish houses in Sana'a were designed differently than those of the Muslims. There was a sharp distinction between the music specific to Jewish synagogiues and that of men outside the synagogue and of women, which is fundamentally a moderate version of Muslim Yemenite music. The same situation pertains regarding dance and cloth.

The singularity of Jewish-Yemenite culture and its ancient features began to be revealed to other Jewish communities and the academic world only with the publication of Ya'aqov Sappir's *Even Sappir* (vol. I, Lyck 1866; vol. II, Mainz 1874), in which he provided a detailed depiction of Yemenite Jewry, based on his stay in Yemen for about eight months in 1859. More was learned only when Yemenite Jews immigrating to the Land of Israel beginning in the 1880s brought with them their old manuscripts. Even in Israel today, Yemeni Jews and their third- and fourth-generation descendants retain their unique traditions more than any other community in Israel.

Folklore and Folklife

The culture of the Jews of Yemen derived from both Jewish and Arabic sources. Scholars know, however, that contacts with Persian, Indian, and Abyssinian folk cultures influenced Jewish culture in Yemen. This influence was naturally not limited to the Jews there but encompassed Muslim culture as well. Jews had lived for so long in the social and economic environment of Yemen that in many respects they can be considered Arabicized Jews. Their language was Arabic, colored, in each district, by the local vernacular.

They were influenced in almost all walks of life by the Arab majority—indeed, they shared that life. Hardly any village, however remote or tiny, failed to have Jewish families or at least one such family. They were intensively and extensively bound up in economic life, not isolated from their Arab neighbors. Thus, for example, no one, except the Jews could repair the broken tools of the farmers or the gun of the warrior tribesmen; not to mention that only Jews could fashion the jewelry, eagerly sought by Muslim women.

Admittedly, Jews and Arab Muslims maintained separate societies from the point of view of religion and politics. Yet the Jewish community nonetheless shared some Arab traits, in addition to language. Jewish folklore and ethnology in Yemen combined Jewish traditions and Arab characteristics. In every sphere, even those that might be considered purely Arab, Jewish uniqueness can still be discerned in clothing, craftsmanship, music, and style of construction. Even the dialect of Arabic spoken by Jews is not the same as that spoken by Arabs.

In cities and townships, where differentiation was clearer and more conspicuous, because they resided in separate neighborhoods, the ethnographic differences were greater than in villages, where Jews and Muslims were more involved in each other's daily lives. Urban Jews were less Arabicized than those who lived in the villages.

Jewish-Yemenite ethnography has benefited from many descriptions and much research, starting with Ya'aqov Sappir's books in the 1860s. But only a little has been accomplished in comparative research with Muslim ethnography in Yemen. Some research of this kind has been conducted recently, but most is still yet to be done.

Amulet for a Jewish groom, used to prevent harm during the wedding. Yemen, ca. 1920. *(Gross Family Collection, Tel Aviv)*

The Jews of Yemen had a folktale tradition both oral and written in Judeo-Arabic. The written tales appear in various manuscripts sometimes as single tales and sometimes in series. So far no single manuscript has appeared that is devoted to folk narratives. At the end of the nineteenth century, Jewish-Yemenite printers started publishing folk narratives in traditional editions. In the twentieth century, these tales have been included in Jewish-Yemenite folk narrative collections, followed by Hebrew translations. The narratives draw upon traditional Jewish themes that are common in exempla (see: Exemplum) and in the accounts of Jewish history. Among them are "The Death of Moses," "The Death of Aaron," "The Conquests of Joshua bin Nun," "Ḥannah and Her Seven Sons," and "The Story of Moses ben Maimon

(Maimonides)." This narrative corpus is closely related to the collections of rabbinic exempla that were common in manuscripts from Yemen and Persia, similar to *The Exempla of the Rabbis,* edited by Moses Gaster (1924).

These written folk narratives became an integral part of the Jewish canonic literature that presented to the members of Jewish community a definite set of spiritual and social values, models of imitable exemplary characters and advocated the supremacy of Judaism. The oral folk narratives were recounted mostly by women. Because they were transmitted from generation to generation through the female line in society, these tales were not part of rabbinical or scholarly discourse. In contrast to written tales, the respective oral narratives, many of which belong to the international folktale tradition of Jews and Muslims, had a great deal of overlap. There are also tales with Jewish-Yemenite themes concerning personalities such as the poet Rabbi Shalom Shabazi, historical events such as the exile of the Jews in Mawza (1678–1679), and relations with Muslim society.

Folk narratives of the Jews of Yemen after their immigration to Israel were collected by Jewish-Yemenite intellectuals, by scholars, and by institutions. The Israel Folktale Archives (IFA) at the University of Haifa holds 1,586 folk narratives recorded by Yemeni Jews in Israel.

Yosef Tobi

See also: Shabazi, Shalom.

Bibliography

Ahroni, Reuben. *The Jews of Aden: The British Crown Colony of Aden: History, Culture and Ethnic Relations.* Leiden: E.J. Brill, 1994.

———. *Yemenite Jewry.* Bloomington: Indiana University Press, 1986.

Eraqi-Klorman, Bat-Zion. *The Jews of Yemen in the Ninteenth Century.* Leiden: E.J. Brill, 1993.

Goitein, Shlomo Dov. *Yemenites: History, Social Order, Spiritual Life, Selected Writings.* Jerusalem: Ben-Zvi Institute, 1983 (in Hebrew).

Nini, Yehuda. *The Jews of Yemen, 1800–1914.* Chur: Harwood Academic, 1991.

Noy, Dov. *Jefet Schwili erzahlt—Hundertneunundsechzig jemenitische Volkserzahlungen aufgezeichnet in Israel, 1957–1960.* Berlin: Walter de Gruyter, 1963.

Tobi, Yosef. "The Comparative Research of the Jewish and Muslim Folk Literature in Yemen." *Jerusalem Studies in Jewish Folklore* 24/25 (2006/2007): 415–433 (in Hebrew).

———. *The Jews of Yemen: Studies in Their History & Culture.* Leiden: E.J. Brill, 1999.

YIDDISH

See: Languages, Jewish

YIVO ETHNOGRAPHIC COMMITTEE

See: Cahan, Y.L.; Poland, Jews of

YOM KIPPUR

Yom Kippur (or Day of Atonement) is a twenty-five-hour fast from sunset to nightfall, falling on the tenth of Tishrei, even if it falls on a Sabbath. The most solemn day in the Jewish calendar, it is observed in accordance with the biblical commandment found in the Book of Leviticus (Lev. 23:26–32). Specifically, verse 27, enjoining that "you shall afflict yourselves," was interpreted by the sages of old as prescribing five forms of mortification: abstinence from food and drink, marital intercourse, bathing, anointment with oil, and wearing of leather shoes. In addition, all Sabbath prohibitions on work apply to Yom Kippur.

In the days of the Temple in Jerusalem, one elaborate ritual of sacrifice took place on this day, consisting of two parts: first, a sacrificial ceremony during which the high priest confessed sins on behalf of himself, the priesthood, and the people of Israel. He then entered the holy of holies (the most sacred place in the Temple) dressed in white linen robes—the only occasion when this visit was permitted—and sprinkled the blood of the offerings on the *parokhet* (curtain covering the holy ark) and offered incense on the golden altar. Second, a scapegoat "bearing upon him all their [the Jews'] iniquities" (Lev. 16:22) was hurled to his death in the wilderness, or from a mountaintop, called Azazel (Lev. 16:26; *m. Yoma* 6:4), symbolically redeeming the people of their sins. In medieval Hebrew illuminated manuscripts, Azazel is portrayed as a devil and identified with Samuel, rather than being understood as a place name. This tradition dates to Byzantine sources (*Pirqe de'Rabbi Eliezer*, chapter 76) and medieval biblical commentators (e.g., Ibn Ezra, Ramban). A detailed description of the entire ceremony is recorded in the Mishnah tractate *Yoma* and in the Talmud. Since the destruction of the Temple, this ancient ceremony has been commemorated in an elaborate *piyyut* (liturgical poem) based in the Mishnah, and included in the Musaf prayer service.

The night of Yom Kippur begins with a very emotionally moving incantation of the "Kol Nidrei," in which vows of the past year (and, according to some, of the future) are annulled and sinners who have been banned from the synagogue are permitted to enter and participate in the services.

Unlike all other festive days, Yom Kippur has five (not four) services, the additional one being the conclud-

Sefer Torah *tas* (breastplate) with inscription "Yom Kippur." Germany, 1700. *(Gross Family Collection, Tel Aviv)*

ing Neilah service, whose dominant item is the closing (Neilah) of the Judgment Day and the sealing of the divine verdicts. The other prayer services stress confession of sins (listed alphabetically) and asking for forgiveness, even for the unworthy. The Šaḥrit morning service includes a Torah reading relating to the sacrificial rituals in the Temple (Lev. 16, 19:7–11), and the *haftarah* (57:14–58) emphasizes that without true repentance ritual is meaningless. In the Minḥa afternoon service, devoted to forbidden marriages, is read, followed by reading the Book of Jonah, with its message of divine forgiveness for true repentance. At the close of the day, usually after the Arvit (Ma'ariv) (from the word for "nightfall") service, the shofar (ram's horn) is sounded, followed by the exhortation "*Le'shanah ha'baah bi'Yerushalayim*," translated as "next year [may we be] in Jerusalem" (with those living in Israel adding: "in Jerusalem rebuilt"), and the congregants greet one another, saying, "*gemar ḥatimah tovah*" (lit., a propitious sealing [of the divine judgment], or, more idiomatically, May you be inscribed [in the Book of Life] for good). And in order to begin the new lease on life with a mitzvah, the male congregants gather outside the synagogue to bless the new moon (*kiddush ha'ḥodesh*).

Many folk customs developed over the generations following the destruction of the Second Temple. Thus, in the absence of the Azazel scapegoat, the Kapparot ceremony came into being, in which a rooster for a male and a hen for a female symbolically served in place of the scapegoat. On the eve of Yom Kippur, they were held by the legs over the head declared to serve as a substitute for their owners, who transferred the burden of his sins upon them. They were ritually slaughtered and usually given to the poor as charity.

Additional forms of mortification were practiced, such as *malkot,* the whipping (thirty-nine times) of a bare-backed male congregant in the synagogue close to the onset of Yom Kippur, a symbolic form of punishment and atonement. Similarly, it is customary to make ritual ablutions in the *mikveh* (ritual bathhouse) on the eve of Yom Kippur, in order to cleanse oneself of one's impurities and sins.

It is a natural human desire to try to ascertain what the future may bring, "who will die, who will live, whose end will come, whose end will not come" (from the *piyyut* "Unetaneh tokef"). In order to do so, some would make an especially long wax candle that would burn for twenty-five hours; it would be brought to the synagogue before Yom Kippur, and the beadle would light it. If the candle stopped burning before the fast ended, its owner would depart this life during the coming year. However, in many communities the various candles had no specific identification of their owners, so if a particular candle went out early, one could not know which congregant would die. The whole congregation would then have an additional incentive to genuinely repent their sins and pray for God's clemency.

Male worshippers, many of whom would spend the entire twenty-five hours in the synagogue in prayer, and the hardiest of whom might even remain standing throughout, would wear white robes (called *kittel* or *sargenes*), evoking the high priest's white vestments. These were variously interpreted as symbolizing the pristine purity of angels, to whom the worshipers wished to be compared, or alternatively (or additionally) they were likened to funerary shrouds, indicating the extreme humbleness of the wearer, who sees himself as having as little value as a corpse.

Although Yom Kippur was a day of fasting and solemnity, mistakenly called "the black fast" by gentiles, it was not seen as a day of sadness but, on the contrary, as one of joyful thanks for the opportunity to be forgiven and granted an additional year of life. Medieval philosophers (such as Judah Halevi, Maimonides, ha'Meiri), following earlier philosophers and the sages, describe it as the day when the soul, freed from corporeal fetters, attains the peak of perfection in the service of God. Thus it has the dual character of a fast day and a festival day. A mishnaic statement (*m. Ta'anit* 4.8) declares Yom Kippur one of the happiest days of the year, when maidens dressed in white danced in the vineyards and sought out their marital partners. What better time to find a mate than on the day of penitence and forgiveness.

Daniel Sperber

See also: Lamps and Candles.

Bibliography

Gaster, Theodor Herzl. *Festivals of the Jewish Year.* New York: W. Sloane, 1953.

Goodman, Philip. *The Yom Kippur Anthology.* Philadelphia: Jewish Publication Society, 1974.

Sperber, Daniel. *Minhagei Yisrael.* Jerusalem: Rav Kook Institute, 1994–2003 (in Hebrew).

"Yom Kippur." *Encyclopedia Biblica* (Mikrait), vol. 3, pp. 595–600. Jerusalem: Bialik Institute, 1965 (in Hebrew).

"Yom Kippur." *Encyclopedia Judaica,* vol. 5, pp. 1376–1387. Jerusalem: Keter, 1974.

"Yom Kippur." *Encyclopedia Talmudit,* vol. 22, pp. 420–574. Jerusalem: Harav Herzog Institute, 1995 (in Hebrew).

"Yom Kippur." *The Jewish Encyclopedia.* New York: Funk and Wagnalls, 1902.

YOSEF DELA REINA, THE STORY OF (*MA'ASEH YOSEF DELA REINA*)

The story of Yosef dela Reina is the account of an attempt by a kabbalist-magician by this name to destroy the Sitra Aḥra ("the other side" of the divinity, that is, Satan and his evil forces) by magical means and thereby to bring about the redemption.

Textual History

The core outline of this narrative underwent a number of transitions. The story, which was apparently originally composed in Spain at the beginning of the sixteenth century, echoed an actual event that had taken place about half a century earlier in either North Africa or Spain. Yosef dela Reina's failed attempt aroused the wrath of contemporary kabbalists and was condemned. The account on it was put in writing by an anonymous kabbalist as an explanation for the delay in the redemption, which was expected to occur in 1489.

In this form, the story reached the Land of Israel, and in 1518 it was told anew by Rabbi Abraham ben Eliezer Halevi in the earliest version known to scholars. It was apparently in this version that the narrative spread and reached the circle of the famous kabbalist Rabbi Isaac Luria (known as Ha'Ari), in Safed. In the writings of his disciple, Rabbi Ḥaim Vital, the story is evoked as testimony to the dangers inherent in the use of "practical Kabbalah" (i.e., the practical use of the power embedded in Kabbalah secrets). At this stage, a conclusion had already been appended to the story in which the punishment had shifted from the national dimension (delaying the redemption) to the individual dimension (Yosef dela Reina's personal fate). Some fifty years later, Rabbi Solomon Navarro wrote down another version of the story, which by then had developed and expanded into a folk magic legend featuring a resident of Safed and set in the Land of Israel. It was this version of the legend that became widely known, starting in the mid-seventeenth century, among the Jewish communities in both the East and the West, in Hebrew, and in translation into Ladino, Arabic, Persian, and Yiddish (in this language there also exists a Sabbatean version of the narrative). In the twentieth century, it was also translated into other European languages.

The Story

According to the most prevalent version of the story, a kabbalist from Safed named Yosef dela Reina set out, together with five trustworthy disciples and equipped with a scribe's inkstand (for writing incantations) and "all kinds of herbs" (for carrying out the required rituals), to eliminate Satan (Samael) and Lilith in order to bring redemption to his people. Various figures appear to him along the way: Rashbi (Rabbi Shimeon Bar Yoḥai, who is traditionally considered the author of the Zohar); the prophet Elijah; and the angels Sandalfon, Akatriel, and Metatron. All warn him against the aspired deed, yet all encourage him and guide him for the rest of his journey. Rashbi and Elijah instruct him on how to bring the angels down to earth, whereas the angels reveal to him the information required for his mission: the path to Samael's location, the obstacles in the way and the incantations that nullify them, and the way to trap Samael and Lilith (by means of lead plates upon which is written the tetragrammaton). Likewise, they warn Yosef dela Reina against succumbing to Samael and Lilith's shrewdness and their pleadings to grant their requests.

The group indeed encounters all the dangers and difficulties of which they were forewarned but overcomes them. They bind Samael and Lilith and deny Samael's pleadings for food while continuing on their way to bring Samael to receive God's judgment on Mount Seir. However, when very close to the mountain, Yosef—arrogant and self-satisfied—is lured into permitting Samael a moment to smell the frankincense that is in his hands. This small pinch of idolatry is sufficient to revitalize Samael. Now strengthened, he burns the ropes that bind him, casts from him the magical lead plates, and attacks Yosef's disciples. Two of them die, and two others become insane. Yosef, however, reaches the city of Sidon, loses his faith, and is caught in the world of demons. He makes a pact with Lilith and delivers his soul to her. With this power, he adjures demons and every night has them bring the queen of Greece from her palace to his bedchamber. When her husband, the king, hears of this, he sends for Yosef, who throws himself into the sea and dies. His last disciple, the account relates, lies bedridden until his death, injured and pursued by evil spirits.

A different version of the story bases the whole journey on the revelation of Elijah to Yosef dela Reina. It sketches the voyage relatively briefly, whereas Yosef's end is told at length. He is cast onto a mountain close to France and reaches the king's city, where he becomes famous for his magical power. When the king realizes that Yosef uses his power for bringing his wife, the queen, to his bedchamber he sends someone to seize him, but Yosef makes himself disappear and flees. The Jews, however, fearing that they will be harmed, entreat him to surrender, and in his distress dela Reina leaps off a tall mountain and dies.

Folkloric Elements

The folkloric elements of this legend of magic and redemption are pronounced. In contrast to the succinct early version, concerned primarily with the danger of trying to bring about the redemption, at the center of the more developed version is the figure of a folk hero who sets out on a hazardous quest in an effort to overcome and destroy, with the aid of magic, the cosmic forces of evil in order to save his community. The heroic plot is developed through means common to the folk legend: the triple format, the repetition of words and situations, and the portrayal of the tribulations of the protagonist developing from minor difficulties to greater ones that reach their climax in a dramatic struggle with the mythical monster. This narrative, however, undermines both the normative view that the redemption should be brought by heaven alone and the common objection to the manipulation of divine names for magical purposes. A tale relating the failure of Yosef dela Reina is not, therefore, merely holding onto the sorrow of an unrealized redemption. It is foremost an exemplum aimed at the condemnation of the use of "practical Kabbalah," especially for messianic purposes. In contrast to the early version of the story, the obstacle to completion of the objective in the legendary version is not the mission that Yosef undertakes but his character. Like the heroes of many legends and fairy tales, Yosef stumbles at the last moment. His courage, determination, magical knowledge, and ability to mobilize supernatural agents for his cause did not save him at that (human) moment of weakness on account of his pride and complacency.

The dread of the cosmic evil forces is embodied in the story as a demonstration that the boundary between attempting to cope with them on their metaphysical magical court and surrendering to them is thin and pregnant with danger. This is the source of the inner tension between the mold of the heroic legend within the plot and its comprehensive moral, which portrays the failure as exemplary. He who aspires to rise up to the level of holy ones in ways other than the normative path (the study of the Torah and the fulfillment of the commandments) will ultimately find himself subordinated to evil and will sink deep into impurity. Thus, the story rejects the popular messianic yearning for an immediate redemption by a charismatic human figure, such as Yosef with his heroic actions, and calls instead for normative obedience.

The magical, demonic, and angelological world of the story of Yosef dela Reina is rich and varied. It reflects a common perception of the power of the angels, alongside a belief in man's ability to bring them down to earth and to gain their assistance through the use of charms and adjurations. At the same time, the story reveals a belief in the role of Satan in the shaping of human life, in general, and in the dejected Jewish existence, in particular, and explicitly links the destruction of Satan (Samael) and the redemption of the nation. This set of ideas and beliefs is anchored in the world of theosophical Kabbalah and in the magical tradition that preceded its rise and integrates them. Lilith is familiar from many medieval Jewish sources (kabbalistic and other). Her figure in the story constitutes a further transformation of a literary motif that expresses the common dread of this malicious demoness, against whom, since antiquity, Jews had used amulets and other means of protection (see: Lilith). The erotic aspect that is often implicated in the Jewish notion of the relations between a man and a female demon is replaced in the story by two factors: subordination to the demoness, on the one hand, and manipulation of her power for the purpose of sinful sexual relations with a woman of flesh and blood, on the other. As regards this last aspect, the story ties practices of erotic magic, which are attested in many contemporary Jewish books of magical recipes together with the literary motif of relations with the king's wife or daughter, aided by Satan, that is found in both European and Middle Eastern sources.

Yuval Harari

See also: Messiah and Redeemer.

Bibliography

Ben Amos, Dan, ed. *Mimekor Yisrael, Classical Jewish Folktales.* Coll. M.J. Bin Gorion, trans. I.M. Lask. Bloomington: Indiana University Press, 1990.

Benayahu, Meir. "Ma'aseh Norah of R. Joseph dela Reina." *Areshet* 5 (1972): 170–188 (in Hebrew).

Dan, Joseph. *The Hebrew Story in the Middle Ages.* Jerusalem: Keter, 1974 (in Hebrew).

Rubashov, Zalman. "The Story of R. Joseph dela Reina in the Sabbeteian Tradition." In *Eder Hayekar: Chapters of Literature and Research in Honour of S. A. Horodetski,* ed. E. Bin-Gorion, pp. 97–118. Tel Aviv: Dvir, 1947 (in Hebrew).

Scholem, Gershom. "The Case-History of Joseph della Reyna." In *Studies in Jewish Religious and Intellectual History,* ed. S. Stein and R. Loewe, pp. 101–108. Tuscaloosa: University of Alabama Press, 1979 (in Hebrew).

———. "The Magid of R. Yosef Taitazak and the Revelation Attributed to Him." *Sefunot* 11 (1971–1977): 69–112 (in Hebrew).

Z

ZEFAT

See: Safed, Legends of

ZIPPORAH

Zipporah is mentioned in the Book of Exodus as Moses's wife and one of seven daughters of Jethro (also called Reuel), the priest of Midian. In one of the most dramatic incidents in the Hebrew Bible, she appears to save Moses's life. Moses met the daughters of Jethro by a well, where they had come to draw water, when he fled Egypt after having killed an Egyptian, an offense for which his own life was at risk. Moses chased away some shepherds who were preventing the daughters from drawing water from the well and stayed to live at Jethro's home; subsequently he married Zipporah (Exod. 2:10–22). Despite her betrothal to Moses, Zipporah is not described in any way that would distinguish her from her sisters; this omission might reflect the fact that her character and relationship to Moses do not play a major role in the remainder of the story. The use of seven—a familiar token in folklore—for the number of daughters attests to the folk origins of the story and to a literary intention to evoke an archaic ambiance.

The Midrash Shemot Rabbah (1:32) locates the root *tzipor* (Heb., bird) in Zipporah's name. When Jethro asks his daughters to invite Moses to dine at his home, she flies off like a bird to bring him back.

Zipporah plays a leading role only in the enigmatic story of the "blood groom": At God's commandment, Moses returns to Egypt with his wife and two children, and en route, according to some interpretations, God meets him and seeks to slay him. Zipporah takes a "flint and cuts off her son's foreskin and touch[es] Moses's feet with it" and declares, "Surely, you are a bridegroom of blood to me!" God relents, and Moses is saved (Exod. 4:24–26).

This enigmatic passage has promoted considerable interpretive controversy, and Zipporah's exact contribution in the biblical narrative remains a matter of debate. According to one account, she saves Moses from God's wrath by carrying out the circumcision on their son. Some commentators propose a different account, suggesting that Zipporah saves her son Gershom, either from some third-party assailant or from his father, Moses, whose anger subsides only after Zipporah carries out the circumcision. According to the Midrash to Exodus, Shemot Rabbah, an angel comes and swallows Moses from his head to his circumcised part, so Zipporah knows that Moses was harmed by the circumcision.

The passage leaves a number of lingering, intriguing questions. How does the specific action Zipporah takes, circumcising her son, prevent disaster? What is the significance of touching the foreskin to Moses's "feet," a common biblical euphemism for genitals? Is there any connection between this act and the sprinkling of blood in the anointing of the priesthood, as described in Exodus 29:20?

This text is unique not only within a biblical framework but also within the context of the ancient Middle East as a whole, where there is no other evidence that women performed acts of blood sacrifice.

Saving Moses from the wrath of God, Zipporah follows in a line of heroines, such as the two midwives to the Israelites in Egypt Shiphrah and Puah (who defy Pharaoh's decree to kill male newborns), Moses's mother, Yocheved, and Pharaoh's daughter. Like her predecessors, Zipporah allays the wrath of a vengeful God in a manner familiar in international and Jewish folklore: partial sacrifice, on the theory of a "part instead of the whole." She offers the foreskin and some blood instead of the sacrifice of her husband. By means of the circumcision ceremony and spilling the drop of blood, Zipporah converts destructive violence into an expression of institutionalized violence; she transforms blood from a symbol of death itself into a symbol to ward off death. Only a woman, who is linked to the life cycle at birth (by giving birth or assisting at a birth as a midwife) and at death (mourner) can assume such a vital role.

The physical heroism displayed by Moses by chasing off the shepherds at the well originally stands as a contrast to the weakness of Zipporah and her sisters. But his prowess appears somewhat transient. In the blood groom sequence, roles are reversed: Zipporah embraces the role of a protective mother not only toward her son but also toward Moses himself, and she saves him from death.

At some point, one not detailed in the biblical narrative, Moses casts off Zipporah and their children. The text refers to this only in Exodus 18:2, in which Jethro hears about the exodus from Egypt: "Now Jethro, Moses's father-in-law, had taken Zipporah, Moses's wife, after he had sent her away and her two sons." Jethro takes them to the desert, to Moses. The text describes at length the meeting between Jethro and Moses, but it is reticent about Moses's meeting with his wife, and "her" (not "their") two sons, Gershom and Eliezer. But in the Midrash the names of the two sons are bestowed by Moses, not by Zipporah (this departs from the custom in tales of mothers and matriarchs). The major national stories that are linked to the fate of the people are what appear central to those who prepared the text; the feelings and status of a woman are neglected, since they do not pertain to the male world of political power.

Moses's brother, Aaron, and sister, Miriam, speak out against Moses because of the "Cushite" woman he married (Num. 12:1). God's furious response to Miriam for having defamed a prophet is described in this passage, along with the punishment Moses's sister receives. The Midrash holds that the Cushite is Zipporah (*Sifrei Bamidbar* 99), explaining that "Cushite" is used to connote difference: "In the same way that Cushite is different in skin color, so too did Zipporah's beauty distinguish her from other women."

In this Midrash, Zipporah hints that Moses has taken to abstinence from conjugal relations. The Midrash praises Zipporah for her vitality and righteousness, and thus emphasizes the injustice done to her as a result of Moses's choice of abstinence.

The Midrash also emphasizes Zipporah's love for and loyalty to Moses. When Jethro first discovers that Moses had fled Egypt, fearing punishment by Pharaoh, he hurls him into a hole; Zipporah tends to him secretly for ten years. Afterward, she asks her father to find out whether Moses is still alive, and Jethro is amazed to discover that he is (*Yalkut Shimoni* Shemot 168). Zipporah then demands her father's consent to become betrothed to Moses (*Midrash Shechem* Shemot 4). She emerges as a righteous woman who follows the trail of the Hebrew matriarchs.

Aliza Shenhar

See also: Moses.

Bibliography

Alter, Robert. *The Art of Biblical Narrative.* New York: Basic Books, 1981.

Boyarin, Daniel. *Carnal Israel: Reading Sex in Talmudic Culture.* Berkeley: University of California Press, 1993.

Dennis, Trevor. *Sarah Laughed—Women's Voices in the Old Testament.* Nashville: Abingdon, 1994.

Kirsh, Jonathan. *The Harlot by the Side of the Road.* New York: Ballantine Books, 1998.

Kosmala, Hans. "The Bloody Husband." *Vetus Testamentum* 12 (1962): 14–28.

Pardes, Ilana. *Counter Traditions in the Bible: A Feminist Approach.* Tel Aviv: Ha'kibbutz Ha'meuḥad, 1996 (in Hebrew).

Robinson, Bernard P. "Zipporah to the Rescue: A Contextual Study of Exodus IV 24–26." *Vetus Testamentum* 36 (1986): 447–461.

Skinner, John. *A Critical and Exegetical Commentary on Genesis.* Edinburgh: T&T Clark, 1963.

Zlotnick, Yeshayahu

See: Poland, Jews of

Appendices

The Hebrew Bible

Pentateuch, Hebrew: *Torah*—Law.

Genesis (Gen.), Hebrew: *Bereshit.*
Includes the creation of the world and humankind; the expulsion of Adam and Eve from the Garden of Eden; the first murder of Abel by Cain; the story of the Ark of Noah; the Tower of Babel; and stories of the Patriarchs—Abraham, Isaac, and Jacob.

Exodus (Exod.), Hebrew: *Shemot.*
The Israelite's departure from Egypt. Includes the rescue of Moses the child from the Nile; the story of the burning bush; the confrontation with Pharaoh and the ten plagues; the miraculous escape from Egypt; the giving of the law and construction of the tabernacle.

Leviticus (Lev.), Hebrew: *Vayikra.*
Deals with ceremonial law—religious regulations and priestly rituals.

Numbers (Num.), Hebrew: *Bamidbar.*
Starts with the census of the people at Sinai and concentrates on the harsh trials of the life in the wilderness.

Deuteronomy (Deut.), Hebrew: *Devarim.*
Includes the words of Moses to the Israelites before his death, the rehearsal of the law, the appointment of Joshua as Moses' successor, and the death of Moses.

Prophets, Hebrew: *Nevi'im.*

Joshua (Josh.), Hebrew: *Yehoshua.*
The story of the conquest of Canaan including the Battle of Jericho. Ends with the death of Joshua.

Judges (Judg.), Hebrew: *Shoftim.*
The history of the biblical heroes known as judges, including the stories of Samson, Gideon, Deborah, Jephthah and his daughter.

1 Samuel, 2 Samuel (1 Sam., 2 Sam.), Hebrew: *Shemuel.*
The first book deals with the story of the nation during the judgeship of Samuel and the beginning of the kingdom—the reign of Saul. The second book concentrates on the reign of David.

1 Kings, 2 Kings (1 Kgs., 2 Kgs.), Hebrew: *Melakhim.*
Contain the history from David's death; Solomon's reign and the construction of the Temple in Jerusalem; the division of Solomon's kingdom into two separate northern and southern nations; the story of the first northern king Jeroboam and his sin and the stories of the prophets Elijah and Elisha. The book ends with the destruction of Jerusalem and exile of the people of Judah to Babylon by Nebuchadnezzar (586 B.C.E.).

Isaiah (Isa.), Hebrew: *Yeshayah.*
Includes prophesies attributed to Isaiah (eighth century B.C.E.).

Jeremiah (Jer.), Hebrew: *Yirmiyaḥ.*
Prophecies attributed to Jeremiah (seventh–eighth century B.C.E.) announcing the captivity of Judah and its sufferings and the final salvation from its enemies.

Ezekiel (Ezek.), Hebrew: *Yeḥezkel.*
Includes messages of warning and prophecies of redemption. It contains several visions, including the vision of the dry bones.

The Twelve Minor Prophets, Hebrew: *Trey Asar.*

Hosea (Hos.)
Joel (Joel)
Amos (Amos)
Obadiah (Obad.)
Jonah (Jon.)
Micah (Mic.)
Nahum (Nah.)
Habakkuk (Hab.)
Zephania (Zeph.)
Haggai (Hag.)
Zechariah (Zech.)
Malachi (Mal.)

Writings, Hebrew: *Ketuvim*

Psalms (Ps.), Hebrew: *Tehilim.*
Sacred poems traditionally ascribed to David.

Proverbs (Prov.), Hebrew: *Mishle.*
A representation of Jewish wisdom literature traditionally attributed to Solomon.

Job (Job), Hebrew: *Yiov.*
A story describing the trials of Job, a righteous man of Edom. Deals with the problem of evil and justice of God.

Song of Songs, Hebrew: *Shir Ha'Shirim.*
A most famous book of love poems, mostly in the form of a dialogue between a man and a woman. In the Jewish tradition it was interpreted allegorically as love between God and the Jewish people.

Ruth, the Scroll of, Hebrew: *Megillat Ruth.*
The story of the foremother of King David, a Moabite woman, Ruth, who follows her mother-in-law back to the Judah tribe territory, and marries Boaz, her deceased husband's kinsman.

Lamentations (Lam.), Hebrew: *Megillat Eikha.*
The book consists of five poems that recount the horrors experienced during the destruction of the first temple and exile to Babylon.

Ecclesiastes (Eccles.), Hebrew: *Kohelet.*
A collection of sayings on the meaning of life. The author presents himself as Solomon, son of David.

Esther, Scroll of, Hebrew: *Megillat Esther.*
The story of a plot to commit genocide against the Jews by Haman in the time of Ahasuerus, the king of Persia. The Jews are saved by Mordechai and the Jewess Esther, queen of Persia. The Esther scroll is the basis for the Purim holiday.

Daniel (Dan.)
The story tells about Daniel, an Israelite who becomes the adviser of Nebuchadnezzar, the ruler of Babylon.

Ezra (Ezra) and Nehemiah (Neh.)
Historiographical books describing the rebuilding of Judah after Babylonian exile.

1 Chronicles, 2 Chronicles (1 Chron., 2 Chron.), Hebrew: *Divrey Ha'Yamim.*
The final book of the Hebrew Bible. Chronicles tell the history also included in the Books of Samuel and the Books of Kings.

Rabbinic Literature

Tannaitic—Early Rabbinic—Works (Third Century C.E.): Palestine, Mainly Hebrew

Mishnah: A collection of mainly religious law (halakhic), attributed to R. Yehudah ha'Nasi; consists of six main divisions or orders (*seder*, pl. *sedarim*). Each order is comprised of tractates (*masachtot*), reaching the overall sum of sixty-three tractates. Although it mainly addresses halakhic matters, the Mishnah includes some aggadic (nonlegal) material. Tractate *Avot*, for example, which appears in *seder Neziqin*, is comprised entirely of rabbinic aggadic maxims and lore.

References to the Mishnah are according to tractate, chapter, and mishnah, e.g. (tractate) *Avot*, (chapter) 1, (mishnah) 1.

Tosefa: A halakhic work that corresponds in structure to the Mishnah, at times interpreting the Mishnah, at times deviating from it. Like the Mishnah, although predominantly concerned with rabbinic law, it includes nonlegal narratives.

Mekhilta de'Rabbi Yishmael, *Mekhilta de'Rabbi Shimeon Bar Yoḥai*: Works that interpret the book of Exodus, each one attributed to a different rabbinic school, respectively.

Sifra (also known as *Torat Cohanim,* the Law of the Priests): A work that explicates the book of Leviticus.

Sifrei on Numbers: A work that explicates the book of Numbers.

Sifrei on Deuteronomy: A work that explicates the book of Deutoronomy.

Tannaitic midrashic works, addressing the five books of the Pentateuch, usually follow the sequence of the biblical books they address. Their compositional framework is thus defined as exegetical. They are mainly, but not exclusively, halakahic in nature.

Amoraic Works (Fifth–Sixth Century C.E.):

Palestine (Hebrew and Aramaic)

Jerusalem or Palestinian Talmud (*Talmud Yerushalmi*): Commentaries on and expansions of the Mishnah, arranged according to thirty-nine of the mishnaic tractates. In additions to halakhic material, the JT (PT) contains much aggadic (nonlegal) discourse. References to the JT (PT) are according to tractate, chapter, and halakhah (and usually with the addition of page and column, referring to the Venice printed edition).

Genesis Rabbah: One of the most important aggadic midrashim that addresses the book of Genesis. Comprised of 100 chapters, arranged according to scriptural sequence, thus described as an exegetical Midrash.

The name "Rabbah," meaning great/big, may have originated in order to distinguish this work from another, smaller, compilation on Genesis. Subsequently, the name "Rabbah" was used for other midrashim on the Pentateuch as well as on the five Scrolls. The entire body of the midrashim called "Rabbah" is of heterogeneous character, comprised of different poetic principles and edited in different contexts, including ones that postdate the rabbinic period. The name that these midrashim share thus does not indicate any essential connection between them.

Leviticus Rabbah: An aggadic midrash that address the mostly legal-cultic book of Leviticus. It is comprised of thirty-seven chapters, each one referring to a portion of the Torah as read in a three-year cycle at the synagogue. In contrast to Genesis Rabbah, whose composition does not appear to have coherent internal principles, Leviticus Rabbah strives for greater coherence within each chapter, both structurally and thematically. Because of its compositional structure, it is referred to as a homiletic midrash.

Lamentations Rabbah: An aggadic midrash that addresses the book of Lamentations. The destruction of the First Temple, which is the subject of the biblical Scroll, serves the rabbis as a template to discuss the more recent, and in some respects more relevant, event of the destruction of the Second Temple. The work is comprised of numerous proems (*petichta'ot*). These are followed by exegesis of the book of Lamentations according to the scriptural sequence (thus, referred to as an exegetical midrash).

Pesiqta de'Rav Kahana (Cahana): A homiletic midrash that addresses portions of scripture that were read in the synagogue on festivals and special Shabbats—the total sum varying according to the edition. There are five chapters that overlap with Leviticus Rabbah (the origin of which is debated).

Esther Rabbah I: Addresses the Esther Scroll, read on Purim. Esther Rabbah I includes sections 1–6 and belongs to the end of the classical midrash period. The continuation, Esther Rabbah II, is possibly an eleventh-century work. The combination of both parts took place in the twelfth or thirteenth century.

Ruth Rabbah: A complete commentary on the book of Ruth, read on Shavuot, comprised of eight sections. It was known as Midrash Ruth until the Venice edition of 1545 renamed it.

Song of Songs Rabbah: An exegetical midrash, offering a typological reading of Song of Songs. Has been dated to the sixth century, or alternatively, to the post-Amoraic period (seventh or eighth century). Either way, it clearly includes early material as well.

Babylonia (Hebrew and Aramaic)

Babylonian Talmud (*Talmud Bavli*): Commentaries on and expansions of the Mishnah, arranged according to thirty-seven of the mishnaic tractates. In contrast to the amoraic literary poly-system in Palestine that included both a Talmud and separate midrashic works, the Babylonian rabbis produced one major work—the Babylonian Talmud (BT)—which is an expansive and elaborated composition encompassing a wide range of materials and whose final editorial process reached into the seventh century. References to the Babylonian Talmud follow tractate, page (in turn divided into a/b, depending on the side of the page).

Late and Post-Amoraic Works (Seventh–Eleventh Century C.E.)

A large variety of works of different nature, scope, and provenance. Composed and edited in both Muslim and Christian environments, throughout the Mediterranean, Southern Europe, and the Near East. The date and place of many of the late midrashim is uncertain. Although considered postclassical midrashim, they also contain material from earlier periods.

Tanḥuma (known also as *Yelamdenu*), a major work of that period, arranged according to the portions of the Pentateuch read in the synagogue, containing early material as well as later starta, maybe as late as of the ninth century. The Tanḥuma circulated in different versions (two of which have been published: the printed edition and the Buber edition). There are numerous midrashim of this period that contain distinctly Tanḥuma material (see below).

Ecclesiastes Rabbah: An exegetical midrash addressing the book of Ecclesiastes. The work discusses an array of topics, rendering it encyclopedic in nature. It may have originated in Palestine in the eighth century, or even earlier.

Pirqe de'Rabbi Eliezer (The Chapters of Rabbi Eliezer): An eighth-century work, probably composed in Palestine or its vicinity, presenting a comparatively continuous narrative that retells events recounted in the Bible, beginning from the creation of the world and ending with the leprosy of Miriam. Its poetics have been described as a combination of the second temple period's "rewritten Bible" and midrash.

Deuteronomy Rabbah: Consists of twenty-seven homilies that relate roughly to the three-year cycle of Torah reading. Probably of an early Palestinian origin but due to its complicated textual history the time of its final redaction remains unclear, anytime between the fifth and ninth century. Two versions exist: the printed version and one published by Saul Lieberman.

Pesiqta Rabbati (the "big" Pesiqta, applied to the work in order to distinguish it from *Pesiqta de'Rav Kahana*): A collection of sermons for the feasts and special Shabbats. A composite work that prevents an overall assessment regarding its time and place of redaction.

Exodus Rabbah: A work that addresses the book of Exodus, comprised of two parts. The first, chapters 1–14, is an exegetical midrash on Exodus 1–10; the second part, chapters, 15–52, is homiletic in nature and belongs to the Tanḥuma tradition. It has been dated to the tenth century but its place has remained obscured.

Midrash on Proverbs: An exegetical, or rather commentary-like, midrash on Proverbs. It is dated roughly to ninth to eleventh centuries. Its place of redaction is unknown. It contains a few novel narratives and mystical themes.

Numbers Rabbah: Consists of two parts. Part one (sections 1–14, about three-quarters of the composition) is an aggadic exegesis of Numbers 1–7. The second part (sections 15–23) is a homiletic midrash that address Numbers 8–36, and is similar to the Tanḥuma tradition. It has been suggested that the text was edited—either only the first part or in its entirety—by R. Moshe ha'Darshan of eleventh-century Provence, but this is far from clear.

Medieval Compilations

Midrash of the Ten Commandments (*Midrash Aseret ha'Dibberot*): A midrash written in the East (Babylon or Persia) during the Gaonic period (eighth to tenth century), explicating the Ten Commandments. The discussion of each biblical verse begins and ends with scanty and unoriginal homiletic sermons. In between, about fifty stories are enclosed, included so as to demonstrate each biblical commandment. The stories comprise the main bulk of the material, and the midrashic aphorisms are secondary. Thus, the compilation is considered to be a transition stage between ancient aggadic literature, in which literary works were an addition to texts of religious (halakhic) law, and medieval literature, in which stories were legitimized for their own right.

The Ben-Sira Story in its two versions—Alphabet of Ben-Sira (*Alfa Beta de'Ben Sira*) and The History of Ben-Sira (*Toldot Ben Sira*): A text written in Babylon or Persia during the ninth to tenth century, and pseudepigraphically attributed to Ben-Sira, the author of Ecclesiasticus. The compilation is divided into four parts: (a) The miraculous conception and birth of Ben-Sira; (b) Ben-Sira and his tutor, who teaches him the alphabet at the age of one year (comprising of twenty-two proverbs on the letters of the alphabet, and relevant stories); (c) Ben-Sira and King Nebuchadnezzar, who asks him twenty-two questions and is answered by aetiological stories; and (d) Homiletic-like discussions between Ben-Sira's son and grandson, who provide commentary and interpretation on twenty-two of his Aramaic proverbs. The work contains bawdy humor, parodies rabbinic learning, and satirizes accepted norms of Judaism. It is considered to be the second stage in the development of the medieval story, already regarding the story as substantive.

The Book of Josippon (*Sefer Yosiffon*): An anonymous composition compiled in 953 in Southern Italy, as if according to Latin translation of the writings of Josephus Flavius. The book pretends to survey the history of the Jewish people, and was highly esteemed by medieval Jewry as such. In fact, it provides "fictional history," including stories taken from Strabo, Lucian, and Eusebius, as well as from Josephus.

The Book of Stories, also known as A Beautiful Composition of Salvation (*Sefer Ma'asiyyot ha'Ḥakhamim vehu Ḥibbur Yafeh meha'Yeshu'ah*): Written at the middle of the eleventh century by Nissim ben Jacob of Kairouan. Written in Arabic yet known mainly by its medieval Hebrew translation, the book is a compilation of Talmudic-midrashic stories combined with Judaized Arabic medieval folktales. It contains diverse stories on many subjects, yet its declared aim is to comfort a suffering friend and to strengthen his faith in God by telling him stories that teach the ways of Providence, exalt God, preach moral behavior, and explain why the righteous suffer and the wicked thrive.

The Book of Genealogy (*Sefer Yoḥasin*), known as The Chronicle of Aḥima'atz (*Megilat Aḥima'atz*, ed. by B. Klar, 1945): Written in 1054 by Aḥima'atz ben Paltiel in Capua, Italy. The book depicts in rhymed prose the history of Aḥima'atz's family and chronicles the early Jewish communities in Italy, from the eighth until the eleventh centuries. Among stories with some historical foundation, the book also consists of realistic stories, legends, and miraculous tales.

The Exempla of the Rabbis (*Sefer Ma'asiyyot*), published from a manuscript by Moses Gaster (1924; repr. 1968): An anonymous work compiled in the East in the eleventh or twelfth century. The book contains above 300 mainly talmudic-midrashic stories, as well as Hebrew medieval folktales, all edited and combined together into narrative sequences.

Book of the Pious (*Sefer Ḥasidim*): A moralistic book written mostly by Judah ben Samuel he'Ḥasid, in Germany of the eleventh to twelfth centuries. The book contains almost 400 mostly original stories, embedded in discussions on diverse historical, social, and religious matters concerning the life of the pious Ashkenazi Jews in the Middle Ages. All stories are exempla, artistically minimalized, serving to demonstrate moralistic, conceptual, and mystic context. A central place is given to stories with demonological and fantastic elements. It was one of the most influential works of the Middle Ages.

The Book of Tradition (*Sefer ha'Kabbalah*): Written by Abraham Ibn Daud (RABD) of Toledo, Spain, in 1161. Ibn Daud attempted to oppose Karaism by establishing the chain of Jewish tradition as a sequence from the age of Moses to his own time. The book includes valuable information about contemporary Spanish Jewry, as well as legends and tales providing "fictional history" (such as the story of the four captive rabbis who were redeemed by four Jewish communities where they spread Jewish culture).

The Book of Delight (*Sefer Sha'ashuim*): Written in Spain by Joseph ibn Zabara (Barcelona, twelfth century). The book is written in rhymed prose, in the nonclassical form of the Hebrew *māqāma* genre. It contains animal stories, fables, proverbs, folk tales, and misogynistic tales—all interwoven among other things into a continuous plot, enabling us to consider the work as the first picaresque novel written in Hebrew.

Fox Fables (*Mishle Shu'alim*) by Berechiah ha'Nakdan (France and England, twelfth–thirteenth century): A book of 107 (119 in another edition) animal fables written in rhymed prose, reminiscent of the Hebrew *māqāma* genre. The fables are gathered from non-Hebrew medieval bestiaries, especially that of Marie de France, and are the main source from which medieval Jews became familiar with Aesop's fables. The book is the first fable collection written in Hebrew, and the greatest to be written in the Middle Ages. It was widely circulated and was translated into Yiddish, Latin, German, and English.

The King's Son and the Ascetic (*Ben Ham'elekh Ve'ha'nazir*): A rhymed prose work of *adab* (morale literature), written in the first half of the thirteenth century by Abraham Halevi ben Samuel Ibn Ḥasdai of Barcelona. The story is a translation-adaptation of the celebrated legend of *Barlaam and Josaphat*, which is based on a second to fourth century Buddhist Sanskrit text about the life of Gautama Buddha.

The Book of Deeds (*Sefer ha'Ma'asim*): Redacted at the middle of the thirteenth century, probably in Northern France. It contains sixty-one stories, many of which are sacred legends and Jewish (Judaized) novels. The origin of eighteen stories is unknown; twenty-four stories have parallels in the writings of the Sages; and nineteen are known from earlier medieval books—mainly Midrash of the Ten Commandments and *Ḥibbur Yafeh me'ha'Yeshu'ah*.

The Fable of the Ancient (*Mashal ha'Qadmoni*) by Izḥak ibn Sahula (Spain 1281): A book of animal fables and moral tales written in rhymed prose, in the nonclassical form of the Hebrew *māqāma* genre. Ibn Sahula's declared aim was to prove that Hebrew was not inferior to Arabic as a literary medium.

Kalilah wa'Dimnah (*Kalila ve'Dimna*, also: The Fables of Bidpai): Indian book of fables, composed in India in about 300 C.E., in its two Hebrew translations (made from the Arabic translation), by Rabbi Joel and by Ya'akov ben Elazar (1283). The book consists of didactical stories aiming to guide the readers in how to live their lives. The Hebrew translation by Rabbi Joel was translated-redacted into Latin by the converted Jew John of Capua, and his variant, titled "Directorium Vite Humane," was the basis for the translations into many vernacular languages.

Anthologies of Jewish Folklore

Early Anthologies. Tenth Century to 1814

Abramson, Shraga. *Nissim Gaon: Libelli Quinque.* Jerusalem: Mekitzei Nirdamim, 1965 (in Hebrew and Judeo-Arabic).

Ben-Amos, Dan, and Jerome R. Mintz, trans. and eds. *In Praise of the Baal Shem Tov {Shivhei ha-Besht}: The Earliest Collection of Legends About the Founder of Hasidism.* Bloomington: Indiana University Press, 1970.

Brinner, William M., trans. and ed. *An Elegant Composition Concerning Relief After Adversity,* by Nissim ben Jacob ibn Shāhīn. Yale Judaica Series 20. New Haven, CT: Yale University Press, 1977.

Cassel, Paulus. *Mischle Sindbad, Secundus, Syntipas: Einleitung und Deutung des Buches der sieben weisen Meister.* Berlin: R. Schaeffer, 1888.

Diederichs, Ulf, trans. *Das Ma'assebuch: altjiddische Erzählkunst ins Hochdeutsche übertragen.* Munich: Deutscher Taschenbuch Verlag, 2003.

Eidelberg, Shlomo. *R. Juspa, Shammash of Warmaisa (Worms): Jewish Life in 17th Century Worms.* Jerusalem: Magnes, 1991.

Elmaleḥ, Avraham. *Mishle Erasto.* Translated into Hebrew by Rabbi Yitsḥak Uziel, the Rabbi of Amsterdam 1606–1622, Sifriyat Mekorot 7. Jerusalem: Mossad Harav Kook, 1945.

Epstein, Morris, ed. and trans. *Tales of Sendebar.* Philadelphia: Jewish Publication Society of America, 1967.

Fishman, Yehudah, Leib ha-Cohen. *Ma'asim 'al 'Aseret ha-Dibrot o Aggadah shel Shavu'ot* (Tales About the Ten Commandments, or Haggadah for Shavu'ot). Jerusalem: "Ha-Tor," 1924.

Gaster, Moses, ed. and trans. *The Chronicles of Jerahmeel; or, The Hebrew Bible Historiale, Being a Collection of Apocrypha and Pseudo-Epigraphical Books Dealing with the History of the World from the Creation to the Death of Judas Maccabeus.* Translation Fund, London; new ser., v. 11. London: Royal Asiatic Society, 1899. Reprinted: New York: Ktav, 1971.

———. *The Exempla of the Rabbis: Being a Collection of Exempla, Apologues and Tales Culled from Hebrew Manuscripts and Rare Hebrew Books.* New York: Ktav, 1968 [first published 1924]. See Philip S. Alexander, "Gaster's Exempla of the Rabbis: A Reappraisal." In *Rashi 1040–1990 Hommage à Ephraïm Urbach,* ed. Gabrielle sed-Rajna, pp. 793–805. Paris: Les Éditions du Cerf, 1990; and Rella Kushelevsky, "Some Remarks on the Date and Sources of *'Sefer ha-Ma'asiyyot'*" (in Hebrew). In *Kiryat Sefer: Collected Essays, Articles and Book Reviews in Jewish Studies,* Suppl. 68 (1998), ed. Y. Rosenberg, pp. 155–157.

———. *Ma'aseh Book: Book of Jewish Tales and Legends, Translated from the Judeo-German.* 2 vols. Schiff Library of Jewish Classics. Philadelphia: Jewish Publication Society of America, 1934.

Grözinger, Karl E., trans. and ed. *Die Geschichten vom Ba'al Schem Tov = Schivche ha-Bescht = Sefer Shivḥe Ba'al Shem Tov.* In collaboration with Ruth Berger and Rachel Elior and an essay by Rachel Elior, "Shivḥe ha- Besht, German, Yiddish & Hebrew." 2 Vols: Vol. 1, Hebrew with German translation, and Vol. 2, Yiddish with German translation. Wiesbaden, Germany: Harrassowitz, 1997.

Habermann, Abraham Meir. *Mishlei Sendedad: Sippur Mezimat Eshet Melekh Hodu ve- Ḥokhmat Sendebad ve-Shiv'at Yo'atzei ha-Melekh.* (Sendedad's Fables: The Story of the Queen's Plot and the Wisdom of Sendebad and the Seven King's Counselors). Tel Aviv: Maḥbarot le-Sifrut, 1946.

Hadas, Moses, trans. *Fables of a Jewish Aesop.* New York: Columbia University Press, 1967. An analytic study of this anthology is Haim Schwarzbaum, *The Mishle Shu'alim (Fox Fables) of Rabbi Berechiah Ha-Nakdan: A Study in Comparative Folklore and Fable Lore.* Kiron: Institute for Jewish and Arab Folklore Research, 1979.

Hasan-Rokem, Galit, ed. *Midrash Aseret ha-Dibrot Nusaḥ Verona T"Z* (Midrash of the Ten Commandments, Verona Version 1647). Jerusalem: Hebrew Literature Department, Hebrew University, 1971.

Hermes, Eberhard, trans. and ed. *The 'Disciplina Clericalis' of Petrus Alfonsi.* trans. P.R. Quarrie. Berkeley: University of California Press, 1977. See Haim Schwarzbaum, "International Folklore Motifs in Petrus Alphonsi's 'Disciplina Clericalis.'" *Sefarad* 21 (1961): 267–299; 22 (1962): 17–59, 321–344; 23 (1963): 54–73. Reprinted in H. Schwarzbaum, *Jewish Folklore Between East and West: Collected Papers,* ed. Eli Yassif, pp. 239–258. Beer-Sheva: Ben-Gurion University of the Negev Press, 1989.

Hershler, Moshe, ed. "*Yalkut ha-Ma'asiyyot ve-ha-Ma'asim*" (An Anthology of Tales and Legends). *Genuzot* 2 (1985): 160–184. (From a 1525 manuscript in Rome [Vatican library]?).

Ḥibbur Yafe me-ha-Yeshu'ah. See Abramson; Brinner; Oberman; and H.Z. Hirschberg, trans. *Ḥibbur Yafe me-ha-Yeshu'ah by Rabbi Nissim ben Jacob ibn Shāhīn.* Sifriyat Mekorot 15. Jerusalem: Mossad Harav Kook, 1953.

Horodezky, Samuel Aba, ed. *Sefer Shivḥei Ha-Besht* (In Praise of the Besht). Berlin: 'Ayanot, 1922. Reprint editions: Tel Aviv: Dvir, 1947, 1960.

Ibn Chaviv, Yaakov. *Ein Yaakov: The Ethical and Inspirational Teachings of the Talmud.* Trans. Avraham Yaakov Finkel. Northvale, NJ: Jason Aronson, 1999. First published: Salonika, 1516.

Ma'aseh Book. See Diederichs; Gaster; Maitlis; Zfatman.

Maitlis, Jacob. *El libro de cuentos de la edición en Basilea, 1602. The Book of Stories Basel, 1602 and Studies on the Jewish Literature.* Musterverk fun Yidisher literature 38. Buenos Aires: Ateneo Literario en el Instituto Científico Judío, 1969 (in Yiddish). [A selection of 84 out of 254 tales in the original edition.] *See* Jakob Meitlis, *Das Ma'assebuch: seine Entstehung und Quellengeschichte, zugleich ein Beitrag zur Einführung in die altjiddische Agada.* Berlin: R. Mass, 1933.

———. *The Exempla of Rabbi Samuel and Rabbi Judah, the Pious (A Study in Yiddish Folklore)*. London: Kedem, 1961 (in Yiddish). [A selection of 27 out of 254 in the original edition.]

Midrash Aseret ha-Dibrot (Midrash of the Ten Commandments). *See* Fishman; Hasan-Rokem; Shapira.

Mintz, Binyamin, ed. *Sefer Shivhei Ha-Besht im Tosafot* (In Praise of the Besht with Additions). Tel Aviv: Talpiyot, 1961. [Based on the Berditchev edition of 1815.]

Mishlei Sendebad. See Cassel; Epstein; Habermann.

Mondstein, Joshua. *Shivhei Ha-Baal Shem Tov: A Facsimile of a Unique Manuscript, Variant Versions and Appendices*. Jerusalem: N.p., 1982 (in Hebrew).

Oberman, Julian, ed. *The Arabic Original of Ibn Shâhîn's Book of Comfort Known as the Hibbûr Yaphê of R. Nissîm b. Ya'aqobh.* Yale Oriental Series, Researches Vol. 17. New Haven, CT: Yale University Press, 1933.

Rubinstein, Avraham, ed. *In Praise of the Ba'al Shem Tov {Shivhei Ha-Besht}*. Jerusalem: Rubin Mass, 1991 (in Hebrew).

Schwarzbaum, Haim. *The Mishle Shu'alim (Fox Fables) of Rabbi Berechiah ha-Nakdan: A Study in Comparative Folklore and Fable Lore.* Kiron: Institute for Jewish and Arab Folklore Research, 1979.

Shapira, Anat, ed. *Midrash Aseret ha-Dibrot (A Midrash on the Ten Commandments): Text, Sources and Interpretation*. Jerusalem: Bialik Institute, 2005 (in Hebrew).

Shivḥei Ha-Ba'al Shem Tov. Compiled by *Dov Baer ben Samuel of Linits.* See Ben-Amos and Mintz; Horodezky; Mintz; Mondstein; Rubinstein. For a bibliography, see I. Raphael {Isaac Werfel}, *"Shivhei ha-Besht," Areshet: An Annual of Hebrew Booklore*, II, pp. 358–377. Jerusalem: Mossad Harav Kook, 1960; and *"Shivhei ha-Besht"* (Supplement) *Areshet: An Annual of Hebrew Booklore*, III, pp. 440–441. Jerusalem: Mossad Harav Kook, 1961.

Yassif, Eli, ed. *The Book of Memory That Is the Chronicles of Jerahme'el*. Tel Aviv: Chaim Rosenberg School of Jewish Studies, 2001 (in Hebrew). Discussed in Malachi Beit-Arie, "Ms. Oxford, Bodleian Library, Bodl. Or. 135." *Tarbitz* 54 (1985): 631–634 (in Hebrew); and Eli Yassif, "Sefer ha-Ma'asim." *Tarbitz* 53 (1984): 409–429 (in Hebrew).

———. *The Tales of Ben-Sira in the Middle-Ages: A Critical Text and Literary Study.* Jerusalem: Magnes, 1984.

Zfatman, Sara. "The Mayse-Bukh: An Old Yiddish Literary Genre." *Ha-Sifrut/Literature* 28 (1979): 126–152 (in Hebrew).

Late Anthologies. Middle of the Nineteenth Century to the Present

National Anthologies

Ben-Yeḥezki'el, Mordekhai. *Sefer Ha-Ma'asiyyot.* 3 vols. Tel Aviv: Dvir, 1925–1929. Expanded edition in 6 vols. Tel Aviv: Dvir, 1957.

Bialik, Ḥayyim Naḥman, and Yehoshua H Rawnitzki. *Agada: Skazania, pritchi, izrechenia, Talmud ait Midrasheci.* Odessa: S.G. Fruga, 1910.

———. *The Book of Legends. Sefer Ha-Aggadah: Legends from the Talmud and Midrash,* trans. William G. Braude. New York: Schocken Books, 1992.

———. *Di Yidishe Agodes* (The Jewish Legends). 2d ed. Berlin: Moriya, 1922.

———. *Kenjatachi no "Seisho" densetsu. Sefer ha-aggadah/jo.* Tokyo: Mirutosu, 2001.

———. *Sefer ha-Aggadah: Mivehar ha-Aggadot she-ba-Talmud u-ve-Midrashim.* (The Book of Legends: A Selection of Legends from the Talmud and the Midrashim). 3 vols. Krakow: Fisher, 1908–1911.

Bin Gorion (Berdyczewski), Micha Joseph. *Der Born Judas: Legenden, Märchen und Erzählungen,* trans. Rahel Bin Gorion (Bamberg). 6 vols. Leipzig: Insel, 1916–1923.

———, ed. *Mimekor Yisrael*, ed. Emmanuel Bin Gorion. 6 vols. Tel Aviv: Dvir, 1939–1945; 2d ed., 1952; 3d ed., 1966.

———. *Mimekor Yisrael: Classical Jewish Folktales*, ed. Emanuel Bin Gorion and trans. I.M. Lask. 3 vols. Bloomington: Indiana University Press, 1976.

———. *Mimekor Yisrael: Classical Jewish Folktales* (Abridged and Annotated), ed. Emanuel Bin Gorion and trans. I.M. Lask. Prepared with an "Introduction" by Dan Ben-Amos. Bloomington: Indiana University Press, 1990.

———. *Mimekor Yisrael: Selected Classical Jewish Folktales*, ed. Emanuel Bin Gorion and trans. I.M. Lask. Prepared with an "Introduction" and headnotes by Dan Ben-Amos. Bloomington: Indiana University Press, 1990.

Jawitz, Ze'ev. *Siḥot mini Kedem* (Ancient Talks). Warsaw: A. Boymritter and N. Gonshor, 1887.

Jellinek, Adolph. *Bet ha-Midrasch: Sammlung kleiner Midraschim und veremischter Abhandlungen aus der ältern jüdischen Literatur. Nach Handschriften und Druckwerken*. 6 vols. Leipzig: F. Nies, 1853–1877 (in Hebrew).

Kuttner, Bernhard. *Jüdische Sagen und Legenden für jung und alt.* 5 vols. Frankfurt am Main: J. Kauffmann, 1906.

Levner, Israel Benjamin. *Kol Aggadot Yisrael* (All the Jewish Legends). 5 vols. Pietrokov: Tushiyah, 1898–1903.

Margulies, Isaac. *Erzählungen Jeschurun's characterbilder und sage aus dem Talmud Bawli, Jerushlmi, Midrasch, Jalkut und Sohar.* Berlin: Editor's edition, 1877.

———. *Sippure Yeshurun al pi Sippure ha-Soferim, ha-Ketubim be-Sifere ha-Talmud ha-Bavli ve-ha-Yerushalmi, Midrash, Yalkut ve-Zohar* (Jewish Tales According to Scribes' Stories Which Are Written in the Books of the Babylonian and the Jerusalem Talmuds, Midrash, Yalkut and the Zohar). Berlin: Sittenfeld, 1877.

Nadich, Judah. *The Legends of the Rabbis.* Vol. 1: *Jewish Legends of the Second Commonwealth.* Vol. 2: *The First Generation After the Destruction of the Temple and Jerusalem.* Northvale, NJ: Jason Aronson, 1994. (Vol. 1 appeared first as *Jewish Legends of the Second Commonwealth.* Philadelphia: Jewish Publication Society of America, 1983.)

Pascheles, Wolf. *Gallerie des Sipurim: eine Sammlung jüdischer Sagen Märchen und Geschichten, als ein Beitrag zur Völkerkunde.* Prag: W. Pascheles, 1847. Alternative title and further volumes: *Sippurim: eine Sammlung jüdischer Volksagen, Erzälungen, Mythen, Chroniken, Denkwürdigkeiten und Biographieen berümten Juden aller Jahrhunderte, besonders des Mittelalters.* 5 vols. Prague: Wolf Pascheles, 1853–1864. See Frédéric Garnier, "La vie juive à Prague à travers les 'Sippurim.'" *Tsafon* (Lille) 52 (2006–2007): 51–64.

Patai, Raphael, ed. *Gates to the Old City: A Book of Jewish Legends.* Detroit: Wayne State University Press, 1981.

Rappoport, Angelo S. *Myth and Legend of Ancient Israel.* 3 vols. London: London Gresham, 1928 [Reprinted with an "Introduction" by Raphael Patai. New York: Ktav, 1966.]

Hasidic Folktale Anthologies

Note: For a bibliography of Hasidic folktale anthologies, published locally in Hebrew and Yiddish in East European towns, see Gedalyah Nigal, *The Hasidic Tale*, 343–359. This bibliography lists many of the source-books upon which many later Hasidic anthologies and narrators drew.

Band, Arnold, J., trans. and ed. *Nahman of Bratslav: The Tales.* The Classics of Western Spirituality. "Preface" by Joseph Dan. New York: Paulist, 1978.

Buber, Martin. *Die Chassidischen Bücher.* Berlin: Schocken, 1927. Later published as *Die Erzählungen der Chassidim.* Zurich: Manesse, 1949; in English as *Tales of Hassidim,* trans. Olga Marx. 2 vols. New York: Schocken, 1947–1948, 1961, 1966; and in Hebrew as *Or ha-ganuz* (Hidden Light). Tel Aviv: Schocken, 1946.

Eliach, Yaffa. *Hasidic Tales of the Holocaust.* New York: Oxford University Press, 1982.

Mintz, Jerome R. *Legends of the Hasidim: An Introduction to Hasidic Culture and Oral Tradition in the New World.* Chicago: University of Chicago Press, 1968.

Newman, Louis I., ed. and trans. *The Hasidic Anthology: Tales and Teachings of the Hasidim. The Parables, Folk-Tales, Fables, Aphorisms, Epigrams, Sayings, Anecdotes, Proverbs, and Exegetical Interpretations of the Hasidic Masters and Disciples; Their Lore and Wisdom.* In collaboration with Samuel Spitz. New York: Bloch, 1944.

Nigal, Gedalyah. *The Hasidic Tale,* trans. Edward Levin. The Littman Library of Jewish Civilization. Oxford: Littman, 2008.

Zevin, Shelomoh Yosef, ed. *Sipure Ḥasidim: Mekhunasim mi-Pi Sefarim umi-Pi Sofrim* (Hasidic Tales, Culled from Books and Authors). 2 vols. Tel Aviv: A. Tsiyoni, 1956–1957.

The Israel Folktale Archives Anthologies

General

Avitsuk, Jacob, ed. *The Three That Absorbed Tears: 36 Folktales Collected from 12 Narrators.* Israel Folktale Archives Publication Series 7. Haifa: Haifa Municipality, Ethnological Museum and Folklore Archives, 1965.

Baharav, Zalman, ed. *Mi-Dor le-Dor: One Generation to Another. Seventy-one Folktales Collected in Israel*, ed. Dov Noy. Tel Aviv: Tarbut Ve-ḥinukh, 1968.

Cohen, Malka, ed. *Mi-Pi ha-Am: Sippurei-Am mi-Pi Edot Yisrael* (From Folk Tradition: Folktales of Ethnic Groups in Israel). 3 vols. Tel Aviv: Alef, 1974–1979.

Jason, Heda, ed. *Märchen aus Israel,* trans. Schoschana Gassmann. Die Märchen der Weltliteratur. Düsseldorf: Eugen Diederichs Verlag, 1976.

Marcus, Eliezer, ed. *Min Ha-Mabua* (From the Fountainhead)*: Forty-Four Folktales Collected by the "Mabuim School-Pupils."* Israel Folktale Archives Publication Series 12. Haifa: Haifa Municipality, Ethnological Museum and Folklore Archives, 1966 (in Hebrew).

Nanah, Reuven, ed. *Otzar ha-Ma'asiyyot* (A Treasury of Tales). 3 vols. Jerusalem: Author's publication, 1979.

Noy, Dov, ed. *Folktales of Israel,* trans. Gene Baharav, with Dan Ben-Amos. Folktales of the World. Chicago: University of Chicago Press, 1963.

Rabbi, Moshe, ed. *Avoteinu Sipru: Sippurim u-ma'Assiyyot she-Nirshemu mi-Ziknei ha-Dor* (Our Fathers Told: Tales and Stories That Were Written Down from the Elders). 3 vols. Jerusalem: Bakal, 1970–1975.

Vigiser, Moshe. *Haḥalom Ufishro: Anthology of Folk Stories*, ed. Shmuel (Vigi) Vigiser. Tel Aviv: Tammuz, 2006 (in Hebrew).

Annual Harvest of Tales

Cheichel, Edna, ed. *A Tale for Each Month 1967. Twelve Selected and Annotated IFA Folktales.* Israel Folktale Archives Publication Series 22. Haifa: Haifa Municipality, Ethnological Museum and Folklore Archives, 1968 (in Hebrew).

———, ed. *A Tale for Each Month 1968–1969. Twelve Selected and Annotated IFA Folktales.* Israel Folktale Archives Publication Series 26. Haifa: Haifa Municipality, Ethnological Museum and Folklore Archives, 1970 (in Hebrew).

———, ed. *A Tale for Each Month 1972. Twelve Selected and Annotated IFA Folktales.* Israel Folktale Archives Publication Series 30. Haifa: Ethnological Museum and Folklore Archives, 1973 (in Hebrew).

Kagan, Ziporah, ed. *A Tale for Each Month 1963. Twelve Selected and Annotated IFA Folktales.* Israel Folktale Archives Publication Series 6. Haifa: Haifa Municipality, Ethnological Museum and Folklore Archives, 1964 (in Hebrew).

———, ed. *A Tale for Each Month 1964. Twelve Selected and Annotated IFA Folktales.* Israel Folktale Archives Publication Series 9. Haifa: Haifa Municipality, Ethnological Museum and Folklore Archives, 1965 (in Hebrew).

Noy, Dov, ed. *A Tale for Each Month 1961. Twelve Selected and Annotated IFA Folktales.* Israel Folktale Archives Publication Series 1. Haifa: Haifa Municipality, Ethnological Museum and Folklore Archives, 1962 (in Hebrew).

———, ed. *A Tale for Each Month 1962. Twelve Selected and Annotated IFA Folktales.* Israel Folktale Archives Publication Series 13. Haifa: Haifa Municipality, Ethnological Museum and Folklore Archives, 1963 (in Hebrew).

———, ed. *A Tale for Each Month 1965. Twelve Selected and Annotated IFA Folktales.* Israel Folktale Archives Publication Series 11. Haifa: Haifa Municipality, Ethnological Museum and Folklore Archives, 1966 (in Hebrew).

———, ed. *A Tale for Each Month 1966. Twelve Selected and Annotated IFA Folktales.* Israel Folktale Archives Publication Series 18. Haifa: Haifa Municipality, Ethnological Museum and Folklore Archives, 1967 (in Hebrew).

———, ed. *A Tale for Each Month 1970. Twelve Selected and Annotated IFA Folktales.* Israel Folktale Archives Publication Series 27. Haifa: Ethnological Museum and Folklore Archives, 1971 (in Hebrew).

———, ed. *A Tale for Each Month 1971. Twelve Selected and Annotated IFA Folktales.* Israel Folktale Archives Publication Series 28. Haifa: Haifa Municipality, Ethnological Museum and Folklore Archives, 1972 (in Hebrew).

———, ed. *A Tale for Each Month 1974–1975. Twenty Four Selected and Annotated IFA Folktales.* Israel Folktale Archives Publication Series 36. Jerusalem: Hebrew University. Folklore Research Center, 1978 (in Hebrew).

———, ed. *A Tale for Each Month 1976–1977. Twenty Four Selected and Annotated IFA Folktales.* Israel Folktale Archives Publication Series 39. Jerusalem: Hebrew University. Folklore Research Center, 1979 (in Hebrew).

———, ed. *A Tale for Each Month 1978. Twenty Four Selected and Annotated IFA Folktales.* Israel Folktale Archives Publication Series 40. Jerusalem: Hebrew University. Folklore Research Center, 1979 [1980] (in Hebrew).

Local Anthologies

Baharav, Zalman. *Sixty Folktales Collected from Narrators in Ashkelon,* ed. Dov Noy. Israel Folktale Archives Publication Series 5. Haifa: Haifa Municipality, Ethnological Museum and Folklore Archives, 1969 (in Hebrew).

Gutter, Malka. *Honor Your Mother: Twelve Folktales from Buczacz,* ed. Aliza Shenhar. Israel Folktale Archives Publication Series 23. Haifa: Haifa Municipality, Ethnological Museum and Folklore Archives, 1969 (in Hebrew).

Noy, Meir, ed. *East European Jewish Cante Fables.* Israel Folktale Archives Publication Series 20. Haifa: Haifa Municipality, Ethnological Museum and Folklore Archives, 1968 (in Hebrew).

Pipe, Samuel Zanvel. *Twelve Folktales from Sanok,* ed. Dov Noy. Israel Folktale Archives Publication Series 15. Haifa: Haifa Municipality, Ethnological Museum and Folklore Archives, 1967 (in Hebrew).

Shenhar, Aliza, ed. *A Tale for Each Month: 1973.* Israel Folktale Archives Publication Series 32. Haifa: Haifa Municipality, Ethnological Museum and Folklore Archives, 1974 (in Hebrew).

Shenhar, Aliza, and H. Bar-Itzhak, eds. *Sippurei 'Am me-Bet-She'an* (Folktales from Bet She'an). Haifa: Haifa University Press, 1981.

———. *Sippurei 'Am me-Shelomi* (Folktales from Shelomi). Haifa: Haifa University Press, 1982.

Sider, Fishl. *Seven Folktales from Boryslaw,* ed. Otto Schnitzler. Israel Folktale Archives Publication Series 19. Haifa: Haifa Municipality, Ethnological Museum and Folklore Archives, 1968 (in Hebrew).

Ethnic Anthologies

Aminoff, Irit. *The Emir and the Widow: Twelve Folktales from Bukhara Related by Benjamin Hiatt Aminoff,* ed. Otto Schnitzler. Israel Folktale Archives Publication Series 31. Haifa: Ethnological Museum and Folklore Archives, 1974 (in Hebrew).

Attias, Moshe. *The Golden Feather: Twenty Folktales Narrated by Greek Jews,* ed. Dov Noy. Israel Folktale Archives Publication Series 35. Haifa: Haifa Municipality, Ethnological Museum and Folklore Archives, 1976 (in Hebrew).

Babay, Rafael. *A Favor for a Favor: Ten Jewish-Persian Folktales,* ed. Batya Maoz. Israel Folktale Archives Publication Series 41. Jerusalem: Magnes, Hebrew University, 1980 (in Hebrew).

Bar-Itzhak, Haya, and A. Shenhar, eds. *Jewish Moroccan Folk Narratives from Israel.* Jewish Folklore and Anthropology Series. Detroit: Wayne State University Press, 1993.

Ben-Ami, Issachar. *The Apple of Conception: Jewish Moroccan Folk Narratives.* Jerusalem: Lugassy, 2000 (in Hebrew).

———. *A Flower to Resuscitate the Dead: Jewish Moroccan Folk Narratives.* Jerusalem: Lugassy, 2000 (in Hebrew).

Ben-Amos, Dan, ed. *Folktales of the Jews. Volume 1: Tales from the Sephardic Dispersion.* Edited with commentary. Dov Noy, consulting ed.; Ellen Frankel, series ed. Philadelphia: Jewish Publication Society, 2006.

———, ed. *Folktales of the Jews. Volume 2: Tales from East Europe.* Edited with commentary. Dov Noy, consulting ed.; Ellen Frankel, series ed. Philadelphia: Jewish Publication Society, 2007.

———, ed. *Folktales of the Jews. Volume 3: Tales from Arab Lands.* Edited with commentary. Dov Noy, consulting ed.; Ellen Frankel, series ed. Philadelphia: Jewish Publication Society, 2011.

Bribram, Gershon. *Jewish Folk-Stories from Hungary: Fourteen Folktales,* ed. Otto Schnitzler. Israel Folktale Archives Publication Series 10. Haifa: Haifa Municipality, Ethnological Museum and Folklore Archives, 1965 (in Hebrew).

Falah, Salman, and Aliza Shenhar, eds. *Druze Folktales: Thirty Druze Folktales Collected in Israel, Annotated and Indexed.* Israel Folktale Archives Publication Series 37. Haifa: Haifa Municipality, Ethnological Museum and Folklore Archives, 1978 (in Hebrew).

Fus, Dvora. *Seven Bags of Gold: Seven Yiddish Folktales from Lithuania,* trans. Israel Rosenthal and ed. Otto Schnitzler. Israel Folktale Archives Publication Series 25. Haifa: Haifa Municipality, Ethnological Museum and Folklore Archives, 1969 (in Hebrew).

Keren, Abraham. *Advice from the Rothschilds: 28 Humorous Stories from Poland,* ed. Otto Schnitzer. Israel Folktale Archives Publication Series 43. Jerusalem: Magnes, Hebrew University 1981 (in Hebrew).

Mizrahi, Hanina. *With Elders Is Wisdom: Forty Jewish-Persian Folktales Collected in Israel.* Israel Folktale Archives Publication Series 16. Haifa: Haifa Municipality, Ethnological Museum and Folklore Archives, 1967 (in Hebrew).

Nehmad, Moshe. *The New Garment: Five Folktales from Jewish Persian Tradition,* ed. Otto Schnitzler. Israel Folktale Archives Publication Series 14. Haifa: Haifa Municipality, Ethnological Museum and Folklore Archives, 1966 (in Hebrew).

Noy, Dov, ed. *Jewish Folktales from Libya: Seventy-One Tales from Oral Tradition.* Jerusalem: Bi-Tefutsot ha-Golah, 1967 (in Hebrew).

———, ed. *Jewish Folktales from Morocco: Narrated and Collected in Israel.* Jerusalem: Publishing Department of the Jewish Agency for Israel, 1964; 2d ed., 1967 (in Hebrew).

———, ed. *Jewish Folktales from Tunisia.* Jerusalem: Bi-Tefutzot ha-Golah, 1966 (in Hebrew).

———, ed. *Jewish-Iraqi Folktales.* Tel Aviv: Am Oved, 1965 (in Hebrew).

———. *Moroccan Jewish Folktales.* Foreword by Raphael Patai. New York: Herzel, 1966.

Pinhasi, Jacob. *Folktales from Bukhara*, ed. Dov Noy. Israel Folktale Archives Publication Series 38. Haifa: Haifa Municipality, Ethnological Museum and Folklore Archives, 1978 (in Hebrew).

Rabach, Berl. *The Kept Promise: Six Folktales from Galicia*, ed. Otto Schnitzler. Israel Folktale Archives Publication Series 13. Haifa: Haifa Municipality, Ethnological Museum and Folklore Archives, 1966 (in Hebrew).

Seri, Rachel. *The Holy Amulet: Twelve Jewish-Yemenite Folktales*, ed. Aliza Shenhar. Israel Folktale Archives Publication Series 21. Haifa: Haifa Municipality, Ethnological Museum and Folklore Archives, 1968 (in Hebrew).

Tsedaqa, Ratson. *Samaritan Legends: Twelve Legends from Oral Tradition*, ed. Dov Noy. Israel Folktale Archives Publication Series 8. Haifa: Haifa Municipality, Ethnological Museum and Folklore Archives, 1965 (in Hebrew).

Yehoshua, B.Z. *The Father's Will: Thirteen Folktales from Afghanistan, Related by Rafael Yehoshua-Raz*, ed. Ziporah Kagan. Israel Folktale Archives Publication Series 24. Haifa: Haifa Municipality, Ethnological Museum and Folklore Archives, 1969 (in Hebrew).

Yeshiva, Miriam. *Seven Folktales* [from Rumania], ed. Dov Noy. Israel Folktale Archives Publication Series [2]. Haifa: Haifa Municipality, Ethnological Museum and Folklore Archives, 1963 (in Hebrew).

Narrators' Anthologies

Haviv, Yifrah. *Never Despair: Seven Folktales Related by Aliza Anidjar from Tangiers*, ed. Edna Cheichel. Israel Folktale Archives Publication Series 13. Haifa: Haifa Municipality, Ethnological Museum and Folklore Archives, 1966 (in Hebrew).

Noy, Dov, ed. *Jefet Schwili Erzählt: Hundertneunundsechzig jemenitische volkserzählungen aufgezeichnet in Israel 1957–1960.* Supplement-Serie zu Fabula Zeitschrift für Erzählforschung Reihe A Band 4. Berlin: Walter de Gruyter, 1963.

Weinstein, E. *Grandma Esther Relates. . . .* , ed. Ziporah Kagan. Israel Folktale Archives Publication Series 4. Haifa: Haifa Municipality, Ethnological Museum and Folklore Archives, 1964 (in Hebrew).

Zohar, Ilana. *Kinor Eliyahu: H"Y Sippurei-'Am mi-Pi Flora Cohen* (Elijah's Violin: Eighteen Tales Told by Flora Cohen). Kiryat-Tivon: N.p., 1991.

Thematic Anthologies

Haimovits, Zvi Moshe. *Faithful Guardians: Eighteen Folktales from Thirteen Narrators*, ed. Dov Noy. Israel Folktale Archives Publication Series 34. Haifa: Haifa Municipality, Ethnological Museum and Folklore Archives, 1976 (in Hebrew).

Noy, Dov, ed. *The Jewish Animal Tale of Oral Tradition.* Israel Folktale Archives Publication Series 29. Haifa: Haifa Municipality, Ethnological Museum and Folklore Archives, 1976 (in Hebrew).

Stahl, Abraham, ed. *Stories of Faith and Morals: 36 Jewish Folktales.* Israel Folktale Archives Publication Series 17. Haifa: Haifa Municipality, Ethnological Museum and Folklore Archives, 1976 (in Hebrew).

Translated or Retold Folktales

General:

Ben-Zvi, Hava, ed. and trans. *The Bride Who Argued with God: Tales from the Treasury of Jewish Folklore.* New York: iUniverse, 2006.

Nagarajan, Nadia Grosser. *Jewish Tales from Eastern Europe.* Northvale, NJ: Jason Aronson, 1999.

Rush, Barbara. *The Book of Jewish Women's Tales.* Northvale, NJ: Jason Aronson, 1994.

Sadeh Pinḥas. *Jewish Folktales,* trans. Hillel Halkin. New York: Doubleday, 1989.

———. *Sefer ha-Dimyyonot shel ha-Yehudim: Sippurei-'Am* (The Book of Jewish Imaginaries: Folk-Tales). Jerusalem: Schocken, 1983.

Schram, Peninnah. *Jewish Stories One Generation Tells Another.* Northvale, NJ: Jason Aronson, 1987.

———. *Stories Within Stories: From the Jewish Oral Tradition.* Northvale, NJ: Jason Aronson, 2000.

Schwartz, Howard. *Elijah's Violin and Other Jewish Fairy Tales.* New York: Harper & Row, 1983.

———. *Gabriel's Palace: Jewish Mystical Tales.* New York: Oxford University Press, 1993.

———. *Lilith's Cave: Jewish Tales of the Supernatural.* San Francisco: Harper & Row, 1988.

———. *Miriam's Tambourine: Jewish Folktales from Around the World.* New York: Seth, 1986.

Sephardic Folktale Anthologies:

Alexander, Tamar, and Dov Noy, eds. *The Treasure of Our Fathers: Judeo-Spanish Tales.* Jerusalem: Misgav Yerushalayim, 1989 (in Hebrew).

Alexander, Tamar, and Elena Romero. *Erase una vez . . . Maimónides: cuentos tradicionales Hebreos:* Córdoba: Ediciones el Almendro, 1988.

———. *Once Upon a Time . . . Maimonides,* trans. Rhoda Henelde Abecasis. Lancaster, CA: Labyrinthos, 2004.

Crews, Cynthia Mary Jopson. *Recherches sur le judéo-espagnol dans les pays balkaniques.* Paris: E. Droz, 1935.

Elbaz, André E. *Folktales of the Canadian Sephardim.* Toronto: Fitzhenry & Whiteside, 1982.

Grünwald, Max. *Tales, Songs and Folkways of Sephardic Jews*, ed. Dov Noy. Folklore Research Center Studies 6. Jerusalem: Magnes, 1982 (in Hebrew).

Koen-Sarano, Mathilda. *De Saragosa a Yerushaláyim: Kuentos Sefaradís.* Zaragoza: Iberecaja, 1995.

———. *Djoha ke dize? Kuentos populares djudeo-espanyoles.* Jerusalem: Kana, 1991.

———. *King Solomon and the Golden Fish: Tales from the Sephardic Tradition.* Translated and annotated by Reginetta

Haboucha. Raphael Patai Series in Jewish Folklore and Anthropology. Detroit: Wayne State University Press, 2004.

———. *Konsejas i konsejikas del mundo djudeo-espanyol*. Jerusalem: Kana, 1994 (in Hebrew and Judeo-Spanish).

———. *Kuentos del folklor de la famiya Djudeo-Espanyola*. Jerusalem: Kana, 1982 (in Hebrew and Judeo-Spanish).

———. *Lejedas i kuentos morales dela tradisión djudeo-espanyola*. Jerusalem: Nur Afakot, 1999.

Larrea Palacín, A. de. *Cuentos populares de los judíos del norte de Marruecos*. 2 vols. Tetuán, Morocco: Marroqui, 1953.

Luria, Max A. "A Study of the Monastir Dialect of Judeo-Spanish Based on Oral Material Collected in Monastir, Yugo-Slavia." *Revue Hispanique* 79 (1930): 323–583.

Meyuḥas, Joseph. *Ma'asiyyot Am li-Bnei-Kedem* (Oriental Folktales). Tel Aviv: Dvir, 1938.

Wagner, Max Leopold. *Beiträge zur Kenntnis des Judenspanischen von Konstantinopel*. Schriften der Balkankommission, Linguistische Abteilung. Vienna: A. Hölder, 1914.

Ashkenazic Folktale Anthologies:

Almi, A. *1863: Yidishe povstanye-mayselekh* (1863: Jewish Tales of Polish Insurrection). Warsaw: Goldfarb, 1927.

Ayalon-Baranick, Benzion Ḥayyim. *Antologia le-Folklore Yehudi be-Artzot Mizraḥ Eiropa: Hayoh Haya Ma'aseh: Shirim, Sippurim, Masorot, Minhagim, Hanhagot, Bediḥot, Pitgamim, Emunot Tefelot, Parpera'ot, Ḥidot* (Anthology of Jewish Folklore in East-Europe: Once Upon a Time: Songs, Tales, Traditions, Customs, Ordinances, Jokes, Proverbs, Superstitions, Anecdotes and Riddles). Tel Aviv: Folklore, 1946.

Cahan, Yehydah Leib. *Jewish Folklore*. Publications of the Yiddish Scientific Institute 9, Philological Series 5. Vilnius, Lithuania: Yiddish Scientific Institute, 1938 (in Yiddish).

———. *Yidishe folksmasiyyot: oys demfolksmoyl gezamlt* (Yiddish Folktales: Recorded from Oral Tradition). Yidishe Folklor-Bibliyotek, 1. New York/Vilna: Yidishe Folklor-Bibliyotek, 1931. Expanded ed. in Cahan, *Gesamlte ktovim* (Collected Writings), vol. 5. Vilna, Lithuania: Yiddish Scientific Institute, 1940.

Dymchitz, Valery, ed. *Contes populaires juifs d'Europe orientale: contes merveilleux Légendes et traditions contes de mœurs histoires et anecdotes*. Collection Merveilleux 25. Paris: José Corti, 2004.

Gross, Naftoli. *Mayselech un Mesholim: Tales and Parables*. New York: Forewerts, 1955. [An analytic study of this anthology is Haim Schwarzbaum, *Studies in Jewish and World Folklore*. Supplement-Series to *Fabula* series B, vol. 3. Berlin: Walter de Gruyter, 1968.]

Raĭze, Efim Samoĭlovich. *Contes populaires juifs d'Europe oriental: contes merveilleux, légendes et traditions, contes de mœurs, histoires et anecdotes*, trans. Sophie Benech and ed. Valery Dymchitz. Collection Merveilleux 25. Paris: Corti, 2004.

———. *Evreĭskie narodnye skazki: Predanii , bylichki, anekdoty*, ed. Valerii Dimshits. St. Petersburg: Symposium, 1999.

Stephani, Claus, ed. and trans. *Ostjüdische Märchen*. Die Märchen der Weltliteratur. München: Eugen Diederich, 1998.

Wanwild, M., ed. *Bay untz Yidn: Księga zbiorowa folkloru i filologji* (Among Us Jews: An Anthology of Folklore and Philology). Warsaw: Graubard, 1923 (in Yiddish).

Weinreich, Beatrice Silverman, ed. *Yiddish Folktales*, trans. Leonard Wolf. Pantheon Fairy Tale and Folklore Library. New York: Pantheon and YIVO Institute for Jewish Research, 1988.

Zfatman, Sarah, ed. *Ma'asiyyot Kesem mi-Pi Yehudei Mizraḥ Eiropa/Yidishe vunder-Ma'asiyyot fun Mizrakh-Eirope* (Yiddish Wonder Tales from East Europe), trans. Yosel Birstein and Ido Basok. Tel Aviv: Hakibbutz Hameuchad, 1998 (in Hebrew and Yiddish).

Anthologies of Tales from Countries of Islam:

Arakie, El'azar. *Sefer ha-Ma'asiyyot* (Book of Folktales). Calcutta, 1842.

Avishur, Yitzhak, trans. and ed. *The Folktales of Jews of Iraq: Thirty Stories in Judeo-Arabic from 19th Century Manuscripts*. 2 vols. Haifa: University of Haifa, 1992.

———. *The Ḥakham from Bagdad in Calcutta: Ḥakham Shelomo Twena and His Works in Hebrew and Judaeo-Arabic*. 2 vols. Tel Aviv: Archaeological Center and "Magen Aboth" for Calcutta Jews, 2002 (in Hebrew).

Caspi, Mishael. *Mi-Zkenim Ethonan* (I Will Observe the Elders). Sedeh-Boker, Israel: Midreshet Sedeh Boker, 1968.

Gamlieli, Nissim Benjamin. *The Chambers of Yemen: 131 Jewish-Yemenite Folktales and Legends*. Tel Aviv: Afikim, 1978 (in Hebrew).

———. *Hevion Teman: From the Depth of Yemen Memoirs, Folktales and Legends*. Ramleh: Author's publication, 1983 (in Hebrew).

Goitein, S.D. *From the Land of Sheba: Tales of the Jews of Yemen*, trans. Christopher Fremantle. New York: Schocken Books, 1947.

Ha-Kohen, El'azar ben Aharon Sa'adya. *Sefer ha-ma'asiyyot* (A Book of Tales). Calcutta, 1842.

Ha-Kohen, Yosef Eliahu *'Ajab al-'ajab* (Wonder of Wonders). Bombay, 1889 (in Judeo-Arabic).

Ḥayyim, Yosef. *Sefer Niflaim Ma'asekha* (Book of Your Wonderful Acts). Jerusalem, 1912.

Ḥuzin, Shelomoh. Bekhor. *Sefer Ma'aseh Nissim* (Miracles). Baghdad, 1890.

———. *Sefer Ma'asim Tovim* (The Book of Good Acts). Baghdad, 1890.

Kokhavi, Shelomoh. *Mivḥar me-Sippurei Yehudei Teiman: mi-Pi ha-Am u-min ha-Midrash* (A Selection of Jewish-Yemenite Tales from Oral Tradition and from the Midrash). Tel Aviv: Afikim, 2006.

Yarimi, Aharon, ed. *Me-Aggadot Teman: Me-Sippurei Rabbi Yehuda ben Rabbi Aharon Yarimi*. Jerusalem: Author's publication, 1978.

Folksong Anthologies

Sephardic Folksong Anthologies

Armistead, Samuel G. *El romancero judeo-español en el Archivo Menéndez Pidal (Catálogo-índice de romances y canciones)*.

Selma Margarettern, Paloma Montero, and Ana Valenciano, collaborators; Israel J. Katz, musical transcription. Vol. 3: "Anthology of Rare Ballads," pp. 7–73. Madrid: Cátedra-Seminario Menéndez Pidal, 1978.

Armistead, Samuel G., and Joseph H. Silverman, eds. *The Judeo-Spanish Ballad Chapbooks of Yacob Abraham Yoná.* Folk Literature of the Sephardic Jews I. Berkeley: University of California Press, 1971.

———. *Judeo-Spanish Ballads from Bosnia.* In collaboration with Biljana Šljivić-Šimšić. Philadelphia: University of Pennsylvania Press, 1971.

———. *Judeo-Spanish Ballads from Oral Tradition I. Epic Ballads.* Folk Literature of the Sephardic Jews II. Berkeley and Los Angeles: University of California Press, 1986.

———, eds. *Romances judeo-españoles de Tanger* (Judeo-Spanish Ballads of Tangiers). Zarita Nahón, recorder; Oro Anahory Librowicz, collaborator; Israel J. Katz, musical transcription. Madrid: Cátedra-Seminario Menédez Pidal, 1977.

Armistead, Samuel G., Joseph Silverman, and Israel J. Katz. *Judeo-Spanish Ballads from Oral Tradition II. Carolingian Ballads (1): Roncevalles.* Folk Literature of the Sephardic Jews III. Berkeley and Los Angeles: University of California Press, 1994.

———. *Judeo-Spanish Ballads from Oral Tradition IV. Carolingian Ballads (2): Conde Claros.* Folk Literature of the Sephardic Jews IV. Newark, DE: Juan de la Cuesta, 2008.

———. *Judeo-Spanish Ballads from Oral Tradition IV. Carolingian Ballads (3): Gaiferos.* Folk Literature of the Sephardic Jews V. Newark, DE: Juan de la Cuesta, 2005.

Attias, Moshe. *Cancionero judeo-español: canciones populares en judeo-español.* Jerusalem: Centro de Estudios sobre el Judaísmo de Salónica, 1972.

———. *Romancero sefaradí: romanzas y cantes populares en judeo-español.* Jerusalem: Kiryat Sefer, 1961.

Hemsi, Alberto. *Cancionero sefardí*, ed. Edwin Seroussi. Jerusalem: Music Research Center, Hebrew University of Jerusalem, 1995.

Levy, Isaac. *Chants judéo-espagnols.* 4 vols. London: World Sephardi Federation [1959]–1973.

Ashkenazic Folk Song Anthologies

Cahan, Yehudah Leib. *Jewish Folklore.* Publications of the Yiddish Scientific Institute 9, Philological Series 5. Vilnius, Lithuania: Yiddish Scientific Institute, 1938 (in Yiddish).

———. *Yiddish Folk Songs with Melodies,* ed. Max Weinreich. New York: YIVO Institute for Jewish Research, 1957 (in Yiddish).

———. *Yiddish Folk Songs with Their Original Airs. Collected from Oral Tradition.* 2 vols. New York: International Library, 1912 (in Yiddish).

Dobrushin, Yeḥezkel, and A. Yudiski. *Yidishe Folkslider.* Moscow: "Der Emes," 1940.

Ginzburg, S.M., and P.S. Marek. *Yiddish Folk Songs in Russia: A Photo Reproduction of the 1901 St. Petersburg Edition*, ed. Dov Noy. Ramat-Gan: Bar-Ilan University Press, 1991 (in Yiddish).

Gorali, Moshe, Gideon Almagor, and Moshe Bick, eds. *The Golden Peacock: Yiddish Folksongs* Haifa: Haifa Music Museum and A.M.L.I. Library, 1970 (in Yiddish with Hebrew translation and succinct English summaries).

Lehman, Shmuel. *Ganovim Lider mit melodis* (Songs of Thieves with Melodies). Warsaw: Graubard, 1928.

Mlotek, Chana, and Mark Slobin, eds. *Yiddish Folksongs from the Ruth Rubin Archive.* Detroit: Wayne State University Press, 2007.

Pipe, Shmuel Zanvel. *Yiddish Folksongs from Galicia / The Folklorization of David Edelstadt's Song "Der Arbeter" / Letters*, ed. Dov Noy and Meir Noy. Folklore Research Center 2. Jerusalem: Folklore Research Center, Hebrew University, 1971 (in Yiddish).

Prilutski, Noah. *Yiddishe Folkslider* (Yiddish Folk Songs). 2 vols. Warsaw: Bikher far Aleh, 1911 and Nayer Ferlag, 1913 (in Yiddish).

Rubin, Ruth, ed. *A Treasury of Jewish Folksong.* New York: Schocken, 1950.

Slobin, Mark. *Old Jewish Folk Music: The Collections and Writings of Moshe Beregovski.* Philadelphia: University of Pennsylvania Press, 1982.

Vinkovetzky, Aharon, Abba Kovner, and Sinai Lichter, eds. *Anthology of Yiddish Folksongs.* 4 vols. Jerusalem: Magnes, 1983.

Warshawski, Mark. *Yidishe Folkslider* (Yiddish Folk Songs). Warsaw: [s.n.], 1901.

Anthologies of Songs from Countries of Islam

Avishur, Yitzhak. *Women's Folk Songs in Judeo-Arabic from Jews in Iraq.* Studies in the History and Culture of Iraqi Jewry 4. Or Yehuda: Iraqi Jews' Traditional Culture Center and Institute for Research on Iraqi Jewry, 1987 (in Judeo-Arabic and Hebrew).

Gamlieli, Nissim Binyamin. *Arabic Poetry and Songs of the Yemenite Jewish Women.* Tel Aviv: Afikim, 1974 (in Hebrew).

Humor Anthologies

Aschkenasy, Isaac. *Oytsre's fun Yidishn Humor, Ḥokhme's, Vitsen, Glekhvertlakh fun Rabonim un fun'm Folk* (Treasures of Jewish Humor, Smart Sayings, Wits, Metaphors of the Rabbis and the Folk). New York: Tel Aviv, 1929.

Ausubel, Nathan. *A Treasury of Jewish Humor.* Garden City, NY: Doubleday, 1951.

Ben-Amotz, Dan, and Ḥaim Ḥefer. *Yalkut ha-Kezavim* (A Bag of Lies). Tel Aviv: Ha'kibbutz Ha'meuḥad, 1956.

Bialostotzky, B.J. *Jewish Humor and Jewish Jesters.* New York: Central Yiddish Culture Organization (CYCO), 1963 (in Yiddish).

Bloch, Chajim. *Ostjüdischer Humor.* Berlin: B. Harz, 1920.

Bronner, Gerhard. *Tränen gelacht: Der jüdische Humor.* München: Amalthea, 1999.

Cohen, Adir, ed. *The Big Book of Jewish Humor: A Treasury of Jewish and Israeli Jokes.* Or Yehuda, Israel: Kinneret, Zmora-Bitan, Dvir, 2004 (in Hebrew).

Davidson, Efraim. *Sehok le-Yisrael: Yalkut le-Folklore Havai, Humor u-Bediḥah al Medinat Yisrael* (Israeli Humor: An Anthology of Folklore, Lifeways, Humor and Jokes about the State of Israel). Ramat Gan: Matmonim, 1958.

———. *Sehok Pynu (Our Mouth's Laughter): Anthology of Humour and Satire in Ancient and Modern Hebrew Literature.* Ramat Gan: Matmonim, 1951 (in Hebrew).

Davidson, Israel, ed. and trans. *Sepher Shaashuim: A Book of Mediaeval Lore by Joseph ben Meir Zabara. Texts and Studies of the Jewish Theological Seminary of America.* Vol. 4. New York: Jewish Theological Seminary of America, 1914. For an analytical study, see Judith Dishon, *The Book of Delight: Composed by Joseph Ben Meir Zabara*. Jerusalem: Mass, 1985 (in Yiddish).

Druyanow, Alter. *Sefer ha-Bediḥah ve-ha-ḥiddud* (The Book of Jokes and Wit). Frankfurt am Main: Omonuth, 1922.

———. *Sefer ha-bediḥah ve-ha-ḥiddud* (The Book of Jokes and Wit). 3 vols. Tel Aviv: Author's publication, 1935–1938.

Geiger, Raymond. "Nouvelles Histoires Juives." *Les documents bleus* 17. Paris: Librairie Gallimard, 1925.

Isaacs, Ron. *Have a Good Laugh: Jewish Jokes for the Soul.* Jersey City, NJ: Ktav, 2009.

Kerman, Danny, ed. *Two Jews Took a Train: The Best of Alter Druyanov.* Tel Aviv: Zmora-Bitan, 1995 (in Hebrew).

King, Alan. *Alan King's Great Jewish Joke Book.* New York: Crown, 2002.

Köhler, Peter. *Das Leben ist ein Hering an der Wand.* Leipzig: Reclam, 2003.

Landmann, Salcia. *Die klassischen Witze der Juden: Verschollenes und Allerneuestes.* Berlin: Ullstein, 1996.

Liacho, Lázaro, ed. *Anecdotario judío: Folklore, humorismo y chistes* (Jewish Anecdote Collection: Folklore, Humor, and Jokes). Buenos Aires: M. Gleizer, 1939.

Lion, Michal, ed. *Mach, was du willst, Mose! Jüdischer Humor.* Gütersloh: Gütersloh Verlagshaus, 2000.

Lipson, Mordekhai. *Di Velt dertseylt: Mayses, Vertlakh, Hanhoges un Mides fun Anshey-Shem bay Idn* (People Tell: Tales, Sayings, Customs and Manners of Famous People Among the Jews). 2 vols. New York: Doyres, 1928.

———. *Mi-Dor Dor* (From Early Days). 3 vols. Tel Aviv/New York: Dorot, 1929–1938; 4 volume edition, Tel Aviv: Achiasaf, 1968.

Mendelsohn, S. Felix. *Here's a Good One: Stories of Jewish Wit and Wisdom.* New York: Bloch, 1947.

———. *The Jew Laughs: Humorous Stories and Anecdotes.* Chicago: L.M. Stein, 1935.

———. *Let Laughter Ring.* Philadelphia: Jewish Publication Society, 1941.

———. *The Merry Heart: Wit and Wisdom from Jewish Folklore.* New York: Bookman Associates, 1951.

Milburn, George. *The Best Jewish Jokes.* Little Blue Book No. 1082. Girard, KS: Haldeman-Julius, 1926.

Minkoff, David. *Oy! The Ultimate Book of Jewish Jokes.* New York: Thomas Dunne Books/St. Martin's, 2006.

———. *Oy Vey: More! The Ultimate Book of Jewish Jokes Part 2.* New York: Thomas Dunne Books/St. Martin's, 2008.

Olsvanger, Immanuel. *L'Chayim! Jewish Wit and Humor.* New York: Schocken, 1949.

———. *Rêjte Pomeranzen.* Berlin: Schocken, 1935.

———. *Rosinkess mit Mandlen. Aus der Volksliteratur des Ostjuden: Schwänke, Erzählungen, Sprichwörter, Rätsel.* Schweizerische Kommision für jüdische Volkskunde. Schriften zur jüdischen Volkskunde No. 1. Basel: Verlag der Schweizerischen Gesellschaft für Volkskunde, 1920 (2d ed., 1931; 3d ed., 1965.) Translated into German as *Jüdische Schwänke,* trans. Max Präger and Siegfried Schmitz. Vienna and Leipzig: R. Löwit Verlag, 1928, 1964.

Oring, Elliott. *Israeli Humor: The Content and Structure of the Chizbat of the Palmah.* Albany: State University of New York Press, 1981.

Ouaknin, Marc-Alain, and Dory Rotnemer. *Tout l'humour juif.* Paris: Assouline, 2001.

Rawnitzki, Yehoshua H. *Yudishe Vitsen* (Yiddish Jokes). Berlin: Moriyah, 1921/22.

Richman, Jacob. *Jewish Wit and Wisdom.* New York: Pardes, 1952.

———. *Laughs from Jewish Lore.* New York: Behrman's Jewish Book House, 1926.

Rochmes, Wolfgang, ed. *Gegen's Heimweh: Judische Witze, Anekdoten und Geschichte.* München: Wilhelm Heyne Verlag, 2008.

Sadan, Dov. *Ke'arat Egozim o elef bedihah u-bedihah: asufat homor be-yisrael* (A Bowl of Nuts or A Thousand and One Jokes: An Anthology of Humor in Israel). Tel Aviv: Neuman, 1953.

———. *Ke'arat Tsimukim o elef bedihah u-bedihah: asufat homor be-yisrael* (A Bowl of Raisins or A Thousand and One Jokes: An Anthology of Humor in Israel). Tel Aviv: Neuman, 1952.

Sherer, Zalman. *Jewish Folk Wisdoms.* Tel Aviv: Kavvim, 2008 (bilingual, Yiddish-Hebrew edition).

Shua, Ana María. *El pueblo de los tontos: Humor tradicional judío* (The People of Folly: Traditional Jewish Humor). Buenos Aires: Alfaguara, 1995.

Spalding, Henry D. *Encyclopedia of Jewish Humor.* New York: Jonathan David, 1969.

Teitelbaum, Elsa. *An Anthology of Jewish Humor and Maxims.* New York: Pardes, 1945.

Tsuker, Yitsḥak (Bunim). *Lakhn iz Gezunṭ: Anekdoṭn, Aforizmen* (Laughter Is Healthy: Anecdotes and Aphorisms). Tel Aviv: Published with the assistance of Keren Tel-Aviv le-Sifrut ule-Omanut, 1997.

Anthologies for Holidays and Festivals

Bar-Itzhak, Haya, and Edna Kremer. *Mishloaḥ Manot—Holiday Folktales.* Tel-Aviv: Sifriyat Poalim, 1986.

Estin, Colette, ed. *Contes et fêtes juives* (Jewish Tales and Holidays). Paris: Beauchesne, 1987.

Goodman, Philip, ed. *The Hanukkah Anthology.* Philadelphia: Jewish Publication Society of America, 1976.

———, ed. *The Passover Anthology.* Philadelphia: Jewish Publication Society of America, 1961.

———, ed. *The Purim Anthology.* Philadelphia: Jewish Publication Society of America, 1949.

———, ed. *The Rosh Hashanah Anthology.* Philadelphia: Jewish Publication Society of America, 1970.

———, ed. *The Shavuot Anthology.* Philadelphia: Jewish Publication Society of America, 1974.

———, ed. *The Sukkot and Simhat Torah Anthology.* Philadelphia: Jewish Publication Society of America, 1973.

———, ed. *The Yom Kippur Anthology.* Philadelphia: Jewish Publication Society of America, 1971.

Lewinski, Yom-Tov, and Yitshak Leib Barukh, eds. *Sefer ha-Mo'adim* (Book of Holidays). 8 vols. Tel Aviv: Agudat 'Oneg Shabat (Ohel Shabat), 1947.

Marcus, Eliezer. *Jewish Festivities.* Jerusalem: Keter, 1990 (in Hebrew).

Rush, Barbara, and Eliezer Marcus, eds. *Seventy and One Tales for the Jewish Year: Folk Tales for the Festivals.* New York: A.Z.Y.F., 1980.

Miscelleneous and Ethnic Anthologies

Moreen, Vera Basch, ed. and trans. *In Queen Esther's Garden: An Anthology of Judeo-Persian Literature.* Yale Judaica Series 30. New Haven, CT: Yale University Press, 2000.

Nemoy, Leon, ed. and trans. *Karaite Anthology.* Yale Judaica Series 7. New Haven, CT: Yale University Press, 1952.

Rivlin, Yosef-Yoel. *Shirat Yehudei ha-Targum: Pirkei Alilah u-Gevurah be-Fi Yehudei Kurdistan* (The Poetry of Targum Speaking Jews: Heroic Poetry of the Jews of Kurdistan). Jerusalem: Bialik Institute, 1959.

Sabar, Yona, ed. and trans. *The Folk Literature of the Kurdistani Jews: An Anthology.* Yale Judaica Series 23. New Haven, CT: Yale University Press, 1982.

Stern, David, and Mark Jay Mirsky, eds. *Rabbinic Fantasies: Imaginative Narratives from Classical Hebrew Literature.* Philadelphia: Jewish Publication Society, 1990. Reprinted in Yale Judaica Series 29. New Haven, CT: Yale University Press, 1998.

Wolf, Leslau, ed. and trans. *Falasha Anthology.* Yale Judaica Series 6. New Haven, CT: Yale University Press, 1951.

INDEX

Page numbers in italics indicate illustrations.

D

G

H

J

L

Midrash *(continued)*
on Sarah, 2:471
on stones, 2:516
on Sukkot, 2:517
on Tamar, 2:522
on Western Wall, 2:560
on Zipporah, 2:575, 576
Midrash Aseret ha'Dibberot (*Midrash of the Ten Commandments*), 1:41, 44, 152, 184, 327; 2:338, 365
Midrash Rabba, 2:365, 438, 466
Midreshei ha'tannaim, 2:364
Mieder, Wolfgang, 1:132
Mihaielanu, Radu, 2:501
Mikdash-Shamialov, Liya, 1:159
mikdashyah, 1:248, 277
Mikhali, Rabbi, 1:131
mikveh, 2:464, 484, 550, 572
military parades, Israel and, 1:255
milk products, 1:195, 226, 227; 2:488
Milkham, myth of, 1:26
Milner, Moshe, 1:172
Milton, John, 1:8
Mimuna Festival, 1:137, 172; 2:365–67, *366*
Minḥa, 2:410, 425, 572
minhag (custom), 2:368–69, 425
minhag books, 1:230, 320; 2:369–70
Minor Yom Kippur, 2:373
Mintz, Alan, 1:54
Mintz, Jerome, 1:74, 328
minyan, 1:102, 110, 111; 2:370–71
miracle tales, 1:262–63
miracles
magic and, 2:342, 343, 348
Moses and, 2:376
Pinto family and, 2:409–12
Rabbi Meir and, 2:356, 357
Rachel and, 2:442
Rambam (Maimonides) and, 2:442, 512
the sea and, 2:476
Western Wall and, 2:560
miranda de hanuka (Ḥanukkah festal board), 1:227
Miriam, 1:1, 163; 2:374, 375, 576
Miriam (Berdyczewski), 1:76–77
Miriam (Tanḥum's daughter/Nahtom's daughter), 2:377, 378
Miron, Dan, 2:381, 500
Mirsky, Mark Jay, 1:49
Mishle Shu'alim (Fox Fables), 1:42, 155, 185, 320; 2:353, 474
mishloaḥ manot, 1:146; 2:430
Mishnah, 2:364, 437, 438
on age and the aged, 1:19

Mishnah *(continued)*
on corpses, 1:120
on first fruits, 2:487
folk narratives, 1:178, 180
Haggadah and, 1:218
Hebrew and, 1:314
magic and, 2:343–45
on months, 2:372–73
on Passover, 2:403, 404
Rabbi Meir and, 2:355, 356
on Rosh Ha'Shana, 2:452
on Sabbath, 2:483–84
on Sabbath lamp, 1:311
on Seder, 2:404
on Sukkot, 2:519
on Tu Be'Shvat, 2:502, 503
Mishneh Torah (Maimonides), 1:16, 144, 251; 2:362, 442, 485, 539
mitat neshiqah. See death by kiss
mitnagdim, 1:290–91; 2:454
mitpaḥat, 2:534–36
Mitteilungen der Gesellschaft für Jüdische Volkskunde (journal), 1:205, 216, 328; 2:479
Mitzvah dance, 1:163, 164
mitzvoth, 1:123; 2:368, 437, 548, 572
mizbe'aḥ, 2:464
mizraḥ, 1:156, 278; 2:371, 399, 491, 531
Mizraḥi (Zionist party), 2:420
Mizrahi, Moise, 1:214
Mizraḥim, folk beliefs, 1:161, 162, 167, 168
mizug galuyot, 1:92
Mlotek, Chana, 1:48
Mlotek, Eleanor Gordon, 1:175
modesty, 1:114, 163
mofleta, 2:366, 367
Mohammad Reza Shah, 1:262
Mohammed/Muhammad, 1:2; 2:543
Mohar, Yeḥiel, 1:194
mohels, 1:108, 110, 111, 258, 300; 2:550
amulets and, 1:305
Georgian customs, 1:202
Hasidic, 2:554
Mohilev synagogue (Belarus), 1:278
Moldavia, 2:449, 450–51, 528, 529
Molkho, Solomon (Shlomo), 1:106; 2:361
Mongols, 1:260, 264
monotheism, 1:2, 3–4
Monsonego family, 2:391
monsters and mythological creatures, 1:37; 2:347, 371–72, 475, 476
month, 2:372–73, *372*
moon, calendar and, 2:372, 373
Morael (angel), 1:33
moral, of stories, 1:34, 155; 2:512

Moran, Ann, 1:100
Moravia, 1:116, 221, 242
Esther scrolls, 1:146
illuminated manuscripts, 1:253, 278
Seder plates, 2:478
tombstones, 2:527, 528
Torah ark curtains, 2:533
Mordechai, 1:143–46, 260; 2:430, 431
Mordechai di Segni, 1:272
Moreen, Vera, 1:49
moreh, 2:540
Moriah (publisher), 2:446
morning prayer, 1:3, 15; 2:491
Morocco, 1:187, 264; 2:389, 390, 391–92
anthologies, 1:47
bar mitzvah/bat mitzvah in, 1:66
Canadian Jews from, 1:97
Chelm stories and, 1:108
childbirth, 1:82
circumcision in, 1:112
dress restrictions, 1:115
Esther scrolls, 1:146
folk art, 1:159
folk dance, 1:165
folk music and song, 1:174
folk songs and poetry, 1:190, 191, 192; 2:545
Ḥanukkah lamps, 1:228, 229, 230
immigration by Jews, 1:97; 2:367, 412, 554
instinzal technique, 1:123
Internet folklore resources, 1:259
Judeo-Arabic, 1:315
ketubbot, 1:296, 297
lulav, 2:518
magic, 2:348
mezuzah, 2:363–64
Mimuna Festival, 1:137, 172; 2:365–67
Pinto family, 2:409–12
riddling-tales, 2:448
Seder baskets, 2:478
Seder plates, 2:479
sukkah, 2:520
Sukkot, 2:519
Torah finials, 2:540
Torah mantles, 2:537
Torah pointers, 2:540
wedding customs, 1:137, 191, 312
women's hair covering, 1:*223*, 224
Mortara-Ottolenghi, Luisa, 1:158
mortification, 2:572
Moscona, Yitzhak, 2:515
Moses, 1:37, 55, 138, 155; 2:373–77, *374*, 389, 519, 558
Aaron and, 1:1; 2:341–42, 402, 576
alchemy and, 1:24

O

P

T

U

V

Z